FOREIGN AND COMMONWEALTH OFFICE

DOCUMENTS ON BRITISH POLICY OVERSEAS

EDITED BY

G. BENNETT, M.A.

AND

K.A. HAMILTON, Ph.D.

SERIES III

Volume II

LONDON: THE STATIONERY OFFICE

First published 1997

ISBN 0 11 591 6970

Published by The Stationery Office and available from:

The Publications Centre
(mail, telephone and fax orders only)
PO Box 276, London SW8 5DT
General enquiries 0171 873 0011
Telephone orders 0171 873 9090
Fax orders 0171 873 8200

The Stationery Office Bookshops
59-60 Holborn Viaduct, London EC1A 2FD
temporary until mid 1998
(counter service and fax orders only)
Fax 0171 831 1326
68-69 Bull Street, Birmingham B4 6AD
0121 236 9696 Fax 0121 236 9699
33 Wine Street, Bristol BS1 2BQ
0117 9264306 Fax 0117 9294515
9-21 Princess Street, Manchester M60 8AS
0161 834 7201 Fax 0161 833 0634
16 Arthur Street, Belfast BT1 4GD
01232 238451 Fax 01232 235401
The Stationery Office Oriel Bookshop
The Friary, Cardiff CF1 4AA
01222 395548 Fax 01222 384347
71 Lothian Road, Edinburgh EH3 9AZ
(counter service only)

Customers in Scotland may
mail, telephone or fax their orders to:
Scottish Publications Sales
South Gyle Crescent, Edinburgh EH12 9EB
0131 622 7050 Fax 0131 622 7017

The Stationery Office's Accredited Agents
(see Yellow Pages)

and through good booksellers

Printed in the UK for The Stationery Office

J31678 C15 11/97 9385 7167

Series III, Volume II

The Conference on Security and Cooperation in Europe, 1972-75

DOCUMENTS ON BRITISH POLICY OVERSEAS

Editorial Team

G. Bennett, M.A. (Head of FCO Historians and Senior Editor)

K.A. Hamilton, Ph.D. (Senior Editor)

I. Warner, Ph.D. (Assistant Editor)

R. Bevins, M.A.

G. Quinn, Bsc.Econ.

E. Kane, D.Phil.

PREFACE

The signing on 1 August 1975 of the Final Act of the Conference on Security and Cooperation in Europe (CSCE) was an event of undoubted diplomatic significance. Thirty-five delegations, representing Canada, the United States and every European state except Albania and Andorra, attended the ceremony in the Finlandia Hall, Helsinki. Amongst the delegates were the Presidents of eight countries, the Prime Ministers and Heads of Government of seventeen, the Party Secretaries of six, and the Foreign Ministers of almost all the participating countries. Their presence in the Finnish capital constituted the third and final stage of negotiations which had begun almost three years earlier, and the gathering has since been seen as a symbolic highpoint of a journalistically popular, though ill-defined, process of East/West *détente* in Europe. While the Final Act went some way towards confirming, without legally endorsing, the territorial *status quo* in Europe, it also offered new opportunities for transcending the ideological divide imposed on the continent in the aftermath of the Second World War. This volume documents the United Kingdom (UK)'s policy towards, and role in, the CSCE from the period preceding the opening of Multilateral Preparatory Talks (MPT) at Dipoli (near Helsinki) in November 1972, through the formalities of Stage I in Helsinki and the protracted negotiations of Stage II at Geneva, until the aftermath of Stage III. In addition, it charts British endeavours to achieve a common negotiating stance within NATO, and parallel efforts to coordinate and harmonise policy with the UK's new partners in the European Community (EC) through the recently-established Davignon machinery for European Political Cooperation (EPC). The documents reveal a diplomacy which was both multilayered and multilateral, and whose subject matter, which extended from the problems of divided families to those of divided nations, was ultimately as broad as it was diverse.

As is apparent from the documentation in Volume I of this series, the British were reluctant converts to the cause, long-advocated by the Russians, of a European security conference. This was hardly surprising given the mutual antagonism prevailing between London and Moscow in the autumn of 1971, and British suspicions of Soviet intentions in Europe. But at a time when three of Britain's principal allies, France, West Germany and the United States, were each engaged in bettering their bilateral relations with the Soviet Union, the Foreign and Commonwealth Office (FCO) could not ignore widespread public support for *détente*. Moreover, although the Americans were even more sceptical than the British about the prospects for a conference, the White House, in face of demands for military retrenchment abroad, were ready to trade acceptance of the CSCE for a Soviet commitment to talks on Mutual and Balanced Force Reductions (MBFR). The FCO responded by seeking to transform the rhetoric of pan-European cooperation into practical measures for broadening and 'normalising' relations amongst peoples on both sides of the East/West divide. Along with the representatives of other Western governments, British diplomats thereby

v

helped extend the scope of *détente* beyond the narrower notion of easing tensions between *blocs*. The strategy fulfilled a triple function: it provided a positive and popular cause on which participants in EPC could unite; it won the sympathy and support of the neutrals and non-aligned; and it shifted the diplomatic agenda, forcing the Russians and their allies to negotiate on an unfamiliar terrain. By highlighting Soviet reservations about subscribing to international accords on human contacts and information, the West were also able to focus public attention on the shortcomings of the East.

Preparing for preparatory talks

Early in 1972 the FCO's Western Organisations Department (WOD), working in close conjunction with Eastern European and Soviet Department (EESD), became lead department on CSCE matters. An undated draft position paper, which its Head, Mr. C.C.C. Tickell, circulated to posts on 25 February, reflected the Office's still rather less than enthusiastic attitude towards the conference idea. It thus reaffirmed the broad conclusions of a 1970 Planning Committee paper: 'that a Conference was unlikely to do the West much good; that the harm it might do could probably be contained; and that there was no reason for Britain either to encourage or to oppose the movement towards a Conference which seemed to be increasingly inevitable' (No. 1). Mr. J.N. Henderson, HM Ambassador at Warsaw, questioned the relevance and validity of conclusions reached at a time when West Germany was still negotiating its Eastern treaties, and when HMG was anxious not to impair Bonn's support for the UK's entry into the EC (*ibid.*). But the verdict of Mr. C.D. Wiggin, WOD's superintending Assistant Under-Secretary, was almost certainly more representative of opinion within the Office. 'The Conference', he minuted on 14 March, 'is (probably) inevitable rather than desirable, and our primary aim defensive' (No. 3). Such reasoning was based on the assumption that the Soviet Union intended to use the Conference to reinforce its hegemony in Eastern Europe, retard the economic and political integration of Western Europe, and weaken NATO. The Russians evidently wished to 'formalise the "results of the Second World War"', particularly as they related to the political and territorial *status quo*, and British officials believed that they were seeking to generate an atmosphere of *détente* which would sap the will of Western countries to maintain effective defence arrangements and ultimately undermine long-established military links between the United States and its European allies. There was also good reason to suppose that the East hoped to secure commercial advantages and greater access to Western scientific and technological achievements.

Nevertheless, few British diplomats had any doubts about the need to respond positively to Soviet proposals for a CSCE. Public opinion in Western Europe and Congressional opinion in the United States seemed both to favour and expect further progress towards *détente* with the East. The war in Vietnam had, in Mr. Tickell's words, 'caused a profound revulsion and the virtual alienation of a generation' in the United States, and in Denmark the very idea of defence had become 'slightly absurd'. In a melancholy minute of

6 March, in which he reflected upon the strains placed upon defence policy by the increasing disparity between NATO and the Warsaw Pact and 'widespread cynicism in the West about the possibilities of military power', Mr. Tickell observed that people wanted to hear that the Cold War was coming to an end, that the German treaties, the Strategic Arms Limitation Talks (SALT) and the projected CSCE, would create a more rational and stable system in Europe, and that defence expenditure would be cut as a result of mutual and balanced force reductions along the line of the old Iron Curtain. 'In short', he added, 'Czechoslovakia notwithstanding, East and West can kiss and make friends.' At the same time, Mr. Tickell cautioned his colleagues against being manoeuvred by fear of transient unpopularity into accepting an agenda or endorsing objectives drawn up by Warsaw Pact countries or 'our own more knockkneed allies'. Mr. Wiggin agreed. 'When in doubt', he noted, 'we must continue to err on the side of being branded cold warriors, whatever one or two of our Representatives in Eastern Europe may suggest to the contrary' (No. 2).

Unfortunately, from the British point of view, the Russians had so far seemed far more successful than the West in promoting the idea of a conference for their own propagandistic ends. And if Western countries were to draw any advantage from the CSCE, they must, as the FCO position paper recognised, maintain their unity and frustrate Soviet objectives 'without appearing to sabotage *détente*'. They would have to avoid unjustified euphoria, make it clear that the dialogue with the East could advance 'at the same time as, but without prejudice to, the construction of Western Europe', and persuade Western public opinion that they were striking the right balance between flexibility and caution. Meanwhile, the FCO felt that the West should do nothing that might suggest their endorsement of the Brezhnev doctrine of limited sovereignty, and that they might have to resort to plain speaking if they were not to play into Russian hands by seeming to accept the Soviet contention that the problems of European security could be solved by the abolition of *blocs* and the adoption of pan-European mechanisms. There was, however, as the position paper indicated, always the danger that if British delegates spoke out too robustly, they would come to be regarded in NATO and elsewhere as so negative that their views need not be taken into account. 'The Russians', it asserted, 'will certainly take every opportunity they get to try to isolate us in this way' (No. 1).

The FCO also appreciated the importance of achieving with Britain's allies and partners an understanding covering the kind of conference they wanted, its agenda and organisation, and their specific aims and objectives. It was from the start only too apparent that the Americans were, at best, indifferent towards a security conference. Dr. H. Kissinger, President R.M. Nixon's Assistant for National Security Affairs, did not, according to Mr. M. Butler, Counsellor at the British Embassy in Washington, 'regard the CSCE as being a "serious" affair' (No. 6). And on 28 July President Nixon told Sir B. Trend, the Cabinet Secretary, that the United States (US) Government 'had never wanted the conference', and that it was some of the European countries, 'not least the United Kingdom, who had originally pressed for it' (No. 12). Moreover, the Americans considered that any preparatory talks should involve substantive negotiations, and that the West could use the threat of refusing to go to a conference in order to extract concessions from the Warsaw Pact. This British officials thought 'unrealistic'. In their opinion, once preparation for a conference had begun, 'it would be politically extremely difficult for the West to withdraw from it' unless there were a serious deterioration of East/West relations for other reasons, such as a Soviet invasion of Romania, then the most recalcitrant of Russia's European allies. They preferred proposals put forward by the French in the autumn of 1971 for MPT which would concentrate on the agenda and procedures, and a short ministerial meeting which would remit problems of substance to expert sub-committees. Detailed agreements might then be referred back to a second ministerial conference if desirable. But, unlike the French, the British in the first instance favoured keeping the agenda vague so that the West could raise such issues as they liked once a conference assembled (No. 1).

The attitude of other NATO countries towards the CSCE varied considerably. In a letter of 25 April, in which he briefly summarised positions adopted within the Alliance, Mr. R.Q. Braithwaite of WOD underlined Bonn's commitment to a conference which West Germans hoped would improve intra-German relations. 'They suspect', he observed, 'that our view of the conference is negative and that we regard it as primarily an occasion for judicious political warfare (which of course we do).' Moreover, while the French official analysis of the usefulness of a conference resembled that of the FCO, French Ministers were inclined in private to argue that the Conference would enable NATO to pursue 'peaceful roll-back' through the loosening of the Soviet Union's grip upon its East European allies. The Italians took the opposite view. Italian officials were, according to Mr. Braithwaite, 'particularly sceptical' about the value of a conference which they saw as a Soviet device to disrupt Western Europe, and he found the Dutch, Greeks and Turks equally 'hard-headed'. By contrast, Norway, Denmark, Belgium and Canada were 'known to the irreverent as the "wet front"', because their Ministers tended to believe the Conference would be a 'Good Thing', that it would be capable of negotiating a genuine *détente*, and that the West must therefore avoid provoking the Russians (No. 8). It was for this reason that they, the West Germans, and briefly, the French, were doubtful about pressing the East for the inclusion in the agenda of an item on freedom of movement. Despite the fact that this, in Mr. Wiggin's estimate, ought to have been 'one of the main cards' in Western hands, they seemed to prefer to seek such improvements piecemeal when negotiating about cooperation in particular fields (No. 3). By June the French had moved closer to the British, and both took the lead in arguing that the West should put forward an agenda formula which would permit Ministers to deal with the matter as they wished, but avoid premature argument in the preparatory talks. There remained, however, a deep gulf between these positions and that adopted by the Americans and the Dutch, who wanted the 'West to assume an unequivocal stance from the outset, modifying it as necessary later in discussion with the other side (No. 10).

Another idea, which some in the FCO regarded as a 'positive and concrete proposal which [they] could advocate in the Alliance and in public as a contribution to East/West *détente*', was the proposal for the establishment of some kind of permanent machinery (No. 1). The British had long shown an interest in the creation of such mechanisms. But the Americans had reservations about adopting such a course, and discussions with Britain's European partners soon revealed that attitudes towards the idea of a permanent body with wide-ranging responsibility for general political questions ranged from cool to strongly hostile. Some feared that it might be used by the Russians to impede the development of Western European institutions. There was, however, sympathy for the idea of setting up other types of machinery, limited in function and not permanent, to deal with various practical problems arising from the CSCE (No. 3). NATO and EC countries were similarly divided over what should constitute the security content of the CSCE. The US Government wished to avoid any move within the CSCE context which might complicate or delay the opening of MBFR talks, and the French, who, along with the British, disliked MBFR because of the military disadvantages likely to result from it, were opposed to any linkage between the two sets of negotiations. Meanwhile, NATO members without troops or territory on the Central Front wanted to safeguard their interests by establishing a clear link between MBFR and the CSCE in order to ensure they had some say in the outcome of the former. In these circumstances the FCO, in consultation with the Ministry of Defence, suggested that the CSCE might: (1) negotiate a declaration on force levels so general that all participants could sign it; and (2) agree on certain 'politico-military' confidence building measures (CBMs). In addition, British officials foresaw a CSCE security commission setting up sub-groups to negotiate force reductions in particular areas (No. 9). Proposals on these lines could, as the UK Deputy Permanent Representative to NATO recognised, serve as 'bargaining counters' with which to extract concessions from the East, and should put the West in a favourable position at the outset of any subsequent MBFR talks. They might even ease Congressional pressure for force cuts and delay the whole process of MBFR (No. 7).

Such hopes soon proved illusory. The White House were determined to have MBFR, and at a NATO ministerial meeting on 30-31 May it was agreed that member states would participate in the MPT for the CSCE, and that exploratory discussions for MBFR talks should be undertaken either before, or in parallel, with these (No. 9). During September the Russians indicated to Dr. Kissinger their willingness to begin preliminary consultations for MBFR in January 1973, and this opened the way for allied acceptance of a Finnish invitation to begin MPT in Helsinki on 22 November (No. 13). Yet, despite the West's acceptance of preparatory talks, the FCO remained uncertain about the course on which they were embarking. Indeed, Mr. N.M. Lunkov of the Second European Department of the Soviet Foreign

Ministry, seemed only to confirm their worst fears of Russian motives when, on 15 and 18 September, he visited the Office for talks with Sir T. Brimelow, Deputy Under-Secretary of State, Mr. Wiggin and Mr. Tickell. Mr. Lunkov indicated that his Government were not interested in discussing at the CSCE any part of the military aspects of security, that they had few practical ideas about economic and technological cooperation, and that they hoped to exclude serious discussion of the items grouped under freer movement (No. 14). 'In a nutshell', Mr. Tickell observed, 'they see the Conference as an occasion for declarations, statements of principles and propaganda of all kinds designed to better establish their hold on the East and weaken the coherence of the West; while we see it as a means for lowering East/West barriers, improving confidence and adopting practical measures to improve cooperation' (No. 13). Moreover, Mr. Lunkov did not, as expected, emphasise Russian interest in creating permanent machinery—a notion which, given the doubts expressed by other EC governments, the British had had come to view with increasing scepticism (No. 14).

Throughout 1972 consultations continued with, and amongst, Britain's partners and allies on the CSCE and the strategy and tactics to be adopted by the West. One paper which the FCO drafted for consideration by the EPC Political Committee's CSCE Sub-Committee analysed in detail the attitude of East European states to the Conference. It argued that while moves to secure the general recognition of frontiers would command widespread support, the attitude of East European states to the formalisation of Soviet hegemony was likely to vary considerably. There would, according to the paper, be strong pressure for conformity which East European countries would find it difficult to resist and, where differences affected motives rather than the policy advocated, the West was likely to find itself confronted with a 'high degree of apparent unity in the Warsaw Pact camp, masking the real differences of approach'. This would be difficult to exploit, not least because policies designed to increase freedom of manoeuvre in the East might weaken the cohesion of the West. Moreover, the extent to which Warsaw Pact countries would allow their citizens to have contact with the West was clearly limited by their fear of provoking Soviet intervention and by the interest of Party leaders in excluding influences which could undermine their own positions. The FCO was, however, in no doubt about the significance of this issue. 'If', the paper concluded, '. . . one looks at the matter not through the eyes of the Party leaders but through the eyes of a broad section of the educated population in Eastern Europe, progress on freer movement becomes one of the criteria by which the success of the Conference will be judged' (No. 5).

The whole subject of the freer movement of people and ideas was examined by an FCO working party on the cultural aspects of the CSCE which began work at the end of July. In a letter of 4 August, covering the records of the working party's first meeting, Mr. G. Walden of EESD insisted that 'in our aim to secure genuine improvements in reducing barriers within Europe and "generally to spread the contagion of liberty" we should not shrink from asserting western beliefs in the freedom of movement, information, and cultural contacts'. But, as Mr. Walden noted, while the presentation of Western ideals would be a matter of careful drafting, it would be far more difficult to establish a realistic fall-back position. Where information was concerned, he thought the Russians would find it difficult to turn down out of hand proposals for the mutual establishment of reading rooms and libraries in each other's capitals, the publication of an East/West magazine, the annual publication in national newspapers of statements emanating from participating countries, and improved exchanges in the field of films, radio and television (No. 11). Subsequent discussions within NATO and the Davignon machinery revealed a broad consensus on the need to enlarge the definition of 'cultural' to include many activities not hitherto strictly regarded as such, and the desirability of increasing non-governmental exchanges in preference to official ones. British officials also thought it right to link freer movement with cultural relations as one agenda item so that Eastern countries, who were evidently opposed to including any reference to extending human contacts, would have to give proper examination to both subjects. Nevertheless, when the MPT began in November the West still had few concrete proposals to put forward in the cultural sphere. 'The fact is', one of Mr. Walden's colleagues noted, 'the Western shop window still lacks solid merchandise and contains too much tinsel' (No. 18).

Multilateral Preparatory Talks

The NATO steering brief for the MPT, which was based upon a British draft, made the reduction of barriers within Europe, especially by promoting freer movement of persons, information and ideas and by developing East/West cooperation, one of the West's three 'positive' aims. The other two were the achievement of appropriate CBMs (discussion of which was now seen as a means of bringing it home to public opinion that 'the balance of forces in Europe [was] the real question affecting security'), and an increase in the freedom of manoeuvre of East European countries by reducing the scope for application of the Brezhnev doctrine (No. 17). Britain and its allies were also careful not to commit themselves to a conference unless the results of the MPT were such as to justify it. They wanted the talks to establish that enough common ground existed amongst participants to warrant reasonable expectations that a conference would produce satisfactory results. From the Western point of view the problem was to ensure agreement on an agenda which would allow Ministers to raise at the Conference proper the points to which they attached importance, and a Conference structure which would ensure that the various items on the agenda received detailed examination before any decisions were taken. The Russians were clearly unhappy about discussing commission mandates at the MPT. But participants in the Davignon machinery insisted that the talks must agree terms of reference for the commissions and sub-commissions which would constitute Stage II of a three-stage Conference (No. 16); and the FCO recognised that these would have to be sufficiently explicit to allow the Western delegates to say what they wanted without being restricted by procedural objections from the East. A draft brief prepared for British delegates to the talks emphasised this point. 'We do not', it affirmed, 'want to arrive at the first stage of the Conference proper without a clear idea of what is to be discussed, and of how the work is to be handled.' British officials hoped that if the West remained united, the Russians would agree to discuss terms of reference. Even then, however, they thought they would have to ensure that these discussions were carried out in parallel with those on the agenda, and that they must withhold agreement to the formulation of agenda items until appropriate terms of reference for commissions had been settled (No. 17).

Whilst the British expected the talks to consider in detail the framework of a conference, they nonetheless hoped that they would not deal with questions of substance. The FCO maintained that the MPT were not, and should not become, a 'pre-conference'. Yet officials were only too well aware that if Western proposals on the agenda and terms of reference were opposed, questions of substance would 'not be very far from the surface', and that they would have to keep Conference objectives 'firmly in view' (*ibid.*). Indeed, within the next three months the talks assumed a rather different pattern from the 'informal consultations amongst Ambassadors' which had once been envisaged. As Mr. T.A.K. Elliott, British Ambassador in Helsinki and Head of Delegation, later recalled, the talks began at a 'leisurely pace' with business conducted in a single daily plenary meeting, but by the spring of 1973 had taken on all the characteristics of a major international conference (No. 37). This transformation was in large part a consequence of persisting differences between East and West over what the talks were intended to achieve. During the first session, which ended on 15 December, rules of procedure were agreed. But the desire of Warsaw Pact countries to give priority to deciding the date and location of the Conference, the list of participants and its general organisation, and the Soviet Union's opposition to the elaboration of terms of reference for commissions and sub-commissions (henceforth more usually referred to as committees and sub-committees), impeded efforts to draft a work programme (No. 19). Western delegates were, for their part, concerned lest agreement on the agenda should leave the Russians free to claim that the main work of the talks had been accomplished without any consideration having been given to those particular issues with which Western, along with neutral and non-aligned, countries wanted the CSCE to deal.

This tactical problem was considered within NATO and amongst the Nine EC countries during the Christmas recess, and on 15 January 1973 Western delegations tabled proposals on agenda items and terms of reference in such a way as to make it clear they were to be considered together. These covered security problems, economic and environmental cooperation, and cultural and human relations. A week later the Russians showed signs of adopting a more conciliatory approach when they indicated their readiness to consider 'Certain measures for strengthening stability and confidence', and to treat cultural relations, human contacts and the dissemination of information as a separate item. Of greater significance for the structural development of the CSCE was, however, Mr. Elliott's contribution to the plenary meeting on 24 January, when, following agreement amongst NATO representatives, he spoke in favour of an Austrian recommendation for the grouping of agenda proposals in broad subject areas or 'baskets'. The Swiss were also encouraged by the Nine to prepare a catalogue of proposals so far submitted, and this document, which was accepted on 29 January, grouped proposals into four numbered baskets dealing respectively with: (1) political and security matters; (2) economic and related issues; (3) human contacts, culture and information; and (4) follow-up to the Conference (No. 20). Meanwhile, the Russians, apparently with a view to increasing the momentum of the talks, signalled their readiness to discuss draft assignments for Stage II committees and then proceeded to table these for committees on each of the four baskets. Mr. Elliott inferred from their recent speeches that the Russians were ready to discuss the substance of Western proposals. They, nevertheless, still maintained their opposition to the drafting of terms of reference for sub-committees, though they suggested that they might eventually acquiesce in the subdivision of assignments according to subject matter (No. 21).

Much of the credit for this apparent Soviet retreat was, in Mr. Elliott's opinion, due to the Nine, who had maintained their unity throughout the MPT's first and second sessions (*ibid.*). But Mr. Elliott was also aware that neutral and non-aligned delegates, whose support the West wished to retain, were becoming impatient with the lack of results, and that the Warsaw Pact countries would soon begin pressing to begin drafting, probably in working groups. There were obvious dangers in this course. As had long been apparent, the West, once faced with even a provisionally agreed agenda and brief descriptions of committees' tasks, would be in a weak bargaining position to seek agreement on terms of reference and the establishment of sub-committees for an effective Stage II. Mr. Elliott recommended that they therefore start the drafting process 'from the bottom up', considering individual subjects in each basket, seeking agreed formulations for each of them, and building up a number of smaller subject areas corresponding to sub-committees and finally complete agenda items (No. 22). This inductive approach was supported within the Alliance and the EC and, following the acceptance in plenary on 26 February of a French proposal for the creation of a single open-ended working group, it was effectively adopted by other delegations (No. 23). Progress, however, remained slow until on 8 March the British introduced a framework document on principles which allowed for the insertion of further detail. The Working Group remitted this to an informal drafting group, more usually referred to as the Mini-Group, thereby setting a precedent which allowed for the emergence of a more flexible organisational structure for the MPT. 'This', Mr. Elliott noted on 14 March '. . . is likely to be followed for the other baskets, and will enable us to secure full discussion of those items on the agenda to which we attach importance (particularly the economic and cultural baskets) before we give formal agreement to formulations on Basket I (security) which the East favour' (No. 26).

The British proposal for a framework document for Basket I foresaw a text which would clearly indicate those principles governing relations amongst states to which attention should be paid (*ibid.*). A Western draft on principles, tabled by the Italians on 15 January, had already been severely criticised by Soviet delegates, who objected to its coupling of the inviolability of frontiers with the non-use of force and its references to human rights and national self-determination (No. 21). But the British regarded with equal disdain a Soviet draft declaration on principles, a copy of which they received from the Americans. Its advocacy of a system of collective security aimed at overcoming existing divisions in Europe was seen as an endorsement of the Brezhnev doctrine, and Mr. Walden claimed that it was 'replete with alien concepts expressed in unwieldy formulations', and that, if released to the British press, 'it might well be portrayed as a blueprint to transform Western Europe into a sort of Soviet Disneyland' (No. 24). The Russians were, however, determined to secure an international and unqualified endorsement of the principle of inviolability (which they seemed sometimes to interpret as meaning something closer to immutability) of frontiers, and they evidently wanted a formula which would disallow territorial claims by one European state upon another. This, as Mr. Walden pointed out, was unlikely to be acceptable to either the Irish Republic or Spain, given their respective claims on Northern Ireland and Gibraltar. It also posed serious difficulties for the West Germans who, though ready to acquiesce in the textual separation of frontier inviolability from the non-use of force, were insistent that the former should not be held to preclude peaceful change and even the abolition of frontiers by mutual agreement. The Russians claimed not to understand German objections since the inviolability of frontiers was mentioned in both the Federal Republic's treaties with Moscow and Warsaw. Bonn, nevertheless, maintained that there was an important difference of degree between these accords and the kind of multilateral document which the CSCE would produce and, along with the British Government and other allied governments, opposed using bilateral agreements as quarries for principles, especially as this might lead to the emergence of 'some sort of European regional law' (No. 27).

Western acceptance of the decoupling of inviolability of frontiers from the non-use of force was in effect traded for the East's agreement to the separate listing, amongst the principles to be considered by the Conference, of the peaceful settlement of disputes, respect for human rights and fundamental freedoms, and the fulfilment in good faith of obligations under international law. The Russians had been particularly critical of the reference to human rights which, they argued, did not constitute a principle governing relations amongst states, and self-determination, which they held to be relevant only in colonial situations (No. 21). However, on 23 March they indicated that, subject to order and precise formulation, they would accept a list of ten principles informally circulated by the Swiss convenors of the Mini-Group (No. 27). Disagreement over the ordering and inter-relationship of principles, their field of application and source documents to be cited in any mandate persisted until the end of May. Even then, it was necessary to devise a formula which would satisfy the Romanians who wanted separate references to sovereignty and the equal rights of states (Nos. 30, 34 and 35).

Soviet delegates meanwhile managed to overcome some of their initial doubts about the two CBMs, the prior notification of military manoeuvres and movements and the exchange of observers at military exercises, which the West wished to include in Basket I. Reluctant to accept any reference to 'movements', by mid-May the Russians seemed ready to concede a formulation which would allow their discussion in the CSCE, but 'without the degree of commitment as to the outcome in the text on manoeuvres' (No. 34). Much, however, of the fourth session's debate on the military aspects of security was focused upon the contentious issue of whether the terms of reference should establish, or imply, any linkage between the CSCE and MBFR. The question divided allies with the Americans, Russians and French resisting, and the Dutch, Romanians and Yugoslavs demanding, linkage. The British, for their part, wanted to avoid any decision in the CSCE which might complicate negotiations on MBFR (No. 33). But it was the French who finally upset efforts to achieve a compromise. On 31 May they made it clear to other members of the Nine that the most they could accept was a vague preambular reference to participants 'bearing in mind the fact that efforts aimed at disarmament complement political *détente*' (No. 34)—a phrase which, while it committed no one to reaching any agreed conclusions, could still open the way to potentially far-reaching discussions.

The EC Nine and the NATO Fifteen were more obviously at one when it came to dealing with the contents of Basket III. They had from the start to cope with the very restrictive interpretations which the East endeavoured to place upon texts relating to human contacts and the freer dissemination of information. Mr. V.F. Maltsev, the Soviet Ambassador in Helsinki, made it clear on 22 January that these should not allow for the 'dissemination of anti-culture, ie pornography, racism, fascism, cult of violence, hostility among peoples and false and slanderous propaganda' (No. 20). And when on 8 February Mr. V.A. Zorin, who was assumed to have been sent to Dipoli to take care of matters of KGB interest, put forward draft proposals which, in Mr. Elliott's words, were 'empty of content and long on qualifications', he too insisted that preparatory work on Item III must proceed in accordance with generally accepted norms for dealing with questions falling within the internal competence of states (Nos. 21 and 37). Mr. Zorin subsequently contended that delegates should concentrate upon drafting a preamble which would include aims and principles, and he attacked the prominence given in a Danish paper, put forward on behalf of the West, to marriage and reunification of families. Such delicate problems, he added, could only be solved bilaterally (No. 30). None of this came as any great surprise to Mr. Walden. He thought it most unlikely that the Russians would make any concessions of substance on freer movement, and that only in the information field did there seem any likelihood at all of securing concrete improvements. Even then, he thought such gains would be limited. Nevertheless, Basket III was regarded in Helsinki as the only issue on which a breakdown in the talks could be effectively justified, and Mr. Walden considered it necessary to keep up the pressure on the Russians. 'We must', he minuted, 'squeeze the Russian lemon very hard to demonstrate to public opinion how little juice there is in *détente à la russe*' (No. 31).

Amongst the West's basic requirements for Basket III was the establishment of separate sub-committees for the consideration of human contacts and information. This, by April, the Russians seemed ready to concede, but only on condition that sub-committee mandates were effectively circumscribed by a preambular reference to the principle of 'non-interference'. The Nine refused to bargain on this basis and, even after the Russians had indicated that they might be ready to agree instead to a general preambular reference to principles guiding relations between states and a specific mention of sovereignty and human rights, the Dutch, supported by the Italians and the Belgians, were reluctant to compromise (Nos. 30, 32 and 33). What Mr. Elliott termed the 'most radical shift in the Soviet negotiating position' came on 17 May. Then, evidently with a view to avoiding further delay, the Russians offered to abandon their demand for reference to 'non-interference' in return for a package which included the insertion into the preamble of a phrase emphasising that Committee III's proposals should be based on full respect for the principles agreed in Committee I, and the introduction into the human contacts mandate of a sentence stating that relevant matters should be examined and settled by 'states concerned' (No. 34). The offer opened the way to agreement on the Basket III preamble and to the settlement during the following three weeks of the mandates for the four Committee III Sub-Committees.

It proved far easier to reach agreement in Basket II. The subject matter was less controversial and the experts representing the main participants were already well-experienced in handling the economic issues dividing East and West. There were, however, parallels with Basket III discussions. As Mr. J.K. Gordon of the FCO's Trade Relations Department (TRED) explained, Western tactics 'concentrated on securing a minimum of references to wide-sweeping "principles" and to stressing the need for "concrete measures"', and the East 'tended to do the opposite, pleading . . . the doctrines of non-interference and respect for existing legislation' (No. 36). Moreover, until the end of the third session, Eastern delegates insisted that the Committee's mandate should contain a commitment to a 'European programme of specific projects' and allow for the development of economic relations on the basis of non-discrimination and most favoured nation (MFN) treatment. From informal discussions with the newly-appointed Soviet representative, Mr. V.S. Pozharski, fresh and more generally acceptable formulae emerged after the Easter break. Yet, by the end of May, delegates were engaged in another round of verbal gymnastics, this time to ensure that a preambular reference to 'conditions of reciprocity', which the West required, was balanced, but not qualified, by a preceding mention of the 'diversity of economic and social systems' (*ibid.*). And the resulting preamble was further complicated by the stipulation that the Committee's proposals would be based on full respect for the principles in Basket I. Mr. Elliott was, nevertheless, pleased with terms of reference which he felt provided 'the basis for a business-like examination of economic questions' and placed a 'useful emphasis on reciprocity, and on information and contacts' (No. 37).

The achievements of Western diplomats in discussions on the first three baskets could be measured against the draft agenda items originally tabled by the Belgians, Danes and Italians (No. 20). But until the final session of the talks no specifically Western proposals were submitted on follow-up. The FCO, despite the positive approach adopted in the draft position paper of February 1972 (No. 1), had by the autumn come to the conclusion that follow-up should not be considered as a separate agenda item. Instead, they subscribed to the NATO line that although there was nothing to be gained from establishing new permanent machinery, non-permanent institutionalised arrangements could prove useful if progress were made on subjects of interest to the Alliance, and that these could carry forward the process of negotiation and give effect to Conference decisions (No. 17). On 22 January the Russians, who, along with their allies, had long favoured some kind of permanent international machinery for European security, tabled a fairly modest proposal for the establishment of a consultative committee (No. 20). Neutral and non-aligned delegations were sympathetic to the idea of continuing machinery. And while Mr. Elliott thought it still valid for the West to argue that they could not decide what new machinery might be necessary until they had a clearer idea of what would result from the Conference, and that there were good tactical reasons for holding to this position, he also felt it necessary to give urgent consideration to the draft terms of reference for a committee on follow-up (No. 22). Other Western delegates were thinking along similar lines, and on 5 March the French argued in the Davignon (EPC) CSCE Sub-Committee that if a coordinating committee were created for the Conference, it might concern itself with Eastern requests for a consultative committee. Mr. Tickell was inclined to agree and, on a submission of 22 March in which Mr. Tickell reiterated the arguments for and against such continuing machinery, Mr. Wiggin noted that if they had to have such machinery 'the more we can keep it to some sort of Ambassadorial teaparty . . . the better' (No. 28). In the event, the East refrained from pressing the matter until the final session of the MPT when, somewhat to the surprise of British delegates, they accepted terms of reference for what was now designated Item IV. These required the Conference Coordinating Committee to consider, 'on the basis of the progress made at the Conference', measures which might be necessary to give effect to its decisions (No. 34).

The West, in Mr. Elliott's opinion emerged from the MPT in a 'position of clear advantage'. They had secured a three-stage Conference, an agenda which would allow Ministers to raise at Stage I points to which they attached importance and, in effect, terms of reference which would assure that agenda items were thoroughly examined in committees and sub-committees during Stage II. This success Mr. Elliott attributed to the detailed preparatory work of the Nine, the cohesion of the Western allies, the sympathy of the non-aligned and neutrals for the Western position, and the Nine's refusal to accept an opening date for the Conference until the talks had produced satisfactory results. The Russians had fought hard for more restrictive texts, particularly in Basket III, and had given way only when they realised they must pay the price of accepting those agreed in order to have a Conference at all. And the decision of the US delegation to maintain a low profile, evidently with the object of reconciling their desire to avoid both public confrontations with the Russians and accusations of collusion between the superpowers, 'thrust the main burden of defending Western positions upon the Nine'. The latter, Mr. Elliott concluded, had 'passed the first real test of their ability to develop and execute a common policy with flying colours'. The negotiations had also allowed the British delegates to assume a more positive role in confronting the East. Mr. Elliott and his colleagues had, despite the poor state of Anglo-Soviet relations, been able to demonstrate to the Russians at Dipoli that their underlying attitude to the CSCE was constructive and, lacking some of the peculiar concerns of their EC partners, the British had been encouraged to take a lead amongst the Nine. Yet, whilst drawing satisfaction from this, Mr. Elliott added a rider. 'If Britain is not to act as a major European Power in the context of the CSCE', he observed, 'she can hardly hope to be a Power anywhere' (No. 37).

The long hard slog

Some within the FCO remained dubious about the CSCE. Mr. Wiggin was always inclined to regard it as essentially a propaganda battle. 'I shall', he minuted on 20 June, 'be pleasantly surprised if, at the end of the whole cycle, anything of real and positive value emerges.' Even Mr. Elliott harboured doubts about prospects for the Conference. Progress in the MPT had, in his opinion, seemed to suggest that the Russians had misjudged the situation. They had only been able to count on the regular support of their East European allies, and had sometimes given the impression of being in a state bordering on panic 'as they found themselves in a negotiating position rather less strong than they had enjoyed in the UN in the early 1950s'. But he also admitted that there could be no guarantee that the results of the Conference proper would justify the expectations raised by the wording of the terms of reference: some of the formulae evolved had, after all, done little more than 'paper over major differences of principle' (*ibid.*). Sir J. Killick agreed. The Russians had, he thought, given a 'good deal of verbal ground' in order to win Western support for the holding of a Conference, but he felt sure they would regard these concessions as of a purely tactical nature and that the West must expect them 'to fight hard to try to retrieve what they [seemed] to have given up'. Much as he welcomed the diplomatic 'springboard' established by the MPT, he predicted a 'long hard slog', with the Russians attempting to trade on the West's 'comparative lack of patience'. In a letter of 27 June he advised Mr. Tickell: 'we must play it as long and as hard in the Commissions as necessary, and I only hope that the Americans . . .

will not join the Russians in pressing for speed. It is we who must exploit Brezhnev's sense of urgency and desire for a concluding "summit" in order to drive hard bargains' (No. 38).

Stage I appeared only to confirm Sir J. Killick's gloomy prognosis. The Foreign Ministers who met in Helsinki during 3-7 July witnessed a determined endeavour on the part of the Soviet Foreign Minister, Mr. A. Gromyko, and his Eastern *bloc* colleagues 'to put the clock back to 1972' (No. 42). 'The Russians', noted Mr. J.L. Bullard, Head of EESD, 'seem to have decided that although they have lost a battle (the MPT) they have definitely not lost the war.' Both in their speeches and in draft texts which they tabled, Eastern delegates made it plain that they were still hoping for a declaratory Conference, with a propagandistic final document, which would create the illusion of a new era in Europe without conceding any changes that could endanger the Soviet system. To that end they were resolved that any action under Item III should be subject to the principles of non-interference and individual sovereignty. Moreover, in placing renewed emphasis on the inviolability of frontiers, Mr. Gromyko and his Czechoslovak counterpart appeared to indicate that the frontiers in which they were particularly interested were those that separated East from West. 'This concept of a revived Iron Curtain or extended Berlin Wall', Mr. Bullard observed, 'fits the very toughly ideological cast of Gromyko's presentation and effectively disproves many of the rosier hopes expressed at the Conference about the elimination of obstacles throughout Europe' (No. 40). Yet, while the Russians publicly adopted rigid attitudes, they did not, as Mr. Elliott pointed out, 'defend them very hard when it came to the crunch'. Stage I was, after all, in many respects a formality. Its primary purpose was to register the Final Recommendations prepared by the MPT, and the Russians gave the impression that they were less interested in the substance of the Conference than in the smooth completion of its proceedings. They could, Mr. Elliott predicted, be expected 'to fight a good deal harder in Stage II, and to repeat many of the skirmishes that we hoped had been concluded on the Dipoli terrain' (No. 42).

Soviet conduct during Stage I did not suggest that the Russians would necessarily succeed in subsequent engagements. Western delegates had expected that the Soviet Union and its allies would seek a propaganda victory at Stage I, but the reactionary tone of their speeches and the paucity of their proposals denied the East any such advantage. Moreover, Mr. Gromyko, who treated the gathering as though it were a regular East/West confrontation, seemed wholly insensitive to the role of the neutrals and non-aligned in the process of *détente* (*ibid.*). This was only too apparent in his reaction to the endeavours of the Maltese Prime Minister, Mr. D. Mintoff, to persuade the Conference to hear the views of the Algerian and Tunisian Foreign Ministers. Mr. Mintoff was supported by other Mediterranean countries, including France, Italy and Spain, but consideration of the matter was deadlocked when the Israelis requested a hearing, and subsequent Maltese efforts to have this disagreement recorded in the Conference *communiqué* infuriated the Russians. In truth, the British were even more wary of a course which could easily embroil the CSCE in the problems of the Middle East. Nevertheless, Mr. Gromyko, who attached considerable importance to having an agreed *communiqué*, revealed the Soviet Union's 'cloven hoof' when he threatened that if Maltese resistance persisted, he would advise changing the rules of consensus to allow the Conference to proceed even if one country objected. Russian 'bullying tactics', Mr. Elliott recalled, 'caused resentment among all the smaller countries for whom, whatever the merits of the present dispute, the rule of consensus is their essential safeguard' (No. 41).

The Maltese episode also revealed significant differences amongst the Nine and the Fifteen. The French and Italians had evidently wished to ingratiate themselves with Algeria and Tunisia and, without consulting their allies, they aligned themselves with Malta. Meanwhile, the Canadians, Dutch, Danes and Norwegians ranged themselves alongside the Americans, who had 'cautiously raised' the Israeli aspect, in insisting that other non-participating Mediterranean states be accorded the same treatment (*ibid.*). The issue continued to divide partners and allies and, despite the endeavours of the Nine to agree a common position (No. 42), when the Conference Coordinating Committee assembled at Geneva for its first meeting during 29 August-3 September they failed to act in unison. Representatives of the non-aligned nations were due to meet in Algiers on 5 September and, possibly with this in mind, both the French and Russians were prepared to give priority to the Mediterranean question, with the result that the work of the Committee was delayed for several days. An arrangement, which granted the Israelis treatment equal to that afforded to the Algerians and the Tunisians, was eventually agreed, and a committee structure which met Western requirements was established for the following stage. But Mr. Elliott found the whole business 'a pretty dismal experience'. Delegates had failed to show a spirit of compromise, successive chairmen had failed to apply the rules of procedure fairly, and debates had been characterised by a lamentable long-windedness. It all, he feared, boded ill for Stage II (No. 44).

Developments in the Soviet Union meanwhile cast a shadow over the CSCE and the future of *détente*. Attacks in the Moscow press on two leading dissidents, the nuclear physicist, Dr. A. Sakharov, and the author, Mr. A. Solzhenitsyn, and the opening of a long-forecast 'show trial' of two Russians human rights activists, led Sir J. Killick to conclude that the Soviet Government intended 'to demonstrate beyond doubt in deeds as well as words both to the West and to the Soviet people that relaxation of tension on the international plane need not and will not be accompanied by relaxation at home or by ideological *détente*'. In a telegram of 5 September he warned the Foreign Secretary, Sir A. Douglas-Home, that if the West went ahead with the CSCE as if nothing had happened and ended up accepting 'minimal concessions' in Basket III in return for allowing the Russians what they wanted in Basket I, it would appear in the Soviet Union and throughout Eastern Europe that 'we have ignored the challenge and come to terms with the newly revealed "ugly face" of communism'. Sir A. Douglas-Home thought they might well have to make it clear to the Russians that Western negotiators operated within the 'framework of public opinion' and that any further action against dissidents might seriously prejudice the atmosphere for the CSCE. Yet neither he nor Mr. Elliott appear to have felt the need for an any more drastic reaction: Mr. Elliott could see no advantage in fighting a propagandist battle over current events instead of pressing for the long-term improvements envisaged at Dipoli (No. 45). As the steering brief for the UK delegation to Stage II admitted, the CSCE would 'at best be only a step in the right direction'. The FCO hoped for small but tangible improvements in the field of human contacts and information coupled, more significantly, with 'a general recognition of the relevance of these subjects to the strengthening of security and development of cooperation'. British officials regarded agreement on Basket III issues both as a precursor of change in the Soviet system, and as a measure of the Soviet commitment to their view of *détente* (No. 46).

The CSCE also remained for the British 'something of a test case for the development of foreign policy co-ordination among the Nine' (*ibid.*) and, as Mr. Elliott subsequently recalled, the first three months of the second stage provided a training period during which methods of consultation among EC partners, and with NATO allies, were adapted to the circumstances of Geneva (No. 57). With twelve working bodies to take into account, it was obviously more difficult for delegates to harmonise policy and conduct than it had been at Dipoli, and the degree of discipline which the Dutch and Belgians demanded was rarely attainable. The French had already demonstrated during the first meeting of the Coordinating Committee their capacity for independent action, and although Mr. Elliott recognised their 'valuable and loyal role', he understood that they liked to 'play out front', and that, as the 'preferred interlocutors' of the Russians in the Western camp, they were more inclined than their partners to display a flexible attitude. 'They could', he noted in a summary despatch of 15 December, 'break loose if the issues in question are not thoroughly explored and agreed upon by the Nine, with French views taken fully into account' (*ibid.*). Where Basket II issues were concerned, a further complication was presented by the inclusion in the delegation of the country holding the EC Presidency of representatives of the EC Commission. This allowed the latter their first opportunity to engage in long informal discussions with the Russians, but it also raised problems of diplomatic competence. Moreover, within the CSCE Ad Hoc Group, the body responsible for coordinating EC policy on economic issues, Commission representatives were, along with the Belgians and French, reluctant to work closely with non-EC NATO allies. They also tended to favour making an offer of future commercial negotiations with the Eastern *bloc* as a way of securing diplomatic recognition from the East (Nos. 50, 53 and 55). The Americans, a key element in any effective cooperation amongst the Nine and NATO, meanwhile maintained their reserve and, as British delegates were well aware, could easily be tempted, for reasons connected with their bilateral relationship with the Soviet Union, to work for an early and possibly premature conclusion of Stage II (No. 46).

During the autumn of 1973 discussions at Geneva were dominated by essentially procedural matters. Western delegations wanted to ensure a proper balance between progress in all three substantive Committees. Otherwise, it was feared the Russians would seek to give priority to the drafting of a Declaration of Principles, and that once that was achieved they would press for the speedy completion of work in Committees II and III. In British eyes it therefore seemed sensible to promote working methods analogous to the 'inductive approach' adopted in the MPT, and to resist all drafting of texts before the in depth examination of agenda items in the sub-committees (No. 43). An Eastern manoeuvre evidently designed to lead to the early and separate discussion of preambular, and therefore qualifying, provisions of Basket III, was successfully countered by the West (No. 47). But consideration of sub-committee mandates remained very general and, following a visit to Geneva in late October, Mr. B.J.P. Fall of EESD reported that he had found that everyone was expecting Stage II to last at least until March 1974, and that delegations 'with greater or lesser reluctance [were] reconciling themselves to a long haul' (No. 52). Even the Russians, though 'robustly negative on a great number of points of interest to the West', seemed to be desisting from efforts to accelerate the work of sub-committees, and Mr. Elliott reported on 17 November that they appeared to have given up their hope of forcing an early conclusion to Stage II (No. 54).

When at the beginning of the Christmas recess Mr. Elliott assessed Western achievements he concluded with some satisfaction that the West had succeeded both in moderating the tempo of work generally, and in postponing moves towards drafting before the completion of detailed agenda discussions in the sub-committees. In Committee I Western delegates had managed to keep discussions going long enough on principles to allow for the thorough examination of all aspects of Basket III. A large number of Western papers had been tabled in Committee III Sub-Committees very much with the object of exploring areas of possible agreement on mutual measures for 'extending and normalising' human contacts. Yet, as Mr. Elliott explained, there was a wide gap between East and West. 'The Communist States', he noted, 'wish to confirm the political and ideological division of Europe; but the expansion of contacts which we are seeking, whatever our intentions (and they deeply distrust them), could have a directly contrary, and perhaps ultimately greater political effect.' While, however, Mr. Elliott thought it unlikely that the West would be out-manoeuvred if they stuck to their guns, he also accepted that the successful conclusion of the Conference according to Western criteria might not be possible, and that the West might have eventually to choose between accepting an unsatisfactory result and assuming responsibility for declaring the Conference a failure (No. 57).

Officials in London appreciated that Western governments would find this choice easier to make than they might have done a year before. The popular euphoria once associated with the CSCE had disappeared, and the public seemed to see the Conference more as a test of Western ability to hold firm on human contacts and information, and less as an indication of government attitudes towards *détente*. Indeed, Sir A. Douglas-Home, felt they could afford to take a strong line on the future of the Conference. 'If it comes to the point', he minuted, 'we should declare it a failure. A phoney result would be worse than useless . . . But having said that we must play for a success & if we can't get it, play for a break which is on the popular ground of human rights. Possibly the right answer would be a public adjournment until the Russians are willing to come along with the rest.' For the moment, however, British officials remained relatively optimistic (No. 58). The West had retained the advantage gained in the MPT, and when the Nine's CSCE Sub-Committee and the Ad Hoc Group met in Bonn during 7-9 January 1974 there were few signs of any fissures. Despite the strong opposition of the Russians to a French draft Declaration of Principles which linked the inviolability of frontiers to a provision for their peaceful change, the Nine agreed to maintain their support for it, and they were united in insisting that it was still premature to consider follow-up (No. 60). Nevertheless, as Mr. Tickell had already pointed out, once drafting began and allies and partners had to distinguish the essential from the less important in the proposals tabled, their cohesion would be severely tested (No. 58).

British diplomats were resolved: (1) that it was essential that the Nine should oppose deadlines or even target dates for the end of Stage II; and (2) that they should not allow drafting to start on 'easy points first' basis where this might leave the Nine *demandeurs* at a later stage in the Conference (No. 60). On both points they soon found themselves at odds with Soviet policy. In a letter delivered to the Prime Minister on 11 January, Mr. L.I. Brezhnev, General Secretary of the Soviet Communist Party, warned Mr. E. Heath that 'unduly prolonging' the CSCE could 'only damage trust and common interest existing between the Soviet Union and Great Britain' (No. 62). And after the Conference reconvened the Russians began pressing for the drafting of preambular introductions for Item III and each of its sub-sections (Nos. 61 and 63). The Prime Minister, in his reply to Mr. Brezhnev, rejected 'both artificial delays and artificial deadlines' (No. 62), and on 6 February agreement was reached in Committee III allowing for the parallel drafting of a covering preamble and substantive provisions (Nos. 63 and 65). Nevertheless, Committee III Sub-Committees were still beset by procedural disputes, and in a paper of 15 March, which he prepared to brief Mr. L.J. Callaghan, Sir A. Douglas-Home's successor in the new Labour Government, Mr. Tickell noted that in Committee III there had 'so far been little to show for six months' detailed work in Geneva'. The Russians and their allies continued to maintain a restrictive interpretation of the Helsinki terms of reference; they sought to avoid detail and commitment on points of most interest to the West; and they were trying to qualify the results of Committee III with a preamble which would include 'wording designed to provide them with an excuse for maintaining their present restrictive practices (and any others they may decide to introduce) and with a pretext for insisting that

Western Governments should control the activities of broadcasting authorities, publishers and the like' (No. 68).

Progress was barely more impressive in Committee I. In the Principles Sub-Committee the texts of only two of the ten principles had been registered by 20 March, and even these were, in the words of Mr. Elliott, 'larded with square brackets' (No. 69). Moreover, continued Soviet resistance to any linkage in the third principle between acceptance of the inviolability of frontiers and provision for their peaceful change had deadlocked further discussion. A compromise proposal involving the registration on a separate sheet of paper of a text on peaceful change and the postponement of a decision on where this should feature in the Declaration seemed likely to win broad support. Both the Americans and the Russians appeared to favour such a solution, and reports from Bonn and Geneva indicated that the West Germans (whose particular interests were most obviously at stake) might be persuaded to adopt the procedure. For tactical reasons the British delegates opposed it. Peaceful change was in their estimate the 'one real bargaining counter' which the West possessed and, once detached from inviolability of frontiers, the West would never be able to reattach it. 'We have', they reported on 26 March, 'urged our partners and allies not to concede an issue of such fundamental importance to the East at this point, when all we shall get in return will be valueless undertakings that progress will follow in Committee III' (No. 70). But, much to Mr. Tickell's regret, other Western delegations were ready to accept a package on this basis and, rather than risk isolation, on 5 April the British acquiesced in the separate and provisional registration of texts (No. 72). Meanwhile, in the Military Sub-Committee the Russians seemed in the opinion of one British official 'to be making almost as much a meal of CBMs as they [were] of Committee III subjects' (No. 74). A British draft resolution on CBMs had been tabled in January (No. 59), and subsequent drafting had resulted in the provisional registering of a mosaic of alternative and square-bracketed proposals. The Russians were, however, determined to exclude as much of their territory as possible from the application of CBMs, and took a similarly minimalist view of both the size of military manoeuvres to be notified and the length of prior notice to be given (No. 74).

Faced by the prospect of the West making little further headway at Geneva, British diplomats reconsidered their negotiating strategy. In a letter of 22 February Mr. Tickell postulated that on present form the results of Stage II were unlikely to justify the summit-level Stage III desired by the Russians to confirm that the CSCE was an 'historic event of great significance in itself'. The alternatives were either a Stage III at foreign-minister level, or a failure to agree on a final stage, with or without some provision for the future resumption of talks. Adoption of the latter course would almost certainly depend upon a Western initiative. Yet, as Mr. Tickell argued, Western governments would then have to demonstrate to their own and neutral public opinion that their aims had been frustrated and that differences could not be overcome, and the 'burden of proof would be a heavy one'. He was, in any case, against trying to define a 'minimal Western position' since it would be difficult to avoid either tying negotiators down to 'unrealistically rigid positions on detail', or setting down fall-back positions to which they would all too quickly retreat (No. 66). Mr. Elliott was of much the same opinion. In a stocktaking telegram of 20 March he contended that, although Soviet tactics were not easy to analyse, the overriding interest of the Russians appeared to be a July summit, and their attitude might reflect a reluctance to make concessions until the latest possible date and a calculation that their June deadline for the end of Stage II would be tacitly accepted by the Conference as a whole and work in their favour. He did not, he added, share the view of some delegates that the West should be ready to ask for a summer break in order to continue the Conference in the autumn. The Conference might then become a 'permanent gathering', and he feared the West could lose the leverage they derived from the Soviet desire for its early conclusion, and that their unity would be menaced by transatlantic tensions and differences amongst the Nine (No. 69).

Western delegations had, however, to reckon that even if they denied the Soviet Union a summit, they would, if they accepted a July Stage III, still have to squeeze the greater part of the CSCE negotiations into barely more than a couple of months. Furthermore, as was to become apparent when the Conference resumed after the Easter break, the East were, despite their having achieved an agreed text on the inviolability of frontiers, not prepared to make any concessions in the sensitive Basket III areas of human contacts and information (No. 76). Much to the frustration of other delegates, the Russians quite flagrantly adopted delaying tactics and on CBMs remained 'uncompromisingly negative' (No. 79). Moreover, Mr. Gromyko, after having blamed the British for being 'more receptive of ideas of slowness', confessed to Sir T. Garvey, Sir J. Killick's successor as British Ambassador in Moscow, that where Item III was concerned he 'sometimes wished that he could cut the bottom out of the Basket and let all the accumulated details in it fall out'. Mr. Elliott, in a speech to the Coordinating Committee on 16 May, made the point that if the deadlock were not broken within the next two weeks there would be little chance of ending the Conference that summer (No. 81). Nevertheless, in the face of Russian intransigence, Western options were limited. As Mr. Elliott explained, it was now easier for the West to expose the Russian position for what it was on CBMs and Basket III, and Western delegates could hope to maintain the support of the neutrals and non-aligned if they showed the maximum flexibility over language and a willingness to drop fringe proposals. He also thought it essential for the West to cling to what 'bargaining counters' they had, including the provisional nature of the agreement on inviolability of frontiers, the level of the third stage, and follow-up (No. 82), though, where the latter was concerned, Mr. Callaghan had already indicated a readiness to take a more positive stance than his Conservative predecessor (No. 80).

On the timing of the final stage Mr. Elliott remained firm. He observed in a telegram of 22 May that he did not believe that a Stage II which lasted beyond July would be in the interest of the West, and that he could see no grounds for thinking that they would receive from the Russians in September what they failed to give in July. The West, he thought, should let it be known that, unless a satisfactory Final Act had been agreed by late July, they would reluctantly have to accept an indefinite recess until the climate improved (No. 82). Neither Mr. Callaghan nor his officials in London were swayed by this argument. Mr. Callaghan doubted if it would be helpful to put public pressure on the East by threatening to break off or suspend the Conference, especially as it 'might easily boomerang', and Mr. Fall thought it would be better to concentrate on how the West could make the best of a resumed Conference in the autumn (No. 84). Yet, as Mr. Elliott had previously implied, further protracted negotiations at Geneva threatened to expose latent divisions within NATO. It had long been feared that at some point one of the allies might 'decide to cut and run' and the United States, which had so far taken the least interest in the CSCE, seemed the most likely candidate (No. 77). At a NATO ministerial meeting at Ottawa during 18-19 June Dr. Kissinger, who since the previous August had been US Secretary of State, denied that the United States wished to accelerate the negotiations, but a joint *communiqué* issued on 3 July at the end of a visit by President Nixon to Moscow announced that he and Mr. Brezhnev favoured an early conclusion of the CSCE and a Stage III at the highest level. Moreover, although Dr. Kissinger subsequently informed the NAC that the United States had no bilateral agreement with the Soviet Union on the CSCE negotiations, he urged the allies to consider what was 'the essential aim of Basket III' and what they could hope to achieve. The allies, he said, 'should stop talking in general terms and get down to drawing up a list of aims . . . that were to be reckoned as attainable' (No. 89).

The American performance in Moscow and Dr. Kissinger's proposal for a review of Western negotiating priorities had a dispiriting effect upon the Nine (No. 91). Mr. Tickell, who was particularly irritated by Dr. Kissinger's assertion that the 'negotiating process in Geneva had become over-bureaucratic, with each individual country promoting its own shopping-list of measures especially under Basket III', still had grave doubts about the wisdom of the West preparing a list of their minimum requirements. On the assumption that such a list would soon leak to the other side, he feared that it risked having two effects: (1) the abandonment of all requirements not included in the list; and (2) a failure to achieve even these minimum requirements since the Russians would regard them as the starting point for further negotiations (No. 89.). Others amongst the Nine disliked a proposal which looked as though it would ignore the interests of the neutrals and non-aligned, and which meant that the West would be setting priorities when they were still unable to assess Soviet positions on a number of important issues which had yet to be examined at Geneva (No. 91). And, although the Nine were ready to engage in a review of Alliance objectives, a process which continued until mid-September, the Americans were impatient for results and irritated by the insistence of their European allies that there must be a point by point examination of the Helsinki Recommendations before any final trade-off and that the West's minimum requirements should not be previously communicated to the Russians (No. 92). Indeed, Mr. Elliott wondered if Dr. Kissinger had really grasped the significance of the Russians having, in effect, accepted that relations between governments and their citizens should be the subject of international discussion. 'To him', Mr. Elliott added, 'it is axiomatic that more liberal practices in the Eastern bloc cannot be induced by direct pressure, but will come about as a natural concomitant of *détente* in inter-Governmental relations.' It seemed, Mr. Tickell suggested, as if Dr. Kissinger did not understand 'the genuinely idealistic element' in the European approach to the CSCE and, like 'his hero Metternich, [wanted] stability and *détente* . . . for their own sakes' (No. 94).

Sir T. Garvey shared some of Dr. Kissinger's doubts about the impact of the Geneva negotiations on domestic developments in the Soviet Union. The machinery of control there he thought so strong that no document signed was likely to improve significantly the access of ordinary Russians to the West. He, nevertheless, agreed with Mr. Elliott that it was not a waste of time to go on 'hammering away at the East in Geneva on the points which [were] proving so sticky'. The West, he presumed, were fighting for a *locus standi* for those within and without the communist East who were trying to promote a 'more normal' flow of information and, however limited might be the immediate results, the position of those involved would thereby be bettered (No. 95). But by the end of July, when the Conference adjourned for a six-week summer break, the Declaration of Principles was not yet half complete, and the Russians seemed determined to postpone any significant concessions on CBMs until the negotiations were nearer to their end. Meanwhile, in Basket III, they and their allies had maintained their tactic of proposing restrictive preambular passages aimed at depriving the operative ones of all practical significance. Even after the East's acceptance of a neutral compromise package, which provided for the incorporation in Basket III's preamble of a general reference to the Declaration of Principles and a guarantee that the latter would include an assurance that all countries would respect the rights of others to decide their own political order, Mr. Elliott thought the outlook far from certain. 'The autumn', he observed, 'will show whether we have achieved a break-through or have merely transferred the battle on this central issue to other ground' (Nos. 93 and 94).

Hesitation rather than impasse

In September 1974 Mr. D.H.T. Hildyard, the UK Permanent Representative to the Office of the UN at Geneva, formally succeeded Mr. Elliott as Head of Delegation to the CSCE. He was far from optimistic about the prospect of bringing the Conference to an early and successful conclusion. 'There is', he noted on 12 September, 'a widespread hope but no general expectation that Stage II will be completed by Christmas.' The Russians evidently wished to avoid giving the impression that they were under any time pressure, and during the early autumn little or no progress was made towards settling those Basket I and III issues in which the West were interested. Indeed, it seemed to representatives of the Nine as if the East, encouraged by Western initiatives to accelerate work and the efforts of the Americans to persuade their allies 'to set their sights lower and "more realistically"', were concentrating upon testing the unity and determination of the West. The Russians might also try to exploit the frustration felt by neutral and non-aligned delegations over the slow pace of negotiations (No. 97). This, in the opinion of the FCO, made it all the more important to achieve a 'clear demonstration of Western cohesion', and to ensure that neutral initiatives were 'steered in the right direction'. Fortunately, from the point of view of the Nine, the Americans were ready to acquiesce in European demands for a first reading of Basket III texts. Dr. Kissinger, while still arguing that the West should work out a common position for presentation to the Russians, assured Mr. Callaghan on 26 September that he did not want 'accusations from the Europeans that they were being "raped" by the Americans', and a week later US delegates joined their European colleagues in the Coordinating Committee in what Mr. Hildyard described as 'an impressive display of Western resolve' (No. 98).

The readiness of the Americans to join with the Nine in pressing for a first reading, in the sense of a first drafting, in each sector, may, as Mr. Hildyard supposed, have persuaded the Russians that 'they would have to go along with this procedure' (No. 105). Certainly, during the first fortnight of October some 'substantive progress' was made in Basket III Sub-Committees, and neutral and non-aligned delegations began work on a further package deal covering all five elements of human contacts (No. 101). But the Russians soon lowered the boom again and, by 2 November, Mr. Hildyard had 'little progress to report', though he added that the atmosphere was 'one of hesitation rather than impasse'. Western and neutral delegations were uncertain about the East's willingness to move, and such evidence as there was suggested that the Russians were looking for a way forward but had not yet made up there minds how to proceed (No. 102). Another explanation, one that had already occurred to Mr. Bullard, was that the Russians 'might be seeking to establish a link between the CSCE and MBFR, and calculating that Western eagerness for results in the second would make [them] ready for concessions in the first' (No. 99). The Russians had previously hinted that the prospects for MBFR might be improved by a satisfactory conclusion of the CSCE, and Mr. Tickell thought that they reckoned on using the American desire for progress at Vienna in order 'to persuade the all-too-easily persuadable Dr. Kissinger' of the need to make haste at Geneva. The US representative to the North Atlantic Council (NAC) even suggested that the Alliance consider 'reversing this link', and that the West might argue that there could be no satisfactory conclusion of the CSCE unless Warsaw Pact delegations in Vienna were prepared to move from the rigid positions they had adopted there. But there was little support in either Brussels or London for a strategy which threatened to divide the Alliance and alienate the neutrals, and on 27 November the NAC were informed that Washington had 'no predisposition in favour of any form of reverse linkage'. Discussion of the issue, nevertheless, served to highlight the importance of maintaining allied unity and the value of what Mr. Tickell termed the 'one major asset' the West possessed—'Soviet interest in the development of the US/Soviet relationship' (No. 100).

It was also still necessary to take account of public opinion in the West. After his return from a fortnight's visit to Geneva, Mr. Fall, in a minute of 11 November, suggested two radical alternatives to the policies presently being pursued there: the West could propose Stage II's interruption until 'conditions improved', or they could 'try to get it over with as quickly as possible on terms which would be readily acceptable to the East'. Yet, he saw no cause for pursuing either. 'The fact of the matter', he observed, 'is that we are not in a situation where the West can be convincingly represented as holding up the conclusion of the second stage.' East/West differences over Basket III issues and CBMs remained unresolved, but it was the particular concerns of the neutral and non-aligned delegations which were delaying consideration of the last three principles in Basket I and, as was generally accepted, the Conference could move no faster than the drafting of the Declaration of Principles (No. 103). Indeed, there seemed no good reason to suppose that there would be anything to be gained from the West abandoning the line it had assumed in September. Given the scale and composition of the Conference, the West had, in Mr. Tickell's words, 'to proceed carefully across a broad front registering agreements where possible and working on the principle of the coral reef rather than the prefabricated house'. FCO officials recognised that the results of the Conference would fall short of original Western requirements, but by the close of 1974 it also seemed likely that they would exceed the most optimistic expectations of a few years before. The CSCE, which had once been considered by the West an 'exercise in damage limitation', was now focused upon issues which both the Western and neutral participants regarded as important factors in *détente*. Texts on family reunification and marriage would not change the rules in force in Eastern Europe, but they might lead to their more flexible application, and could provide a useful point of leverage for Western governments wishing to take up individual cases. And, though it might not be possible to deal with radio jamming or make all the Western press accessible to Soviet readers, the arrangements being worked out on the dissemination of information might allow Western governments to intervene. on behalf of broadcasters and publishers (No. 104).

The British felt themselves in a good position to play an active part in working for acceptable compromises. 'We', noted an FCO briefing paper of 27 November, 'have a major asset in that we are free from the commitment to individual hobby horses which distorts the perspective of a number of participants; and we are therefore able to take the overall view' (*ibid.*). Other NATO delegations were, like the British, anxious to speed-up the momentum of the Conference. But while the Dutch and the Italians remained hardliners and the West Germans could be erratic and inflexible, the French, whose clear thinking and efficacy Mr. Hildyard admired and with whom he favoured forming a 'ginger group', were inclined to intrigue (No. 105). A visit by Mr. Brezhnev to Paris in early December appears to have allowed them the opportunity to settle secretly with the Russians the terms a new mini-preamble for the human contacts section of Basket III. The resulting text, which the French persuaded the Austrians to table, was coolly received by France's partners and allies. They judged it unduly restrictive and, as the Russians resisted amendment, the autumn session ended in disappointment and deadlock in the Human Contacts Sub-Committee. Nevertheless, Mr. Hildyard still thought it might be worthwhile the British taking the initiative in bilaterals with the Russians. The British had thus far 'not lost credibility', and the fact that Mr. Callaghan and the Prime Minister, Mr. H. Wilson, were due to visit Moscow in February 1975 made it increasingly possible that the Russians would seek to use them as interlocutors. If they were 'considerably more frank and willing to take the views of other into account' than the French had been, then Mr. Hildyard believed the British might be able to make a 'substantial and constructive contribution'. Other officials were more worried by the attendant risks. Sir J. Killick, who was now Deputy Under-Secretary in the FCO, thought it unwise for HMG to take any such initiative, especially as the Russians would use it 'to divisive effect in Geneva' and judge the UK 'a potentially soft touch and raise their price accordingly' (No. 107).

The Soviet intent may, as Mr. Callaghan surmised, have been to use the Moscow visit to bring the British into line with the position of other Western countries (No. 113). In other respects it was probably of somewhat less significance for the CSCE. The British Ministers assured their Soviet hosts that they favoured a summit in the summer and that agreement on CBMs would be 'essentially voluntary in character'. And, after Mr. Gromyko had reiterated the familiar Russian case on the special significance of agreement on the inviolability of frontiers and the location of any reference to their peaceful change, Mr. Wilson confessed 'that he was an amateur on these matters, and that the discussion had been very educational for him' (No. 112). Mr. Tickell, who accompanied Mr. Callaghan to Moscow, nevertheless, felt the Russians to be 'in more of a hurry to complete the CSCE than they generally liked to admit', and he correctly predicted that 'the next few months might be less of a slogging match and more of a war of movement than people . . . seemed to expect' (No. 113). Within a month the Russians moved on two issues which were generally considered the most important and difficult in the CSCE, notably the peaceful change of frontiers and CBMs. The Americans succeeded in winning Soviet acceptance of a German-approved text on peaceful change for insertion in Principle I (No. 114). Then, on 13 March, Mr. A.G. Kovalev, the Soviet Head of Delegation, appeared to suggest that the USSR would accept prior notification of manoeuvres to all participants, that this should cover national and multinational manoeuvres, and that it should be on a voluntary basis (No. 115). Only in Basket III did the Conference mark time with the Russians seeming to have renewed difficulties with their allies over how best to reflect

Western and neutral demands for clear commitments to improving the lot of the individual in the field of human contacts and information. Yet, as the recently-knighted Sir D. Hildyard explained, the Russians had vowed so often that they could 'never consent' that if they ever reached 'any genuinely final positions' when the West were hoping for more it would not be easy to 'distinguish the signals' (No. 117).

The West's bargaining position was improved by the apparent desire of Mr. Brezhnev to bring the negotiations to an early conclusion. On 8 March he wrote to Mr. Wilson proposing that the 'final stage of the Conference at the highest level' should open on 30 June (No. 115). His message, which was also sent to other Western leaders, once more put the Soviet delegation in what Mr. Tickell described as 'the invidious position of working against a self-imposed deadline' (No. 117). Soviet tactics seemed, he thought, to fit a 'classic pattern', that of seeking to generate irresistible momentum towards an early Stage III summit whilst reducing the outstanding number of issues to which they attached real importance in the hope of forcing a showdown in which it would be the Western and neutral delegations which had to sacrifice essential objectives, especially in Basket III (No. 118). The Russians were indeed clearly reluctant to make any concessions of substance in Basket III for fear, Sir D. Hildyard supposed, that these might be simply swallowed up by the West and doubt cast upon Soviet resolve in other sectors. In these circumstances Mr. M. Alexander of the UK delegation recommended that the West adopt a new strategy. He thought that for the time being they should continue to take a hardline on Basket III issues, but that they should try to capitalise on the Soviet desire for a July summit and consider offering the East the option of a 'global solution' to outstanding problems relating to human contacts and information. Texts, he suggested, should be supplied to Mr. Y.V. Dubinin, senior Soviet delegate in Committee III, as a single document, and he should be informed that this would be withdrawn in its entirety if Soviet demands for amendment were regarded as excessive (No. 119). But the West's adoption of this approach was delayed by the Dutch, who were reluctant to offer any concessions before a final trade-off, and it was not until 15 May that a package on the lines suggested by Mr. Alexander was put to the Russians (Nos. 120-122).

The Soviet reply, delivered on 21 and 22 May, was judged 'highly unsatisfactory' by most of the Nine. While the Russians accepted the Western preamble on human contacts with its emphasis on humanitarian considerations, they adopted a far more negative attitude towards the text on travel and rejected the extension of rights granted to journalists to their technical staff. Mr. Alexander nevertheless regarded their response as evidence of a 'real effort' on their part to 'move'. It turned out to be the prelude to a rather disorderly retreat. Impressed, perhaps, by the unity of the West and possibly concerned about the outcome of an impending NATO summit, on 28 May the Soviet delegation signalled their readiness to withdraw over a third of their proposed amendments. They seemed, according to Mr. Alexander, 'to be firmly on the hook' (No. 123), and the following week witnessed remarkable progress in settling outstanding problems in Basket III. The Russians abandoned the pretence that they were not under any time pressure and urged upon all occasions that the tempo of work be speeded up. On 6 June Mr. Kovalev produced in the CBMs Sub-Committee three combinations of area and troop threshold parameters for the prior notification of manoeuvres, and there was every indication that the Russians wanted to begin serious negotiations in Basket II. Mr. Alexander found it 'hard to believe that anything other than an almost desperate Russian wish to have the Summit in July would have led them to make such abrupt concessions' (No. 124).

There were, however, still serious obstacles to overcome before a date could be set for Stage III. Agreement had yet to be reached on the parameters for the prior notification of military manoeuvres on Soviet territory. This for the British was almost as much an intra-allied, as an East/West, issue, for having agreed to take the lead amongst the Western delegations in negotiating on CBMs, they found themselves exposed to Soviet criticism when Dr. Kissinger unexpectedly indicated US readiness to accept parameters which undercut those previously agreed in NATO. Mr. Callaghan rightly dismissed the Soviet Ambassador's complaints that the British were being uncooperative and delaying agreement as 'complete rubbish': HMG, he explained, had to carry their friends and allies with them and could not order them what to do. Already on 16 June Sir D. Hildyard had reported that the Dutch had 'bolted' and made it clear that they could not be counted to go along with CBMs on a voluntary basis (No. 126). It took another two weeks before the Nine and Fifteen could be shepherded back into line, and a compromise arranged which involved German concessions on area parameters and the Soviet acceptance of a lower troop threshold than that they had originally demanded. Even then final agreement on CBMs was complicated by the Turks, who, like the Russians, had frontiers with non-participating states in Asia. They evidently wished to exclude the greater part of Anatolia from the provisions of the agreement, including those bases from which they had, in the previous year, launched their invasion of Cyprus. The delegations of other Mediterranean countries, including Cyprus, protested, and it was not until the early hours of 19 July, after a fifteen-hour negotiating marathon, that a formula was at last found which in effect applied to Turkey the same kilometric exclusion limits as had been accepted by the Soviet Union, but stated that notification need not be given in those areas contiguous to a non-participating state (Nos. 127, 129, 133 and 134).

Amongst the other matters which remained for settlement during the first fortnight of July was a suitable Basket I text which would safeguard the quadripartite rights and responsibilities of Britain, France, the USA and USSR in Germany, but which would neither refer specifically to Germany, nor seem to provide cover for the evasion of other undertakings. A solution was finally achieved on 6 July, but only in the wake of a good deal of legalistic wrangling which, at one stage, left the four occupying powers ranged against an ill-assorted coalition of Romania, some Western allies, and the neutrals and non-aligned (Nos. 120, 129 and 130). Equally difficult to draft were follow-up texts concerning possible further meetings of senior officials, and Basket II provisions relating to reciprocity. The former were of particular interest to the British who, for the previous eighteen months, had been urging their partners and allies, including a somewhat reluctant France, to assume a more constructive approach to continuing the multilateral process (No. 116). But the draft agreed in the Follow-up Working Group on 9 July hardly appeared to meet Western requirements that follow-up should be conditional on the effective implementation of Conference decisions. It committed a ministerial review conference, planned for 1977, to defining the 'appropriate modalities for the holding of other meetings', and thereby implied that these would take place. 'In the final stage of negotiations', one British delegate recalled, 'the lack of realism, failure to identify objectives precisely, and tactical ineptitude of the West's laggards, the Dutch, the Belgians and above all the French, denied the Alliance a final result which would have been more satisfactory than the compromise which actually emerged' (No. 131). Basket II negotiations were also beset by intra-allied differences, especially when the Americans perceived that the Nine might be prepared to drop any link between MFN treatment and reciprocity in return for a relatively strong definition of the latter. Pressure of time seems, however, to have worked in Western favour, and on 17 July formulae were provisionally accepted giving recognition in the operative part of the commercial exchanges section to the value of MFN treatment, and back-referencing this to a preambular commitment to reciprocity (No. 135).

Three days earlier, on 14 July, the Coordinating Committee had agreed to invite the Finns to begin preparations for the opening of Stage III at Helsinki on the 30th. But this decision was only reached after the Maltese had once more demonstrated the diplomatic leverage derived by even the smallest of states by the application of the consensus rule. Already in the previous summer, after the West Germans had succeeded in persuading the Americans to put aside their misgivings about a process which seemed likely to impinge on Dr. Kissinger's Middle Eastern diplomacy, a Working Group had been established to prepare a Mediterranean Declaration (Nos. 75, 81 and 90). Mr. Mintoff was determined to make the most of this opportunity, and he sought to broaden the scope of this document so as to incorporate in it his own proposals for a Euro/Arab federation and the withdrawal of the Soviet and US navies from the Mediterranean. He also hoped to extract from the Conference a commitment to promote peace in the Middle East. In these respects the draft Declaration which emerged from the Working Group clearly failed to meet his requirements and, on 9 July, the Maltese made it quite plain that they would block further progress in the CSCE until they received satisfaction. A compromise was offered, but the Maltese would not be hurried, and during the afternoon and evening of 10 July all the other delegates were left to 'sit around in increasing rage and humiliation' before learning that Mr. Mintoff was 'in bed with a slight fever, and could not discuss the question until he had held further consultations'. Mr. Kovalev vowed revenge and, according to Sir D. Hildyard, the Finnish delegate, Mr. J. Iloniemi, 'only just managed to restrain himself from hitting the Maltese Ambassador'. Nevertheless, the Conference had in the end to accept a Mediterranean Declaration which spoke of lessening tension in the area and 'reducing the armed forces in the region' (Nos. 129, 130 and 132).

The final meeting of the Coordinating Committee on 20 July was, if not as farcical, almost certainly as ill-tempered an occasion. After a prolonged debate it was eventually decided that the follow-up conference would assemble in Belgrade. Turkish and Cypriot representatives then clashed over the composition of the Cyprus delegation to Stage III, and before the meeting broke up at 03.40 on the morning of 21 July the Romanians and the Russians engaged in an undignified argument over the motion of thanks to be addressed to the Finns, the Swiss and the Yugoslavs. 'By the time that this wrangle was finished', Sir D. Hildyard observed, 'everyone had had enough and the Conference ended abruptly without any of the gestures of friendship or the plethora of congratulatory speeches which we had all expected' (No. 136).

Stage III and after

The three-day summit, which opened in Helsinki on 30 July, was a far more orderly affair than the discussions which had preceded it in Geneva. Mr. Mintoff was, despite his recent diplomatic triumph, the one notable absentee from an assembly which Mr. Elliott described as 'the only European Summit Conference of this century' (No. 139). Since the major decisions had already been taken and documents drafted, Conference sessions consisted in the main of set speeches from Heads of Government. Mr. Wilson, who spoke first, pointed out that *détente* meant little if it was 'not reflected in the daily lives of our peoples' and, he continued, there was no reason why in 1975 'Europeans should not be allowed to marry whom they want, hear and read what they want, travel abroad when and where they want, meet whom they want'. The Prime Minister's words encapsulated a vision of *détente* which was shared by the leaders of other West European countries. But during the bilateral meetings that took place at Helsinki continuing ideological differences and rivalries soon surfaced. When Mr. Wilson met Mr. Brezhnev on 1 August he impressed on the Soviet leader his anxiety over recent developments in Portugal. The revolutionary events which had followed the collapse of Dr. M. Caetano's dictatorship in 1974 and the fears of some Western observers that they were about to witness a communist takeover in Lisbon raised the spectre of possible Soviet involvement. Ironically, at the time of the signing of a Final Act, whose terms seemed to imply the general acceptance of the political *status quo* in Europe, political instability in the most westerly region of the continent threatened to become a fresh source of tension in East/West relations. 'One test of *détente*', Mr. Wilson informed Mr. Brezhnev, 'was the position of Portugal' (No. 138). His warning was pertinent for, although communism in Portugal was soon in retreat, the collapse of the Portuguese empire in Africa and the civil strife which followed in Angola did much to sour relations between the superpowers, and seemed destined to open a new front in a continuing Cold War.

British diplomats were indeed already beginning to wonder what, if anything, had changed in relations with the Soviet Union. In a letter of 12 August Sir J. Killick speculated on whether the Cold War was over, or whether it had 'only taken a new shape'. He feared that it would 'still involve a great deal of time and effort on the part of a number of Whitehall Departments . . . before [they found] out' (No. 135). A month later, in a despatch of 9 September, Sir T. Garvey emphasised that for the Russians the key importance of the Helsinki Final Act lay in the multilateral acceptance of frontiers and the political *status quo*. The Act's non-binding character and its reservation on the peaceful change of frontiers would not, he thought, prevent the Soviet Union from interpreting Western signatures as confirmation that NATO would not try to set back the map of Europe. 'Moscow', he added, 'intends that note should be taken of this in Eastern Europe in case anyone there had hoped for change.' As a result of Helsinki the Soviet Government had gained an international success useful for internal propaganda, and a quarry of texts to use against those whom they classed 'enemies of *détente*' in the West. Nevertheless, Sir T. Garvey also recognised that the Russians had been forced to pay a price, and that for them it was a 'major setback' even to have to discuss some of the humanitarian subjects in Basket III. The implementation of the human contacts and information provisions were likely to place new strains on relations between the USSR and some of its more liberal allies, and the follow-up conference in 1977 would allow the West to focus upon these issues. In any event, Western governments now had their *locus standi* for pressing for practical changes in the Communist East. 'Mishandled by the West', Sir T. Garvey reasoned, 'the pursuit of *détente* could lead to a Soviet walkover in Europe. But if Western countries continue, negotiation by negotiation, to stick together, to keep their guard up and to settle for nothing less than a fair balance of concrete advantage, they need not shrink from it' (No. 141). *Détente* still had much to offer even if, as Mr. Walden had earlier remarked on the MPT, it sometimes seemed like the 'continuation of Cold War by other, more subtle means' (No. 37).

Acknowledgements

In accordance with the Parliamentary announcement, cited in the Introduction to the Series, the Editors have had the customary freedom in the selection and arrangement of documents including full access to all classes of FCO documentation. There have, in the case of the present volume, been no exceptional cases, provided for in the Parliamentary announcement, where it has been necessary on security grounds to restrict the availability of particular documents, editorially selected in accordance with regular practice.

The main source of documentation in this volume has been the archives of the FCO held, pending their transfer to the Public Record Office, by the Records Management Services of the Library and Records Department, and I should like to thank the RMS staff for responding so expeditiously to all our numerous requests. I am also grateful to the Historical and Records Section of the Cabinet Office and the Public Records Officer at No. 10 Downing Street for their permission to cite documents in their custody; to the former Head of the FCO's Library and Records Department, Mr. Ian Soutar, and the Head of Records and Historical Services, Mrs Heather Yasamee, and their staff for their help and support in the preparation of this volume; to Research Analysts, Mr. Paul Bentall and Ms. Sally Morphet, for their valuable comments upon the typescript; and to my colleagues, Mrs Diane Morrish and Miss Elaine Flynn, for their secretarial assistance. To my Assistant Editor, Dr. Isabel Warner, and my Research Assistant, Mr. Gregory Quinn, B.Sc.Econ., I am particularly indebted for their hard work, patience and resilience. Special thanks are likewise due to the Head of Historians, Ms. Gill Bennett, M.A. who, despite other competing and heavy demands upon her time, has always been ready to offer advice and guidance.

KEITH A. HAMILTON

August 1997

CONTENTS

PAGES

CHAPTER I   Multilateral Preparatory Talks,   I
1972-3

CHAPTER II   The Long Haul, 1973-4   152

CHAPTER III   Concluding Stage II, 1974-5   327

CHAPTER IV   Stage III, 1975   461

APPENDICES   480

INDEX   493

LIST OF PLATES

Sir Alec Douglas-Home.
Supplied from FCO photographic collection

(*a*) Mr. (later Sir) Charles Wiggin; (*b*) Mr. (later Sir) Crispin Tickell; (*c*) Mr. Anthony Elliott; (*d*) Sir David Hildyard.
Supplied from FCO photographic collection

(*a*) Sir Terence Garvey; (*b*) Miss (later Dame) Anne Warburton; (*c*) Mr. Peter Maxey; (*d*) Mr. (later Sir) Michael Alexander.
Supplied from FCO photographic collection

President G. Ford, Mr. H. Wilson, Dr. H. Kissinger and Mr. L.J. Callaghan at Helsinki on the moring of 30 July 1975.
Reproduced by permission of the Associated Press

ABBREVIATIONS FOR PRINTED SOURCES

Annual Register	H.V. Hodson (ed.), *The Annual Register. World Events in 1973*, vol. 215, (London: Longman, 1974).
Cmnd. 1552	*Selected Documents on Germany and the Question of Berlin 1944-1961* (London: HMSO, 1961).
Cmnd. 4675	*Agreement between the Government of the United Kingdom of Great Britain and Northern Ireland and the Government of the Union of Soviet Socialist Republics on Relations in the Scientific, Educational and Cultural Fields for 1971-73* (London: HMSO, 1971).
Cmnd. 6201	*Selected Documents on Germany and the Question of Berlin 1961-1973* (London: HMSO, 1975).
Cmnd. 6932	*Selected Documents Relating to Problems of Security and Cooperation in Europe 1954-77* (London: HMSO, 1977).
Human Rights	I.I. Kavass, J.P. Granier & M.F. Dominick (eds.), *Human Rights, European Politics, and the Helsinki Accord: The Documentary Evolution of the Conference on Security and Co-operation in Europe 1973-1975*, 6 vols. (Buffalo: William S. Hein & Co., 1981).
Kissinger	H. Kissinger, *Years of Upheaval* (London: Weidenfeld & Nicolson, 1982).
Parl. Debs., 5th ser., H. of C	*Parliamentary Debates (Hansard), Fifth Series, House of Commons, Official Report* (London, 1909f.).
Public Papers	*Public Papers of the Presidents of the United States. Richard Nixon, 1971-1974* (Washington: GPO, 1972, 1974 & 1975).
Series III, Vol. I	*Documents on British Policy Overseas*, Series III, Volume I, 'Britain and the Soviet Union, 1968-72', (London: TSO, 1997).
UNGA, A/PV, No. 1301	*Records of the 19th Session of the United Nations General Assembly* (New York: 1964).

ABBREVIATED DESIGNATIONS

AFP/AP	Associated Foreign Press	
BBC	British Broadcasting Corporation	
CBMs	Confidence Building Measures	
CCP	Common Commercial Policy	
CDU	*Christlich Demokratische Union* /Christian Democratic Union (FRG)	
CED	Cultural Exchange Department, FCO	
COREPER	*Comité des Représentants Permanents* /Committee of Permanent Representatives, EC	
Coreu	EC telegraphic correspondence	
CRD	Cultural Relations Department, FCO	
CSU	*Christlich Soziale Union/* Christian Social Union (FRG)	
CMEA/ COMECON	Council for Mutual Economic Assistance	
CPSU	Communist Party of the Soviet Union	
CSCE/CES	Conference on Security and Cooperation in Europe	
DDR	*Deutsche Demokratische Republik*	
DTI	Department of Trade and Industry	
EC	European Community/ Communities	
ECE	Economic Commission for Europe	
EEC	European Economic Community	
EESD	Eastern European and Soviet Department, FCO	
EID	European Integration Department, FCO	
EPC	European Political Co-operation	
FCO	Foreign & Commonwealth Office	
FDP	*Freie Demokratische Partei /* Free Democratic Party (FRG)	
FRG	Federal Republic of Germany	
GATT	General Agreement on Tariffs and Trade	
GDR	German Democratic Republic	
GIPD	Guidance and Information Policy Department, FCO	
HMG	Her Majesty's Government	
IRD	Information Research Department, FCO	
KGB	*Komitet Gosudarstvennoi Besopasnosti*	
MAC	Mutually Acceptable Conditions	
MBFR	Mutual and Balanced Force Reductions	
MFA	Ministry of Foreign Affairs	
MFN	Most Favoured Nation	
MIFT	My Immediately Following Telegram	
MIPT	My Immediately Preceding Telegram	
MPT	Multilateral Preparatory Talks	
NAC	North Atlantic Council	
NAD	North America Department, FCO	
NATO	North Atlantic Treaty Organisation	
NNA	Neutral and Non-Aligned	
OECD	Organisation for Economic Co-operation and Development	

OPEC	Organisation of Petroleum Exporting Countries
PCF	Peaceful Change of Frontiers
PUS	Permanent Under-Secretary
PUSD	Permanent Under-Secretary's Department, FCO
QRs	Quantitative Restrictions
QRR	Quadripartite Rights and Responsibilities
RFE	Radio Free Europe
SALT	Strategic Arms Limitation Talks/Treaty
SCEWR	Standing Committee on East-West Relations
SPC	Senior Political Committee (NATO)
SPD	*Sozialdemokratische Partei Deutschlands*/German Social Democratic Party (FRG)
SWB	Special Working Body
TRED	Trade Relations and Exports Department, FCO
TUR	Telegram Under Reference
UKDEL	United Kingdom Delegation
UKMIS	United Kingdom Mission
UN	United Nations
UNESCO	United Nations Educational, Scientific and Cultural Organisation
VOA	Voice of America
WED	Western European Department, FCO
WOD	Western Organisations Department, FCO

CHAPTER SUMMARIES

CHAPTER I

Multilateral Preparatory Talks
25 February 1972 - 27 June 1973

	NAME	DATE	MAIN SUBJECT	PAGE
1	Draft FCO Position Paper	Feb.	CSCE: The Next Phase. Outlines role UK might play in preparing Conference.	1
2	Mr. Tickell Foreign & Commonwealth Office	6 Mar.	Minute to Mr. Wiggin on Western defence policy and European security.	15
3	Mr. Wiggin Foreign & Commonwealth Office	14 Mar.	Minute to Sir T. Brimelow comments on No. 1: 'Conference is (probably) inevitable rather than desirable, and our primary aim defensive'.	18
4	Sir J. Killick Moscow Tel. No. 362	15 Mar.	Reports conversation with Mr. Lunkov on preparations for CSCE.	21
5	FCO Paper	20 Mar.	East European attitudes to CSCE.	24
6	To Mr. Butler Washington	27 Mar.	Letter from Mr. Tickell discusses European and American views on CSCE.	34
7	Mr. Thomson UKDEL NATO	5 Apr.	Letter to Sir T. Brimelow suggests how to put UK views on CSCE/MBFR in NATO.	37
8	To Mr. Allan Luxembourg	25 Apr.	Letter from Mr. Braithwaite describes national positions on CSCE within NATO.	40
9	Mr. Tickell Foreign & Commonwealth Office	23 May	Discusses link between Security Conference and MBFR.	43
10	To Sir G. Millard Stockholm	6 Jun.	Letter from Mr. Tickell on coordination with the neutrals.	46
11	To Mr. Staples UKDEL NATO	4 Aug.	Letter from Mr. Walden sets out UK approach on cultural aspects of CSCE.	50

	NAME	DATE	MAIN SUBJECT	PAGE
12	SIR T. BRIMELOW Foreign & Commonwealth Office	14 Aug.	Minute to Mr. Wiggin reports talk with Dr. Kissinger on CSCE, MBFR and SALT.	56
13	MR. TICKELL Foreign & Commonwealth Office	20 Sept.	Minute to Private Secretary outlines position on CSCE and MBFR.	58
14	To SIR J. KILLICK Moscow	29 Sept.	Letter from Sir T. Brimelow on Soviet approach to CSCE.	61
15	SIR E. PECK UKDEL NATO	17 Oct.	Discusses political consultation among the Nine and the Fifteen.	62
16	To SIR E. PECK UKDEL NATO Tel. No. 355	9 Nov.	Sir A. Douglas-Home comments on administrative arrangements for CSCE.	70
17	DRAFT BRIEF FOR UKDEL To MPT	13 Nov.	CSCE.	73
18	To MR. STAPLES UKDEL NATO	24 Nov.	Letter from Mr. Brown outlines position on cultural and human relations at onset of MPT.	81
19	MR. TICKELL Foreign & Commonwealth Office	21 Dec.	Suggests points for discussion with partners before resumption of MPT on 15 Jan.	84
20	MR. TICKELL Foreign & Commonwealth Office	1973 25 Jan.	Takes stock of MPT ten days into second session.	87
21	MR. ELLIOTT Helsinki Tel. No. 147	10 Feb.	Summary of position reached at end of second session of MPT.	91
22	MR. ELLIOTT Helsinki Tel. No. 149	10 Feb.	Recommends drafting in working groups to start from 'bottom up' rather than with 'easy points', as favoured by Russians, when talks resume.	94
23	MR. ELLIOTT Helsinki Tel. No. 184	28 Feb.	Reports setting up of open-ended Working Group for Basket I.	98
24	To LORD CROMER Washington	8 Mar.	Letter from Sir T. Brimelow with FCO reactions to Soviet draft 'General Declaration'.	99
25	MR. GRAHAM Washington	12 Mar.	Letter to Mr. Bullard comments on US attitude: CSCE is viewed as unimportant in the overall scheme of things.	102

	NAME	DATE	MAIN SUBJECT	PAGE
26	Mr. Elliott Helsinki Tel. No. 1 to Brussels	14 Mar.	Summary of position reached mid-way through third session; reports Russian acceptance of 'bottom up' approach.	104
27	Mr. Brown Foreign & Commonwealth Office	20 Mar.	Discusses Russian desire to list 'inviolability of frontiers' as an independent principle.	106
28	Mr. Tickell Foreign & Commonwealth Office	22 Mar.	Considers advantages and disadvantages of Soviet demand for creation of permanent machinery to follow the CSCE.	108
29	To Mr. Elliott Helsinki Tel. No. 178	28 Mar.	Guidance on UK tactics at MPT.	114
30	Mr. Elliott Helsinki Tel. No. 361	7 Apr.	Reports results of third session and considers general approach to next round, including outline of a possible bargain to be indicated to Russians before talks resume.	116
31	Mr. Walden Foreign & Commonwealth Office	16 Apr.	Minute to Mr. Tickell considers Western tactics on Human Contacts and warns that end product on Basket III could be 'embarrassingly thin'.	120
32	Mr. Elliott Helsinki Tel. No. 434	5 May	Reports on opening of fourth session; growing readiness to assume the Conference will begin end June/early July.	121
33	Mr. Elliott Helsinki Tel. No. 2 to Brussels	13 May	Briefing on progress in Helsinki for Mr. Wiggin's use at Political Directors' meeting.	123
34	Mr. Elliott Helsinki Tel. No. 495	19 May	Comments on momentum of MPT and date/site of CSCE.	128
35	Mr. Elliott Helsinki Tel. No. 522	23 May	Elaboration of the 10 Principles.	131
36	Mr. Gordon Foreign & Commonwealth Office	24 May	Minute to Mr. Fretwell summarising state of play in Basket II discussions.	133
37	Mr. Elliott Helsinki	13 June	CSCE: The First 200 Days. Analyses results of the MPT.	136

NAME	DATE	MAIN SUBJECT	PAGE
38 Sir J. Killick Moscow	27 June	Letter to Mr. Tickell comments on No. 37 with particular reference to the Soviet Union.	146

CHAPTER II

The Long Haul
25 June 1973 - 29 July 1974

NAME	DATE	MAIN SUBJECT	PAGE
39 To Sir J. Beith Brussels Tel. No. 152	25 June	Reports that meeting of CSCE Sub-Committee of the Nine to prepare for Stage I made good progress.	152
40 Mr. Bullard Helsinki	5 July	Letter to Mr. Wiggin assesses Soviet attitude to CSCE: Russians seem to have decided they 'may have lost a battle (the MPT)', but not the war.	157
41 Mr. Elliott Helsinki Tel. No. 742	8 July	Stage I: Mediterranean aspect.	160
42 Mr. Elliott Helsinki	16 July	Reflects on implications of Stage I for Stage II of CSCE.	163
43 To Mr. Stark Copenhagen Tel. No. 171	23 July	UK paper on organisation of Stage II.	168
44 Miss Warburton UKMIS Geneva Tel. No. 377	3 Sept.	Meeting of the Coordinating Committee, 29 Aug.-3 Sept.	173
45 Sir J. Killick Moscow Tel. No. 1014	5 Sept.	Considers timing of Soviet campaign against dissidents: relaxation of international tension 'need not and will not be accompanied by relaxation at home or by ideological _détente_'.	176
46 Steering Brief For UKDEL To Stage II of CSCE	13 Sept.	Sets out HMG's general strategy for Stage II.	179
47 To Mr. Hildyard UKMIS Geneva Tel. No. 264	20 Sept.	Basket III.	187
48 Mr. Hildyard UKMIS Geneva Tel. No. 417	29 Sept.	Reviews situation on eve of 1 Oct. meeting of Coordinating Committee.	188

NAME	DATE	MAIN SUBJECT	PAGE
49 To Mr. Hildyard UKMIS Geneva Tel. No. 279	5 Oct.	Advocates adoption of procedural arrangements which preserve right degree of 'parallelism' between work in Baskets I and III.	191
50 Mr. Hildyard UKMIS Geneva Tel. No. 441	9 Oct.	Briefing on CSCE/EEC for Political Directors' meeting (11-12 Oct.); considers Community competence and Commission participation in Basket II.	193
51 Miss Warburton UKMIS Geneva Tel. No. 496	20 Oct.	Despite 'uncertain personal calibre of some of our colleagues', West's performance has generally been satisfactory.	195
52 Mr. Fall Foreign & Commonwealth Office	25 Oct.	Minute to Mr. Tickell records impressions of visit to Geneva.	198
53 Mr. Hildyard UKMIS Geneva Tel. No. 560	8 Nov.	Up-date for Political Directors' meeting (12-13 Nov.) on work in Baskets I, II and III.	201
54 Mr. Hildyard UKMIS Geneva Tel. No. 596	17 Nov.	Comments on Eastern attitude to pace of work at the Conference.	204
55 Mr. Hildyard UKMIS Geneva Tel. No. 599	17 Nov.	Basket II: European Community offer.	206
56 Mr. Maxey UKMIS Geneva	21 Nov.	Letter to Mr. Tickell examines Russian tactics on inviolability of frontiers.	210
57 Mr. Elliott UKMIS Geneva	15 Dec.	CSCE: The Second Stage so far. After 3 months of uninterrupted session the 'real negotiation' has yet to begin.	213
58 Mr. Tickell Foreign & Commonwealth Office	20 Dec.	Takes stock of the situation outlined in No. 57 and looks at the way forward for the West.	222
59 To Sir E. Peck UKDEL NATO Tel. No. 471	21 Dec.	CBMs: British paper on future tactics in Geneva.	226
60 Sir N. Henderson Bonn Tel. No. 44	1974 9 Jan.	CSCE Sub-Committee of the Nine met in Bonn (7-9 Jan.) to coordinate positions for Stage II.	230
61 To Mr. Hildyard UKMIS Geneva Tel. No. 19	18 Jan.	Guidance on procedural questions in Basket III.	234

	NAME	DATE	MAIN SUBJECT	PAGE
62	Mr. Tickell Foreign & Commonwealth Office	18 Jan.	Analyses message from Mr. Brezhnev to the PM on CSCE of 11 Jan.	235
63	Mr. Hildyard UKMIS Geneva Tel. No. 68	2 Feb.	Reports on neutral efforts to resolve deadlock over procedure for drafting in Basket III.	238
64	Mr. Hildyard UKMIS Geneva Tel. No. 71	4 Feb.	Up-date for Political Directors' meeting (6-7 Feb.): West 'well placed tactically with a multitude of detailed proposals on the table against a thin and unconvincing Eastern contribution'.	241
65	Mr. Hildyard UKMIS Geneva Tel. No. 78	7 Feb.	Committee III: acceptance of neutrals' compromise package enables drafting to proceed.	244
66	To Mr. Staples UKDEL NATO	22 Feb.	Letter from Mr. Tickell discusses Soviet desire for a Stage III 'at the highest level'.	245
67	Mr. Hildyard UKMIS Geneva Tel. No. 145	28 Feb.	Briefing on CSCE for EC Ministerial meeting (4 Mar.).	248
68	Mr. Tickell Foreign & Commonwealth Office	15 Mar.	Basket III: background and way forward.	250
69	Miss Warburton UKMIS Geneva Tel. No. 218	20 Mar.	Comments on general situation and registers concern about rate of progress at Geneva.	254
70	Mr. Hildyard UKMIS Geneva Tel. No. 247	26 Mar.	Basket I: Principles. Russians exerting pressure to detach sentence on peaceful change from principle on inviolability of frontiers.	257
71	Sir. T. Garvey Moscow Tel. No. 337	29 Mar.	Considers Soviet tactics at CSCE to be following 'traditional' pattern.	260
72	Mr. Tickell Foreign & Commonwealth Office	4 Apr.	Discusses merits of text proposed for registration on inviolability of frontiers.	262
73	Mr. Hildyard UKMIS Geneva Tel. No. 288	6 Apr.	Reports adjournment of Conference until 22 Apr. and reviews progress since No. 69.	265
74	Mr. Hildyard UKMIS Geneva Tel. No. 293	8 Apr.	Basket I: military aspects of security.	269

	NAME	DATE	MAIN SUBJECT	PAGE
75	To Sir E. Peck UKDEL NATO Tel. No. 80	19 Apr.	Political Directors' meeting (18-19 Apr.) considered report of the Nine's CSCE Sub-Committee.	271
76	Mr. Burns UKMIS Geneva Tel. No. 334	27 Apr.	Basket III: East unmoving on human contacts and information but wish to move ahead on culture and education.	275
77	Mr. Tickell Foreign & Commonwealth Office	30 Apr.	Minute to Private Secretary discusses reply to Dr. Kissinger's message to Mr. Callaghan regarding desirability of early decision on Stage III.	277
78	To Sir P. Ramsbotham Washington Tel. No. 1035	8 May	CBMs: although Alliance should not settle 'prematurely for less than might be obtained with persistence later in Stage II', UK ready to show 'selective flexibility' to keep work moving.	279
79	Mr. Hildyard UKMIS Geneva Tel. No. 404	11 May	CSCE state of play: 'virtual impasse since Easter' on areas of interest to West. Russians making 'little attempt to hide their delaying tactics'.	281
80	To Sir P. Ramsbotham Washington Tel. No. 1126	17 May	Instructions to sound out Americans on British ideas re. CSCE follow-up.	284
81	Mr. Tickell Foreign & Commonwealth Office	20 May	Records general impressions of two-day visit to Geneva.	286
82	Mr. Hildyard UKMIS Geneva Tel. No. 458	22 May	Up-date for Political Directors' meeting (27-28 May): Russians continue to 'drag their feet' on CBMs and Basket III, only on drafting of principles and Basket II are there any signs of 'willingness to make progress'.	288
83	Mr. Hildyard UKMIS Geneva Tel. No. 500	31 May	Basket III Sub-Committees.	291
84	Mr. Fall Foreign & Commonwealth Office	4 June	Minute to Mr. Tickell on timing of Stage III.	292
85	Sir T. Garvey Moscow Tel. No. 627	7 June	Reports a call on Mr. Gromyko to discuss CSCE.	294

	NAME	DATE	MAIN SUBJECT	PAGE
86	Mr. Fall Foreign & Commonwealth Office	17 June	Minute to Mr. Tickell outlines remaining points of East/West difference on CSCE.	296
87	Mr. Hildyard UKMIS Geneva Tel. No. 583	24 June	Non-intervention in internal affairs. Emergence of Finnish/neutral compromise package.	300
88	Mr. Cloake Foreign & Commonwealth Office	3 July	Minute to Mr. Marshall reviews progress in Basket II: 'we have gained little but we have lost nothing'.	301
89	Sir E. Peck UKDEL NATO Tel. No. 350	4 July	Briefing by Dr. Kissinger on US attitude to CSCE: Alliance should 'stop talking in general terms' and get down to drawing up a list of 'attainable' aims.	304
90	Mr. Hildyard UKMIS Geneva Tel. No. 617	6 July	Reports that Soviet 'obduracy' has led to virtually total paralysis—'this does not seem to be the moment for a general reappraisal of Western strategy'.	307
91	To Sir E. Tomkins Paris Tel. No. 310	12 July	Political Directors' meeting (11 July) considered CSCE against background of Dr. Kissinger's proposal reported in No. 89.	311
92	Mr. Hildyard UKMIS Geneva Tel. No. 692	24 July	US policy towards CSCE.	313
93	Mr. Hildyard UKMIS Geneva Tel. No. 730	27 July	Basket III Sub-Committees.	315
94	Mr. Elliott Helsinki	29 July	CSCE: The Long Haul. Considers Stage II unlikely to conclude before end of year and argues that earlier ending unlikely to suit Western interests.	317

CHAPTER III

Concluding Stage II
20 August 1974 - 28 July 1975

	NAME	DATE	MAIN SUBJECT	PAGE
95	Sir T. Garvey Moscow	20 Aug.	Letter to Mr. Tickell comments on No. 94 with particular reference to the Soviet Union.	327

	NAME	DATE	MAIN SUBJECT	PAGE
96	To Sir. P. Ramsbotham Washington Tel. No. 1842	5 Sept.	Transmits Mr. Callaghan's reply to a message from Mr. Kissinger of 1 Sept. on CSCE.	330
97	Mr. Hildyard UKMIS Geneva Tel. No. 894	20 Sept.	CSCE state of play: outlook is 'not encouraging'.	333
98	To Mr. Hildyard UKMIS Geneva Tel. No. 398	30 Sept.	Agrees UK delegation should seek to maintain US support for West's position and persuade neutrals to 'hold firm'.	335
99	Mr. Bullard Foreign & Commonwealth Office	1 Oct.	Minute to Sir J. Killick on CSCE and the Conference of European Communist Parties.	337
100	Mr. Fall Foreign & Commonwealth Office	18 Oct.	Minute to Sir O. Wright on CSCE/MBFR link.	339
101	Mr. Hildyard UKMIS Geneva Tel. No. 945	19 Oct.	Basket III Sub-Committees: 'Having taken three paces forward last week, the Russians took two smart paces backward at the beginning of this week'.	343
102	Mr. Hildyard UKMIS Geneva Tel. No. 964	2 Nov.	CSCE state of play: 'little progress to report, but the atmosphere is one of hesitation rather than impasse'.	345
103	Mr. Fall Foreign & Commonwealth Office	11 Nov.	Minute to Mr. Tickell following visit to Geneva. Sees 'no reason to despair of the prospects for the Conference, or to look for short cuts'.	347
104	FCO Paper	27 Nov.	CSCE: implications and prospects for British policy.	351
105	Mr. Hildyard UKMIS Geneva	29 Nov.	Letter to Sir J. Killick on how prospects look from Geneva.	358
106	Mr. Fall Foreign & Commonwealth Office	20 Dec.	Minute to Mr. Tickell on CSCE follow-up.	361
107	Mr. Hildyard UKMIS Geneva	24 Dec.	Letter to Sir J. Killick records impressions of last session, the attitudes of main participants and the UK delegation's role.	363
108	To Sir A. Galsworthy Dublin Tel. No. 24	1975 17 Jan.	Meeting of the Nine's CSCE Sub-Committee (16-17 Jan.) to prepare report on outstanding problems.	368

L

NAME	DATE	MAIN SUBJECT	PAGE
109 Mr. Tickell Foreign & Commonwealth Office	24 Jan.	Minute to Private Secretary updating Mr. Callaghan on CBMs.	371
110 Mr. T. Alexander Foreign & Commonwealth Office	5 Feb.	Minute to Mr. Popplewell on Basket II.	374
111 Sir E. Peck UKDEL NATO Tel. No. 73	8 Feb.	NAC meeting (7 Feb.) reviewed progress at CSCE, in particular on CBMs and follow-up.	376
112 Western Organisations Department Foreign & Commonwealth Office	15 Feb.	Note of meeting between Mr. Callaghan and Mr. Gromyko at the Kremlin on 14 Feb. which discussed CSCE.	378
113 Mr. Tickell Foreign & Commonwealth Office	21 Feb.	Minute to Sir J. Killick reports briefing of the Nine on PM/Secretary of State's visit to Moscow and his talk with Mr. Mendelevich on how Anglo-Soviet cooperation at the CSCE might now be followed up.	382
114 Sir D. Hildyard UKMIS Geneva Tel. No. 132	28 Feb.	CSCE state of play: reports Russian 'tightening up' on individual contacts in all sectors.	385
115 Sir D. Hildyard UKMIS Geneva Tel. No. 172	14 Mar.	Despite movement on CBMs and PCF Russians 'may now be regarding the other main outstanding issues, particularly in Basket III, as interdependent'.	387
116 Mr. Burns Foreign & Commonwealth Office	26 Mar.	Minute to Mr. Tickell discusses latest version of a report on follow-up prepared by the Nine's CSCE Sub-Committee.	390
117 Mr. Tickell Foreign & Commonwealth Office	27 Mar.	Summary of position reached in Geneva before the Easter break.	393
118 Sir D. Hildyard UKMIS Geneva Tel. No. 262	19 Apr.	CSCE state of play.	396
119 Mr. M. Alexander UKMIS Geneva	25 Apr.	Letter to Mr. Burns on Basket III: human contacts and information.	399
120 Mr. Burns Foreign & Commonwealth Office	29 Apr.	Minute to Mr. Tickell records that 'not a single word has been registered since the Easter break and attitudes have hardened on all sides' in Geneva.	401

	NAME	DATE	MAIN SUBJECT	PAGE
121	Sir D. Hildyard UKMIS Geneva Tel. No. 330	8 May	CSCE state of play: signs of movement towards conclusion of Stage II.	405
122	Mr. Tickell Foreign & Commonwealth Office	16 May	Reports that UK delegation in Geneva has presented Russians with a package deal of texts on human contacts and information.	408
123	Mr. M. Alexander UKMIS Geneva	30 May	Letter to Mr. Burns on Russian response to 'global approach' outlined in No. 122.	410
124	Sir D. Hildyard UKMIS Geneva Tel. No. 392	7 June	CSCE up-date: 'improved prospects' for agreement on CBMs, but 'remain stuck' on QRR and only making 'slow progress' on Principles.	413
125	Mr. Burns Foreign & Commonwealth Office	12 June	Minute to Mr. Tickell outlines position reached in Basket III: human contacts and information.	415
126	To Sir D. Hildyard UKMIS Geneva Tel. No. 214	19 June	Reports conversation between Mr. Callaghan and Mr. Lunkov on CBMs.	419
127	To Mr. Roper Luxembourg Tel. No. 30	24 June	Comments on CBMs, compromise package emerging in Geneva.	422
128	Mr. Tickell Foreign & Commonwealth Office	25 June	Basket III. Summary of situation on broadcasting, the 'only outstanding issue in the information texts'.	423
129	Mr. Tickell Foreign & Commonwealth Office	3 July	Minute to Mr. Weston summarises state of play in Geneva for Mr. Callaghan.	426
130	Sir D. Hildyard UKMIS Geneva Tel. No. 504	6 July	CSCE up-date: 'achieved remarkable progress yesterday' and there seems no reason why outstanding issues, apart from Maltese proposal and Turkish case on CBMs, should not be resolved next week.	430
131	Sir D. Hildyard UKMIS Geneva Tel. No. 529	9 July	Reports discussion of follow-up text.	433
132	Sir D. Hildyard UKMIS Geneva Tel. No. 540	11 July	Timing of Stage III and Malta.	435

	NAME	DATE	MAIN SUBJECT	PAGE
133	SIR D. HILDYARD UKMIS Geneva Tel. No. 554	14 July	Timing of Stage III and state of play in Geneva.	438
134	SIR D. HILDYARD UKMIS Geneva Tel. No. 586	19 July	Agreement on outstanding issues and confirmation on the date of 30 July for Stage III.	440
135	DR. FIELDER UKMIS Geneva	21 July	Letter to Mr. T. Alexander on the closing stages of Basket II.	444
136	SIR D. HILDYARD UKMIS Geneva	25 July	CSCE: The Conclusion of Stage II.	447
137	TO CERTAIN MISSIONS Guidance Tel. No. 120	28 July	FCO guidance on CSCE.	454

CHAPTER IV

Stage III
2 August - 9 September 1975

	NAME	DATE	MAIN SUBJECT	PAGE
138	TO SIR T. GARVEY Moscow Tel. No. 725	2 Aug.	Discussions at Helsinki between Mr. Wilson, Mr. Callaghan, Mr. Brezhnev and Mr. Gromyko.	461
139	MR. ELLIOTT Helsinki	12 Aug.	The CSCE Summit: Finland's place in the sun. Summary of Stage III.	464
140	MAJ.-GEN. SCOTT-BARRETT Berlin	15 Aug.	The implications for Berlin of the CSCE.	470
141	SIR T. GARVEY Moscow	9 Sept.	CSCE and Soviet Westpolitik.	474
APPENDIX I ORGANOGRAM			Organisational structure for Stage II of the CSCE (1973-75).	480
APPENDIX II MR. PAKENHAM UKMIS Geneva		1974 26 July	CSCE: Basket III.	481
APPENDIX III MR. PARSONS Budapest		1978 13 Mar.	The Belgrade CSCE Follow-up Meeting.	486

CHAPTER I

Multilateral Preparatory Talks
25 February 1972 - 27 June 1973

No. 1

Draft Position Paper

[EN 2/5]

Confidential   FCO,[1] *[February] 1972*
The Conference on European Security: The Next Phase[2]

1. This paper[3] is intended to sum up where we have got in the move towards a Conference.[4] It suggests the basic objectives which the West will need to bear in mind, both in preparing for a Conference and at the Conference itself. In particular it outlines the role which Britain might play. Attached to the paper are a number of Annexes,[5] discussing aspects of the

---

[1] Foreign and Commonwealth Office.

[2] This undated draft position paper was sent by Mr. C.C.C. Tickell, Head of Western Organisations Department (WOD), to Mr. C.D. Wiggin, one of WOD's Superintending Under-Secretaries, under cover of a minute of 25 February 1972. It was circulated to overseas posts under a covering letter of the same date to Mr. J.A. Thomson, United Kingdom (UK) Deputy Permanent Representative to the North Atlantic Council (NAC). Mr. Tickell explained in his minute that for some weeks WOD and Eastern European and Soviet Department (EESD) had been working on a series of papers about the strategy and tactics to be adopted during the preparation of a Conference on European security and at the Conference itself. He added that the line set out in the paper had been endorsed in general terms by Sir T. Brimelow (Deputy Under-Secretary of State), Mr. J. Cable (Head of Planning Staff), Mr. C.M. James (Head of Western European Department (WED)), and Mr. J.L. Bullard (Head of EESD). Problems connected with the Conference were henceforth handled by WOD, whilst EESD retained a general interest in its Soviet and East European aspects and was specifically responsible for 'cooperation' items, including the free movement of peoples.

[3] In a letter to Mr. B.E. Bellamy (Department of Trade and Industry (DTI)) of 28 February, enclosing this draft position paper, Mr. Bullard stated that it 'should not be taken as a firm expression of FCO views', and that neither it nor its Annexes had yet been cleared by all interested FCO departments. He also pointed out that the FCO were not committed to issuing the document in a final form, and that the 'most sensible course' might be to use it and any comments on it as the basis for briefing British delegations to meetings on the Conference.

[4] See Volume I, No. 85: cf. also No. 50.

[5] Not printed. Annexes A, B, C, E and F dealt respectively with the Brezhnev Doctrine, Principles governing relations between states, East/West Cooperation, Coordination and Consultation, and Standing Machinery for East/West relations. Annex H was the text of a

problem in greater detail. These Annexes are intended to provide policy guidance on individual problems. In certain indicated cases they are suitable for transmission to Allies.

Background

2. A 1970 Planning Committee paper (PC(70)14) set out the arguments for and against a Conference.[6] Its broad conclusions, which remain valid, were that a Conference was unlikely to do the West much good; that the harm it might do could probably be contained; and that there was no reason for Britain either to encourage or to oppose the movement towards a Conference which seemed to be increasingly inevitable.[7]

3. Since then the problem has primarily been one of timing: at what point could the West safely agree to begin East-West preparation of a Conference without prejudicing the outcome of current negotiations, i.e. the talks on Berlin and the Federal Government's *Ostpolitik* negotiations.[8] In these negotiations, it has primarily been German national interests which have been at stake. We have therefore been content to be guided by German views on timing.

4. The problem of timing is now, however, on the way to solution. The Federal Government's Eastern treaties will probably be ratified, and the Berlin agreements concluded, by the middle of 1972. The German interest in delay will be diminished, although complications arising out of the continuing negotiations for a *modus vivendi* with the DDR may still arise. However, barring unforeseeable accidents, NATO will have, early in the second half of 1972, to meet its public commitment to begin East-West preparation of a Conference; the Conference itself might take place early in 1973.

5. Meanwhile, the Alliance has done a great deal of work in preparation for a Conference. Voluminous studies have been completed over the past three years: on 'Issues for Possible Negotiations with the East'; on 'Possible Procedures for Negotiations with the East', on the economic and cultural aspects of a Conference; on a possible document on principles governing the

possible main speech. Annex D on administrative arrangements for a Conference, and Annex I, on possible links between the projected talks on Mutual and Balanced Force Reductions (MBFR) in Europe and a Conference on Security and Cooperation in Europe (CSCE), were still in preparation.

[6] See Volume I, pp. 262-3.

[7] Mr. J.N. Henderson, HM Ambassador in Warsaw, questioned the relevance and validity of conclusions reached in 1970. In a letter to Mr. Tickell of 17 March 1972 he argued that several posts had not agreed with the Planning Committee's paper and that a great deal had happened since its preparation. He observed that in 1970 'one of our main preoccupations on this subject was not to get ahead of the FRG [Federal Republic of Germany] for fear of impairing their support for our entry to the EEC [European Economic Communities]' and the FCO was then convinced that Moscow was 'not at all interested in *détente* and that the whole manoeuvre was designed to make NATO [North Atlantic Treaty Organisation] drop its guard' (WDW 1/1).

[8] Quadripartite negotiations on Berlin and interlinking FRG negotiations with the GDR [German Democratic Republic], Poland and the Soviet Union are documented in Volume I: see p. 426 for the situation at the beginning of 1972.

relations between states.[9] This mountain of work has not, however, yet produced clear or agreed policy directives: a vast number of possibilities has been analysed, but few conclusions drawn. This is not surprising: the Alliance is notoriously unable to make up its mind except under the extreme pressure of events. But over the next six months, as the Conference approaches, the need for the Alliance to make up its mind on some basic questions of tactics is likely to become inescapable.

6. In this situation the need and the opportunity for Britain to play an active role is perhaps greater than in the past. We could afford to be relaxed about the question of timing. But it is an important British national interest that the Alliance should have a clear and agreed strategy for the Conference, and adopt procedures and tactics which will minimise the disadvantages to the West of a Conference, and maximise its advantages.

Soviet Aims at a Conference

7. The somewhat grandiose title of the Conference suggests a traditional function: to negotiate specific agreements, to avert a war, or to tidy up after a war. But the proposed Conference is clearly incapable of doing these things (although the Russians may hope that it would give them some of the advantages of a formal peace settlement in Europe). It is agreed only that the Conference should talk about 'Security in Europe' and 'Cooperation in Europe'—phrases which are defined extremely vaguely in the communiqués issued by NATO and the Warsaw Pact. Questions (such as MBFR)[10] which could become the subject of genuine negotiation under the first head are hardly appropriate to a Conference of more than 30 Foreign Ministers. And detailed negotiations on cooperation could clearly be better undertaken within the permanent machinery of the Economic Commission for Europe or bilaterally.[11]

8. That such an unpromising and impractical idea has got so far must be accounted a success for the Russians.[12] The Conference was their idea.

[9] See Volume I, Nos. 31, 35, 39, 46 and 62.

[10] See Volume I, *passim*, e.g. Nos. 10, note 9, 45, note 11, pp. 343-5 and 478, and No. 107, note 5. A draft of Annex I, enclosed in a letter of 14 April from Mr. Tickell to Mr. Thomson, stated that the 'broad line' laid down by British Ministers was that a CSCE should tackle in general terms the problems of military security in Europe, but that NATO's proposal for MBFR was 'too complex to be handled in the Ministerial Session of a Security Conference, although it could perhaps be negotiated in machinery set up by a Conference, if this seemed appropriate'. The Annex concluded that HMG should continue to advocate with its allies 'the advantages in certain circumstances of linking MBFR and the conference' (WDW 1/1).

[11] The Economic Commission for Europe (ECE) is a regional agency of the United Nations (UN). Established in 1947 to assist in the coordination of the work of European economic reconstruction after World War II, in 1972 it was the only European body in which representatives of states of both East and West met on a regular basis.

[12] In his letter to Mr. Tickell (see note 7 above) Mr. Henderson criticised this 'pained expression'. He contended that HMG seemed to be doing itself a disservice by adopting 'too weary a note' when it had a 'great many good ideas to which much thought [had] evidently been applied'. He tended to think it 'a little old-fashioned to assume automatically that the relaxation of tension in Europe must willy-nilly redound to Soviet advantage'. Sir J. Killick,

Unpalatable though it may be to have to admit it, Western countries have had to accept it largely because of domestic political pressure: they have had, in effect, to accept the Soviet thesis that support for a Conference is the only acceptable evidence of willingness to work for *détente*. Some of the Russians' original motives in promoting a Conference now seem less important. Their campaign for a Conference can no longer be attributed to a desire to restore the Soviet image in the aftermath of Czechoslovakia and to divert the world's attention from the invasion, though a general desire to project a peace-loving image remains. The progress of the Berlin Agreement and the talks between the 2 Germanies have somewhat lessened the importance of the Conference as a device for exerting pressure on the West, and particularly the FRG, to accept the GDR into the international community, though the GDR government and their friends will doubtless continue to exploit preparations for the Conference to pursue their aims. But although the prestige they will gain from seeing their proposal become reality is probably an important motive, long-term objectives probably now predominate in Russian thinking about the Conference. They hope to encourage an atmosphere in Europe in which the presence of American troops appears increasingly unnecessary, and in which all-European cooperation seems more attractive than West European integration. They will wish at a Conference:

(*a*) to formalise the 'results of the Second World War'; i.e. the *status quo* in that part of Europe which is controlled by the Warsaw Pact Governments, with particular emphasis on frontiers (possibly as a substitute for a formal peace settlement);

(*b*) to generate an atmosphere of *détente* which will weaken the West's determination to maintain effective arrangements for its defence;

(*c*) to undermine the Atlantic link, with the particular aim of encouraging the progressive withdrawal of American troops;

(*d*) to weaken NATO, by undermining belief in its usefulness and by pressing for the 'abolition of blocs';

(*e*) to undermine the drive towards greater economic, political and military integration in Western Europe by advocating 'all-European cooperation' and a 'new security system';

(*f*) to gain in the more political atmosphere of a CSCE advantages in the fields of trade, science and technology, etc, which they have not been able to secure bilaterally or through negotiations in the Economic Commission for Europe.[13]

HM Ambassador in Moscow, was pleased with the position paper, but also agreed in large measure with Mr. Henderson's 'presentational comment'. He wrote to Mr. Tickell in a letter of 7 April: 'While I do not suppose that the Russians are likely to stop putting us in the dock with the Americans as the least positive in our approach to the CSCE I am naturally anxious to deprive them of gratuitous ammunition' (WDW 1/1).

[13] In Moscow telegram No. 333 of 7 March Mr. J.A. Dobbs (HM Minister in Moscow) expressed his general agreement with this description of Soviet aims in the CSCE. But he also thought that the paper needed to make it plain that the Russians did not want a formalising of the *status quo* for its own sake, but because it would signify the formal international acceptance

Western Aims at a Conference

9. Because the practical utility of a Conference is so doubtful, and because it is so clear that a Conference will be primarily a *political* occasion rather than one for doing business, the West's main aims at the Conference itself, as in the manoeuvres leading up to it, are likely to be basically defensive. Thus we shall want:

(*a*) to maintain Western unity, on which our security chiefly depends;

(*b*) to avoid unjustified euphoria;

(*c*) to make it clear that we want the East/West dialogue to go forward at the same time as, but without prejudice to, the construction of Western Europe;

(*d*) to persuade public opinion in the West that we are striking the right balance between flexibility and caution in our dealings with the East.

10. But in the judicious political warfare which is likely to be the main characteristic of the Conference, the West will also have opportunities to counter attack (see paragraphs 14 and 15 below). There may, moreover, be scope for agreement on practical measures of East/West co-operation. The Conference might even give a fresh impetus to existing work, or help to get round obstacles which have previously prevented progress. In any case, we should try to ensure that the Conference is as businesslike as possible, and that there is a minimum of duplication with the work of existing bodies.

The Tactical Problems for the West

11. In the light of this statement of Soviet and Western aims, the main tactical problems for the West are

(*a*) how to maintain its own unity;

(*b*) how to frustrate Soviet objectives without appearing to sabotage *détente*.

12. The problem of maintaining Western unity arises generally, not only in the context of a Conference. The further development of that unity remains, for most of the Governments of countries belonging to NATO and the EEC,[14] of more importance than marginal improvements in the not particularly bad relations which now exist between East and West in Europe.

of the Soviet sphere of influence in Europe, its inviolability, and the permanent division of Germany. 'Their primary reason for wanting these things', he observed, 'is their concern for the stability and continuance of the Soviet system inside the USSR for which they regard the maintenance of their hegemony in Eastern Europe as a necessary condition.' In addition, he thought that the Russians hoped that the Conference would 'provide a controllable safety valve for the European aspirations of [their] East European partners', and that they wanted a genuine reduction of tensions in Europe in order 'to avoid being faced with simultaneous challenges from the West in Europe and from China'.

[14] On 22 January 1972 the Prime Ministers of Denmark, the Republic of Ireland, Norway and the UK signed, at Brussels, the Treaty of Accession committing their countries to become full members of the EEC, the European Atomic Energy Community and the European Coal and Steel Community on 1 January 1973: see Volume I, No. 87, note 12. Since their administrative merger in 1967 these institutions were known collectively as the European Community or Communities (EC).

As long as this remains true, we have little to fear from a Conference. But the Russians will clearly seek to bring about a reversal of this order of priorities. We would need to take vigorous remedial action if individual Western governments began to place their hopes of long-term security and prosperity in East-West arrangements, rather than in the institutions which the West has been developing in the last two decades.

13. Apart from the general question of unity, it will also be necessary to maintain harmony among the Western delegations to the Conference itself. This will not be so easy, largely because the Allies disagree about the nature and value of a Conference, and about how hard a line to adopt on matters which might embarrass the Russians. Firm leadership will be needed within the Alliance over the next six months if we are to achieve agreement on a sufficiently robust line. We cannot expect in negotiations with the East to win back tricks we have lost in preliminary discussions within the Alliance; and we shall have to take an overall view of the issues at stake if we are to ensure that any concessions made in one field are matched by gains in another.

14. The problem of how hard a line to take with the Russians will arise both in the period leading up to a Conference, and at the Conference itself. The Russians will seek to exploit the Conference for propaganda purposes, and (apart from the MBFR issue, which is a two-edged weapon) they have so far had rather the better of the game. They are already orchestrating a renewed campaign in an increasing number of international and parliamentary bodies. NATO cannot afford to ignore the propaganda aspects of the Conference. It is important that we do not leave it to the Russians and their allies to define the obstacles to European security and co-operation which it is the assumed object of the Conference to reduce or remove. The tactical problem is: how explicitly should the West spell out what it sees as the real dangers to the security of Europe; the Soviet politico-military domination of Eastern Europe, the Brezhnev Doctrine,[15] Soviet subversion in the West? It would clearly be wrong to act as if these dangers do not exist. But to invoke them too directly would be to lay oneself open to accusations by the Warsaw Pact, by certain sections of Western public opinion, and possibly by the non-aligned and even some members of NATO, of wanting to wreck the Conference and sabotage *détente*. This is not at all an easy dilemma to resolve.

15. The solution may be to approach the problem indirectly, both in the pre-Conference period, and at the Conference. It seems clear that the (opening) Ministerial session of the Conference will more resemble the General Debate in the UN General Assembly than a businesslike progress item by item through a concrete agenda. Ministers will make highly political speeches, of a general kind. It would be natural for Western Ministers, in their speeches, to set out, in general terms, their views on the underlying causes of tension in Europe. They could refer to the very large numbers of

[15] See Volume I, Nos. 22, note 2 and 62. Mr. L.I. Brezhnev was General Secretary of the Central Committee of the Communist Party of the Soviet Union (CPSU).

6

troops in Central, and particularly in Eastern Europe. They could refer in general terms to the desirability of limiting conventional arms in Europe; but a detailed discussion of NATO's MBFR proposal would be impracticable and possibly impolitic, given NATO's continuing confusion on the subject. (See Annex I).[16] They could describe in detail what the West means by the principles of non-use of force and non-interference in the internal affairs of others and stress that these principles must be applied not only between East and West, but between countries of similar social systems. They could underline the desirability of removing existing barriers to the free movement of peoples and ideas if *détente* is to become a reality. In none of this would they point the finger directly at the Russians.

16. The purpose of speaking thus firmly but unprovocatively would not be to compel the Russians to withdraw the Brezhnev Doctrine or open their frontiers to the free flow of Western newspapers. Hopes that they would do so would almost certainly be vain (further discussion of these problems can be found in Annex A 'The Brezhnev Doctrine';[17] Annex B 'Principles governing relations between states';[18] Annex C 'East-West cooperation'[19] and Annex G 'Freer movement of peoples and ideas').[20] But plain speaking by at least some members of the Western Alliance will be necessary if we are not to play into the Russians' hands by seeming to accept their contention that the problems of European security can be painlessly solved by the 'abolition of *blocs*' and the adoption of 'pan-European' (and in the long run Russian domination) mechanisms for security and cooperation. Those members of the Alliance who do not wish to indulge in plain speaking should at least not too

[16] See notes 5 and 10 above, and No. 9.

[17] 'We want', Annex A stated, 'to avoid doing anything which would suggest Western acceptance of the Brezhnev doctrine; and to make it clear that in our view relations between states should be based on principles incompatible with it.' But the Annex also recognised that a 'frontal attack' was unlikely to succeed in changing the doctrine, and that a confrontation on this issue 'might lead to the isolation of a small group of "hard line" Western delegations'.

[18] As Annex B explained, the inclusion of this subject in the agenda of a CSCE had first been suggested by the NAC in the spring of 1970; as a rejoinder to the 'Prague documents', circulated after the Warsaw Pact Foreign Ministers' meeting of 30-31 October 1969. See Volume I, pp. 196-8 and 238-9.

[19] Annex C pointed to the West's need to avoid: (1) agreeing to anything in the interests of 'all-European co-operation' which would hinder the integration of Western Europe; and (2) giving the countries of Eastern Europe the impression that they were being cut off from the West, and thereby affording the Soviet Union the opportunity to impose a greater degree of integration upon them. It also emphasised the importance of focusing attention in the EC and NATO on the value of trade-offs that might be achieved between different items, and between technical and wider political considerations.

[20] A draft of Annex G, which was prepared by the UK delegation (UKDEL) to NATO, was communicated to the Alliance's Political Directorate on 28 February. It argued that the West should most probably seek to secure a mixture of both real improvements and propaganda advantages in so far as freer movement was concerned. There seemed, for example, to be little likelihood of the East conceding greater freedom of movement for people, but the Annex suggested that the West could, nevertheless, gain from drawing attention to the fact that the inhabitants of the Eastern Europe could not travel freely outside the Soviet bloc (EN 2/13).

obviously contradict the more robust line.[21] One of the main problems in the next phase of preparation within NATO will be to secure the agreement of the Alliance as a whole that this is the best tactic to pursue.

The Organisation of the Conference: Participation

17. Participation in the Conference—and in preparation for it—will presumably be open to all members of the Alliance and of the Warsaw Pact, and to 'all [other] interested States' (to use the language of NATO communiqués). We and other NATO members may receive approaches in the next few months from various neutrals asking us to support their participation in the Conference. We should presumably tell them that, in our view, the Conference is open to all European countries plus Canada and the United States, and to suggest that they speak to the country organising the preparatory sessions, namely the Finns.

18. French Procedural proposals[22] still seem the most sensible, and we should support them. It is now practically certain that NATO will accept the Finnish offer to provide facilities in Helsinki for the preparation of a Conference.[23] The main advantage of Helsinki is that both the German Federal Republic and the DDR have Missions there (Consulates General). Preparatory discussions at the level of Heads of Missions would thus limit any premature improvement in East Germany's status: and it should be our objective to resist any attempt to raise the level of the talks. The Warsaw Pact may repeat their proposal that preparations should be conducted by 'plenipotentiaries', who might include a very senior East German. This proposal could probably be successfully resisted if the Alliance were sufficiently determined; (the Bonn Group[24] have however been examining an appropriate disclaimer by the Western Allies to minimise the ill-effects should the East Germans attempt this particular manoeuvre).

[21] In a letter to Mr. Tickell of 17 April Mr. R.A. Hibbert (HM Minister in Bonn) wrote that he did not think it would be easy to bring the West Germans round to follow British views on plain speaking. They, he explained, had developed their own diplomatic tactic which they would like to have adopted widely in the Alliance. This consisted firstly of establishing agreement on a non-controversial procedural framework of a very general nature which could accommodate the differing approaches of the various participants.

[22] In the autumn of 1971 the French tabled a paper in NATO proposing that East/West multilateral preparation for a security Conference should concentrate on agenda and procedures, and that problems of substance should be remitted by Ministers at a short Conference to sub-committees of experts who would negotiate solutions. This contrasted with the American view that multilateral preparation should involve the preliminary negotiation of substantial East/West agreements which would be endorsed at a Ministerial Conference. The Americans believed that this procedure would enable the West to control the rate of progress towards a Conference, and the West would be able to break off preparatory talks at any point (minute from Mr. R.Q. Braithwaite (WOD) to Mr. Wiggin of 26 October 1971, WDW 1/1).

[23] On 5 May 1969 the Finnish President, Mr. U.K. Kekkonen, had proposed Helsinki as a venue for the Conference: see Volume I, No. 35, note 7.

[24] The Bonn Group was formed in 1959. It was made up of Counsellors of the British, French and US Embassies in Bonn and senior officials of the West German Foreign Ministry, and met regularly to coordinate policy regarding Berlin.

19. Assuming NATO takes the final decision to move to multilateral East/West preparation at the Foreign Ministers' Meeting at the end of May, it seems likely that the first full meeting in Helsinki would take place after the summer holidays, possibly in September. But preliminary contacts might take place earlier, and many Western countries (including the 'Six' under French leadership) will wish to move quickly. We should go along with them. But even if the business of preparation is conducted expeditiously, it is possible that the preparatory meetings may go on for several months: a security conference is therefore unlikely to meet until 1973 (which would in any case fit in better with the American electoral timetable).[25] This time lag should give the Federal Government sufficient time to negotiate its *modus vivendi* with the DDR before a Conference begins. If not, it may be necessary to drag out the preparatory period: the modified French proposals now before the Davignon Committee[26] (which have evidently been tailored to meet German preoccupations), would make this possible.

20. The preparatory meetings in Helsinki should not attempt to negotiate agreements to be endorsed by Ministers at the subsequent conference. This procedure is advocated by the Americans, who believe that the West can use the threat of refusing to go to a Conference in order to extract concessions from the Warsaw Pact. But this seems unrealistic. Once preparation for a Conference has begun, it would be politically extremely difficult for the West to withdraw from it unless there were a serious deterioration in East-West relations for other reasons, e.g. a Soviet invasion of Romania. This could become a point of some disagreement between the 'Six' and the Americans. We should seek to persuade the Americans, both bilaterally and in NATO, of the logic of the Six's position: the Americans will in any case be cross if their arguments are simply ignored.

21. The object of the preparatory work in Helsinki should therefore be limited. The aim should be to secure agreement on:

(*a*) Administrative arrangements for the Ministerial Conference, e.g. Chairmanship, Secretariat, venue, languages, finances.

(*b*) The agenda.

[25] Presidential elections were due to be held in the United States in November 1972.

[26] The Davignon machinery for European Political Cooperation (EPC) was established by EC states in November 1970 on lines recommended in a report prepared by a Committee under the chairmanship of the Viscount E. Davignon, the Political Director of the Belgian Foreign Ministry. With the object of coordinating and harmonising their foreign policy, Foreign Ministers of member states met twice yearly, and a Political Committee, composed of their Political Directors, assembled four times a year. Two Working Groups were set up to deal with matters relating to the proposed security Conference: the Sub-Committee on the CSCE, which was concerned primarily with the political issues; and the Ad Hoc Group, which focused on the economic and 'cooperation' aspects of the Conference, and with which the EC Commission was associated. The UK participated in EPC from February onwards. See note 14 above.

(*c*) Method of business at a Conference, e.g. agreement that Commissions[27] should be set up by a Conference as required to negotiate detailed agreements for reference back to a second Ministerial Conference if desirable.

22. A detailed discussion of possible administrative arrangements for a conference is at Annex D.[28] The questions of the Chairmanship, Secretariat and venue could be particularly contentious, because of their political, as well as practical, implications. The simplest solution would almost certainly be to build on the experience gained in the preparatory phase, and to hold the Ministerial Conference at Helsinki also, probably under Finnish chairmanship (though we need not say so publicly until we see how the Finns deal with the preparatory stages).

Agenda

23. The question of the Agenda could be the most difficult of all on which to reach agreement. This is partly because, for the reasons set out earlier, it is difficult to devise a concrete or practical Agenda for this particular conference but also because the Russians in particular will be on the look-out for attempts by the West to spell out too specifically in the Agenda their intention of raising subjects embarrassing to the Russians. The ideas of the two sides on Agenda were last formally set out in NATO's Rome *communiqué* of May 1970 and the Warsaw Pact Memorandum of June 1970.[29] These two statements overlapped to some extent, and an Agenda which covered the proposals of both sides would look something like this:

Security

(*a*) 'Ensuring European security'. (Warsaw Pact proposal).
(*b*) 'The renunciation of force, or the threat to use it in relations between States in Europe' (Warsaw Pact proposal).
(*c*) 'The principles which should govern relations between States, including the non-use of force' (NATO).
(*d*) 'The creation . . . of a body on questions of security and cooperation in Europe' (Warsaw Pact).

Cooperation

(*a*) 'Free movement of people, ideas and information' (NATO).
(*b*) 'Expansion of trade, economic, scientific, technical and cultural ties on an equitable basis' (Warsaw Pact).
(*c*) 'Cooperation in the field of human environment' (NATO).

[27] The Commissions and Sub-Commissions eventually established for what became Stage II of the Conference were alternatively referred to as Committees and Sub-Committees.

[28] See note 5 above. In his letter to Mr. Thomson of 14 April (note 10 above), Mr. Tickell stated that WOD were not at present intending to produce an Annex on administrative arrangements (WDW 1/1).

[29] See Volume I, pp. 238-9.

24. So far the arguments put forward in NATO and in the Davignon Committee have favoured defining the Agenda more precisely during the preparatory phase. But there are in fact definite advantages in leaving the Agenda as vague as it now is. As it stands, the West could raise all the issues set out in paragraph 15 without being ruled out of order. A comparatively unclearly defined Agenda of this type would also be more compatible with the character which we expect the Ministerial Conference to assume; and the case for such an approach has been strengthened by the Declaration on Peace, Security and Co-operation in Europe issued by the Warsaw Pact Political Consultative Committee in January 1972.[30] The declaration listed seven 'fundamental principles of European security and relations among states in Europe' which together with a number of specific topics in the co-operation field and the idea of a standing body, should 'form the fundamental contents' of the agenda. The reference to principles extends the apparent overlap between the two alliances' proposals on the general outline of an agenda. But the principles themselves, and the co-operation items selected, contain much which would be unacceptable to the West. An attempt in these circumstances to draw up a detailed agenda would inevitably cause difficulties with the East, without in any way adding to our possibilities of raising at the Conference proper the subjects to which we attach importance. We should seek to persuade our Allies accordingly.

25. If it appeared during the Ministerial session of the Conference that there was in fact concrete business to be done, the problems could be referred, as the French have suggested, to 'Commissions' of experts set up to consider particular aspects of East/West relations, e.g. security, economic cooperation, and cultural cooperation. These Commissions could report back to a reconvened Ministerial Conference if this seemed appropriate. It would no doubt be right to let at least some of them meet in neutral capitals other than Helsinki in order to meet the desire of the Swiss, Austrians and others also to provide facilities for these exchanges.

The Role of the Eastern European Countries

26. It is sometimes argued that a Conference will give the non-Soviet Warsaw Pact countries freedom for manoeuvre that they do not at present enjoy. For example, the network of obligations created by a 'declaration on the non-use of force', or the creation of a permanent European security body, to which they could, if necessary, complain, would help to protect them against Soviet pressures. These arguments are open to doubt. Existing International bodies, and existing International obligations to refrain from the use of force, have not helped the East Europeans in the past. Moreover the Russians will certainly be ready to prevent any excessive display of initiative by the Allies in the preparation and holding of a Conference. Nevertheless, some of the East European countries (notably Romania) themselves believe that a Conference could give them additional security. The Conference could offer opportunities for the more adventurous members of the Warsaw Pact to

[30] See Volume I, No. 87, note 12.

widen their freedom of manoeuvre, if only by a little. It is in the West's interest to encourage these aspirations.

The Role of the Neutrals

27. The neutrals and non-aligned are broadly sympathetic to the West. But some of them may be inclined to accept at its face value the idea that the Conference could be a major step towards removing the causes of East/West tension and promoting East/West economic cooperation. There is already evidence that the neutrals are talking to one another in order to coordinate their positions at a Conference (the Swiss last month arranged to talk to the Austrians and the Swedes). It will be highly desirable for the NATO countries to build up the closest possible relations with the neutrals both before and during the Conference, in the hope of influencing them to support the Western line generally. It will be, in particular, important that NATO countries should not appear as cold warriors. Over the next months we should increasingly talk to the neutrals in Capitals, in order to build up a relationship which we can exploit in the corridors of the Conference itself. The neutrals would doubtless welcome such approaches from us. We should argue in favour of such exchanges both in NATO and in the Davignon Committee. (See Annex E: Coordination and Consultation).[31]

The Role of existing International Bodies

(a) *General Organisations* (membership drawn from both East and West).

28. Various such bodies have already indicated their interest in the Security Conference. The most important of these is the Economic Commission for Europe (ECE), which is closely concerned with the likely subject matter of the 'co-operation' part of the Conference. This body already deals with the business of promoting economic and technical co-operation in Europe, and it is arguable that everything that can be done to overcome the barriers to East/West exchanges is already being done through the ECE, where it is not being done bilaterally. However, the ECE's environmental activities have been marred by GDR difficulties; we can hope these will have been resolved by the time the CES takes place. Another International body which has already attempted to get a foot in the Conference door is UNESCO.[32] UNESCO is organising 'a European cultural conference' in Helsinki in June 1972;[33] and it has offered to provide working papers for the Security Conference. The Inter-Parliamentary Union is also working in the field, and there is a proposal for a special Conference in advance of the CSCE. The West must be careful that important passes in the Conference context are not sold in advance through such other organisations.

---

[31] Annex E recommended that HMG should consider with their Allies 'whether and how best to associate the OECD [Organisation for Economic Cooperation and Development] countries not members of NATO with as much as possible of the pre-Conference work being done within the Alliance'. It also noted that henceforth the UK would be participating in pre-Conference consultations within the Davignon machinery, and that HMG had much to gain from a fairly wide-ranging discussion of CSCE matters within the enlarged EC.

[32] United Nations Educational, Scientific and Cultural Organisation.

[33] See Volume I, No. 99.

29. It should be a major aim of the West to prevent or limit duplication between the work done by the Conference, and the Commissions which may be set up by Ministers, and bodies already in the field. In particular, it is highly desirable that the Commissions created by the Conference should draw fully on the existing expertise of the ECE. Two ways of doing this would be:

(i) to have observers from the ECE (and possibly UNESCO) at the Conference itself; and

(ii) to ensure that the terms of reference of subsidiary bodies created by the Conference contain firm instruction that they are to avoid duplicating work being done elsewhere and cooperate to the fullest practicable extent with bodies working in the field. (This would argue in favour of the 'economic' commission set up by the Conference working in Geneva, where the ECE has its Headquarters).

(b) Limited Organisations (membership limited to East or West)

30. On the Western side, it is possible that the OECD would wish to be associated with the work of the Conference. It might be useful in the light of the aims in paragraph 29 above for the Secretariat to be represented by an observer during the discussion of subjects in which the OECD has an interest. This would seem even more appropriate if the Organisation had previously been involved in the Western preparations for a Conference (see Annex E).[34] If this were accepted, it would presumably encourage a similar application on the part of the CMEA,[35] and possibly also of other international organisations. There may be objections to such applications from some of our allies. For our part, we need not object to anything which is likely to improve the effectiveness of the Conference or avoid duplication with other bodies.

31. A far more important question under this head is the extent to which the EEC participates in the Conference. The implementation of the Common Commercial Policy on the one hand, and the attitude of the Warsaw Pact countries (and especially the Soviet Union) on the other, is likely to cause considerable difficulty at the Conference.

32. It is not possible at this stage to state clearly how far the Conference will deal with matters falling within the competence of the Community: the detailed agenda of the Conference is still unknown: and the position of the Community is complicated by uncertainty over the (overdue) completion of the Common Commercial Policy from which the Eastern countries have so far been largely exempt.[36] The extent to which the Soviet Union will

[34] See note 31 above.

[35] Council for Mutual Economic Assistance, sometimes referred to as COMECON. The CMEA was formed in Moscow in January 1949 at a conference attended by delegates from Bulgaria, Czechoslovakia, Hungary, Poland, Romania and the USSR in order to broaden economic cooperation amongst its participants.

[36] A summit meeting of EC Heads of Government in Paris on 19-20 October reaffirmed the Community's intention to pursue a common commercial policy towards Eastern Europe with effect from 1 January 1973 with a view to promoting *détente*. This policy of cooperation was to be founded on reciprocity with these countries. See *Selected Documents Relating to Problems of*

maintain its opposition to dealing with the Community as such is unclear; and the member countries have not yet decided how they would handle Community participation institutionally on their side.

33. These questions have already been touched upon in the EEC machinery, and will need to be considered there in greater detail. We shall be consulted under the interim procedures pending our accession. We shall also be fully involved in the discussions in Davignon. We shall no doubt wish to proceed with caution on questions which involve the balance of power within the Community. But there are wider issues involved, on which we should make clear our views.

The Role for Britain

34. For reasons set out at the beginning of this paper, it is now time for us to take a more active rôle in the Alliance's discussions, in order to promote the objectives set out above. We shall find ourselves arguing at times against the Americans, who will tend to believe that a Conference can be prevented from happening at all; and against those who believe that a Conference could usher in a brave new world. Until they are satisfied that they have reached an adequate *modus vivendi* with the East Germans, we shall have to continue to take account of German views on timing. At the Conference itself, we will almost certainly have to be among those willing to speak robustly about the realities of the security problem in Europe. We shall doubtless make ourselves slightly unpopular in doing so; and it will be necessary to avoid being regarded both within the Alliance and elsewhere, as so negative that our views need not be taken into account. The Russians will certainly take every opportunity they get to try to isolate us in this way.

35. For this reason we should continue to take great care not to be closely associated with moves over the next few months which will slow down the rate of progress towards a Conference. We should, on the contrary, as far as possible, be seen to be amongst those who are working for the Conference to take place soon. We shall have to give careful thought not only to the substance but to the presentation of our policy. The draft speech at Annex H[37] is intended to illustrate the line which Ministers might take in public between now and the Conference, in order to

(a) Counter Soviet propaganda;
(b) Influence our Allies in the right direction;
(c) Prepare opinion in this country and in Western Europe for the line which we shall take at the Conference itself.

36. It is also arguable that we should adopt at least one positive and concrete proposal which we could advocate in the Alliance and in public as a

Security and Cooperation in Europe 1954-77, Cmnd. 6932 (London: HMSO, 1977), pp. 135-7 for extracts of the Declaration issued at the summit.

[37] Amongst the main themes of this draft speech were the dangers inherent in high force levels in Europe and ideologies which regarded conflict as a necessary element of inter-state relations, the importance of freer movement of people, ideas and information, the advantages of greater economic cooperation, and the scope for 'continuing machinery' in the security field.

contribution to East/West *détente*. The obvious candidate is the Secretary of State's proposal for permanent machinery for East/West relations.[38] This has always been regarded as primarily a British idea.[39] We have not recently been promoting it vigorously partly because in its original form our Allies disliked it.[40] But it could now be desirable to re-launch it. Annex F sets out the arguments more fully.[41]

[38] See Volume I, No. 39, note 8. On 20 July 1970 Sir A. Douglas-Home, Secretary of State for Foreign and Commonwealth Affairs, had, in responding to a Parliamentary question from Mr. M. Stewart, his Labour predecessor, indicated that he thought the idea of establishing standing machinery concerned with force reductions in Europe merited careful study (*Parl. Debs., 5th ser., H. of C.,* vol. 804, cols. 7-8). Annex F suggested that continuing machinery could either be specifically set up by a Ministerial session of the CSCE, or a Commission created to examine the security aspects of East/West relations during the Conference could be given a continuing role. Its functions would be: (1) to provide a forum to explore possibilities for negotiating on East/West issues; (2) to serve as a forum for negotiating, and subsequently supervising, an MBFR agreement; and (3) to act as a 'crisis management' body.

[39] Mr. Braithwaite later questioned the validity of this assumption. In a minute to Mr. Tickell of 4 April he maintained that there was 'some verbal confusion here' since Ministers in the present British Government had never suggested that a Conference might 'create permanent machinery for its own sake', and that they had emphasised that HMG had 'no wish to set up a body which was not needed and which had no precise function' (WDW 1/8).

[40] In a letter of 28 January, commenting on an earlier draft of the position paper, Mr. Thomson warned Mr. Braithwaite that this proposal might prove 'rather controversial' in NATO: the White House apparently had doubts about it, and the Canadian Permanent Representative at Brussels was fond of denigrating the idea (WDW 1/1).

[41] According to Annex F the main advantage of establishing such permanent machinery would be 'that it could provide continuous contact between East and West, and enable discussions to proceed away from the glare of publicity and the pressures of Ministerial timetables which attend a conference'. Other advantages cited were: (1) it would provide a further court of appeal for East European countries being 'bullied' by the Russians; (2) the West would have a plausible justification for commenting publicly on Soviet 'misbehaviour' in eastern Europe; (3) it could act as a monitoring body for force reductions; and (4) it might prove more effective than a further Conference in negotiating any 'follow-up action'. Disadvantages were considered to be: (1) it might result in 'more unnecessarily time-consuming international machinery'; (2) there was a risk of duplication unless it could be made clear that the new machinery was not to concern itself with the 'cooperation' aspects of East/West relations; and (3) participation 'could make it much harder for the West to avoid reacting to Russian military operations in Eastern Europe, in a way which might contribute to a serious breakdown in East/West relations in Europe'.

No. 2

Minute from Mr. Tickell to Mr. Wiggin

[*WDW 1/1*]

Confidential   FCO, *6 March 1972*

Western Defence Policy and European Security

Western Organisations Department is responsible for work on both Western defence policy and European security. As a newcomer to the

Department, I am conscious that our thinking on these problems is pulling us in two directions.

Western Defence Policy

2. The defence policies we have pursued since the war are coming under increasing strain. This arises from both external and internal factors.

3. The *external factor* is the increasing disparity between the military strengths of the North Atlantic Alliance and the Warsaw Pact (whatever purposes they are designed to serve). The credibility of the US strategic nuclear deterrent is no longer total: this particularly affects the US nuclear commitment to the defence of countries outside the American homeland. There are likewise increasing doubts, military as well as political, about the value of tactical nuclear weapons in the spectrum of deterrence against aggression in Europe. These weapons were first devised as a substitute for conventional forces. But now far from strengthening their conventional forces, some of the governments of the Alliance are seeking means of reducing them. There is recurrent pressure from the United States for the American military establishment in Europe (already at a low point) to be further cut down. The Danes, Belgians , Turks—to mention only the most notorious—are thinking on similar lines. If the Danish defence bill now before the Folketing were to pass in anything like its present form, it would not only damage the NATO defence system at a critical point but—worse—set a precedent which would probably be followed by other countries.[1]

4. At the same time the military capabilities, both nuclear and conventional, of the Warsaw Pact countries are steadily increasing. They have their problems too. But their military power on land and sea and in the air is probably greater in relation to that of the Alliance than ever before. In the last two years we have seen the successful assertion of Russian naval power world wide.

5. The *internal factor* arises from widespread cynicism in the West about the possibilities of military power and the meaning of defence, at least where the super powers are concerned. This feeling is compounded partly of hopelessness, partly of wishful thinking, partly of reluctance to face the social consequences of providing for effective defence policy. This sapping of the national will varies from country to country. In the United States the Vietnam fiasco has caused a profound revulsion and the virtual alienation of a generation. In Denmark the very idea of defence has become slightly absurd: in 1971 30% of those called up were conscientious objectors and 20% contrived to be medically unfit. By contrast in countries with strong traditions and national pride—such as Britain and France—defence continues to make sense. But even there tradition is stronger than conviction. After a quarter of a century of peace in Europe, most people do not take the military threat from the East as genuine. They regard policies which carry the threat of nuclear

[1] The Danish Defence Bill, which was introduced in the Folketing on 14 December 1971, proposed substantial cuts in Denmark's armed forces and, in the eyes of other NATO countries, threatened to call into question Denmark's capacity to fulfil its defence commitments.

devastation to both sides as manifestly unreal. They certainly would not draw the conclusion that the West should have any more men under arms. If the Communist countries choose to arm themselves to the teeth, then—so the argument goes—that is their affair. They will find it expensive and pointless in the end.

European Security

6. So strong is the prevailing current of opinion that few Ministers in the West make speeches about the nature of the threat or the need to counter it. Those who do so speak find that their words are so largely unreported or fall on deaf ears. What people want to hear is quite different. In so far as they think about these things, they want to be told that the twenty five years of the cold war are coming to an end; that the German treaties, Berlin agreement, S[trategic]A[rms]L[imitation] talks[2] and eventual European security conference will produce a more rational and stable system in Europe; and that to crown this we shall all be able to cut defence expenditure through mutual and balanced force reductions along the line of the old Iron Curtain. In short, Czechoslovakia notwithstanding, East and West can kiss and make friends.

7. In many ways we are accomplices in promoting the illusions which bedevil popular thinking on this subject. Governments do not, for example, say that *détente* is highly relative and a product of particular and ephemeral international circumstances. They do not admit that a European security conference would probably turn out to be a jamboree of propaganda, whose result could strengthen the Russian grip on Eastern Europe while weakening the cohesion of Western Europe. They do not say that every model of an MBFR agreement so far constructed works to the military disadvantage of the Alliance. Privately we can afford to be sceptical. Dr. von Weiszäcker[3] (of the German CDU) described the security conference to the Chancellor of the Duchy[4] last November as 'the intellectual disarmament of the West'. At the signing of the treaty of our accession to the Community M. Jean-Francois Deniau[5] said to me that he thought it was the biggest threat so far to the continued integration and development of Western Europe.

The Future

8. What if anything is to be done? The heart of the problem is one of mood, and the present mood in the West arises from fundamental doubts about the nature and purposes of industrial society. It cannot therefore be lightly or quickly changed. But there are three things we can do.

(*a*) We can recognise the problem for what it is. If there is a real contradiction between the needs of defence and those of domestic politics, let us define it and stop deceiving ourselves. Last week I heard the Dutch

[2] See Volume I, No. 78, note 13.

[3] Dr. R. von Weizsäcker was Chairman of the Christian Democratic Union (CDU)/Christian Social Union (CSU) Parliamentary Group.

[4] Mr. A.G.F. Rippon.

[5] European Commissioner.

Minister of Defence[6] talking about the worsening defence prospects on one hand and the security conference and MBFRs on the other, as if there was no connexion between them. We all tend to put problems into compartments, and half believe our own propaganda. The more optimistic officials and experts who are for example set to work on schemes for MBFRs (as their predecessors on a Multilateral Nuclear Force) could rise so well to the intellectual challenge that they could in the end bamboozle their Ministers as well as themselves.

(*b*) We can set out our objectives for a security conference in realistic terms so that people can realize our minimum terms for attendance and see more clearly what is at stake. At all costs we do not want for fear of transient unpopularity to be manoeuvred into accepting an agenda or endorsing the objectives drawn up by the Warsaw Pact countries or our own more knock-kneed allies.

(*c*) We can reduce the gap between our public and private utterances. This process might begin in dealings between Governments, in particular in the Alliance, and lead to Governments making a greater effort to put the problem to their Parliaments and public opinion. This would be far from easy and could have international as well as national consequences. But it would lead over a period of time to a change in public attitudes and to debate of the real rather than the false issues.[7]

C.C.C. TICKELL

[6] Heer H.J. de Koster.

[7] Mr. James agreed with the thrust of Mr. Tickell's argument, but in a minute of 7 March he also pointed out that the British were already regarded by many of their Allies as 'fairly hard liners' and that the danger of widening this 'persuasion gap' was one reason why HMG had to go along with the CSCE. He, nevertheless, thought that this should not deter HMG 'from trying to inject as much steel into the demands of the Conference as possible'. Mr. Wiggin, who 'brooded' on Mr. Tickell's minute for over a month, was of much the same opinion. 'When in doubt', he minuted Mr. Tickell on 18 April, 'we must continue to err on the side of being branded cold warriors, whatever one or two of our Representatives in Eastern Europe may suggest to the contrary.'

No. 3

Minute from Mr. Wiggin to Sir T. Brimelow[1]

[EN 2/15]

Confidential FCO, *14 March 1972*

1. The Departments concerned are to be congratulated on the thought and work they have put into these papers.[2] I will seek to confine my comments to a number of basic points.

[1] This minute was also addressed to Mr. T.L.A. Daunt, Private Secretary to Sir D. Greenhill, the Permanent Under-Secretary of State (PUS).

[2] See No. 1.

2. The main position paper refers (without much hope) to the possibility of reaching agreement on practical measures. I see no prospect of any significant agreement emerging, and if any concrete agreements at all emerge they could doubtless have been achieved elsewhere. The Conference is (probably) inevitable rather than desirable, and our primary aim defensive. This does not, however, mean that we should leave the initiative entirely to the other side. The PUS saw an advance copy of the paper. I attach a copy of his minute of 8 March which is relevant to this point.[3] (The Department will be submitting separately on the points raised by the PUS.)[4]

3. When one gets to specific proposals the difficulties become apparent. For example, 'freedom of movement' ought to be one of the main cards in our hand. But the Federal German Government are shaky on this, and the French, who used actively to promote the idea (surprisingly, in view of their habitual reluctance to annoy the Russians) have lately shown signs of going into reverse (doubtless because they have now decided that they do not want to annoy the Russians after all).[5] Then again, the Secretary of State's idea for permanent machinery has latterly encountered increasing opposition within the Alliance. The Americans have long been at best reserved, and now there is opposition in the Davignon machinery, with the Italians in the lead.[6]

[3] This evidently refers to Sir D. Greenhill's manuscript minute of 7 March, in which he observed: 'I read all these pps with great interest. The work has been very well done. My own feeling is that the Russians are well on the way to establishing the type of document which they want the Conference to produce and to give its blessing. Unless some rivals enter the field pretty soon the game will be half won before the Conference opens. We know that the Yugoslavs have a draft which we will see soon. Ought we, at this stage, to try to produce something which we could accept and in which we could, if possible, see positive merit. If the task proves too difficult, we might consider trying from the outset to prevent the production of any document—at least at the first conference.'

[4] *V. ibid.* Mr. Tickell doubted the value of trying to achieve agreement in NATO on a text for submission to the proposed Conference. Any such text, he minuted, was almost bound 'to represent a very low common denominator' which would leave few bargaining counters. In minutes of 28 March both Sir T. Brimelow and Sir D. Greenhill indicated that they shared this point of view (WDW 1/1).

[5] Mr. J.N. Allan (Head of Chancery, HM Embassy in Luxembourg) reported in Luxembourg telegram No. 86 that when the Davignon CSCE Sub-Committee (see No. 1, note 26) met on 28-29 February both the French and Germans were inclined to think the West should not propose free movement as a specific agenda item for the Conference because of the danger of confrontation with the Russians, and that it would be better to seek such improvements piecemeal when negotiating about cooperation in particular fields (WDW 1/8).

[6] See No. 1, notes 38, 39, 40 and 41. According to Mr. Allan's report (*v. ibid.*): 'Attitudes towards the idea of a permanent body with wide-ranging responsibility for general political questions ranged from cool to strongly hostile'. But, while many thought that such a body could well be used by the Russians to impede the growth of Western European institutions, there was some sympathy for the idea of setting up other types of machinery, 'limited in function and not permanent', to deal with various practical problems arising from the CSCE. Mr. Braithwaite, who also attended this meeting, minuted Mr. Tickell on 1 March that he thought the FCO should now abandon the proposal for permanent machinery in paragraph 36 of their draft position paper (No. 1). 'It seems clear', he noted, 'that this would not meet with the

4. Similar problems arise over aims as distinct from specific proposals. For example, the paper suggests that it is in the West's interest to encourage the more adventurous members of the Warsaw Pact to widen their freedom of manoeuvre, if only by a little. But carried too far this process could be dangerous; and I do not myself believe the Russians will allow it to be carried any material distance at all without clamping down. Then again in the propaganda field we wish to be in a position to debate Czechoslovakia but to prevent debate of Northern Ireland, much easier said than done.

5. I find one or two of the recommendations possibly disadvantageous as distinct from difficult to attain. For example, we should be wary of making tangible one-sided concessions in fields such as scientific and technological exchanges and easing restrictions on imports from Eastern European countries, in return for less tangible benefits such as 'even a small amount of progress on the freedom of movement question' and 'improving facilities for Western firms and businessmen in Eastern Europe.'

6. On timing, I am hesitant about the recommendation in paragraph 35 of the main position paper, that we should as far as possible be seen to be amongst those working for a conference to take place soon. I can see that we do not want to be classed as leading the cold warrior brigade. But I would prefer to continue with our traditional policy of seeking to go no faster and no slower than the Federal German Government. (Even the Russians now accept in practice that for various reasons the Conference cannot come about before 1973.) Of course, if the *Ostpolitik* collapses then we will all have to think again anyway.

7. I have discussed with Mr. Tickell what use we should put these papers to in the future. Inevitably they are already a little dated in some respects. We agreed that it would be impracticable to seek to keep them up to date day by day but that equally it would be wrong to 'finalise' them. The Department will arrange to review them periodically circulating amendments to those interested at home and abroad.

8. I think the papers are too bulky to put to Ministers at this stage and that we should seek specific decisions from Ministers case by case as necessary. In addition to the questions arising from the PUS' minute referred to above, I think we ought fairly soon to submit to the Secretary of State on the difficulties which we are encountering on the permanent machinery idea.

C. D. WIGGIN[7]

approval of our European allies, and the short term attractiveness of the proposal is therefore diminished. We can reserve the arguments for deployment at a later stage if this seems useful' (WDW 1/8).

[7] At a meeting of the Davignon CSCE Sub-Committee on 23-24 March UK representatives claimed that a Belgian paper, summarising the views expressed on permanent machinery at the previous Sub-Committee meeting (*v. ibid.*), exaggerated advantages the Russians might expect to derive from such a body (Luxembourg telegram No. 117 of 24 March). Nevertheless, in a submission of 4 April Mr. Braithwaite observed that he thought the Belgian paper 'commendably sceptical of Soviet motives', and that there seemed little reason why HMG should not agree with the paper's argument that 'any machinery set up by a Security

Conference should be technical, probably of limited duration and with narrowly defined functions'. The subject was discussed at a meeting held by Mr. J. Godber, the Minister of State, with Sir D. Greenhill and others on 10 April, and later that day Sir T. Brimelow, who was attending a meeting of EC Political Directors, was instructed, in telegram No. 44 to Luxembourg, to make it clear that HMG was not committed to the establishment of permanent machinery 'for its own sake'. If, however, 'there were to be any need for machinery to do a specific job on a continuing basis' HMG should look at the question 'on its merits' (WDW 1/8).

No. 4

Sir J. Killick (Moscow) to Sir A. Douglas-Home

No. 362 Telegraphic [ENS 3/548/6]

Priority. Restricted   MOSCOW, *15 March 1972, 6.30 a.m.*

Information to Routine Washington, Paris, Bonn, UKDEL NATO and UKDEL EEC. Saving to Warsaw, Prague, Sofia, Belgrade, Budapest and Bucharest.

M[y] I[mmediately] P[receding] T[elegram].[1]

1. Following this exchange with Lunkov (Second European Department MFA)[2] on Anglo-Soviet relations (not telegraphically to all) I continued that the desire for a return to normal did not apply only to trade relations. It was now time that I began my programme of calls on other Soviet Ministers. On the subject of CSCE, the NATO *communiqué*[3] had indicated that the time was right for bilateral contacts to begin. Lunkov said that a number of countries were already in contact with the Finnish Government and that the sum of these amounted to multilateral contact. I pointed out that bilateral contacts with the Finnish Government would only cover procedural and administrative arrangements for the CSCE. HMG attached great importance to the substance. The NATO *communiqué* had referred to contacts with all interested parties, and on the substance no contact was more important than with the Soviet Government. Though I had no instructions to see Gromyko,[4] it was possible that I might receive them: I was in any case at his disposal at any time. At all events I needed henceforth to be in regular and normal contact with senior Soviet officials.

2. Lunkov asked whether we were really as pessimistic about the timing of a CSCE as you had seemed to indicate in your talk with Smirnovsky (your

---

[1] In this telegram of 14 March Sir J. Killick reported a meeting that day with Mr. N.M. Lunkov (Head of Second European Department), during which the Ambassador, after referring to HMG's belief that 'it was time to return to normal working relations', had discussed with Mr. Lunkov the scope for improving Anglo-Soviet commercial relations. Cf. Volume I, No. 91.

[2] Mr. Lunkov was appointed Soviet Ambassador to the UK in 1973.

[3] See Cmnd. 6932, pp. 104-7.

[4] Mr. A.A. Gromyko was Soviet Minister for Foreign Affairs.

tel[egram] No. 224).[5] I replied that you were not pessimistic but realistic. You would not necessarily in principle have excluded an earlier date, but did not believe in practical terms that it was realistic. The FRG Government had made it clear that their Parliamentary situation would not allow of multilateral preparations simultaneously with ratification of the Eastern Treaties.[6] Even so there were difficulties in Bonn, which we regretted, furthermore, we were now well into election year in America. If the CSCE was to be productive there was nothing to be gained by pushing the US Government in an election year.

3. Lunkov said that when in London[7] he had read statements in the British press to the effect that only the Soviet Government had anything to gain from a CSCE. This was a big misunderstanding: the relaxation of tension was in the general interest. He felt sure that we would agree that the USSR was strong enough economically and militarily to fear nobody. I replied that such press statements did not reflect the view of HMG. Smirnovsky had expounded to you the contents of the Warsaw Pact Declaration,[8] and you had replied that our general approaches to the security aspects of CSCE were similar, although it would be difficult to put them into practical effect. You had raised with Smirnovsky the equally important 'co-operation' aspect of the agenda and in particular the possibility of dealing with the free movement of people and ideas in Europe, a subject on which the Prague Declaration said little. Lunkov said that no declaration could be expected to cover everything. I agreed, but said that Smirnovsky had appeared unhappy about the idea that free movement of people should appear on the agenda of a CSCE.[9] Yet the Prague Declaration had referred to the elimination of

[5] In this telegram (WDW 1/1) of 8 March Sir A. Douglas-Home reported that the Soviet Ambassador, Mr. M.N. Smirnovsky, had informed him that his Government hoped that the CSCE would take place in 1972, and that multilateral preparations would start as soon as possible. Sir A. Douglas-Home told Mr. Smirnovsky that HMG's 'approach to the CSCE was similar', adding that it would be impossible to tell what could come out of it without a meeting, that a single Conference would not do much good, and that for this reason he was 'inclined to favour a permanent body'. But the next day, *The Times* reported, apparently in connexion with this conversation, that the Russians had 'accepted a date in the spring of 1973'. The Soviet Embassy was subsequently informed that this statement was not based on anything said by an FCO official (telegram No. 227 to Moscow of 9 March, WDW 1/1).

[6] See No. 1, note 8.

[7] Mr. Lunkov accompanied a Soviet trade delegation to Dublin during 29 February-4 March. On his return journey to Moscow he stopped over in London for the weekend of 4-5 March (Moscow telegram No. 364 of 15 March, ENS 3/548/1).

[8] See Volume I, No. 87, note 12. The Prague Declaration of the Warsaw Pact Political Consultative Committee 'On Peace, Security and Cooperation in Europe' was signed on 26 January 1972. Relevant extracts can be found in Cmnd. 6932, pp. 107-12.

[9] According to telegram No. 224 to Moscow (see note 5 above), when Sir A. Douglas-Home had asked Mr. Smirnovsky what he thought about putting the free movement of peoples and ideas on the Conference agenda, the latter had replied: 'The Berlin agreements had been a start. In time, with an improved political climate and a better security system, it might be possible to go further. But to begin with freedom of movement would not be useful.'

artificial barriers of which the Berlin Wall was an obvious example. This seemed a suitable subject for bilateral discussion between us. Lunkov said that the broadening of scientific, cultural and other links had already been proposed for inclusion in the agenda.

4. I said that whatever the press might say HMG approached the Conference with a positive attitude. Lunkov replied that the NATO *communiqué* seemed unnecessarily pessimistic on the subject of multilateral preparations. Some European Governments were already prepared to proceed in Helsinki. If HMG really supported the Conference, the Soviet Government hoped they would move 'without great delay' to bilateral talks in Helsinki: this would be 'a contribution of great importance'. I replied that this was in my personal view by no means excluded and you were no doubt considering what Smirnovsky had said. But HMG were equally concerned about proper preparations of the substance: any Helsinki exchanges should only be part of a network of bilateral contacts. I had made a bet with Smirnovsky that we would be the best prepared participant on the Western side: we were more concerned to make proper preparations than speeches. Working contracts with the Soviet Government were essential for this. Lunkov said that it was of great importance that the UK should be seen not to be dragging her feet in Europe but to be making the running.

5. I pointed out that far from dragging their feet, HMG had naturally been giving first priority to our entry into the EEC. Lunkov replied that this was HMG's own business. An old Russian proverb said: 'God has joined them together and God will also drive them asunder'. I said I hoped that the Soviet Government would leave it to God and not try to help him.

6. I said that the Soviet Government should realise that HMG were realistic, emphasising action rather than words: this went far to explain their concern that the Conference should be well prepared. As the PUS had remarked to Smirnovsky, some other Governments sought to give the impression of favouring an early CSCE but of being held back by their allies.[10] Yet their attitude was in fact no different from ours. The proof of our position would be seen in events as they developed through the resumption of normal diplomatic contacts between our countries.[11]

7. At this point I raised the question of visas.
See M[y] I[mmediately] F[ollowing] T[elegram] (FCO only).[12]

[10] See Volume I, No. 90, para. 7.

[11] On 16 March Sir A. Douglas-Home minuted on a copy of this telegram: 'We can I suppose talk to the Finns now about procedural matters' (WDW 1/1).

[12] This telegram (ENS 3/548/1) of 15 March reported Sir J. Killick's discussion with Mr. Lunkov of problems relating to the granting of visas to British and Soviet diplomats: cf. Volume I, Nos. 88, 90 and 91.

No. 5

Paper by the Foreign and Commonwealth Office
[EN 2/5]

Confidential   FCO, *20 March 1972*
East European Attitudes to the CSCE[1]

1. The attitudes of the East European countries to the CSCE are difficult to analyse. The official positions of individual countries may differ from what even quite important members of the hierarchy may say in private. And sections of the educated population will have their own hopes for the future, to which they would like the CSCE to contribute. But we shall be dealing at the Conference with officials on duty, who will be required to take up positions in the presence of the Soviet delegation. East European attitudes will therefore inevitably have much in common with that of the Soviet Union. Our interest is concentrated on the extent to which they differ. The paper therefore starts with a brief assessment of Soviet objectives; and then examines East European attitudes to them. A short separate section deals with Soviet and East European attitudes to the freedom of movement questions likely to be raised by the West; and there is a brief general conclusion. Further notes on individual countries are annexed.[2]

Soviet Union

2. We believe that the first priority of Soviet policy in Europe is to maintain its hegemony in Eastern Europe, which the Soviet leaders regard as essential to the continuance of the Soviet system inside the USSR, and of the World Socialist System also. The Soviet desire to formalise the *status quo* in that part of Europe which is controlled by the Warsaw Pact Governments (known in the jargon as 'recognising the results of the Second World War') stems from this. The Russians hope for the formal acceptance by all European countries and the United States and Canada of the Soviet sphere of influence in Eastern Europe; of its inviolability; and of the permanence of the division of Germany as guaranteed by recognition of the GDR as a sovereign state.

3. In the longer term the Russians, who have never indicated their acceptance of the political *status quo* in Western Europe, and have never

[1] This paper was drafted following agreement at the February meeting of the Davignon CSCE Sub-Committee (see No. 3, note 5) that the British would produce an analysis of East European attitudes towards the CSCE. A covering note of 20 March stated that the paper had not been cleared with 'all those concerned' and that it did 'not necessarily reflect the considered views of HMG'. As Mr. B.J.P. Fall (EESD) explained to Mr. H.A.J. Staples (Head of Chancery, UKDEL NATO) in a letter of 28 March, there had not been time, prior to the March meeting of the Sub-Committee, to receive comments from posts in Eastern Europe, but the authors had tried to incorporate their views. FCO officials were surprised and irritated by the unauthorised leaking of the document to Mr. R. Norton-Taylor of *The Guardian* and the newspaper's publication on 12 May of an article quoting from it at length.

[2] Not printed.

concealed their aim of progressively changing the balance of power in favour of the socialist system, would like:-

(*a*) to weaken the West's determination to maintain effective arrangements for its defence;

(*b*) to undermine the Atlantic link, with the particular aim of encouraging the progressive withdrawal of American troops;

(*c*) to weaken NATO, by undermining the belief in its usefulness and by pressing for the 'abolition of blocs' and their replacement by a 'new security system';

(*d*) to undermine the drive towards greater political and economic integration in Western Europe, *inter alia* by offering a vision of 'all-European co-operation'.

4. Soviet support for the idea of a European Security Conference, which was first publicly put forward by the Polish Foreign Minister Rapacki[3] at the United Nations General Assembly in December 1964[4] and endorsed by the Political Consultative Committee of the Warsaw Pact in January 1965,[5] must be seen in this context. The Russians must have calculated that if the West were to accept the call for a Conference it would contribute to the various objectives described above. (They also, no doubt, hoped that in the more political atmosphere of a Conference they might be able to win advantages in the fields of trade, science and technology, etc, which they had not been able to secure bilaterally or through negotiations in the Economic Commission for Europe. If, on the other hand, the West were not to take up the idea, the Russians and their allies would be left with a propaganda line which they would be able to use to good effect.

5. The invasion of Czechoslovakia put an end to the first stage in the campaign for a Conference.[6] The proposal was re-launched by the Warsaw Pact in 1969, partly in order to hasten the rehabilitation of the Soviet Union after the invasion. It is difficult to assess how far the marked deterioration of Sino/Soviet relations in the course of 1969 has affected Soviet thinking towards the Conference and towards other manifestations of their *Westpolitik* (the Four-Power Talks on Berlin, the FRG/Soviet Treaty and the 'peace offensive' after the 24th Party Congress). The China angle cannot be

[3] Mr. A. Rapacki was Polish Foreign Minister, 1956-68.

[4] See *Records of the 19th Session of the United Nations General Assembly*, A/PV, No. 1301.

[5] See Cmnd. 6932, p. 4.

[6] In his NATO Annual Review for 1971, despatched to the FCO on 7 January 1972, Sir E. Peck, UK Permanent Representative on the NAC, speculated, evidently with the events of 1968 in mind, that during 1972 the Russians would 'take some action (in Yugoslavia, Romania or elsewhere) which could serve to convince the weaker brethren in NATO that a strong defence is more important to the West than the Soviet version of *détente*' (WDN 1/1). But Mr. Bullard thought that the Russians would do everything in their power to avoid any move that might cast doubt on their desire for *détente*, and he informed Mr. Thomson in a letter of 8 March that, though he would like to associate himself with Sir E. Peck's prediction, he felt 'hesitant to do so, even speculatively' (ENS 2/4).

ignored, because it is clearly to the Soviet advantage not to be pressed on 2 fronts at once. But there is no evidence to suggest that the Russians are prepared, because of China, to conclude with Western countries agreements which they would not regard as satisfactory in the purely European or East/West context; and Soviet objectives at the Conference are probably much the same now as they were in 1965/66, although priorities have varied. Perhaps the most significant difference is that the importance to the Soviet Union of undermining the drive towards Western European integration has increased with the enlargement of the European Community.

Eastern Europe

6. Turning now to Eastern Europe, it may be useful first to explore attitudes in the light of the Soviet objectives suggested above.

A. Maintaining Soviet Hegemony in Eastern Europe

7. The Soviet insistence on 'recognising the results of the Second World War' is supported by the other countries of Eastern Europe as far as frontiers are concerned. For example:

(*a*) Poland would welcome multilateral confirmation of the agreements reached in the FRG/Polish Treaty,[7] particularly as regards the Oder/Neisse line;

(*b*) East Germany sees in the campaign for a CSCE a means of accelerating its progress towards recognition; and in the Conference itself a means of ensuring multilateral confirmation of such a status;

(*c*) Czechoslovakia may similarly see the run-up to the Conference as encouraging the speedy conclusion on satisfactory terms of a bilateral treaty with the FRG, whose terms could then secure a degree of multilateral endorsement at the Conference itself;

(*d*) and, from a very different standpoint, Yugoslavia has also emphasised the importance of recognition of frontiers in the Conference context, (no doubt hoping thereby to strengthen its hand against Bulgarian claims in Macedonia).

It would seem, therefore, that moves at a Conference to secure the general recognition of European frontiers would receive widespread support in Eastern Europe, though for a mixture of reasons.

8. To the extent that what the Russians wish to formalise is not only existing frontiers but Soviet hegemony in Eastern Europe, the attitude of the East European countries differs considerably.

(*a*) At one end of the spectrum, Yugoslavia will insist on its non-aligned status and hopes that the Conference will serve to confirm this. The Yugoslavs are particularly anxious that the Declaration of Principles Governing Relations Between States, which they hope the Conference will adopt, should be clearly incompatible with the doctrine of limited sovereignty. They have already privately expressed their doubts about the

---

[7] See *Selected Documents on Germany and the Question of Berlin, 1961-1973*, Cmnd. 6201 (London: HMSO, 1975), pp. 226-7.

drafting of the Declaration issued by the Warsaw Pact Consultative Committee in January.[8]

(*b*) Romania, as a member of the Warsaw Pact, does not lay claim to non-aligned status; but where Soviet influence in Eastern Europe is concerned it sees its interests in much the same light as Yugoslavia. The Romanians will be just as concerned as the Yugoslavs to avoid language in the declaration on Principles which might be regarded as endorsing the Brezhnev doctrine.

(*c*) At the other end of the scale, the East Germans are likely to do whatever they can to demonstrate a rigid *Abgrenzung*[9] both between the GDR and the Federal Republic and between Eastern and Western Europe. They will resist for this reason anything which might lead to a weakening of Soviet influence in the area.

(*d*) Where the other members of the Warsaw Pact are concerned, differences between them are too nuanced to reflect properly in an outline paper. They are likely to adopt with varying degrees of enthusiasm an orthodox Warsaw Pact position; and they will have to bear in mind the extent to which their own continuation in power depends upon Soviet support. But as far as the Brezhnev doctrine is concerned their public attitude may best be summed up in the old Common Law maxim: 'Thou shalt not kill but needst not strive officiously to keep alive'. In private, some of them no doubt feel that it is not only their Western frontiers which they would like to have regarded as inviolable.

9. The negotiation at a CSCE of a declaration on Principles will thus be a matter of considerable interest to the countries of Eastern Europe. The section on Principles in the Warsaw Pact document issued this January in Prague[10] is unsatisfactory to the West in a number of respects, and it is not surprising that the Yugoslavs should have shown their concern. But, taken as an opening position, the Prague document is not too discouraging; and it does not appear to commit the Warsaw Pact countries irrevocably to texts which are unnegotiable. Once the Conference gets under way, not only the Romanians, but also the Poles and Hungarians, can be expected tacitly to welcome efforts by the West to secure a balanced statement of all the relevant basic principles of the UN Charter, and to emphasise their application irrespective of differences in political, economic and social systems. The extent to which these countries will be able to make their views known in public will undoubtedly be limited; and they will have to rely on the West and on the neutrals to ensure that the final text of the Declaration makes more rather than less difficult any future Soviet attempt to interfere openly in their

[8] During a meeting with Sir D. Greenhill on 6 March 1972 the Yugoslav Deputy Foreign Minister, Mr. J. Petric, was reported as having said 'that the text [on principles] in the recent Warsaw Pact Declaration contained many ambiguities' (WDW 1/1). See No. 4, note 8.

[9] A term used to describe the GDR's policy of seeking to emphasise its separate international and political identity.

[10] See note 8 above.

affairs. But it seems reasonable to conclude from what we know of their private views that at least these three countries, together of course with Yugoslavia, hope that the Conference will achieve something in this direction.

B. *Weakening NATO*

10. The attitude of the Eastern European countries to the long-term Soviet objectives aimed at the weakening of the Western defence capability, the undermining of the Atlantic link and the weakening of NATO, will vary in accordance with their basic loyalty to the Warsaw Pact. Yugoslavia, as a non-member of the Pact, is clearly a case apart; and the Yugoslavs would regard as a danger to their security any outcome of the Conference which were to shift the balance of power in Europe in a direction unfavourable to the West, or disturb the present equilibrium which makes their neutrality possible. The Romanians have occasionally given some indication that they share this basic calculation of national security interest, but they will be inhibited by their membership of the Warsaw Pact from promoting this line of thought. They will be mainly interested in ideas which they think will reduce the Soviet pressure upon them in the short term and they will not be unduly worried if these are likely still more to reduce the strength of the West. Indeed, they may calculate that only in these circumstances are the Russians likely to agree to a particular package; and they are prone to exaggerate the extent to which they can hope successfully to play off the blocs against each other. The positions of the middle range of Warsaw Pact countries are again difficult to distinguish. Insofar as they differ from that of the Soviet Union, they are likely to have much in common with the attitude of the Romanians outlined above. Perhaps only the East Germans are really convinced that successful Soviet moves to weaken NATO would strengthen their own security.

11. The idea of a 'new security system' put forward by the Warsaw Pact countries in connection with the Conference should be considered in the light of this analysis.[11] The rather crude notion of dissolution of blocs has featured in Soviet propaganda for many years. It has never been spelt out in any

[11] The paper is here footnoted: 'For example, the Bucharest Declaration of July 1966 states: "The real guarantee of the security and progress of each European country lies not in the existence of military groupings, who do not correspond to the sound present-day trends of international life, but in the establishment in Europe of an efficient security system based on relations of equality and mutual respect among all the states of this continent, on the joint efforts of all European nations. The signatory countries to this Declaration maintain that the time is ripe for undertaking measures for the lessening of the military tension in Europe. The radical way to do this would be the simultaneous abolition of the existing military alliances: the present situation makes this possible".

'The Prague Declaration of January 1972 states: "At the all-European Conference the participants could work out practical measures for the further lessening of tension in Europe and lay the foundations for a building of a system of European security.

'Participants at the meeting are of the opinion that European security and co-operation require the creation of a system of obligations which would eliminate any use of force and threat of force in mutual relations among European states, which would provide all states with a guarantee against acts of aggression and which would contribute to the welfare and prosperity of each nation".'

convincing detail. The proposal would, if translated into practice, be obviously one-sided in its effect: the West would lose thereby the arrangements which had been found necessary to correct the 'natural' balance of power in Europe, which leaves the Soviet influence preponderant; and the Russians themselves would lose virtually nothing, thanks to the network of bilateral treaties which link them to the individual members of the Warsaw Pact. This notion of dissolution of blocs, which has featured in Soviet propaganda in the past and was emphasised in the 1966 Bucharest Declaration,[12] is not mentioned in the 1972 Prague Declaration.[13] This is probably because the Consultative Committee wished to issue a studiously moderate document in order to encourage the convocation of a conference; but the Yugoslavs have suggested that the dissolution of blocs might now be regarded by the Russians, who are seeking to emphasise multilateral links in the Warsaw Pact and in the CMEA, as likely to have an unsettling effect in Eastern Europe.[14] To the extent that this is true, it may serve to explain support for the idea from certain East European countries: because the bloc system means for them subservience to Moscow, they would like to see it abolished.

12. The idea of a 'system of obligations' referred to in the Prague Declaration may be more attractive to the East Europeans, though here again we have little knowledge of what the Russians have in mind. Yugoslavia, while regarding the maintenance of Western power as important to its security, may genuinely see the creation of such a system as an additional safeguard of its freedom from interference. Others, while recognising and, to a greater or lesser extent, sharing the Soviet motives for putting forward an idea likely to induce a sense of euphoria in the West, may nevertheless see in it a degree of protection against physical imposition of the Brezhnev doctrine, or some encouragement to a withdrawal of Soviet troops from Eastern Europe. The Romanians in particular seem optimistic in this regard; and it is clear, *inter alia* from the current emphasis in Eastern Europe on the security role of continuing machinery to be established by the Conference, that other countries too are attracted by the idea.

13. The Russians have given no concrete indication of what they mean by this 'new system', other than suggesting that it would involve a series of bilateral or multilateral agreements on the non-use of force. The Poles may see in the idea an opportunity to revert to their previous proposals for a treaty on the renunciation of force and for some kind of authority to back it up; and the Romanians and Yugoslavs have both referred favourably to the idea of non-nuclear zones in Europe which might be incorporated in or built upon such a 'new system'. It seems likely that the smaller countries of Eastern Europe, for whom the present system of security in Europe is primarily associated with the presence of Russian troops and limitations on their sovereignty, will be keen to explore the possibilities for change. Those who

[12] See Cmnd. 6932, pp. 38-43.

[13] See No. 4, note 8 above.

[14] Mr. Petric expressed this view to Sir D. Greenhill on 6 March (see note 8 above).

genuinely wish to increase their freedom of manoeuvre will tend to argue in the same way as those who are concerned to further Soviet objectives against NATO, and it will be more than usually difficult as a result to make an accurate assessment of how these countries see their own interests. The East Germans may be alone in hoping that the 'new system' will do nothing to inhibit the stationing of Soviet troops on their territory in something very like their present strength. But there is no sign in what the Poles and Hungarians have said about the system that they are thinking differently from the Russians as far as the effect on the West is concerned.

C. Undermining the Drive towards Western Integration

14. Soviet opposition to the EEC has been expressed on economic, ideological and political grounds. The Soviet Union, with a relatively low dependence on external trade in general and on agricultural trade in particular, has not been significantly affected by the Common Market as far as its trade is concerned; and the rapid growth of Soviet/EEC trade since 1958[15] has much reduced the credibility of Soviet protests against 'closed economic groupings'. Ideological attacks against the Common Market as a bastion of monopoly capitalism appear from time to time in the Soviet media. But, possibly because of the attitude to the EEC of the French and Italian communist parties, they have recently been directed largely towards opinion in the candidate countries. There is no doubt that the main reason for Soviet opposition to the EEC is a political one. They are concerned that the successful development of the Community, and indeed its enlargement, will strengthen Western Europe; they are worried about the attraction of the Community for the neutrals and, in the longer term, for the countries of Eastern Europe; and they are particularly concerned to prevent integration within the enlarged Community from spreading into the political and defence fields. They will therefore seek to do what they can to slow up the process; and their emphasis on 'all-European co-operation' is based upon this rather than on technical factors.

15. As far as the ideological and political arguments against the EEC are concerned, the attitudes of the countries of Eastern Europe vary in much the same way as their attitudes to the security questions discussed above. But the East European countries are also more dependent than the Russians on trade with the West, and some of them clearly attach considerable political importance to limiting the extent of their economic dependence on the Soviet Union. For them, the question of 'all-European co-operation' at the CSCE has an importance which goes beyond Soviet objectives with regard to the EEC.

16. In their dealings with the EEC, the East Europeans find themselves operating within two constraints which give them little freedom for manoeuvre: on the one hand, there is the Treaty of Rome and in particular the Common Agricultural Policy; on the other, there is the attitude of the

---

[15] In 1958 Soviet exports to the EEC valued 472 million ecus, and by 1973 had risen to 2.3 billion ecus.

Soviet Union which has so far prevented any CMEA member country from formally recognising the EEC. The only exceptions to this general rule are East Germany and Yugoslavia. On the one hand, East Germany, though subject to the Soviet constraint, has to some extent escaped from the Treaty constraint through the special arrangements for inter-zonal trade. It is difficult to predict how far this special position will affect the East German attitude at the CSCE. On the other hand, Yugoslavia, having escaped from the Soviet constraint, has been able to recognise the EEC, and has signed with the Commission a trade agreement which provides *inter alia* for preferential access for baby beef, which is of considerable importance to the Yugoslav economy. The main Yugoslav concern at the CSCE in this field will be to avoid any hardening of group positions which would affect her ability to continue to trade freely with both East and West on the best terms available.

17. The other countries in the group find themselves affected by the EEC largely in proportion to their dependence upon foreign, and especially agricultural trade. Bulgaria is probably content with the Soviet line; and Czechoslovakia at present shows virtually no signs of independence. But others, who have already had talks with the Commission at technical level, would probably like to follow the example of Yugoslavia. Poland and Hungary are among those who have had such talks; but Romania, which has recently addressed to M. Thorn[16] in his capacity as Chairman of the Council of Ministers a request that Romania should be included in the Community offer of Generalised Preferences, has travelled furthest along the road. These countries will wish at the CSCE to avoid any results which would harden the economic divisions in Europe and encourage the Russians to seek to match the pace of integration in the West by pressing for corresponding measures in the CMEA. In particular, while they are unlikely to have any real objection to bilateral dealings with the Commission, they will wish to avoid having to negotiate trade agreements with the EEC through any form of CMEA machinery having real powers of co-ordination in the field of East/West trade.

18. The East Europeans can be expected at the CSCE to support the Russians with varying degrees of enthusiasm in attacking the EEC along lines already familiar from discussions in the ECE, and in pressing the advantages of all-European co-operation. To some extent, however, they will do so from motives which are different from those of the Soviet Union. Their concern with the EEC is not so much directed against the West as designed to ensure the degree of access which they require for economic reasons; and they have a political interest in the expansion of East/West trade as a means of limiting their dependence on the Soviet Union. It is a nice question how far these differences of motive will be apparent at the Conference; and there is no doubt that the East Europeans will be just as active as the Russians in pursuing advantages in technical fields which they have failed to gain bilaterally or through negotiations in the ECE.

[16] M. G. Thorn was Luxembourg Foreign Minister.

Freer Movement

19. The extensive restrictions imposed by the Soviet Union in areas which would be covered by the Freer Movement discussions as a CSCE are regarded by the Soviet leaders as essential to the preservation of their political system. There have been minor fluctuations in the rigour with which they are maintained, and the CSCE may result in a certain relaxation at the margin. But it would be unrealistic to believe that any radical chances will be forthcoming. Recent developments in the Soviet Union suggest a tightening of the reins, partly perhaps in order to make it clear that propaganda in favour of *détente* in Europe would not be regarded as permitting relaxation at home.

20. The Soviet leaders are conscious also of the dangers to them of internal relaxation in Eastern Europe. Western emphasis on freer movement in the context of the CSCE confronts them with an awkward problem. They are anxious to present in a light attractive to the West their ideas of security and co-operation; but they are very limited in what they can offer, or safely allow their allies to offer, in order to encourage the changes which they would like to see in Western attitudes.

21. Similar restrictions are maintained by the other Warsaw Pact member states, but practice varies from country to country. There is a basic identity in the general approach, but there are also significant shadings of difference which need to be taken into account. The extent to which the Warsaw Pact countries will permit contacts with the West is limited (apart from technical considerations such as the restricted availability of foreign exchange) by their fear of provoking Soviet intervention and by the interest of the respective Party leaders in shutting out influences which could undermine their position. Which of these two constraints is the dominant one will vary from country to country and from time to time; but East European sources will refer only to the former in explaining their difficulties to Western interlocutors.

22. It seems clear that certain Warsaw Pact countries will adopt a hard-line attitude to this question at the CSCE. The East Germans will wish to maintain their policy of *Abgrenzung*; the Bulgarians will follow the Soviet line as closely in these matters as in others; and recent press comments in Czechoslovakia have referred to the free movement of ideas as a Trojan Horse intended to slow down preparations for a conference, and as an instrument of subversion. The other countries in Eastern Europe will probably be largely concerned with maintaining their existing degree of freedom in these matters, and in avoiding any undue exposure *vis-à-vis* the Soviet Union. But insofar as their practice is more liberal, they may welcome Western concentration on areas where the laggards in Eastern Europe could be encouraged to take steps forward which would lead to a consolidation of position nearer the liberal end of the present spectrum.

23. If, however, one looks at the matter not through the eyes of the Party leaders but through the eyes of a broad section of the educated population in Eastern Europe, progress on freer movement becomes one of the criteria by which the success of the Conference will be judged. Interest in such progress

is not confined to a narrowly defined 'intelligentsia', but extends also to the 'technocrats' who would gain professionally from easier contact with the West. They will be too realistic to expect any major developments at the CSCE; but they will hope that it will contribute to gradual improvements in the fields of particular interest to them.

Conclusions

24. The main conclusion to emerge from this analysis is that the attitudes of the East European countries differ both as between themselves and also from that of the Soviet Union. But the practical importance of these differences is limited because:

(*a*) there will be strong pressures for conformity during the Conference which the East Europeans will find difficult to resist, even where on the substance they might wish to do so; and

(*b*) where the differences affect the motives rather than the policy advocated (eg 'the new security system' and 'all-European co-operation') the West is likely to find itself confronted with a high degree of apparent unity in the Warsaw Pact camp, masking the real differences of approach. From the point of view of Western tactics at the Conference it will be important to bear the differences in mind, particularly when it comes to framing practical proposals; but attempts openly to exploit them may increase the pressures for group loyalty on the Eastern side and thus prove counter-productive. The East Europeans will be aware of our desire to do nothing which would tighten the reins in Eastern Europe and they will probably urge upon us various policies which they claim would increase their freedom of manoeuvre. Insofar as these policies seem likely to weaken the cohesion of the West, or divert attention from the pursuit of integration within the enlarged Community, we shall have to weigh very carefully the suggested advantages for the East Europeans. In the last resort we shall have to make our own assessment of the costs and benefits, bearing in mind that whatever machinery and developments result from the CSCE will be more important in the long run than the Conference itself.[17]

---

[17] This paper was favourably received by other delegates when on 23-24 March it was circulated to the Davignon CSCE Sub-Committee. The Germans were the exception, and, according to Luxembourg telegram No. 117 of 24 March, 'were more reticent and did not volunteer any comment of substance' (see No. 3, note 7). Mr. Bullard stated in a letter to Sir J. Killick of 21 March that he hoped to be in a position to submit this paper officially to the EC Political Directors meeting on 11-12 April if required.

No. 6

Letter from Mr. Tickell to Mr. M.D. Butler[1] (Washington)

[*WDW 1/1*]

Confidential   FCO, *27 March 1972*

CSCE

Thank you for your letter of 2 March about our documents on the CSCE.[2] I delayed replying to your letter until the American Embassy had made the approach to Tom Brimelow which has been so long foreshadowed. Galloway[3] came in to speak to Brimelow on 14 March, and I enclose a copy of the record.[4]

2. I think that this record, and the minute of 2 March by Rodric Braithwaite recording his discussion with the American Embassy,[5] set out our present views reasonably fully. We do indeed want to avoid any European/American row about CSCE, and we agree that the avoidance of such a row is more important than abstract arguments about how a hypothetical conference might be prepared. But there are two important political points which tend to be undervalued:

[1] Mr. Butler was Counsellor at HM Embassy in Washington. In July 1972 he was appointed Head of European Integration Department (EID) in the FCO.

[2] In this letter Mr. Butler gave his views on the 'voluminous documents' relating to the CSCE (see No. 1) which had been copied to him. He explained that although the American handling of the CSCE would be decided by the US President, Mr. R.M. Nixon, and his Special Assistant for National Security Affairs, Dr. H.A. Kissinger, both of whom were to visit the Soviet Union during 22-30 May, the White House were not at the moment taking any interest in the subject. 'This', he suggested, 'is partly because Kissinger does not regard the CSCE as being a "serious" affair, partly because he is busy with other things and partly because he probably does not yet know what kind of tone he will wish to give to US/Soviet relations after the Moscow visit.' He suspected, however, that the White House would continue to take 'a very hard line' about the timing and content of multilateral preparations, and that they would want these preparations to be thorough.

[3] Mr. W.J. Galloway was Counsellor at the US Embassy in London.

[4] Not printed. During this meeting Mr. Galloway emphasised the importance Americans attached to 'substantive preparations' for a Conference and, in a note he gave Sir T. Brimelow, he expressed the US Government's concern lest the Conference's outcome increase pressures in Congress and from the public for a unilateral withdrawal of American forces from Europe and erode support in allied countries for necessary force improvements. For his part, Sir T. Brimelow made plain his view that the Warsaw Pact would not be prepared to engage in 'difficult discussions' at a preparatory stage, that the Russians wanted 'propaganda and political gains' from a Conference, and that it was necessary to convince Western opinion that 'the Alliance was prepared to talk to the East as well as to defend itself' (WDW 1/304/1).

[5] Mr. Braithwaite reported in this minute on a conversation he had on 2 March with Mr. G.G. Oplinger of the US Embassy on British and American attitudes towards the CSCE. 'In practice', Mr. Braithwaite had said, '. . . the differences seemed to be that while we were equally sceptical of the Conference, the Americans thought that for tactical reasons we should attempt to negotiate on substantive matters before Ministers met; while we thought that such negotiations should take place afterwards' (WDW 1/304/1).

(a) No European government, once multilateral preparation for a conference has begun, will wish to incur blame for preventing the conference from taking place. This means that the most likely reason for a breakdown at the multilateral preparatory stage would be action by the Russians (e.g. an invasion of Romania) or action by the Americans (e.g. a flat refusal to go to a conference on the grounds that preparations were unsatisfactory). The latter case would place considerable strains on the unity of the Alliance. It is no doubt for this reason that American officials admit in private that they too regard a conference as practically inevitable. (b) There is a growing political consensus among the members of the enlarged Community, born of a natural feeling of shared interest and coming alive in the workings of the Davignon Committee. The passive attitude of the Americans in NATO discussions have caused no check to the growth of this consensus. Moreover the Americans do not seem to have used their bilateral links with the French and the Germans to try and influence them. They have instead concentrated on trying to convince us. The procedural ideas to which the Americans object are not of British origin; but we see no reason to disagree with the consensus emerging around French and German views in the Davignon Committee.

3. We believe that maintenance of the unity of the Alliance is the West's most important single requirement in connexion with the Conference. But if we have to understand the American position, the Americans have to understand the European one. Our colleagues in the Davignon Committee could well resent it if the Americans failed to take European views into account because they regarded the discussions in NATO and Davignon as 'mildly useful as far as they keep everybody busy'.

4. You will see that Brimelow spoke of our concern to the American Embassy and suggested that the problem could be discussed both when von Staden[6] visited Washington and in the margin of the Senior Officials' meeting in Washington in the spring.[7] The aim of these exchanges would be to ensure that the White House, in briefing President Nixon for his Moscow visit,[8] was aware of the possibility of a divergence between American and European views, and recognised that both sides might have to make adjustments to reach a common position.

5. Incidentally you should know that Oplinger of the US Embassy here approached us on 21 March. He said that the State Department were pleased with what the Prime Minister had said in his speech to the Foreign

[6] Herr B. von Staden was Assistant State-Secretary at the West German Foreign Ministry.

[7] On 7 March Sir T. Brimelow had noted on Mr. Braithwaite's minute of 2 March (see note 5 above) regarding differences between the EC and the USA over the CSCE: 'Herr von Staden is going to discuss this general question in Washington later this month. He thinks there should be a Directors' meeting in Washington before the NATO May meeting, & that an effort should be made to reach agreement in the margin on the handling of this question in NATO.'

[8] See note 2 above.

Press Association.[9] They regarded his emphasis on the need for practical results in a Security Conference as close to their own views. They wondered if it would be useful for our two Delegations to NATO to attempt a first draft of the *Communiqué* which Ministers might issue after the NATO Ministerial Meeting in May. This would be a way of devising public language to which we could both subscribe.[10]

6. We have not yet replied to Oplinger but intend to do so soon. We shall then say that we have given careful thought about how best to prepare for the forthcoming NATO meeting. Brimelow discussed it with Ted Peck in Brussels on 19 March, and both thought little purpose would be served by trying to begin work on the *Communiqué* until early May, in other words, after the Baden-Württemburg [*sic*] elections[11] on 23 April and the Bundestag debate on 2-4 May.[12] They strongly felt that any work done before this would be wasted.

7. We shall also tell Oplinger that Brimelow talked to von Staden on 17 March following his return from Washington. Von Staden seemed fairly confident that the divergences of view between the Europeans and the Americans about the preparation of the Security Conference could be reconciled. Brimelow also spoke to Gaja[13] of the Italian Foreign Ministry on 20 March. He too thought that things were too uncertain to permit the preparation at this stage of the next NATO Ministerial Meeting.[14]

8. It may well be that Ministers will then have to play for time on the question of the Berlin precondition and the opening of the multilateral phase of the preparation of the Security Conference. This would happen if the

---

[9] In this speech, delivered on 16 March, the Prime Minister, Mr. E.R.G. Heath, spoke of his expectation that over the next ten years the common interests of Western Europe would be translated into 'effective common foreign policy'. He added, with regard to the CSCE, that the Warsaw Pact seemed 'more concerned with propaganda than with practical results', and HMG wished to develop contacts and cooperation with the East so that 'gradually we may dissolve the unnecessary barriers between us'.

[10] When Mr. Oplinger telephoned this proposal to Mr. Braithwaite on 21 March, Mr. Braithwaite told him that he thought they would have to 'bring in the French and the Germans informally at an early stage' since a text which did not command their agreement was 'unlikely to stick'. But Mr. Tickell subsequently minuted that it seemed 'churlish to rebuff an American approach of this kind'. He added: 'The Americans are feeling pretty sensitive about new working methods in the Davignon Committee, and would probably like to think they were cooperating closely with us on the drafting of the *communiqué*' (WDW 1/304/1).

[11] The Baden-Württemberg *Land* elections were regarded by the coalition Social Democrat (SPD)/Free Democrat (FDP) Government in Bonn as a test of the popularity of its treaties with Poland and the Soviet Union. In the event, the opposition CDU gained 53% of the votes cast and an absolute majority in the *Land* assembly. But the ruling parties regarded the 46% that they polled as a satisfactory result.

[12] See Volume I, No. 94.

[13] Sig. R. Gaja was Secretary-General of the Italian Foreign Ministry.

[14] Mr. Braithwaite spoke on the basis of paragraphs 6 and 7 when, on 30 March, he informed Mr. A.G. James of the US Embassy of British views on the drafting of a NATO *communiqué* (minute by Mr. Braithwaite of 30 March, WDW 1/304/1).

Treaties had not been ratified by then. In any case there seems no need for there to be a step forward at every Ministerial meeting.[15]

9. Apart from all this is the question of whether or not points of substance could be negotiated in the preparatory phase of a conference. We believe that no really interesting points are likely to be negotiated in a conference of more than thirty states, either at the Ministerial Session or in the preparations for it. In three years of bureaucratic activity NATO has been unable to identify any serious issues which might yield to negotiation in such a forum. Nor have the Americans suggested any. If events were to prove us wrong, and a conference led to practical agreements of genuine value to the West, nobody would be more pleased than ourselves.

C.C.C. TICKELL

[15] See No. 9, note 2 and Cmnd. 6932, pp. 120-22.

No. 7

Letter from Mr. Thomson (UKDEL NATO) to Sir T. Brimelow

[*WDW 1/1*]

Confidential   BRUSSELS, *5 April 1972*

Dear Tom,

1. In my Saving telegram No. 3 I set out in simplified terms the results so far of the negotiations in NATO on CSCE and MBFR.[1] I said that the negotiations here had been carried about as far as they could be unless some of the delegations received new instructions. It is clear that in the next 3 or 4 weeks all the capitals concerned will be looking again at their positions on these questions and not only in the light of what has happened at NATO but also with other considerations in mind such as President Nixon's visit to Moscow, European/American relations, the progress of *Ostpolitik* etc. I know that you are considering using some of the forthcoming international meetings, e.g. talks with the Germans in Bonn[2] and the Senior Level meeting in Washington,[3] for discussion of these subjects. It may be useful if I set out

[1] This telegram of 5 April reported major differences in NATO over the amount of agreement on substance necessary to justify Western assent to a CSCE at Ministerial level, and the timing of such a Ministerial meeting. Whilst the Americans thought Ministers should meet simply to ratify agreements on substance reached at a multilateral preparatory stage, the British considered it unrealistic 'to expect to get off the escalator once it is moving', and wished to preserve full flexibility at any Ministerial gathering. This, Mr. Thomson assumed, meant restricting the preparatory phase to agreement on agenda headings, machinery for subsequent substantive discussion, and 'agenda papers' elaborating headings and providing terms of reference. Mr. Thomson also pointed out that the majority in NATO favoured some link between CSCE and MBFR.

[2] These bilateral talks were held at senior official level on 9 June.

[3] See No. 6, note 7.

below some of the nuances of the situation which I omitted for the sake of simplicity from my Saving telegram No. 3 and some personal suggestions about how we might best press our own views on some of our allies.

2. First of all, the range of opinions within the Alliance is still fairly wide. There is some risk of a clash between the US and the Davignon countries but it has not come to that yet and it is important to see that it does not. What matters is that there should be a common allied position on substance. If that can be achieved it may be no bad thing that we should speak in slightly differing tones of voice. I suggest we are well placed to take a leading part in trying to establish the largest possible area of common ground.

3. I hope it is apparent from my Saving telegram No. 3 what are the main points on which it would be advantageous to move our principal partners. The following are some suggestions, based on our experience here, of arguments which may carry weight with certain of the allies.

4. The French have shown some sensitivity to tactical considerations. I believe that the argument which is most likely to move them closer to our position on the 'security' content of a CSCE is the thought that it will be useful to put up some ideas as bargaining counters which would not be damaging to us to withdraw in exchange for Soviet concessions. To meet French susceptibilities we have moved from speaking about a link between CSCE and MBFR and instead refer to confidence building measures and to general principles relating to force levels in Europe unconnected with any particular geographical area.[4]

5. The US Delegation here profess to have been converted to the following views which they say they have pressed on Washington:

(*a*) Once the multilateral preparatory phase has started it will be nearly impossible for the West to break off East/West negotiations short of some startling extraneous event.

(*b*) The security item on the CSCE agenda should comprise 2 sub-items as described in my Saving telegram No. 3.[5]

The argument in pressing the Americans to accept the consequences of (*a*) is that if we take a tough line about needing to get agreements on substance at the multilateral preparatory phase and then find ourselves moving into the next phase without having achieved much it will look as if our bluff has been called and both the East and the neutrals may be encouraged to believe that

[4] In his Saving telegram No. 3 (see note 1 above) Mr. Thomson remarked that the French were opposed to linking the CSCE in any way with the MBFR, but that they could probably agree to discuss confidence building measures (CBMs).

[5] These two sub-items were (1) a joint declaration relating to the level of armed forces in Europe, and (2) CBMs. In telegram No. 170 to UKDEL NATO of 14 April Sir A. Douglas-Home informed Mr. Thomson that while HMG favoured discussing 'military security' in 'general terms' at a Conference, they saw a difference between this and a 'specific link' between the CSCE and the MBFR. Moreover, he felt that more study needed to be given to CBMs 'which often look better than they are'.

they need not take Western stated positions too seriously. On (*b*) the arguments which have been most effective have been:

    1. that we need bargaining counters;
    2. that if, surprisingly, there was an East/West agreement this would put us in a favourable position at the outset of any subsequent MBFR talks;
    3. discussion of security in a CSCE might help to hold off both Mansfield[6] and real MBFR talks. The latter on the grounds that it would not be useful to get into more details until such time as comparatively simple things like a joint declaration and confidence building measures have been agreed.

6. If left to themselves the German Delegation here appear to be prepared to accept our views on virtually every question. I have dealt in separate correspondence with the important point of whether 'Freer Movement' should appear as such on the agenda of a CSCE.[7] If Bonn comes round to our view as expressed robustly by the Prime Minister in his speech of 16 March[8] (and the Germans here believe that at the top level in Bonn this view is likely to be accepted) then we here doubt whether any other delegation (including the French) will stand out against it. As regards the content of the security item at a CSCE the Germans seem to be quite sensitive to the argument that we do not want to give all 35 countries a pretext for intervening in force reduction talks which relate only to the Central Front. The 3 arguments at the end of paragraph 5 above also seem to carry weight. We think the Germans might well rally to the draft Joint Declaration enclosed in Lever's letter to Braithwaite of 4 April.[9] It is after all largely German language. Finally, on the crucial question of how much substance should be discussed at the multilateral preparatory phase the Germans seem attracted by the idea of 'agenda papers' (paragraph 5 of my Saving telegram No. 3).[10] We have suggested that these like the Nixon-Chou *communiqué*[11] might turn

---

[6] On 11 May 1971 the Senate Majority Leader, a Democrat, Mr. M. Mansfield, introduced an amendment to the Draft Extension Act with a view to cutting US forces in Europe by 150,000 men. This move, which was opposed by the Administration, was defeated in the Senate, but Mr. Mansfield continued to advocate military retrenchment.

[7] Mr. Thomson reported in Saving telegram No. 3 (see note 1 above) that the Germans, 'possibly supported by the French', opposed the British and Americans over whether 'freer movement' should feature on the CSCE agenda on the grounds that it would antagonise the Russians (cf. No. 3, note 5). However, at Anglo-German talks on 9 June (see note 2 above) Herr von Staden agreed that NATO should aim at its inclusion as a separate agenda item (minute from Mr. Braithwaite to Mr. Wiggin of 14 June, WDW 1/309/1).

[8] See No. 6, note 9.

[9] This draft Joint Declaration sent by Mr. P. Lever (UKDEL NATO) affirmed that talks on the level of armed forces in Europe would be useful, and outlined the objectives of such talks and the principles upon which force reductions should be implemented (WDN 27/1).

[10] See note 1 above.

[11] See *Public Papers of the Presidents of the United States. Richard Nixon, 1972*, (Washington: GPO 1974), pp. 376-9 for the joint statement issued following Mr. Nixon's discussions with leaders of the People's Republic of China, including Premier Chou En-Lai, from 21-28 February. See also Volume I, pps. 446-7.

out to be in 3 parts—a Western statement, an Eastern statement and common ground. Thus there could be some substance without there having to be a debate leading to either agreement or disagreement. It would be an agreement to differ pending the meeting at Ministerial level.[12]

J.A. THOMSON

[12] Sir A. Douglas-Home told Mr. Thomson in telegram No. 170 to UKDEL NATO (see note 5 above) that, 'barring accidents', HMG did not believe it realistic to think there could be any going back on a Conference once multilateral preparations for it had begun, and that this was likely fairly soon after the signature of the Berlin Final Protocol (see Cmnd. 6201, pp. 259-60). He pointed out that HMG remained 'sceptical about the practical value of a conference', and were concerned mainly (1) to maintain allied unity, and (2) to ensure that British Ministers retained freedom of action to speak at it as they might wish on European security and the barriers between East and West. 'We do not', he noted, '. . . want the Alliance to adopt any line which could lead to futile and possibly damaging East-West confrontations between officials at the preparatory stage, leading possibly to constraints on the agenda.' And, he added, HMG was cautious about handing detailed 'agenda papers' to the other side during the preparatory stage since this could lead to 'premature confrontation'.

No. 8

Letter from Mr. Braithwaite to Mr. Allan (Luxembourg)

[*WDW 1/1*]

Confidential   FCO, *25 April 1972*

Dear James,

CSCE: National Attitudes

1. The following is a hasty attempt to produce encapsulated descriptions of national positions within the Alliance, in response to the request in your letter of 20 April.[1]

Federal Republic of Germany

2. The Germans regard themselves (rightly) as having the biggest national stake in the conference. This is because Germany is divided and because they hope that a conference could produce some improvement in cooperation between East and West Germany as well as between East and West Europe as a whole. They therefore neither wish nor wish [*sic*] to be seen to be delaying the move to a conference. Nor are they prepared to speak about it in less than guardedly optimistic tones. They suspect that our view of the conference is negative and that we regard it as primarily an occasion for judicious political warfare (which of course we do). They fear that such an attitude, if adopted by the Alliance, would wreck whatever chance the conference may have of producing an amelioration in East/West relations

[1] In this letter Mr. Allan requested basic information on the positions of the other Alliance members on the CSCE to enable him to produce 'a summary of national positions' for his Ambassador.

from which they would benefit.[2]

3. The Germans have known from the beginning that a conference could only take place if the DDR participated on an equal basis with others; and that Soviet pressure for a conference is also pressure for the West to recognise the DDR. They have therefore been grateful for devices (such as the Berlin precondition) which slow down the rate of movement for the conference while they try to negotiate their *modus vivendi* with East Germany. In this question of timing they have our full support.

United States

4. The Americans think (as we do) that nothing good or sensible is likely to come from the conference. They believe that the Russians want the conference, and therefore thought that we can get the Russians to make concessions (in areas they have failed to define) in return for Western agreement to go to a conference. This is why they believe that the multilateral preparatory phase should be used in order to negotiate Russian concessions.

5. They fear that the Russian objective for seeking a conference is sinister: to divide the Alliance. Even though they (like we) may think that the danger of the Russians succeeding is not very great, they resent the idea that the Russians will gain a prestige success once their long standing proposal for a conference is accepted.

6. However recently the Americans appear to have been coming round to our own view that, like it or not, a conference is politically inevitable barring some major external event e.g. the invasion of any Warsaw Pact country, or some other incident leading to a serious worsening of East/West relations.[3] Much will depend on what President Nixon brings back from Moscow.[4]

France

7. The French official analysis of the usefulness of a conference resembles our own. French Ministers are however inclined in private to argue that a conference would enable the Allies to pursue what M. Schumann[5] described to the Secretary of State last autumn as 'peaceful roll-back'[6] i.e. that the

---

[2] Mr. Hibbert remarked in a letter to Mr. Wiggin of 5 April that in a recent conversation with Herr von Staden the latter had emphasised that the CSCE was inevitable, should be regarded positively as a suitable vehicle for Western *détente* diplomacy, and should not be approached with a primarily defensive attitude. 'I have', Mr. Hibbert observed, 'the impression that von Staden would find the tone of the British position paper [No. 1] uncomfortably cool' (WDW 1/309/1).

[3] On 4 May Mr. W.P. Rogers, the US Secretary of State, met Sir A. Douglas-Home in London. He said that the Americans attached importance to having a clear idea of what would emerge from a Ministerial Conference before it started. 'He did not however', according to telegram No. 191 to UKDEL NATO of 4 May, 'dispute that once the multilateral band-wagon had begun to roll it would gather its own momentum.'

[4] See No. 6, note 2.

[5] M. M. Schumann was French Foreign Minister.

[6] Sir A. Douglas-Home met M. Schumann on 11 November 1971 during a visit by the latter to London (WRF 3/548/10): see Volume I, No. 83, note 9.

conference would lead to a loosening of the Soviet Union hold on East European countries. (We doubt if French officials really think that this is very likely in the foreseeable future.) In public French Ministers are even more optimistic, because of their 'special' role in relations with Eastern Europe (and, no doubt, to appease left-wing opinion in France).

8. While participating fully in the Alliance's discussions about the conference, (but not about MBFR) the French take care not to tie their hands nor to commit themselves to any particular Alliance formula. Their ideas on procedures are however winning a growing number of adherents in the Davignon machinery. These ideas are that the conference should be organised as follows:

(*a*) multilateral preparations, probably in Helsinki, designed to seek agreement on procedures and agenda, but not to negotiate substance;
(*b*) a short ministerial meeting, at which the Ministers would make broad political speeches and agree to set up commissions of officials to pursue individual problems. These commissions would deal with security; economic cooperation; cultural cooperation etc (including 'freer movement');
(*d*) [*sic*] the commissions would report back to a second Ministerial conference once they had reached conclusions suitable for decisions.

We think the French proposals are practical and sensible. But we are not blindly committeed [*sic*] to them: much will depend on developments in the tactical and political situations.

Italy

9. Italian officials are particularly sceptical about the value of a conference, which they see in a very sinister light as a Soviet device for disrupting Western Europe. They are very active in Davignon discussions and less active (because less well represented) in NATO. In Italy however *détente* is electorally attractive and Italian Ministers therefore avoid taking up clear positions. But so far they have stuck loyally to the line agreed in NATO communiques.

The Netherlands, Greece and Turkey

10. I lump these nations together because at least on official and private Ministerial occasions they take a hard-headed view of the prospects of a conference.

Norway, Denmark, Belgium and Canada

11. These countries are known to the irreverent as the 'wet front' because their Ministers tend to believe—in spite of the evidence—that the conference would be a Good Thing. M. Harmel is particularly dedicated to the pursuit of *détente* since he invented it when he wrote the 'Harmel Report' for NATO in 1967.[7] The characteristics of the wet front are that they believe that a conference could negotiate a genuine *détente* and that the West must avoid being provocative either before or during the conference (especially on

---

[7] M. P.C.J.M. Harmel was Belgian Foreign Minister. See Cmnd. 6932, pp. 5-6 and Volume I, No. 10, note 9.

things like free movement of people on which they know the Russians are vulnerable).

Yours ever,

R.Q. BRAITHWAITE

No. 9

Minute from Mr. Tickell on the link between a Security Conference and MBFR[1]

[*WDW 1/1*]

Confidential   FCO, *23 May 1972*

1. The Alliance is at the moment much exercised with the problem of how far there should be a direct link between the proposed Conference on Security and Co-operation in Europe and the negotiation of Mutual and Balanced Force Reductions. The present submission sets out the views of officials in the Foreign and Commonwealth Office and Ministry of Defence. The Secretary of State may wish to see it before the NATO Ministerial Meeting in Bonn, at which the problem may well be raised.[2]

2. The discussion in the Alliance is obscured by confusion over the meaning of words. But there are three different sets of considerations which lead individual members of the Alliance to take up differing positions:

(*a*) The Americans do not want the rate of progress towards East/West exploration of MBFR to be impeded by any procedural complication, of the kind which a link between MBFR and the CSCE might entail. This is for well-known domestic political reasons. Nor do they want countries not directly concerned (and particularly neutrals) to exercise any jurisdiction over the course of negotiations;

(*b*) Members of the Alliance who do not have troops or territory on NATO's Central Front (and whose claim to participate directly in the detailed negotiation of MBFR is therefore rather small) nevertheless fear

[1] This minute was addressed to Mr. Wiggin, Sir T. Brimelow and the Private Secretary (Mr. A.A. Acland). On 30 May Mr. Wiggin minuted to Mr. Tickell: 'Sir T. Brimelow and Mr. [M.O'D.B.] Alexander [Assistant Private Secretary] have seen. They both felt it was unnecessary to put this paper to the Secretary of State at this stage.'

[2] This meeting was held on 30-31 May. Its final *communiqué* committed NATO to entering Multilateral Preparatory Talks (MPT) after the signature of the Berlin Protocol, although, as Sir A. Douglas-Home reported in Bonn telegram No. 741 of 31 May, Mr. Rogers stated that the Americans would not in practice be ready for these until after their Presidential elections. A formula was also found, to which the French could subscribe, 'to distinguish military measures which would be examined at the Conference itself (i.e. confidence building measures) and MBFR', and it was agreed that multilateral explorations for MBFR negotiations should be undertaken either before or in parallel with the MPT. Sir A. Douglas-Home added that the Americans did not seek to establish a link between the CSCE and MBFR exploratory talks, but that 'the thought was clearly at the back of their minds'. See also Volume I, pps. 477-8.

that the negotiation would affect their interests. They evidently believe that a clear link between MBFR and the Security Conference (in which they would participate with full rights) would help to ensure that they could take some direct part in the negotiation of force reductions. The Italians,[3] Norwegians, Greeks and Turks have all expressed firm views about the desirability of a clear link (so have the Germans, for reasons which are obscure)[4];

(*c*) We and the French fall into neither of the previous categories. We both dislike the idea of MBFR because of the military disadvantages. The French choose to opt out entirely. We believe that the domestic political pressures on both the Americans and the flank members of the Alliance (i.e. the countries motivated by the considerations in (*b*) above) are strong. In the interests of Alliance unity, both need to be taken into account.

3. Officials in the Foreign and Commonwealth Office and the Ministry of Defence have therefore been examining various proposals for linking MBFR and the CSCE. Our aim has been to find possible devices, which might meet the political requirements of the Americans and the flank countries, without gratuitously accelerating the move towards MBFRs or allowing outsiders to dictate the course of any eventual negotiation. These devices fall into two categories:

(*a*) Proposals which would give the discussion at a Security Conference of 'aspects of military security' (suggested by NATO as a possible agenda item) some real content; and which might be negotiated among all participants at a Security Conference, including the neutrals;

(*b*) Procedural arrangements, which would provide some link between the Security Conference and any body set up to negotiate MBFRs, without giving the 34 countries participating in a Security Conference any jurisdiction over the negotiations themselves.

4. Officials' ideas are set out in the attached copy of a draft paper,[5] which is in a form suitable for handing to selected Allies.[6] Briefly they are as follows:

[3] In a letter of 18 May Mr. Thomson informed Mr. Wiggin the 'Italians have embarked on quite a campaign' in support of a CSCE/MBFR link.

[4] Bonn telegram No. 724 of 29 May reported a radio interview given by the West German Defence Minister, Herr H.H.W. Schmidt, on 28 May in which he said: 'I cannot conceive of a conference about the security of Europe at which there was no discussion whatever about mutual troop reductions.'

[5] Not printed. This draft paper was a revised version of Annex I of the FCO's CSCE Position Paper (see No. 1). The original draft of Annex I had been sent to Mr. Thomson on 14 April (see No. 1, note 10).

[6] The proposals outlined in the draft paper rested on the assumption that MBFRs 'could well damage the Alliance militarily'. But the paper recognised that for political reasons, and in order to avoid the unilateral reduction of national forces in NATO, HMG might have to negotiate on the subject. It further asserted that a CSCE/MBFR link could depend on political developments, including the coincidence in time between the start of the CSCE and domestic pressure in the USA for early MBFR talks, and the need to devise a procedural

(*a*) The Security Conference might agree to negotiate (perhaps in a Security Commission of officials set up for the purpose) (*a*) a 'declaration' on force levels in Europe so general that all participants in the Conference could sign it; and (*b*) certain 'politico-military confidence-building measures'. These might for example impose an obligation to notify in advance the movement of large bodies of troops; they would be simple to negotiate and operate, and their effect would be political rather than military;

(*b*) The Security Commission might set up sub-groups to negotiate reductions in particular areas. The sub-group on Central Europe would negotiate reductions in Central Europe (i.e. MBFRs). It would inform the Plenary Commission of progress as appropriate, without accepting that the plenary meeting had any direct authority over the negotiations.

5. These ideas are of course very hypothetical, and we would not want the Alliance to commit itself to them prematurely. Much further study is necessary, and decisions will be much influenced by political developments. It is not yet clear whether a link between the CSCE and MBFR is politically inevitable, or whether the Americans, as their own ideas become clearer, will continue to insist that there should be *no* substantive link. However the ideas set out in the attached memorandum seem, on present form, to represent a possible meeting-ground between the opposing views of the Americans and the flank countries, and might also find acceptance with the French.

Recommendation

6. I therefore *recommend* that we deploy the arguments set out in the paper with our Allies[7] as an illustration of the way we think a link between the Conference and MBFRs might sensibly emerge, while for the time being resisting any attempt to commit the Alliance prematurely to a public position (e.g. in the forthcoming NATO *Communiqué*). I have inserted an appropriate passage in the Secretary of State's draft statement for the NATO Ministerial Meeting for use if desired.[8]

C.C.C. TICKELL

framework to take account of the desire of neutral and non-aligned states and certain allied countries, not directly involved, to be associated in some way with force reduction negotiations.

[7] A final version of this paper, which omitted references to the political reasons for MBFR and the danger of unilateral force reductions (*v. ibid.*), was approved by Sir T. Brimelow and subsequently distributed to posts. Mr. Thomson was requested, in a covering letter of 7 June, to circulate the paper to allied representatives in Brussels (WDN 27/1).

[8] On 23 May Mr. Wiggin noted on this submission: 'I agree in principle, but all this is highly theoretical at this moment . . . For their own domestic reasons the Americans *may* on MBFR insist on something much more "streamlined", at the risk of seriously upsetting their Allies and some of the neutrals. We must, as Mr. Tickell suggests, keep our options open.'

No. 10

Letter from Mr. Tickell to Sir G. Millard[1] (Stockholm)

[*WDW 1/373/1*]

Confidential   FCO, *6 June 1972*

My dear Ambassador,

   Conference on European Security (CSCE): Coordination with the neutral countries

   1. We were most grateful to you for your letters of 17 and 26 May[2] about your exchanges with the Swedes about the European Security Conference (CSCE). Swedish views are reassuringly similar to our own in most respects. Bearing in mind the caveat in the last sentence of your letter of 26 May,[3] we can only hope that their courage will not fail them on the night. It might be useful for your next encounter if I were to comment on the main points raised with you by Wachtmeister.

   2. You will have seen from the NATO *Communiqué* of 31 May[4] that the Alliance has now formally accepted the Finnish offer to provide facilities in Helsinki for the multilateral preparatory talks. The Swedes should by now have received a Finnish memorandum on the subject giving administrative details. A copy is enclosed.[5]

   3. No decision has been taken about the place for the Conference itself. This is presumably one of the points which would have to be settled at the preparatory stage. In some ways it would make sense to have the Conference at Helsinki; but the Americans have expressed reservations on the subject to the Russians as well as to their own Allies, and others have similar reservations. The particular convenience of Helsinki in regard to the problem

---

[1] HM Ambassador in Stockholm.

[2] These letters recorded Sir G. Millard's conversations, on 17 and 25 May, with Count W.H.F. Wachtmeister, the Head of the Political Division of the Swedish Foreign Ministry. On 25 May Count Wachtmeister informed Sir G. Millard of recent discussions between Dr. K. Wickman, the Swedish Foreign Minister, and M. P. Graber, his Swiss counterpart, on CSCE (WDW 1/1 and 1/373/1).

[3] In the final paragraph of this letter (*v. ibid.*) Sir G. Millard reported that Dr. Wickman had emphasised the importance the Swedes attached to the cooperation aspects of CSCE and the need to avoid challenging the East. 'I rather suspect', Sir G. Millard concluded, 'that in the end we shall find the Swedish politicians somewhat less resolute in pressing the Russians, both on the Agenda and on basic principles, than the quite robust line taken by Wachtmeister with me on 17 May would seem to suggest.'

[4] See No. 9, note 2.

[5] Not printed. Commenting on this memorandum in a letter to Mr. Thomson of 19 May, Mr. Braithwaite said that at first glance the arrangements 'seem entirely adequate'. He doubted, however, if they were suitable for the long-drawn out process the multilateral conference was likely to be (EN 2/15).

of German representation should of course disappear when both German states enter the United Nations.[6]

4. You will see from the Finnish memorandum that no decision has yet been taken about Conference languages. The Germans feel very strongly about this, and Scheel[7] made a particular point of it at the NATO Ministerial Meeting. The Germans are anxious to avoid the sort of translation difficulties on questions of especial importance to them which arose during the recent Four Power talks on Berlin.[8] In addition, as Scheel said, it would be deplorable for the East and West Germans to communicate with each other in a foreign language. There would, I think, be little difficulty about accepting German as a Conference language if the Italians had not put in a comparable claim for Italian. At the NATO Meeting Moro[9] made a slightly shamefaced reference to Italian claims, although he must know that they have little justification. We have no wish to get involved in this dispute although we have told the Germans that we are sympathetic to their claim. We hope that the Germans and Italians will be able to sort matters out between them. If they could produce a compromise, no doubt the other NATO countries would gladly accept it.

5. It may not be easy to reconcile the differences within the Alliance on Western tactics over the item on freer movement of people, ideas and information. There is a school, headed by the Americans and Dutch, who think it would be right for the Conference to take up an unequivocal position on this at the outset, modifying it as necessary later in discussion with the other side. The other school, headed by the French and ourselves, would prefer to use subtler tactics and to put forward a formula for use on the agenda which would permit Western Ministers to deal with the matter as they wished at the Conference itself but avoid a premature argument, in which we could emerge the losers, at the preparatory talks. The particular formula we have in mind is: 'the development of contacts between peoples, the wider dissemination of information and the strengthening of cultural co-operation'. Others, particularly the Germans, believe that there should not be a separate agenda item at all but that we should seek to obtain piecemeal concessions on this point when dealing with other items on the agenda. In addition Scheel suggested at the NATO Meeting that freer movement might be one of the principles in a declaration on the principles governing relations between states. We see no objection to this provided it is not merely an alternative to negotiations. It is good that the Swedes attached importance to the substance of this question, and appear to be aware of the difficulties

[6] Sir G. Millard had told Count Wachtmeister on 17 May (see note 2 above) that Helsinki was a particularly good venue for preparatory talks because both East and West Germany were represented there. On 21 June 1973 the UN Security Council approved the entry of the two Germanies into the UN and they were formally admitted on 18 September.

[7] Herr W. Scheel was West German Foreign Minister.

[8] See Volume I, No. 79.

[9] Sig. A. Moro was Italian Foreign Minister.

involved in approaching it bald-headed.[10] Provided they and other neutrals can maintain this attitude, they could play a useful part in bringing the Russians to negotiations.

6. There were a number of confused references to disarmament during the Ministerial Meeting in Bonn. The consensus seemed to be that the CSCE should not be turned into a disarmament conference although it could discuss certain confidence-building measures (e.g. notification of troop movements and prohibition of manoeuvres in areas close to international boundaries) whose effect would be chiefly political. It will be interesting to know in due course precisely what disarmament questions the Swedes consider that the Conference might usefully discuss. NATO has hitherto limited its 'disarmament' studies to the question of MBFR and 'certain military aspects of security' (those described above).[11]

7. On MBFR, the Alliance is divided in a number of ways. The French, as you know, have opted out of the debate altogether. The others divide between the American view that any link between the Conference and MBFR should be 'minimal' and the opposite view, espoused in particular by the Italians, that MBFR should be closely associated with the Conference and that those participating in the Conference who wished also to participate in MBFR should be entitled to do so. We, as you know, take a middle view. We shall shortly be sending you a revised version of Annex I to our draft position paper on the Conference, which sets out in some detail our views on the nature of a link between the Conference and MBFR.[12] We shall be showing this paper to our Allies. There would be no objection to your drawing on it when talking to the Swedes, but it would be as well to explain that the subject remains hypothetical and our ideas are only among a range of possibilities.

8. We received a more detailed exposition of the Swiss proposals on the arbitration machinery a Conference might set up when the Swiss Ambassador called on Tom Brimelow on 24 May. The record of their conversation is contained in Allan Ramsay's letter of 1 June to Miss Brown[13] in Berne (copied to you).[14] Our impression of the Swiss proposals remains that they are not

[10] Count Wachtmeister had told Sir G. Millard on 17 May (see note 2 above) that Sweden wanted to go 'as far as possible in using the Conference to secure greater freedom of movement of persons, ideas and information'. But he warned the British Ambassador 'there was a limit to what would be practicable'.

[11] See No. 9.

[12] *V. ibid.*, notes 5, 6 and 7.

[13] Mr. A.J. Ramsay was First Secretary in WOD and Miss G.G. Brown was Head of Chancery at HM Embassy in Berne.

[14] Not printed. This letter reported that the Dr. A. Weitnauer, the Swiss Ambassador in London, had informed Sir T. Brimelow of his Government's proposal for the establishment of two permanent European organs: an arbitration tribunal and a commission of enquiry, mediation and conciliation, which would be respectively responsible for dealing with justiciable and non-justiciable disputes. Sir T. Brimelow agreed that 'the proposal for compulsory arbitration had respectable antecedents', such as those put forward by the Duc de Sully and the Abbé de Saint Pierre, but added that no-one had been able to carry them out, and that

altogether realistic. We await the Legal Adviser's opinion,[15] but it would be interesting to know in due course what the Swedes think about them.

9. We agree with Wachtmeister's warning against permitting outsiders, e.g. the Mediterranean Arab countries, to participate in a Conference. This is an issue with dangerous implications. A variation of the idea, put forward by Moro at the NATO Ministerial Meeting, is to have a Mediterranean Security Conference in succession to the European one. We do not like this idea either.

10. I conclude on a general point. For the reasons given in my letter of 20 April to Patricia Hutchinson, we attach particular importance to remaining in close contact with the neutral countries before and during the Conference.[16] At the NATO Meeting both the Secretary of State and Maurice Schumann laid particular emphasis on this point. The Secretary of State said that we must never overlook the fact that in many respects the views of the neutral countries were identical with those of the Alliance, and that many of their aims were similar. Whatever procedures for consultation the Alliance might set up during the multilateral preparatory phase should therefore be sufficiently flexible to allow for the participation of neutrals from time to time. No-one challenged this point and I think it was generally accepted. I see no reason why you should not inform the Swedes in confidence that the Secretary of State spoke on these lines on 30 May. The neutrals will no doubt be unwilling to be seen to associate themselves too closely with NATO during the preparatory talks and the Conference itself. But we want to develop a relationship with them which will enable consultation to take place continuously if unobtrusively. Your own exchanges with Wachtmeister seem to us an admirable first step in this direction.

Yours ever,
C.C.C. Tickell

now the Russians were a problem since they had 'a very restricted interpretation of international law'.

[15] In a paper of 11 September Mr. H.G. Darwin, Legal Counsellor in the FCO, recommended qualified acceptance of the Swiss proposal. He thought the East Europeans likely to oppose it, and that there was clear advantage in supporting the Swiss at the opening and demanding that the item should be included separately on the CSCE agenda for serious substantive discussion.

[16] In this letter to Miss P.M. Hutchinson (Head of Chancery, HM Embassy in Stockholm) Mr. Tickell argued that: (1) the West might wish to enlist neutral support in raising important issues at the Ministerial stage of the CSCE; (2) HMG's hand with their 'more pliant Allies' would be strengthened if they could obtain the neutrals' understanding for British views; and (3) the Russians would certainly soon try to woo the neutrals to their cause (EN 2/15).

No. 11

Letter from Mr. G.G.H. Walden[1] *to Mr. Staples (UKDEL NATO)*

[*EN 2/13*]

Confidential   FCO, *4 August 1972*

Cultural Aspects of the CSCE

1. I attach a summary record of the first meeting of the Working Party on Cultural Aspects of the CSCE.[2] In reading the back papers in preparation for this meeting, and at the meeting itself, I became increasingly aware of the danger of losing sight of our broad strategy in the morass of detail. Bearing in mind that we shall be called upon in the near future to formulate our approach more succinctly (e.g. in the document we have undertaken to provide for the next meeting of the D'Avignon [*sic*] sub-committee),[3] I think the time has come to attempt to establish the framework in which we are going to work rather more realistically than has been done hitherto. This letter is a first attempt, on which we should welcome your comments,[4] as well as those of Moscow.[5]

2. As you point out in paragraph 6 of your letter to Braithwaite of 28 July, the propaganda aspects of the Conference will inevitably be paramount in this field.[6] We shall have to avoid appearing to lead the pack and the

[1] Mr. Walden was First Secretary in EESD.

[2] Not printed. Mr. Bullard suggested the establishment of a small FCO Working Party to consider cultural (including freer movement) aspects of the CSCE in a minute of 30 June. The Working Party, which included representatives of EESD, WOD, Cultural Exchange Department (CED), Cultural Relations Department (CRD), Information Research Department (IRD) and the Permanent Under-Secretary's Department (PUSD), met for the first time on 26 July.

[3] At the Davignon Political Committee meeting on 18 July the British were asked to produce a paper summarising the preparatory work done both by the CSCE Sub-Committee and by NATO in this field. The paper was sent under cover of a letter from Mr. R.J.T. McLaren (WOD) to Miss J.J.d'A. Collings (HM Embassy in The Hague) of 25 August (WDW 1/8).

[4] In letters to Mr. Walden of 9 and 10 August Mr. Staples expressed his concern over the prospect of 'an enlarged dossier on cultural exchanges', such as the Italian paper appeared to favour, replacing freer movement as an agenda item. He also wondered whether Mr. Walden might not be 'dismissing too lightly some of the possible Soviet tactics to head us off free movement proposals'.

[5] Mr. K.B. Scott (Head of Chancery, HM Embassy in Moscow) wrote to Mr. Walden in a letter of 24 August that he thought that the Russians would inevitably describe the Western line on culture as 'provocative, unjustified and designed to wreck *détente*'. 'This', he maintained, 'is why it is important that the initial western presentation should, without pulling punches or pussy-footing, be transparently reasonable in the eye of any unbiased observer.'

[6] This letter summarised recent US proposals regarding cultural relations in the CSCE. But Mr. Staples also emphasised that though it would be wrong for the West to go to the Conference seeking only a propaganda victory, it would be foolish to ignore the fact that propaganda was bound to play a part. Western countries should not, he thought, be inhibited

'provocative' presentation of our views. But in our aim to secure genuine improvements in reducing barriers within Europe and 'generally to spread the contagion of liberty' we should not shrink from asserting western beliefs in the freedom of movement, information, and cultural contacts. Neutral opinion will be of great importance. Despite probable Soviet tactics to head us off, e.g. by proposing visa abolition agreements, and the counter-arguments that they may produce (which have already been anticipated in US and other papers on this subject) we should not have too much difficulty in coming out on top. Soviet arguments are likely to be unconvincing, particularly in the light of their own recent arrest of dissidents and the Czechoslovak trials.[7] There will be little need for the West to point this up at the Conference; it will no doubt be done very efficiently in the Press (discreetly aided by ourselves if need be).

3. But we must also seek to salvage some practical improvements in the present situation from whatever verbiage the Conference produces.

The reasons for this are:

(*a*) practical improvements (whether qualitative or quantitative) are desirable in themselves;

(*b*) the Russians should be made to pay a price for the West agreeing to hold the Conference at all;

(*c*) Ministers will presumably wish to demonstrate to domestic opinion here not only their ability to get the better of the Russians in ideological disputation, but to negotiate practical measures to increase close contacts.

4. The presentation of Western ideals will be a matter of careful drafting. Far more difficult will be the establishment of a realistic fall-back position, i.e. the identification of areas of potential agreement between ourselves and the East. What we need here is a carefully composed list of hardheaded proposals which:

(*a*) it would be difficult for the Russians to decline;

(*b*) can be agreed with our allies;

(*c*) appeal to the popular imagination;

(*d*) are workable in practice;

(*e*) involve a minimum of Government finance;

(*f*) will attract sufficient numbers of Western participants (e.g. in any increased exchanges);

(*g*) introduce another germ of freedom into the East.

Cultural Exchanges

5. Clearly, few of the proposals so far advanced satisfy all the above criteria. In the cultural field in particular it is most important to take full stock of our

from putting forward proposals which they believed would improve the situation in Europe by fear that the East would describe this 'as a purely propaganda initiative'.

[7] Between 17 July and 11 August forty-six people were jailed in Czechoslovakia on charges of subversion, anti-state propaganda and sedition.

present position before promoting further officially sponsored exchanges. The main fact to bear in mind is that the UK was for a long period the front runner in this field (Mr. Macmillan's visit in 1959),[8] and has amassed considerable expertise in implementing a complex and comprehensive network of cultural and other exchanges with the Soviet Union and other East European countries. We are in danger of taking too much for granted what has already been achieved, and of ignoring what is already being done. I attach a copy of our latest Cultural Agreement with the Soviet Union;[9] a quick glance will suffice to show how extensive the field already covered is. I should emphasise here that we are in general well satisfied with the way this Agreement works. The second point to be clear about is the scope for intensifying these exchanges, either numerically or by seeking to cover a wider field. The experience of the last few years has shown convincingly that this scope may be very narrow. In particular, the abortive Anglo/Soviet Consultative Committee on the development of bilateral relations, which sought to identify new areas for exchanges, produced a large number of recommendations (attached) which in the event either proved impractical, or encountered simply no demand.[10] As far as we could identify them, the reasons were disenchantment with the Soviet Union; a reluctance to become enmeshed in the difficulties of administering exchanges with the Russians; and lack of finance. The plain fact is therefore that in so far as we and the experts in this field—Cultural Exchange Department and the British Council—are able to judge, we have probably reached a temporary plateau of interest in the Soviet Union in this country, and it would be unrealistic and indeed subsequently embarrassing if we were to undertake at a CSCE to increase exchanges, only to discover that there were insufficient takers. This is in fact precisely what happened in the case of the Anglo/Soviet Consultative Committee, where the Russians made some play with our alleged failure to act on the Committee's recommendations.

6. On the other hand we do not wish to take a negative line on cultural exchanges at the Conference. We therefore think that the basis of our position should be to draw a distinction between governmental and non-governmental exchanges. Our initial position would be to note with satisfaction the high level of exchanges already achieved under bilateral Cultural Agreements, and to make non-committal noises about developing and expanding these where possible. At the same time we would press for increased contacts in the non-governmental field (i.e. directly between

[8] See H. Macmillan, *Riding the Storm, 1956-1959* (Macmillan: London, 1971), pp. 557 f.

[9] Not printed. See *Agreement between the Government of the United Kingdom of Great Britain and Northern Ireland and the Government of the Union of Soviet Socialist Republics on relations in the Scientific, Educational and Cultural Fields for 1971-73*, Cmnd. 4675 (London: HMSO, 1971); also Volume I, p. 331.

[10] See Volume I, No. 45, note 1.

universities and other independent bodies).[11] This would serve both our ideological and practical purposes. It would be more in keeping with the Western, and particularly the British way of doing things, to encourage autonomous organisations to establish their own contacts with their Soviet counterparts, though they would of course need guidance from e.g. the British Council. It would also avoid financial difficulties, which are very real. The Soviet reaction to this tactic would no doubt be one of suspicion, but they could hardly denounce us for proclaiming a principle which they have already accepted in practice in one or two cases. On this subject therefore we would anticipate only a discreet tussle over drafting rather than a polemic. The main difficulty might be to substantiate our position on non-governmental exchanges by suggesting fields besides universities where this could be usefully encouraged. CED are looking into this.

7. We must not expect our detailed positions to coincide with those of our Allies, since existing arrangements will vary from country to country. This is obviously an argument for keeping the discussion at the Conference on general lines, leaving any detailed points to be worked out bilaterally. It may well be that some NATO countries will see areas for expansions.

8. There are some signs that the Russians themselves may favour a general approach. I note for example that *Pravda* of 26 July (Barder's[12] letter to Fall of 27 July) in reporting the Brussels Assembly of Representatives of Public Opinion for Security and Cooperation in Europe, said that

> 'The Assembly came to the conclusion that it was necessary to draw up an international cultural exchange convention that would serve as the basis for wider cultural exchanges among all European nations.'[13]

I think the negotiation of any such document (providing we were willing to accept it in principle) would clearly be a delicate matter. The Russians may well turn up with a draft including unacceptable passages, e.g. stipulating that cultural exchanges should not be used to spread 'inhumane' values. We on our side would no doubt wish to insert a reference to 'freedom' in some form or other. In other words any such negotiation would be likely to follow the ritual we perform every two years when the foreword of our cultural agreement is re-negotiated with the Russians; and the result would no doubt be an anodyne document inoffensive to both sides.

[11] In his letter to Mr. Walden of 24 August (see note 5 above) Mr. Scott questioned whether it was 'indeed possible to have a truly "non-governmental" exchange with the S[oviet] U[nion]' given the all-pervading nature of the Soviet state.

[12] Mr. B.L. Barder was First Secretary at HM Embassy in Moscow.

[13] This article by Mr. A.P. Shitikov, the Chairman of the Soviet Committee for European Security, also recalled that 'people working in the cultural field' had emphasised that cultural contacts should not be used for causing damage to any country, and that there should be 'no compromising attitude towards the attempts of implanting anti-popular, anti-communist ideas in the socialist countries' (EN 2/15).

Freedom of Information

9. Freedom of information is a separate but clearly related item. Here we see little reason to equivocate on our principled position, and there should be no difficulty in drawing the Russians and others into making ham-fisted statements in favour of censorship by enunciating our own ideals in a non-polemical way. But it is also in the information field, we think, that our most significant and tangible gains might be secured, and we should work hard at establishing a series of practical proposals which stand a good chance of being accepted. There is clearly no question of the Russians or East Europeans agreeing to the unrestricted circulation of Western Books and newspapers in their countries. But the following proposals may be difficult for them to turn down out of hand:

(*a*) the mutual establishment of reading rooms and libraries in each other's capitals, (in our case we shall have to bear in mind the need to keep Russian official representation in Britain below its ceiling, but this is strictly a bilateral matter which can be pursued if necessary after the conference).

(*b*) The establishment of an East/West magazine, which could grow out of the publication of the CSCE minutes, and become a sort of international and more specialised version of '*Angliya*'.[14] This would have a joint, and perhaps rotating editorship (one East, one West, one neutral) and cover 'cooperation' subjects, e.g. economic collaboration, pollution, etc. (We are still working on the details of this proposal and would prefer you not to mention it to our Allies for the time being.)

(*c*) A mutual commitment to publish in full in one or two national newspapers a statement of agreed length provided by each country on it's [*sic*] National Day.

(*d*) Improved exchanges in the field of films, radio and television. (We are still looking into this; there may well be insuperable commercial obstacles.)

We are not hopeful about persuading the Russians to discontinue jamming of the BBC or of other Western broadcasts (although there is an outside chance that they may do so unilaterally, perhaps for the duration of the Conference itself). They may well demand an unacceptable *quid pro quo* either in the form of an understanding that Western broadcasts will be 'toned down' or even that Radio Liberty and Radio Free Europe will be closed down[15]. Paradoxically the West's interests would be best served if the Russians were to emerge from the Conference with jammers still blaring, given that these are by no means 100% effective. A deal would almost certainly leave us the net losers.[16]

[14] See Volume I, No. 11, note 8.

[15] Cf. Volume I, No. 92, note 19.

[16] In their letters of 10 August and 24 August (see notes 4 and 5 above) Mr. Staples and Mr. Scott respectively supported the proposals in this paragraph and agreed with Mr. Walden's assessment of how they would be perceived by the Soviets. However, Mr. Scott also noted 'the problems of editing an East/West magazine to create a readable paper seem formidable' and the exchange of films, radio and television programmes could 'encounter commercial problems'.

Freedom of Movement

10. Again we see little difficulty in discreet but persistent presentation of our views in favour of unrestricted freedom of movement between East and West. We are however extremely pessimistic about the prospects of securing any significant concessions from the Russians or the more hard-line Eastern Europeans here. For example, we think that it is inconceivable that the Russians will agree to abolish exit visas. As I argue in my letter to Sheridan[17] in Oslo of 4 August we shall not be short of counter-arguments to any Soviet proposals for entry visa abolition agreements and should not allow Soviet tactics to deflect us from our general line.[18] But we cannot at present think of any worthwhile practical proposals on which agreement might be reached. We foresee a situation where the Russians might once again succeed in saving their faces by making a few well judged face saving concessions, e.g. on marriages (of [*sic*] the Brooke affair)[19] and re-uniting families, which would have publicity value, but would be insubstantial in themselves.

11. To sum up:

(*a*) our approach to the cultural aspects of the Conference should be designed to secure both practical improvements and propaganda advantage; however we shall only achieve the improvements by agreeing with our Allies a series of realistic fall-back proposals which the East may accept.
(*b*) There is little scope for the expansion of officially sponsored cultural exchanges, and we should concentrate on encouraging non-governmental arrangements. We should recognise however that it may be difficult to coordinate the Western position on this and should keep the discussion general.
(*c*) We should try to extract substantial concessions from the Russians on freedom of information.
(*d*) We do not expect much progress in freedom of movement, but this should not dissuade us from pressing the East on this.

Our overall aim would thus be to emerge from the Conference with the smallest possible loss of ground along the whole front, some small but worthwhile gains in the cooperation field and, if possible, bearing the propaganda trophy. We shall thus be in a good position both to lament the fact that the East was not more forthcoming, and to demonstrate that we had not been gulled into attending a Conference which proved totally

[17] Mr. R.G. Sheridan was Head of Chancery at HM Embassy in Oslo.

[18] As Mr. Walden explained in his letter to Mr. Sheridan, the Bulgarians, the Hungarians and the Poles had recently taken the offensive in criticising Western entry visa restrictions, and it seemed increasingly clear that they were acting as front-runners in an Eastern attempt to dissuade the West from pressing the freer movement issue by threatening to propose visa abolition agreements which Western countries were unable to accept. Mr. Walden cited, as Western counter-arguments, the facts that entry visa requirements did not 'prevent the free movement of bona fide East European and Soviet citizens into the UK', and that the 'most significant obstacle to freer movement' was the East's insistence on exit visas.

[19] See Volume I, No. 35.

unproductive in fields to which we attach importance. Finally and perhaps most important, we shall be able to let it be known that the UK played a constructive role in securing a sensible compromise and some practical results.

G.G.H. WALDEN

No. 12

Minute from Sir T. Brimelow to Mr. Wiggin

[*WDW 1/304/1*]

Secret. Eclipse[1]   FCO, *14 August 1972*
Talk with Dr. Kissinger in Washington, 10 August 1972.[2]
CSCE, MBFR, SALT

1. Very little time was available for the discussion of these three subjects.

2. Dr. Kissinger, when I raised the question of further talks about a Conference on Security and Co-operation in Europe, said that the USA had never wanted such a Conference.[3] If they had been able to get the support of two or three European countries, they might have prevented it. The next four years might be more dangerous than the last. The Conference could do harm. I said that I had noticed in Sir Burke Trend's record a comment by President Nixon to the effect that it was not least the United Kingdom that had pressed for the Conference.[4] When Mr. Michael Stewart had been Foreign and Commonwealth Secretary, he had taken the line that NATO's response to the Warsaw Pact proposal for a Conference should not be negative. He had held that if NATO refused to discuss security and *détente*, it would forfeit the support of the young.[5] But this was not the same thing as actively pressing for a Conference; and once the major issues of European security had come to be discussed in other fora (e.g. SALT and the Berlin negotiations), the United Kingdom Government had been careful not to support any suggestions in favour of the early opening of the Conference. I

---

[1] A security caveat denoting that the document contained information not to be communicated to the US, or to other countries except, on a 'need to know' basis, Canada, Australia, and New Zealand.

[2] Sir T. Brimelow visited Washington to discuss with Dr. Kissinger Soviet proposals for an American-Soviet Agreement on the prevention of nuclear war. See H. Kissinger, *Years of Upheaval* (London: Weidenfeld & Nicolson, 1982), pp. 278-86.

[3] Cf. H. Kissinger, *Diplomacy* (London: Simon & Schuster, 1994), pp. 758-9.

[4] Sir B. Trend was Secretary to the Cabinet. On 28 July, during a visit to Washington, he had discussions with both Mr. Nixon and Dr. Kissinger. According to Sir B. Trend's record of this meeting, a copy of which was sent to Sir A. Douglas-Home on 1 August, Mr. Nixon had said with regard to the CSCE that the US Government 'had never wanted the conference—it was some of the European countries, not least the United Kingdom, who had originally pressed for it'. Mr. Nixon added that the 'wisest thing to do now . . . was to try and slow it down as far as possible', and that this was what the preliminary discussions were intended to do (AMU 3/548/12).

[5] See Volume I, No. 10, note 8.

had myself visited a number of capitals in Eastern Europe to put the arguments in favour of letting the real negotiations be concluded first. We had just circulated in NATO a draft steering brief which set out our current thinking.[6] Dr. Kissinger said that he was aware of all this; but the President's views of our attitude had been formed in his last interview with Mr. Michael Stewart, which had overshadowed everything else.[7] He (Dr. Kissinger) would like us to have talks with the White House on CSCE and MBFR.[8] But he regarded it as up to us to suggest a time.[9] Our ideas could be conveyed through Mr. Tebbit,[10] who should deal with General Haigh[11] (or, in the last resort, with Mr. Rodman).[12] On MBFRs, the United States ideas would probably be put to NATO about the third week in September. The United States could do with some support on MBFRs. When they failed to make proposals, the Europeans were critical. When they did make proposals, the Europeans were critical and alarmed. The choice of participants on the United Kingdom side would be up to us.

3. On SALT, Dr. Kissinger said that the White House would not be ready for talks before the beginning of September. It was possible that their thinking might not crystallize till October.[13]

4. As regards the place of talks on MBFR, the CSCE and SALT, Dr. Kissinger said it was possible that they might have to be held on the West Coast.[14]

THOMAS BRIMELOW

[6] See No. 17, note 2.

[7] In May 1970: See Volume I, No. 46, note 13.

[8] Mr. Acland minuted Sir T. Brimelow on 21 August that Sir A. Douglas-Home had noted alongside this sentence: 'I will do so when I see the President. ADH.' When Sir A. Douglas-Home met Mr. Nixon in Washington on 29 September neither referred to the CSCE. But Mr. Nixon assured Sir A. Douglas-Home that 'he would not withdraw any American forces from Europe without a *quid pro quo*' (annex to minute from Mr. Acland to Mr. H.T.A. Overton (Head, North American Department (NAD) of 3 October, AMU 3/548/14).

[9] Whilst doubtful about what they might usefully discuss with the White House on the CSCE and MBFR at this stage, Mr. Wiggin favoured proceeding with such talks. He remarked in a minute to Sir T. Brimelow of 15 August: 'The Americans' ideas tend to present more difficulties for a number of our Allies than they do for ourselves. But a visit might help to steer the White House in the right direction. And if Dr. Kissinger is looking for "support" from us on MBFR we may be able to discreetly to supply some.' Sir T. Brimelow noted that in principle he agreed. See No. 13, note 12.

[10] Mr. D.C. Tebbit was HM Minister in Washington.

[11] Gen. A.M. Haig, Jr. was Deputy Assistant to the President for National Security Affairs.

[12] Mr. P. Rodman was aide to Dr. Kissinger.

[13] In his minute to Sir T. Brimelow of 15 August (see note 9 above) Mr. Wiggin reported that the FCO was keen to 'handle CSCE/MBFR on the one hand and SALT on the other separately'.

[14] Sir A. Douglas-Home noted on this minute: 'If we co-ordinate our speeches to the Security Conference, not only need we fear nothing but our case is far better and more attractive than that of the Russians. MBFR is much more dangerous and it is for that the Americans seem to be pressing. ADH.'

No. 13

Minute from Mr. Tickell to the Private Secretary

[*WDW 1/1*]

Secret. Eclipse   FCO, *20 September 1972*

1. Dr. Kissinger briefed the Secretary of State on his talks in Moscow at their meeting on 14 September.[1] You told me that the Secretary of State would be interested to have a note to explain where we were on CSCE and MBFR. The position is broadly as follows:

CSCE

2. During the summer the Finns proposed that multilateral preparatory talks should start in Helsinki on 22 November.[2] The Alliance as a whole delayed a reply to this proposal while the Americans sought to persuade the Russians to agree to the start of MBFR explorations at roughly the same time.[3] Dr. Kissinger seems now to have resolved this difficulty[4] (although the Alliance has yet to adopt a common view) and preparatory talks should begin on 22 November. This date causes no difficulty for us.

3. Much preparatory work has already been done in NATO and in the Davignon machinery of the Ten.[5] There are naturally some differences of

---

[1] During 11-13 September Dr. Kissinger visited Moscow for wide-ranging talks with Mr. Brezhnev and Mr. Gromyko. When he called on Sir A. Douglas-Home at the FCO on 14 September, he said, with regard to the CSCE, that he thought the Russians had a double aim: 'to sustain a mood in Europe in which Defence became progressively less important, and gradually to insinuate the idea of alternative security organisations' (record of conversation between Sir A. Douglas-Home and Dr. Kissinger on 14 September, AMU 3/548/15).

[2] On 19 July Mr. M. Tuovinen, Director of Political Affairs at the Finnish Foreign Ministry, asked Mr. B.W.J. Ledwidge (HM Ambassador in Helsinki) if HMG would accept an invitation to participate in preparatory talks beginning in Helsinki on 22 November (Helsinki telegram No. 409 of 20 July).

[3] Sir A. Douglas-Home informed Sir E. Peck in telegram No. 232 of 25 July that HMG remained ready to participate in MPT at any time convenient to its allies. At an NAC meeting on 26 July it was generally accepted that HMG might indicate informally to the Finns that 22 November would be a suitable starting date (UKDEL NATO telegram No. 331 of 26 July).

[4] Whilst in Moscow (see note 1 above) Dr. Kissinger explained to the Russians 'that the two conferences need not run exactly together, but fairly close', and the Russians handed to him a paper which, in effect, proposed that MPT should begin on 22 November and that the CSCE itself should start in late June 1973. Preliminary consultations for MBFR would begin in January 1973 and be followed by negotiations 'on a non-block basis' in October. The US Government responded positively to this paper in a note handed to Mr. A.F. Dobrynin, the Soviet Ambassador in Washington, on 27 October. But the note stressed that the date for convening the CSCE should be decided by all participants when they were satisfied that sufficient progress had been made in the MPT (UKDEL NATO telegram No. 441 of 24 October and Moscow telegram No. 1690 of 27 October, WDN 27/1).

[5] Norway also participated in the Davignon machinery until the Norwegian referendum of 23-24 September produced a clear majority against the country's entry into the EC, and the 'Ten' were reduced to the 'Nine'.

approach but they are not of major importance and they are unlikely to cause real difficulties once the preparations start.

4. We have also held talks with the Swedes, the Austrians and the Swiss during the past month. Our main purpose in doing so was to enlighten them about the work in progress in NATO and Davignon, and persuade them of the inexpediency of their forming a sort of neutral bloc with a neutral role in matters where their interest was squarely with the West. We found their views generally close to our own, and none seemed tempted towards balancing or compromise positions. We have, I hope, laid the foundation for co-operation with them at least during the preparatory phase.

5. We have also had bilateral talks with the Russians. Over the last couple of months HM Ambassador in Moscow has had a number of conversations with Soviet Ministers and officials,[6] and discussions with visiting Soviet officials took place in London on 15 and 18 September.[7] We found we were not far apart on most questions of procedure but on points of substance we spoke a different language. We are clearly going to have a struggle over the agenda, and then, if and when the Conference starts, over the whole range of issues which we think should be dealt with at the Conference. In a nutshell they see the Conference as an occasion for declarations, statements of principles and propaganda of all kinds designed better to establish their hold on the East and weaken the coherence of the West; while we see it as a means for lowering East/West barriers, improving confidence and adopting practical measures to improve co-operation.

MBFR

6. The Russians proposed to Dr. Kissinger that 'preliminary consultations' on MBFR (or, as the Russians put it, 'the problem of reducing armed forces and armaments, first of all in Central Europe') should start in January 1973. This date is likely to be acceptable to the Alliance as a whole and there seems no reason why we should not agree to it. We are less happy with the Soviet proposal that an MBFR Conference should take place in September/October 1973. The present Alliance position is that agreement to exploratory talks on MBFR does not involve commitment to a Conference. We want to hold to this position.

7. A number of questions will have to be resolved before the opening of exploratory talks on MBFR. The question of participation is among the most delicate but, more important, it will also be necessary to reach agreement on how to handle the substance of the question. To judge from what Dr. Kissinger said to the Secretary of State on 14 September, the Americans are

---

[6] In a minute to Mr. Bullard of 25 August, summarising points made in recent conversations Sir J. Killick had had with Mr. Gromyko, Mr. A.Y. Nesterenko (Head of the International Economic Organisations Department of the Foreign Ministry), Mr. Lunkov and Mr. V.V. Kuznetsov (1st Deputy Foreign Minister), Mr. R.H. Brown (EESD) noted that 'one gets the feeling . . . they [the Russians] are beginning to realise that they will not have things all their own way and to appreciate the West's determination to make some progress on the "cooperation" items' (EN 2/15). Cf. Volume I, No. 101.

[7] See No. 14.

taking a sensibly firm line and fully understand the dangers of MBFR.[8] We still know of no arrangement likely to be negotiable with the Russians which would not diminish Western security.[9] But the Americans are continuing to work on various models and are expected to table further papers in NATO shortly. We hope to gain a clearer idea of American thinking at the end of this week when a team of officials— Mr. Wiggin, with Mr. Nash (Ministry of Defence),[10] General Lloyd[11] and myself—hold talks with members of the White House staff in Washington (we have particularly been asked not to mention the fact of these talks to the State Department or other American officials).[12]

C.C.C. TICKELL

[8] Dr. Kissinger insisted to Sir A. Douglas-Home (see note 1 above) that 'MBFR must be conducted from the *security* point of view . . . taking account of what NATO could afford to do.' He added that the 'problem was to create a reasonably equitable-looking proposal to put to the Russians', and that the best scheme might be for NATO cuts of 10-15% followed by Warsaw Pact cuts down to a common ceiling.

[9] On 14 September Mr. W.G. Hyland, who was on the staff of the National Security Council, told Mr. M. Mackintosh (Assistant Secretary in the Cabinet Office) that Dr. Kissinger, whom he had accompanied to Moscow, wished 'to "enmesh" the Soviet Union' in a series of accords which would limit its freedom of manoeuvre, whilst leaving the United States with more flexibility because of its wealth and better relations with other world powers and groupings. In a minute of 18 September covering Mr. Mackintosh's record of this conversation, Mr. P. Cradock, the Head of the Cabinet Office's Assessments Staff, warned Sir B. Trend: 'The implications of this enormously expanded bilateralism for America's allies could be serious, since an Administration obsessively concerned with engaging the Soviet Union at all points will be more inclined to neglect the worries of NATO' (AMU 3/548/15).

[10] Mr. K.T. Nash was Assistant Under-Secretary (Defence Staff) at the Ministry of Defence.

[11] Maj.-Gen. R.E. Lloyd was Assistant Director of the Arms Control and Disarmament Research Unit.

[12] These talks took place at the White House on 22 September. On the American side, they were attended by four of Dr. Kissinger's staff, Mr. H. Sonnenfeldt, Mr. Hyland, Mr. P. Odeen and Mr. D. Aaron. During eight hours of discussion a lot of ground was covered. Whilst Mr. Odeen explained that, with a Presidential election pending, there was no enthusiasm in Washington for either the CSCE or MBFR, Mr. Sonnenfeldt stressed that for domestic political reasons the Administration wanted 'to nail down MBFR negotiations'. He also complained that the Europeans had 'hustled the United States into accepting the CSCE' (a charge Mr. Wiggin did not think 'quite fair'), and Mr. Hyland stated that 'the Americans would not be taking the lead at the Conference on anything'. For his part, Mr. Wiggin expressed British scepticism about both the CSCE and MBFR. 'We believed', he added, 'that while the CSCE, properly handled, could be relatively harmless, MBFR were potentially dangerous' (minute from Mr. Tickell to Sir T. Brimelow of 27 September, covering record of Anglo-American talks on CSCE and MBFR, WDN 27/1).

No. 14

Letter from Sir T. Brimelow to Sir J. Killick (Moscow)

[*MWE 2/24*]

Confidential   FCO, *29 September 1972*

Dear John,

Soviet Approach to the CSCE

1. I enclose in final form the records of our talks with Lunkov on 15 and 18 September.[1] Copies of the draft have already reached you, and you will have seen our telegram No. 958 (copy enclosed for posts to whom it was not sent at the time).[2]

2. Lunkov's instructions were evidently very tight. He had a brief, and he stuck to it. This brief did not include much guidance on points of substance (for example confidence-building measures and handling of freer movement). Nor, perhaps more surprisingly, did it tell him how to cope with fairly elementary points about procedure. This made him sound evasive and insubstantial.

3. Lunkov's whole approach confirms the scepticism which we have been inclined to feel all along about Soviet motives in promoting the Conference. He indicated that his Government were not interested in discussing at the CSCE any part of the military aspects of security (which should, he thought, be lumped together with MBFR and dealt with separately);[3] that they had few practical ideas about economic and technological cooperation (or if they had any such ideas they were keeping them to themselves); and that they obviously hoped to exclude serious discussion of the items we group under freer movement. It was, in fact, clear that the Russians expected the Conference to be mainly concerned with drafting declarations and exchanging propaganda. Judging from Lunkov's remarks, the Russians want chiefly to have the Conference held soon, to keep everything awkward off the agenda and to provide Brezhnev with the opportunity for a triumphant entry with a suitable fanfare of trumpets.

4. Lunkov did not emphasise as much as we had expected the Russian interest in creating permanent machinery to follow the Conference. We have once or twice had the impression that the Russians themselves are less keen on the 'organ' than some of the East Europeans. It is true that Lunkov's

[1] Not printed. These talks between Mr. Lunkov and an FCO team led by Sir T. Brimelow, and including Mr. Wiggin and Mr. Tickell, concentrated on CSCE, MBFR and Anglo-Soviet bilateral relations. Sir D. Greenhill also met with Mr. Lunkov on 19 September.

[2] This telegram of 19 September reported that 'Lunkov did nothing to dispel the impression that the Soviet Government are mainly interested in propaganda and atmosphere' (EN 2/28).

[3] 'As regards "confidence-building measure"', Mr. Lunkov contended, 'if the military aspects of security were touched upon at a CSCE even minimally this would surely divert the Conference from its proper course and overload its agenda. It was more expedient, logical and useful to discuss such confidence-building measures together with proposals for arms reductions.'

remarks at various points seemed to imply that the Russians may envisage a series of Conferences stretching far into the future, but I am not sure that this was anything more than an excuse for not putting the awkward questions on the agenda for the first one.[4]

6. I am giving this letter and the enclosures a wide distribution. HM Representatives may feel free to draw on what was said on the British side during the talks, but they should emphasise that we were speaking only for ourselves and not for the Alliance or the Ten.[5]

Yours ever,

THOMAS BRIMELOW

[4] Mr. Lunkov indicated on 15 September that the creation of a permanent body to deal with questions of security and cooperation in Europe should be an agenda item. But Sir T. Brimelow and Mr. Tickell both made it clear that HMG would regard new permanent machinery with scepticism, though they said that HMG would be prepared to consider the creation of *ad hoc* bodies if these were shown to be necessary.

[5] In a letter to Sir T. Brimelow of 12 October Sir J. Killick suggested that Mr. Lunkov's expression of Soviet interest in working with HMG indicated 'a welcome, if perhaps belated, recognition on the Soviet side of the importance of the British role in CSCE and consequently of the need to carry HMG along'. He thought the Russians 'probably under no illusion that the inclination of HMG will be to act as a brake on the sort of "progress" they would like to make', and he argued that HMG 'should certainly exploit their present approach for all it is worth' (EN 2/15).

No. 15

Sir E. Peck (UKDEL NATO) to Sir A. Douglas-Home

[WDW 1/9]

Confidential   BRUSSELS, *17 October 1972*

Summary . . . [1]

Sir,

NATO and Davignon: The Ways and Means of Political Consultation

It was, I believe, Lord Melbourne who, in speaking of the collective responsibility of the Cabinet, said: 'It doesn't matter what we say as long as we all say the same thing'. The same phrase might be used, with about equal justice, to define the object of political consultation between allies. A truly credible alliance is one which speaks with one voice. The point was rather less cynically formulated, in words of which Ambassador de Staercke[2] frequently reminds us, by NATO's first Secretary-General, Lord Ismay: 'The NATO Council is a place where friends can dissent but must in the end agree'. Within the North Atlantic Alliance, it was recognised from the beginning that NATO could fulfil its role as the cornerstone of Western defence with full

[1] Not printed.

[2] M. A.M. de Staercke was Belgian Permanent Representative to NATO.

success only if its members sought at the same time to co-ordinate and harmonise their foreign policies on matters of concern to the Alliance as a whole. And so from its very beginning the North Atlantic Council practised political consultation.

2. The Report of the Three Wise Men (Pearson, Spaak and Lange)[3] which was accepted by the Ministerial Meeting in December 1956 laid down the following guidelines for political consultation:

Members should inform the Council of any development significantly affecting the Alliance. They should do this not as a formality, but as a preliminary to effective political consultation;
Both individual member Governments and the Secretary-General should have the right to raise in the Council any subject which is of common NATO interest and not of a purely domestic character;
A member Government should not, without adequate advance consultation, adopt firm policies or make major political pronouncements on matters which significantly affect the Alliance or any of its members unless circumstances make such prior consultation obviously and demonstrably impossible;
In developing their national policies, members should take into consideration the interests and views of other governments, particularly those most directly concerned, as expressed in NATO consultation, even where no community of view or consensus has been reached in the Council formation of national policies. When for national reasons the consensus is not followed, the Government concerned should offer an explanation to the Council. It is even more important that when an agreed and formal recommendation has emerged from the Council's discussions, governments should give it full weight in any national action or policies related to the subject of that recommendation.

3. Over the years these principles have continued to form the basis of political consultation in NATO. Consultation has been practised with greater or lesser success. There have been, for example, those among our allies who have felt that the briefings they have been given on the work of the Bonn Group have been less full and frank than might have been desirable. On the other hand there has been general satisfaction with the trouble to which the Americans have gone to keep their allies informed of the progress of the Strategic Arms Limitation Talks (SALT). Still very fresh in the minds of all of us here are the many rounds of consultation over the Malta problem, on which I can say that we had good co-operation from our allies, with the

---

[3] NATO Foreign Ministers decided in May 1956 to set up a 'Committee of Three Wise Men', Mr. L.B. Pearson, the Canadian Secretary of State for External Affairs, Professor G. Martino, the Italian Foreign Minister, and Hr. H.M. Lange, the Norwegian Foreign Minister, 'to advise the Council on ways and means to improve and extend NATO co-operation in non-military fields and to develop greater unity within the Atlantic community'. The Committee's report was approved by the NAC in the following December. Meanwhile, M. P-H. Spaak, the Belgian Foreign Minister, was elected to succeed Lord Ismay as NATO Secretary-General.

deplorable exception of the Italians.[4] All the time NATO has been the main multilateral instrument through which the European countries have been able to influence the policies of their most important ally, the US.

4. The importance of exercising influence with the US has increased not declined since the Three Wise Men's report. The world balance of power has been significantly realigned, and it is no longer to be taken for granted that the US and Western Europe will see their interests in the same light when it comes to manoeuvring with the Soviet Union, China, Japan and the Third World. A number of pressures are combining to lessen the American commitment to Europe. These include the lowered perception of a common threat, the American preoccupation with other areas, the tensions in international financial affairs symbolised by President Nixon's statement of 15 August, 1971,[5] the political pressures in favour of protectionism, and the problems of burden-sharing and of 'Mansfieldism'.[6] There is evidence of an increasing tendency for the Americans to deal bilaterally with the Russians over the heads of the Europeans. All these developments heighten the need to maintain, indeed to improve, trans-Atlantic political consultation. NATO is essential for this purpose.

5. We are now witnessing the development of a new forum for political consultation, the so-called 'Davignon' machinery. This of course is still in its embryonic stages, and at present, although it groups the countries who will form the enlarged European Economic Community, it has no formal links with the existing Community organs, established under the Treaty of Rome. Yet it represents the first step towards a Western European community which will have its own common foreign policy. Despite its immense potential importance, it none the less poses a number of immediate problems for the overall pattern of Western political consultation, and it is these problems which are examined in the following paragraphs.

6. The problems which I have in mind arise almost entirely out of the overlap between political consultations in the Davignon machinery and in NATO. Eight countries (Belgium, Denmark, France, the Federal Republic of Germany, Italy, Luxembourg, the Netherlands and the UK) take part in both sets of consultation, and a ninth, Norway, also did so until the

---

[4] In June 1971 the new Maltese Prime Minister, Mr. D. Mintoff, announced the cancellation of the Anglo-Maltese Defence Agreement of 1964 under which the UK had paid £5 million per annum for the right to station troops on the island and for air and naval bases which were also available for NATO use. Mr. Mintoff demanded up to £30 million per annum, the British threatened complete withdrawal, and both the US and Italian Governments exhibited alarm at the prospect of the Russians seizing the opportunity to extend their influence in the Mediterranean. Only after tortuous negotiations was a new seven-year defence agreement concluded in March 1972, which provided Malta with £14 million per annum as a joint British-NATO contribution.

[5] See *Public Papers of the President: Richard Nixon, 1971* (Washington: GPO, 1972), pp. 886-91. This speech effectively signalled the end of the Bretton Woods system.

[6] See No. 7, note 6.

Norwegians turned their faces against the EEC in the recent referendum.[7] The two sets share a great deal of the same subject-matter. The Davignon Political Directors have regularly been discussing the formulation of the Western negotiating approach to the Conference on Security and Co-operation in Europe (CSCE) and have moreover set up two subordinate bodies to discuss specifically the member countries' attitudes to this:

(*a*) the Sub-committee on the CSCE (dealing with political aspects);
(*b*) the Ad Hoc Group (dealing with economic aspects).

It is recognised by the Davignon countries that the security aspects of the CSCE are primarily a matter for NATO. As a counterpart to this it is coming to be accepted in NATO that on questions of East-West economic co-operation (especially where Community responsibility may be involved) the Davignon member countries must reach agreement among themselves before they can have useful discussions with their other allies. There remains however a large area of subject-matter related to possible East-West political co-operation which has in recent months been the subject of discussion both in Davignon and in NATO. This has led to duplication of effort. Several national papers (for example on Western ideas for the discussion at the CSCE of the freer movement of people, ideas and information) have been tabled in both bodies, and there have been occasions when discussion of a particular topic in the one body has followed almost exactly the same lines as a previous exchange in the other. As against this, there is for the eight members of NATO who also take part in Davignon consultations the considerable potential advantage that views can be harmonised in the smaller forum before the same ideas are tried out in NATO. In practice, however, this process of harmonisation has seldom been completely effective, because it has not often been possible to achieve complete unanimity. There is also the problem that the much greater frequency of meetings in the NATO framework means that the two sets of consultations have to be managed very carefully if they are not to get out of step (see also paragraph 14 below).

7. For the other seven members of NATO (Canada, Greece, Iceland, Norway, Portugal, Turkey and the US) the position is rather different. They tend, perhaps inevitably, to view the Davignon consultations with varying degrees of suspicion, from an unsubstantiated anxiety that the Davignon countries are somehow going behind NATO's back, to a more rational fear that there will be a growing tendency for the Davignon countries to agree on positions and then present them to NATO as *faits accomplis* on a take-it-or-leave-it basis. Some of them are afraid that the result will be the division of NATO into different groups.

8. The precise nature of the worries among the seven non-Davignon countries varies from one country to another. The Americans are mainly worried by the idea that it will be impossible to persuade the eight to budge in NATO once they have agreed their line in Davignon. They are ready

[7] See No. 13, note 5.

enough to admit how hard it is to change an American position once it has been through the mill of the Washington bureaucracy and they fear that Davignon may produce a similar or worse situation in Europe. This fear is coloured by the impression that the actual effect of the Davignon consultations will be to bring all the eight into line with the French, whose position on many issues is the furthest removed from that of the Americans. It is not altogether unfair to say that the Americans' real concern is that they may find it more difficult than in the past to persuade the Europeans to agree with them, though they lay themselves open to the argument that in the past they have often complained about the failure of the Europeans to speak with one voice. Nevertheless, the fact remains that for the foreseeable future the security of Western Europe will continue to depend on the American commitment, and there is no need to emphasise again the interrelationship between the defence commitment and the political commitment. The Americans have on the whole a good record in taking seriously their obligation to consult with their allies, and it would clearly be contrary to our interests and indeed to European interests generally as understood by most West Europeans to antagonise the US in this matter.

9. Canadian worries are similar to those of the Americans, but take perhaps a more acute form. Obviously, whatever the future of political consultation within the framework of the Atlantic Alliance, no one can ignore the views of the US. But the same is not true of Canada. Her membership of NATO has been one of her best opportunities to attempt to exert her influence in the non-American world, and since she does not fail to make full though not always effective use of these opportunities, anything which appears to threaten to reduce her influence in NATO is bound to cause her concern.

10. The Greeks and Turks share the Canadian worry about losing the ability to influence events, but the main point for both of them, especially the Turks, is that they are anxious to avoid any development which might call into question their credentials as good Europeans. Both are associate members of the EEC, under agreements which envisage progress in due course to full membership. In the Greek case this provision has been put into cold storage for political reasons; but the Turks take very seriously their position as future full members, and are exerting considerable pressure to be associated in a special way with the Davignon consultations and even in 1973 to participate in them. They are by no means wholly satisfied with the response. I suspect in fact that the Turks will be the most difficult to satisfy of all the non-Davignon members of NATO. The Portuguese share some of the same feelings, but are unlikely to make much of a fuss. As for the Icelanders, I think that in this context at least they may safely be ignored.

11. A new factor is the special position of the Norwegians, who had been participating in the Davignon consultations, but who are now excluded because of the vote against joining the EEC in the recent referendum. Having for a time participated in Davignon, Norwegian politicians and diplomats are bound to be acutely conscious of the disadvantages they will suffer from being outside it. However, even though they will be quick to

notice any instance in which it may seem that the Davignon members are not consulting properly with their NATO partners, they will be reluctant to make a fuss about such cases; for to do so would be to lay themselves open to the retort that their exclusion from Davignon is the result of their own choice. But there is a risk that such instances could create resentments which, perhaps illogically, but by a process which is psychologically understandable, could make more difficult any further move for Norwegian entry into the EEC. If, as I believe, it is a British interest that Norway should in the end join the EEC after all, then we should do our best to avoid creating such resentments. I should add that as seen from here, there is every sign that Norway will continue to value the link with NATO, and even to increase the importance she attaches to it.

12. The Irish, as usual, pose a problem all of their own. They participate in the Davignon consultations, but they are not members of NATO. So far this anomaly has not attracted any great attention, but it is conceivable that it might in future serve to exacerbate the resentment felt at the existence of the Davignon machinery by the non-Davignon members of NATO. There are two possible dangers here:

(*a*) Discussions in the Davignon sub-Committee have made frequent references to NATO papers, and, although no political or politico-military NATO papers have been passed to the Irish, the latter will naturally have gained a fair idea of their contents. We may well at some stage be faced with complaints from the non-Davignon members of NATO that NATO secrets are being leaked without authorisation to a non-member of the Alliance.

(*b*) If the impression gains ground that the members of the enlarged Community are taking the Davignon consultations more seriously than those with NATO as a whole, the non-Davignon members could well object to what they would see as our taking the neutral Irish more closely into our confidence than our NATO comrades-in-arms.

At present I do not wish to over estimate these risks, in large part because the Irish themselves are adopting 'a low posture' and have sought to make their participation in Davignon consultations as unobtrusive as possible. But it is right that we should keep an eye on these points for the future.

13. The degree to which we are able to allay the misgivings of the non-Davignon countries will depend to a considerable extent on the handling of issues which are discussed by both NATO and Davignon. If over such questions we can ensure that the non-Davignon countries are kept properly informed of what has been decided in Davignon, and if the Davignon countries display reasonable willingness to modify their positions in order to obtain a consensus in NATO, then in time many of the existing suspicions will vanish. Here a great deal will depend on procedure and presentation. Some progress has been made in agreeing among the Davignon countries on arrangements for the communication to NATO of the results of Davignon discussions. At the meeting of Davignon Foreign Ministers in Luxembourg on

26 and 27 May of this year, you Sir, and your Ministerial colleagues authorised the Chairman-in-office to communicate unofficially to the members of NATO not members of the Enlarged Community, and to the Secretary-General of NATO, such documents (or self-contained parts of documents) as had been agreed. At subsequent meetings at NATO headquarters of the Permanent Representatives to NATO of the Davignon countries, this agreement was elaborated. It was decided that the transmission of documents agreed either by Ministers or by the Davignon political committee should be decided on a case-by-case basis; that the non-Davignon countries should also be informed in a general way of the progress of Davignon consultations; that the Permanent Representative to NATO of the country in the chair in Davignon should convene meetings of the non-Davignon Permanent Representatives to give them the information; and that he should brief the Secretary-General separately. The briefing of the Secretary-General is, incidentally, of considerable importance. The Secretary-General has authority to bring questions before the NATO Council on his own initiative, and if Dr. Luns,[8] who has harboured suspicions of the disruptive effect of the Davignon machinery, were to feel that he was not being kept properly informed, he would be quite capable of bringing the whole question of NATO/Davignon relations to the Council, and thus possibly precipitating a major wrangle.

14. These arrangements will no doubt go some way towards ensuring smooth and efficient interaction between political consultations in Davignon and in NATO. I believe however that it would be useful now to take a closer look at the way in which—ideally at least—we think that the two machines should interact. I have already drawn attention (paragraph 6 above) to the difficulty arising from the greater frequency of consultation in NATO. During the summer of 1972, this problem threatened to assume quite serious proportions as far as preparation of the economic dossier for the CSCE was concerned, with the Americans complaining that the Work of the Alliance was being seriously held up by the Davignon Ad Hoc Group's methods of work. A pragmatic solution to this particular problem has been found in the formation at the NATO headquarters of a caucus of the eight Davignon members of the NATO Economic Committee; this caucus meets in order to harmonise views before each meeting of that Committee. It has come to be accepted by the non-Davignon members, and has, I believe, made a positive contribution to the work both of the Alliance and of the Ad Hoc Group itself. I find it hard to believe that efficient interaction between Davignon and NATO would not similarly be improved by the establishment here of a caucus to handle political matters also. The process of harmonising and of modifying positions in order to obtain a consensus is of the essence in allied consultation. The Davignon machinery was not intended to and must not be allowed to prevent this from happening. Informal meetings of the kind suggested for political as well as for economic questions constitute the simplest

[8] Dr. J.M.A.H. Luns was NATO Secretary-General.

way of keeping the two sets of consultations in harmony. Several of our Davignon allies however have serious reservations about any such proposal on the grounds that it would lead to institutionalising a split within the Alliance, though they are prepared to accept the economic caucus on the grounds that this deals with matters especially appropriate to members of the Community as such. Such fears are in my view unfounded. The existence of political consultation within the Enlarged Community is a fact of life with which the other members of NATO are prepared to come to terms, provided that their own interests and the interests of the Alliance as a whole are taken into proper account. In a sense, the division in NATO is an accomplished fact, in that eight members are actual or candidate members of the Enlarged Community and seven are not. But the problems that arise from this division will not be resolved by pretending that it does not exist. It is far preferable to adopt sensible measures which are seen to take account as far as possible of the interests of all those concerned. It is also worth pointing out that there is precedent in NATO for the existence of a caucus in the shape of the Eurogroup[9] (of Defence Ministers or their representatives), the value of which has come to be accepted not only by its members, but also by its most important non-member, the US.

15. Like all new machinery, the Davignon mechanism needs running in, and during the running-in period there are bound to be problems. These problems are temporary in nature; it is simply a matter of adapting our habits on the lines suggested above in order to avoid serious damage to NATO, the existing vehicle for Western political consultation. If the affluent family of to-day may be said to require both a town runabout and a long-range touring car, then, whatever teething troubles there may be in the new acquisition, these should not be such as to cause a collision between two vehicles belonging to the same family; nor, in the best regulated families, should there be a clash of interests between users. The emergence of Western Europe as a political entity is a great achievement but it could set up new strains. This makes it even more important to have a forum where Europe and the US can consult together, and that forum can, in present circumstances only be NATO.

16. I am sending copies of this despatch to Her Majesty's Representatives at Ankara, Athens, Bonn, Brussels, Copenhagen, Dublin, The Hague, Helsinki, Lisbon, Luxembourg, Moscow, Oslo, Ottawa, Paris, Reykjavik, Rome and Washington, and to the UK Ambassador to the European Communities, Brussels. [10]

I have, etc.,

EDWARD PECK

[9] See Volume I, p. 90.

[10] In a letter to Sir E. Peck of 20 November Mr. Tickell thanked him for his 'most useful survey' with the conclusions of which the FCO were 'broadly in agreement'. He added that there was one major difference between NATO and Davignon meetings. Whilst the former were conducted by officials posted to NATO, the latter were made up of officials sent from capitals. 'This', he wrote, 'cannot but affect the character of the meetings. In our view they do not therefore duplicate each other and should be regarded as complementary.'

No. 16

Sir A. Douglas-Home to Sir E. Peck (UKDEL NATO)
No. 355 Telegraphic [EN 2/15]

Priority. Confidential   FCO, *9 November 1972, 8.15 p.m.*

Information priority to Bonn, Paris, Washington, Rome, Helsinki.

Your telegram No. 476.[1]

CSCE

1. You raised some points on Moscow telegrams Nos 1725[2] and 1726.[3]

(*a*) Mandates for Commissions. There is general agreement in Davignon that we should present for discussion at the preparatory talks draft terms of reference for the Commissions and Sub-Commissions. The idea was first spelled out in documents tabled by the French, who as you know take a minimalist view of the scope of the talks. Nothing less would be regarded by most other members of the group (including ourselves) as satisfying the conditions of paragraph 9 of the Bonn *Communiqué*.[4] Although the Russians are clearly unhappy about the idea, we must work for terms of reference to be agreed at the preparatory talks. They would have to be confirmed by Ministers at the first stage of the Conference proper, but under our scenario this would be essentially a formality.[5]

(*b*) Site of CSCE. Discussion of the site at an early stage of the talks would inevitably tend to prejudice the position in paragraph 9 of the Bonn

[1] This is evidently in error and should refer to telegram No. 467 of 6 November, in which Sir E. Peck sought clarification of HMG's views on matters raised recently by Mr. Lunkov regarding the CSCE (see notes 2 and 3 below). Sir E. Peck also reported that 'in the corridors' at Brussels there was 'increasing recognition that if we insist on our item on freer movement we shall probably have to admit a discussion in some way of the idea of permanent machinery' (WDW 1/1).

[2] Dated 3 November, this recorded a discussion that morning between Sir J. Killick and Mr. Lunkov about arrangements for the MPT and the CSCE.

[3] This telegram of 3 November contained the text, given by Mr. Lunkov to Sir J. Killick, of the latest Soviet formulation for the CSCE agenda. It foresaw negotiations on three items: (1) 'the ensuring of European security and the principles governing relations among European states'; (2) 'expansion of commercial, economic, scientific-technological and cultural relations on a basis of equal rights, including cooperation on questions of the environment'; and (3) 'establishment of a body on questions of security and cooperation in Europe'.

[4] See No. 1, note 22 and Cmnd. 6932, pp. 120-2.

[5] During his meeting with Sir J. Killick on 3 November (see note 2 above) Mr. Lunkov reviewed the Soviet concept of a three-stage Conference. He said that one of the MPT's functions would be to work out agreed recommendations on 'procedure and agenda', and that at Stage I Foreign Ministers would approve the agenda and 'set up working groups or Commissions' for Stage II. This led Sir E. Peck to speculate, in his telegram No. 467 (see note 1 above), on whether the Russians expected to negotiate the mandates for Commissions at the MPT, or whether, as information from other sources suggested, they intended to avoid discussion of the issue in these talks.

Communiqué. Furthermore a decision on the suitability of various sites could not be taken until we had a clearer idea of the structure of the Conference, and in particular of the second stage. For your own information we continue to have considerable doubts about Helsinki and see strong arguments in favour of Vienna.

(*c*) Languages. We are committed to support Italian, and we understand that the Russians told Andreotti[6] that they would at least not oppose it. The Spanish mentioned this problem on an equal treatment for Spanish and Italian basis at the Anglo/Spanish bilateral talks here yesterday.[7] We made no commitment on Spanish and pointed out the technical difficulties of dealing with more than five languages.

(*d*) Secretariat. We agree for the reason you give that the Secretariat should be provided by the host country.[8]

(*e*) Chairmanships. We agree that the general approach to the question should be settled at the preparatory talks.

2. Inscription of items on the agenda. You will have seen from our telegram No. 335[9] that the Davignon Sub-Committee agreed that we should avoid any procedure which gave any participant an effective right of veto. The Political Directors have since approved the conclusion that, in the last resort and provided the subject falls within the scope of the CSCE, an item should be included on the agenda even if all participants do not agree.[10] There will clearly be a good deal of haggling over agenda items, in particular freer movement and the permanent organ. On Belgian suggestion we are now examining in Davignon what sort of wording we would find least objectionable for discussion of the idea of a permanent organ. (Incidentally the qualification about the scope of the CSCE is partly designed to guard against the introduction of a special 'Mediterranean' item on the agenda,

[6] Sig. G. Andreotti was Italian Prime Minister.

[7] Anglo-Spanish talks on the CSCE took place in London on 8 and 9 November (WDW 1/317/1).

[8] Sir E. Peck explained in his telegram No. 467 (see note 1 above) that, although this subject had not been discussed in NATO, he believed that most delegations would oppose a new international secretariat on the grounds that the host country could provide an adequate one and that such a secretariat might 'too easily be transposed into a permanent organ'.

[9] This telegram of 2 November relayed to the FCO the conclusions of a meeting on 31 October-1 November of the Davignon CSCE Sub-Committee. These affirmed that a report prepared for EC Political Directors should: (1) state that the length of the Conference should be determined by what was necessary to give its work useful and practical effect, and not by any external timetable; (2) set out the arguments in favour of a three-stage Conference with a second committee-stage; (3) make clear that the question of how far the MPT went into substance must largely depend on Russian reactions to Western views on the agenda and terms of reference for Commissions and Sub-Commissions; and (4) deal with the tactical handling of the agenda, including, for example, opposition to 'the inscription of points which dealt with extra European questions or went beyond the scope of the Conference as at present envisaged' (EN 2/14).

[10] This agreement was reached at the EC Political Directors meeting on 6-7 November.

though some CSCE participants no doubt will argue that the Mediterranean does qualify.)[11]

3. The Russians are evidently working hard at present to create the impression that the West is swinging to their way of thinking on a wide variety of CSCE aspects and to minimise the differences which persist. The line which Lunkov took with Sir J. Killick in their conversation on 3 November illustrates this.[12] The Russians will doubtless continue to seek to exploit their bilateral discussions with individual Western countries to try and pick them off one by one calculating that in multilateral discussions they or their allies may find themselves at a relevant disadvantage if the allies stick together. We see advantage in continuing the Anglo/Soviet dialogue on the CSCE. But we do not wish to encourage the Russians to believe that important questions concerning the Conference can be settled bilaterally rather than multilaterally.

4. Sir J. Killick may wish to draw on the above as appropriate in conversation with Soviet officials.[13] On the question of general items he should not of course divulge the Davignon position described in paragraph 2 above (though we realise that it will doubtless leak to the Russians sooner or later). He should take the line that our approach to agenda items remains as Sir T. Brimelow explained it to Lunkov and his colleagues in London.[14]

5. The Soviet formulation of agenda Item 1 (Moscow telegram No. 1726)[15] corresponds to that proposed by Bondarenko[16] to the Germans (record sent to you under cover of Tickell's submission of 24 October).[17] It must be assumed to represent the Soviet opening position at the preparatory talks.

[11] See note 9 above.

[12] Sir J. Killick reported in his telegram No. 1725 (see note 2 above) that Mr. Lunkov had said that as a result of his visit to London 'and subsequent bilateral exchanges it was clear that the Soviet and British positions on many aspects of CSCE were similar or identical'.

[13] Mr. Tickell informed Sir J. Killick in a letter of 13 November that he doubted if there were any need for him to have another general exchange with Mr. Lunkov before the MPT began on 22 November. But he noted that it would be useful if Sir J. Killick would let the Russians know that it was HMG's 'firm view that the terms of reference for commissions and sub-commissions at the CSCE should be dealt with at the preparatory talks'. He added that he could see no prospect of the West being able to keep proposals for permanent machinery off the CSCE agenda.

[14] See No. 14.

[15] See note 3 above.

[16] Mr. A.B. Bondarenko was Head of the Third European Department of the Soviet Foreign Ministry.

[17] The West Germans had bilateral talks with the Russians on CSCE and MBFR between 10 and 12 October, and a full record of these was subsequently communicated to HM Embassy, Bonn. In his submission Mr. Tickell observed that the Germans thought the Russians at least ready to talk about CBMs, though they remained 'tough on freer movement'.

No. 17

CSCE: Draft Brief for the United Kingdom Delegation to the Multilateral Preparatory Talks[1]

[*EN 2/29*]

Confidential   FCO, *13 November 1972*
Introduction

1. The United Kingdom attitude to the CSCE is broadly reflected in the steering brief (based on a British draft) which is at present under discussion in NATO. The text is attached at Annex I to this brief,[2] and should serve as general guidance to the delegation.[3]

2. We have been careful not to commit ourselves to attend a Conference unless the results of the Multilateral Preparatory Talks (MPT) are such as to justify it. This is formally the position of the Alliance. NATO objectives at the MPT remain as stated in paragraph 9 of the Bonn *Communiqué:*[4] Ministers wish to ensure that their proposals will be fully considered at the Conference, and to establish that enough common ground exists among the participants to warrant reasonable expectations that a Conference will produce satisfactory results.[5]

[1] This brief was despatched under cover of a minute from Mr. Fall to Mr. McLaren of 13 November and was circulated within WOD, EESD and News Department. Mr. Fall suggested that given the need to prepare a brief for the delegation to the MPT this draft 'could serve the basis for a discussion which we should have very soon'.

[2] Not printed. This steering brief was based on a British draft of 21 July and contributions and comments made by other delegations during discussions in the NATO Senior Political Committee (SPC). It was discussed by the NAC on 16 November when it was decided to recommend it to allied Governments for the guidance of their representatives at Helsinki and to submit it to Ministers for consideration (WDW 1/1).

[3] The NATO steering brief (*v. ibid.*) defined three 'positive' Western aims: (1) to secure genuine improvements in reducing barriers within Europe, especially by promoting freer movement of persons, information and ideas and by developing East/West cooperation; (2) to achieve appropriate CBMs; and (3) to increase, at least to some extent, the freedom of manoeuvre of East European countries *vis-à-vis* the Soviet Union by reducing the scope for the application in practice of the 'Brezhnev Doctrine' of limited sovereignty. In addition, the brief cited five 'defensive' Western aims: (1) to maintain Western unity; (2) to seek to avoid unjustified reactions that would undermine parliamentary and public support in allied countries for necessary defensive measures; (3) to persuade Western public opinion of the need for caution at the CSCE and for a balance of mutual advantage to be struck in whatever emerges from it; (4) to frustrate any attempt to slow down or prejudice the movement towards Western European integration; and (5) to refute the Soviet concept that peaceful coexistence called for an unremitting ideological struggle, and to maintain that all the principles of equality between states and non-interference in internal affairs must apply to relations between states with the same political and social systems.

[4] See Cmnd. 6932, pp. 120-2.

[5] At this juncture, the NATO steering brief (see note 2 above) asserted, it was hard to judge which countries would do better at a Conference. 'The Eastern countries', it argued, 'have the advantage of greater internal discipline, and the power to appeal over the heads of

3. These objectives can best be pursued by seeking agreement at the MPT to:

(i) an agenda which will allow Ministers to raise at the Conference proper the points to which they attach importance; and,

(ii) an organisation structure for the Conference which will ensure that the various items on the agenda receive detailed examination before any decisions are taken.

These considerations are spelled out in more detail in Davignon document CP(72)57, which has been submitted to Ministers for their approval. The main section of the document, which is attached at Annex II,[6] should serve as a steering brief for the delegation.

4. We think that the Conference should take place in three stages, the second of which will allow for a detailed examination by officials of the points on the agenda in a number of commissions and sub-commissions. The MPT should in our view endorse this method of work; and recommend (in the light of agenda to be agreed) appropriate terms of reference for the commissions and sub-commissions.

5. The document at Annex II is supplemented by three annexes, of which:

- the first sets out an agreed position of the Nine on the agenda and terms of reference for the commissions which we shall wish to propose at the MPT;[7]

- the second summarises the position reached in Davignon and in NATO on the issues of substance which will be considered at the Conference;[8] and,

- the third recommends the line to take on a number of practical questions on the functioning of the MPT[9] (this should be read together with NATO

governments to Western public opinion. On the other hand the Western countries exercise an attraction and dynamism through their political system and economic achievements. The Western countries can be more easily divided and thus weakened among themselves, but in the long run they may run lesser risks in going to a Conference.'

[6] Not printed. This paper, dated 2 November, is the Davignon CSCE Sub-Committee report referred to in No. 16, note 9. It stressed that the MPT must not constitute a pre-conference and that participants should avoid 'une formalisation excessive' which could obstruct work and prolong the talks without good reason (WDW 1/8).

[7] Not printed. This proposed the establishment of three commissions dealing with: (1) security; (2) economic, scientific and technical cooperation; and (3) the strengthening of cultural cooperation, the development of human contacts, and the broader dissemination of information. Commission I was to have two sub-commissions, and Commission III, four sub-commissions (WDW 1/8).

[8] Not printed. This British-drafted paper (CSCE(72)48 UK 2nd Revise), dated 16 October, treated the various Conference agenda items subject by subject (WDW 1/8).

[9] Not printed.

document CM (72)47[10] on the rules of procedure of the MPT, and should serve as briefing for the delegation).

A separate paper (CP (72)54)[11] covers the ground on the first annex with regard to the economic and technical items proposed for the Conference agenda. These documents will be available to the delegation in a separate folder.

6. Our proposals for the agenda and the terms of reference are based on detailed work in NATO and in Davignon on the substance of the issues. The delegation should draw on these papers for guidance where necessary. We hope that the MPT will not deal with questions of substance: it is not, and should not become, a pre-conference. But if there is opposition to our proposed agenda and terms of reference, it is clear that questions of substance will not be very far from the surface. We shall have to keep firmly in view our objectives at the Conference itself, as they emerge from the preparatory work done with our partners and allies.

7. A draft speech for the general debate which is likely to take place at the opening stage of the MPT is attached at Annex III.[12]

The Agenda

8. We have agreed in Davignon the conditions which should be applied to proposals for the inscription of an item on the agenda. They are set out in paragraph 13 of Annex II. Essentially, we have concluded that to make inscription conditional on consensus would given an effective right of veto, from which we would be likely to lose more than we would gain. The criteria which we propose therefore tend more towards the position that a consensus is required to *exclude* an item, although this is necessarily subject to certain qualifications (in particular as regards what we see as the proper scope of the Conference). The Russians are likely to conclude that they stand to gain from a consensus rule for inclusion, and to press for its acceptance.

9. The following are the points likely to cause difficulty in the elaboration of an agreed agenda:

(a) *Principles Governing Relations between States.* It is generally agreed that the subject should be discussed at the CSCE, but this formulation is the one favoured by the West. The Russians speak of 'guaranteeing' or 'ensuring'

[10] The final version of this paper (CM(72)47 (Final)) was sent to Mr. McLaren under cover of a letter from Mr. Lever of 18 October. The memorandum provided for two courses of action: (1) the communication to the Finnish and other governments of a 'tentative list of questions' that needed to be resolved before the beginning of MPT; and (2) a procedure for sounding out the Finnish and other governments 'on the basis of the consensus plus voting model for Rules of Procedure' (WDW 1/1).

[11] Not printed. This report by the Ad Hoc Group was in part inspired by the notion that the Nine shared a common interest in taking the initiative and presenting an attractive and well-balanced offer in the sphere of economic cooperation. It did not, however, foresee negotiations leading to concrete and reciprocal engagements (WDW 1/8).

[12] The first draft of this speech was written by Mr. Fall and sent by him under cover of a minute to Mr. McLaren of 9 November (WDW 1/1).

security in Europe, and emphasize in particular the non-use of force and the integrity of present frontiers. They will seek:

(i) to give the impression that a declaration on non-use of force and on frontiers can solve the basic problems affecting security in Europe, and,

(ii) to suggest the need for a declaration in legally-binding form.

We shall wish to secure a formulation which makes it clear that 'principles' are only one aspect of security; and which leaves open the form in which the conclusions of the Conference on this question are expressed.[13]

(b) *Military Aspects of Security.* Our partners and Allies are agreed that MBFR should not be discussed at the CSCE. But they wish (with varying degrees of emphasis) to bring home to public opinion that the balance of forces in Europe is the real question affecting security. We shall wish to get an agenda item which allows us to do so, by discussing certain confidence-building measures and, possibly a declaration on force levels.[14] The Russians will oppose this, ostensibly on the grounds that this is the proper function of the talks on MBFR.[15]

(c) *Peaceful Settlement of Disputes.* The Swiss will put forward as a separate item on the agenda their proposals for new arbitration machinery. Our partners and Allies view the substance of these proposals with varying degrees of enthusiasm. We see much merit in them and have told the Swiss that we will support them. The Russians are likely to oppose the substance of the Swiss ideas and may wish to prevent their inscription as a separate item on the agenda.[16]

(d) *Disarmament.* Neither the NATO nor the Warsaw Pact countries will propose disarmament as such as an item for the Agenda. The Swedes may well do so, however. The Romanians, and perhaps the Poles and Bulgarians, may propose measures such as nuclear-free zones, which are clearly closely related to disarmament. We shall wish to consider any such proposals on their merits, bearing in mind that:

(i) disarmament questions are best discussed in a global context, such as that provided by the UN machinery;

(ii) the agenda should maintain a balance between items of interest to us and those put forward by others:

[13] The NATO steering brief (see note 2 above) also stated that 'it would be preferable to have no Declaration rather than one which enunciated undesirable doctrine'. A declaration, it added, 'should be clearly incompatible with any doctrine of limited sovereignty'.

[14] The second annex of Annex II (see note 8 above) stated that NATO was now agreed that allied negotiators at the CSCE should propose: (1) the advance notification of manoeuvres and troop movements; and (2) the invitation on a generally equitable basis of observers to military exercises. There was, as yet, no agreement within NATO on the nature or desirability of a joint declaration on mutual and balanced measures relating to the levels and activities of armed forces in Europe.

[15] Cf. No. 9.

[16] See No. 10, notes 14 and 15.

(iii) the formulation of agenda items should not prejudice in a way unacceptable to us the decisions to be taken by the Conference.

In the last resort, however, we may have to accept some discussion of disarmament, subject to there being general agreement to our views on conditions for inscription.

(*e*) *Middle East.* The Austrians are likely to propose that the Middle East be discussed, but are unlikely to press the point in the face of the expected opposition from both NATO and Warsaw Pact countries. We regard the Middle East as a question going beyond the proper scope of the Conference, and will therefore oppose its inscription on the agenda.

(*f*) *Mediterranean.* Malta is likely to propose an item on security in the Mediterranean, and may get sympathy and perhaps support from Yugoslavia and even Italy. The Romanians and Bulgarians may make common cause with them, in the hope of getting some specific reference to security in the Balkans. We shall wish to oppose as beyond the scope of the Conference any item which would inevitably result in requests for the participation of countries other than the 35 at present invited; and we do not wish to encourage the discussion at a general conference of issues of interest only to a minority of the participants.

(*g*) *Economic and technical cooperation.* There is general agreement as to the items which should be discussed, and the problem will be to get a satisfactory formulation which:

(i) gives due weight to particular points of interest to us and reflects our wish to deal subject by subject with the question at issue; and,

(ii) avoids prejudging issues of substance (the Russians, by inserting the phrase 'on a basis of equality' in their proposal, may hope thereby to provide an opening to attack the EEC as a discriminatory bloc).[17]

(*h*) *Cultural and Human Relations (Freer Movement).* The Davignon and NATO position is that these questions should be dealt with under a separate item of the agenda. The Russians will oppose this. They wish to limit discussion to 'cultural cooperation', and to deal with it with economic and technical cooperation. This is a point of major importance to us. Although (with a large majority of our partners and allies) we see advantage in presenting the former and less polemical formulation, we shall insist on getting an agenda item under which we can raise questions of interest to us in the freer movement field. We have let it be known that we would not be willing to go to the Conference if we do not get satisfaction on this point.

(*i*) *Environment.* There is general agreement that the environment should

---

[17] The NATO steering brief (see note 2 above) maintained, with regard to this item, that in almost every case the West had potentially more to give than to receive and was therefore in a strong bargaining position. It also contended that there was political advantage in reducing autarky in Eastern countries, although there was a corresponding risk that they might become more efficient competitors in the process. 'Throughout the negotiations', the brief stated, 'it will be essential not to make concessions at the expense of Western European integration.'

be discussed at the Conference. The Russians have proposed that it be dealt with under the catch-all 'cooperation' item which has been put forward by the Warsaw Pact. We would prefer to deal with it as a separate item, largely for the tactical reason that we want to break down the Warsaw Pact 'cooperation' item in order to ensure separate treatment for the freer movement item.

(*j*) *Permanent Organ.* The Russians want a separate item to deal with 'the establishment of a body on security and cooperation in Europe'. We do not think that the question of what machinery, if any, is required to follow up the work of the Conference should be discussed under a separate item of the agenda. Our position, that the case for continuing machinery can only be considered on the merits of the particular case, would best be maintained if the question of follow up work were discussed as necessary in connection with the relevant substantive issues on the agenda. But we may, as a last resort, have to accept a separate agenda item as the price of Soviet agreement to a separate item on cultural and human relations. We shall in that case wish to avoid a formulation which prejudges the desirability of a new body covering the field proposed by the Russians; and we shall be considering further with our partners in Davignon the details of our fall back position.[18]

Commissions and Sub-Commissions

9. There is general agreement to the setting up of commissions at the second stage of the Conference. But the Russians, who wish to limit the length of the second stage and to avoid too detailed an examination of the questions under discussion, may oppose the creation of sub-commissions. We shall have to make it clear that we regard it as essential that the MPT should reach agreement on the establishment of sufficient commissions and sub-commissions to allow for detailed consideration of all the points on the agenda.

10. The Russians have indicated that they will oppose the consideration of terms of reference for the commissions at the MPT. They have argued that this would involve questions of substance which can only be dealt with at the first stage of the Conference proper. This again is a point of major importance to us. We regard it as essential that the MPT should recommend in some detail what the commissions and sub-commissions will do. We do not want to arrive at the first stage of the Conference proper without a clear idea of what is to be discussed, and of how the work is to be handled.

11. If, as we hope, this position is firmly maintained by our allies, the Russians will no doubt agree to the discussion of terms of reference. We shall,

---

[18] In general, NATO Governments had serious reservations about establishing any permanent organ such as the Warsaw Pact had proposed. It was, according to the NATO steering brief (*v. ibid.*), their view that more could be achieved through better cooperation in the context of existing international institutions. The West, the brief stated, did not want 'a political court of appeal, which might give the Russians scope to interfere in our affairs'. But the allies also recognised that non-permanent institutionalised arrangements could prove useful if progress were made at the CSCE on subjects of interest to them, and that these might carry forward the process of negotiation, and/or give effect to Conference decisions.

however, have to ensure that these discussions are carried out in parallel with those on the agenda itself; and we should not give final agreement to the formulation of an agenda item until appropriate terms of reference have been agreed for the commission which is to deal with it at the second stage of the Conference proper.

12. The points likely to cause difficulty over the agenda (see paragraph 8 above) will no doubt be reflected in the negotiations on the terms of reference. The question is not one which can be dealt with in summary form, and the delegation should be guided by the background documents referred to above. Just as on the agenda we cannot realistically expect to inscribe the items to which we attach importance while excluding those proposed by other participants, so on the terms of reference we shall have to accept provision for points of interest to the East. Our major objective will be to ensure that our points will be fully considered at the Conference, and that the terms of reference do not prejudice its decisions in a way unacceptable to us.

Date, Place, Duration and Level of the Conference

13. The Russians will propose that the date, place and duration of the Conference, and the level of the third stage, should be decided upon at the outset of the MPT. They are likely to prefer a relatively short Conference, with a third stage 'at the highest level'. We shall wish to oppose this procedure on the grounds that:

(i) we do not want to commit ourselves to a Conference until we are satisfied that the objectives in paragraph 2 above have been met;[19]
(ii) we cannot decide on the site of the Conference until we have had time to assess the facilities available in the light of the type of Conference involved (the structure of the second stage is of particular importance in this respect); and,
(iii) we cannot decide on the duration of the Conference until we have a clearer idea of the work to be done at the second stage, and of the way it will be handled; and,
(iv) we cannot decide on the level which would be appropriate for the third stage until we are able to judge the results of the second stage.

Procedures, Technical Organisation and Financing of Conference

14. These questions will have to be agreed upon at the MPT and they might usefully be remitted for discussion in working groups. Separate briefing will be provided as necessary. The delegation should bear in mind that the decisions to be taken will depend in large part on the overall organisation of the Conference, and in particular of its second stage. It would not therefore be appropriate to begin discussion in working groups until a clearer picture of what may be required has emerged from the discussion of the substantive items considered above.

[19] The NATO steering brief (*v. ibid.*), nevertheless, recognised that once the MPT had started there would be 'certain political difficulties for the West in disengaging from them'.

Western Coordination

15. We shall wish to maintain at the MPT the close consultation with our partners and Allies which has marked the detailed preparatory work in Davignon and in NATO. We shall also wish to keep in close touch with the neutrals, whose position on many issues is basically much nearer to the West than to the East. We do not want to encourage them to set up a 'neutral bloc', which would see virtue in adopting positions distinct from those of the West.

16. To some extent, this consultation can be conducted on an informal basis. Where the neutrals are concerned, this will be necessary as no institutional machinery for consultation has been established. In the case of NATO and Davignon, however, we hope that the process will be one of coordination rather than consultation, and we should exploit institutional means to this end.

17. The ideal solution would no doubt be to have regular caucus meetings of the Nine and the Fifteen at Helsinki. In practice, however, it may not be possible to run two sets of Western coordination meetings; and there is the additional problem that the French, with whom we shall have to maintain the closest contact if Western coordination is to be a reality, are unlikely to agree to meetings *à quinze* in Helsinki (they have, however, agreed to regular meetings of the Nine).

18. The question has still to be decided upon in NATO, and further guidance will be sent to the delegation if necessary. It seems probable, however, that we shall:

(i) have regular meetings of the Nine in Helsinki, and
(ii) use the NATO machinery in Brussels (perhaps with some coordinated reporting procedure from Helsinki) to ensure that the Alliance is able to consider and where necessary react to developments in the MPT.

If such is the case, the delegation, while playing a full part in the meetings of the Nine, should keep in close touch with the other members of the Alliance, and particularly with the Americans. The work done so far in Davignon to prepare for the CSCE has marked an encouraging first step in the coordination of the foreign policies of the Nine. We should do what we can to maintain this progress at the MPT and thereafter at the Conference itself. But it will be at least equally important to ensure that this developing unity does not prove divisive of the Alliance.

No. 18

Letter from Mr. Brown to Mr. Staples (UKDEL NATO)

[*EN 2/13*]

Confidential   FCO, *24 November 1972*

Dear Justin,

CSCE: Cultural and Human Relations

1. You have been closely concerned in the progress which has been made on these aspects of the Conference within NATO and the Davignon machinery since George Walden wrote his letter of 4 August,[1] but as the multilateral preparatory talks begin I think it may be useful to set out the present position here so that other interested posts can see where we have got to.

Formulation of Agenda Item

2. Our main concern is to ensure that all agenda items, but especially this one, are formulated in a way which is open yet also explicit enough to allow us to say what we want without the East being able to object that we are out of order. In the West, formulae for this item have been proposed as follows:

Dutch: *Libre mouvement des personnes, des idées et des informations.*

French: *Développement des contacts entre les hommes, élargissement de la diffusion de l'information et renforcement de la co-opération culturelle.*

Belgian: *L'amélioration de la circulation des personnes et des rapports humains, l'élargissement de la diffusion de l'information et des idées et l'augmentation des échanges culturels.*

Ministers agreed last April to accept the French formulation. This remains our position. If there should eventually turn out to be a general preference for the Belgian suggestion, we could accept it but would like the last four words replacing by: '. . . et le renforcement de la co-opération culturelle' because we have doubts about the value of a *quantitative* increase in the number of existing cultural exchanges for its own sake. At present, the Dutch are sticking to their proposed wording. They are supported in NATO by the Americans.

One Commission or Two?

3. We agree with the French that there should be one commission to deal with cultural co-operation, contacts and information. The Dutch, supported by the Belgians, think that contacts and information should be dealt with by a separate commission. The Americans have some sympathy with this view. We and the French, with considerable support, believe that such a procedure carries the risk that the Russians will accept one commission (on cultural co-operation) and oppose the other, thus producing at the multilateral preparatory talks the confrontation which we wish to avoid. Even if both commissions were established, such an arrangement would help the East take a forthcom-

[1] No. 11.

ing attitude on cultural exchanges and an obstructive one on other matters.

4. Although in the main the Russians continue to oppose the inscription of freer movement as an Agenda item in any form some Eastern Europeans, including the Czechs and Poles, have recently indicated willingness to see it on the Agenda in some guise. And there have been one or two small signs lately that the Russians are realising that some sort of deal may have to be done if they are to get their proposed 'permanent organ' on the agenda.[2] A reasonable (but not weak) Western formulation would render this easier, while a tough one would risk bringing all the Eastern countries together to oppose an attempt at 'open subversion'. As our basic purpose is to allow Ministers to pursue the substance of the matter at the Conference itself a moderate wording of the Agenda item would give us what we wanted. We therefore think it right to link freer movement with cultural relations in one Agenda item and one commission so as to ensure that the Eastern countries have to give proper examination to both subjects.

5. We and the French are drawing the attention of the Dutch and Belgians to the risks which we see in their present policy and the dangers of adopting a hard-line position prematurely, modification of which could look like retreat from a point of principle. At present the Russians are saying that they do not want the formulation of agenda items and the mandates for commissions to be discussed at the multilateral preparatory talks. We intend that they should be. It remains to be seen what will happen.

Proposals

6. The French have produced a useful document on what they think the Cultural and Human Relations commission should do,[3] and NATO has now more or less finalised its cultural relations dossier.[4] We agree with much of what is said in both documents and each reflects a lot of our thinking. In particular, proposals which we have put forward for internationally linked East/West television discussion programmes and a joint East/West magazine about European affairs appear in the NATO dossier. It also contains a number of other useful proposals designed to improve and increase exchanges between East and West of people, information and ideas. Many of the proposals are framed with two basic ideas—accepted by most of the partners and allies—in mind

—the need to broaden the definition of culture to include many activities

---

[2] See No. 16.

[3] Mr. Tickell received a copy of this paper, dated 23 October, at the EC Political Directors meeting on 7 November.

[4] One of the issues which delayed completion of the NATO cultural relations dossier was the British proposal for a joint East/West magazine (see No. 11). This was opposed by the Americans on the grounds that the magazine might be exploited by the Russians, that its publication could have an adverse affect upon the circulation of existing Western periodicals in Eastern Europe, and that further consideration needed to be given to the details of the proposal. Finally, on 22 November, the NAC agreed to the proposal's insertion in the dossier in a square-bracketed paragraph, indicating the absence of consensus (letter from Mr. Staples to Mr. Brown of 22 November).

not hitherto thought of as being strictly 'cultural';
—the desirability of increasing non-governmental exchanges in preference to official ones.

The fact is, the Western shop window still lacks solid merchandise and contains too much tinsel. But we hope to be able to take one or two real steps to reduce barriers by increasing the spread of Western information and ideas, both written and broadcast, and of 'communicators' of various kinds and other people.

A Declaration

7. The indications are that the Russians, now that they have achieved in other ways (the various German agreements etc) much of what they originally hoped to get out of a CSCE, increasingly see the Conference as being both shorter and more declaratory than we want and they first intended. The West, while not objecting to the idea of declarations, believes that they are not in themselves sufficient, and wants detailed negotiations on practical improvements. In the resulting inevitable compromise it is unlikely that we shall be able to avoid some sort of declaration on e.g. the principles of relations between states. Work had been done in NATO and the Davignon machinery on this and on a declaration of the principles of economic co-operation. We should perhaps start now to give consideration to the text of a declaration (or even convention) about international cultural affairs. This is not to suggest that such documents would be a good thing in themselves, but there are indications that the Russians may press for them, and we do not wish to be forced into negotiating on the basis of Soviet drafts which, besides being unacceptable in content, are also likely to be couched in Soviet bureaucratic cultural jargon which would make it a most unappetizing offering to Western public opinion.

Tactics

8. Most of the posts which replied to George Walden's letter agreed with the view that the Western countries will have the best of the argument over the cultural and human relations item so long as it can be got on to the agenda in a form which allows us to deploy our strength effectively.[5] Some good suggestions were put forward about how to deal with Eastern proposals for visa abolition,[6] and we should not have too much difficulty in making our

[5] See No. 11, notes 5, 11 and 16. In a letter to Mr. Walden of 8 September Mr. P. Yarnold (HM Embassy, Bucharest) argued that in the area of freedom of information the Romanian viewpoint was significantly different from that of the Soviet Union, and that this difference could be exploited 'in order to screw more concessions out of the Soviet Union'. He thought the Romanians could well be attracted by the idea of an East/West magazine. 'But', he observed, 'it could very easily degenerate into the sort of jargon-stuffed propaganda vehicle, bristling with high-sounding sentiments and in reality saying nothing at all, which the Romanians and the other communists are expert in producing.'

[6] These were generally accepted as being an East European 'ploy' which should not be allowed to cloud discussions on issues which would have a real effect on freedom of movement. In a letter of 8 September, Mr. R.H. Baker (Head of Chancery, HM Embassy, Warsaw) suggested to Mr. Walden: 'It should be easy enough to expose the absurdity inherent in the

points tell. (You may be interested to know that we are looking into visa procedures for Eastern Europe to see whether there is any scope for speeding them up—e.g. by using computers.) One potential difficulty is that practices on this and other aspects of freer movement do in fact vary quite widely between the Warsaw Pact countries, and it will be neither easy nor political to tar, say, the Rumanians with the same brush as the East Germans. 'Trade-offs', including inter-sectoral ones whereby we would hope for freer movement concessions in return for economic/technological ones, could be tricky things to handle.

9. What we hope for, at the end of the day, is a small step forward in the long process of bringing about in the Warsaw Pact countries the kind of conditions in which the provisions of our existing cultural relations agreements with them (which already allow in theory for most of what we want) can be more fully implemented.

Yours sincerely,
R.H. BROWN

position of a country which will not grant its own citizens freedom to move abroad but agrees to visa abolition with others; the difficulty is to play on it in a way which stands some chance of getting them to budge a little.'

No. 19

Submission from Mr. Tickell on CSCE: Multilateral Preparatory Talks[1]

[WDW 1/1]

Confidential   FCO, *21 December 1972*

I submit (i) Helsinki telegram No. 846,[2] in which HM Ambassador gives his impressions of the first session; and (ii) a short paper where we analyse some of the issues to be faced when the multilateral preparatory talks resume in Helsinki on 15 January.[3] Before then there will be a meeting of the Davignon Sub-Committee and Ad Hoc Group early in January, leading up to a meeting of the Political Directors of the Nine on 16 and 17 January; and

[1] This submission was addressed to Sir T. Brimelow and the Private Secretary.

[2] Not printed. Mr. T.A.K. Elliott, who in October was appointed HM Ambassador at Helsinki, reported in this telegram of 18 December that the MPT, the first session of which ended on 15 December, had made 'reasonable progress'. But while rules of procedure had been agreed, attempts to set out a work programme had so far failed because of the Russian refusal to accept any specific mention of terms of reference for the Commissions of the main Conference. Moreover, although Mr. Elliott thought that tactically the session had gone well for the West (the Russians, had 'failed in their attempt to settle the site, place and participation of the Conference before we had discussed the agenda and related questions'), he predicted that the next session was 'going to be more difficult' and that it would 'no doubt need a more carefully elaborated and longer-term tactical approach' than was possible in the first (EN 2/29).

[3] Not printed. The main points of this paper are summarised in paragraph 3.

NATO meetings will continue as usual. We shall therefore have a full opportunity to discuss with our partners and Allies the line which we should take at the resumption of the talks.

2. In making the following comments, I am indebted to Mr. Fall (EESD) and Mr. Adams (WOD) who supported Mr. Elliott[4] throughout the first session of the talks and did most of the co-ordination among the Nine and the Fifteen behind the scenes. I agree generally with Mr. Elliott's impressions. The description of the rôle played by the United States (paragraph 6 of the telegram) is particularly important.[5] There are however two points in which I would have placed the emphasis rather differently:

(i) The first (paragraph 5) concerns the rôle of the French.[6] I think that the Russians may have been rather more ready to do business with the French than Mr. Elliott suggests. But so far as I can judge the French have stuck loyally to the Davignon line. It is very much in our interests that they should continue to do so. According to Sir E. Tomkins,[7] with whom I discussed this point last week, the French attach particular value to Community co-operation over the CSCE (even if they—characteristically—see this in terms of the Eight falling into line with them). This of course cuts both ways, and I think we can make good use of it. The fact that the French have either not attended or played little part in meetings of NATO countries in Helsinki has made it more difficult than it need have been to keep in touch with the non-EEC members of the Alliance. But, albeit at some cost in duplication of meetings, we have so far been able to consult effectively.[8]

(ii) I think it is too early to draw any firm conclusions from the fact that the Russians were left to play their hand more or less alone during the closing stages of the session (paragraph 7 of the telegram).[9] This was indeed a

---

[4] As Ambassador to Finland, Mr. Elliott was UK Head of Delegation to the MPT. He subsequently headed the UK delegation to Stage II of the CSCE at Geneva.

[5] Mr. Elliott wrote (see note 2 above) that, though always helpful when asked for support, the Americans had 'been passive to a fault'. As a matter of principle, they seemed anxious to let the Europeans make the running, and, Mr. Elliott deduced, they wished 'to avoid major confrontations with the Russians'. This, he observed, had 'left the Canadians sensitive and uncertain; while the Greeks, Turks and Portuguese [had] sometimes sounded a bit confused by the course of events'.

[6] Mr. Elliott reported in paragraph 5 of his telegram No. 846 (*v. ibid.*) that the French had maintained closer contacts than other Western delegations with the Russians. But he also noted that they had 'generally played fair by the Nine', and that, although they had sometimes been too keen to put forward their own views in plenary without proper consultations with their partners, their 'deviations' had been 'more procedural than substantial'.

[7] HM Ambassador in Paris.

[8] The coordination of Western views had, according to Mr. Elliott (see note 2 above) so far proceeded smoothly with the Nine's group of experts functioning as the main forum for consultation. French reluctance to attend regular meetings of NATO delegations had, however, to some extent hampered coordination amongst the Fifteen.

[9] Apart from the Romanians, only the Poles, amongst the Warsaw Pact countries, had, Mr. Elliott reported (*v. ibid.*), 'shown any measure of independent thought and activity'.

notable feature of the proceedings, but the subject of terms of reference is one on which the Russians may well have warned their allies that they were occupying ground that they did not intend to hold for long. I have little doubt that the Russians will be able to mobilise effective support when they need it on the substantive issues which will follow.

3. The paper attached is not designed to recommend new lines of policy, but in it we suggest a number of points which could usefully be discussed with our partners between now and the resumption of the talks. These are the following:

(i) that we should maintain the line that a decision on who should participate in the Conference should not be taken until we have a clearer idea of the agenda of the Conference. In the meantime we must of course deal (either in the Davignon machinery or in the committee of the Nine Permanent Representatives examining the European Commission's papers) with the problem of the representation of the Community at the Conference itself.[10]

(ii) that we should maintain the position that the preparatory talks should consider in detail the terms of reference of the Committees and Sub-Committees which will meet at the second stage of the Conference proper. We need not necessarily insist on pursuing the discussion of the work programme of the preparatory talks until agreement has been reached on a text incorporating a satisfactory mention of terms of reference. It would be just as satisfactory, and might prove tactically more desirable, to bypass discussion of the work programme and table proposals on the agenda and on the terms of reference in such a way as to make it clear that we intend the two to be considered together.[11]

(iii) that we should do our best, both in Davignon and in NATO, to ensure that what is tabled in Helsinki represents an agreed position of the Nine and the Fifteen. But in the last resort we should do whatever we reasonably can to ensure that the French remain committed to a common position of the Nine which is already broadly acceptable to NATO.

(iv) we should give early consideration to the question of the site of the Conference. Pressures in favour of Helsinki are gaining strength and if we prefer an alternative we should begin to make our position clear in

---

Nevertheless, Mr. Elliott observed that during the last week of the session the Russians had 'been left to defend their less reasonable positions increasingly alone', and he had detected 'an occasional touch of panic' when they realised on how little firm and effective support they could depend.

[10] WOD did not, according to the attached paper (see note 3 above), think it wise to press for the EC Commission to participate in the Conference, if the Community could be effectively represented by the country holding the Presidency of the Council of Ministers.

[11] This was a course advocated by Mr. Elliott in his telegram No. 846. The WOD paper (*v. ibid.*) commented with regard to this point: 'The Russians might find it easier to discuss the substance of what they might choose to call "pieces of paper", than to accept in principle the idea that we should decide on the terms of reference at the preparatory talks.'

informal discussion. My own view is that we should indicate a readiness to accept Helsinki for the first stage, but that we should press for the Committees which will constitute the second stage to meet elsewhere.[12] The site of any third—or resumed Ministerial—stage should be left open.

4. These are not points on which we should take decisions before we have had time to discuss them with our partners. But I recommend that our delegation to the meeting of the Davignon Sub-Committee on the CSCE on 4/5 January should be instructed to deploy the arguments in the paper where appropriate. I have already had a word with the Belgians, who will be chairing the next meeting, and suggested that we should then concentrate on tactics at Helsinki when the talks are resumed and on the problem of the site. I also suggested that it might not be a bad idea for the Nine to think and perhaps discuss among themselves (without the presence of the Commission) what to do about the problem of Community participation at the Conference itself.

C.C.C. TICKELL[13]

[12] WOD thought that Western interests at Stage II would be best served by a fairly complex structure of Committees and Sub-Committees, and that it was difficult to see how these could all be effectively serviced in Helsinki where conference facilities and the size of Western missions imposed limitations (*v. ibid.*).

[13] On 22 December Sir T. Brimelow minuted the Private Secretary on this submission that he thought it would make a satisfactory brief for UK representatives at the forthcoming meeting of the Davignon CSCE Sub-Committee. Sir A. Douglas-Home subsequently noted on it: 'I think 3 answers are clear. 1. Attendance should be at Foreign Minister level for a few days. Then Ministerial substitutes should go. 2. The place should be Helsinki. 3. We should go for the settlement of the Agenda; after that Committees and their terms of reference will or should fall into place. ADH.' Uncertain as to how to interpret this third point, Mr. McLaren reminded Mr. Wiggin in a minute of 2 January 1973 that the West wanted clear terms of reference for Conference Committees and Sub-Committees, and if the Russians continued to resist this 'we would see tactical advantages in by-passing discussion of the work programme and tabling proposals on the agenda and on the terms of reference in such a way as to make it clear we regard the two as going together'. Sir T. Brimelow agreed, and Sir A. Douglas-Home commented on the minute: 'Yes. I see the value of the link. ADH' (WDW 1/2).

No. 20

Minute from Mr. Tickell on CSCE Preparatory Talks[1]

[*WDW 1/2*]

Confidential   FCO, *25 January 1973*

The second session of the preparatory talks in Helsinki is now ten days old and this may not be a bad moment to take stock. Helsinki telegram No. 79[2]

[1] This minute was addressed to Sir T. Brimelow and the Private Secretary. Sir A. Douglas-Home noted on it: 'So far so good. The Russians will have to be careful how they oppose an item dealing with better contacts or they will reveal themselves in all their rigidity. ADH 28/i'.

[2] Mr. Elliott reported in this telegram of 25 January that the consultations continued to go well for the West; that the East had unexpectedly accepted the broad lines of the West's

provides an assessment of the position on the spot. It may also be helpful to summarise developments as seen from here.

2. When the talks resumed in Helsinki on 15 January, the proposals for the agenda and terms of reference for Committees which had been worked out by the Nine and in NATO were tabled in three parts corresponding to the main areas of work of the Conference (political/security; economic and environmental co-operation; cultural and human relations). By previous agreement the proposals were introduced by the Belgian, Italian and Danish delegations who each dealt with a separate area of the agenda.[3] Heads of other Western delegations (including HM Ambassador) then spoke in support.

3. Neutral and non-aligned delegations welcomed these proposals in general terms and added further ideas of their own, particularly in the security field.

4. On 22 January the Soviet delegation offered amendments to the agenda proposals they had put forward in the first session of the talks. The amendments were clearly designed to have greater appeal for the Western countries and the neutrals. The revised Soviet proposals[4] differ from the earlier ones in the following ways:

(*a*) 'Certain measures for strengthening stability and confidence' is now included in the title for the political/security item;

(*b*) The co-operation item is divided into two, with a separate item on 'extension of cultural co-operation, of contacts between organisations and people and of dissemination of information';[5]

agenda proposals without forcing similar concessions from the West; and that the neutrals and non-aligned had played their part in this by discreet support for the West.

[3] Agreement was reached in Brussels on 9 January at a meeting of EC country Ambassadors and subsequently in the NATO SPC on a formula for the tactical handling of agenda and mandate items in the resumed MPT (UKDEL NATO telegram No. 20 of 9 January). The Western delegations aimed at tabling proposals on the agenda and terms of reference in such a way as to make it clear that they were to be considered together. On 15 January the Belgians tabled the Western agenda proposals and terms of reference for the Committee dealing with economic and related questions, and the Italians and Danes tabled the terms of reference for the Committees dealing with security questions and human contacts, culture and information respectively.

[4] Mr. V.F. Maltsev, the Soviet Ambassador to Finland, prefaced these proposals with the statement that the agenda should ensure that all problems of common interest would be discussed, that there should be no 'surprises' in the submission at the Conference of new agenda items, and that the wording of the agenda should be as brief as possible 'with no excessively detailed clarification which could lead to "the creation of the notorious procrustean bed"'. The consultations should not, he said, be turned into a pre-conference (Helsinki telegram No. 65 of 22 January). As Mr. Elliott commented in a letter to Mr. Tickell of 25 January, the Soviet Ambassador had obviously not realised that his reference to no surprises 'provided a clear justification for the agreement of "mandates" in advance'.

[5] According to Helsinki telegram No. 65 (*v. ibid.*) Mr. Maltsev insisted that under this item there was no room for the 'dissemination of anti-culture, i.e. pornography, racism, fascism, cult of violence, hostility among peoples and false slanderous propaganda'.

(*c*) The permanent organ is now described as 'a consultative committee'.[6]

5. We have suggested, with wide support from Western and neutral countries, that the proposals on the table should now be grouped together so that they can be considered in detail on a sector by sector basis. It seems likely that this procedure will be agreed, although we should have to accept the consultative committee as a separate grouping of its own.

6. The main points of difficulty which remain are the following:

(*a*) We must ensure that the terms of reference for the Committees and Sub-Committees are dealt with in a satisfactory way.[7] We may be obliged to shorten or otherwise modify the draft terms of reference which we and our partners and Allies have put forward, but we would be giving away a major point of principle if we were to abandon our position on this point. The Russians have so far given no indication that they will be prepared to agree to the elaboration of terms of reference during the preparatory talks. Their informal suggestions (paragraph 2 of Helsinki telegram under reference) that terms of reference might be worked out bilaterally after the talks are over or at the first stage of the Conference, are clearly unsatisfactory.[8]

[6] The Committee's functions, the Soviet Ambassador explained (*v. ibid.*), 'might include the preparation for subsequent all-European conferences, exchange of information on a multilateral basis on matters concerning European security and cooperation, and other questions which might be entrusted to it by the Conference'.

[7] At the plenary session of the MPT on 24 January Mr. Elliott, following agreement in the previous day's NATO meeting and in close coordination with the Austrians, spoke in support of an Austrian recommendation for the grouping of agenda proposals in broad subject areas or 'baskets'. He did not suggest a subject group for follow-up to the Conference, but said that this was of a 'somewhat special nature because it was bound to depend upon the results of the Conference'. The Swiss were meanwhile encouraged by the Nine to prepare a catalogue of proposals so far submitted on the agenda and terms of reference. As anticipated, this catalogue, which was accepted on 29 January as a working paper for the talks, grouped the proposals into four numbered baskets, dealing respectively with: (1) political and security matters; (2) economic and related issues; (3) human contacts, culture and information; and (4) follow-up to the Conference (Helsinki telegrams Nos. 73 and 74 of 24 January and No. 86 of 29 January).

[8] In Helsinki telegram No. 79 (see note 2 above) Mr. Elliott reported that in conversations with the Americans the Russians had indicated that terms of reference could be worked out bilaterally after the preparatory talks were over, and that Mr. Maltsev had recently suggested tentatively that experts accompanying Ministers to Stage I of the Conference should do the work. 'Both ideas', Mr. Elliott observed, 'are unrealistic and probably reflect the failure of the Russians to think their rigid ideas through.' He also noted that in their oral explanations of their agenda items the Eastern delegates had provided some useful potential material for terms of reference and that, theoretically, there was scope for compromise. The Western proposal that they should move on to discuss broad subject areas would, he thought, probably be accepted and: 'With luck the need for terms of reference [would] then become self-evident without an argument of principle'. Moreover, he felt it possible that agreement to accept a fourth agenda item on the Soviet proposal for a consultative committee could be another bargaining counter. However, in telegram No. 67 of 30 January to Helsinki, Sir A. Douglas-Home cautioned Mr. Elliott against giving the Russians any encouragement in their apparent desire to increase the momentum of the talks.

(*b*) We shall need to reach an acceptable compromise on the security content of the CSCE. The outcome will naturally be influenced by the eventual decision on participation in the MBFR exploratory talks.

(*c*) There is considerable pressure from the Mediterranean countries to include a specific reference in the agenda to Mediterranean aspects of European security. We shall have to seek agreement to a formula which will meet their legitimate concern without widening the present scope of the Conference or giving rise to demands for participation by countries not represented in Helsinki.

(*d*) Although the Russians have now agreed to a separate agenda item to deal with cultural and human relations, we must expect them to express strong opposition to the ideas expressed in the Western terms of reference in that respect.

7. The talks have continued to go reasonably well for the West. The members of the Community and the Alliance have generally stuck together, and (according to the Finns who mentioned this point to me specifically on 24 January) have thereby made an unexpectedly impressive contribution. We shall have to watch the French who are not always as open as we should like and fancy themselves as East/West bridge builders. The neutrals have co-operated well and generally taken positions nearer to ours than to the other sides. For their part the Russians have shown some signs of being in a hurry. It may not be a coincidence that they have chosen to be conciliatory at Helsinki while creating problems over MBFR.[9] If the Russians were to stick to their present position on MBFR, the Americans (and others with them) could feel that the basic Russo-American agreement of last autumn, which set the CSCE and MBFR processes in train, was in question, and might be disposed to slow things up or otherwise retaliate in Helsinki.[10] A major row over MBFR would anyway adversely affect the atmosphere and proceedings at Helsinki. But if the MBFR difficulties can be resolved, and we continue to work effectively with our Community partners and NATO Allies (in consultation with the neutrals), we should be able to continue pushing things the way we want.

C.C.C. TICKELL

[9] A brief prepared by WOD on 26 January for the Prime Minister's meeting with President Nixon at Camp David on 31 January summarised the state of play regarding MBFR. On 18 January the Warsaw Pact had accepted NATO's invitation to 'exploratory talks', commencing on 31 January, but suggested that these should take place in Vienna, rather than Geneva, and that participation should be wider than the Central front and flank powers originally proposed by NATO. While it was finally agreed that talks would begin in Vienna, the Warsaw Pact 'reserved the right to raise the question of participation . . . during the exploratory talks' (telegram No. 286 to Washington of 30 January, WDN 27/1).

[10] On 6 February Mr. Tickell wrote to Mr. C.J. Audland (Counsellor, HM Embassy in Bonn) that the Americans had evidently wished to avoid doing anything in the CSCE which might upset MBFR prospects, and they had not wished 'by taking a major role themselves, to provoke the Russians into acting correspondingly'.

No. 21

Mr. Elliott (Helsinki) to Sir A. Douglas-Home

No. 147 Telegraphic [WDW 1/2]

Priority. Confidential   HELSINKI, *10 February 1973, 10.20 a.m.*

Repeated for information Priority UKDEL NATO and Vienna, Routine Moscow, Washington, Bonn, Paris, The Hague, Brussels, Rome, Copenhagen, Dublin and Luxembourg, Saving Sofia, Athens, Budapest, Valetta, Oslo, Warsaw, Bucharest, Madrid, Stockholm, Berne, Ankara, Belgrade, Ottawa, Nicosia, Lisbon, UKREP Brussels, Reykjavik, Prague, UKMIS Geneva and UKDIS Geneva.

My telegram No. 144.[1]

CSCE/MPT

1. The second stage of the preparatory talks concluded on 9 February. Plenary sessions will resume on the afternoon on 26 February.

2. All delegations who intended to do so have now tabled proposals on the agenda and on the work of the committees. The proposals have been grouped in four subject areas referred to simply as numbered baskets to avoid prejudging decisions on the agenda of the Conference.[2] Each basket has been the subject of a preliminary exchange of views in plenary which has served to indicate more clearly the points of difficulty which lie ahead.

3. I set out below a summary of the position reached on the main points. An assessment of the performance of delegations at this session and suggestions on how we should approach the next are contained in my two immediately following telegrams.[3]

Terms of Reference and Sub-Committees

4. The Russians have moved a considerable way on terms of reference. They have tabled brief 'assignments' for committees on each of the four baskets and their most recent speeches suggest that they are prepared to discuss the substance of the Western proposals. They still maintain that the preparatory talks should not deal with terms of reference for the sub-

---

[1] This and Helsinki telegram No. 145, both of 9 February, summarised the final plenary meeting of the second stage of the MPT, which concentrated upon continuing machinery or follow-up, now designated Item or Basket IV.

[2] See No. 20, note 7.

[3] In Helsinki telegram No. 148 of 10 February Mr. Elliott stated that the session had 'gone well for the West', and that the Nine, who had remained united, could claim much of the credit for signs of Soviet flexibility. But, he also explained that, while the performance of other NATO countries had been affected by the Americans' adoption in plenary of a posture which varied 'between the low and the undetectable', the Soviet Union had made the running on the Warsaw Pact side. 'Our own position', Mr. Elliott observed, 'is made more difficult by the low posture of the Americans and the continuing tendency of the Russians to see the worst in what we say in plenary.' Helsinki telegram No. 149 is reproduced at No. 22. Mr. Fall speculated in a minute to Mr. Tickell of 14 February: 'The Americans may see these preparatory talks as in some ways a political test for the Nine, and they may have decided to follow the logic of the scientific method and to keep their fingers out of the test-tube' (EN 2/6).

committees which they claim it will be for the Conference itself to establish. But they have said that they have nothing against sub-committees in principle and they have indicated informally that they might eventually acquiesce in drafting assignments for committees that would be divided into separate paragraphs which might eventually correspond to sub-committees.

Principles Governing Relations between States

5. The Russians have been highly critical of the Western draft[4] which speaks of 'refraining from the threat or use of force, particularly as regards the inviolability of frontiers'. They argue that the inviolability of frontiers is a principle in its own right and that by coupling it with the non-use of force the Germans are going back on their bilateral agreements.

6. The Russians have not included in their list of principles references to the peaceful settlement of disputes, human rights, fundamental freedoms, equal rights and self-determination of peoples and the fulfilment in good favour of obligations under international law (all of which appear in the Western draft). Their main criticism has been directed against the references to human rights, which they argue is not a principle governing relations between states, and to self-determination, which they suggest is relevant only in colonial situations.

Security Content of the Conference

7. There are no major differences in the short texts on confidence building measures in the Western draft and in the proposal tabled by the GDR[5]. But the neutral and some Western countries would like to go considerably further. It is not yet clear how much flexibility the Russians (and for that matter the Americans) will be prepared to show.

8. Proposals designed to increase the security content of the Conference differ in detail but reflect the same basic idea. Their supporters would like to emphasise the indivisibility of political and military aspects of security and many hope that the Conference will produce a declaration which would cover the general principles which negotiations for force reductions should take into account.

Peaceful settlement of disputes

9. The Swiss proposal that the Conference should formulate a system for the peaceful settlement of disputes has been supported by many of the neutral and by a number of NATO countries.[6] The Russians have been

[4] The Western draft terms of reference on principles were tabled by the Italians (see No. 20, note 3). These had been worked out by the Nine on the basis of a French draft and were subsequently agreed in NATO (draft report of the UK delegation to the MPT of 9 June, covered by minute from Mr. Fall to Mr. Tickell of 13 June, EN 2/1).

[5] On 5 February the East Germans tabled a text which referred to 'certain measures for strengthening stability and confidence having in mind mutual notifications about large military manoeuvres in stipulated areas and the possibility of the exchange of observers according to an invitation at such manoeuvres'. However, by the end of the second session the Russians had still not given formal support to this formula (*ibid.*).

[6] The Swiss, after extensive bilateral consultations before the MPT (see No. 10, note 14), indicated in the opening session of the talks that they wanted an explicit reference to machinery for the peaceful settlement of disputes included in the security items of the agenda, and in January they proposed that this matter be referred to a separate sub-committee. The

careful so far not to oppose the proposal publicly or outright. But their own draft links the settlement of disputes to other measures designed to promote the implementation of the agreed principles and emphasises the development of multilateral and bilateral political consultations. The East Germans have made it clear that they regard as premature any attempt to establish a system involving compulsory jurisdiction.

Mediterranean

10. The Austrians are alone in pressing for a specific role for the CSCE in the Middle East context. But the Mediterranean littoral countries including NATO members seem determined to ensure that Mediterranean aspects of security and cooperation in Europe are considered by the Conference.[7] Some at least are likely to press for the principles and possibly the confidence building measures to be extended in some way to non-participating Mediterranean countries. The Russian attitude is negative.

Economic and Technical Cooperation

11. The Western proposals are regarded as a good basis for discussion by the large majority of participants.[8] The East European members of CMEA have all made speeches emphasising the importance of economic cooperation and going into considerable detail. They have also however expressed support for the short Soviet proposal which contains very little by way of illustration of the 'draft final document containing a European programme' which they have proposed. The CMEA countries have predictably taken the line that the Conference should consider general principles including MFN[9] and non-discrimination.

Cultural and Human Relations

12. The Soviet draft proposal is as was to be expected empty of content

UK delegation made it clear that they would want to amend this project. But, as the delegation's draft report (*v. ibid.*) stated, there was a 'strong tactical element' in the British position 'in that the Swiss proposal seemed likely to point up the contrast between Soviet lip-service to the principle of peaceful settlement of disputes and their dislike of specific arrangements'.

[7] Algeria and Tunisia had, since the beginning of the MPT, pressed for their association with the CSCE and, in January 1973, the French drafted a paper urging the Nine not to take a negative attitude towards their case. The UK delegation took the line that, 'while we had no objection to a general formula requesting the Conference to bear in mind Mediterranean aspects of European problems, we would rather not have specific references to specific aspects of the agenda mandates' (*v. ibid.*).

[8] The Belgian draft agenda item and mandate for economic cooperation (see No 20, note 3) proposed the study 'under conditions of reciprocity and mutual benefit, ways and means of developing commercial exchanges as well as co-operation in the various economic fields' and referred to the possibility of 'newer forms of co-operation, especially in the fields of industry, raw materials and energy resources'. The proposed Committee would be assisted by four Sub-Committees on: (1) the development of commercial exchanges; (2) industrial cooperation and cooperation in the development of raw materials and energy resources; (3) cooperation in other areas of economics, notably transportation, communications and tourism; and (4) cooperation in the field of the environment (*v. ibid.*).

[9] Most favoured nation.

and long on qualifications.[10] A very negative introductory speech in plenary by the Poles which emphasised Eastern views on state control[11] led to vigorous responses by a number of Western and neutral participants which brought out clearly the fundamental differences of approach in this area.

Continuous Machinery

13. The Russian proposal for a Consultative Committee[12] has been described by them as meeting Western objections to too ambitious a permanent organ. The idea of some form of continuing machinery has been supported by a number of neutral and non-aligned countries.

[10] The Soviet delegate, Mr. V.A. Zorin, put forward this very restrictive assignment for Item III at the plenary session on the 8 February. He insisted that preparatory work on the subject must proceed in accordance with generally accepted norms for dealing with questions falling within the internal competence of states (Helsinki telegrams Nos. 137 and 138 of 9 February).

[11] In this speech delivered on 7 February the Polish representative emphasised the responsibility of individual states and claimed that no state could 'decline responsibility for what [took] place on its own territory and prejudices the international atmosphere' (Helsinki telegrams No. 133 of 8 February).

[12] See No. 20.

No. 22

Mr. Elliott (Helsinki) to Sir A. Douglas-Home

No. 149 Telegraphic [*WDW 1/2*]

Priority. Confidential   HELSINKI, *10 February 1973, 11.15 a.m.*

Repeated for information Priority UKDEL NATO and Vienna, Routine Moscow, Washington, Bonn, Paris, The Hague, Brussels, Rome, Copenhagen, Dublin and Luxembourg, Saving Sofia, Athens, Budapest, Valetta, Oslo, Warsaw, Bucharest, Madrid, Stockholm, Berne, Ankara, Belgrade, Ottawa, Nicosia, Lisbon, UKREP Brussels, Reykjavik, Prague, UKMIS Geneva and UKDIS Geneva.

My two IPTs.[1]

CSCE/MPT

1. When the talks resume we shall come under pressure from the Warsaw Pact countries[2] to get down to drafting probably in working groups. The Russians would like us to start with the 'easy points' by which they mean the titles of the agenda items and a short and fairly general description of the tasks of the committees.[3] We should not underestimate the attraction of this

[1] See No. 21 and note 2 below.

[2] In Helsinki telegram No. 148 (see No. 21, note 3) Mr. Elliott noted that it was clear the Russians intended 'to exercise tight control over the pace of movements towards compromise', though they still gave 'every sign of wanting a speedy conclusion'.

[3] At a buffet supper on 5 February Mr. L.I. Mendelevich, a leading member of the Soviet delegation, suggested to Mr. R.C. Beetham (First Secretary, HM Embassy in Helsinki) that when the MPT resumed they 'should set up working groups, perhaps one on baskets 1 and 4

approach for many of the neutral and non-aligned delegations who would like to see some results emerging from the talks.[4]

2. There are clear dangers in this approach for our position. Once faced with even a provisionally agreed agenda and brief description of the committees' tasks we should be in a weak bargaining position in trying to get agreement to more detailed terms of reference and to the establishment of sufficient sub-committees to ensure an effective second stage of the Conference. Without such detail it will be difficult to achieve our aim of establishing that enough common ground exists among the participants to warrant reasonable expectations that a Conference would produce satisfactory results.

3. In my view the better procedure for us would be to start the drafting process from the bottom up. In this way we would consider the individual subjects in each basket and seek agreed formulations of them and then build up first a number of smaller subject areas (which would correspond to sub-committees) and finally a composite agenda item. We have circulated informally to Western delegations here a paper (my telegrams numbers 142 and 143) which sets out these arguments more fully.[5]

4. There are a number of points on the substance of the subjects in the various baskets which are likely to cause difficulty when the talks resume. The most immediately important one concerns the security content of the Conference. The neutrals, having resisted the Soviet suggestion that they should transfer their attention to Vienna, clearly hope for some degree of Western support here.

5. The question is one on which there is still no agreement either in the Nine or in NATO,[6] and it will clearly be difficult to reach a common position.

and one on baskets 2 and 3, and have fewer plenaries' (letter from Mr. Beetham to Mr. C.C.W. Adams (WOD) of 6 February, EN 2/2).

[4] The Soviet proposal for working groups, though not raised in plenary before the end of the session, became a major subject for informal consultations at Helsinki. At a meeting of the Fifteen on 7 February, both the Norwegians, who had long advocated the establishment of working groups, and the Americans, who had suggested the idea informally to UK delegates, supported the proposal. But the French argued that it would be tactically unwise to establish working groups before agreement had been reached in plenary on the general principles which should guide their work (Helsinki telegram No. 142 of 9 February).

[5] Mr. Elliott discussed this paper with American, Belgian, Canadian and West German delegates at a working dinner on 8 February. In the paper he contended that, while the formal establishment of working groups would offer the best opportunity for all those interested to contribute to the drafting of the agenda and terms of reference, it would wrongly imply that there was already a wide degree of agreement which merely required formulating. He therefore proposed that it would be better to speak of 'specialised committees'; and that, rather than follow the Russian approach, which involved provisionally accepting agenda items and some sort of mandates for committees without having agreed either to sub-committees or the questions covered by their mandates, they should attempt to reach agreement 'from the bottom up' (Helsinki telegrams Nos. 142 and 143 of 9 February). These proposals were well received by NATO's SPC when it met on 13 February (UKDEL NATO telegram No. 139 of 13 February, WDW 1/1).

[6] At the NATO SPC meeting on 13 February (*v. ibid.*) the US representative announced that, though his authorities still had reservations about the introduction into the CSCE of too

Our own position lies somewhere between the two extremes but I am not clear exactly where we would like to draw the line. I am being increasingly pressed by my neutral colleagues to give a more precise indication of where we stand.

6. There is obviously no point in our parading a position which is unacceptable to the Americans, French and Russians but I nevertheless hope that we can show some flexibility on this point.[7] Given the difficulty of drafting terms of reference which would include a draft declaration along the lines of the Anglo-German one discussed in NATO but exclude the Benelux ideas which go further, we may have to think of other ways of reaching a compromise. An idea which occurs to me is that we might give to a sub-committee terms of reference which would allow for an exchange of views on certain military aspects of security in addition to the confidence-building measures but which would make it clear that no formal recommendations were expected from it on this subject.

7. There are a number of other points on which it is clear that the West will come under pressure to modify its opening position. I do not think that we need be in any great hurry to offer concessions and we should no doubt exploit the apparent Soviet desire to get the preparatory talks over as soon as possible. But it may be useful during the break to give consideration to the following points:

(a) *Principles*. The arguments (which I deployed in plenary) that one cannot pick and choose from the generally accepted principles of the Charter and the UN Declaration is [*sic*] accepted by a large majority of the participants. But there is also some sympathy among the neutral delegations for the Soviet argument that inviolability of frontiers should be accepted as a separate principle and that bilateral as well as multilateral texts can be drawn upon where appropriate in the discussion of principles. This is very much a point for the German delegation[8] and my impression is

much military content, they had been impressed by the strength of feeling of the neutral countries on this issue and the need to find a position acceptable to the rest of the Alliance, and they were therefore prepared to envisage the inclusion of a reference to military security in a declaration of principles guiding relations between states. Mr. Lever welcomed this move, and the French representative indicated that, even if his Government could not directly support such an inclusion, they might not openly oppose it.

[7] Mr. Tickell thought that the UK should seek agreement in the EC and NATO to a 'fairly forthcoming line' on this, a subject on which the majority of the neutrals and non-aligned had made it clear they wanted an opportunity to air their views. 'An agenda which allowed scope for general discussion of the military aspects of security would', he noted, 'lend support to our position on participation in MBFR and help neutralise the neutrals.' Sir T. Brimelow agreed (minutes by Mr. Tickell and Sir T. Brimelow of 14 February).

[8] In a letter to Mr. E.A. Burner (HM Embassy in Bonn) of 2 March Mr. R.A. Burns (WOD) explained the FRG's position succinctly. He stated that while the West Germans claimed they could not accept the present frontiers as necessarily the legitimate or final ones, the only way to 'violate' them would be by using force and disturbing the peace, and since they had renounced the use of force and agreed to settle disputes by peaceful means, they were prepared to accept the inviolability of frontiers as an aspect of the principle of the non-use of

that they will eventually accept a formulation on inviolability which is satisfactory to the Russians.[9]

(*b*) *Mediterranean.* There is strong pressure to include references to the Mediterranean both in the security and cooperation items of the agenda. A French paper to be considered again in the Sub-Committee of the Nine offers a basis for a flexible response to the suggestions which have been made.

(*c*) *Economic Cooperation.* We shall as expected have to agree to discuss science and technology in the economic text. There is no problem of substance here but we should seek to gain what tactical advantage we can in meeting East European demands on this subject. We shall also have to agree a formula covering obstacles to trade which will deal with the East European points on MFN and non-discrimination while allowing us to put forward for discussion the barriers on the other side. We may also have to cover the question of financial and monetary cooperation. In this as in other cases there seems no reason for us to make a significant step forward until the East have agreed to terms of reference sufficiently detailed to reflect the content of their speeches.

(*d*) *Cultural and Human Relations.* Positions are still so far apart that it is difficult to see how the detailed discussion will go. We shall have to shorten what are generally regarded as over-lengthy terms of reference and I welcome the work which has already been done on this subject. We should also consider whether it is realistic to expect the Conference to work out a 'long term programme' on cultural exchanges as we at present recommend. It is interesting that Zorin should have raised the matter from the practical point of view in his speech and it may be that the Russians see the possibility of a bargain to drop both this long term programme and the one which they themselves have proposed in the economic field.

(*e*) *Continuing Machinery.* The argument that we cannot decide what (if any) new machinery will be required until we have a clearer idea of the results of the Conference remains valid. There are good tactical reasons for sticking to it. But neutral and non-aligned delegations have sufficient sympathy for the idea of continuing machinery to make it impractical for us to seek to exclude a separate agenda item or even a separate committee to deal with the question at an appropriate stage during the Conference. I

force. This he considered a view to which HMG was bound to give a certain amount of support. But, he added that the Germans were likely to come under strong pressure to moderate their attitude, especially as in their treaty with the Soviet Union of August 1970 they had achieved a connexion between the principle of the non-use of force and inviolability of frontiers by what was 'barely more than juxtaposition within the same article' (WDW 1/6).

[9] At meetings of the Davignon CSCE Sub-Committee on 3 March and of the NATO SPC on 6 March, the German delegates indicated that they no longer insisted on an explicit link between the non-use of force and the inviolability of frontiers in the mandate for the Sub-Committee on Principles (UKDEL NATO telegram No. 194 of 7 March). The SPC also agreed that the UN Charter and the UN Declaration on Friendly Relations should be retained as the main sources for principles, and proposals for including references to bilateral agreements should be treated with caution (letter from Mr. Lever to Mr. Burns of 13 March).

think that we need to give urgent consideration to draft terms of reference for such a committee. These should make it clear that we were not committed to new machinery, still less to any particular proposal, but there would seem no harm in saying that the committee should consider all proposals put forward for the follow up of the Conference including those already on the table here. It will be necessary also to do further work either in the Nine or in NATO on the substance of the Soviet proposal for a consultative Committee which has been cleverly designed to allay the suspicions of the neutral and non-aligned delegations that something far too ambitious was being proposed.

No. 23

Mr. Elliott (Helsinki) to Sir A. Douglas-Home

No. 184 Telegraphic [WDW 1/2]

Priority. Confidential   HELSINKI, *28 February 1973, 3.30 p.m.*

Repeated for information Priority UKDEL NATO Routine UKREP EEC Brussels, Moscow, Paris, Washington, Bonn and Vienna, Saving Sofia, Copenhagen, Athens, Budapest, Luxembourg, Valetta, The Hague, Oslo, Warsaw, Bucharest, Madrid, Stockholm, Berne, Ankara, Belgrade, Ottawa, Nicosia, Dublin, Lisbon, Reykjavik, Prague, Rome, UKMIS Geneva and UKDIS Geneva.

My telegram No. 179 (not to all).[1]

CSCE/MPT

1. It has now been agreed to establish one open-ended Working Group[2] which will start work tomorrow on Basket number one (political and security questions).

2. It became clear as a result of the debate on Tuesday[3] that an attempt to agree precise objectives or methods of work for the Working Group would

---

[1] Dated 26 February, this recorded a meeting of the Nine that day at which it was decided, in line with agreement reached by EC Political Directors on 20 February (telegram No. 45 to Brussels of 21 February, WDW 1/3), 'that there would be tactical advantage in proposing the inductive (bottom up) approach to the future work of the consultations and the creation of a single Working Group rather than react to suggestions which might be put forward by others'. M. G. André, French Ambassador at Helsinki, proposed this arrangement at the plenary meeting on 26 February. He explained that the Working Group 'would work successively on the four Baskets without necessarily exhausting one before passing to the next', emphasising that this would not be a drafting group, and that the Group would work informally without publicity.

[2] British delegates later recalled in their draft report (see No. 21, note 4) that Western consultations during the second break 'were influenced by the belief that if the rate of progress could not be increased the neutral and non-aligned countries would tend to become impatient with the amount of detail contained in the Western proposals'. They also pointed out that while the inductive approach, which Mr. Elliott had proposed (cf. No. 22), was never formally accepted by the Russians, it 'was accepted by them in practice when the Working Group began its examination of the proposals in the various baskets'.

[3] i.e. 27 February.

lead to a lengthy and unproductive debate. Participants in the Working Group will take into account a draft on the tasks of the group distributed by the French Ambassador (text in MIFT)[4]: his introductory statement (in which he set out the case for an inductive approach): and statements made by the Russians and other Warsaw Pact countries emphasising the need to get down to detailed drafting. Warsaw Pact countries who spoke expressed a preference for four working groups which would each deal with one of the baskets, and have said that they regard the present arrangements as experimental.

3. The procedural arrangements for the Working Group are based on those for the Plenary Sessions, subject to certain modifications which I proposed informally and which proved generally acceptable (text by bag to FCO and UKDEL NATO).[5] The Chairmanship will rotate daily. The first Chairman will be provided by the Soviet Union who were successful in a draw, the results of which were greeted with more amusement than surprise.

4. The Warsaw Pact countries appear concerned to ensure that the momentum of the consultations is maintained and that consideration of Basket IV (continuing machinery) is not unduly postponed. They have suggested that the Working Group should (at least in the first instance) spend only a short time on each basket (the Bulgarians proposed three days for the first) and have made it clear that they retain the option to propose the creation of additional groups.

[4] Not printed.

[5] These procedural arrangements were sent under cover of a letter from Mr. Adams (UKDEL MPT) to Mr. Burns of 1 March.

No. 24

Letter from Sir T. Brimelow to Lord Cromer[1] *(Washington)*

[*WDW 1/6*]

Confidential   FCO, *8 March 1973*

CSCE: Soviet Draft Declaration

1. During the Prime Minister's visit,[2] Kissinger gave Burke Trend a copy of the Soviet draft of a 'General Declaration' which Dobrynin had earlier given Kissinger.[3] Kissinger told Dobrynin that the document would have to be

[1] HM Ambassador in Washington.

[2] Mr. Heath visited Washington between 30 January and 2 February.

[3] On 2 February Mr. Dobrynin gave Dr. Kissinger a copy of a Soviet draft General Declaration on Foundations of European Security and Principles of Relations between states in Europe. Later that day, during a conversation with Dr. Kissinger at Camp David, Mr. Heath remarked that the CSCE had 'probably been originally envisaged by the Soviet Government as a means of dealing with the German problem', and that since that had been bypassed by the success of the *Ostpolitik* of the West German Chancellor, Herr W. Brandt, what were they 'likely to think up now, as their next device for blocking the interests of the

discussed with America's Allies; and he mentioned specifically that he was showing it to us. We were enjoined not to discuss it further.

2. During our talk with Kissinger on 5 March,[4] I told him we had prepared some comments on the Soviet paper and he expressed interest in receiving them. I attach a copy of our paper for transmission to his office and a second copy for retention by you.[5] If Kissinger or his staff dissent from any of our comments, we should of course be glad to learn what alternative considerations should, in their opinion, be preferred.

3. In the circumstances of our talk, where this was only a peripheral issue, I thought it would be inopportune to pursue a number of questions which interest Western Organisations Department. Was the Soviet draft handed over simply to indicate the present lines of Soviet thinking? Or was it to be the bait leading to bilateral US/USSR discussions? Did Dobrynin invite comments? In our view the text itself has puzzling features. For example there is a reference to 'the right of peoples to determine without impediment their own destiny' on page 5: yet the Russians have strongly opposed at Helsinki the inclusion of a reference to the principle of self-determination in the mandate for the Sub-Commission on Principles (to be set up for the second stage of the CSCE).[6] As you will see from our analysis, we find a good deal to take exception to.[7] Our objections to the use of the phrase 'peaceful

West'? Dr. Kissinger replied that 'they would simply go on trying to undermine NATO by every means they could' and that this was clear from the General Declaration, a copy of which he passed to the Prime Minister (extract record of conversation PM/Nixon at Camp David on 2 February). A substantially amended version of this draft General Declaration, dated 4 July, was tabled by the USSR at Stage I of the CSCE. See I.I. Kavas, J.P. Granier and M.F. Dominick (eds.), *Human Rights, European Politics, and the Helsinki Accord: The Documentary Evolution of the Conference on Security and Co-operation in Europe 1973-1975* (Buffalo, NY: William S. Hein & Co., 1981), vol. i, pp. 357-61.

[4] Sir T. Brimelow was in Washington for further discussions of the Soviet proposal for an American-Soviet Agreement on the prevention of nuclear war. Cf. No. 12, note 2.

[5] Amongst the several points to which the FCO objected in the Soviet draft was its preambular reference to the 'difference of socio-political systems' not being 'an obstacle for all-round development of relations between states on the basis of peaceful co-existence'. The Russians had not included 'peaceful co-existence' in the short list of principles cited in their draft assignment for the security Committee in Helsinki, and it was felt that if the Nine stood firm on this issue, they should be able to achieve a more satisfactory formulation such as 'fruitful co-operation'. The FCO paper also noted that the reference to socio-political differences avoided the important point 'that such differences should not prevent all participating states from benefiting fully from generally recognised principles of international law' (undated paper, CSCE: detailed comments on the draft General Declaration given by the Soviet Ambassador in Washington to Dr. Kissinger).

[6] The FCO paper (*v. ibid.*) pointed out that the Russians had previously accepted far more explicit language on national self-determination (e.g. UN Declaration Concerning Friendly Relations Among States, see No. 27, note 8), and concluded 'we should not accept their argument that it is not applicable in the European context'.

[7] Mr. Walden complained that the Soviet draft was 'replete with alien concepts expressed in unwieldy formulations', adding that if it were available to the British press, 'it might well be

co-existence' may not be entirely shared by the Americans, but to judge from recent correspondence our objections will be strongly upheld by other Europeans.[8] What I myself regard as the most objectionable aspect of the Soviet draft is the philosophy which underlies the whole document and which looks towards the establishment of a new system of 'collective security' in Europe.[9]

4. The approach of the Russians in Helsinki to the question of 'principles' has so far been highly selective. The aim of the alliance in dealing with the question of a Declaration is to focus discussion on our own draft rather than any Soviet one. I enclose a copy of the latest NATO draft Declaration of Principles Governing Relations Between Participants[10] which, although not yet agreed, shows the outlines of what we intend to propose when the time comes. In our view it would be unwise to get into any discussion with the Russians about their draft until we reach the second stage of the Conference. As suggested above, we would in any event want on the table a Western draft of equal status. It is the Russians, not we, who want a declaration, and we must make them work for it at this point and, we hope, extract from them concessions in other fields as a price for eventual agreement.[11] (We know that the Secretary of State agrees with this.) If we were to begin exchanging views on a bilateral or other basis with the Russians now, we should not only reduce the possibility of more effective leverage later, but also accelerate a process which it could be in our interest to prolong. There is the additional danger that if we reached agreement on some sort of declaration before the Conference, the Russians might try to persuade Ministers to try to sign it at the end of the first Ministerial Meeting. This would of course emasculate the

portrayed as a blueprint to transform Western Europe into a sort of Soviet Disneyland' (minute to Mr. Fall of 13 February).

[8] After consultations with other Community capitals, Mr. Burns minuted that the UK's partners took a 'commendably robust attitude' towards the use of 'peaceful co-existence'. He noted: 'They all dislike the phrase, and condemn it, in more and less explicit terms, as a hangover from the cold war' (minute to Mr. McLaren and Mr. Tickell of 23 March, WDW 1/1). See also Volume I, No. 104.

[9] The preambular draft declaration referred to the desirability of effecting a transformation of relations amongst states in Europe which would permit them to overcome the continent's division into military political blocs and replace these 'with a system of collective security'. In his minute of 13 February (see note 7 above) Mr. Walden commented that this was 'pie in a Soviet dominated sky. "Collective security" = Brezhnev doctrine'. He also drew attention to an article which obliged participants to consider introducing legislation to give effect to other provisions of the Declaration. It could, he thought, 'easily be exploited to bolster the Finlandisation thesis'.

[10] Not printed.

[11] Mr. Bullard, who reckoned the draft declaration to amount to 'an endorsement of the Soviet vision of Europe, in which the Russians and their friends would have a free hand to interfere in the affairs of the West, while the apparatus of Party control would guarantee that nothing whatever was changed in the East', argued that HMG's initial attitude towards it should 'be one not simply of reserve but of total rejection' (minute to Mr. McLaren of 16 February).

Committee stage and again cause us to lose leverage.

5. It is obviously for the Americans to decide what to do with the document. At our talk, Kissinger said that he thought that the French and the Germans had copies, but did not state, nor even hint, how or from whom they had acquired them.[12] We ourselves think it would be helpful if at some stage the Americans would circulate their copy of the Soviet text within NATO. Further work on the NATO draft could be facilitated if we could collectively consider the Soviet one. But such a suggestion might be unwelcome to the White House. If you decide to raise the question at all, it might be better to do so interrogatively—have they considered whether the North Atlantic Council should be allowed to see and comment on the Soviet draft at some stage?[13] Kissinger's comment to Dobrynin that the document would have to be discussed with America's allies should provide a lead-in.

THOMAS BRIMELOW

[12] On 19 April Dr. Kissinger told Sir T. Brimelow that 'the Americans knew that the French and Germans had also received copies', and this seemed to substantiate reports which had reached the FCO in the autumn of 1972 that Soviet drafts on principles had been communicated to the French and Germans. Mr. Tickell thought it 'not surprising that the Russians should have tried on the French and Germans (then considered to be somewhat softer than the British over Principles) and later the Americans the draft of a Declaration which might emerge from the Conference' (minute to Mr. Wiggin of 8 May).

[13] Mr. R.A. Sykes (Minister, HM Embassy in Washington) thought it best to discuss the Soviet draft General Declaration with Mr. Sonnenfeldt as Senior Staff Member for Europe and East-West Relations of the National Security Council. But the opportunity to do so did not occur until the end of March. Mr. Sonnenfeldt then said that the Americans had not considered circulating the draft to NATO, and that if they decided to do so they would have 'to clear it with the Russians first so as to preserve the confidentiality of their channels'. Mr. Sykes observed that it was apparent from Mr. Sonnenfeldt's attitude that the draft had 'a pretty low priority on Kissinger's agenda'. The draft surfaced again, in May, during talks between Mr. Kissinger and Mr. Brezhnev in Moscow (letters from Mr. Sykes to Sir T. Brimelow of 30 March and 22 May).

No. 25

Letter from Mr. J.A.N. Graham[1] (Washington) to Mr. Bullard

[EN 2/6]

Personal and Confidential   WASHINGTON, *12 March 1973*

Dear Julian,

Brian Crowe[2] tells me that you were rather alarmed by what Jim Sutterlin[3] told you at dinner about the new American line in CSCE. Brian undertook to look into this. We may not be reporting on this for a while,

[1] Counsellor and Head of Chancery at HM Embassy in Washington.

[2] Mr. B.L. Crowe was First Secretary at HM Embassy in Washington.

[3] Mr. J.S. Sutterlin was Country Director for Germany at the US Department of State.

however, so I thought I had better let you have this personal line so that you know where things stand.

2. As you know, CSCE was one of the subjects discussed between Tom Brimelow and Kissinger a few days ago.[4] I do not know what distribution Tom Brimelow will be giving to this part of the record, but if you see it, you will know that Kissinger professed to accept that his strategy of the CSCE was consistent with our tactics in Helsinki. (I personally believe, though I was not present, that there is in fact a rather more substantial difference than the conclusion of the discussion suggests.)

3. Kissinger's general attitude was, not surprisingly, reflected in conversation between Bill Hyland, John Wilberforce[5] and Brian Crowe at dinner on 7 March. Hyland took the line that CSCE was not important. In response to the argument that we should try to get what we could out of it, he did not dissent but said that he could not conceive that the Russians would agree to anything disadvantageous to them and there was therefore no point in having a showdown about it. Nor should there be any linkage between the CSCE and the MBFR talks; it would be disastrous if both conferences went down the drain in a short space of time. Hyland commented that the MPT now taking place in Helsinki were not at the stage at which anything real could be done. That would follow in the second stage after the foreign ministers' meeting. There was therefore no point in drawing things out. But he volunteered that proceedings were going very satisfactorily in Helsinki. He thought that the US Delegation were behaving extremely well in maintaining their low profile position and leaving the lead with the EEC countries. He thought that the latter had worked very effectively and played a useful role. Altogether he gave the impression that the Americans were quite relaxed about the CECE [*sic*] and the way it was being handled and gave no impression that they were thinking of throwing a spanner in the works.

4. One last point made by Hyland—not exactly a new one; he said that nobody at the top of the Administration had really focussed on CSCE. By this he clearly meant the details of tactics for the talks. Kissinger's views as expressed to Tom Brimelow and earlier to Gaston Thorn[6] and HM

---

[4] See No. 24.

[5] Mr. W.J.A. Wilberforce was Counsellor at HM Embassy, Washington.

[6] On 1 March, at a working dinner of the Nine in Helsinki, the Luxembourgers briefed their colleagues on M. Thorn's recent meeting with Dr. Kissinger in Washington. According to Helsinki telegram No. 196 (WDW 1/2) of 2 March, Dr. Kissinger had apparently criticised the Europeans for being 'thoroughly unhelpful' over the CSCE and MBFR. He had said with regard to the CSCE that they 'should let the Russians, as sponsors, have what they wanted, a short snappy Conference with little substance', and accept that little progress was possible. 'Freer movement', he remarked, 'had tactical uses but would lead to nothing'. Mr. G. Vest, the US delegate at the MPT, subsequently told Mr. Fall that he regarded M. Thorn's report as 'basically accurate', but added that he did not believe Dr. Kissinger had 'given very deep thought to the question', and that 'the President would want the American delegation to remain committed to the line agreed in NATO' (letter from Mr. Fall to Mr. Tickell of 8 March, WDW 1/2).

Ambassador reflected his strategic view of the unimportance of CSCE in the overall scheme of things (this is the reason for my personal doubt expressed in para 2 above).[7]

Yours ever,

J.A.N. GRAHAM

[7] In a letter of 19 March Mr. Bullard thanked Mr. Graham for his letter, noting that it made 'a number of things much clearer'.

No. 26

Mr. Elliott (Helsinki) to Sir J. Beith[1] *(Brussels)*

No. 1 Telegraphic [*WDW 1/2*]

Priority. Confidential   HELSINKI, *14 March 1973*

Repeated for Information Priority FCO and UKDEL NATO, Routine Paris, Bonn, Washington, Rome, Vienna and UKREP Brussels, Saving Sofia Copenhagen, Athens, Budapest, Luxembourg, Valetta, The Hague, Oslo, Warsaw, Bucharest, Madrid, Stockholm, Berne, Ankara, Moscow, Belgrade, Ottawa, Nicosia, Dublin, Lisbon, Reykjavik, Prague, UKMIS Geneva and UKDIS Geneva.

For EC Political Directors Meeting.

CSCE/MPT

1. The meeting of Political Directors of 15 March and of Ministers on 16 March will no doubt wish to consider what has so far been achieved at the MPT and what lies ahead. The third session is currently in mid-stream but the following is a summary of where we stand.

2. The third session began slowly. The Russians were persuaded to accept the Nine's proposal for the creation of a single Working Group. They also accepted the so-called 'bottom up' approach of discussing all proposals in each category before attempting to draft the terms of reference for the committee in question. We realised that we would come under increasing pressure to start drafting after the establishment of the Working Group, either in more working groups (opposed by the French) or through some other informal mechanism. This became particularly clear as the rate of progress was regarded as insufficient not only by the Russians, but also by the neutrals and a number of NATO countries. Through our proposal of agreeing in the Working Group on a framework document on the first part of the security basket (principles) which was then remitted to an informal group for more detailed drafting,[2] this difficulty was overcome and a useful precedent established.

[1] HM Ambassador in Brussels.

[2] The paper which the British delegates circulated informally to the Working Group on 8 March foresaw a Basket I text which would include: (1) a brief job description; (2) a basic premise; (3) summary references to UN principles which the committee or sub-committee should bear in mind; (4) an indication of the principles to which special attention should be paid; (5) a reference to the interrelationship of principles; (6) a formula enabling the committee

3. We thus now have a more flexible working structure within which to operate. The plenary continues to meet and to deal with general proposals for any part of the proposed agenda and with organisational questions concerning the consultations and the Conference. Beneath it the Working Group ploughs a patient furrow through the baskets, probing and elucidating and, if it proves generally acceptable in future, handing a framework document on each separable subject to an informal drafting group. The drafting group then embarks on the drafting work and, if the Nine have their way, will hold any agreed drafts to a later stage.

4. This working structure is likely to be followed for the other baskets, and will enable us to secure full discussion of those items on the agenda to which we attach importance (particularly the economic and cultural baskets) before we give formal agreement to formulations on Basket I (security) which the East favour. The Russians by accepting an outline for the terms of reference on principles clearly based on the original Western proposal, have taken a further step towards our ideas. Eastern countries have told us privately that for them the framework approach is a valuable face-saver, enabling them to work informally on the basis of western drafts without being seen too publicly to be doing so.

5. Due to this search for a more flexible organisational structure progress on substance has been slow. The Working Group have however given exhaustive treatment to the principles and are now discussing confidence building measures. Discussion in the Working Group so far has indicated that the East can probably be persuaded to accept the greater part of the Western proposals with a leavening of their own and neutral ideas. They are also talking in terms of drafting substantial terms of reference for commissions and may eventually go along with the Nine's compromise proposal on sub-commissions. We must accept however that the real political test has yet to come in the informal drafting group which has just begun to meet.

6. The signs of restlessness however which appeared among the neutrals and within the Alliance before we made our framework proposal last week (para 2 above) may well re-appear. The Nine must continue to keep in close touch with the other members of NATO and with the neutrals and to show flexibility in negotiating on points which do not affect the substance of our position. I believe that effective coordination and the substance of our common position can be maintained but this will require general willingness to take tactical decisions on the spot. The main danger is that the Russians by exploiting the capacity which they now seem to have for quick decision taking could undermine the support of the neutrals for Western positions and open up differences within the Alliance.

7. The future timetable is not easy to forecast, though it seems clear that we shall have a break from early April until just after Easter, with a fourth

or sub-committee to consider additions to or clarifications of the principles; and (7) a statement of objectives. On 9 March the Working Group accepted the paper as a general framework for the text to be produced on principles by an informal drafting group, henceforth usually referred to as the 'Mini-Group' (Helsinki telegrams Nos. 215 and 219 of 8 and 9 March).

and—one hopes—final session ending in late May. This would enable the first stage of the Conference itself to take place at the end of June (a date which has retained a certain mystique and is certainly the assumption of all the East Europeans, most of the neutrals and a number of members of the Alliance). Certain delegations among the Nine and Fifteen, notably the Belgians and Dutch, seem to be operating on the assumption that the first stage of the Conference cannot begin before September, most other delegations here however assume that the second stage will begin in September, after the European holidays.

No. 27

Minute from Mr. Brown on CSCE: Principles[1]

[EN 2/1]

Confidential   FCO, *20 March 1973*

1. Today, discussion in the working group of the MPT will be switched away for a time, at least, from the question of what the CSCE should discuss under the question of principles governing relations between states. This may therefore be a good moment to review the position.

Frontiers

2. The Russians are insisting that the inviolability of frontiers be listed as an independent principle in the terms of reference for the second stage committee.[2] Everybody else wishes to give endorsement in some form to this principle, but the question has areas of extra sensitivity for some. These are principally the Germans[3] and to a lesser extent the Irish and Spanish.[4]

[1] Copies of this minute were sent to Mr. Bullard, Mr. Walden and Mr. S.J.L. Wright.

[2] There was some discussion within the FCO over the exact meaning of the word used by the Russians to convey the idea of inviolability. By the end of March the Russians had settled for the use of 'nenarushimost' rather than 'nerushimost', the term used in the Russian text of the Soviet/FRG Treaty of August 1970 and in the Prague Declaration of 26 January 1972. As Mr. K.A. Bishop of Research Department explained in a minute of 30 March, while 'nerushimost' suggested indissolubility or immutability, 'nenarushimost' was derived from the adjective meaning 'that which can or may not be violated' and would therefore 'appear slightly less uncompromising than the former'.

[3] On 6 April Herr G. van Well, the Political Director of the West German Foreign Ministry, told Mr. Hibbert, with regard to a forthcoming visit by Mr. Brezhnev to Bonn, that it 'was of the greatest importance from the Federal Government's point of view that the principle of inviolability of frontiers should not be held to preclude peaceful change and even abolition of frontiers by mutual agreement' (Bonn telegram No. 428 of 6 April).

[4] Article I of the Soviet draft General Declaration (see No. 24) proclaimed 'that borders existing between European states are inviolable, that territorial integrity of all European states in their present borders should be recognized, and unconditionally respected, that territorial claims by some European states against others should be completely excluded and that any attempt of encroaching upon the inviolability of existing borders will be regarded as an act of aggression'. This, as Mr. Walden noted in his minute of 13 February (see No. 24, note 7) was unlikely to be acceptable to either the Irish Republic or Spain, given their respective

3. The Russians say they cannot understand German objections since the inviolability of frontiers is mentioned in the FRG treaties with Moscow and Warsaw. The Germans claim that there is an important difference of degree between bilateral treaties and the kind of document which the CSCE should produce, and that the Moscow and Warsaw treaties do not, in this case, constitute precedents. The allies agree, both to support the Germans and because they would prefer bilateral treaties not to be used as quarries for principles. They fear that to do so might enable the Russians to use the CSCE to create some sort of European regional law.[5] In allied consultations Britain has been taking the line that we can go along with anything the Germans accept. The French, however, have recently shown signs of impatience.

4. In fact, this issue should resolve itself fairly easily because:

—there appears to be some softening in the original German position[6]
—we can insist that inviolability has nothing to do with immutability
—we can emphasize the last point by juxtaposing the principles of inviolability and non-use or threat of force.[7]

Sources

5. The West says that the principles should be quarried only from the United Nations Charter and the Declaration concerning Friendly Relations

territorial aspirations with regard to Northern Ireland and Gibraltar. It might also, as Mr. B.M. Mawhinney of the Canadian High Commission in London, indicated to Mr. McLaren, imply the *de jure* recognition of the Soviet Union's incorporation of Estonia, Latvia and Lithuania (minute from Mr. McLaren to Mr. Burns, 9 March, WDW 1/6).

[5] Mr. Darwin thought that HMG should, if possible, seek to avoid references to bilateral agreements in any accord emanating from the CSCE, and that they must certainly avoid anything which might give the appearance of committing the UK to texts to which it was not party. Soviet attempts to create some form of European international law could, he argued, 'have the disadvantage of encouraging other regions to produce their own versions' (minutes by Mr. Fall and Mr. Darwin of 5 and 6 March).

[6] Cf. No. 22, notes 8 and 9. At a meeting of NATO delegations in Helsinki on 22 March it emerged that the West Germans regarded 'an outcome with ten distinct principles (i.e. selling inviolability of frontiers in return for human rights and self-determination) as an acceptable outcome' (Helsinki telegram No. 268 of 22 March, WDW 1/6). But the Italians objected to this decoupling of principles and delayed the West's formal acceptance of this compromise until after the Easter break (draft report of the UK delegation, see No. 21, note 4).

[7] The Swiss had grouped the various proposals made on principles on ten sheets of paper covering: sovereign equality, non-use of force, inviolability of frontiers, territorial integrity, peaceful settlement of disputes, non-intervention in internal affairs, respect for human rights and fundamental freedoms, equality of rights of people and their right to self-determination, fulfilment in good faith of obligations under international law and cooperation. At the NATO meeting on 22 March (*v. ibid.*) it was agreed that the allied aim should be to have any references to inviolability of frontiers and respect for territorial integrity appear after the non-use of force. At the meeting of the principles mini-group on the 23 March Mr. Mendelevich confirmed implicitly that he would be prepared to accept this list of ten principles (Helsinki telegram No. 281 of 24 March).

among States.[8] The East wishes to include other sources such as bilateral documents and the UN Declaration on the Strengthening of International Security.[9] We have resisted this (i) because bilateral documents—especially some of those which the Soviet Union has signed with neutral and Western countries—contain much unsatisfactory language (including 'peaceful co-existence') which it would be both dangerous and unworthy to dignify by referring to it, or including it in the kind of document which we hope the CSCE will produce; (ii) because the Declaration on International Security is a less satisfactory document than that on Friendly Relations and has less status.

6. Some compromise will be necessary and the Western position at present is tending towards:

—re-examining the Declaration on International Security to see whether it might not prove acceptable as a quarry after all (it exorcises the Brezhnev doctrine, reaffirms those parts of the Charter to which we attach special importance and is only really objectionable—if at all—in its references to apartheid and colonialism)

—conceding that discussion on principles may be 'illuminated' in some fashion by bilateral documents.

R.H. BROWN

[8] UN Declaration Concerning Friendly Relations Among States, GA Resolution 2625 (XXV), as recommended by the Sixth Committee A/8082 and adopted by the General Assembly on 24 October 1970.

[9] UN Declaration on the Strengthening of International Security, GA Resolution 2734 (XXV), as recommended by the First Committee A/8096 and adopted by the General Assembly on 16 December 1970.

No. 28

Submission from Mr. Tickell to Sir T. Brimelow

[*WDW 1/10*]

Confidential   FCO, *22 March 1973*

CSCE: *Continuing Machinery*[1]

1. We shall soon have to make up our minds about how to cope with the long-standing Soviet demand for the creation of permanent machinery to follow the Conference on Security and Co-operation in Europe.

2. The present Soviet proposal is a modified and weaker version of a proposal which has been present in Warsaw Pact thinking for as long as the idea of the Conference itself. At Helsinki the Russians have proposed the establishment of a Consultative Committee

[1] In preparing this submission Mr. Tickell appears to have drawn heavily upon views expressed in a minute to him from Mr. Fall of 23 February.

'to deal with questions of security and co-operation in Europe, open for participation to all European states, the USA and Canada. This Committee will have a consultative status. Its functions may include such tasks as matters relating to European security and co-operation; preparation of further all-European conferences; and any other questions which might be entrusted to it by the Conference. The Committee will work on the basis of consensus'.[2]

The wording of this passage is looser than had been expected, and may still not represent the final Soviet position. The Russians want their proposal to be treated as a separate agenda item and discussed in Fourth Committee at the second—or Committee—stage of the Conference.

Background

I The British Attitude

3. Her Majesty's Government's attitude towards some sort of permanent machinery has undergone change in the last four years. Mr. Michael Stewart favoured a Standing Committee of East/West relations (SCEWR).[3] In doing so he had in mind as much a device for preparing a conference as permanent machinery to follow it. When Mr. Gromyko came to London in October 1970, the present Secretary of State indicated to him that we had an open mind on this subject, and the *communiqué* subsequently published referred to the 'possible establishment of permanent machinery for further consideration of these matters' (i.e. matters of common interest).[4] Our partners in the Community and the Alliance have generally taken a more hostile line and, in the course of current preparations for the CSCE, we ourselves have come round to the view that the right way to deal with work arising from the CSCE is either to farm it out to existing bodies (for example the Economic Commission for Europe) or to create specific ad hoc machinery with a mandate in time and function. We have made no secret of this view to the Russians or anyone else. In Britain the Labour Party, and in particular Mr. Michael Stewart, have continued to take a more favourable attitude towards continuing machinery as such. To judge from my own contacts with MPs who take an interest in the CSCE, most think it reasonable that some sort of continuing machinery emerge. It was implicit in the final resolutions of the recent IPU Conference in Helsinki[5] that the process of East-West co-operation would need to be followed up after the CSCE but there was no reference to the creation of specific machinery for the purpose.

[2] The Soviet delegation tabled this draft assignment on 8 February (Helsinki telegrams Nos. 139 and 140 of 9 February, WDW 1/2). Cf. No. 21, note 12.

[3] See Volume I, No. 39, note 7. Cf. No. 1.

[4] See Volume I, p. 53 and D.C. Watt and J. Mayall (eds.), *Current British Foreign Policy. Documents, Statements and Speeches, 1970,* (London: Temple Smith, 1971), pp. 584-6.

[5] The Inter-Parliamentary Union Conference on Cooperation and Security in Europe took place in Helsinki during 26-31 January.

II The Advantages and Disadvantages

4. It may be convenient to draw up a check list of advantages and disadvantages to the West of the proposal now put forward by the Russians. I think we must assume that although it now looks fairly harmless, the Russians would like to use any Consultative Committee which might be set up to further their previous purposes, in other words to have an international mechanism designed to help bring into existence 'an all-European security system' and to promote *détente* and all-European Co-operation in the very selective sense in which they use these terms.

Advantages

(*a*) On the assumption that the Conference is a success and that work arising from it is farmed out to existing or new bodies, there could be a requirement for somebody to co-ordinate progress of work, sort out difficulties, receive complaints from one side or the other, report to Governments as necessary and generally act as a means of continuing multilateral contact between participants at the CSCE. This body need not be more than a co-ordinating committee on the lines we are now proposing for the second stage of the Conference itself.[6] It could for example consist of Ambassadors in an agreed spot, such as Helsinki, meet only when need arose (though this would require careful definition) and, as the Russians themselves suggest, work by consensus. The fields in which such a Committee might best serve Western interests would be in monitoring the execution of confidence-building measures[7] and of any agreements which may be reached on cultural exchanges, freer movement of people, ideas and information etc.[8]

---

[6] Both the French and West Germans favoured the idea of a Coordinating Committee for Stage II of the Conference and, in a minute to Sir T. Brimelow of 1 March, Mr. Tickell gave qualified support to the proposal. At a meeting of the Davignon CSCE Sub-Committee on 5 March the French argued successfully that the early establishment of such a body 'would provide a useful means for dealing with Eastern requests for a Consultative Committee to follow the Conference and make it easier to ensure that the need for a Consultative Committee would be considered in the light of the work of other Committees and not as something good in itself'. Draft terms of reference for a Coordinating Committee, which UK delegates submitted to the Sub-Committee, also included the provision: 'When a specific requirement has been identified in a field where no suitable institutions exist, the Committee may at its discretion recommend to the Conference proposals for the establishment of new consultative machinery to meet this specified requirement for as long as this may be necessary' (telegrams Nos. 56 and 57 to Brussels of 5 March, WDW 1/3 and MT 10/598/2). On 13 March the French tabled terms of reference for a Coordinating Committee insofar as they concerned procedural matters.

[7] Mr. Fall suggested (see note 1 above) that if CBMs were to be effective, some sort of machinery might be required to provide for the exchange of notifications and perhaps to consider complaints, and that if a Consultative Committee were already in existence there would be strong practical arguments for adding this role to its functions.

[8] But, Mr. Fall observed, a Consultative Committee would be unable properly to maintain the momentum of the CSCE in the cultural and human relations field 'if it remained a "*salon des Ambassadeurs*"; and it would tend to expand in less desirable directions if it were provided with a secretariat and certain limited executive functions'.

(*b*) The balance of such a Committee would in normal circumstances be tilted in favour of the West. If the neutral and non-aligned countries supported the Community and NATO countries (as they have done more often than not in their preparatory talks at Helsinki), the West would enjoy a substantial majority.[9]

(*c*) More important, American and Canadian membership of the Committee would tend to engage the United States and Canada both in work arising from the Conference and in continued participation in European security matters generally.

(*d*) The existence of such a Committee would probably recommend itself to public and parliamentary opinion who may expect something of a permanent character to match the pretentions of the CSCE. If such a thing as 'the spirit of the CSCE' ever develops, the Committee could usefully serve as its ghost.

Disadvantages

5. (*a*) The Russians would seek to use a Consultative Committee to give them a licence to interfere in the affairs of Western Europe. Although in theory it could give us an equal right to interfere in the affairs of Eastern Europe, such interference—based on appeals to public opinion—could only be effective in the open society of the West and not in the closed society of the East. Consensus-based machinery would not necessarily give us adequate protection.[10] Thus a Consultative Committee could well find itself handling persistent complaints about the activities of Radio Free Europe and Radio Liberty, and perhaps even British policies in Ulster, without being able to do anything about the Soviet attitude towards emigration of Jews, the victimisation of liberals in Czechoslovakia or the jamming of Western broadcasters.

(*b*) The Russians would almost certainly try to make the Consultative Committee generally responsible for carrying into effect whatever broad principles were agreed in a declaration of principles guiding relations between states. They have already spoken about the need for domestic legislation in participating countries to put these principles into effect,[11] and we could expect them to use the Consultative Committee as a sort of ginger group to urge legislation upon recalcitrant governments.

(*c*) The Russians would use the existence of a Consultative Committee to block progress on the Swiss proposal for specific machinery for the peaceful settlement of disputes (an idea which we have discreetly encouraged) or other proposals of the same kind.

[9] Mr. Fall also thought that there would be 'an added stimulus to continuing coordination among the Nine and in NATO'.

[10] In his minute Mr. Fall argued that, although consensus-based machinery would not allow the Russians to take decisions opposed by one or more participants, they would be able 'to mobilise public opinion in the member states in such a way as to make it difficult for a particular government or governments to maintain policies unattractive to the majority'.

[11] See No. 24, note 9.

(*d*) The Russians would seek to expand the responsibilities, functions and organisation of a Consultative Committee. Their terms of reference for it are already sufficiently clear in this respect.[12]

(*e*) The existence of such a Committee might nurture public illusions about *détente* and East/West relations generally on the lines which the Russians are assiduously propagating.

(*f*) In practice many of the tasks of the Committee might well tend to be European regional issues such as transport and energy schemes and the protection of the European environment. This might cause the Americans and Canadians to take interest.

III *The views of other participants*
(*1*) *Eastern Europe*

6. The Yugoslavs and Romanians (occasionally supported in informal conversations by other East Europeans) argue that continuing machinery would help them preserve and even increase their independence of the Soviet Union. It must be assumed that these arguments are known to the Russians and that they have discounted them. The most that can be realistically expected of a Consultative Committee is that its existence might give the Romanians and others a little extra psychological reassurance. It could not protect them against a real Soviet threat.

(*2*) *Neutrals and Non-aligned*

7. Most of the neutral and non-aligned countries would support some form of continuing machinery in the hope that it would enable them to maintain the role on the European stage which they have played with every appearance of enjoyment during the preparatory talks so far.[13]

(*3*) *The Community and NATO*

8. The idea of a permanent body of a political or general nature has been rejected as unacceptable by the Nine and NATO.[14] Our partners and Allies are however more or less resigned to the fact that there will have to be some

[12] The Soviet draft assignment provided that the functions of the Committee should include 'any other questions which might be entrusted to it by the Conference'. Mr. Fall assumed from Soviet Basket assignments that such 'other questions' might include roles for the proposed Consultative Committee in the peaceful settlement of disputes and the development of economic cooperation. In the latter role, he feared that a purely Consultative Committee would be unsatisfactory since machinery already existed for work considered worthwhile and it would not be in Western interests to give the Russians added scope for interfering in the development of the EC (see note 1 above).

[13] 'The most extreme sufferers from this disease', Mr. Fall noted with regard to this point, 'are the Spaniards who see in proposals for continuing machinery a way of maintaining political contact with Eastern Europe and the Soviet Union should their campaign for the establishment of bilateral relations not yield the fruit they desire.' But Mr. Fall also insisted that neither the views of neutrals nor the assertions of the Romanians and the Yugoslavs provided sufficient reason for the West's accepting continuing machinery.

[14] When, on 21, 22 and 23 February, NATO's SPC discussed tactics for the next phase of the MPT several delegates expressed concern over whether French proposals for a Coordinating Committee 'went too far in the direction of sanctioning continuing political machinery' (UKDEL NATO telegram No. 160 of 23 February, WDW 1/1).

discussion of continuing machinery at the Conference. In this respect there is agreement among the Nine (but not yet in NATO) on the tactical handling of the Soviet proposal. We shall wish to ensure that the wording of the agenda on this point, and the arrangements made for studying it at the Conference, do not prejudge the issue in the Russians' favour.

Conclusions

9. We shall almost certainly be obliged to discuss permanent machinery at the Conference. I believe that it will in practice be difficult if not impossible to resist the establishment of some form of Consultative Committee, though we should be able to delay giving our agreement until fairly late in the proceedings when it may earn us some *quid pro quo*. We might suggest that it should be set up for a limited period (say two years) in the first instance.

10. We should be able to keep the activities of such a Committee within reasonable bounds. To do so we will need to resist any effort to give the Declaration of Principles legal force or a status which would require some international body to monitor its application. We will also have to ensure that, whatever declaration is negotiated or confidence-building measures are agreed, we do not give the Russians scope for arguing that they constitute useful occupations for more elaborate and powerful continuing machinery.

Recommendations

11. I recommend that for the present we abide by the agreed NATO position, which is that we should decide what new continuing machinery of an ad hoc nature is necessary only when we have seen the detailed recommendations of the Committees of the Conference and established that the tasks cannot be fulfilled by an existing international body. We should express ourselves ready to examine any proposals for such machinery when the time comes, on the basis that it is right for the Conference to consider any matter which is thought to be important by a number of delegations. This could be done either in a separate committee, provided the terms of reference were tightly drawn, or else in a Steering-Co-ordinating Committee (as the Nine have now agreed).

12. Mr. Bullard agrees.[15]

C.C.C. TICKELL

[15] On 26 March Mr. Wiggin minuted Sir T. Brimelow: '1. I agree with the view expressed in Mr. Tickell's minute of 22 March to you. If at the end of the day we have to have continuing machinery the more we can keep it to some sort of Ambassadorial teaparty in, e.g., Helsinki, the better. 2. The drawbacks of continuing machinery apply whether or not the Conference is eventually termed a success—whatever that may mean—though the pressure will doubtless be heavier if it is. Success is an ambiguous definition in this field; to the Russians it means softening up the West while maintaining their grip on the East.' Sir T. Brimelow noted his agreement.

No. 29

Sir A. Douglas-Home to Mr. Elliott (Helsinki)
No. 178 Telegraphic [*WDW 1/2*]

Priority. Confidential   FCO, *28 March 1973, 5.50 p.m.*

Info Priority UKDEL NATO, Routine Vienna (for Roberts).

Your telegram No. 282.[1]
CSCE/MPT

1. Thank you for this useful assessment. The momentum of the talks seems about right. We agree with the analysis in para 3 of your tel[egram] under reference.[2]

2. Our views on linking progress between the preparatory talks in Helsinki and the exploratory talks on MBFR in Vienna have not changed.[3] In present circumstances we do not think it would be practicable or desirable to hold up the proceedings in Helsinki as a means of putting pressure on the Russians to go faster in Vienna. So far as our current tactics in Helsinki are concerned, we are guided by three broad considerations:

(*a*) The Russians and their allies have made the holding of a CSCE a major objective of policy. On the Western side we have agreed to participate in preparatory talks in the hope that we shall be able to recommend to our respective Ministers that the Conference can take place. In the words of your own statement of 30 November, 'before we can do so we shall have to be sure that this recommendation is based on reasonable expectations of success and not on wishful thinking. In short we need to establish that enough common ground exists between us to justify a

[1] In this telegram of 24 March Mr. Elliott assessed the momentum of the MPT, a subject discussed at a NATO Permanent Representatives' lunch on 20 March and reported on in UKDEL NATO telegram No. 234 of 21 March. Mr. Elliott subsequently confessed to Mr. Tickell, in a letter of 26 March, that he had sent telegram No. 282 in what 'might be described as an attempt to smoke out your views'. He had, he explained, gained the impression from recent telephone conversations with WOD that he and Mr. Tickell might be 'diverging' in their views on 'the basic philosophy of the talks'. Mr. Tickell was quick to reassure him in a letter of 29 March that they were 'thinking in the same terms'.

[2] Mr. Elliott stated in paragraph 3 (*v. ibid.*) that he thought most of the Western allies assumed that they should continue to work towards the achievement of common texts at Helsinki, using the end of June as a working hypothesis for the opening of the Conference. He added that working backwards from this date, it would be advantageous to have by the end of the current session of MPT as clear an idea as possible of the points of major difficulty which would have to be resolved during the next round.

[3] In his telegram No. 282 (*v. ibid.*) Mr. Elliott insisted that he was not qualified to enter into the possible links between progress in the MPT and progress at Vienna, though he recognised that this was at the back of the minds of those delegations who were concerned about the rate of progress at Helsinki. He assumed that HMG's position was still as stated to him by Sir T. Brimelow during the February recess and that they did not envisage trying to slow down proceedings in the MPT for reasons connected with the MBFR.

Conference, and that the points to which our Ministers attach importance will be fully debated and considered there'. In these circumstances it is generally for the Russians and their allies to move towards our requirements rather than for us to move towards theirs. Provided we can stick together and generally bring along the neutrals with us, we see no need to make real concessions of substance to meet Eastern views.

(*b*) Now that preliminary drafting of the agenda and terms of reference for committees and sub-committees is taking place, we need to ensure that any proposals for change in positions agreed in the Alliance and among the Nine should be carefully considered by all concerned. We are reassured that you do not think we are in danger of losing control. But this is a point which we shall have to continue to watch.

(*c*) The performance of the Nine at Helsinki has, partly due to your own good work, been extremely effective, and represents the first such achievement in the field of foreign policy. We attach great importance to maintaining cohesion, however difficult it may be to reconcile the footdragging of some of our partners with the pacesetting of others. Although other members of the Alliance, notably the Americans, have so far been less active, we are equally anxious to maintain the cohesion of the Alliance.[4] We also want to retain the sympathy of the neutrals which has served us well so far. We recognise that these objectives may sometimes conflict.

All this means easier said than done. But it is encouraging that we have so far managed as well as we have.[5]

3. [A member of the US Embassy][6] . . . today showed us a telegram of instructions to your US colleague which showed that American views on the momentum of the talks at present correspond to our own. The Americans believe that the Allies should now proceed with all deliberate speed and continue to set themselves a target of finishing the preparatory talks in time for the Conference itself to start at the end of June.

---

[4] According to Mr. Elliott (*v. ibid.*), the Americans were increasingly showing signs of impatience and seemed 'prepared to be fairly flexible on the drafting'. He also noted that the Canadians and Norwegians had expressed similar views, but that the Benelux countries (primarily the Netherlands) professed themselves unhappy with the way things were going and tended 'to regard slowness as a virtue in itself'. This, he added, was unfortunately not reflected in a willingness on their part to defend Western positions in the working groups, with the result that the main burden of discussion in the Working Group and the Mini-Group on Basket I had fallen on the British, French, Germans and Italians.

[5] Mr. Elliott thought that the West had 'so far managed to avoid yielding any significant point' and that he did not think they were in danger of 'losing control'.

[6] A name has here been omitted.

No. 30

Mr. Elliott (Helsinki) to Sir A. Douglas-Home
No. 361 Telegraphic [WDW 1/2]

Priority. Confidential   HELSINKI, *7 April 1973, 2.30 p.m.*

Information Priority UKDEL NATO, Routine Paris, Bonn, Washington, Rome, Vienna, Moscow, Saving to Brussels, Sofia, Copenhagen, Athens, Budapest, Luxembourg, Valetta, The Hague, Oslo, Warsaw, Bucharest, Madrid, Stockholm, Berne, Ankara, Belgrade, Ottawa, Nicosia, Dublin, Lisbon, UKREP Brussels, UKMIS Geneva, Reykjavik, Prague and UKDIS Geneva.

My tel[egram]s Nos. 360,[1] 341,[2] 359[3] and 349.[4]

CSCE Third Round of the Preparatory Talks

1. The unduly lengthy session which ended on 6 April has involved detailed consideration of the first three Baskets and the points of difficulty which remain are now more clearly exposed. But as there is no very direct connection between many of the subjects under discussion, it has not been easy to maintain the overall view required for the meetings with our partners and Allies which will take place between now and the resumption of the talks on 25 April. I have tried in my tel[egram]s under reference to bring out the main issues on principles, military aspects, co-operation and human relations respectively. The purpose of this telegram is to consider our general approach to the next round of the preparatory talks, and to put forward some

[1] Mr. Elliott reported in this telegram of 7 April on the results of the Mini-Group (see No. 26, note 2) discussion of principles. This he thought had clarified the main areas of agreement and disagreement and 'indicated the broad lines along which compromise texts could be found'. Disagreements with the East existed over: the list of principles, their order, the inter-relationship between them, their field of application, and the source documents to be mentioned in the mandate (WDW 1/6).

[2] Dated 5 April, this telegram provided an update on MPT discussions on the military aspects of security. On CBMs three points remained outstanding: the prior notification of military 'movements', to which the East were resisting making reference; a Romanian suggestion that CBMs were 'measures of a preliminary nature', words to which the Americans, the French and to a lesser extent the Russians, objected; and a Yugoslav proposal for 'restraints' on movements and manoeuvres. With regard to other military aspects Mr. Elliott observed agreement could not be reached 'until the Americans and, if possible, the French are prepared to show greater flexibility' (WDW 1/22).

[3] In this telegram of 6 April Mr. Elliott gave his impressions of the state of play on Basket II. He noted that most of the East Europeans had tried to be helpful, but that they were, except for the Romanians, very much under Soviet control and he accused Mr. Zorin of having been 'typically heavy handed' in his tactics. On coordination amongst the Nine, which he thought good, he added: 'The French ([M. G.] Bochet) have been loyal colleagues and spoken out firmly in defence of our position. The Dutch continue to be negative and the Belgians rigid. The Italians have in general occupied a middle position. The Germans, when led by [Freiherr G.] von Groll, were erratic and slightly uncontrollable, but on his departure [Herr R.] Lucas was a more amenable colleague.'

[4] Mr. Elliott reported in this telegram of 6 April on Working Group discussions regarding Basket III items.

ideas with the aim of provoking the fundamental thinking that seems necessary at this stage.

2. Our objectives at the talks were recently restated in para 2 of your tel[egram] No. 178,[5] in which it was said that 'provided we can stick together and generally bring along the neutrals with us, we see no need to make real concessions of substance to meet Eastern views'. The provisos are likely to have increasing importance during the next round of the talks, and we shall need to think hard about the situation we shall face at the resumption.

3. I hope it is clear from my tel[egram]s under reference that the East have already moved some way towards us on a number of issues. On the first two Baskets, and in parts of Basket III, they have either accepted a framework or tabled drafts which indicate their readiness to accept terms of reference for the three main Committees whose general outline corresponds fairly closely to our ideas. They have not yet accepted that the sub-committees which we have proposed should be established at the preparatory talks, but the point is one which they are likely to concede if the West stands firm. We should therefore be able to ensure a substantial second stage of the Conference.

(A) [sic] Principles

4. On the substance of the mandates, the picture varies from subject to subject. On principles (my tel[egram] No. 30 [*sic*])[6] there is the makings of a package which seems acceptable in political terms: the list of principles would include respect for human rights and self-determination (at the cost of conceding inviolability of frontiers as a separate principle): and it would be stated that the principles should apply to all states, irrespective of their political, economic or social systems. The solution likely to be reached on military aspects of security (my tel[egram] No. 341)[7] will be a disappointment to a number of delegations, but we should be able to get enough to ensure that the question is not ignored by the Conference. On Basket II (my tel[egram] No. 356)[8] the mandate should be sufficient to allow a detailed discussion at the Conference, but it is unlikely to suggest anything more promising than the sort of discussion with which we are already familiar in the Economic Commission for Europe.[9] Basket IV has not yet been dealt with in

[5] No. 29.

[6] Presumably telegram No. 360. See note 1 above.

[7] See note 2 above.

[8] Dated 6 April this recorded the main points of interest in the previous day's Working Group meeting on Basket II. Discussion centred on the environment, and trade and industrial cooperation (SMF 2/579/1).

[9] According to Helsinki telegram No. 359 (see note 3 above) Basket II mandates on science and technology and the environment had been provisionally agreed. The main problem areas on Basket II were: Eastern demands for the mention of a long-term programme and principles and refusal to accept any reference to reciprocity in the *chapeau* of the terms of reference; Eastern insistence on the inclusion of most-favoured nation and non-discrimination provisions and objections to references to improved administrative procedures and business contacts; the East's presupposition that the Conference would agree on joint all-European projects; and

any detail, but it is a fair guess that a mandate which provides for a discussion of the follow-up to the Conference without prejudging the issue will eventually prove acceptable.

5. There should be no great difficulty in ensuring in these sectors that we are able to raise at the Conference the points to which we attach importance. But I do not know whether you would regard a result such as that suggested in paras 3 and 4 above as offering 'reasonable expectations of success' in the specific sectors mentioned. I think that the Americans would be prepared to do so, and they are probably not alone. Putting the question the other way round, I find it difficult to envisage our Allies refusing to go to a Conference on those conditions.

6. We are, however, in a very different situation on Basket III (my tel[egram] No. 349).[10] The Soviet position on human contacts and information falls far short of what we want, and we have no clear indications of how far the Russians would be prepared to go to reach a compromise.[11] As seen from here, this is the only issue on which a breakdown in the talks could be effectively justified.

7. I think that this analysis would find a wide degree of support among Western delegations here. It is much harder to decide what conclusions should be drawn and I recognise that the view from Helsinki is not a complete one. Nevertheless, I would put forward the following ideas:

(*a*) We should be careful not to reach a stage on the first two Baskets (and on the cultural and educational aspects of Basket III) at which we could be said to have agreed (albeit provisionally) to mandates covering both security and co-operation before we have a reasonable assurance of satisfactory results on human contacts and information.

(*b*) The right way to avoid this difficulty is not repeat not to stonewall in the working groups. It is now generally recognised that the drafting stage has been reached or is very near on virtually all subjects except human contacts and information. If we participate in this work, we should do so with the intention of getting results. Stonewalling irritates not only the East,

Spanish and Yugoslav proposals on tourism and migratory labour and a Bulgarian proposal on agriculture.

[10] Mr. Elliott observed in this telegram (see note 4 above) that on Basket III Mr. Zorin's manner and tactics had been aggressive, but that these might have been 'designed to disguise a weak hand'. Eastern drafts on culture, education and information were, he wrote, more detailed than their previous offerings, 'though they naturally attempt to defuse Western proposals on freer movement and information while giving prominence to cultural questions as a whole'. The East, he noted, had not yet produced a draft on human contacts.

[11] On 2 April Mr. Zorin made a lengthy speech to the Working Group in which he claimed general support for his suggestion that they should first concentrate on drafting a preamble, including aims and principles, for Basket III. He strongly attacked the prominence given in the Danish paper (see No. 20, note 3) to marriage and the reunification of families, adding that such delicate problems could only be solved bilaterally. He also proposed that the principle of non-interference be written into the preamble to Basket III (Helsinki telegram No. 330 of 4 April).

but also the neutrals and some of our partners and allies, and it gives the impression that the Nine are incapable of taking decisions.[12]

(c) It would be possible however to approach the problem quite openly by making it clear to the Russians that we could not hope to make substantial progress on Basket I and II until further progress had been made on III. To be effective, such a position would have to command the support of the Nine and the alliance as a whole. I think that there is a reasonable chance that we could get such agreement from the neutrals provided that the issue is not seen as merely a delaying tactic.

(d) The proviso mentioned above brings us back to the question of momentum. As I understand it the Belgians and Dutch think that the interests of the West would best be served if the Conference was put off until September.[13] In practice it will be a tough job for us to complete our work in time for a meeting earlier than September, especially given that a number of the neutrals and non-aligned have already expressed their opposition to too much over-lapping of work on different subjects. But it does not seem likely that dragging out the negotiations on the mandates will produce better results on the substance. Quite apart from the dangers of such a course for the cohesion of the Nine and the alliance, a good case can be made for seeking to exploit Soviet pressure for a June Conference in a concentrated negotiating session of the resumption.

(e) There is I think the makings of a bargain which might usefully be indicated to the Russians by one or more Western countries, preferably including the French before the resumption of the talks. Its main elements would be:

(i) Further real progress on substance will depend on our reaching a satisfactory understanding on human contacts and information.

(ii) The basic requirements are that these subjects should be considered at the Conference in sub-committees distinct from that which will deal with cultural and education matters, and that the terms of reference (on the formulation of which we are prepared to negotiate) should not be restrictive but express a willingness to consider new ideas in the fields we

[12] Mr. Elliott had informed Mr. Tickell in his letter of 26 March (see No. 29, note 1): 'The difficulty is that solidarity here tends to be eroded if the Nine get into a position of immobility.' In such circumstances, he explained, the Russians were inclined to seize the initiative and were then able 'to stampede the neutrals and non-aligned', the Americans became impatient, and the risks increased of the French and Germans, both of whom were in regular contact with the Russians, breaking ranks 'overtly or covertly, to pursue their own bilateral ploys'. The 'underlying thought' in his mind was, he admitted, 'that we shall face trouble in the Alliance— and worst of all perhaps find ourselves in a time-squeeze with the Russians and Americans working in parallel against us—if we do not try to keep the Nine moving ahead gently and persistently'.

[13] Mr. Elliott complained in Helsinki telegram No. 349 (see note 4 above) of the reluctance of the Dutch and Belgians to face 'the inevitability of negotiations' combined with 'a total failure to speak up in the Working Group for the agreed position of the Nine'.

have suggested.[14]

(iii) Once we had reached an acceptable solution on these points, we would be prepared to press forward actively on all other questions in the hope of reaching agreement in time for the first stage of the Conference to take place in Helsinki at the end of June: and

(iv) We would accept that such an agreement should include the listing of inviolability of frontiers as a separate principle in Basket I, and should make provision for a full discussion in Stage II of the follow-up to the Conference.[15]

8. I do not underestimate the difficulties of getting these ideas agreed by our partners and allies. But it seems to me that at this stage both the Nine and NATO should be considering fundamental strategy as well as points of detail: and a working paper along the lines indicated above should serve to concentrate their minds on the basic issues that need to be decided before the next session begins. As seen from here it would be very useful if a working paper on these lines could be produced for the meeting of the Sub-Committee of the Nine[16] on 12 April and subsequently for NATO.[17] I am sure that the question of human contacts and information is by far the most important one left open and that it is only by tackling it directly that we shall reach a satisfactory solution.

9. If we did decide to go ahead on this general basis, it would be necessary to give the major neutrals (notably the Swiss, Swedes and Austrians) as much notice as possible.

[14] In Mr. Elliott's opinion the West should be prepared, if necessary, to consider the preamble of Basket III first. He argued in his telegram No. 349 that in the special circumstances of Basket III what the Russians were prepared to accept on individual subjects might well 'depend on a satisfactory formulation being found for the preamble' (*v. ibid.*).

[15] Sir A. Douglas-Home informed Sir J. Beith in telegram No. 100 to Brussels of 9 April that the FCO accepted Mr. Elliott's analysis in paragraphs 1 to 6 of this document and were attracted by the idea of a bargain as outlined in paragraph 7(*e*).

[16] i.e. the Davignon or EPC CSCE Sub-Committee.

[17] This proposal was agreed by the FCO (see note 15 above).

No. 31

Minute from Mr. Walden to Mr. Tickell

[*EN 2/4*]

Confidential   FCO, *16 April 1973*

CSCE: Human Contacts

1. Basket three is becoming the focal point of our tactics. I note that our Allies seem inclined to play it tough and do not even wish to contemplate fall-back positions at this stage.

2. This is not necessarily to be discouraged. But there is perhaps a danger of losing sight of the concrete concessions we eventually hope to extract from the Russians on human contacts. They are exceedingly modest. Comprehen-

sive preparatory work in NATO and now amongst the Nine has shown that:

(*a*) 'Cultural Exchanges' on the traditional pattern are already covered in bilateral agreements, and have very little relevance to our main aims at the CSCE.

(*b*) The Russians are most unlikely to make any permanent concessions of substance on freer movement. Experience shows that they are likely to go for a carefully selected series of highly publicised gestures (e.g. a few marriages and family reunifications). They might also sign exhortatory pieces of paper promising to consider future cases in a humanitarian spirit. But, (as Zorin has already stated),[1] they are not going to sign any firm agreements on this subject. They are certainly not going to abolish exit visas.

(*c*) It is only in the information field that there seems any likelihood at all of securing concrete improvements. The Russians may stop jamming the BBC (before the Conference if they have any tactical nous) though the West may come off worst if the Germans and Americans collapse under Soviet pressure to close down Radios Liberty and Free Europe. If either of our own proposals for a magazine or linked television programmes comes to anything, that will be the most substantial gain.[2] Reading rooms are also a possibility, though they reach a much narrower public. For the rest, there will be more exhortatory pieces of paper and a few showy gestures, e.g. tours for Western press men (maybe to the Russian space centre).

3. I am not suggesting that we and the Allies are on the wrong track. We must squeeze the Russian lemon very hard to demonstrate to public opinion how little juice there is in *détente à la russe*. But in manipulating basket three we should be constantly aware that the end product, even of successful Western tactics, could be embarrassingly thin.[3]

G.G.H. WALDEN

[1] See No. 30, note 11.

[2] See No. 11.

[3] On 17 April Mr. Tickell noted on this minute: 'I am much aware of this point and glad it should have been thus emphasized'.

No. 32

Mr. Elliott (Helsinki) to Sir A. Douglas-Home

No. 434 Telegraphic [*WDW 1/2*]

Priority. Confidential   HELSINKI, 5 *May 1973, 11.30 a.m.*

Information Priority UKDEL NATO, Routine Paris, Washington, Bonn, Rome, Moscow and Berne. Saving to Vienna, Brussels, Sofia, Copenhagen, Athens, Budapest, Luxembourg, Valetta, The Hague, Oslo, Warsaw, Bucharest, Madrid, Stockholm, Ankara, Belgrade, Ottawa, Nicosia, Dublin, Lisbon, UKREP Brussels, Reykjavik, Prague, UKMIS Geneva, UKDIS Geneva and East Berlin.

CSCE/MPT

You may find it useful to have the following general impressions of where we stand at the end of the second week of the fourth round of the preparatory talks.[1]

2. We have succeeded in our tactical aim of ensuring that there should be intensive discussion of Basket III while the Mini Group on Basket I deals as far as possible with subjects other than principles. We have had daily meetings on Basket III and only one on principles. (My telegram No. 433.)[2]

3. We shall continue next week to have daily meetings on Basket III but we must expect pressure for more active consideration of principles to build up. The Mini Group will consider the Swedish paper again on Wednesday[3] and it is likely that at least one further meeting will have to be accepted before the end of the week.

4. The negotiating position on Basket III remains broadly as stated in my telegram No 424.[4] Main new feature is that the Russians (while continuing in public to take a hard line on references to non-interference and respect for national laws) have sought unattributably to persuade a neutral delegation to propose a compromise formula for the preamble which would include a general reference to the principles to be agreed by the Conference and a specific reference to sovereignty and human rights. This seems the most likely basis for a compromise solution.[5]

5. It is probable that the Russians, having tacitly accepted the Western case that intensive work on Basket III was required to restore a degree of parallelism with the work on other Baskets, will now seek to link concessions on their part in Basket III with further progress on principles. It seems clear that a solution will have to be found on the basis of the Swedish introduction and the list of ten principles which have been worked on in the Mini Group. As seen from here it is essential that at the latest by the meeting of the Nine scheduled for 14 May in Brussels, delegations should be given a negotiating brief which allows them to work for the best solution attainable within that

[1] The fourth session of the MPT began on 25 April and lasted until 8 June.

[2] Dated 5 May, this telegram reported the discussion of a Swedish preambular paper on principles. Although Western delegations had reservations about its weak formulation, particularly with regard to the application of points relevant to the Brezhnev doctrine, Mr. Elliott recognised that it 'must now be regarded as the basis for further work' (WDW 1/6).

[3] i.e. 9 May.

[4] Helsinki telegram No. 424 reported that a Working Group meeting on 3 May had done much to clarify the negotiating position with regard to Basket III, with the Russians insisting on the inclusion in an Austrian draft preamble, the terms of which had already gained Western backing, of 'specific references to sovereignty, non-interference, and respect for national laws'.

[5] On 7 May the Working Group began drafting on Basket III. Mr. Elliott subsequently reported that he thought Mr. Zorin had been instructed to expedite progress, and that the UK delegation would be discussing in the Nine and the Fifteen whether agreement on the preamble as a whole was within their grasp 'on the basis of a *quid pro quo* whereby the West would accept a reference to "sovereignty and human rights" (coupled perhaps with a general reference to respect for principles guiding relations among participating states), in return for Soviet acquiescence on the listing of sub-commissions'. He added that the feeling was emerging amongst the Western Allies that this would be an acceptable compromise (Helsinki telegram No. 438 of 7 May).

framework.

6. Western delegations have so far maintained a satisfactory degree of solidarity on substantive issues but there are increasing signs of tension between the Belgians, Dutch and Italians on the one hand and the Danes and Norwegians on the other. The Americans have been active and helpful on Basket III but remain clearly committed to a fast rate of progress. We continue to find ourselves between the two extremes in company with the French and Germans.

7. There is a growing readiness among delegations here to assume that the Conference will begin at the end of June or early in July.[6] The Russians show every sign of being in a hurry and we should be able to exploit this to our advantage if we are able to show sufficient flexibility to keep the neutrals on our side. Some fairly difficult negotiations lie ahead. There will inevitably be some friction between the faster and slower moving of our partners and allies, but it should be possible to keep this to a minimum if all are prepared to show a genuine willingness to negotiate.

[6] A meeting of EC Political Directors on 25 April reaffirmed their determination not to accept the conclusion of the MPT until an agreement satisfactory to all delegations had been reached. Telegram No. 111 to Brussels of 26 April recorded: 'It was agreed that the date of end June for the beginning of the Conference could be a hope but was not a constraint'.

No. 33

Mr. Elliott (Helsinki) to Sir J. Beith (Brussels)

No. 2 Telegraphic [*WDW 1/2*]

Immediate. Confidential   HELSINKI, *13 May 1973, 7.30 a.m.*

Information immediate FCO and UKDEL NATO.

Following for Wiggin.

You may find it useful to have some general indications of the position as it appears from here before your meeting on Monday.[1] I apologise for the length of this telegram, but it is not easy to foresee what your colleagues may wish to raise.

Basket I

Principles

2. We are in the middle of the drafting process on a number of important questions on the principles mandate and it is not easy to give a concise account of where we stand. I recommend that you take as your general guidance Fall's minute of 11 May and the notes attached.[2]

3. I consider that the text on the application of principles textatively [*sic*]

[1] EC Political Directors were due to meet on Monday, 14 May.

[2] This minute described the current situation with regard to the Swedish paper (see No. 32, note 2) and the application of the Swiss proposal on the peaceful settlement of disputes (WDW 1/6).

agreed for the introduction of the mandate is fully sufficient to meet our requirements. This reinforces the view (paragraph 5 of my telegram No. 434)[3] that it is now essential that Western delegations should be given a negotiating brief which allows them to work for a text incorporating the list of ten principles which have been worked on in the Mini Group.

Swiss Proposal

4. There remains [*sic*] difficulties on the Soviet and Romanian texts, which have been linked with the Swiss proposal.[4] The arguments in FCO telegram No. 284[5] are very much in accord with the line we have been taking here. I think that many of these points will be met if this whole area can be clearly separated off from the section of the mandate dealing with principles (paragraph 2 of Fall's minute of 11 May).[6]

5. We must, however, assume that the Russians will insist on some reflection of their ideas as the price for accepting a reference to the Swiss proposal and that the Romanians will not accept a text on 'practical measures' which does not enable them to raise the questions to which they attach importance. I think that the majority of Western Delegations would if necessary be prepared to go along with the present formulation of the Romanian idea on the grounds that it does not commit us to supporting any particular idea although the formulation in FCO telegram No. 284 would clearly be preferable.[7]

6. As far as the link between the Soviet idea and Basket IV is concerned I do not think that the Russians regard their formulation as an alternative to a separate mandate. It may, however, make it easier for them to accept a mandate for Basket IV which does not prejudge the issue. The indications are

[3] No. 32.

[4] See No. 21, note 6. The Russians introduced into their draft 'assignment' for the Committee dealing with security questions measures to implement principles, including the settlement of disputes by 'peaceful means chosen and agreed upon by the parties and the development of multilateral and bilateral political consultations'. Early in the third session of the MPT the Romanians also proposed that the security Committee study appropriate measures for the peaceful settlement of disputes. The British initially encouraged the Swiss to pursue their ideas, but they, the French and the Italians objected to a composite text, which the Swiss introduced during the second week of May, and which added to their original proposal the requirement that the CSCE further 'bilateral and multilateral political consultations among states' and promote 'undertakings on a bilateral and multilateral basis concerning the elimination of the threat or use of force'. This, Mr. Elliott thought, would prejudge the Western position on Basket IV and give the impression that the application of principles was dependent on new developments in bilateral and multilateral consultations (Helsinki telegrams Nos. 422 and 453 of 3 and 10 May, WDW 1/6).

[5] This telegram of 11 May informed Mr. Elliott that the FCO considered it important to avoid any context which implied that machinery was to be set up to settle disputes arising out of the interpretation and application of the principles guiding relations between states (WDW 1/373/1).

[6] See note 2 above.

[7] See note 5 above. This foresaw a combined Romanian and Swiss text which would begin by requiring the Committee also to examine 'practical measures aiming at inhibiting the threat or use of force by one state against another'.

that they will agree to the question being referred to the Co-ordinating Committee.

Confidence Building Measures/Military Aspects

7. The situation remains as stated in my telegram Nos. 463 and 464[8]. The square brackets which remain in the text represent differences of view which will be discussed further between interested delegations here. I doubt whether it would be worthwhile spending much time on them at the meeting on Monday.

8. A matter of greater concern to the Nine is the position of the French who seem likely to maintain their opposition to sections of the text even if a compromise can be found between the Americans and the Russians on the one hand and the Dutch and the neutrals on the other.[9] The question arises how this position can be expressed without introducing reservations of the kind which could be exploited by other delegations on other sections of the terms of reference. You may wish to ask your French colleague for his views.

Basket II

9. Negotiations on the terms of reference for economic and related questions are proceeding satisfactorily and the Nine are working effectively together. As seen from here there is no reason why Political Directors should get involved. If specific points are raised I hope that you will agree to recommend that they be remitted to the Ad Hoc Group in Helsinki for study in the light of the tactical situation here.

10. Political Directors will be asked to approve the text of a declaration to be made by the Belgians on behalf of the Community. I take it that briefing will have been provided by the FCO. Position here remains as stated in my telegram 458.[10]

[8] These telegrams of 12 May reported a Mini Group meeting of 11 May from which emerged a text on CBMs integrated into a draft sub-committee mandate covering the military aspects of security. But the Russians declined to yield to Western pressure for a textual reference to the prior notification of military 'movements', in addition to military 'manoeuvres' (WDW 1/22).

[9] The British, while conceding that it might be necessary for the CSCE to discuss MBFR, wanted to avoid any decision in the former which might complicate negotiations on the latter. But the French had consistently opposed the holding of MBFR talks and adamantly refused to agree to any linkage between the two sets of negotiations. Their position was challenged by the Dutch who argued, with some neutral support, that the CSCE should discuss the indivisibility of the military and political aspects of security and produce a declaration on force levels in Europe which would enable those not directly involved in MBFR to express their views. Both the Americans and the Russians indicated their readiness to accept reference to disarmament and MBFR and, by 12 May, the Mini Group had produced a compromise preambular text which foresaw this possibility. Nevertheless, as Mr. Elliott reported in Helsinki telegram No. 488 of 17 May, the French continued to insist that they could not accept anything more than a passing reference to disarmament (WDW 1/22).

[10] This telegram of 11 May related to the ongoing discussions in the Ad Hoc Group on Community competence in the CSCE and the role of the Commission.

Basket III

11. I am grateful for the instructions contained in FCO tel[egram] No. 279.[11] You may wish to limit discussion on this subject to a minimum. Much depends on the Soviet reaction to the Yugoslav proposal, which will not be known until Monday at the earliest. Our main objectives in the Political Directors meeting should be:

(*a*) To confirm that 'non-interference' (or 'non-intervention') is unacceptable to all the Nine.

(*b*) To secure Dutch, Italian and Belgian agreement to go along with the majority in accepting a compromise based on a general reference to principles guiding relations between states and a specific mention of sovereignty and human rights.

12. Some recrimination may be unavoidable if the Dutch or others maintain their opposition to this solution, or consider that they are being bounced into accepting it by the French who have already spoken openly in its favour. You may wish to avoid involvement in any postmortem, particularly since we have been active in trying to conciliate the two wings both in the Nine and the Fifteen. But the fact is that the Dutch, who have performed a useful service as anchorman, have failed to see that the time has come to lift the anchor. They appear to believe (probably rightly) that this issue is the key to progress not only in Basket III but in the MPT as a whole, and are in no hurry to meet a June or July 'deadline'.[12] Both they and the Italians underestimate the significance of the concessions we have already secured on the preamble to Basket III (listed in paragraph 2 of my tel[egram] No. 455).[13] In my view these concessions satisfy our main criteria which are:

(*a*) to demonstrate to public opinion that we are serious about achieving some concrete results in the field of human contacts and information.

(*b*) to enable us to raise points of interest to us at the Conference itself.

---

[11] Dated 11 May, this telegram signalled FCO approval of a compromise suggested by Mr. Elliott for the preamble to Basket III. His formula involved the amendment of a Yugoslav proposal to substitute 'the sovereign rights of states and the rights of individuals' for the reference to the principle of 'non-interference' which the Russians wanted. The new text also referred to cooperation on such subjects as contacts between people, information and human rights,.and included a list of sub-committees which placed human contacts first and culture last. This, Mr. Elliott thought, 'would satisfactorily offset any disadvantages of "sovereignty" and the general reference to principles and would enable the West to raise anything it wished during the second stage of the Conference' (Helsinki telegram No. 455 of 10 May).

[12] Despite Dutch objections that it was too early to concede any reference to principles in the preamble to Basket III, EC Political Directors agreed on 14 May to accept a reference to sovereignty and human rights if the East agreed to satisfactory mandates for such items as human contacts and information (telegram No. 295 to Helsinki of 16 May, MWE 2/8).

[13] See note 11 above.

Basket IV

13. There has been no discussion of this question. It is generally assumed that the Russians will accept that it should be dealt with at the Conference by the Coordinating Committee.

Momentum

14. Political Directors are likely to reflect the conflicting views of their delegations here on whether the talks are proceeding too fast. I think that the rate of progress is right and that the time pressure for an early Conference has so far worked largely in our favour in producing concessions of substance from the East.

15. The main question is whether the Russians will agree early next week to a formula in the preamble of Basket III which is acceptable to us. It is generally assumed that they will. But if they do not the question will arise of how far we should allow progress on the other baskets to continue. If the Russians remain obdurate on Basket III I think there would be a case for proposing an interruption of work on the other baskets (but not for stonewalling or introducing purely obstructive amendments). This is a question to which the Political Directors ought to give their attention. From the tactical point of view here it would be useful to have it generally agreed that we cannot proceed much further without agreement to the preamble of Basket III.

Organisation of Conference

16. *(a) Level of Third Stage*

Please see my telegram No. 467 to FCO.[14] I hope that the Political Directors will agree that we should not go further than the formula in the paper previously agreed by the French, the Poles and the Romanians ('either at the level of Ministers for Foreign Affairs or at a higher level').

(b) Site of Conference

The Portuguese are lobbying actively against Helsinki but have so far received more indications of sympathy than of support. The Germans have indicated that they will raise the matter at your meeting. There is widespread belief among Western Delegations here that if the break from Helsinki is to be made it should be made after the first stage, but the Americans have told us that they would like it to be made after the second. No one to whom I have spoken however, regards the idea of postponing a decision on the site of the second stage as being in any way easy to achieve.[15]

[14] Helsinki telegram No. 467 of 12 May reported that the MPT had not yet touched upon the level of Stage III.

[15] At their meeting on 25 April (see No. 32, note 6) the Political Directors had agreed that a decision on the date and place of Stage II should be left for Ministers to decide at Stage I. The place of Stages II and III was left open, but most Directors thought Helsinki inevitable, and the French and Danes regarded themselves as committed to supporting it.

No. 34

Mr. Elliott (Helsinki) to Sir A. Douglas-Home

No. 495 Telegraphic [WDW 1/2]

Priority. Confidential   HELSINKI, *19 May 1973, 6.05 p.m.*

Repeated for information Priority UKDEL NATO, UKREP Brussels, and to Routine Paris, Washington, Bonn, Rome, Moscow, Berne, Vienna and to Saving Brussels, Sofia, Copenhagen, Athens, Budapest, Luxembourg, Valetta, The Hague, Oslo, Warsaw, Bucharest, Madrid, Stockholm, Ankara, Belgrade, Ottawa, Nicosia, Dublin, Lisbon, Reykjavik, Prague, UKMIS Geneva, UKDIS Geneva, and East Berlin.

CSCE/MPT

You may find it useful to have some general impressions of the stage reached in the preparatory talks with specific reference to the question of their momentum (Vienna telegram No. 366, not to all).[1]

Basket I

2. The major points outstanding are the formulation and order of the principles to be listed. This will be taken up in the Mini Group on 23 May.[2] There are indications that the Russians will not insist on an order unacceptable to the Germans and progress may therefore be relatively rapid. There are a number of points on the formulation of the principles which could cause difficulty but they should not prove major stumbling blocks. The Russians have indicated to us privately that they will not seek to transfer their 'non-interference' argument from Basket III to Basket I and that they will accept 'non-intervention' as the Basket I formulation.[3]

3. On confidence building measures, the major difficulty continues to be the reference to 'movements'.[4] The Russians have given hints that they might be prepared to consider a formulation which allows the question of prior notification of movements to be discussed at the Conference but without the degree of commitment as to the outcome in the text on manoeuvres. Mendelevich is returning to Moscow for consultations on Monday and Tuesday[5] and has told us that this is one of the questions on which he will seek new instructions.[6]

[1] This telegram of 16 May reported on the MBFR exploratory talks at Vienna and a Soviet request for postponement of the discussion of the agenda. Mr. Thomson suspected that the Russians might 'be procrastinating with developments at Helsinki in mind' (WDN 27/11).

[2] See No. 35.

[3] See No. 33, note 11.

[4] *V. ibid.*, note 8.

[5] i.e. 21 and 22 May.

[6] During his visit to Moscow Mr. Mendelevich appears to have encountered opposition from the Soviet military authorities to a more conciliatory approach to CBMs, and after his return to Helsinki he insisted that any exchange of observers at military manoeuvres must be 'by invitation'. Nevertheless, on 1 June the Russians accepted that the Committee/Sub-Committee dealing with Item I should 'study the question of prior notification of major military movements and submit its conclusions'. This, according to the UK delegation's draft report (see

4. On other military aspects the differences between the Americans and Russians on the one hand and the Dutch, Yugoslavs and Romanians on the other are now fairly narrow and it should be possible to find an acceptable compromise. The French, however, remain intransigent and could cause serious problems.[7]

Basket II

5. The position remains as stated in my telegram No. 491.[8]

Basket III

6. The most radical shift in the Soviet negotiating position has come on Basket III. The dropping of their insistence on 'non-interference' represents a major psychological victory for the West and the preamble to the section of the mandate reads well from our point of view.[9] The main requirement now is that the West should work effectively for a satisfactory text in other parts of the mandate. We may have to move quickly to achieve a reasonable compromise.

Basket IV

7. The Russians have circulated a draft (text in MIFT)[10] on the institutional follow up to the Conference which they are likely to table at a meeting of the Working Group on Wednesday or Thursday. The Nine are generally agreed to take the text approved in NATO as our starting point but the Germans are clearly prepared to go much further.[11] They have told us here that Brandt would indicate to Brezhnev a positive willingness to work for continuing machinery of a political and consultative character.[12] The French and Italians remain cautious on consultative machinery but would be

No. 21, note 4), 'was a considerable Western achievement in view of the earlier Russian attitude and their normal attitude to such sensitive issues'.

[7] See No. 33, note 9. At a working lunch of the Nine on 31 May M. J. Andréani, French Head of Delegation, indicated that the most France could accept was the inclusion in the terms of reference of the statement that Committee I would bear in mind 'the fact that efforts aimed at disarmament complement political *détente* and are essential elements in a process in which all participating states have a vital interest' (Helsinki telegrams Nos. 535 and 577 of 25 May and 1 June, WDW 1/22). The final formula was agreed on the basis of this French draft.

[8] Not printed. See No. 36.

[9] On 17 May the Russians offered to abandon their demand for reference to 'non-interference' in return for a package including: (1) the insertion into the preamble of a phrase emphasising that the Committee's proposals should be based on full respect for the principles in Basket I; (2) the introduction into the human contacts mandate of a sentence stating that relevant matters be examined and settled by 'states concerned'; and (3) the exclusion of a reference to 'travel within' (as opposed to 'travel between') participating states (Helsinki telegram No. 489 of 17 May).

[10] Not printed.

[11] On 12 April NATO's SPC endorsed a proposal that a Coordinating Committee should, before submitting to the Conference the recommendations of other Committees, study such measures, including the creation of new international machinery, as might appear necessary to give effect to these recommendations (enclosure in letter from Mr. Staples to Mr. McLaren of 5 April, WDW 1/10; UKDEL NATO telegram No. 269 of 12 April).

[12] Mr. Brezhnev visited Bonn during 18-22 May.

prepared to accept a reference to the possibility of a second Conference.

8. This is an issue on which we had hoped not to play a major role but given the attitude of some of our partners it will not be easy to secure the sort of text which we would prefer. We may have to agree to a reference to the Soviet proposal for a Consultative Committee and perhaps also to the possibility of a second Conference provided that the context is such as not to imply commitment to either of these ideas.[13]

Date of Conference

9. It is now generally agreed that this round of the preparatory talks should continue until 1 June in the hope of completing the work. The Russians give every indication of wanting to have everything settled by then and will press hard for whatever procedural arrangements (including night sessions) are required. There was no objection at the Plenary meeting on 18 May when the Chairman proposed that the date of 1 June be taken as a guideline and there is a general disposition among Western Delegations here to work in this context.

10. The Czechs proposed at the same meeting that the first stage of the Conference should start on 28 June. There was no discussion of the proposal and it seems unlikely that the East will press for a formal decision at this stage. The French have told the Nine that they would prefer the date of 3 July and this seems likely to prove acceptable to our partners if the work of the preparatory talks can be successfully concluded in the next two weeks.

Site of the Conference

11. The question is likely to arise during the discussion on procedures in the next few days. The Romanians are expected to propose Geneva and if they do so the Germans and Italians have indicated that they will support them. Other members of the Nine seem concerned to ensure that the bandwagon is well under way before they leap on. Positions of the Danes and the French remain unchanged.[14]

Conclusions

12. I do not regard the 1 June 'guideline' as unreasonable but it is too early to say for sure whether it will be met. What is clear, however, is that we shall all be under strong pressure to meet it. The time pressure so far has worked largely in our favour and there is a feeling of satisfaction among most

[13] A mandate for the Coordinating Committee to consider follow-up was subsequently drafted on the basis of a Belgian text, and it was agreed that this should figure as agenda Item IV (see Cmnd. 6932, p. 151). In their draft report (see No. 21, note 4) the UK delegation commented: 'It is by no means clear why the Russians did not fight harder for a punchier text on this subject. One explanation may be that in view of the strong Western attitude they reckoned it would be better to allay neutral and non-aligned suspicions by going for the least controversial text. It may also be that their enthusiasm for the subject has been somewhat dented by the nature of the mandates agreed for the second stage of the conference and that they wish to keep open their options. Whatever the Russian motives, it is interesting that neither the Romanians nor the Yugoslavs made any serious effort to get included references to a second conference, for there seems little doubt they will revert to this idea during the second stage.'

[14] See No. 33, note 15.

Western Delegations at the results which have been achieved. I share this but not the feeling of some of our allies that we can now afford to take a relaxed view of the remaining points of substance, nor the feeling of other allies that we can still afford to raise a multiplicity of points of detail.

No. 35

Mr. Elliott (Helsinki) to Sir A. Douglas-Home
No. 522 Telegraphic [*WDW 1/6*]

Immediate. Confidential   HELSINKI, *23 May 1973, 8.10 a.m.*

Repeated for information Immediate Brussels and to Priority UKDEL NATO, Moscow, Berne and Vienna, and to Routine Paris, Washington, Bonn and Rome, and to Saving Sofia, Copenhagen, Athens, Budapest, Luxembourg, Valetta, The Hague, Oslo, Warsaw, Bucharest, Madrid, Stockholm, Ankara, Belgrade Ottawa, Nicosia, Dublin, Lisbon, UKREP Brussels, Reykjavik, Prague, UKMIS Geneva, UKDIS Geneva and East Berlin.

CSCE/MPT: Meeting of Political Directors on 24 and 25 May
Principles

Mini Group on 23 May reverted to the list of principles. It was generally agreed that the list should include as separate principles on the one hand the inviolability of frontiers and on the other respect for human rights and fundamental freedoms and equal rights and self-determination of peoples.

2. The West Germans (Brunner)[1] stated that they interpreted inviolability of frontiers as meaning the renunciation of force against territorial integrity. The principle did not prevent peaceful changes of frontiers nor restrict the treaty making power of sovereign states. It did not prevent the rectification of frontiers nor their removal if states wished to merge. Brunner referred specifically in this context to Western European unity. He was supported in general terms by the Italians, the Irish and ourselves.

3. The Swiss (by previous arrangement with the Russians) then asked Mendelevich how in his view the principle of inviolability would be affected if Libya and Egypt were to merge and abolish their frontiers. Mendelevich replied that this would be regarded as an exercise of sovereignty. The principle of inviolability of frontiers would not be relevant in this context.

4. The Group then proceeded to a reading of the ten Principles in the Chairman's list.[2] At the end of this the West Germans intervened again and made the following main points:

(i) The task of the Conference was not to make new international law and

[1] Herr G. Brunner headed the West German delegation to the MPT.

[2] Helsinki telegram No. 360 of 7 April listed the ten principles as follows (subject to order and precise formulation): 'sovereign equality: non-use of force: inviolability of frontiers: territorial integrity: peaceful settlement: non-intervention: human rights: self-determination: co-operation: and fulfilment of obligations under international law'. The same order was maintained in the Final Recommendations agreed at Stage I. See Cmnd. 6932, p. 145.

they were glad that this was clear from the terms of reference as now drafted.

(ii) In elaborating upon and formulating the listed principles the Conference should take into account the relationship between certain of them.

(iii) The Germans had consistently maintained that inviolability of frontiers was a form of the principle of non-use of force derived from Article II (IV) of the Charter.

(iv) The principles of respect for human rights and of self-determination were of major importance and the Germans had always made it clear that references to inviolability in the treaties they had signed were not contrary to their constitution.

(In view of the unreliable simultaneous interpretation from German we have suggested to Brunner that it would be useful if he prepared a version of his statement for circulation in the Nine).

5. The East Germans supported by the Russians made in reply a brief reference to Article III of their treaty with the FRG.[3]

6. The Group will meet again on Friday afternoon[4] to discuss the order of the principles and their formulation. The general expectation is that the former point will not cause difficulty although the Russians are likely to make a lengthy statement setting out their views. The question of formulation should be relatively easy, and the Spaniards have told us that they will not insist on a reference to unity.[5] The main difficulty will be the Romanian insistence on splitting the principle of sovereign equality into two to make separate reference to sovereignty and equal rights. They may also continue to insist on independence in this context.[6]

7. There is fairly widespread irritation at the Romanians but it is not clear how strongly they will be opposed. They may get some support from the Yugoslavs. We would propose to take the line on Friday that we have no authority to accept 'sovereignty and equal rights' and that any reference to independence should be qualified by 'political' and linked with territorial integrity as in Article 2 (IV) of the Charter. A compromise on the lines of 'sovereign equality and equal rights' would on the other hand seem to us an acceptable compromise despite its untidiness. Grateful for your views.[7]

[3] See Cmnd. 6201, p. 261.

[4] i.e. 25 May.

[5] The Spanish delegation had sought to combine with the principle of territorial integrity a reference to unity (Helsinki telegram No. 217 of 9 March).

[6] The Romanians were resisting a simple mention of sovereign equality, and demanded separate references to the principles of (1) the right of each state to a free existence to independence and to sovereignty: and (2) the equality of rights of all states (Helsinki telegram No. 281 of 24 March).

[7] Sir A. Douglas-Home informed Mr. Elliott in telegram No. 321 of 24 May that the FCO agreed that he should resist 'sovereignty and equal rights', and argue that any reference to independence should be qualified as he proposed. A compromise was finally reached on a formula 'sovereign equality, respect for the rights inherent in sovereignty' (Helsinki telegram No. 578 of 1 June).

No. 36

Minute from Mr. J.K. Gordon to Mr. M.J.E. Fretwell[1]

[MT 10/3]

Confidential   FCO, *24 May 1973*

CSCE/MPT: Basket II Discussions

1. As of course you know I returned from Basket II discussions in Helsinki on 22 May. The following general comments and summary of the state of play when I left may be of interest.

2. Basket II discussions, both in co-ordination meetings of the Nine, Fifteen and in the Working Group itself, have been considerably less dramatic and 'confrontational' than those for Baskets I and III. This mainly of course reflects the simple fact that economic issues find East and West less far apart than political, cultural and human contact issues, partly the fact that the same economic issues have been already many times thrashed out in the ECE and all those concerned tend to have a sense of 'déja-vu' about further discussions, and is partly because most countries left this Basket to their economic experts rather than the more politically-orientated diplomats who were their spokesmen for the other Baskets.

3. A further difference lies in the far greater practical importance of consultations between the Nine over Basket II than over the other Baskets. In the former, the Ad Hoc Group meets on average perhaps three times as much as NATO, where the consultation process tends to be largely nominal and consists largely of keeping the Americans and Canadians happy. In Baskets I and III on the other hand the most important decisions have been taken within NATO.

4. However, in both the Nine and Fifteen consultation has proceeded smoothly over Basket II and the French have continued to be loyal and effective colleagues. The Belgians have made a particular effort to be effective in the Chair although as always this reflects itself more in a conscientious attempt to take full account of previous decisions by the Political Directors than in a more outward-looking and imaginative response to an ever-changing situation.

5. Western tactics on Basket II have concentrated on securing a minimum of references to wide-sweeping 'principles' and to stressing the need for 'concrete measures'. The East, in accordance with its general philosophy, has tended to do the opposite, pleading against our insistence on the need for specific measures to be adopted the [sic] doctrines of non-interference and respect for existing legislation. A further very strong trend of Eastern argument has been that a number of such measures involve the 'multilateralisation' of commercial and economic relations which are by their nature 'bilateral'.

[1] Mr. Gordon was First Secretary in Trade Relations Department (TRED), and Mr. Fretwell was his Head of Department.

6. At the end of MPT III the East were still insisting that the mandate should commit us to 'a European programme' of specific projects and contain a reference basing the development of economic relations on the 'principles of non-discrimination and MFN'. However, in informal discussions at the beginning of MPT IV Mr. Pozharski (who has taken over from Ambassador Zorin as chief Soviet delegate of Basket II)[2] told us that he was ready to commute the reference to 'programme' into one to 'joint action' and the reference to 'principles' to a neutrally phrased reference to MFN. Since the former had proved the main barrier to drafting a satisfactory 'chapeau', this was able to proceed fairly rapidly once he had indicated that he would accept a reference to 'common efforts' rather than 'joint action'.

7. Once this difficulty was out of the way the two sentences of the 'chapeau' which took up most time were:

(i) The reference to developing countries.
The Romanians, supported by the Yugoslavs and other Mediterranean countries pressed for a more wholehearted reference than we were willing to accept. We were supported in this by the Russians, who argued that this reference could be no stronger than that referring to peace and security in Europe (which came immediately before). After two days intensive debate, in the course of which Soviet-Romanian relations became all too evidently frayed, an acceptable form of working was finally agreed.

(ii) The reference to international organisations.
This was first proposed by the East, but was limited to say that the Committee would take into account 'the work of bodies of the UN system including the ECE'. In private they made clear to us that [in] putting forward this formula they wished to deny us the right to mention non-UN bodies, of which the most important would be the EEC and GATT[3]. In response to our criticisms, they offered to agree a form of wording which would allow the work of non-UN bodies to be taken into account where judged relevant by the Conference. Since this would give any one member state the explicit right of veto, this was also unacceptable to the West. Finally, a compromise form of wording was agreed which read 'it (i.e. the Committee) will take into particular account the work of the UN Economic Commission for Europe'. It was noticeable throughout this discussion that everybody was positively anxious to include a specific mention of the ECE.

8. The text (Flag A)[4] was agreed *ad referendum* subject to a Spanish reservation on a mention of the Mediterranean being included and a Western reservation of the mention of the word 'reciprocity'. This was intended as a purely tactical measure to encourage concessions by the East

[2] Mr. V.S. Pozharski was Deputy Head of the International Economic Department in the Soviet Foreign Ministry.

[3] General Agreement on Tariffs and Trade.

[4] Not printed.

elsewhere in the Mandate. However, complications were introduced when it was agreed that Basket I principles taken from the Declaration on Friendly Relations specifically referred also to Baskets II and III and that a reference of the sort agreed for the Basket III 'chapeau' can also be accepted for Basket II. This agreement is obviously to our advantage in Baskets I and III, but is arguably less so in Basket II. This is primarily because the wording of the references to non-intervention and co-operation contains a commitment not to try and interfere with the economic system of other countries, and not to discriminate against them on the grounds of difference in social and economic system alone. These either work in our favour or, in the case of the former, are balanced by reference to other principles in the political and cultural spheres in Baskets I and III. There are no relevant 'countervailing' principles on the economic side, largely because we had come to an agreement with the East to exclude a reference to principles altogether, with the exception of 'mutual advantage'.

9. As a result, the Ad Hoc Group agreed that a tough line would have to be taken in order to retain a balancing principle on our side, and insisted in the Working Group of 23 May on a reference to 'reciprocity' in the chapeau. The East countered by proposing the mention of 'sovereign equality, non-intervention and non-discrimination'.[5]

10. Drafting of the Trade Sub-Committee mandate nominally started on 17 May. The East made it clear that no new text could be expected from them. The Nine then prepared a new text (Flag B),[6] which was cleared with capitals. Its basic premise was to balance a neutrally worded reference to MFN to which the Russians had told us informally they attached great importance (reading 'it—i.e. the Sub-Committee—could also discuss general problems relating to MFN treatment') in return for the East accepting our references to specific measures. As you know, the Commission representative (M. Meyer)[7] argued very strongly for adding at the end 'in the tariff field'. This was based on the idea that the Mandate was some sort of prelude to trade negotiations at Stage 2 of the Conference and that, unless this qualification was made we would necessarily be admitting that we would be prepared to discuss QRs[8] in the MFN context. All delegations made the point that they accepted the Commission's views on substance, but that as a matter of tactics it was better to leave the insertion out and defend our position at Stage 2. M. Meyer finally agreed in return for an assurance that an oral statement would be made at the end of the MPT maintaining the Community's position in the MFN field. No-one disagreed at the time, although the French entered a formal reservation (my minute to you of 23

---

[5] The Working Group subsequently compromised on a preambular reference to the Committee studying ways 'to facilitate, with due regard for the diversity of economic and social systems and under conditionso fo reciprocity of advantages and obligations, the development of trade and cooperation'. See Cmnd. 6932, p. 147.

[6] Not printed.

[7] Dr. K. Meyer was Deputy Secretary-General of the EC Commission.

[8] Quantitative Restrictions.

May covers this ground in greater detail).[9]

11. Discussion in the Working Group continues on the basis of an Austrian paper which is not very different from our own paper at Flag B.

12. Drafting of the industrial co-operation and 'other areas' mandates has not yet begun, although the German economic delegate (Mr. Lucas) and I worked out a possible redraft of the industrial co-operation mandate which would be discussed in the Nine and Fifteen and then referred back to capitals. There is also a small amount of 'tidying up' on the science, technology and environment mandates still necessary. If the June 1 deadline for the end of the MPT is to be met discussions on Basket II will need to be finished by 30 May, it looks as though the Nine, the Fifteen and the Working Group have a number of late-night sessions ahead.

13. I shall be submitting separately some thoughts on the role of the Commission in the CSCE and others on the wider implications for East/West economic relations based on discussions with both Eastern and Western delegates at the MPT.[10]

J.K. GORDON

[9] This described how an FCO telegram had arrived too late to prevent the UK delegation siding with other national delegations in the Ad Hoc Group in rejecting, largely with a view to preserving tactical flexibility, the Commission's proposal for the inclusion in the trade mandate of a specific reference to tariffs.

[10] Not printed.

No. 37

Mr. Elliott (Helsinki) to Sir A. Douglas-Home

[*WDW 1/2*]

Confidential HELSINKI, *13 June, 1973*

Summary ... [1]

Sir,
CSCE: The First Two Hundred Days[2]

The Multilateral Preparatory Talks for the Conference on Security and Co-operation in Europe began in the resounding concrete halls of the Finnish Students' Union at Dipoli, outside Helsinki, on 22 November, 1972. My colleagues, who vary considerably in their experience of multilateral diplomacy, found themselves sitting around a large hexagon of tables with

[1] Not printed.

[2] On 20 June Mr. Wiggin noted on a submission by Mr. Tickell covering this despatch: 'So far the West has done surprisingly well. But the real battles lie ahead. I shall be pleasantly surprised if, at the end of the whole cycle, anything of real and positive value emerges. We must nevertheless continue to take the exercise very seriously. The underlying propaganda battle alone makes that essential.' The underlining on this manuscript minute was made by Sir A. Douglas-Home.

microphones in front of them, advisers behind, and very little idea of what awaited them. It was fashionable at that time to speak of informal consultations between Ambassadors accredited to the same post; and we were unanimous in saying that our intention was not to have a pre-Conference.

2. When the preparatory talks concluded 199 days later, on 8 June, 1973, they had taken on a different pattern. The leisurely pace of the first two sessions, where the business was conducted in plenary meetings convened only once a day, gave way to a proliferation of formal and informal working groups and drafting committees; delegations were reinforced by various categories of expert advisers; and the final confusion of night sessions, compromise proposals and interpretative statements was in every way typical of a major international conference.[3]

3. The preparatory talks can indeed be regarded as a Conference in their own right. Many issues of major importance in East-West relations received detailed consideration before agreement could be reached on the agenda of the Conference itself and on the terms of reference for the Committees and Sub-Committees which will meet during its second stage. The presence of neutral and non-aligned countries gave a particular flavour to the debates, and their special concerns complicated the task of negotiation, especially at the final stage; but the main issues were between East and West. It is, I believe, the fact that we, with our partners and allies, emerged from the process in a position of clear advantage.

4. The brief for the UK delegation at the outset of the preparatory talks[4] restated the objectives agreed by NATO Ministers: to ensure that the proposals in which they were interested would be fully considered at the Conference, and to establish that enough common ground existed among the participants to justify the reasonable expectation that a Conference would produce satisfactory results. Hence, our aim was to seek agreement at the preparatory talks on:

(i) an agenda which would allow Ministers to raise at the Conference proper the points to which they attached importance,
and
(ii) an organisational structure for the Conference which would ensure that the various items on the agenda received detailed examination before any decisions were taken.

---

[3] Mr. Walden, in a letter of 5 June to Mr. Fall, responded to the latter's suggestion that he should 'jot down some points' on the work of the CSCE for possible inclusion in a despatch. He pointed out that the Conference might be regarded as a 'natural successor to the Congress of Vienna', though he thought that it sometimes seemed like the 'continuation of the Cold War by other, more subtle means'. And whilst he refrained from making comparisons with the social life of the Vienna Congress, he noted that the Finnish Government had hired the site of the MPT from the 'plutocratic Finnish Students Union; and that some of the close diplomatic in-fighting took place in the "Sexy Bar"' (EN 2/1).

[4] See No. 17.

In my view these objectives have been met.

5. A major difficulty in the early part of the discussions lay in convincing the Russians that an agenda drawn up in general terms, even with a separate agenda item covering human contacts and information (a point in effect conceded by Brezhnev in his speech to the 50th Anniversary Congress in Moscow in December),[5] would not be sufficiently detailed to meet the requirements of Western delegations. We insisted that the preparatory talks should also specifically agree terms of reference for the Committees and Sub-Committees which would undertake the detailed work of the Conference at its second stage. The Belgians, Italians and Danes tabled on 15 January draft proposals (previously agreed among the Nine and in NATO) for the agenda and terms of reference.[6] The recommendations that finally emerged from the talks are naturally less satisfactory to us than those original drafts. But it is remarkable how little has been given away.

6. The preparatory talks have in effect endorsed the essential features of the Western approach to the Conference. It will take place in three stages; and it will not produce results until the Committees and Sub-Committees at the second stage have undertaken a thorough examination of the subjects covered in their terms of reference. I have reported on their contents in telegrams to the Department, and the delegation has produced separately a fuller record of the main points of interest.[7] But the following points are worth noting here as successes for the West.[8]

(i) The list of 'principles of primary significance guiding the mutual relations of the participating States' includes:

(*a*) respect for human rights and fundamental freedoms, including the freedom of thought, conscience, religion or belief; and,

(*b*) equal rights and self-determination of peoples.

(ii) The terms of reference on principles contain two important sentences which are clearly incompatible with the Brezhnev doctrine. One refers to 'those basic principles which each participating State is to respect and apply in its relations with all other participating States irrespective of their political, economic and social systems'; and the other provides that the document to be submitted for adoption by the Conference 'shall express the determination of the participating States to respect and apply the

---

[5] Moscow telegram No. 1942 of 22 December 1972 reported that Mr. Brezhnev's remarks about freer movement 'set out authoritatively the reservations and qualifications which the Soviet bloc will seek to impose on any agreements in the field of wider contacts between East and West.' These reservations were couched in such 'vague and sweeping terms that they could (and no doubt will) be used to justify objections to any Western proposals likely to let fresh air into Eastern Europe' (EN 2/15).

[6] See No. 20, note 3.

[7] Not printed. See No. 21, note 4.

[8] The Final Recommendations of the MPT, including the agenda and terms of reference for Committees and Sub-Committees, are printed in Cmnd. 6932, pp. 143-58.

principles equally and unreservedly in all aspects of their mutual relations and co-operation in order to ensure to all participating States the benefits resulting from the application of these principles by all.'

(iii) The terms of reference for the Committee dealing with economic and related forms of co-operation provide the basis for a business-like examination of economic questions at the second stage of the Conference, and they place useful emphasis on reciprocity, and on information and contacts.

(iv) The section of the terms of reference corresponding to the original Western ideas on 'freer movement' contains a preamble which contradicts the traditional Communist line that progress in this field is limited by differences in political, economic and social systems; and which states that the Committee 'shall not only draw upon existing forms of co-operation but shall also work out new ways and means appropriate to these aims'.

(v) In addition, there are agreed references to facilitating freer movement and contacts between persons, as well as institutions and organisations, of the participating States; to marriages between nationals of different States and the re-unification of families; to the freer and wider dissemination of information of all kinds, and to improving conditions for journalists working outside their own countries.

7. There can admittedly be no guarantee that the results of the Conference proper will justify the expectations raised by a reading of the terms of reference. Some of the formulae that were evolved did little more than paper over major differences of principle. Thus, the dispute between the French on one side and the Dutch and Yugoslavs on the other about the relationship between the military and political aspects of security (and so *inter alia* the possibility of a link between the CSCE and the MBFR) was composed by means of a neutral formula that in effect exports the dispute to a later stage of the Conference. Again, the Maltese demand that the Mediterranean Arab States should be permitted to participate in the Conference was deflected on the final day (after it had appeared likely to block a general consensus) by the adoption of wording which keeps open the possibility that these States might present their case to the Conference, and which may be so vague as to give Mr. Mintoff scope for lengthy argument at the first stage.[9] More important, there is still room for months of discussion at

[9] See No. 21, note 7. The desire of Algeria and Tunisia for association with the CSCE was championed by the Maltese who, on 23 March, tabled an amendment proposing that the Arab states bordering the Mediterranean should be entitled to attend the Conference as full participants. This raised the prospect of the CSCE becoming enmeshed in the problems of the Middle East and the proposal was unanimously opposed by all other delegations. Nevertheless, some European powers were sympathetic to giving the Conference a Mediterranean dimension and during the third session of the MPT several informal meetings on the subject were convened by Spain and Yugoslavia. UK, French, Italian and Dutch delegates attended these gatherings, and on 27 April the forum tentatively agreed that: (1) the Middle East should not figure on the agenda; (2) there was no need for specific reference to the expansion of the principles to the Mediterranean (Turkey dissenting); (3) CBMs should not be extended to the

the second stage on the precise decisions to be taken by Governments on the issues covered by the first three major sections of the terms of reference. The Russians fought hard for more restrictive texts, and gave ground only when they realised that they must pay the price of accepting them in order to get any Conference at all. If we are to build effectively on the foundations laid by the preparatory talks we shall have to exert and maintain similar pressure on them during the first and second stages of the Conference. I think it important, therefore, to consider in some detail what have been the main reasons for the relative success of the West so far.

8. The primary reason, I believe, was the careful advance preparation carried out in NATO and in the Political Consultations of the Nine. As a result we were able from the outset to adopt a business-like attitude to the Conference, and thus to win the sympathy of the neutrals and non-aligned. In sharp contrast the Warsaw Pact countries proved unable to produce any evidence of detailed planning for the Conference which they had so long promoted. Our advantage was confirmed when the Western proposals were tabled on 15 January. The East never explicitly accepted them as the basis for negotiation, but as the talks proceeded it proved as a matter of practice that the discussion tended to be based on them rather than on their own much more sketchy drafts. The West were thus able to maintain their ground until acceptable compromises were in sight.

9. The second reason was the success of the West in maintaining its cohesion throughout the long negotiations. Our advance preparations would hardly have been effective if our partners and allies had not been willing and able to put up a persistent defence of their joint proposals. They did so with varying degrees of commitment, and there were inevitably occasions when a delegation departed from the agreed line. But on the whole the West stuck together well, and the fact that they created an impression of harmony rather than of unison contrasted favourably with the rigid discipline of the East. Confusion could have resulted from the evident decision of the US delegation to maintain a low posture with the object of reconciling the two aims of avoiding public confrontations with the Russians and accusations of collusion between the super Powers. But that thrust the main burden of defending Western positions upon the Nine, and they passed the first real test of their ability to develop and execute a common policy with flying colours.

10. The idea that the preparatory talks should take the form of a *salon des ambassadeurs* soon evaporated, as far as the Nine were concerned. Even before the substitution of working groups for the plenary sessions, many of the Ambassadors had dropped out of the picture, lacking either the time or the inclination to acquire the volume of detailed knowledge needed for negotiations whose subject matter ranged from divided countries to divided families, from the social conditions of migrant workers to East/West industrial

Mediterranean (Yugoslavia and Malta dissenting); and (4) the best way of covering the Mediterranean might be the inclusion of a phrase in the preamble to the effect that the relationship between security in Europe and in the Mediterranean should not be overlooked (draft report on the CSCE, see note 7 above).

co-operation. Co-ordination between the Nine in Helsinki thus devolved on a number of deputy heads of delegation who had been involved from an early stage in working out the common positions of the Nine in the Sub-Committee and Ad Hoc Group reporting to the Political Directors. They were used to working together, and felt jointly involved in the papers they were defending. They were as a result able to form a cohesive nucleus which proved resilient to the strains of the negotiations, and to the unpredictable behaviour of the Belgian Presidency, which alternated in Helsinki between King Log and King Stork. Their efforts were co-ordinated by meetings of the Nine in Brussels during the break between the various stages of the preparatory talks; and by detailed discussion of CSCE questions in the regular meetings of Political Directors. The latter were occasionally tempted to think too little about strategy and too much about tactical details which could have been left to delegations on the spot; and the timing of their meetings (perhaps unavoidably) appeared eccentric to those engaged in the day-to-day struggle at Helsinki. Yet without the discipline provided by common instructions from senior officials who were free to concentrate on the broader picture the Nine would have proved far less effective.

11. Much of the credit for the achievements of the Nine must go to the French delegation. Despite occasional lapses, they remained loyal to the positions worked out with their partners and defended them actively not only in debate but in private conversations with the Russians. If they had chosen to act as mavericks they could have confronted their EEC partners with an uncomfortable choice between an appearance of solidarity around the French flag and the maintenance of agreed positions. In the event, the French were especially effective in their deployment of the Western case on principles guiding relations between States and on most of the major issues relating to freer movement.[10] Their attitude contrasted with that of the Dutch and Belgians who, for all their tough noises in meetings of the Nine and the Fifteen, were for the most part unwilling to expose their views in discussions with the East.

12. A third reason for the favourable development of the talks was the extent to which the neutrals gave sympathy and support to Western positions. The Austrians, Swedes and Swiss worked closely together, but without trying to establish a 'neutral *bloc*' that might have made a virtue of taking decisions half-way between East and West. Instead they defended their own conception of a business-like Conference, and made it plain that on most issues, their values were those of the West. (Indeed, the Swiss, and sometimes the Austrians, found themselves often to the right of the NATO centre.) The support of these delegations was especially valuable to us in so far as it formed a focus for other neutral and non-aligned delegations; and we shall no doubt

[10] Mr. Walden noted (see note 3 above) that, overshadowed by the Americans in bilateral dealings with the Russians, only occasionally had the French ingratiated themselves with the 'opposition by going off at a tangent'. Nevertheless, he thought that it might take the Russians some time to 'appreciate that attempts to exercise pressure on the Nine via the US are counter-productive, if only because of the French reaction'.

need to retain their confidence during the Conference itself. Bilateral consultations are time-consuming, but it would patently be useful to arrange an exchange of views with each of these three countries (and if possible also with the Yugoslavs) before the second stage of the Conference begins.

13. One final reason for the success of the Western tactics remains to be mentioned. The Nine refused to accept an opening date for the Conference until it was clear that the preparatory talks had produced satisfactory results. Before the beginning of the crucial fourth session, the Political Directors reaffirmed their determination not to accept an artificial timetable,[11] and we were able to maintain to the end that the preparatory talks would conclude only when the results justified it. Hence, the West continued to exploit the Soviet anxiety to hold the Conference in the middle of the summer without themselves coming under time pressure on points of major importance. The implications for our strategy at the second stage of the Conference itself are obvious.

14. I turn now to the general shape of our dealings with the East during these negotiations. British relations with the Russians were still in an icy stage when the talks began, and this was reflected in our contacts with the Soviet delegation here. During the first and second stages the Russians reacted to most of our interventions as if they were deliberate attempts to obstruct progress towards a Conference, and they concentrated their bilateral attentions on the Americans, French and West Germans, trying to settle as much business as possible with them in the corridors. That they failed is due to the loyalty shown by those three delegations to their partners and allies; and also to the fact that the neutral and non-aligned countries made it crystal clear that they (like the French) would not accept solutions privately concocted by the big Powers. (There is a moral here that might well repay thought in Washington as well as Moscow.) Meanwhile, we did our best to establish in the minds of the Russians the idea that, although we would fight hard in defence of our positions, our underlying attitude to the talks was a constructive one; and that we were in as good a position to influence the opinions of the Nine and the Fifteen as any other delegation. They reacted realistically; and during the third and fourth session of the talks, we were fully accepted as a delegation with whom the Russians thought it necessary and profitable to do business.

15. The other East European countries as a whole failed to make the most of the opportunities the Conference gave them. The Russians kept their allies under strict control and allowed them small discretion on points of importance. The Bulgarians, Czechs and Hungarians neither made, nor tried to make, an individual impact; while the Poles, although better equipped in diplomatic skills, disastrously allowed themselves to be manoeuvered [*sic*] by the Russians into defending an absurdly illiberal (and soon discarded) thesis on

[11] See No. 32, note 6.

human and cultural contacts,[12] and ceased thereafter to play a prominent role. The East Germans deserve a special word. Their main representative, Dr. Siegfried Bock,[13] displayed an irrepressible intelligence and sophistication of manner which one may hope will be repeated at other conferences as the GDR gains in international experience. He was the only East European representative to take an active part in negotiations on questions of substance, and his relationship to the Russians was that of a member of a team rather than that of a subordinate. But often enough, when the Russians decided that the time had come to make another move towards the Western position, they left him stranded.

16. The Romanians were a case apart. They began the preparatory talks with a loud (and to the Russians no doubt embarrassing) advertisement of their independence and sovereignty. Yet as the talks proceeded it became clear that they had done no more than give premature indications of fall-back positions acceptable to the other Warsaw Pact countries; and that they were among the most rigid of the East Europeans on questions of freer movement and human contacts. Their reputation became tarnished, and in the closing stages of the talks their elegant prevarications (expressed in impeccable French) produced apoplectic reactions among both Eastern and Western delegations. They finally achieved a coup of a sort by persuading Mr. Mintoff, on the basis of a formula proposed by the French weeks previously, not to block a final consensus; but they had by then lost much of the general sympathy they had won at the outset of the talks. The Yugoslavs, on the other hand, by maintaining a consistent line and pursuing their major interests with a balance of firmness and flexibility, emerged from the process with a high reputation. The contrast is instructive.

17. I should say a word finally about the Finnish record at the Conference. The vigorous pro-Western performance of their fellow neutrals, the Austrians, the Swedes and the Swiss, placed them in a position of some embarrassment. Finnish neutrality, which has yet to be recognised by the Soviet Union, by definition cannot be pro-Western; and the Finns were careful not to associate themselves with these three delegations. On the other hand, they did not allow themselves to be used as 'Eastern neutrals' to provide a counter-weight. They may well have come under bilateral pressure to do so, as an intervention they made at the outset of the detailed discussions on human contacts and information suggested; but this was a solitary lapse and otherwise they kept resolutely silent. The Chairman of the preparatory talks, Richard Totterman (Secretary-General of the Finnish MFA), and the Executive Secretary, Ambassador Joel Pekuri, performed their difficult tasks impartially

---

[12] According to the UK delegation's draft report on MPT (see note 7 above), on 7 February the Poles were persuaded by the Russians to make 'a remarkably crude attack on the West for allegedly aiming at subverting the social systems of Eastern Europe by pornography, etc.'. Mr. Zorin's own speech on this occasion, the report noted, 'was noticeably more flexible in tone' and included one of the Western papers amongst those which could be examined in working out the mandate for Basket III.

[13] Head of the Policy and Planning Department of the East German Foreign Ministry.

and well, and the general organisation of the long and (for the Finns immensely expensive) talks was seldom faulty. I think it a reasonable reward for these efforts that the first and third stages of the Conference should take place in Helsinki. There was a risk that the decision of many of the Nine to support Geneva as the site of the second stage would cause the Finns offence; but the negotiations that achieved this result were handled with great skill by the Irish chairman, and I was eventually assured by Mr. Sorsa, the Finnish Prime Minister, that the Helsinki-Geneva-Helsinki formula was the 'best possible solution' to the problem.

18. It is to the Conference itself that the West have now to turn their attention. We entered the preparatory talks believing that the Conference was inevitable; that the dangers it comprised could probably be avoided; and that it might provide us with some modest benefits. In the light of the preparatory talks I would take a more optimistic view.

19. The Russians have pressed for the Conference for their own purposes. They hoped no doubt to get its blessing for the Brezhnev doctrine; and to exploit it in other directions as a means of dividing the West. The preparatory talks suggest that they did not judge the situation very accurately. From the first they found themselves in a forum where they could expect the regular support of only six out of thirty-four delegations; and where the neutral countries, because of the consensus rule, had much more incentive to express, and persist in expressing, their individual points of view than is the case in international meetings operating under majority voting procedures. In the early days of the talks I sometimes had the impression that the Soviet spokesmen were in a state bordering on panic as they found themselves in a negotiating position rather less strong than they had enjoyed in the UN in the early 1950s. As time went by they adapted themselves to the new situation, abandoned bullying tactics (which succeeded only in alienating the Swiss, the Maltese, and many other neutrals), and began to deploy their real diplomatic skills and experience.[14] But they still remained in a defensive position; and one where their only hope of making their point was by rational argument rather than by the exercise of pressure. It was a stimulating experience for Western delegations to find the Russians, in the hearing of representatives of all their satellites, obliged to give a detailed defence of their domestic policies on, for example, the increase of human and cultural contacts, in order to answer criticism by Liechtenstein.[15] For the Soviet spokesmen themselves the

[14] Mr. Walden, who considered the MPT 'a diplomatic tournament, in which form was at least as important as content', was particularly scathing in his criticism of the conduct of the Soviet delegate, Mr. Zorin (see note 3 above). The latter, who was ungenerously known to the Western delegates as 'The poisoned Dwarf', had evidently been sent to Helsinki in order to oversee work in fields of interest to the KGB. 'Needless to say', Mr. Walden observed, 'the interest of the KGB as well as of the Soviet Government as a whole would have been better protected if Zorin had stayed at home. His abrasive style exercised a unifying effect on the West, who also gained from his clumsy negotiating tactics.'

[15] The UK delegation's draft report (see note 7 above) described the Liechtenstein delegation in engagingly affectionate terms. 'Liechtenstein', it observed, 'fielded Prince Henri,

experience cannot have been so refreshing. It is no wonder that the Soviet leadership are still pressing for an early end to the Conference.

20. It should nevertheless be possible for the West at the Conference to exploit the psychological advantage gained at the multilateral preparatory talks. I know that we have never set much store by a declaration on principles guiding relations between States; and public opinion in the UK is rightly suspicious of elevated legalistic phrases with little practical content. But the relevant section of the terms of reference[16] provides some encouragement for the view that we should be able to produce a document of political value if we are prepared to make a major effort to elaborate the principles. Perhaps more important, we can work for some improvement in Soviet behaviour in the area covered by the terms of reference on human contacts and information. In this field, which they have always hitherto insisted is appropriate only to bilateral discussion, we now have a means of exerting multilateral pressure on the Russians and their satellites; and we have never had anything of the sort before. At the least, we ought now to be in the position to oblige the Russians either to make some concrete (if modest) advances in this area or to expose the hollowness in practical terms of their professed desire for *détente*.

21. The importance of the Conference is not limited, however, to what it achieves in the field of East/West relations. It has become, as a result of the work done both before and during the preparatory talks, something of a test case for developing the co-ordination of foreign policy among the Nine. Many of our partners have reasons for wanting to go their own way in important aspects of their relations with the East. But they have shown during the preparatory talks a willingness to work as a group and an awareness of the negotiating advantages this provides. It should surely be a major objective of our policy to ensure that this lesson is reinforced in the course of the Conference itself. We shall not get our own way during the second stage without full preparation.

22. There is one final point. As the MPT showed, the Nine cannot be led from behind. In the early days of the talks the still uncertain state of our bilateral relations with the Russians, as well as tactical considerations relating to our position as a newcomer to the EEC, led the British delegation to play a cautious role. But the detached position of the French, the special preoccupations of the Germans, the eccentricity of the Italians and the public silences of Benelux increasingly made it necessary for us to give a lead, if the Nine were to continue to follow a positive line and enjoy the initiative in the talks. I believe that we shall find ourselves in a similar position in the second stage of the Conference itself; we shall have little choice but to act as one of the leaders of the West. And it is reasonable enough that we should do so.

a Count with glasses and a Count with a moustache. The latter two intervened often enough to ensure that Liechtenstein was noticed. They were admirably robust on questions of freedom; extremely pedantic on legal and financial questions; and generally incapable of suppressing the echoes of musical comedy which followed them about.'

[16] See note 8 above.

We can, evidently, make a greater contribution to the collective self-confidence of EEC and the more effective safeguarding and prominence of the Community countries' interests if we take a lead in urging and directing the full preparation of the position of the Nine than if we take a back seat. If Britain is not to act as a major European Power in the context of the CSCE she can hardly hope to be a Power anywhere.

23. I cannot conclude this despatch without expressing my gratitude and admiration for the work of the First Secretaries (including my own Head of Chancery, Mr. Beetham) who bore the whole burden of the detailed work of negotiation on our side. They were younger than any other delegation and more lively, led by Mr. Brian Fall, who played a significant role in shaping the course of the talks, they took a prominent part in working out the agreed terms of reference and the arrangements for the procedure and finances of the Conference. Their ingenuity, drafting ability and resilience during these protracted discussions were alike remarkable. I found it both a piece of good fortune and a pleasure to work with them.

24. I am sending copies of this despatch to Her Majesty's Ambassadors in Paris, Brussels, Bonn, Rome, The Hague, Copenhagen, Stockholm, Moscow, Washington, Bucharest, Belgrade, East Berlin and to Her Majesty's Representatives to NATO and the European Community.

I have, etc.,
T.A.K. ELLIOTT

No. 38

Letter from Sir J. Killick (Moscow) to Mr. Tickell
[*WDW 1/2*]

Confidential MOSCOW, *27 June 1973*

Dear Crispin

The End of the MPT for CSCE

We have been reading with great interest and satisfaction Anthony Elliott's despatch of 13 June about MPT,[1] the draft report of the United Kingdom delegation at the MPT,[2] and the Final Recommendations.[3] It might be helpful to you in preparing the strategy for the conference proper, and in assessing what has been achieved so far, if I offer some comments on those aspects of the Helsinki talks which affect the Soviet Union in particular.

2. To start with the negative, I was particularly struck by Anthony Elliott's remark in paragraph 7 of his despatch that there can be no guarantee that the expectations which might be implied in the terms of reference worked out at the MPT will be justified at the Conference. So far as the Russians are

[1] No. 37.
[2] See No. 21, note 4.
[3] See No. 37, note 8.

concerned I am sure that this is right, and had come to the same conclusion. As the despatch and report clearly show, the Soviet delegation has had to give a good deal of verbal ground in order to get Western agreement to the holding of the conference at all. But I am sure that they will regard these concessions as being of a purely tactical nature, and we must expect them to fight hard to try to retrieve what they seem to have given up. It is striking that the old Soviet language of Basket III about the need for respect for national laws and practices and non-interference in internal affairs is already creeping back into Soviet language, so soon after they agreed to omit it from the terms of reference. For example, it was there on 20 June in *Pravda* in the *communiqué* issued after a CPSU delegation visit to Belgium, as well as in the Labour Party delegation's joint *communiqué*.[4] They also put the Italians on pretty clear notice during Gaja's visit here that, as regards Basket I, they have by no means abandoned their attitude on 'linkage' nor on priority for inviolability of frontiers. We must be prepared to go over every inch of all this ground again, if necessary with endless repetition. The Russians will trade on our comparative lack of patience; we must play it as long and as hard in the Commissions as necessary, and I only hope the Americans (given the language used in the Nixon-Brezhnev *communiqué*)[5] will not join the Russians in pressing for speed. It is we who must exploit Brezhnev's sense of urgency and desire for a concluding 'summit' in order to drive hard bargains. Potential packages will no doubt emerge, but we must not start searching for them or hawking them around prematurely.

3. It will be a continuing long hard slog, but not, as I have always said, necessarily only a negative and defensive exercise (i.e. the avoidance of damage rather than the registering of gain, however modest). In this respect, I agree with paragraph 20 of Anthony Elliott's despatch, and my satisfaction derives from the achievement of MPT in establishing a spring-board which keeps these perspectives open. I was disturbed, in the earlier part of last year, that MPT might overtake us before NATO and EEC (particularly the latter) had been able to prepare themselves properly. I accepted, a little unhappily, that before 1 January, 1973, we could not play a leading role among the Nine. In the event, as paragraphs 8 and 9 of the despatch show, the Nine have withstood the test well, and indeed, as I have also long felt, should perhaps be grateful for the challenge with which CSCE has presented them. However, the challenge is still there, and the necessary cohesion may not be

[4] A Labour Party delegation, led by Mr. W. Simpson and Mr. E. Short, visited the Soviet Union from 4 to 11 June where they had talks with senior political figures including Mr. Gromyko. In a letter to Mr. Bullard of 12 June describing the visit, Sir J. Killick reported that the original Soviet draft of the *communiqué* had contained propositions that were 'too much for the visitors to swallow'. They had commented critically on 'this experience of Soviet "negotiation by *communiqué*"' and some recasting had been undertaken. However, 'the delegation were only able to retain their passage on the exchange of ideas and information etc. at the price of the inclusion of the Soviet phrase "in the spirit of mutual respect and non-interference in each other's affairs"' (ENS 3/548/8).

[5] See Cmnd. 6932, pp. 132-4.

easy to maintain. This brings me to paragraph 22, in which regard I fully support Anthony Elliott's proposition about the British role, not simply on its merits but because, as I have advocated in past correspondence, the best way for us to work for improved Anglo-Soviet working relations is to bring it home to the Russians that we count in Europe and cannot, in the Soviet interest, be ignored and cold-shouldered. Needless to say, our activities in this respect should be constructive and not such as not to lend themselves to plausible charges of provocation or 'anti-Sovietism'.

4. I believe that the MPT have already achieved a good deal in this respect, and my second cause for satisfaction lies in Anthony Elliott's paragraphs 14 and 23. I should like to add a word of congratulation and gratitude to him and the delegation not just for a performance which merits it in its own right, but because it led to explicit (if, as, not yet public) Soviet recognition of the importance and quality of the British role. It is many months since I first told Mr. Gromyko that, whatever he might profess to think of the British attitude to CSCE, he would find the proof of the pudding in the eating. The British delegation would probably be the best-prepared and most effective participant. The delegation have been good enough (in both senses) to prove me as good as my word.

5. Looking a stage further, we must also have in mind the Soviet capacity for divorcing action from words. Even if, as I believe to be entirely possible, we can exploit Brezhnev's desire for speed and success in order to make gains on various fronts, lest the outcome for the Soviet side be to expose 'the hollowness . . . of their professed desire for detente,' we must ensure that the gains are not only paper ones. We must not lose sight of the certainty that the Russians, even if forced to put their names to whatever language we can extort from them as part of the price for what they really want, will then do everything possible to avoid implementing (at any rate for long) those promises which they have been obliged to make. The more watertight the commitments that we can exact from them, the better, but there will still be a need for action to test them and make them effective (see my letter of 12 June to George Walden about Basket III).[6]

6. This is not the place to set out again our estimate of basic Soviet aims at CSCE. I would endorse in general what Anthony Elliott says in paragraph 19, with the reservation that even the Russians can scarcely have hoped for an explicit endorsement of the Brezhnev doctrine unless in the most ambiguous

[6] Sir J. Killick argued in this letter that even if the West succeeded in gaining something concrete from the Russians in the CSCE, little would be achieved in practical terms unless it were followed up by action designed to test how far the Russians, or other East Europeans, were willing to give effect to agreed propositions. Where Basket III was concerned, he thought that the additional Government money required to prod individuals and organisations into action was unlikely to be forthcoming from HMG, and that there was no alternative to letting the French have their heads of this front. 'The French', he contended, '. . . are unique in pursuing an active and expensive cultural foreign policy—and clearly attach great, even though no doubt unrealistic, importance to their role in a sort of cultural roll-back of the Iron Curtain' (EN 2/4).

and indirect terms. Apart from securing general Western acquiescence in their sphere of influence in Eastern Europe (an objective already, as it turned out, largely achieved by the complex of treaties and agreements affecting Berlin and the FRG but which they are now anxious to 'multilateralise'), their over-riding interest seemed to me to lie in the obstruction and diversion of the process of Western European integration in the economic, political and eventually military fields. With the passage of time and events, it begins to look to me as though their hope of making effective use of CSCE to this end, at least in the economic field, has lessened. But they will keep trying. It is this process of western European integration which they must see as the greatest obstacle to realising the dream of a fragmented Europe abandoned by the Americans and dominated by the Soviet Union. In order to deflect Western integration, they claim to offer an alternative vision of 'all-European cooperation', without blocs, and without 'closed' economic groupings; that is to say, groupings which can be criticised as 'closed' in the constitutional sense, as distinct from their own economic bloc, which will remain 'closed' and highly 'preferential' in practice. At the same time, the idea of economic cooperation with the capitalist world has become controversial domestically. As things now stand, we are still confronted by CSCE with dangers and opportunities:-

(a) The *threat*, if such it still be in real terms, is that the Russians will in the end succeed in convincing a sufficient number of influential people in Western Europe that the alternative scenario for Europe which they pretend to offer is indeed better than pursuing the primary aim of Western European integration. This looks less likely than it did. Conceivably the Russians will come up at some point in the CSCE with some sort of ostensibly practical proposals to this end, although we have been unable to gain any indication of what form they might take, and you will recollect past Soviet concern that neither side should confront the other with surprises at CSCE. One possible clue is contained in Brezhnev's passage on CSCE in his Fiftieth Anniversary speech on 21 December, when his expression of conditional willingness to see direct relations between the EEC and CMEA was firmly placed in a CSCE context.[7] A possibility, however remote, for which we ought perhaps to be prepared is that the Russians and their allies will table proposals for the creation of a permanent new all-European organ with sweeping responsibilities for promoting cooperation in every kind of field, including economic, trade, human and cultural contacts, the environment, and so forth. Under such an umbrella EEC-CMEA relations might be established. But this is highly

[7] In Moscow telegram No. 1942 (see No. 37, note 5), Sir J. Killick had commented that this passage in Mr. Brezhnev's speech implied 'the Russians may intend to make concrete proposals at the CSCE in the field of EEC-CMEA relations, including apparently provisions to eliminate what the Russians regard as EEC discrimination against Eastern Europe and to safe-guard "natural bilateral ties". The latter point could well mean a demand for the reversal or modification of the EEC's Common Commercial Policy in relations to Eastern Europe.'

conjectural, and it is equally possible that nothing at all concrete will emerge. All Brezhnev's emphasis in his current activities seems to be on a bilateral economic cooperation.

(*b*) The *opportunities* which Soviet objectives offer to the West are indeed those to which Anthony Elliott has drawn attention in his despatch. I see no reason why we should not energetically follow up (*b*) while still successfully resisting (*a*).

7. Apart from their overall tactical failure with the neutrals and their own allies, in one particular respect I am sure the Russians must have been disillusioned by the experiences of the last year: the small impact made on European public opinion by the concept or slogan of an 'all-European security system'. The European security 'movement' has barely moved; and Mr. Shitikov's[8] Committee has proved a damp squib, although both will no doubt be activated to the greatest possible extent in support of Brezhnev's desire for speed. Soviet efforts to engage British support for this essential anti-NATO enterprise have been singularly unsuccessful, despite advances both to the Labour Party and the Trade Unions; though of course we must expect these efforts to continue. I am not fully informed on the situation in other Western European countries but it seems pretty clear that nowhere will Soviet hopes of influencing public opinion in favour of 'collective security' (in the Soviet concept) have been realised. The fact is, no doubt, that for European public opinion, in non-Soviet Eastern Europe as well as Western Europe, 'cooperation' is a much more effective slogan than 'security': easier human and trade contacts mean much more to the ordinary East of [*sic*] West European than the complexities of different recipes for national defence. But on the cooperation side of the Conference the obvious slogans work in favour of the West (hence Soviet defensiveness on Basket III). Insofar as the Russians conceived the Conference as a public relations and propaganda exercise (which I should think was at least 50 per cent of the motivation) they may well feel, in the light of experience, that the West is getting the better of the bargain and it would now be best to get it over as quickly as possible. And the same is true of the substance if the balance has shifted as I suggest in paragraph 6. But, if we continue to play our cards right, the *demandeur* for speed cannot also be the *demandeur* on substance in the sense of ensuring that he gets what he wants without giving what he does not want to give.

Yours ever,
J.E. KILLICK

PS A thought arising from the last sentences of paragraph 2. If the package approach is to be adopted at some stage, how will packages be put together if they, as seems inevitable, cross the boundaries between the Commissions? I assume there will be some kind of overall delegation leader and coordinator at the centre of the spider's web on the Soviet side with

[8] See No. 11, note 13.

whom contacts will be possible. We shall all need some such person coordinating the activities of all our expert representatives. Is this what we have in mind?[9]

[9] In a letter of 29 June Mr. Tickell wrote that he agreed with Sir J. Killick's comments which reflected 'closely the line we have been taking here'. He also informed him that Mr. Elliott would be leader of the UK delegation at Stage II, and that, though resident in Helsinki, he would pay regular visits to Geneva and would normally represent HMG on the Coordinating Committee. The idea of a Coordinating Committee had, he explained, been first proposed by the French, and the British had agreed to it with two purposes in mind: 'to ensure that the important issues were dealt with on a political level by senior officials able to take an overall view; and to divert demands for early discussion of machinery to follow the Conference'.

CHAPTER II

The Long Haul
25 June 1973 - 29 July 1974

No. 39

Sir A. Douglas-Home to Sir J. Beith (Brussels)

No. 152 Telegraphic [WDW 1/3]

Confidential   FCO, *25 June 1973, 5.40 p.m.*

Repeated for information to immediate Helsinki, UKDEL NATO, Priority UKREP Brussels, Paris, Bonn, Routine Washington, Rome, Copenhagen, The Hague, Tunis, Algiers, Saving to Dublin, Luxembourg, Moscow, Vienna, Sofia, Athens, Budapest, Madrid, Stockholm, Valletta, Oslo, Warsaw, Bucharest, Berne, Ankara, Belgrade, Ottawa, Nicosia, Lisbon, Reykjavik, Prague, UKMIS Geneva, UKDIS Geneva.

Political Co-operation of the Nine: CSCE

1. The CSCE Sub-Committee met in Brussels on 21/22 June to prepare for the first Ministerial stage of the CSCE. Good progress was made. Draft conclusions all in MIFT.[1]

2. At our suggestion the Sub-Committee concentrated upon the following problems:

(*a*) How to resist any attempt to re-open the recommendations agreed at the end of the Helsinki preparatory talks:

(*b*) How to respond if the Russians or others submitted formal proposals designed to take the initiative:

(*c*) How to avoid a substantive *communiqué*:

(*d*) How to ensure the continued cohesion of the Nine and the Fifteen.

Recommendations

3. It was agreed that we should oppose any attempt to reopen the Helsinki Recommendations or to table proposals which ran counter to them. The Finns should therefore be informed of our desire that the recommendations should be approved by all participants at the start of the first stage before the general debate, if possible at the inaugural session. As the Romanians could

---

[1] Telegram No. 153 of 25 June to Brussels summarised information contained in the present document.

be among those who could make trouble, the Germans said they would tackle Ceaucescu[2] when he visited Bonn.[3]

Proposals

4. We spoke on the basis of my telegram No. 145 to Brussels.[4] We then distributed drafts of information papers which could be circulated at the first stage and of a possible discussion paper on the principle of human rights.[5] The ensuing debate reflected a difference of view between those who favoured tabling drafts of final declarations etc., at the first stage if the Russians or their allies did so, and those who opposed the tabling of any papers at all.

5. The French, who took the former view, said that ideally the West should be able to table a Declaration of Principles if the Russians did so: but the state of Western preparations did not permit this (as the present NATO text was defective and out of date).[6] They accordingly felt that we should be ready to counter a Soviet draft in some other way: in order to maintain the Western position in the eyes of public opinion, they proposed to table the text of their own proposal on cultural co-operation. The Dutch argued the other way, maintaining that the Western position would not be damaged either in substance or in public relations terms if we maintained that draft declarations etc., should only emerge from the second stage after a detailed discussion of the substance. It was impossible for good Western proposals to be agreed by 3 July, and to table something at that stage in the form of a draft resolution would compromise our tactical position in subsequent negotiations. The Italians, Danes and Belgians shared these views in various degrees, but were more concerned to provide material to impress the Western case on public opinion. For their part the Germans said that their Minister would feel obliged to make concrete suggestions during his speech and to follow these up by tabling guidelines papers on industrial co-operation, working conditions for journalists and other matters.

6. The Sub-Committee agreed to the following compromise:

[2] Mr. N. Ceausescu was General Secretary of the Romanian Communist Party and President of the State Council.

[3] President Ceausescu visited Bonn during 26-29 June to discuss a variety of subjects, including CSCE, MBFR, and economic and industrial cooperation.

[4] In this telegram of 13 June Sir A. Douglas-Home stressed the importance of not allowing the initiative to pass to the Russians and East Europeans by underestimating the significance of Stage I. There was, he thought, a distinct possibility that they would table proposals at Stage I, hoping thereby 'to gain the initiative in public relations terms: and . . . to try to impose their own concept of the Conference and to pre-empt any inconvenient Western proposals'. He recommended that to counter such an attempt, the West should: (1) avoid allowing Eastern proposals to lie unchallenged between Stages I and II; (2) demonstrate through Western proposals the detailed and practical nature of the Conference envisaged; (3) give the neutral and non-aligned delegations a clear idea of what the West wanted in a form likely to attract their sympathy and support; and (4) ensure that the Russians and East Europeans did not capture the headlines in default of any equally eye-catching Western proposals.

[5] Not printed.

[6] Dated 11 May, this text had been produced at the SPC meeting on 9 May. It was sent to Mr. Adams under cover of a letter from Mr. Lever of 15 May (WDW 1/6).

(*a*) Ministers should, if they wished, make practical suggestions in their speeches:

(*b*) Explanatory national documents giving more details about these suggestions could be tabled thereafter:

(*c*) If the Eastern or neutral countries tabled drafts of final documents, the Nine should consult at Helsinki and decide whether and how to react. (The French however remain attracted by the idea of tabling their cultural proposals in final form and there is some doubt about how far in practice they will abide by this compromise).[7]

Human and Cultural Questions

7. The Sub-Committee briefly examined the draft proposals on human and cultural questions worked out by the experts of the Nine in Helsinki. Most delegations were without authority to give them final approval but they accepted them in principle and agreed that they should be drawn upon for Ministerial speeches and explanatory documents at the first stage of the CSCE. The French produced revised versions of their cultural proposals which were accepted as substitutes for the originals. Our own papers on information (including those on a CSCE magazine and on linked television current affairs programmes) were also accepted. The individual papers will now be introduced in NATO by their authors as national papers which have been discussed in the Nine.[8]

8. It was agreed that the West should emphasise the human and cultural aspect of the CSCE agenda at the first stage.[9] Delegations were invited to volunteer to deal in greater detail with specific subjects and to consider tabling explanatory documents. The Danes, Germans and Italians will agree between them on a division of labour on human contacts. The French will take the lead on culture. We said that we would wish to concentrate on information (and in particular the points on which we had prepared papers). We agreed with the Germans (who pressed us strongly on the point) that they should introduce a paper on working conditions for journalists.

[7] In a submission of 27 June, summarising this compromise, Mr. Tickell explained that the main Western requirements were 'to hold the tactical initiative at Helsinki, emphasise the practical Western approach and postpone until the second stage consideration of detailed texts'. Sir A. Douglas-Home minuted on this: 'I think that papers put in should not be discussed but be fodder for the committees. I am doubtful about anything being in open session other than the set speeches. There could be a lot of wrangling' (WDW 1/17).

[8] See *Human Rights*, vol. i, pp. 384-6 and 399-409..

[9] Sir A. Douglas-Home insisted in his telegram No. 145 to Brussels (see note 4 above) that if there were a general tendency to table proposals on human contacts at Stage I 'we should be ready with texts to show that our intentions are practical rather than propagandist'. He thought it probable that proposals in this area would be the 'most headline-catching' of all Western proposals tabled during the Conference.

Principles guiding relations between States

9. It was generally agreed that the present NATO draft[10] would not do for the first stage, and that more work would have to be done for the second stage. We circulated a text on human rights to illustrate a more detailed approach to one aspect of the declaration.[11] A number of delegations expressed interest in this approach. The Dutch and Germans may produce similar texts on other principles for a meeting of the Sub-Committee shortly after the first stage of the CSCE. The French, who have been trying to produce their own draft declaration, may have a text ready by then.

10. The French tabled papers on the legal status of the document to be adopted by the CSCE[12] which it was agreed would be discussed as a matter of priority at the next meeting of the Sub-Committee.

Political consultation

11. In reply to our plea for the same measure of co-operation and co-ordination of the Nine as during the preparatory talks, the French argued that there was no Ministerial directive in this sense. There were bound to be areas of discussions where the vital interests of some countries were more involved than those of others and where some Governments would judge it possible or necessary to go further than their partners. We strongly resisted this effort to reduce the effectiveness of the Nine and drew attention to the conclusion of the Political Directors in March (on the need to agree common texts at the Conference) which had been subsequently approved by Ministers at their meetings in March and June.[13] The Italians, Belgians and Germans supported us on the texts of final proposals, but were prepared to accept less detailed clearance of explanatory papers. But even the French agreed that none of the Nine should put forward ideas to which any other one objected.

Open Sessions

12. The Sub-Committee agreed that open sessions would help to ensure greater responsibility amongst all participants, and that a Western country should therefore propose at the inaugural session that all sessions should be

---

[10] See note 6 above. In his telegram No. 145 to Brussels (*v. ibid.*) Sir A. Douglas-Home stated that the Russians might well table a draft Declaration on Principles guiding relations between states and that this should not lie unchallenged over the summer. He suggested that the West could table a declaration of its own, but he did not think that prepared by NATO was particularly well-adapted to the terms of reference of the Principles Sub-Committee. Alternatively, he thought, individual Western delegations might table national papers on individual principles 'in such a way as to promote debate and serve as a quarry from which the eventual text of the declaration would be taken'.

[11] This text on respect for human rights and fundamental freedoms recalled that it was one of the purposes of the United Nations to promote universal respect for, and observance of, such rights and freedoms, and committed participating states to encouraging the 'dissemination of and access to information concerning' them (EN 2/23).

[12] Not printed.

[13] Telegram No. 79 to Brussels of 17 March recorded the results of the Political Directors meeting on 15 March. The Political Directors' conclusions were approved by Ministers at their meetings on 16 March and 5 June (telegram Nos. 80 and 81 to Brussels of 17 March and Nos. 363 and 364 to Helsinki of 6 June).

open. It was felt that it would be difficult for any other participant to resist this proposal under the television cameras of the inaugural session, but that it would be necessary first to square the Americans, who had expressed doubts on this subject.[14]

Communiqué

13. The Sub-Committee agreed that the best way to avoid points of substance creeping into a final *communiqué* was to have no *communiqué* at all. A virtue of open sessions was that the verbatim reports envisaged in the rules of procedure could then be published at the end of the first stage. It followed that we should oppose the establishment of any *communiqué* drafting group. Ambassadors of the Nine in Helsinki were asked so to inform the Finns and other participants.[15]

Mediterranean

14. It was agreed that the Algerians and Tunisians should be discouraged from attempting to present their views orally at the first stage, but the French and Italians said that it would be difficult for them to oppose such a proposal if it were made and that if the Algerians and Tunisians consulted them about it beforehand they would at a pinch have to say that they would raise no objection. We argued that the Nine should simply agree to discourage the Algerians and Tunisians, and to concert action if the proposal envisaged were not vetoed by the Russians or anyone else.[16]

Next Meetings

15. The Sub-Committee agreed to meet informally during the first stage. Its next meeting is likely to be 17 or 24 July, depending on the length of the first stage and the date agreed for the Ministerial meeting of the Nine.

Meetings during the second stage

16. The Italians proposed that the Ad Hoc Group[17] should meet in Brussels (but under a Danish President) on the eve of meetings of the NATO

[14] At a meeting of the SPC in Brussels on 25 June to discuss tactics for Stage I, the US delegation (and the Portuguese) justified their opposition on the grounds that 'open sessions would mean a more propagandist and less businesslike Conference' (UKDEL NATO Brussels telegram No. 469 of 26 June, WDW 1/17).

[15] In Helsinki telegram No. 665 of 26 June Mr. Elliott reported that although the Finns had been appraised of the general feeling among missions that no *communiqué* was necessary, they still thought that 'there was a case for forming an open-ended group which should make preliminary recommendations on matters like dates of the opening of the second stage and the first meeting of the Coordinating Committee'. They argued that 'these were not problems that could easily be settled by Foreign Ministers in plenary session and that there was a risk that if there was no working group any attempt to push agreed proposals on these points through the plenary might be resisted (as a Big-Power Diktat) by some of the neutrals and smaller powers'. Mr. Elliott considered that this attitude was 'dominated by their wish to avoid public controversy which would get a bad press for Stage I and also cause delay in the proceedings', and advised that more pressure from EC Ambassadors was necessary if the Finns were to modify these 'instinctive' views (WDW 1/17).

[16] See No. 41.

[17] At a meeting of the Ad Hoc Group in Brussels on 22 June British efforts to involve the EC Commission more fully in CSCE matters were frustrated by the insistence of Dr. Meyer

Economic Committee, but did not press their point in the light of French objections. The Sub-Committee will meet regularly in Geneva during the second stage, and it was agreed in principle that meetings in Copenhagen should take place immediately before the regular meetings of the Political Directors.

Aid to the Presidency

17. The Belgians circulated a paper about the kind of assistance the Presidency would need during the Conference.[18] It was criticised by the Germans for having been the product of discussions among the Correspondants rather than in the Sub-Committee, and by the French for being too rigid and formalistic, and for concentrating on the idea of seconded administrative assistance to the exclusion of other possibilities. The Germans said in this connexion that they were prepared to nominate Brandt's personal interpreter to such a team. Other delegations (including ourselves) indicated their willingness to help in whatever way the Presidency thought most useful. The Danes expressed their thanks and said they would recommend accordingly.

that a Commission representative should speak on behalf of the Nine in the Sub-Committee responsible for trade. Sir A. Douglas-Home commented in telegram No. 154 to Brussels of 26 June: 'As the real business of the CSCE becomes closer and more urgent, it is all the more unfortunate that the Commission still chooses to act as a sort of adversary of the Nine within the machinery of political co-operation.'

[18] Not printed.

No. 40

Letter from Mr. Bullard (Helsinki)[1] to Mr. Wiggin

[*EN 2/6*]

Confidential   HELSINKI, *5 July 1973*

Dear Wiggin,

CSCE: Soviet Attitude

1. You will no doubt have formed your own opinion of the Soviet attitude to the CSCE as revealed in Gromyko's speech of 3 July[2] and the draft

[1] Mr. Bullard was a member of the British delegation to Stage I of CSCE at Helsinki. See No. 42, note 3.

[2] Excerpts from Mr. Gromyko's speech are printed in Cmnd. 6932, pp. 160-6. An EESD assessment of the performance of the Soviet Union and its allies at Stage I pointed out that although the Finns 'could not really have allowed anyone else to speak before Gromyko, even if an official from the Soviet Embassy had not queued up from an early hour of the day when the list opened to book his place', the speech 'was meant to catch most of the limelight on the first day, and his draft declaration of principles was astutely held over until the next morning to make a second lot of headlines' (enclosure in letter from Mr. Bullard to Sir J. Killick of 10 July, EN 2/22).

declaration circulated the following day.[3] Texts of both are being sent to the FCO by this bag, for distribution to other posts concerned. Our own thoughts are as follows.

2. The Russians seem to have decided that although they may have lost a battle (the MPT) they have definitely not lost the war.[4] Their opening position this week has been essentially what it was last November when the MPT began. In some respects the formulation is even stiffer. The supporting comment from the Soviet press, of which we have seen quite full reports, suggests that Soviet Tactics are to mount an offensive in order to cover up the weakness of their position. As forecast by John Killick in his letter to Crispin Tickell last week,[5] the Russians are evidently hoping to claw back in the CSCE what they lost in the MPT. Except at one or two points they have used the Final Recommendations only where these can be quoted to support their own positions.

3. In concrete terms this means that the Russians are still hoping to get a declaratory conference ending in a propaganda document which will create the illusion of a new era in Europe, without conceding any changes which could be dangerous for the Soviet system or for the East European regimes. They have no serious hopes of anything coming out of Item II. They are absolutely determined that any action taken under Item III shall be subject to the principles of non-interference and individual sovereignty i.e. subject to their own veto in anything that could affect the USSR or its allies. They are less sure than they used to be that they want follow-up machinery. They are reconciled to seeing Stage 2 begin in September and last for several months. They regard the summit-level 3rd stage as probably in the bag.

4. The Warsaw Pact have prepared quite efficiently for the present phase, except that Romania as usual has not cooperated. The Soviet draft on Item I, the GDR-Hungarian on Item II, the Polish-Bulgarian on Item III and the Czechoslovak on Item IV[6] effectively blanket the subject matter of the Conference, making it possible for the Russians to argue that we already

---

[3] See No. 24, notes 3 and 12. British suspicions that the French and Germans had received advance copies of the Soviet draft declaration were confirmed when, according to Mr. Tickell, Freiherr von Groll 'made an ass of himself at the Nine's CSCE Sub-Committee on 21 June by contriving to indicate Russo-German exchanges on the subject over several months, and then by trying to implicate the French in these proceedings (minute to Mr. Wiggin and Sir T. Brimelow of 25 June).

[4] A brief for Sir A. Douglas-Home's attendance at Stage I, dated 3 July 1973, argued that although the Russians had conceded wording in the terms of reference for the Conference Committees and Sub-Committees which in some respects went further than had been expected, there was no guarantee that they would 'agree to the steps required to put flesh on the bones'. The Soviet acceptance of a Conference substantially on the lines proposed by the West was, the brief concluded, 'some indication of the strength of their commitment to the Conference, and this provides us with an opportunity to press for real improvements' (MWE 2/8).

[5] No. 38.

[6] See *Human Rights*, vol. i, pp. 357-61, 369-74, 375-8, and 366-7 respectively.

have on the table the working documents necessary to launch the second stage as soon as other participants are ready.

5. The Brezhnev-Nixon meeting and agreements[7] have been pointedly commended by Gromyko and by his allies (again with the exception of Romania), to the point where the US is almost depicted as a better executant of *détente* than even the most favoured states in Western Europe. But it is not easy for the Russians (nor have the Americans made it easy for them) to bring this new lever to bear upon the CSCE.

6. Soviet emphasis on inviolability of frontiers has gone even beyond what had been expected. There is also the rather significant gloss, in Gromyko's speech and especially in Chnoupek's,[8] that the borders whose inviolability they have most in mind are those which coincide with the line between the two political and economic systems in Europe. This concept of a revived Iron Curtain or extended Berlin Wall fits the very toughly ideological cast of Gromyko's presentation and effectively disproves many of the rosier hopes expressed at the Conference about the elimination of obstacles throughout Europe.

7. Altogether the outlook at the end of the second day is not such as to warrant any modification of the estimate we made before the Conference began.[9]

8. I enclose an interesting analysis of the Soviet draft declaration by Brian Fall.[10]

J.L. Bullard

[7] Mr. Brezhnev visited Washington from 18-25 June for talks with President Nixon. See *Public Papers of the President. Richard Nixon 1973* (Washington: USGPO, 1975), pp. 611-19 for the joint *communiqué* issued following these discussions. The text of the US-Soviet Agreement on Prevention of Nuclear War of 22 June 1973 is printed in H.V. Hodson (ed.), *The Annual Register. World Events in 1973* (London: Longman, 1974), vol. 215, pp. 523-4. See also No. 12, note 2 and No. 24, note 4.

[8] Mr. B. Chnoupek was Czechoslovakian Foreign Minister.

[9] On 11 July Mr. Dobbs wrote to Mr. Wiggin registering agreement with Mr. Bullard's appraisal: 'It has been depressing, even if perhaps predictable, to see from the sidelines here how both Gromyko's presentation of Soviet views in his formal intervention and the texts of the East European drafts, have reflected all the familiar preoccupations of the East Europeans with rigidly firm control of East/West contacts.'

[10] Not printed. This analysis was contained in a minute to Mr. Bullard of 4 July, in which Mr. Fall noted the declaration 'confirms our assessment that the Russians want a declaratory and essentially superficial Conference . . . It has to a large extent been designed to avoid controversy, no doubt in the hope of getting a rapid conclusion to this part of the work of the Conference (and thus contributing to the pressure to reduce the length of the Second Stage as a whole).'

No. 41

Mr. Elliott (Helsinki) to Sir A. Douglas-Home

No. 742 Telegraphic [*WDW 1/16*]

Priority. Confidential   HELSINKI, *9 July 1973, 6.15 a.m.*

Repeated for information to Priority UKDEL NATO, Moscow, Bonn, Rome, Paris, Washington, Valletta, Routine to Copenhagen, The Hague, Brussels, UKREP Brussels, Luxembourg, Algiers, Tunis and Tel Aviv, Saving to Vienna, Sofia, Athens, Budapest, Oslo, Warsaw, Bucharest, Madrid, Stockholm, Berne, Ankara, Belgrade, Ottawa, Nicosia, Dublin, Lisbon, Reykjavik, Prague, UKMIS Geneva, UKDIS Geneva and East Berlin.

CSCE First Stage: Mediterranean Aspect

1. The one subject at the Conference which provoked real debate, negotiation and bad temper was the attempt of the Maltese to persuade the Conference to permit the Algerian and Tunisian Foreign Ministers to address it.[1] Mintoff's personal performance served both to enliven and exasperate the Conference, and he and his deputy consumed the time and energy of Ministers, working groups and drafting groups until well past the eleventh hour. At the end Mendelevich (Soviet Union) remarked to one of us that he had previously thought criticism of Mintoff no more than imperialist propaganda. Now he knew better.

2. The affair had three stages. During the first in which the problem was remitted to a working group, the essential issue was the way in which the Algerians and Tunisians might be allowed to make their views known to the Conference. The Maltese proposal had the full support of the Spaniards, who submitted a similar proposal of their own.[2] They were joined by the French, and other Mediterranean countries. None of the remaining participants wished to be the first to say no, but the Russians eventually did so on ingenious but specious procedural grounds. This led to a lively and at times personal exchange between Mintoff and Mendelevich. The Americans cautiously raised the Israeli aspect, mentioning that the Israelis had requested that whatever arrangements should be made for the Algerians and Tunisians should also be made for them. But they did not have to press the point as the original Maltese request was clearly unacceptable to the majority of delegations, whose unspoken desire was to keep the Middle East problem as far as possible away from the CSCE. By 4 July the Maltese had retreated and there was the prospect of a compromise by which Algerian and Tunisian

---

[1] See Nos. 21, note 7 and 37, note 9. Valletta telegram No. 368 of 14 June gave advance warning of Mr. Mintoff's intentions, and in a minute of 18 June Mr. Burns observed 'if such a proposal was made most of the Mediterranean countries would find difficulty in opposing it. We may be sure however that the Nordic countries as well as the Russians and East Europeans will be most reluctant for such a thing to happen'. Nevertheless, he thought that if the proposal found general acceptance in Helsinki HMG would hardly wish to be alone in objecting. See *Human Rights*, vol. i, p. 355.

[2] See *Human Rights*, vol. i, p. 356.

representatives would be permitted orally to introduce written statements of their views before a committee specially set up by the plenary Conference.

3. The second stage began with the arrival of a letter addressed by the Israeli Ambassador to the Danish chairman on 5 July asking for equal treatment for Israel with Algeria and Tunisia. When the Danish representative on the Working Group tried to read out the Israeli communication, there were protests from the Maltese and other delegations on the grounds that the Working Group could not take cognisance of a communication of which the Plenary meeting was ignorant. When the matter was raised in the Plenary by the Danish Chairman, Mintoff called him to order arguing first that he should not read the message as it did not emanate from a participating Government, and secondly that as the message had not been read he could not allow the Working Group to take cognisance of it. This led to some tense exchanges in which Gromyko, certain now that there was no risk of the Algerian and Tunisian Foreign Ministers making a personal appearance, was able to switch his support to Mintoff in resisting German, Canadian, Dutch and other demands for the Israeli communication to be circulated and taken into account. Eventually it was agreed that as there was no consensus to take cognisance of the Israeli request (and no participating Minister was ready to support it by a written proposal of his own), the Working Group should continue with its work as if the request had not been made.

4. Although Mintoff had won this round on points, it was obvious that progress in the Working Group would now be difficult if not impossible. Within a few moments the argument there turned to the problem of whether other (unspecified) non-participating Mediterranean states should be accorded the same treatment as Algeria and Tunisia. On this occasion the Maltese had support from the Russians, East Europeans, Spaniards, French and Italians. They were opposed by the Canadians, Dutch, Danes, Norwegians and Americans. In spite of prolonged and sometimes bitter argument there was never any serious prospect that the deadlock could be broken. As the general debate in Plenary neared its end, time began to run out for the Maltese. Gromyko indicated his exasperation by telling you that the Russians were now inclined to oppose the submission of any statements either orally or in writing from third countries during the Conference. As things worked out he did not have to take this draconian line which would have been in virtual defiance of the rules of procedure. Deadlock was eventually acknowledged in the Working Group and later repeated at Ministerial level on the afternoon of 6 July. In these circumstances the Maltese had for the time being to admit failure.

5. The third stage began when the Maltese submitted a draft paragraph for inclusion in the final *communiqué* of the Conference on 7 July after the rest of the *communiqué* had been approved in the Working Group. The Maltese draft was designed to record Maltese and Spanish efforts to enable the Algerian and Tunisian Foreign Ministers to be heard and to state that no consensus had been reached. The Maltese said that unless this paragraph

were inserted in the *communiqué*, they would block consensus on the rest of the *communiqué*. After a fruitless argument in the Working Group where it was argued either that the paragraph should not go in or if it did go in should record that the problem of other non-participating states had been considered, the debate was remitted to the Plenary session. Here the Maltese had no real supporters. Gromyko, who, unlike many delegations, clearly attached importance to agreement on a *communiqué* of some kind, went so far as to say that if Maltese resistance continued, he would advise changing the rules of consensus to enable the work of the Conference to go ahead even if one country objected.[3] This attempt to use a club on the Maltese made disagreeable impression on the Conference, and did the Maltese more good than harm. Scheel (FRG), with some support, moved the closure of the Conference without a *communiqué*, but it was decided to make one final effort to produce a compromise text. An old formula in new words was produced by the Canadians and Russians, and to considerable surprise the Maltese accepted it.

6. Three main conclusions can be drawn from this affair. First the Maltese have shown what an effective guerrilla campaign can do. The work of the Conference will continue to be bedevilled by this problem. The essential Maltese point that European security problems cannot be disassociated from Mediterranean ones is supported by several countries. Secondly the Nine members of the Community and Fifteen members of the Alliance were in disarray and unable to act as a group. This was principally because the French and Italians did not honour their commitment to consult the other seven, and wished to ingratiate themselves with the Algerians and Tunisians. Thirdly the Russians showed their cloven hoof. Their bullying tactics caused resentment among all the smaller countries for whom, whatever the merits of the present dispute, the rule of consensus is their essential safeguard.

7. Fortunately we were able to avoid playing anything but a mediatory role. Our basic aim was to keep the non-participating Mediterranean States from importing the problems of the Middle East into the first stage of the Conference. Hence the continuing deadlock suited us very well. As it remained unbroken we were able to keep in friendly touch with all sides in the dispute.[4] One important point was registered in the final *communiqué*: that however such non participating states may eventually make their points to the Conference, these should be limited to the items on the Conference Agenda.

[3] 'In private', Mr. Tickell noted, 'Gromyko was equally brutal', and when Sir A. Douglas-Home asked him whether he intended to put forward this idea, he replied 'that he might "get one of my people to do it"' (minute to Mr. Bullard of 9 July, EN 2/22).

[4] During their flight back from Helsinki Mr. Tickell informed Mr. E.V. Saliba of the Maltese delegation that the British position 'was extremely simple: we did not wish to see the problems of the Middle East incorporated into the CSCE where there were problems enough already'. Mr. Tickell further noted for the record that 'although Mr. Mintoff behaved in maverick fashion and tangled in particular with the Russians, he maintained good relations with us, and after one of the meetings of the Working Group thanked me for the role we were adopting' (minute to Mr. Wiggin of 10 July).

No. 42

Mr. Elliott (Helsinki) to Sir A. Douglas-Home
[*WDW 1/17*]

Confidential   HELSINKI, *16 July 1973*

Summary . . .[1]

Sir,

CSCE: Stage I

The first stage of the Conference on Security and Co-operation in Europe took place in Helsinki from 3-7 July.[2] You, Sir, attended the Conference until the last day, accompanied by Mr. Anthony Royle, MP, Parliamentary Under-Secretary of State, Sir Thomas Brimelow, and other officials.[3] Your impressions are recorded in Helsinki telegram number 735.[4] In this despatch I have the honour to add some reflections of my own, in particular on the implications for the second stage of the Conference.

2. The Conference, which was organised by the Finns with their customary efficiency, despatched its initial business with reasonable expedition. After speeches of welcome from the Finnish Foreign Minister, Dr. Ahti Karjalainen, from President Kekkonen, and from the Secretary-General of the UN, it adopted in open session the final recommendations of the multilateral preparatory talks at Dipoli. Contrary to expectation, there was no attempt by delegations with heterodox opinions to make interpretative or qualifying statements. On the first afternoon, however, when the Conference met in closed session for a procedural discussion, the Prime Minister of Malta made his expected proposal that the Algerian and Tunisian Foreign Ministers should be invited to express their views on the agenda to the first stage of the Conference. After an American attempt to draw attention to the fact that Israel had made a similar request had been shelved, the North African issue was smartly referred to a working group; and the 35 Ministers settled down again in plenary to the business of making their general statements, which were not completed until the morning of 8 July. There followed a day's procedural wrangle, which reflected the failure of the working group to reach consensus either on the Maltese proposal or on language to describe that

---

[1] Not printed.

[2] The verbatim records of the open sessions of Stage I are printed in *Human Rights*, vol, i, pp. 33-348.

[3] The British delegation further included Mr. Acland, Mr. M. Alexander, Miss. J.A. Holder (Assistant Private Secretary), Mr. H.H.G. Leahy (Head of News Department), Mr. A.R. Thomas (News Department), Mr. M.R.J. Guest (Private Secretary to Mr. Royle), Mr. Bullard, Mr. Tickell, Mr. P.M. Maxey (WOD), Mr. Fall and Mr. Adams.

[4] In this telegram of 6 July, Sir A. Douglas-Home observed: 'The first phase went quite well for the West, which got the better of the propaganda exchange. But all points of substance are in effect reserved for the second phase, where we shall have to refight many of the battles of the last six months and no doubt some new ones too.'

lack of consensus in a *communiqué*; but the points in dispute were papered over at the last minute, and the first stage finally ended only a little later than the time originally envisaged by the majority of non-Communist delegations.[5]

3. On the face of it, then, the proceedings went relatively smoothly. Your own speech was widely praised, both by the Press and by delegates from all parts of Europe;[6] (even a middle-ranking member of the Soviet delegation remarked to my Head of Chancery that his 'evaluation of the speech was positive'). Other interesting contributions were made by Herr Scheel and M. Jobert[7] (who spoke in terms of undoubted elegance but rather more doubtful meaning); while Mr. Fitzgerald,[8] in speaking of the future of Ireland and of the tasks of the Conference, displayed a tact and statesmanship missing from the references of the Foreign Ministers of Spain and Iceland to the issues respectively of Gibralter [*sic*] and the fishing dispute.[9] The fact remains, however, that even to those who knew that the first stage of the Conference was likely to be largely a formality, the proceedings were something of a disappointment. Few of the speeches other than those I have mentioned measured up to the occasion. A number of Western Ministers said little that was new, while the Ministers from the Warsaw Pact countries said far too much that was old. Mr. Gromyko's speech was written as if nothing had happened in the last nine months, and certainly seemed designed to ensure that nothing happened in the next. Again, too much time had to be spent inside and outside the plenary meetings on dealings with the irrelevant Maltese proposal. To make matters worse, it at length became plain when San Marino took the chair that the combination of a rotating Chairmanship (chosen by lot) with the complicated system of agreement by consensus was a

---

[5] See No. 41.

[6] Extracts from the Secretary of State's speech of 5 July are printed in Cmnd. 6932, pp. 158-160. Sir J. Killick had suggested that this speech should contain a more positive reference to Soviet conduct in the MPT (Moscow telegram No. 734 of 27 June). This, however, was rejected by Mr. Bullard who explained, in a letter to Sir J. Killick of 29 June, 'we think it right to continue to use the watering-can of scepticism with which the Secretary of State's name is personally associated. This is certainly his own wish.' Sir J. Killick continued to think otherwise. 'We are', he wrote to Mr. Bullard on 6 July, 'going to have quite enough difficulty with the Russians at CSCE without offering them additional pretexts for negative reactions or pinning them up against the wall with blunt propositions. If we are genuinely interested in achieving ends internationally, rather than in the applause of the Conservative Women's Association of Lytham St. Anne's, we ought to proceed accordingly!' (EN 2/22).

[7] M. M. Jobert was French Foreign Minister. Of his speech Sir A. Douglas-Home remarked, in Helsinki telegram No. 735 (see note 4 above): 'It was elegant but perhaps rather high falutin'.'

[8] Dr. G. Fitzgerald was Foreign Minister of the Irish Republic.

[9] In July 1971 the Icelandic Government, ignoring a 1961 agreement which recognised its fisheries limit at 12 miles, unilaterally extended this limit to 50 miles. In April 1972 this decision was referred to the International Court of Justice which produced an interim ruling that the Icelandic Government should not impose its new limits. This was ignored and the limit was extended as of September 1972. The International Court insisted that it had jurisdiction in the matter, but by May 1973 it was apparent that no ruling on the dispute was to be expected until 1974 at the earliest (FCO Guidance telegram No. 90 of 29 May 1973, MWE 2/8).

recipe for the inefficient conduct of proceedings. The Conference ultimately, and after your departure, Sir, degenerated into an unseemly argument about a *communiqué* which appeared the more unnecessary and irrelevant the longer the process of its drafting extended.[10]

4. What are the implications of all this for Stage II? I will take the Maltese proposal first. It fortunately proved possible to prevent any of the non-participants from being heard during Stage I; but the wording of the *communiqué* effectively exports the problem to the beginning of the second stage. The Maltese have put us all on notice that they will pursue their case with equal vigour in September in Geneva. There will be no hope then of simply setting the matter aside. It has to be remembered that in the interval between the end of the preparatory talks and the start of Stage I the Maltese succeeded in mustering new and significant support for their case, notably from Spain, France and Italy. Again, although the Russians tried in the final procedural debates in the plenary to give the impression that the Maltese were in a minority of one, they were themselves most careful throughout the week to say nothing that could offend the Arabs, while arguing with consistent disingenuousness against the appearance of the Israelis. All this, however, may look rather worse from Helsinki than from Geneva. The absence of Mr. Mintoff himself from Stage II, and the fact that publicity for that stage will be less glaring than for Stage I, may help in getting the matter settled. Provided that we can restore the unity of the Nine, there may be a case for agreeing promptly to hear the Mediterranean non-participants in the relevant Committees at the outset of the second stage, and thus defusing the problem from the beginning.[11]

5. The implications of the stiff line taken in the East European speeches during Stage I are more serious. We had expected, as I suggested in my despatch of 13 June,[12] on the preparatory talks, to have in Stage II to refight many of the battles of Dipoli. I do not think, however, that we expected the Russians to try quite so firmly to put the clock back to 1972. In his speech Mr. Gromyko indicated that he wishes to keep its hands stuck. Hardline speeches and tactics were *de rigueur*.[13] One of the most instructive experiences of the

[10] The *communiqué* is printed in Cmnd. 6932, pp. 170-1.

[11] The question of contributions from non-participating states was discussed at the first regular meeting of the Nine's CSCE Sub-Committee under the Danish Presidency on 17 and 18 July. It was generally agreed that the Nine should seek a common position. But while the French and Italians argued that the Algerians and Tunisians should be allowed a hearing, the Germans, supported by the Danes and the Dutch, maintained that the requests of all countries should be treated equally. As a possible basis for compromise the British suggested that a decision in favour of the Algerians and Tunisians should be linked to a guaranteed right of reply, if regarded as necessary, by 'another non-participating country', and that the Nine should consider favourably applications from other Mediterranean countries to make known their views on the agenda (telegram No. 162 to Copenhagen of 19 July, WDW 1/18).

[12] See No. 37.

[13] According to Sir A. Douglas-Home (see note 4 above) the Russians, 'having sensed the dangers in the contagion of liberty, have prepared defences in depth against it. Gromyko more or less asserted the right of national veto over any movement of information, ideas or people.

week was to see how Mr. Gromyko and Mr. Kovaliev [*sic*],[14] one of the two Soviet Deputy Foreign Ministers, instinctively turned to bullying tactics when they failed to get their way round the negotiating table. Half an hour of final debate on the Maltese proposal in plenary was too much for Mr. Gromyko; and he promptly proposed the suspension of the principle of consensus.[15]

6. It was ironical that when this drastic move met, as anyone might have calculated, with opposition from the smaller delegations, and there seemed small prospect of consensus on the wording of their precious *communiqué*, the Russians turned as if in desperation to Ambassador Mendelevich, whose flexible negotiating style had probably achieved more at Dipoli than all the other Communist participants put together. He quickly reached a compromise with the Maltese. It was easy enough for other delegations to read the moral; but what will be interesting is whether the Russians will do so. It will be a test of Soviet intentions for Stage II whether M. Mendelevich is given an important negotiating task in Geneva.

7. Yet, though the Soviet line in Stage I was depressingly tough, it was unmarked by imagination or political insight, and it did not achieve any particular success. Mr. Gromyko, for example, showed no more sign than the Soviet negotiators at Dipoli of realising that this was not just a routine East-West Conference and that the non-aligned countries (whom he did not mention in his speech) are also involved in the process of *détente*. His attack on the principle of consensus could hardly have been better designed to arouse neutral countries' suspicions and fears. In the wider field of public relations the Eastern failure was just as obvious. There was some reason to fear that, having given some ground to the West at the preparatory talks, they would at least seek a major propaganda victory in Stage I. But their reactionary speeches, and the repetitive thinness of the proposals they actually tabled, gave the West much the better of the propaganda exchange. Again, the East made no attempt to invest the Conference with any special atmosphere of urgency or significance. In spite of their protestations before arriving in Helsinki, they quickly came to acquiesce in the Western view that Stage I should be a relatively short and formal affair. Although Mr. Gromyko made a half-hearted attempt to prolong the first stage (in the name of 'dignity') by suspending plenary meetings on the third and fourth days, he soon dropped the proposal in the face of a remarkable, and totally spontaneous display of united opposition by the West; and the Russians agreed with little discussion to the Western proposal that Stage II should not start until mid-September.

He clearly has no intention of agreeing to anything which might represent a threat to the Soviet system or to the East European régimes. It was depressing to hear one Communist speaker after another insisting on the two different systems in Europe and the inviolable frontier between them.'

[14] Mr. A.G. Kovalev was appointed Soviet Head of Delegation to Stage II.

[15] According to notes prepared by EESD (see No. 40, note 2): 'This demonstration of the cloven hoof made a most disagreeable impression, and delegations as far east as the Yugoslavs and the Romanians were full of resentment afterwards. From our point of view this last-minute reminder of Soviet attitudes was probably beneficial.'

8. It may be optimistic to comment that, although the Russians publicly adopted rigid attitudes, they did not defend them very hard when it came to the crunch. It was no doubt inevitable that during the first stage they should give the impression of caring less about the substance of what the Conference decided than that the proceedings should be completed without a hitch. We can expect them to fight a good deal harder in Stage II, and to repeat many of the skirmishes that we hoped had been concluded on the Dipoli terrain. But I do not think we need be too apprehensive about the prospect. So long as Mr. Brezhnev is set on having his European summit meeting, he can be expected to pay a price to achieve it. Just as we were able to exploit the Soviet desire for a Conference to ensure that the MPT's final recommendations basically reflected Western plans, we should be able to exploit the Soviet wish for a summit at the third stage to ensure that Stage II concludes in a form that is favourable to us. What is essential is that the Nine should continue their cohesive approach, and maintain as close harmony with the other NATO countries and the non-aligned as they did at Dipoli.

9. It must be admitted that the handling of the Maltese proposal in Stage I created the impression that the Nine may find united action hard to preserve. The French and Italians certainly made little effort during the first stage to be faithful to what elements of unity there were in the Community position on the Mediterranean. But we must hope that they will draw the appropriate moral from the fact that they were roundly defeated, having failed to secure not only an invitation to Algeria and Tunisia, but also the formula for which they were fighting in the *communiqué*. We must hope too that the North African issue will prove to have been a very special case; and that if at the beginning of Stage II the Community can reach agreement on how to handle it, the advantages of united action will again become obvious to all the Nine.

10. The lesson is clear, as was the lesson of Dipoli, and I do not believe that anything that happened during Stage I need change it. In this forum of 35 European countries a Community united in policy can achieve the greater part of what it sets out to obtain. It is true, of course, that the Russians, if they wish, can bring the process of discussion to a halt by denying final consensus; but (to repeat a point in my despatch of 13 June) they can hardly do so, provided that the West maintain a reasonable line, without exposing the hollowness of their own professions of *détente*. They can hardly do so either without putting themselves in the position of obstructing the development of the European idea. No one who has sat through the apparently interminable debates of the last eight months in Helsinki would deny that there was a great deal of cynicism round the table. But no one could fail to notice, either, that there was a vague but genuine sentiment, not only on the part of Western delegates, that the barriers between European countries ought ultimately to become less significant than the links of their common civilisation. Stage I of the CSCE may not have achieved many tangible results; it may have been a demonstration rather than a discussion; but at least it showed that none of the Foreign Ministers of Europe (always excepting Albania) were ready to stand out against the idea of more regular and more orderly contacts between the

Governments of Europe.

11. Mr. Brezhnev, like other Heads of Government, is still free to prevent the development of this idea if he wishes. But each stage of the Conference is likely to make it increasingly difficult for him to contemplate (or indeed calculate) the consequences of withdrawal from the process. We in the West, on the other hand, may find it a difficult task to push the East into adopting a more civilised attitude towards the development of closer human and cultural contacts between the peoples of Europe. If the pessimists are right about the basic Soviet attitude, we may achieve little or nothing. But if we continue to follow the admirably clear lines of your speech to the Conference, we shall have little at risk if we press on with this task at Geneva.

12. I am sending copies of this despatch to the Ambassadors at Moscow, Washington, Paris, Stockholm. Oslo, Copenhagen, Bonn, Rome, The Hague, Brussels and Luxembourg; and to Her Majesty's Representatives to NATO, the European Community and in Geneva.

I have, etc.,
T.A.K. ELLIOTT

No. 43

Sir A. Douglas-Home to Mr. A.A.S. Stark[1] (Copenhagen)

No. 171 Telegraphic [*WDW 1/18*]

Priority. Confidential   FCO, *23 July 1973, 6.15 p.m.*

Repeated for information to Bonn, Brussels, Dublin, The Hague, Luxembourg, Paris, Rome, UKDEL NATO, Saving to Berne, UKREP Brussels, UK Mission Geneva, Moscow, Washington.

MIPT.[2] Following is text of revised draft:

European Political Cooperation: CSCE

Comments are requested on the following revised version of document CSCE (73) 44 UK in accordance with the decision of the Sub-Committee at its meeting on 17 and 18 July.[3]

Organisation of the Second Stage of the Conference on Security and Cooperation in Europe

1. The Coordinating Committee will meet in Geneva on 29 August to prepare the organisation of the second stage. The decisions it is called upon

[1] HM Ambassador in Copenhagen.

[2] Telegram No. 170 to Copenhagen of 23 July instructed Mr. Stark to communicate the paper enclosed in this document to the Danish Foreign Ministry.

[3] The first draft of this paper was submitted to Mr. Tickell by Mr. Fall on 9 July (EN 2/23), and at the meeting of the Nine's CSCE Sub-Committee on 17-18 July (see No. 42, note 11) it was agreed that the British would circulate a revised version which would serve, subject to further comments, as the basis for instructions to the delegations of the Nine at the first session of the Coordinating Committee. It was also decided that a suitably edited version of the paper should be introduced in NATO.

to take are of a procedural nature, but have considerable importance. On them will depend the extent to which the conception of the work of the second stage favoured by the Nine and reflected in the final recommendations is translated into practice at the second stage.

2. The paper lists the questions which are likely to arise, and suggests the answers which we might propose.

I: How many Committees should there be?

3. It is clear from the arrangement of the final recommendations that 3 substantive committees and a Coordinating Committee are envisaged. This corresponds to our views, and is unlikely to cause difficulty.

II: Which Committee should start first?

4. The Coordinating Committee will meet before the beginning of the second stage, and periodically during it. We should try to avoid too frequent meetings of the Coordinating Committee in the early part of the second stage (although we may wish to arrange some informal procedure for planning the schedule of meetings for the week ahead).[4] Our main objective is to ensure that the substantive Committees adopt a consistent practice on matters of importance to the overall development of the second stage. The work of the Coordinating Committee on agenda Item IV is in a different category. We should insist that it begins only when a clearer view has emerged of the 'progress made at the Conference' (para. 53 of the Final Recommendations).

5. The substantive committees should begin on the first day of the second stage, and work in parallel. The main committees of the UN General Assembly provide the correct analogy. The Russians may press for priority to be given to the work of the first Committee, which they may hope to complete quickly in order to put time pressures on the other committees, and in particular on the third. Our best means of countering this will be to insist on effective parallelism in the work of the three substantive Committees. In practical terms, we should propose that at least during the early stages one of the large meeting rooms be allocated to each of the substantive committees, which would then be responsible for their allocation as between the committee itself and the sub-committees for which it is responsible. It would be possible to make two further committee rooms available, but we understand from the Swiss that they would have difficulty in providing interpretation for more than four simultaneous meetings. We should therefore plan on the basis of a maximum of four simultaneous meetings, and seek to

---

[4] It was later explained, in telegram No. 291 to UKDEL NATO of 7 August, that this sentence had to be read in the light of the objective stated in the following one. The FCO accepted that the Coordinating Committee should meet as often as necessary to ensure consistent practice on matters of importance, but did not wish it to call for regular reports from substantive Committees and sub-committees since this 'would tend (especially in the early stages) to prevent the Sub-Committees from getting down to their work and create an artificial need for meetings of the Committees to produce reports for the Coordinating Committee'. It was also felt that this would give the Russians 'a platform at regular meetings of the Coordinating Committee to press for greater speed'.

ensure that this fourth option is used as fully as possible. It should be possible to devise some informal procedure for sharing the fourth meeting room between the committees in the light of their requirements.

III: How many sub-committees should there be: and when should they begin their work?

6. The Russians opposed a decision on the first question at the preparatory talks, and may argue that the point is for the substantive Committees to decide. There is a danger that such a procedure would postpone the establishment of sub-committees and the start of their work: and lead to each Committee dealing *seriatim* with the points on its agenda and setting up sub-committees only when it had had a preliminary discussion of the subject matter (and perhaps even agreed the broad outline of a final document along the lines of those proposed by the East). This would tend to reduce the sub-committees to the status of drafting groups, and make it more difficult for us to ensure a detailed consideration by experts of the specific points in the terms of reference. For this reason we should aim at the first session of the Coordinating Committee to settle the number of sub-committees and their broad areas of responsibility. We want the initial general debate in each Committee to be kept as short as possible, and we hope that the Coordinating Committee will call for an early start to the work of the sub-committees.

7. There is a clear analogy with the inductive approach which the Nine proposed at the preparatory talks. These considerations are equally relevant to our approach to the work of the Committees and sub-committees of the second stage. We should argue that the appropriate sub-committees referred to in paragraphs 16, 30 and 42 of the Final Recommendations are those indicated in the numbered sub-divisions of the corresponding sections of the terms of reference: that they should deal in the first instance with the detailed work on the substance of matters within their field of competence: and that the outcome of the work of the Committees should be in substance the sum of what has been achieved in each of the sub-committees. This was our intention in pressing for such an arrangement at the preparatory talks, and we should not abandon the point now.

8. There may be pressure from the smaller delegations to reduce the number of sub-committees below that implicit in the recommendations. This should be resisted. We want the sub-committees to work as far as possible in parallel, subject to the need to avoid simultaneous meetings when it is clear that the same people will be involved.

IV: How should the work of the sub-committees be organised?

9. The question is likely to cause difficulty, as it involves both practical and political considerations. Practical, in that delegations will differ in the number of meetings which they are able to service on the same day: and political, in that the answer will have a considerable bearing on the amount of detailed work which can be done.

10. We should start by excluding the 2 extremes. All the sub-committees cannot meet on the same morning or afternoon, because neither the conference facilities nor the resources of individual delegations, particularly

those from smaller countries, will be sufficient. On the other hand, a procedure whereby one sub-committee was required to complete its work before another could start would amount in practice to a decision to have only one sub-committee for each Committee, or to concentrate the work in the Committee itself.

11. Between these extremes, there is a balance to be struck: and it is important that the decision taken should reflect our concern to ensure effective parallelism in the work of the various committees. Practical considerations, which may differ from Committee to Committee and which may be given different weight at the beginning and towards the end of the second stage, will of course be relevant, and we should not try to legislate in too much detail at the first meeting of the Coordinating Committee. Each substantive Committee will have to have some discretion in planning its work. But we should recognise that, even without a target date for the completion of the second stage, time pressure is likely to build up as it proceeds. We should therefore seek to establish and maintain a sufficient degree of overall control over the work of the Committees and sub-committees to ensure that this pressure is not distributed in a way contrary to our interests. This is a point of major importance to us, and it is one which will have to be carefully watched throughout the second stage.

12. Our immediate concern will be to ensure an early start to the detailed work on all the main subjects. Should it appear later that the work on one or other subject requires more time, the Committees should be asked to make arrangements accordingly. (For instance, there may well be occasions once all the sub-committees have begun their work when it will be sensible for one sub-committee to meet intensively for a period of up to a week, while another meets less frequently or has a short break to allow time for reflection). The following points are of importance:

(*a*) The 2 Sub-Committees of the first Committee should work broadly in parallel. On most working days, one could meet in the morning and one in the afternoon. If separate arrangements are required to deal with the Swiss proposal, these should be provided for within the facilities allocated to the first Committee.

(*b*) The 4 Sub-Committees of the third Committee should be regarded as separate entities, though we should try to avoid simultaneous meetings on human contacts and information on the one hand and on culture and education on the other. Given the importance we attach to this Committee, we should seek to ensure that it has access whenever necessary to the fourth meeting room.

(*c*) The arrangements to be worked out for the second Committee should take into account the need for regular and detailed coordination which was emphasized at the meeting of the Ad Hoc Group on 17 and 18 July. In addition we should note:

(i) The greater number of sub-committees.
(ii) The fact that the environment Sub-Committee can to a large

extent be allowed to work separately: and,

(iii) The probable need to have relatively short periods of concentrated work on subjects for which specialists will be required.

13. A decision by the Coordinating Committee asking the substantive Committees to make arrangements for their work along the lines suggested in paragraph 12 above would meet our immediate requirements. It would give our representatives on the substantive Committees a framework in which to press for an organisation of work in keeping with the inductive approach, without tying their hands on questions best decided from day to day. Points of difficulty could be reported back to the Coordinating Commitee:

V: How should the Committees supervise the work of the sub-committees for which they are responsible?

14. We should not seek to lay down hard and fast rules at the outset of the second stage. We hope that the substantive work will be done by the sub-committees, and that they will not be required to waste time producing progress reports for their committees. The senior national representatives on each committee will keep in close touch with the work of the sub-committees. This should in most cases be sufficient to ensure that an overall view is taken.

VI: How should the Coordinating Committee coordinate the work of the Committees?

15. Considerations similar to those in paragraph 14 above apply. We should as far as possible avoid formal reports, especially in the early stages, and rely on individual delegations to brief their representatives on the Coordinating Committee.

B: Coordination of the Nine

16. Political Directors have agreed that consultations on day to day matters should take place in Geneva. If the second stage is organised substantially on the lines suggested above, it would seem best to organise meetings of the Nine on a Committee by Committee basis (the second Committee being the responsibility of the Ad Hoc Group). The representative of the Presidency on each substantive Committee could be responsible for arranging with his colleagues whatever meetings were necessary on the substance or tactics of matters under discussion in the particular Committee or in its sub-committees, and for advising when questions should be submitted to a meeting of Heads/Deputy Heads of Delegation. Meetings at this level will have an important role to play in ensuring that we maintain an overall view of the development of the second stage. They will also be required before meetings of the Coordinating Committee and before the regular meetings of the Political Committee of the Nine.

17. We shall have, as during the preparatory talks, to make arrangements for maintaining close contact with other members of the Alliance and with the neutrals.[5]

---

[5] An amended version of this paper, from which were omitted paragraphs 16 and 17, was discussed in the SPC of NATO on 1 August (letter from Mr. Staples to Mr. Fall of 3 August, EN 2/23). The Americans then undertook to draft a supplementary paragraph on NATO coordination, and, with this addition, the paper was subsequently adopted as NATO document C-M (73) 69 (letters from Mr. Lever to Mr. Fall and Mr. Burns of 9 and 22 August).

No. 44

Miss A.M. Warburton[1] (UKMIS Geneva) to Sir A. Douglas-Home

No. 377 Telegraphic [*WDW 1/15*]

Priority. Confidential   GENEVA, *3 September 1973, 5.35 p.m.*

Repeated for information Priority UKDEL NATO, Copenhagen, Helsinki, Berne and Saving to UKREP Brussels, Paris, Bonn, The Hague, Rome, Brussels, Luxembourg, Moscow, Washington, Dublin, Athens, Ankara, Oslo and Reykjavik.

Following from delegation to CSCE.[2]

CSCE Coordination Committee

1. In accordance with the decision taken during the first stage of the Conference the CSCE Coordinating Committee met in Geneva from 29 August—3 September. Although it relatively easily reached decisions on the organisational matters before it, discussions on the problem of 'contributions' from non-participant countries bordering the Mediterranean held things up for several days.

2. The Russians and the other East Europeans fielded weighty delegations headed (except in the cases of Czechoslovakia and the GDR) by Vice Ministers of Foreign Affairs. The Western delegations were generally smaller. Their leaders were mostly officials of ambassadorial or ministerial rank, who have come to Geneva for the duration of the Conference. But they included some heads of resident missions in Geneva, as well as a fair sprinkling of senior officials commuting from capitals or elsewhere.

3. The decisions taken by the meeting of organisational and financial questions were generally satisfactory from the Western point of view. We have obtained an organisational structure for the second stage which is very much on the lines agreed in NATO and among the Nine on these issues.[3] Western coordination worked very well. But the Nine once again fell apart on the Mediterranean problem, after making a promising start by agreeing a draft which the Italians tabled. Substantial differences on how to handle the issue subsequently developed between the Dutch/Scandinavian group on one side and the French and Italians on the other (see our telegram No. 372, not to all).[4]

[1] Counsellor and Head of Chancery, UKMIS Geneva.

[2] The UK delegation to the Coordinating Committee was led by Mr. Elliott, who was assisted by Mr. Maxey, Mr. McLaren, Miss Warburton and Mr. J.W.D. Gray (UKMIS Geneva).

[3] See Appendix 1. The Special Working Group on the Peaceful Settlement of Disputes was established to meet Swiss and Romanian wishes, and on the understanding that it would, for all practical purposes, be treated as if it were a sub-committee. It was also settled that the Coordinating Committee, together with the other working bodies, would meet on 18 September to inaugurate Stage II of the Conference (UKMIS Geneva telegram Nos. 370 and 371 of 1 September, MT 10/18).

[4] UKMIS Geneva telegram No. 372 of 2 September reported that the basic difficulty concerned allowing Israel equal treatment to Algeria and Tunisia. Whereas the majority of the

4. The new Russian team, with Dubinin[5] and Mendelevich bearing the main burden of negotiations, began by oozing sweetness and light and showing a general disposition to be accommodating, even on the Mediterranean issue. Later, as the atmosphere grew more tense, Vice-President Kovaliev made two interventions in crudely bullying terms which are a bad portent for the future. Rather contrary to expectations, the Russians did not approach us to suggest private consultations though their contacts with us were affable. On the other hand (possibly because Dubinin speaks fluent French) they developed a (perhaps alarmingly) close relationship with the French delegation. Like the French, they seem to have thought it a matter of major importance to play up to the North African states at a time when the non-aligned Conference is proceeding in Algiers;[6] and were apparently prepared to give tactical considerations on this issue priority even over the need to start the work of the CSCE second stage in a good atmosphere and on a businesslike basis.

5. Most of the other East European delegations obediently followed the Soviet lead, though contributing little to detailed discussions on any issue. The Romanians, however, went their own maverick way on the organisational points, threatening at one time to cause serious delay in the proceedings through their insistence on a sub-committee to consider the contents of paragraph 21 of the Final Recommendations.[7]

6. Of the neutrals and non-aligned the Yugoslavs made themselves generally unpopular. Many of their interventions in the discussions on the organisation of the Conference were obscure and unhelpful. On the Mediterranean issue they provided a major and very slippery obstacle to consensus. Of the other non-aligned delegations, the Maltese and the Spaniards formed an effective part of the coalition insisting on protracted discussion of the Mediterranean problem but otherwise did their best to be helpful. The Swiss, Swedes, Finns and Austrians established an early alliance to put forward ideas on the organisation of the second stage but this soon

Western and non-aligned countries were ready to accept the French redraft of an Italian text as offering a guarantee of 'fair treatment' for Israel, Denmark, the Netherlands and Canada (supported by Norway) had, according to Mr. Elliott, 'committed themselves to the Herculean task (given the universal application of the consensus procedure) of providing cast-iron guarantees that Israel [would] be heard' (WDW 1/23).

[5] Mr. Y.V. Dubinin was Head of the First European Department of the Ministry for Foreign Affairs. The Soviet Delegation, led by Mr. Kovalev, also included: Ms. Z.H. Miranova, Head of Delegation to the UN at Geneva; Mr. M.A. Kharlov, Head of the Research Department of the Ministry of Foreign Affairs; Mr. V.I. Simakov, Head of the Department for Trade with Western Countries at the Ministry of Foreign Trade; and Mr. K.V. Ananichev, Head of the Department for International Economic, Scientific and Technical Organisations of the State Committee for Science and Technology.

[6] The fourth summit Conference of non-aligned nations was held in Algiers on 5-9 September 1973. It was attended by over sixty heads of state from Africa, Asia and Latin America.

[7] See note 3 above.

came to grief largely because they had made no attempt to consult Western delegations (including our own, with whom they had previously been in close touch). The Swedes played a noticeably ineffective role in comparison with their performance at Helsinki.

7. As hosts the Swiss left something to be desired. The arrangements for the meeting (with the exception at first of the translation system) worked smoothly and the Conference facilities will be adequate for the second stage (though probably no better than those that would have been available in Helsinki). On the other hand the Swiss tried to make too much use of the Chairmanship in the opening sessions to promote their own ill-conceived ideas about organisation. They obviously held the (unwarranted) view that the Executive Secretary should perform a central and directing role in the Conference's work and they will need to develop much greater tact if they are not to become a nuisance as the second stage proceeds.

8. Although it is satisfactory that a decision has at last been reached (apparently much against the odds) on the Mediterranean issue,[8] it would be too much to hope that there will not be further arguments about it when Stage II begins. In general, the last three days of discussion were distinguished by the failure of many delegates to show a spirit of compromise, the lamentable long-windedness of their arguments, and the failure of successive chairmen to apply the rules of procedure fairly, firmly and promptly. This all bodes ill for Stage II.[9]

[8] On 3 September agreement was reached on a formula which provided for the written submission to Committees I and II of the views of Algeria and Tunisia on the agenda, and the Committees' reception of their representatives. These arrangements, if effected, were to be applied equally to any other Mediterranean state whose request to make its views known was communicated to the Chairman of the Coordinating Committee through a participating state no later than 18 September (UKMIS telegram No. 376 of 3 September; letter from Miss Warburton to Mr. McLaren of 4 September; WDW 1/23).

[9] With particular reference to this telegram Mr. Elliott wrote to Mr. Tickell on 6 September: 'As you will have gathered from my telegrams . . . I found the Coordinating Committee Meeting a pretty dismal experience. This was partly because the coordination of the Nine totally broke down on the Mediterranean issue. Maybe that was a special case and we shall be able to work together successfully on other items on the agenda (as we did on the organisational issues at Geneva), but I do not feel very happy about the way in which the French rushed after the Russians . . . I also think that we as a Delegation are going to be hard put to it to make as much of an impact during Stage II as we did at the MPT. Obviously if I am not going to be in Geneva all the time I can hardly hope to exercise much influence on the day to day discussions in individual committees, though I will of course do everything I can to see that a proper balance is maintained in the rates of progress in each of them. I see my own principal role, however, as being to maintain contact with the leadership of the other Delegations . . . exercising what influence I can in that way, and in general trying to ensure that we adopt an effective and consistent strategy.'

No. 45

Sir J. Killick (Moscow) to Sir A. Douglas-Home

No. 1014 Telegraphic [ENS 1/4]

Priority. Confidential   MOSCOW, *5 September 1973, 8.30 a.m.*

Repeated for information to Routine Washington, Bonn, Paris, UKDEL NATO, UKMIS Geneva, UKREP Brussels, Helsinki, Vienna, and to Saving Prague, Warsaw, Budapest, Bucharest, Sofia, East Berlin, Rome, Brussels, The Hague, Luxembourg, Copenhagen, Berne, Stockholm.

My tel[egrams] Nos. 980, 990, and 995 (not to all).[1]

Campaign against Sakharov and Trial of Dissidents

1. It is not easy to interpret these ugly developments. The following comments are of necessity highly speculative and I offer them with all due reserve.

2. There are three main elements in the current situation and it is important, though difficult, to assess their inter-relationship correctly. They are:

(i) The trial of Yakir and Krasin, its attendant publicity and the naming of Sakharov and Solzhenitsyn in evidence:[2]

(ii) Sakharov's interviews with Swedish television and with Western correspondents:[3]

(iii) Solzhenitsyn's interview with A[ssociated] P[ress] and *Le Monde*.[4]

[1] These telegrams of 29 August, 1 and 3 September reported the publication of an open letter from forty members of the Soviet Academy of Sciences denouncing the Academician and nuclear physicist, Dr. A. Sakharov. This coincided with the opening of the long-forecast 'show trial' of Mr. P.I. Yakir and Mr. V.A. Krasin, two leading members of the Action Group for the Defence of Human Rights, on whose behalf Dr. Sakharov had interceded. On 31 August thirty-one 'leading establishment writers' published another open letter attacking both Dr. Sakharov and the author, Mr. A. Solzhenitsyn, for 'in effect calling on the West to continue the Cold War'.

[2] At a news conference on 5 September Mr. Yakir and Mr. Krasin, who in the previous week had been sentenced to imprisonment and exile for anti-Soviet activities, publicly recanted. During the same news conference, Mr. M. Malyorov, First Deputy Prosecutor, warned Dr. Sakharov that he, Mr. Solzhenitsyn, 'and others like them' were not immune from Soviet law, which he accused them of disobeying.

[3] On 3 July the Swedish press published the text of a television interview in which Dr. Sakharov denounced Soviet socialism as nothing more than empty words and propaganda. Then, on 21 August, he told Western correspondents at a news conference in his Moscow apartment that in his opinion a Western accommodation with the Soviet Union on Soviet terms posed a serious threat to the world, and that the Russians would take economic and technological help from the West while operating domestically behind a wall of secrecy and suppressing individual rights.

[4] In August Mr. Solzhenitsyn claimed that the lives of he and his wife had been threatened, and suggested that the KGB might be planning his death. Moscow telegram No. 990 (see note 1 above) reported a claim by *Pravda*, which referred indirectly to an interview given by Mr. Solzhenitsyn to a representative of *Le Monde* which was published on 29 August, that the public

The Soviet authorities determined the timing of (i), which required careful planning and preparation. They did not determine the occurrence or timing of (ii) and (iii); but (ii) and (iii) were probably triggered off by Sakharov's and Solzhenitsyn's awareness that (i) was imminent and motivated by their desire to make a possibly final statement of their plight and views. The authorities must have reckoned with the possibility that they would speak out if they felt the net closing on them. The circumstances of the Solzhenitsyn interview certainly, and of Sakharov's actions probably, were such that the authorities must have known about them in advance. There must be a strong presumption that the failure to take preventative measures was deliberate. It is even conceivable that Sakharov and Solzhenitsyn were deliberately tipped off about their implication in the Yakir/Krasin trial in order to provoke a reaction.

3. All this points to a considered decision by the authorities to have a public and comprehensive show-down with the dissidents, on the eve of Stage II of CSCE and before the re-assembly of the US Congress and Western Parliaments. The timing implies that the Soviet purpose is to demonstrate beyond doubt in deeds as well as words both to the West and to the Soviet people that relaxation of tension on the international plane need not and will not be accompanied by relaxation at home or by ideological *détente*. The trial of Yakir and Krasin, classically Stalinist in all but the severity of the sentences (though nobody should be under any illusion about their practical effect, in the light of Amalrik's experience),[5] provides the 'justification' for a number of recent statements by the leadership and major press commentaries to the effect that reactionary forces will attempt to use *détente* to undermine the positions of socialism and that increased vigilance is a necessary corollary of the new international climate. Although a public campaign against Sakharov was a likely consequence of his interview with Swedish television in July and of his being named in the Yakir case, its scale and virulence is probably attributable to the fact that his latest interview, succinct and going right to the heart of the matter, warned the West against *détente* on Soviet terms and thus trampled the sacred ground of Brezhnev's 'personal contribution'; this has enabled the authorities, in a classic and nauseating demonstration of doublethink, to label Sakharov as the enemy of peace and *détente*, thus facilitating the mobilisation of the intellectual establishment in condemning him. Solzhenitsyn, in his recent interview, took a more personal line and has not so far been brought into the centre of the denunciatory campaign.[6]

statements of Dr. Sakharov and Mr. Solzhenitsyn, 'made on the eve of the opening of stage two of CSCE, [had been] seized upon to organise a campaign against *détente*'.

[5] In 1970 the Soviet dissident historian, Mr. A.A. Amalrik, was sentenced to three years in a restrictive régime camp for 'deliberate defamation of Soviet State'. He was not released at the end of this term, but sentenced to a further three years confinement (minute from Mr. G.D.G. Murrell (Research Department) to Mr. Bullard of 19 July, EN 2/15).

[6] The appearance in *Pravda* on 4 September of an article which combined a restatement of the Soviet position on cultural exchanges and human contacts with a vicious attack on Dr. Sakharov and Mr. Solzhenitsyn confirmed Sir J. Killick in this assessment of Soviet policy. He pointed out, in Moscow telegram No. 1027 of 6 September, that the article was 'evidently

4. We are thus witnessing the realisation of the bargain which was struck at the April Plenum of the Central Committee (para. 7 of my despatch of 11 May).[7] I cannot judge whether Brezhnev hoped or believed that this might remain an 'optical' transaction. He may not be altogether happy at having to stand by it and may indeed be apprehensive of the implications, particularly of the timing of the crack-down, for his external policies; but we must assume that the campaign has his full if reluctant backing.[8] However this may be, the fact is that the West has been served with a brazen and defiant restatement of the Soviet concept of *détente*. Having been made aware of the challenge, the Soviet and East European peoples will watch closely for the Western response. Paradoxically, therefore, Soviet actions have reinforced the validity of Sakharov's warning of the consequences of the West being seen to acquiesce in the Soviet double standard.

5. The conclusion is stark. If the West goes ahead with CSCE as if nothing had happened and ends up accepting minimal concessions under Basket III in return for letting the Russians have more or less what they want under Basket I, it will appear here and throughout Eastern Europe that we have ignored the challenge and come to terms with the newly revealed 'ugly face' of communism. It is less easy to draw policy conclusions, in terms of how to avoid this by adjusting our line significantly under Basket III.[9] The Soviet response

designed to consolidate the opening Soviet stand on Agenda Item III—acquiescence only in selective cultural contacts, carefully controlled within the framework of intergovernmental agreements—and to fasten the stigma of opposition to detente and (in the case of Sakharov and Solzhenitsyn) of anti-patriotism on to those who differ from it' (EN 2/4).

[7] During the April Plenum of the Central Committee Mr. Brezhnev announced the promotion of Marshal A. Grechko, the Soviet Defence Minister, and Mr. Y. Andropov, the Minister for Internal Security, to full membership of the Politburo. This, Sir J. Killick thought, could be seen either as an initiative designed to disarm conservative critics of Mr. Brezhnev's foreign policy line and to commit more deeply to its support the two interest groups most likely to constitute the base for any opposition to it; or as a concession which Mr. Brezhnev was obliged to make to his critics and doubters in order to secure their endorsement. In his despatch of 11 May Sir J. Killick stated that he gave most credence to the latter interpretation. 'Mr. Brezhnev', he reasoned, 'evidently found it necessary to provide a firm guarantee that considerations of both internal and national security would continue to be given full weight in the formulation of policy' (ENS 1/5).

[8] One explanation of Russian conduct offered in telegram No. 682 to Moscow of 14 September was that the Soviet authorities, faced by the difficulty of delaying the trial of Mr. Yakir and Mr. Krasin, had tried to conclude it before the opening of Stage II. But, the telegram suggested, they had at the same time 'judged it best to try to steer negotiations on Item III in the direction they [wanted] by taking up in public a very tough stance on freer information etc.'. Sir J. Killick agreed in general with this assessment (Moscow telegram No. 1084 of 19 September).

[9] On this point Mr. Elliott commented: 'My initial feeling is that there is really not much need to make short-term "adjustments" in our time [*sic*] to deal with immediate developments in Soviet policy; I presume we have never in any case thought of asking only for "minimal" concessions under Basket III in return for letting the Russians have "more or less what they want" under Basket I. It certainly would be a pity if we got involved in fighting a propagandist battle over current events instead of pressing steadily for the sort of long-term improvements in

to this would no doubt be to brand us, like Sakharov, as the enemies of peace and *détente*, but I hope such accusations would be so transparent in the eyes of public opinion as not to worry us. We cannot very well raise such questions as the trial, which are undeniably Soviet internal affairs, at Geneva directly. But it is hard to swallow a situation in which apartheid has become a major issue in international relations with the Soviet Union leading the pack, while their own shortcomings are allowed to pass. Much presumably depends on the strength and expression of feeling in Western parliaments and press (particularly perhaps the US Congress), and the consequent effect on governments. I would hope at least that governments would be willing and in a position to adduce this at Geneva (much as has been the case over Soviet Jews) and in addition to nail the accusations that the dissidents have been in league with, and aided and encouraged by, those in the West who favour continuing the 'Cold War'. Indeed the Russians have now presented us with sufficient evidence that it is they who are open to this charge.

6. Of course I do not underestimate the difficulties. For HMG in particular, for us to play a major role in this sense would put the further development of Anglo-Soviet relations at risk. More generally, there may be room for doubt about the robustness of some of our European partners and the Americans (who may feel they have more at stake in terms of trade etc. than we); not to mention the European neutrals (although Dr. Kreisky's[10] reported defence of Sakharov is encouraging) and, in terms of world opinion, the non-aligned countries.[11]

the situation which Dipoli encouraged us to think were desirable and possibly attainable' (letter to Mr. Tickell of 6 September, WDW 1/15).

[10] Dr. B. Kreisky was Chancellor of Austria.

[11] Sir A. Douglas-Home thought it 'unfortunate that the concerted move against the remaining Soviet dissidents [had] coincided with a more encouraging trend in Anglo-Soviet relations'. He added, in telegram No. 681 to Moscow of 14 September, 'the events in Moscow can only strengthen the validity of the line which I took in Helsinki, about the emphasis on Item III . . . We may well have to make it plain to the Russians that the Western negotiators operate within the framework of public opinion and that any further action against Soviet dissidents might seriously prejudice the atmosphere for the CSCE as a whole.'

No. 46

Steering Brief for the United Kingdom Delegation to Stage II of the CSCE[1]

[WDW 1/18]

Confidential   FCO, *13 September 1973*
Introduction

1. The second stage of the CSCE will open in Geneva on 18 September.

[1] This brief was submitted to the Private Secretary under cover of a minute on 13 September by Mr. McLaren. Sir A. Douglas-Home noted that it 'well expressed' British aims and tactics.

We regard it as important that it should conduct its work in accordance with the Final Recommendations of the Helsinki Consultations, which were adopted by Ministers during the first stage. They take satisfactory account of the Western approach to the Conference, and constitute a collective commitment by the participants on the basis of which the Western countries agreed to participate in the conference.

2. Arrangements for the organisation of the second stage were agreed by the Co-ordinating Committee at its meeting from 29 August to 2 September.[2] These are generally satisfactory, although a number of Western countries are concerned that the intensive schedule of meetings agreed for the first two weeks should not constitute a precedent for the second stage as a whole.

3. Detailed briefs have been provided on the subjects likely to be discussed during the second stage,[3] together with copies of the more important papers to which the delegation[4] may need to refer.

4. The purpose of this brief is to provide guidance on our overall approach to the second stage, in the light of our objectives and those of the other participants.

Soviet Aims

5. Soviet aims for the Conference have almost certainly changed over the years, but they still see it as contributing to the main objectives of their *Westpolitik*. In broad terms, we believe these to be as follows:

(*a*) to formalize the *status quo* in Europe, including in particular the Soviet sphere of influence in the East; the inviolability of present frontiers (which they seek to imply means immutability, Northern Ireland and Gibraltar apart); and the permanence of the division of Germany;

(*b*) to generate an atmosphere of *détente* which would leave the way open for the Soviet Union to expand its political influence in Western Europe, and thereby undermine NATO and weaken Western (and in particular European) determination to maintain effective defence arrangements;

(*c*) to create political conditions in which the Russians could benefit from increased trade and technological co-operation with the West at a minimal cost in hard currency;

(*d*) to gain credit both for the Soviet Union and for Mr. Brezhnev personally for the promotion of *détente*, while keeping to a minimum commitments to take practical measures towards genuinely greater security and co-operation in Europe; and (somewhat more speculatively)

(*e*) to stabilize the Soviet Union's Western front in preparation for a period

[2] See No. 44, note 3.

[3] Not printed.

[4] The British delegation at Stage II, which was lead by Mr. Elliott, initially included: Mr. J.M. Edes (Counsellor), Miss Warburton and Mr. Maxey, who were responsible for Committees I, II and III respectively; and Mr. Adams, Mr. Burns, Mr. Bishop, Mr. J.C. Kay (TRED), Mr. Gordon, Mr. D.I. Miller (British Military Government in Berlin), Mr. Gray, Mr. R. Reeve (First Secretary) and Dr. M. Fielder (DTI).

of intensified confrontation with China in the East.

6. The Russians were forced at the Preparatory Talks to pay a higher price than they would have wished for Western agreement to the Conference. They conceded wording in the terms of reference for the Committees and sub-Committees which in some respects goes further than we had expected to achieve; and they are now faced with the prospect of a detailed examination of a large number of questions, especially in the human contacts and information fields, which they have never previously admitted as proper subjects for multilateral discussion.

7. It is clear both from the performance of the Soviet delegation at the first stage, and from public statements by the Russians, that they are anxious to limit the damage to their own interests which could result from a second stage as we and our partners and allies envisage it. This aim is likely to colour their whole approach. They will work for a non-controversial and indeed perfunctory second stage, followed by an early Summit. They will press hard for a declaration of principles which they can represent as a multilateral endorsement of the frontier provisions in the FRG's Eastern Treaties; and they remain interested in machinery to ensure the continuation of multilateral consultations after the Conference. On other questions they will try to promote quick broad agreements on a low common denominator basis, in order to limit the possibilities for detailed discussion and practical results, particularly on human contacts and information.

8. The Russians can expect loyal support for this strategy from all their Warsaw Pact allies except the Romanians, who will have ideas of their own to put forward which are likely to irritate their allies almost as much as Western countries. The other five countries joined the Soviet Union at the first stage in a carefully orchestrated tabling of proposals designed to cover all items of the agenda at the level of generality thought tactically appropriate. Any desire on the part of the countries of Eastern Europe to explore the possibilities of progress on economic and related issues, where they are traditionally the *demandeurs*, was subordinated to the overall aim of securing a short second stage.

Western Aims

9. Western aims for the Conference as a whole are partly positive and partly negative. On the positive side they are:

(*a*) to secure the widest possible acceptance of the view that *détente* cannot be secured through declarations alone but requires practical improvements in specific areas;

(*b*) to encourage the lowering of barriers within Europe, especially by promoting freer movement of people, ideas and information and by developing co-operation in its various aspects between the two halves of Europe, not forgetting the neutrals;

(*c*) to contribute to conditions which may in the long term somewhat increase the freedom of manoeuvre of the East European countries with regard to the Soviet Union.[5]

10. Western defensive aims are the converse of the Soviet aims set out in paragraph 5 above. They are in order of priority:

(*a*) to maintain Western unity on which our security chiefly depends;
(*b*) to prevent the creation of an atmosphere of euphoria which would weaken political resistance to Soviet aims in Europe and undermine parliamentary and public support for necessary defence measures; and
(*c*) to frustrate any attempt to slow down or prejudice the movement towards Western European integration.

11. Much will depend on the extent to which the West is able to secure, in the second stage, practical improvements in the development of human contacts and information, which we regard as an essential element of both security and co-operation. If no improvements were forthcoming, and we nevertheless agree to proceed to the third stage of the conference on Soviet terms, our positive aims would be frustrated. We should be exposed to serious criticism from public opinion, which has reacted strongly against the current campaign against dissidents in the Soviet Union.[6] Furthermore, Western ability to maintain its defensive aims in the aftermath of the conference would also be weakened. The West should therefore seek at the second stage to convince the Russians that they are faced with two alternatives: either to achieve a successful conclusion to the Conference, at the price of committing themselves to concrete measures designed to secure genuine improvements in relations in Europe; or to have their policies of *détente* exposed as hollow.

12. In this connection the level and timing of the third stage will be important bargaining counters. Under the terms of the Final Recommendations we are virtually committed to a third stage of some kind; we are not committed to any particular level or date. (The relevant sections of the Final Recommendations read: '(10) In the light of the recommendations drawn up by the Co-ordinating Committee, the Conference will meet for its third stage. (11) The level of representation at the third stage will be decided by the participating States during the Conference, before the end of the second stage. (62) The date of the opening of the third stage shall be decided during the second stage by agreement among the participating States on the basis of the recommendations of the Co-ordinating Committee.') Western Governments should aim to defer any discussion of arrangements for the third stage until comparatively late in the second stage. It is important that delegations should avoid any action during the opening months which might prejudge the eventual decision.

[5] In a letter of 31 August to Dr. M.W. Holdgate of the Department of the Environment Mr. Wiggin confessed that those in the FCO who had been dealing with the CSCE for some time could not be 'described as starry eyed about it'. He would, he wrote, 'be pleased and surprised if concrete benefits resulting from it even [began] to match up in terms of cost-effectiveness to all the effort that [had] been put into it' (WDW 1/20).

[6] Cf. No. 45.

Attitude of the Neutrals

13. The neutral and non-aligned countries were on the whole sympathetic to the Western case during the Preparatory Talks, and this did much to contribute to our success. The Austrians, Swedes and Swiss provided particularly effective support. The attitude of these countries will be equally important during the second stage and their basic sympathies are likely to remain with the West. But their active support cannot be taken for granted.

14. It is possible that the Swiss will feel constrained by their position as hosts to act more as brokers than principals on subjects other than their own proposal on the peaceful settlement of disputes; there are indications from the meeting of the Co-ordinating Committee on 29-31 August that the Swedes will prove less robust than in Helsinki;[7] and the fact that the Finns are now likely to play a more active rôle may encourage the formation of a neutral bloc keeping some distance from the West. This would clearly suit the Russians very well, and they will no doubt seek to encourage the neutrals in this direction. Both the Soviet draft on principles and the Czech contribution on continuing machinery seem designed to attract support from the middle ground.[8]

15. On other points, however, the Soviet approach is unlikely to appear satisfactory to the neutrals, who would like to see the Conference produce practical results. The Swiss have put forward detailed proposals on the peaceful settlement of disputes,[9] referred to above; the Swedes will probably have something to offer on disarmament; and other neutral and non-aligned countries, e.g. the Yugoslavs, may have contributions to make—which, although not necessarily acceptable to the West may well correspond in their degree of detail to the Western rather than the Eastern approach to the second stage.

Tactics

16. The Russians will no doubt seek to give priority to the Declaration of Principles, hoping that the lengthy discussions at the Preparatory Talks and their own relatively uncontroversial draft will permit agreement to be reached fairly quickly. They would then, having achieved their major substantive objective, argue that the work on the other 'less important' items should be concluded by a named date or as soon as possible, with outstanding issues left to interested parties to pursue bilaterally or in the continuing machinery. They can be expected to do their utmost to evade or cut short substantive debate on human contacts and information; and they will probably argue that the outcome of the second stage should be confined to the production of general declarations corresponding in form to those which

[7] In a letter of 11 October Sir G. Millard warned Mr. Bullard that he had derived the impression from a talk with the Political Director of the Swedish Foreign Ministry that the Swedes had decided to present a lower profile at Stage II, especially on Basket III, and that they would concentrate on their own ideas on disarmament. They hoped that this and their status as a neutral would allow them to play 'a rewarding role as honest brokers' (EN 2/6).

[8] See *Human Rights*, vol. i, pp. 357-61 and pp. 366-7.

[9] *V. ibid.*, vol. iii, pp. 185-265.

they and their allies tabled during the first stage. They can also be expected to press hard for an early commitment to the third stage being held as soon as possible and at Summit level.

Western Tactics

17. Western delegations should seek to prevent such an outcome. In particular, we should:

(i) continue to resist artificial deadlines for the conclusion of the second stage;

(ii) emphasize that the Final Recommendations require the Committees and sub-Committees to prepare or consider proposals over a wide range of specific subjects;

(iii) argue in consequence that the form of the decisions of the Conference on any specific subject should be whatever is most appropriate to the particular case (the Final Recommendations speak of 'declarations, recommendations, resolutions or any other final documents');

(iv) seek to ensure a sufficient degree of parallelism in the work on all major subjects to make it difficult for the Russians to land their fish first; and

(v) insist that all the other work must be done properly before a decision can be taken on the timing and level of the third stage.

18. The attitude of the neutral and non-aligned countries will be particularly important. We hope that they will support a thorough and detailed second stage of the sort envisaged in the Final Recommendations. It may be tactically advisable to encourage them by expressing sympathy for 'worthy' initiatives on individual subjects (e.g. on the military aspects of security) even though in substance these may be somewhat unreal, or unnegotiable, or of little interest to us. We should undertake to consider on their merits any neutral or non-aligned proposals falling within the terms of reference.

Specific British Considerations

19. We share the Western objectives stated above but it may be useful to consider in more detail points of particular interest to the United Kingdom. The CSCE is important to us both as a major development in East/West relations and because it has become something of a test case for the development of foreign policy co-ordination among the Nine. These points are considered separately below, together with the question of co-ordination within the Alliance.

(a) East- West Relations

20. From the point of view of East/West relations we regard the Western defensive aims as being the most important at least in the short term, since failure to achieve them would be immediately damaging. Our positive aims are essentially longer term, and the CSCE will at best be only a step in the right direction. Taking an optimistic view one could perhaps see its main positive results as being (in Agenda item order):

(a) a declaration on principles which is clearly incompatible with the

Brezhnev doctrine, which emphasizes the importance in a European context of human rights and self-determination, and which sets a useful precedent for future bilateral declarations or communiques;

(b) some useful though modest confidence building measures of a politico-military kind;

(c) an undertaking to take practical measures to facilitate East/West trade and economic co-operation;

(d) increased self-confidence among the East European states and a weakening rather than a tightening of the Soviet grip upon them; and,

(e) some small but tangible results in the field of human contacts and information, coupled with a general recognition of the relevance of these subjects to the strengthening of security and the development of co-operation.

Of these, we regard the last as the most important.

21. We do not expect the Russians and their allies to make radical changes in their political systems; and it would be unrealistic to think that as a result of the CSCE '*The Times*' will be freely available in Moscow. But we consider the Soviet attitude to human contacts and information to be a fair test of the sincerity of the Russians in pursuing a policy of *détente* as we understand it, and we believe that there are modest but useful measures which they should be pressed to take as the price for a successful conclusion to the Conference. We do not regard our own proposals for linked television discussion programmes or for a new international magazine as in themselves essential to the success of the Conference.[10] But they afford examples of the sort of measure to which we would expect a successful Conference to agree.

22. Our general approach to the second stage will clearly affect our relations with the Soviet delegation, which is even stronger than that which they fielded at the Preparatory Talks and once again greatly senior to our own. Since the first stage in Helsinki the Russians have indicated that British co-operation with them in Geneva (which in practice would mean acting as their accomplices in achieving the kind of second stage they want) would bring us rewards in the bilateral context. It will be necessary to demonstrate at the outset that these are not our intentions and that in Geneva as at Helsinki we shall be loyal members of the Alliance and energetic exponents of *détente* as we define it. This means on the one hand speaking up firmly in defence of our own interests and of procedural correctness, exposing Soviet tactics where necessary; and at the same time working patiently and constructively for agreed solutions where these are attainable without sacrifice of principle.[11] There are no specific circumstances or reasons for adopting any other line than this.

[10] *V. ibid.*, vol. i, pp. 384-5.

[11] Mr. P.S. Preston (Deputy Secretary at the DTI) wrote to Mr. Wiggin on 5 October 'we should make certain we do not get out of line with our Western partners in being excessively anxious to pinpoint the weaknesses in the Russian and Eastern European case'. While he

(b) Co-ordination of the Nine

23. We wish to maintain and if possible improve on the satisfactory co-ordination among the Nine which was a notable feature of the Preparatory Talks. This will not be easy. The French, in particular, have shown distinct impatience at the degree of harmonization urged upon them by their partners; they may become increasingly difficult to restrain; and the Belgians, often with Dutch support, tend to make matters worse by going too far in the other direction and insisting on a discipline far beyond what is attainable. Morale among the Nine has recently been adversely affected by their failure to agree on how to handle the question of contributions from non-participating States; and the French and Italians on the one hand and the Dutch and Danes on the other can all be faulted for short-cutting or evading the normal processes of consultation.

24. We hope that effective though not necessarily over-formal methods of consultation will rapidly become established in Geneva; and that the Nine will play as effective a rôle during the second stage as they did during the Preparatory Talks. The delegation should treat the co-ordination of policies and tactics with our partners as a task of major importance.

(c) Co-ordination in the Alliance

25. We do not wish the development of co-ordination among the Nine to take place at the expense of effective consultation within the Alliance, and we hope that the Nine and the Fifteen will work in harmony. It may not always prove easy to avoid difficulties of the sort which appeared during the Preparatory Talks, but experience suggests that the main requirement is that our non-EEC allies should be quickly and fully informed of what is being discussed in the Nine. This again is a subject to which the delegation should attach importance, although they should seek to ensure that the burden of maintaining relations between the Nine and the Fifteen is not shouldered by the United Kingdom alone.

26. The key to an effective working relationship between the Nine and NATO will again be the Americans. They have hitherto taken little real interest in the CSCE and they may be tempted for reasons connected with their bilateral relationship with the Russians, to work for an early conclusion to the second stage. This would not only weaken the Western position generally, but would almost certainly give rise to a serious dispute between the Americans and the Nine. The Delegation should discreetly encourage the Americans to play an active rôle in promoting agreed Western initiatives, especially on Agenda Item III.

thought that the East should not be allowed to get away with 'misleading or fallacious arguments', he hoped it would not always be the UK which had 'to rush first into the breach'.

No. 47

Sir A. Douglas-Home to Mr. D.H.T. Hildyard¹ (UKMIS Geneva)

No. 264 Telegraphic [EN 2/4]

Priority. Confidential   FCO, *20 September 1973, 6.30 p.m.*

Repeated for information to Priority UKDEL NATO and to Routine Paris, Bonn, Washington, Moscow and to Saving Copenhagen, Helsinki, The Hague, Brussels, Luxembourg, Dublin, Athens, Ankara, Oslo, Reykjavik, UKREP Brussels, Berne.

Your tel[egram] No 393:²

CSCE: Third Committee

We agree with your assessment that the Russians will continue to press for work on a declaration to be done at the same time as discussion proceeds in the Sub-Committees. While we recognise that the Swiss proposal would have been very difficult to oppose (especially in view of the earlier Swiss support for the Western position) we are concerned that it gives the Russians too much ammunition for the meeting of the Coordinating Committee on 1 October.³

2. We do not exclude consideration of an overall declaration at the appropriate time. But work on an anodyne text of the sort which would satisfy the East is all too likely to proceed more quickly than the negotiation of specific proposals put forward by the West. We think it will prove extremely difficult to control the pace of work in the Committee once it gets under way. We naturally wish to avoid a situation where the East could point to 'results' from the third Committee before our points had been met: and we think that the best way of doing this will be to try to postpone the start of work on a

¹ HM Ambassador and Permanent Representative to the Office of the UN and other International Organisations in Geneva.

² This telegram of 18 September described how in Committee III the Soviet Union and its allies had mounted a coordinated attempt to secure separate and early discussion of paragraphs 42-44 of the Final Recommendations, evidently with a view to ensuring that a forum existed for tabling in its entirety a Polish/Bulgarian draft declaration on the basic guidelines for the development of cultural cooperation, contacts and exchanges of information (see *Human Rights*, vol. i, pp. 375-8). The Nine and the Swiss opposed this tactic, arguing that 'work must begin in and be confined to the existing Sub-Committees'. The ensuing deadlock was broken by the East's acceptance of a Swiss proposal that the Coordinating Committee be asked when organising the work of Committee III and its subsidiary organs, as from 1 October, to take into consideration the Committee's wish to deal with these paragraphs 'selon un rhythme qui sera fonction du travail des sous-commissions'. In Mr. Hildyard's opinion this formula met the essential Western interest since it ensured that progress made in the Sub-Committees would determine the pace of work in Committee III (WDW 1/18).

³ Mr. Fall considered that the compromise proposal (*v. ibid.*) gave the Russians 'their point on "separate", and leaves them the "early" to fight for in the Coordinating Committee'. He was concerned that the West had now accepted the Soviet thesis that the outcome of Agenda Item III would be more than the sum of the agreements reached in the Sub-Committees and hoped that when the point was taken up in the Coordinating Committee Western delegations 'will refuse to "deal with" paragraphs 42 and 43 until the work of the sub-committees is very much further advanced' (minute to Mr. Tickell of 19 September).

general declaration until we have a much clearer idea of what the Sub-Committees will produce.

3. The Soviet argument that there is something in preambular paragraphs 42 and 43 which requires discussion other than in the context of the Sub-Committees does not stand up to examination. Moreover, it is difficult to see how the contents of a general declaration reflecting the work of the Conference could usefully be discussed until the Sub-Committees have had sufficient time to examine the proposals before them. We cannot prevent the Warsaw Pact countries from introducing their draft declaration in each of the four Sub-Committees, where the relevant parts could be taken into account as appropriate. But we think this would be preferable to premature consideration of the draft as a whole in the Committee.

4. We hope that you will be able to persuade our partners and allies to take a robust line at the next meeting of the Coordinating Committee.

No. 48

Mr. Hildyard (UKMIS Geneva) to Sir A. Douglas-Home
No. 417 Telegraphic [*WDW 1/18*]

Immediate. Confidential   GENEVA, *29 September 1973, 8.34 a.m.*

Repeated Priority UKDEL NATO and Routine Washington, Paris, Bonn, Moscow, Copenhagen, Rome, UKREP Brussels and Saving other NATO Posts, Dublin, Stockholm, Belgrade, Vienna, Berne, Madrid, Warsaw, Prague, Helsinki.

From UKDEL to CSCE.
My telegram Number 411:[1]

CSCE

1. The situation on the eve of the meeting of the Co-ordinating Committee is as follows.

Committee I

2. In Sub-Committee I on principles general discussion began today with a number of Western speakers including ourselves, firmly making three points:

(*a*) The decision on the form of a document must follow and not precede discussions on the substance:

(*b*) We are not aiming to create a special body of international law relating to Europe:

(*c*) The primacy of the UN Charter should be explicitly stated.

[1] This telegram of 26 September reported agreement that day, in an informal working group, on a procedural formula for adoption by Committee III Sub-Committees providing for the point-by-point examination of participants' directives and the subsequent formulation of final proposals. Sub-committee work had hitherto been blocked by the East's resistance to Western draft agenda, and Mr. Hildyard considered acceptance of the new text 'a distinct gain for us' since the Russians thereby acknowledged the need for working bodies to proceed in orderly fashion through the points in the relevant paragraphs of the Helsinki Recommendations and accepted the clear distinction between discussion and drafting stages (WDW 1/15).

3. There was no significant contribution from the East. The Greeks requested circulation of a form of words on indivisibility of principles (text follows by bag).[2]

4. In Sub-Committee II work is now well advanced, with a large number of new proposals on the table (see my telegrams numbers 418, 419, 420).[3] There is thus plenty of meat for discussion which, if Sub-Committee I begins to run out of material, should stand us in good stead in resisting any attempt to cut short work in Committee III.

5. In the Special Working Body today the Swiss gave an oral *exposé* and circulated a summary (text by bag),[4] of their proposal. The Swiss delegate, who is the author of the proposal, revealed that he would be unable to attend further meetings until 15 October. As a result, it was agreed that discussion of the Soviet and Romanian proposals[5] would start next week and continue for a fortnight, to be followed by a fortnight on the Swiss proposal. The periods of alternation will be reviewed at the end of October. This procedure may not in fact prove too disadvantageous for us. For a variety of reasons it may well not be possible to hold many meetings before 15 October. We suggest that legal adviser should stand by to leave at any time after that date.

Committee II

6. Western Heads of Delegations decided yesterday to seek prompt agreement on procedural questions even at the cost of dropping the detailed agenda, so that this issue would not go to the Co-ordinating Committee. Agreement was reached in the commercial exchanges Sub-Committee this afternoon to use the formula reached in Committee III,[6] together with a statement read by the Austrian (but drafted and negotiated largely by US for the Nine) which indicated that there will be rotation of items, that effectively discussion will be on individual elements of the mandate, and that the goal will be two meetings on each item in the initial stages. This should preserve our main interests in this matter, especially as the Russians have repeatedly assured us that in practice they accept our ideas on procedure. Substantive business is to start at the next meeting. Science and technology Sub-Committee then quickly agreed on a variant of this formula and the industrial Co-operation Sub-Committee is expected to do so at its next meeting.

Committee III

7. The Committee III working bodies have had several sessions on the substance of their mandates which have been mainly general in character. The Russians and East Europeans have adopted a highly restrictive and defensive posture. In all the working bodies they have urged that discussion

[2] Not printed. See *Human Rights*, vol. iii, p. 94.

[3] These telegrams of 29 September commented on the latest proposals tabled on disarmament and MBFR questions by Sweden, Yugoslavia and Romania, and on CBMs by Spain and Sweden (WDW 1/22).

[4] Not printed. See No. 46, note 9.

[5] See No. 40, note 6, and *Human Rights*, vol. iii, pp. 266-70.

[6] See note 1 above.

should focus on the appropriate parts of the Polish/Bulgarian draft resolution.[7] They have mainly confined themselves to generalities, emphasised the importance of observing strictly the principle of non-interference and respect for different social systems and given priority to institutional over personal contacts. Our main intervention was made in the Sub-Committee on information yesterday in which we underlined the importance which HMG attach to the results achieved in Committee III and pointed out the relationship between genuine *détente* and progress in the humanitarian field. We took the line that the task of the Sub-Committee was to identify and remove barriers and drew attention in unambiguous terms to Eastern restrictions on the importation of printed matter and to interference with broadcasts. We also demonstrated the irrelevance of Eastern references to non-interference. There was no immediate reaction to this statement. But it had the desired effect of bringing the discussion down to the real issues and in this Sub-Committee the East Europeans (the Russians are typically leaving the running to them) are now explicitly defending the rights of their authorities to control the flow of information to their peoples so that disruptive and corrupting influences are excluded.

Western Coordination

8. Intentions as regards Western co-ordination are good but, largely because of the present pace of work in the Conference, the system has not been working particularly well in practice. The effect on the cohesion of the Nine of the earlier clash between the French and Italians on the one hand and the Dutch and the Danes on the other over the contributions of Mediterranean states has not been entirely overcome.[8] The Dutch representative at a meeting of the Nine this morning firmly rebuked the French for an article in *Figaro* of 24 September which quoted criticism by the French delegation of the Dutch and Italian delegations, apparently for taking an unreasonably hard line at the Conference. The fact that the French are straining at the leash to table their principles paper,[9] and differences over the role to be accorded to the Commission[10] are not helping. While in NATO Norwegian failure to clear their paper on confidence building measures[11] properly has had a bad effect.[12] We have every confidence however that as

[7] See No. 47, note 2.

[8] See No. 44, note 4.

[9] For the text of this French draft Declaration on Principles, as eventually tabled, see *Human Rights*, vol. iii, pp. 105-8. The British did not initially favour its tabling, preferring for tactical reasons to press either for discussion of individual principles on the basis of Western papers or to fill out the French draft with language from them (telegram No. 270 to UKMIS Geneva of 25 September). It was felt in the FCO that once the French had tabled their paper it would be impossible 'to persuade the Russians to take seriously any Western texts which went beyond the French draft' (telegram No. 718 to Paris of 28 September, WDW 1/6).

[10] See No. 50.

[11] See *Human Rights*, vol. iii. pp. 296-8.

[12] Mr. Tickell informed the Norwegian Embassy on 27 September that Norway's action had 'cut across the present NATO discussions and set a thoroughly bad precedent'. It seemed as

the many new faces get to know each other better the practical difficulties will be overcome (especially if the future pace of work of the Conference is less intense than hitherto). And everybody recognises the importance of maintaining Western cohesion.

Prospects

9. We do not share Andréani's gloom about the present state of play (Paris telegram number 1279).[13] We foresee problems over maintaining parallelism between Committees I and III. The Eastern attitude in Committee III working bodies is depressing and there is clearly a long struggle ahead if we are to achieve anything worthwhile here. But we would not agree that the Conference is off to a bad start. On procedure and substance we are in a good posture in all the working bodies except perhaps because of the delay in the appearance of the Swiss document, in the Special Working Group. The neutrals are generally taking a helpful line. Nor do we accept the implication of Andréani's remarks about unrealistic Western proposals. Our assessment is that we stand to achieve more in the face of the negative Eastern stance in Committee III by making a high bid in the early stages of the Conference.

though the Russians were intent on robbing CBMs of any substance, and Mr. Burns felt the West would need to display 'much stubborn patience' before the Russians recognised they could not succeed. He feared that any indication of Western differences would only encourage their intransigence (letter from Mr. Burns to Mr. Adams of 1 October, WDW 1/22).

[13] This telegram of 27 September reported that M. Andréani, who headed the French delegation to Stage II, had, in conversation with a member of HM Embassy in Paris, insisted on the importance of there being another draft on principles on the table in Committee I. M. Andréani further stated that the West 'could not artificially drag out the discussion of Item 1 for very long and that whatever [was done] it would be over long before [they] were ready to agree on Item 3' (WDW 1/6).

No. 49

Sir A. Douglas-Home to Mr. Hildyard (UKMIS Geneva)
No. 279 Telegraphic [WDW 1/18]

Priority. Confidential   FCO, *5 October 1973, 5.35 p.m.*

Repeated Priority UKDEL NATO and Routine Paris, Bonn, Moscow, Helsinki, Copenhagen, Rome, UKREP Brussels, Berne and Saving Washington, Ottawa, The Hague, Brussels, Luxembourg, Lisbon, Ankara, Athens, Oslo, Stockholm, Vienna, Dublin, Reykjavik, Madrid, Prague, Warsaw, Budapest, Bucharest, Sofia, Belgrade, Nicosia, Valletta, BMG Berlin, UKDIS Geneva, UKMIS NY, Holy See, East Berlin.

For UKDEL to CSCE. Your telegram No. 433[1] and telecon Elliott/Tickell.
CSCE Coordinating Committee

1. We are glad that agreement has been reached on a less intensive programme of meetings. We are less happy with the detailed arrangements

[1] This telegram of 4 October reported on the work of the Coordinating Committee during 1-4 October.

set out in paragraphs 2 and 3 of your telegram under reference.[2]

2. Our main objective is to ensure that work on the declaration of principles in Committee I and work on human contacts and information in Committee III proceed as far as possible in parallel. It is therefore important that we should not agree to procedural arrangements which make this more difficult.

3. The programme for the first fortnight of the second stage which was agreed at the meeting of the Coordinating Committee at the end of August provided for an equal number of meetings of all the working bodies involved. This arrangement was acceptable though less than ideal. The present agreement to give equal time to each of the three Committees for the next six weeks will make it much less easy to preserve the right degree of parallelism. We therefore regret that the working group allowed itself to be 'rail-roaded' in the way you describe. We are surprised that other Western delegations did not provide more effective opposition.

4. It is unfortunate that the Swiss, for their own reasons, should have joined with the Russians in advocating procedural arrangements which are not in the general Western interest. You might take a suitable opportunity to make this point gently to Bindschedler[3] and remind him that progress on the Swiss proposals for the peaceful settlement of disputes will depend to a considerable extent on continued Western benevolence.

5. We note that you consider it possible to take corrective action at the meeting of the Coordinating Committee on 18 October and within the working bodies. We think that this is a task to which the Nine and the Fifteen should give priority.[4]

[2] These paragraphs described a wrangle over the future work programme of the CSCE with 'the Russians pressing for a continuing rapid pace (about nine meetings per day) and the West and certain neutrals for a substantial reduction (six meetings per day)'. A compromise was eventually reached through the medium of a working group under Swiss chairmanship involving roughly seven meetings per day. Mr. Hildyard considered this solution satisfactory, although the disadvantage of the agreed programme was that it involved an equal amount of time being allocated to the work of each Committee as a whole. Since there were more Sub-Committees under Committee III than under Committee I, this could lead to Committee I subjects getting ahead of Committee III. The working group had, according to Mr. Hildyard, been 'railroaded' into this by the Russians, who wanted swift progress on Basket I, and the Swiss, who had the same interest in the Special Working Body. The Nine had concluded that given 'the days of exhausting argument' spent elaborating the compromise, it would not be profitable to persuade the Coordinating Committee to reverse the working group's recommendation.

[3] Herr R.L. Bindschedler headed the Swiss delegation to Stage II.

[4] When at a meeting of NATO Heads of Delegation on 17 October Mr. Elliott suggested that the West should press for a review of the present arrangements, he received no support from any of the other delegates. The unanimous feeling was that the present work programme had not in practice led to a serious imbalance in the rate of progress in Committees I and III and that an awkward precedent might be set. Any attempt to reopen the issue at the forthcoming Coordinating Committee was regarded as premature (UKMIS Geneva telegram No. 471 of 17 October, WDW 1/15).

No. 50

Mr. Hildyard (UKMIS Geneva) to Sir A. Douglas-Home
No. 441 Telegraphic [WDW 1/18]

Immediate. Confidential   GENEVA, *9 October 1973, 11.35 a.m.*

Repeated for information to Immediate UKREP Brussels, Copenhagen and to Priority Helsinki, and to Saving EEC Posts, Moscow, East Berlin, Warsaw, Budapest, Bucharest, Sofia, Prague.

From UKDEL to CSCE.
Your tel[egram] No. 258 to Copenhagen (not to all):[1]
Meeting of Political Directors: CSCE/EEC

1. Questions of Community competence and the participation of the Commission, of interest essentially in Committee II of the CSCE, have pre-occupied the Ad Hoc Group so far and are likely to be raised at the Political Committee even though little needs immediate decision.

2. Our brief is to use the CSCE for developing the CCP[2] and encouraging the East to deal with the Commission. The CSCE is clearly not the place to evolve new common policies or to extend competence. There is, however, so much unclarity about the precise limits of Community competence that we shall inevitably be engaged in interpretation case by case, with consequent decisions about who takes the lead. It is too early to say whether the first case, resolved by COREPER's[3] judgement of Solomon sharing responsibility between the Commission and the Presidency, will avoid real difficulties in the future but it should help.[4]

3. There is, of course, no question but that the Presidency speaks on questions of common interest. Although there has been no explicit agreement in the Ad Hoc Group on the merits of the Presidency speaking for the Nine where competence is doubtful or mixed, it has emerged that where there is Community interest without agreement on competence this is the most likely compromise solution (even the Commission representative privately accepts this). It seems to us that the main criterion is that the Community should not damage itself in the CSCE because of internal theological disputes but be ready to operate pragmatically when necessary. In practice, we would normally be on middle ground with the FRG, Netherlands and Italy.

4. There is a latent problem over the possible Community offer, which the

---

[1] This telegram of 8 October transmitted the agenda received from the Danes for the meeting of Political Directors in Copenhagen, scheduled for 11-12 October. It also requested points for briefing (WDW 1/15).

[2] Common Commercial Policy.

[3] Committee of Permanent Representatives (Comité des Représentants Permanents) to EC.

[4] On 3 October COREPER agreed that at Stage II: (1) the country holding the EC Presidency would speak first in tabling papers on matters of Community competence; (2) Commission representatives in the Presidency delegation would set out the substance of the document; and (3) delegations of any other member state could then contribute within the framework of the Community's position (UKREP Brussels telegram No. 4633 of 3 October, MT 10/598/2).

Commission seem still to hanker after making explicitly and fairly early in the Conference.[5] This reflects the apparent difference between their concept of the CSCE (or its second Committee) as an economic negotiation (privately they have spoken of their negotiating role in a last-minute drafting trade-off) and our own view of the Conference as political and our line that in the Commercial Exchanges Sub-Committee any Eastern concessions are in their own interest and should not be paid for. The formulation of any such offer is, we understand, the main business of the Ad Hoc Group of COREPER but both Ad Hoc Groups may both be involved in its timing. These issues have not yet come to a head and it might be useful to reaffirm understandings on them at Copenhagen this week.[6]

5. Further differences are most likely over competence on 'obstacles to trade', where competence is arguably mixed and there might be a risk that the Commission, if given its head, would project its own view of the Conference as a negotiation. However, the Community offer itself cannot be made without the consent of the Nine. Perhaps the CSCE experts should therefore consider whether this risk is acceptable, given the help the Commission can give in criticizing Eastern obstacles as well as in defending the Community from attack (where their role is undisputed).

6. The relationship between COREPER and the political machinery in regard to issues arising on the economic side of the Conference may well be raised in Copenhagen. In the light of the acceptance last week of the Commission's reference to COREPER this may be a dead issue already—and we much hope that it will not be necessary to refer other issues anywhere. But some may still think it useful to consider the hypothetical question whether economic issues unresolved here go to COREPER or to the political machinery. The question is only likely to arise on the commercial exchange front and it seems to us in practice hard to imagine such issues on which the Commission could be excluded at that stage.

[5] In November 1971 Ministers of the six original members of the EEC agreed in principle that it would be in the Community's interest if, with the support of prospective members and other allies, an 'attractive and well-balanced' trade offer were made to the Eastern Bloc at the CSCE. The EPC (Davignon) CSCE Sub-Committee stated, in a report approved by Political Directors in September 1972, that 'the subject should not be looked at in terms of "buying recognition" of the Community by the East'. But, as Mr. Fall observed in a note covered by a minute to Mr. Maxey of 16 July 1973, the 'general idea' appeared to be to use the offer 'to express, in as bold and imaginative a way as possible, the constructive willingness of the Nine to develop their economic and commercial relations with the East, and thus incidentally to persuade the CMEA member countries of the advantages of dealing with the Community on matters within its competence'. Mr. Fall added that, while the FCO did not consider the CSCE 'an appropriate forum for trade negotiations' and was against using it to work out final documents which by their nature could not be endorsed by all participants, it wanted to 'indicate the willingness of the Community to negotiate with the East, in an appropriate forum and at the appropriate time after the CSCE' (EN 2/5).

[6] In his minute of 10 October (see note 4 above) Mr. Burns commented on this passage: 'It is very tedious that the Commission should be persisting on this matter and that delegations of the Nine in Geneva seem to be incapable of taking a firm line with the Commission.'

7. Finally, there are the difficulties over who speaks for the Community, exacerbated by the unique arrangement of Commission representatives sitting in the Danish delegation, which the Danes find very uncomfortable (see also our tel[egram]s 425 and 426).[7] We doubt whether this need be discussed in Copenhagen. If the Danish paper on Commission participation is agreed here and mutual confidence can be developed, this should become less important, but it will take a lot of goodwill. Both will probably want to avoid the dual speaker device used for 'general provisions', especially as the East dislike it. We have supported the general view that major Commission speeches should be cleared in the Ad Hoc Group in advance but the pre-clearance is not necessary for subsequent interventions, which require Danish agreement on timing. As to tactics, we consider that these are more for member Governments than for the Commission and the latter have so far acted on this basis: we hope they will continue to express any views only in the Ad Hoc Group.[8]

[7] These telegrams of 2 October reported that the Ad Hoc Group had not yet succeeded in defining the scope of Community competence. The Commission held that this included everything covered by the mandate of the Commercial Exchanges Sub-Committee, but a Danish paper, apparently supported by the French, insisted that Community competence was limited to the trade policy field of paragraph 31 of the Final Recommendations. The Danes feared that if the Commission could speak on all issues in the Sub-Committee 'it might in effect do so as a "tenth power" which [would be] both incompatible with the political and sovereign state-oriented nature of the Conference and could also lead to the Danish delegation appearing to speak with two voices' (WDW 1/15).

[8] As the meeting of the Nine's Political Committee in Copenhagen did not discuss the Commission's role in the CSCE, Sir A. Douglas-Home outlined HMG's views on this and related issues in telegram No. 297 to UKMIS Geneva of 16 October. Aware of the dangers of establishing the 'wrong precedents' on Community competence, he thought the 'ideal solution would be for all to agree that the question of who speaks in Geneva on a subject in the grey area should not be regarded as involving a formal decision of competence' (WDW 1/15).

No. 51

Miss Warburton (UKMIS Geneva) to Sir A. Douglas-Home

No. 496 Telegraphic [*WDW 1/18*]

Priority. Confidential   GENEVA, *20 October 1973, 4.50 p.m.*

Repeated for information to Priority UKDEL NATO, and to Routine Brussels, Copenhagen, Dublin, Rome, Helsinki, Luxembourg, The Hague, Paris, Washington, Moscow and to Saving other NATO Posts.

From UKDEL to CSCE: Your telegram No. 478 paragraph 1:[1]

[1] This is evidently an erroneous reference to telegram No. 298 to UKMIS Geneva of 16 October, in which Sir A. Douglas-Home requested an assessment of the Western performance so far. 'Once or twice', he remarked, 'we have had the impression from your telegrams of Western disarray and willingness to accept hasty or unnecessary compromises. We are under no time pressure. Press and parliamentary opinion (so far as it focuses on the CSCE) seems largely

Western Performance

1. Coordination among the Nine is a crucial factor. Arrangements for this are adequate but the system inevitably does not work as smoothly at Geneva, where there are twelve working bodies, as it did at Helsinki, where there were three or four. The difficulty of keeping delegations in line when they want to make a special point is increased and will increase further no doubt since final documents and not merely mandates will be in preparation. The burden upon the larger countries moreover becomes relatively much heavier when there are many working bodies. At Geneva the smaller delegation can do little more than keep abreast.

2. There is unfortunately some question about the role and effectiveness in the longer term of the bigger delegations of the Nine. The Germans cause some anxiety. They are uncertainly led: Brunner has been here only once and von Groll, who is in any case erratic, comes only occasionally. There have also been signs of a certain degree of softness, or at any rate readiness to move faster than we think advisable. The Italian leadership too is uncertain. Ferraris[2] is nearly always sensible but often not here. And there are indications that the Italians may not want to stick their necks out quite so far as they did at Helsinki. The French attitude is at present sound. They no longer appear to want to give the impression of maintaining particularly good contacts with the Russians and although they are at some pains to appear conciliatory in debate they are adhering loyally to agreed Western positions on substance. (Their attitude over their Declaration of Principles is a special case.)[3] But in the longer term they could prove ready to move further and sooner than we might consider desirable in order to achieve a compromise. Andréani is the most able of Elliott's colleagues but he too is often absent and he has no single deputy.

3. In these circumstances, a greater role than would otherwise be the case could be assumed by the smaller delegations, such as the Dutch and Danes, who have Ambassadors as Heads of Delegations permanently in Geneva. Huydecoper[4] is, however, erratic and is not making much of a contribution. Mellbin[5] of Denmark, is unimpressive and is heavily occupied dealing with the chores of the chairmanship.

4. Among the Fifteen the Americans have just changed their Head of Delegation and are generally still lying pretty low.[6] The Portuguese, Turks and Greeks are very much on the margin. The Norwegians and Canadians are sound but uninspired.

favourable to the Western case, but could become critical if we were seen to fail in our publicly stated objectives.'

[2] Sig. L.V. Ferraris was a senior member of the Italian delegation.

[3] See No. 48, note 9. Further attempts to restrain the French from tabling their draft declaration had failed and on 16 October the French announced their intention of tabling it on 19 October (UKMIS Geneva telegram No. 468 of 16 October, WDW 1/6).

[4] Jonkheer J.L.R. Huydecoper van Nigtevecht headed the Dutch delegation.

[5] Herr S.G. Mellbin headed the Danish delegation.

[6] See No. 52.

5. At the level of the working bodies the calibre of the individual delegates is a vital factor. With scattered exceptions the quality of our colleagues among the Nine and Fifteen is not high and some are reluctant to play their full part in the discussions. Consequently, over the Conference as a whole, we have been playing a more or less prominent role.[7] This is generally all to the good. In Basket III, however, it has inevitably resulted in our being looked upon as the leaders of the opposition to the Russians and East Europeans. And there is at present nobody visibly to the right of us in the Western group. Informal contacts with the Russians are sporadic and they seem to have no preferred interlocutor among the Nine. Our own contacts with them are meagre. They may decide that their interests would best be served by dealing more with us. Or they could conclude that they should try to isolate us.

6. The attitude of the neutrals on procedural matters has not been helpful. The latest instance was in Committee III on 19 October (our telegram No. 490).[8] The Swiss are inclined to give undue emphasis to the need for rapid progress and the others tend to go along with them. Bindschedler's interest in peaceful settlement of disputes leads him to adopt attitudes that can be prejudicial to our interests in parallelism. And when the East secures any substantial degree of support from the neutrals it tends to get its way. On the other hand, the neutrals are with us on most matter of substance, especially in Basket III, and their role in the sub-committees has generally been helpful. Arrangements are in operation for co-ordinating with the neutrals in all Baskets but there may be room for improvement and we shall be reviewing the matter with our partners.

7. Western co-ordination has undoubtedly improved and Elliott's view is that it is about as effective in practice as it was in Helsinki. And despite the uncertain personal calibre of some of our colleagues the Western performance in the working bodies has generally been satisfactory. We have secured no indication from the East of any readiness to make concessions on the matters of importance to us but that was hardly to be expected at this stage. Nor have we given any ground: and in our judgement the West's tactical position is satisfactory. Problems of a different order will however arise for the West when the stage of preparing texts, i.e. of genuine negotiation, is

[7] As the UK delegation pointed out in UKMIS Geneva telegram No. 166 Saving of 17 October, coordination between the Nine and Fifteen in Committee II was also made difficult by the heavy programme of meetings of the Nine and the weekly rotation of chairmanship. Moreover, there was, according to this telegram, a 'reluctance among some of the Nine to make the effort' (WDW 1/20).

[8] UKMIS Geneva telegram No. 490 of 20 October reported the previous day's disagreement in Committee III between Eastern delegations, who were pressing for consideration of paragraphs 42-44 of the Final Recommendations, and the West, who considered work in the Sub-Committees insufficiently advanced to merit this. But the neutrals, despite their having been informed of Western ideas, adopted a more accommodating line and, as Miss Warburton admitted, their attitude further weakened the West's position and 'continued Western stonewalling in the Committee would not be easy to justify' (WDW 1/21).

reached. This is not imminent anywhere (although discussion in some of the Basket III[9] Sub-Committees may be hard to prolong). The need for Western co-ordination will be far greater than in the discussion phase, where our task is basically limited to presenting and defending the opening Western positions, and the task of maintaining it more complex. The Eastern delegations are strongly staffed, especially the Soviet delegation and Dubinin and Mendelevich, in particular the latter, have advocates and tacticians of the highest quality who will be quick to exploit Western disarray. From this point of view too the importance and urgency of the West's working out agreed views on long term objectives and strategy and the possible form and content of the final documents is becoming increasingly apparent.[10]

[9] UKMIS Geneva telegram No. 497 of 22 October pointed out that this should read 'Basket II'.

[10] A meeting of the Nine's CSCE Sub-Committee on 25 October soon stalled over the forms of a final document. Mr. Hildyard reported that separate British and Italian papers were before the meeting, the main difference between them being 'the Italians envisaged a more optimistic outcome to the CSCE with a number of binding agreements while ours addresses itself to the more likely practical results' (UKMIS Geneva telegram No. 513 of 27 October, MT 10/598/2).

No. 52

Minute from Mr. Fall to Mr. Tickell

[EN 2/23]

Personal and Confidential   FCO, *25 October 1973*

CSCE: Second Stage

1. I found my visit to Geneva very useful. The sub-Committee on principles had three meetings while I was there so that I was fairly fully employed as a substitute for Mr. Edes. But I also had time to move around.

General Impressions

2. Perhaps the strongest impression I got from my three days is that everyone is expecting this stage of the Conference to last at least until March of next year. Indeed, there is a tendency to assume that the serious drafting work will not start until after Christmas. Delegations with greater or lesser reluctance, are reconciling themselves to a long haul. The Finns who have reasons of their own for trying to predict the length of the second stage fairly accurately, have made their predictions fairly clear: the leader of their delegation has his children at school in Geneva and his junior colleagues have bought cars on which they will have to pay hefty taxes if they cannot keep them out of Finland for a year.

3. The second stage with ten or more working groups in action is inevitably more amorphous than the preparatory talks. Delegates in one Committee have little working contact with their colleagues in others. It is therefore not easy to form an overall picture; or, having formed it, to apply the lessons to all

the relevant working bodies. This is a problem faced by each individual delegation; and more particularly by the Nine and the Fifteen as they try to maintain and develop a common approach to the second stage as a whole.

Western Coordination

4. This seems to be working reasonably well at present. Coordination among the Nine seems fairly good on a committee by committee basis. The more important meetings of the sub-Committee at head of delegation level, one of which is taking place today, may develop into a useful management tool and I think we should do our best to encourage them. The fact that Mr. Vest[1] has now left Geneva will inevitably leave a gap which may affect coordination among the Fifteen. His successor, Mr. Boster,[2] is an experienced Soviet hand and personally extremely pleasant to do business with. But he has little multilateral experience and does not have the benefit of Vest's personal position in NATO and in dealing with the Community.

British Delegation

5. The delegation are in good spirits and seem to have settled down well. I certainly got the impression that we were effectively represented across the board and that each of the three Counsellors is well placed to exert influence in their respective committees.[3] On questions of tactics I think we will see an increasingly confident performance.

6. As far as overall leadership is concerned the arrival of Mr. Pike[4] should take some of the day to day burden of Committee III off Mr. Maxey and allow him more time to look around. But I think we should recognise that there are limits to how much he will be able to do. Committee III will generate a lot of important work and the three officers involved will be hard pressed. It is I think inevitable that during Mr. Elliott's absences from Geneva the British delegation will appear to have three deputy heads each with functional responsibilities.

7. This is likely to work fairly well in the early stages; and I do not think that we need urge Mr. Elliott to increase the frequency of his visits to Geneva in the near future. After Christmas, however, it will be much more important to have a senior head of delegation on the spot. He will be needed both to add weight to the counsels of the Nine and the Fifteen and to provide an influential point of contact with the senior Eastern and neutral representatives. This is a point which you may wish to discuss with Mr. Elliott at an appropriate time.

8. There is a further point which may be worth thinking about. Most of our partners maintain a regular personal contact with their capitals by bringing out senior officials to Geneva for meetings of the Coordinating Committee and for the more important coordination meetings of the Nine. In many cases these officials are Mr. Elliott's opposite number, and we are obviously

[1] Mr. G.S. Vest was US Head of Delegation to the CSCE, 1972-1973.

[2] Mr. D.E. Boster, special assistant to the Assistant Secretary of State for European Affairs.

[3] See No. 46, note 4.

[4] Mr. M.E. Pike was First Secretary, HM Embassy in Washington. He had been seconded to UKDEL CSCE for the final quarter of 1973 to deal with Item III issues.

not able to kill two birds with one stone in the same way. I think it may prove increasingly useful for visitors from London to participate in the proceedings in Geneva where circumstances warrant; and I hope that we can take a fairly flexible line on this.

Delegation subsistence

9. The delegation forbore to lobby me on this subject, but would clearly like an early favourable answer to their request for better financial terms. In view of the current expectations of the length of the second stage I think we should do our utmost to provide them with better conditions. A rate of subsistence appropriate to a short visit to Geneva, or even to a four or five week stay, begins to look seriously inadequate when one finds oneself living away from one's family for a period of months. The fact that a number of other delegations have secured for themselves the same terms as their colleagues permanently posted in Geneva, and have in many cases brought their families, serves to emphasize the inadequacy of our own arrangements. In the longer term it is bound to affect the morale of the delegation if they find themselves seriously out of pocket and are unable either to fly back for a weekend or to bring their wives out without going deeper into the red.

Swiss foot-note

10. The Swiss Ambassador in London did nothing to lessen the impact of your talk with him when he reported back to Berne.[5] We thrashed the matter out on an amicable basis with the Swiss delegation (with the exception of Bindschedler, who was either too angry or too senior to join us). There was inevitably a lot of special pleading on the Swiss side, but we came to the satisfactory conclusion that each should keep the other much more closely informed. The Swiss will continue to be selfish on matters affecting their own proposal, and claim to see substantive as well as tactical advantages in the Romanian proposal.[6] But they have assured us that they will be solid on the substance of Item III. Brunner told us incidentally that Bindschedler had been very angry that the paper produced by the Nine at the meeting of the Coordinating Committee last August had made no separate provision for a working body to consider the Swiss proposal;[7] and the resultant pique may

[5] At Mr. Tickell's request the Swiss Ambassador in London called at the FCO on 19 October. Mr. Tickell then told him of his fears that the Swiss, 'sometimes in their understandable desire to promote their ideas on the peaceful settlement of disputes . . . did not give full weight to the wider interests' they shared with the UK. He further complained that: (1) despite the fact that the British delegation had reluctantly agreed to the establishment of the Special Working Body to consider the Swiss proposal, the Swiss had not been willing to introduce it with the result that Romanian and Russian ideas, to which HMG strongly objected, had been given pride of place; (2) the Swiss had advocated a timetable which had given priority to Committee I over Committee III; (3) they had indicated their support for the Romanian draft on the non-use of force; (4) they had promoted a compromise which helped the Russians to press for separate discussion of the preambular paragraph relating to the work of Committee III; and (5) they had publicly expressed a preference for a 'legally binding' Declaration of Principles (telegram No. 309 to UKMIS Geneva of 19 October, WDW 1/373/1).

[6] See No. 48, notes 4 and 5.

[7] See No. 44, note 3.

explain some of the difficulties we have had with him over the priority to be given to different working bodies. If the Second Committee continues to get through its work fairly quickly, we may be able to solve this problem in practice by borrowing from II to pay III.

B.J.P. FALL

No. 53

Mr. Hildyard (UKMIS Geneva) to Sir A. Douglas-Home

No. 560 Telegraphic [WDW 1/15]

Immediate. Confidential   GENEVA, *8 November 1973, 7.22 p.m.*

Repeated for information to Priority UKDEL NATO, Helsinki, UKREP Brussels, Paris, Brussels, Bonn, and Saving to Copenhagen, Rome, Washington, Mosow, Dublin, Luxembourg, The Hague, Berne, Ottawa, Oslo, Ankara, Athens, Lisbon, Warsaw, Budapest, Bucharest, Prague, Sofia, UKDEL Vienna, East Berlin.

From UKDEL to CSCE: My tel[egram] No. 548:[1]
CSCE: Meeting of Political Directors

1. It may be convenient for you to have our assessment of the present situation.

2. The report of the Sub-Committee[2] is sensible and useful, though it has become regrettably long because of the need to take account of the susceptibilities of the more intransigent members of the Ad Hoc Group. The paper as it stands is primarily the work of the French, who have been constructive in discussion. The paper also reflects a welcome community of view amongst the Nine here, not only on questions of overall strategy but also on more immediate questions of tactics and substance. It does, however, conceal one or two potentially serious disagreements, of which the question of follow-up machinery[3] and the Community offer[4] are perhaps the most significant.

[1] This telegram of 7 November up-dated the FCO on work in progress on a draft report then being prepared by the Nine's CSCE Sub-Committee and the Ad Hoc Group for the meeting of EC Political Directors at Copenhagen on 12-13 November.

[2] *V. ibid.*

[3] In a minute to Mr. J.O. Wright, Deputy Under-Secretary of State, of 9 November Mr. Tickell noted that, where the question of follow-up was concerned, the report was cautious and reflected disagreement between the French, who were now negative about the subject, and the West Germans, who were ready to envisage some kind of consultative committee meeting from time to time in European capitals. He thought that if the Conference were successful the German idea would be a good way of following up results without running the risks involved in too formal an institution. But he suspected the Germans of being 'ready to indicate their agreement to the East too early', and believed that the West could use the Soviet desire for new consultative machinery to extract more concessions from the USSR (MT 10/4).

[4] See No. 50, note 5. In its initial section the Sub-Committee report made what Mr. Tickell termed an 'unfortunate reference' to the offer as an objective of the Nine at the CSCE. This, Mr. Tickell insisted, the British would seek to have removed or toned down at Copenhagen (see notes 1 and 3 above).

First Committee

3. The Sub-Committee on principles has been discussing the fourth principle and is likely to move on to the fifth principle[5] next week. With luck, the general discussion can probably be maintained until the Christmas break. The French draft, however, has been criticised in respect of the third principle and may be losing its potential as a compromise text in favour of that tabled by the Yugoslavs.[6]

4. In the Sub-Committee on military aspects discussion is tending to falter in the face of a restrictive and defensive Soviet line. The neutrals and non-aligned are disenchanted and silent, and the NATO countries are finding it difficult to press forward in the debate in the absence of any clear agreed guidance from Brussels on many points of detail. We shall discuss this problem in a separate telegram.[7]

5. In the Special Working Body it has become apparent that, while the Russians do not accept the underlying principles of the Swiss proposal, they will not kill off the discussion. We are taking an active part in what has become a fairly sterile debate but it is apparent that not all of our partners and allies share our reluctance to give serious attention to the Romanian and Soviet proposals. These difficulties are discussed further in our tel[egram] No 557.[8]

Second Committee

6. The most important Sub-Committee in Committee II is that on commercial exchanges, but here, as in other Sub-Committees, there have

[5] The fourth principle related to the territorial integrity of states, and the fifth to the peaceful settlement of disputes.

[6] See No. 51, note 3, and *Human Rights,* vol. iii, pp. 95-9. The third principle concerned the inviolability of frontiers.

[7] The West, Mr. Hildyard explained in UKMIS Geneva telegrams Nos. 585 and 586 of 15 November, had succeeded in focusing discussion on one of the principal causes of insecurity in Europe, notably the Soviet tendency to exert military pressure on other states. Nevertheless, he thought the Sub-Committee on CBMs was 'beginning to run out of steam'. Where Western tactics were concerned, he considered the main difficulty to be that NATO delegations had little scope to speak in great detail about the modalities of CBMs without entering into matters which were not fully agreed within the Alliance. The Americans had already indicated their concern over the inclusion in CBMs of the prior notification of major military 'movements' which, they argued, would adversely affect movements of forces of NATO countries from Europe to crisis areas. They also thought that such a provision would impinge upon the negotiation of movement constraints in the MBFR context (WDW 1/22).

[8] In this telegram of 8 November Mr. Hildyard reported that the East had made their negative attitude towards the Swiss proposal as clear as they were ever likely to do, and that by insisting that resort to systems of peaceful settlement of dispute must always be made on a voluntary basis they had, in effect, rejected the fundamental principle of the Swiss proposal i.e. compulsory arbitration of legal disputes after the exhaustion of all other peaceful means (see No. 46, note 9). Without acceptance of this principle by at least one East European state, the proposed convention would, in Western eyes, serve no useful purpose, and amongst the Nine and the Fifteen there was, according to Mr. Hildyard, 'almost unanimous dislike of the Swiss proposal in anything like its present form' and a belief that no useful convention would emerge (WDW 1/29).

been few excitements and few initiatives. This is largely because, with the exception of the East on MFN and the West on information and contacts, the participants are reluctant to appear as *demandeurs*. The result is a definite air of *déja vu*, reducing still further the significance of Committee II in the Conference.

7. Our main current problems are intra-Western:

(i) The deep-seated reluctance of some members of the Ad Hoc Group (in particular Belgium, France and the Commission) to co-ordinate positions with our NATO Allies. This is partly the result of the Ad Hoc Group spending so much time reaching agreement among themselves that there is little time or energy left over for broader consultations: but it also reflects an underlying suspicion of our NATO partners not shown by their colleagues in Committees I and III. We are trying to make more sensible counsels (your telegram number 342)[9] prevail through action at head of delegation level (we continue, however, to have reservations on the French idea of informal NATO consultations in the cafeteria). Meanwhile, it would be helpful if our representatives at the Political Directors meeting could expound the ideas in your telegram under reference and try to have them reflected in the conclusions of the meeting. Brussels may wish to comment on how far the rigid attitude of the Belgians stems from Davignon himself.[10] The effectiveness of the Nine in the CSCE is dependent to a considerable extent on the support of our NATO allies which some of the Ad Hoc Group are needlessly jeopardising.

(ii) The question of the Community offer and the economic outcome of the CSCE. We are telegraphing separately on this issue,[11] which is not ready for discussion in Copenhagen next week.

Third Committee

8. All the Sub-Committees are nearing the end of the first reading of their terms of reference without our having gained any clear indications of how far the East may be prepared to go towards accepting Western proposals on the most important items. The discussions between now and the Christmas break must be more structured and positive and we are hopeful that the French discussion papers, if they are accepted by the East (our tel[egram] No. 534)[12] may help to achieve this and to clarify the possible areas of accord.

[9] In this telegram of 6 November Sir A. Douglas-Home maintained 'there should normally be consultation with the non-Community allies before the positions of the Nine are communicated to other delegations' (WDW 1/20).

[10] Viscount Davignon told Sir J. Beith that he accepted that Belgian representatives at Geneva were 'operating under very firm instructions' designed to ensure that any idea of what he called an 'open-ended group of 16' made no progress. He added that once the idea of constituting such a group, which he thought would be a 'real dog's breakfast', was dropped, 'the Belgians would be found to be much more flexible' (Brussels telegram No. 515 of 9 November, MT 10/579/1).

[11] See No. 55.

[12] Mr. Hildyard reported in this telegram of 3 November a French idea for 'cutting up and regrouping all the papers on the table under the relevant headings of the Final

Follow-up

9. There has not been any new pressure from the Russians to open discussion on follow-up machinery although they have threatened to import the subject into the SWB. The Fifteen agreed today that any move to include meetings of the Working Body on Item IV in the programme of the Conference before the Christmas break should be firmly resisted: and that it should be made clear to the East that the question of meetings thereafter is dependent upon adequate progress on Item III in the next month. The dubious element as regards the principle of follow-up machinery are the Germans who are showing a far more positive attitude than the rest of the Nine towards such machinery (see also para. 5 of our tel[egram] No. 557).[13] Any guidance that you or Bonn could provide on the Germans' views and motives would be helpful in determining how far the Western position is likely to be weakened by this difference of view.

The standing of the UK

10. In a situation in which coordination amongst the Nine has much improved, we remain prominent in debate but less exposed as hard-liners. There is little to add to the assessment of Western performance in my tel[egram] No. 496,[14] but coordination *à neuf* is tighter and the French are being helpful. Our contacts with the Russians remain sporadic. Those of the French seem to be closest and most frequent.

Recommendations'. The resulting document would be discussed point by point and would thus serve to focus attention on the Western papers'. The French launched their initiative in Committee III on 9 November, and on 17 November it was agreed that compendia would be prepared in consultation with delegations which had submitted proposals (UKMIS Geneva telegrams Nos. 565 and 593 of 10 and 17 November, WDW 1/21).

[13] See note 8 above. According to Mr. Hildyard, the Germans, unlike other Western powers, had appeared to find in the Swiss proposal for the peaceful settlement of disputes 'arrangements for formal bilateral discussions' which they found attractive.

[14] See No. 51.

No. 54

Mr. Hildyard (UKMIS Geneva) to Sir A. Douglas-Home

No. 596 Telegraphic [*WDW 1/18*]

Priority. Confidential   GENEVA, *17 November 1973, 8.10 a.m.*

Repeated for information to Priority UKDEL NATO, Moscow, and Saving to Helsinki, Warsaw, Prague, UKDEL Vienna, all NATO and EEC capitals, Budapest, Bucharest, Sofia, Belgrade, Berne, Stockholm, Vienna, Madrid.

From Elliott, UKDEL to CSCE:

CSCE: Eastern Attitude

1. The Russians are taking a more relaxed attitude to the pace of work at the Conference. They remain robustly negative on a great number of points of interest to the West and have conceded nothing of substance. In recent

weeks however they have shown themselves ready to desist from efforts to accelerate the work in the Sub-Committees when they have met opposition.

2. It seems clear that the Russians have now given up their hope of forcing an early conclusion to the second stage and are now thinking in terms of working until the spring. This was the strong impression I gained from Mendelevich at lunch yesterday.[1] He appeared reconciled to the fact that drafting in the Sub-Committees could not begin until the new year, though he said that Moscow would react very badly (and might even make difficulties about the beginning of the Christmas recess) if it were suggested that examination of the principles in Sub-Committee I should continue after Christmas. In conversation he threw out the idea that the drafting stage need not last more than 2 or 3 months at the most, and that on this basis it would be possible to envisage Stage II ending in April and Stage III beginning after a 4-week break perhaps in mid May or June. He made the final point that from the Soviet point of view what was important was to avoid deferring Stage III until after the summer holidays: this would have serious implications for *détente*.[2]

3. Nonetheless, the Russians and their allies appear to feel a need for some public affirmation that the Conference is proceeding satisfactorily. At the end of the Coordinating Committee on 14 November the Poles, Czechs and Russians made statements which appeared more designed for home consumption than for effect in Geneva. The Pole drew our attention to the unique character of the Conference and to our task of consolidating peace and promoting peaceful coexistence. The task of concentrating on what united rather than divided us was helped by the constructive atmosphere, the seriousness with which the Helsinki Recommendations were respected and the smart pace of work in the Sub-Committees (despite the difficulties for some). It was regrettable however that this good atmosphere was not always used to speed up work. There had been too much waste of time, especially initially for procedural reasons. This was particularly true of Committee III where some delegations were trying to discriminate between the papers tabled. The Czechs then called for discussion of agenda Item IV (follow-up), and the Russians wound up with a cry for greater productivity in the present generally constructive atmosphere.

4. There is no doubt that at the next Coordinating Committee meeting there will be further discussion of the follow-up. If as we expect certain non-aligned countries (like the Finns and the Maltese) give steady support to the Eastern proposal to begin discussion of agenda Item IV before Christmas, we may well come under greater pressure. But so far the Russians have taken a

[1] On 15 November Mr. Hildyard hosted a lunch for Mr. Elliott and Mr. Mendelevich.

[2] Mr. Elliott wrote to Mr. Tickell on 16 November that Mr. Mendelevich had also used this occasion to suggest that the British delegation 'was unduly tough and less constructive than it had been at Dipoli'. In a minute to Mr. Maxey of 15 November, which he enclosed with this letter, Mr. Elliott explained that he had rejected Mr. Mendelevich's assertion, adding that the 'simple fact was that now, as then, we had been insisting on following the inductive ("bottoms up") method'.

relatively relaxed attitude on this issue.

Conclusions

5. This adapted approach to the timetable seems to be echoed in what other material comes our way from you and Moscow. It is obviously a step towards realism on the part of the Russians, but it could still have its dangers for the West. Keeping the Nine and NATO united sometimes proves less easy in practice when Eastern pressures relax. We shall need to ensure that, in reacting to the Russians, the West does not concede that drafting is dependent on the date of Christmas (or upon the pause for reflection which the holidays afford) rather than on progress in Committee III. Fortunately the West here seems reasonably firm and realistic in its attitudes.

No. 55

Mr. Hildyard (UKMIS Geneva) to Sir A. Douglas-Home

No. 599 Telegraphic [MWE 2/8]

Priority. Confidential   GENEVA, *17 November 1973, 9.30 a.m.*

Repeated for information to UKREP Brussels, Copenhagen, and Saving to UKDEL NATO, all EEC posts and Helsinki.

From UKDEL to CSCE.
My telegram No. 567.[1]

CSCE: Committee II: Community Offer[2]

1. Discussions on the Community offer have aroused strong feelings in the Ad Hoc Group.[3] From subsequent private discussions on a bilateral basis with other members of the Group (but not so far the Commission representative), it appears that divisions are less fundamental than initially appeared the case. We are further encouraged by the relatively relaxed attitude taken by the Political Directors in Copenhagen.[4] Nonetheless, until the Nine have reached

---

[1] In UKMIS Geneva telegram No. 567 of 10 November Mr. Hildyard reported that recent discussions in the Nine on economic objectives had brought to the surface differences between the British delegates and most of the other members of the Ad Hoc Group, including the Commission. These concerned, not only the timing, but also the nature of the proposed Community offer and its relationship to broader CSCE objectives (WDW 1/20).

[2] See No. 50, note 5.

[3] See No. 53, note 4. In a minute of 13 November Mr. Kay explained to Mr. P.H.R. Marshall, his Department's Superintending Under-Secretary, the differences arising over the Sub-Committee report's reference to the Community offer as an objective of the Nine. 'Our principal aim on the economic item is', he observed, 'for the Nine to be seen to be operating as an effective force and we shall not wish to split the Nine on a largely theological point.' Mr. Marshall noted on the minute: 'This has the makings of a real shambles!' (MT 10/598/2).

[4] The document on the objectives and strategy agreed by EC Political Directors at their Copenhagen meeting (see No. 53, note 1, and note 3 above) stated that the Nine had yet to decide on whether the final CSCE documents should refer to future negotiations on commercial matters (RM (73) 20 CP: *Objectives et Stratégie des Neuf à la CSCE* of 13 November, WDW 1/15).

agreement on the basic problems involved it will be impossible for us to agree on objectives for the Commercial Exchanges Sub-Committee, and therefore to prepare draft final documents. Since these should be cleared in the Nine and Fifteen in time for tabling when the Conference re-convenes, in January, we are under some time pressure. We therefore consider that further thought should be given to the issue in capitals as soon as possible, and put forward the following analysis and proposals.

2. The offer is interpreted differently by various members of the Nine in Geneva (approximate positions acceptable to individual delegations indicated in brackets):

(a) Indicating at the Conference a willingness to negotiate subsequently with the East, but not writing anything to this effect in the final documents (UK and possibly France):

(b) Writing in a specific reference in the final document to the possibility of subsequent negotiations on the basis of reciprocity (FRG, Belgium, Italy and as a fall-back position possibly UK and France):

(c) Writing in this reference and then adding in general terms the grounds that would be covered, i.e., further liberalisation on our part in return for guarantees on prices, acceptance of safeguards, and quantitative trade commitments by the East (FRG, Belgium, Italy, Ireland and possibly the Commission):

(d) As at (c) but spelling this out further in providing a detailed list of the points on which we would be prepared to negotiate and the possible *contre-parties* we would expect in return on the basis of the COREPER *aide mémoire* of 9 March[5] (the Commission).[6]

3. The main arguments in favour of an offer, however defined, are:

(a) It would allow the CSCE to be used to strengthen the Community position *vis-à-vis* the East and in particular to develop the CCP more rapidly than would otherwise be the case:

[5] The COREPER *aide-mémoire* of 9 March, which was sent to EC Political Directors as an interim report, examined the possibility of an EEC offer to the East on the basis of an expressed readiness to negotiate tariffs and quantitative restrictions. The UK delegation to the CSCE doubted the commercial value of the proposals outlined in the paper. However, Mr. Hildyard observed in UKMIS Geneva telegram No. 618 of 26 November that, given sufficient political will on both sides, 'something cosmetic on the lines indicated in the *aide mémoire* could provide a basis for some future agreement signifying a new politico/economic climate between the EEC and Eastern European countries' (MT 10/598/2).

[6] During a meeting of the Ad Hoc Group on 2 November M. L. Kawan, the Commission's senior representative, had seemed to envisage a final document which would state that the basic problem of East/West economic relations could be solved by further liberalisation, counterbalanced by Eastern concessions on contacts and information, and by the East agreeing to give undertakings on safeguards and prices. But UK delegates gathered from subsequent discussions with Mr. Kawan that his views were less 'maximalist' than they had previously inferred and that he would prefer positions (b) or (c) (UKMIS Geneva telegrams Nos. 536 and 605 of 3 and 20 November, WDW 1/20).

(*b*) Initially at least we would be dealing with the individual countries of the East rather than with the CMEA:

(*c*) It would indicate that the East can only negotiate with us on our terms. (i.e. on the basis of effective reciprocity and directly with the Commission).

4. The main arguments against are:

(*a*) It is inappropriate to pursue at the CSCE the idea of an offer relevant only to two groups of participating states.

(*b*) Originally, a main objective of the offer was seen as persuading the East to recognise the Community. In the light of subsequent developments (notably the Fadeyev initiative)[7] it is questionable whether this need still exists and whether, by making an offer now, the Community risks appearing as demandeur.

(*c*) Since the offer was decided, difficulties have arisen in agreeing a common line on the common commercial policy. Sir C. Soames suggests (UKREP Brussels telegram No. 5351 para 8)[8] that decisions have not yet been taken in the Nine which would enable us to offer to negotiate.

(*d*) There is a risk that the East may seek to make agreement to negotiate the abolition of our remaining QRs a pre-condition for negotiations, and neither the UK nor most of the Nine are yet ready to go this far.

(*e*) An offer to negotiate later would provide the East with an excuse to avoid specific commitments in the economic Committee (notably on information and business contacts). This would probably emasculate the work of Sub-Committee 3 and possibly 4 (commercial exchanges and industrial co-operation). We see no prospect of subsequent commercial gain for ourselves to offset such political loss as this entails in terms of our CSCE objectives, since it is doubtful whether the East have anything to give of genuine value in purely economic terms. This emasculation might also damage our relations at the Conference with non-EEC NATO allies and the neutrals, some of whom would be disappointed if this area of the CSCE produced nothing.

5. This analysis of the broader context suggests that the balance of argument is against the Community making an offer of any kind at the CSCE and that therefore it would be in the interest of the UK (and the Nine) to dissuade our allies from pursuing this idea. However, our colleagues of the

---

[7] In August Mr. N.V. Fadeyev, Secretary-General of the CMEA, had approached the EC Council with a view to finding out 'whether it could accept official negotiations or discussions of how to improve relations or secure concrete results concerning trade' (UKREP Brussels telegram No. 4384 of 20 September, EN 5/1).

[8] This telegram of 6 November reported on the discussion that day in the European Council of liberalisation measures with regard to state-trading nations. Sir C. Soames, Vice-President of the EC Commission, advocated 'urgent progress' in the framing of a common commercial policy, without which, he said, 'there was no possibility of negotiations between the Community and the state trading countries' (MWE 1/22).

Nine here argue that Ministers are committed by CP(72)54[9] (the idea of an offer is known to other members of NATO and probably beyond). If we want to change the line agreed in the past, perhaps the best approach would be to urge consideration of the whole problem in Brussels. The UK might therefore focus attention on the opposing arguments at para 3 and 4 above, without stating any conclusion at first.

6. If it were decided after further consideration in Whitehall and Brussels that we must go along with the line that an offer be made then we would recommend the following approach as a fallback position:

(*a*) We should seek agreement in the Nine to an offer as near as possible to the UK position at 2(*a*) above and certainly no further than that at 2(*b*).

(*b*) The Nine should at an agreed time undertake informal discussions of this sort of offer with the East Europeans individually, but no written commitment to it would appear in any Western first draft of a final document/documents.

(*c*) If Eastern reactions were favourable, a scenario would be worked out with them (keeping our NATO allies and the neutrals appropriately informed) for handling the offer and any response to it by the East. This would present difficult problems, notably if our aim were still to avoid taking discussion of paragraph 32 of the final recommendations (business contacts and information) out of the CSCE.

(*d*) If it were necessary to have a reference in the final document/documents, the wording might be:

'The participating states recognise the necessity for bilateral and multilateral consultations. In this connection the participating states take note of the offers of negotiation made by certain states and groups of states during the course of discussion at this Conference'.[10]

7. Following recent discussion in Copenhagen, Heads of Delegations of the Nine have gone along with a Belgian proposal to discuss this subject further

[9] The Ad Hoc Group's report CP(72)54 (revised) was approved by Community Ministers on 21 November 1972. While accepting that the CSCE was an inappropriate forum for trade negotiations, it recommended that the Nine should consider indicating their readiness to negotiate with the East on tariffs and trade restrictions. Nevertheless, as Sir A. Douglas-Home recalled in telegram No. 369 to UKMIS Geneva of 21 November 1973, the report had done no more than repeat the agreement of Ministers of May 1972 'that the idea of the offer was one of the principles on which the Ad Hoc Group should continue to base its work'. The Secretary of State did 'not therefore regard British Ministers as committed to the proposition that the Community should make an offer of post-Conference trade negotiations' (WDW 1/20).

[10] In his telegram No. 369 to UKMIS Geneva (*v. ibid.*) Sir A. Douglas-Home instructed Mr. Hildyard to 'work for a consensus somewhere between the positions outlined in paragraphs 2(*b*) and 2(*c*)'. The FCO thought that, while the position in 2(*c*) was 'too specific as a great deal of work still [had] to be done before the brief could be agreed for post-CSCE negotiations', they could not 'reasonably expect to get away with a reference in a final document to negotiations which made no mention of what they were to be about'.

on 26 November.[11] We would see advantage in getting it inscribed on the agenda of the COREPER before then, in which case it might be best to confine discussions here to the implications for our CSCE objectives.[12]

[11] An informal joint meeting of delegates of the Nine on 22 November agreed that it was still premature to decide whether or not the Community should indicate at the Conference its readiness to negotiate afterwards. Mr. Hildyard thought it 'satisfactory' that others of the Nine, notably France, had taken the lead in arguing for this (UKMIS Geneva telegrams Nos. 611 and 622 of 22 and 27 November, WDW 1/20).

[12] Mr. Fall minuted to Mr. Kay on 28 November: 'We should not "strive officiously to keep alive" the idea of the offer; but neither should we try to kill it in its present fairly modest form'. Mr. W. Marsden (EID) noted on this telegram: 'I am very relaxed about this. If the Nine (or the Community in its narrow sense) needs to show willing on quotas for good CSCE reasons I would expect that the COREPER could agree to some waffly undertaking to discuss or negotiate on this after the conference. After all it has already agreed a vague commitment to work for the removal of all but a hard-core of quotas by the end of 1974. A statement in the CSCE could reflect this. W. Marsden, 21/11.'

No. 56

Letter from Mr. Maxey (UKDEL CSCE) to Mr. Tickell
[*WDW 1/6*]

Confidential   GENEVA, *21 November 1973*
CSCE: Inviolability of Frontiers
1. Since Anthony Elliott will not now be back in Geneva until Monday 26 November, I am replying to your letter of 15 November about Semenov's call.[1]

2. I am glad you replied robustly to Semenov's complaints about the unhelpful and unconstructive attitude which he says we are taking in Committee I. We quite agree with you that the Russians are trying to use the Secretary of State's visit to Moscow to persuade us to take a more pliant attitude in Geneva.[2] This is a crude gambit but one that sometimes works with our partners and allies here e.g. the West Germans. Nonetheless Semenov's remarks are interesting to the extent that they confirm the primary importance which the Russians attach to inviolability of frontiers (as did those of Mendelevich at Toby Hildyard's lunch—record attached to Elliott's letter of 16 November).[3] Moreover the details of his complaints

[1] In this letter Mr. Tickell reported that Mr. Y.A. Semenov, Political Counsellor at the Soviet Embassy in London, had called on him on 15 November to discuss what the Russians termed the 'unhelpful and unconstructive attitude' of the UK delegation to CSCE on the principle of the inviolability of frontiers.

[2] Sir A. Douglas-Home visited Moscow during 2-5 December (cf. No. 57, note 15). Mr. Tickell thought the Russians might 'also see some opportunities for wedge-driving between the Nine' (see note 1 above).

[3] See No. 54, notes 1 and 2. To Mr. Elliott's remark that the British fully supported the proposals on inviolability in the French draft declaration (see No. 51, note 3), Mr. Mendelevich

suggest that many of our arguments have struck home and that our role in the successful Western campaign to intensify and prolong the general debate on principles has annoyed the Russians.[4]

3. We have already sent to Christian Adams the detailed records of the discussions in the Principles Sub-Committee.[5] Michael Edes' own interventions have been trenchant and to the point, very much in the spirit of paragraph 22 of the steering brief.[6] But, whatever the Russians may say, they have not been polemical—rather 'suaviter in modo, fortiter in re'. The Russians have only themselves to blame if, as a result of their own insistence that the Principles Sub-Committee should meet more frequently than any other sub-committee, they have exposed themselves to more critical examination of their own ideas than they like.[7] It is they who have placed such importance upon the declaration of principles and, as the records of discussion show, almost all the non-Warsaw Pact delegations have been active in questioning and analysing the underlying intentions of the Soviet draft.[8] (But while this probing in depth may have been galling to Russian self-esteem, it has all been handled by Mendelevich with customary aplomb though without, I think, convincing many other delegations).

4. We have also had to take upon ourselves more than our fair share of the burden in the procedural arguments which have enabled the Nine and the West generally to prevent any move to drafting before Christmas: On both substance and procedure, therefore, we have assumed in this first round of Stage II our old Helsinki role of Western anchor man. Our beneficial result has been to encourage the more timid members of the Conference to speak up vigorously on the matters that concern them.

5. On the individual criticisms to which you refer in your paragraph 4,[9] I

had replied that for the Soviet delegation 'it would be unacceptable to include any reference to the idea of peaceful changes of frontiers in what was said on inviolability' (WDW 1/18).

[4] Mr. Semenov had informed Mr. Tickell (see note 1 above) that the Russians believed any qualification of the principle of the inviolability of frontiers could 'be used by German and other revanchards to effect a change of frontiers by any but peaceful means (as in the case of the Anschluss)'. He added that the Soviet Union did not exclude territorial rectifications by agreement of the parties or integration in Western or Eastern Europe.

[5] Not printed. In UKMIS Geneva telegram No. 538 of 3 November Mr. Hildyard reported that throughout the previous week Warsaw Pact countries had taken an 'uncompromisingly hard line in favour of the Soviet wording' on the inviolability of frontiers. They had particularly stressed that 'all existing frontiers in Europe should be collectively and unequivocally recognised as inviolable "on a permanent basis": that there should be a categorical prohibition of territorial claims: that there was no need to provide specifically for the possibility of peaceful changes of frontiers: and that the principle in question should not in any way be subordinated to any other principle'. However, the Soviet draft received no support among the neutral or other Western delegations.

[6] See No. 46.

[7] Mr. Tickell here noted in the margin: 'This is *not* a real point'.

[8] See No. 46, note 8.

[9] Mr. Semenov also complained to Mr. Tickell (see note 1 above) about British opposition to a Soviet formula covering the 'inadmissibility of territorial claims', and the UK delegation's

would only add the following comments to your own effective rejoinders recorded in your paragraph 5:[10]

(a) It is of course the French draft declaration which proposes specific language to allow for the peaceful change of frontiers by the mutual consent of those concerned. There can be no doubt that this has hurt the Russians very considerably. They have repeatedly stated their refusal to contemplate any change to the formulation in their own text and will have been much dismayed at the extent to which the French position has found support not only among the Nine but among other delegations. There is no reason, in this context at least, why we should be linked with the Italians and the Dutch in an unholy trinity of reactionary opposition.

(b) Again it is not true that we have been alone in questioning the Soviet formula on the inadmissibility of territorial claims. The Americans, Canadians and the Belgians were particularly prominent in debate but many others played an active part.

(c) The Russians are being deliberately disingenuous about the discussion on territorial integrity. They repeatedly tried to side-track discussion onto questions of separatist movements. They consistently refused to answer our own question (phrased in delicate and unpolemical language) whether this principle ruled out the right of the Soviet Union to give material support to the Communist Party of Great Britain. The whole subject rose naturally from previous Soviet interventions. What probably hurt the Russians particularly were the exchanges on Czechoslovakia. It was in fact Mendelevich himself who first raised that (rather relevant) subject, when he attacked our record in 1938. We naturally had to reply.[11]

6. We are no longer as prominent as we were, now that the Nine are pulling together better. We are however conscious that, in words of the steering brief, 'having spoken up firmly in defence of our own interests and of procedural correctness, exposing Soviet tactics where necessary', we should at

reference to the need to cope in the territorial integrity principle with 'circumstances in which participating states belonging to the same social system should claim the right to interfere in each other's affairs'.

[10] In response to Mr. Semenov Mr. Tickell (*v. ibid.*) emphasised that the British position on the inviolability of frontiers was the same as that of other members of the EC, and that HMG believed it should be closely associated with the preceding principle on refraining from the threat of force. He said that he could not, in the light of the Eastern treaties, understand Mr. Semenov's reference to German *revanchards*, and he reminded Mr. Semenov that HMG had not forgotten the Soviet intervention in Czechoslovakia and wanted to be sure that 'we all understood the same thing by respect for territorial integrity'.

[11] When, during a meeting of the Principles Sub-Committee on 6 November, Mr. Edes questioned Soviet intentions regarding foreign support for political parties seeking to change the structure of states and abolish frontiers, Mr. Mendelevich referred to Nazi support for separatists in Czechoslovakia and subsequent British involvement in the Munich settlement of 1938. Two days later, on 8 November, Mr. Edes stated that Mr. mendelevich 'had not expressed similar concern regarding events in Poland in 1939 and Czechoslovakia many years later' (records of Sub-Committee I meetings on 6 and 8 November).

the same time 'work patiently and constructively for agreed solutions where these are attainable without sacrificing principle.'[12] I am sure that once again the Russians will find, as in Helsinki, that when we get down to drafting, we are a delegation who talk constructively and can carry their partners and allies with them.[13]

P.M. MAXEY

[12] See note 6 above.

[13] On 28 November Mr. Tickell saw Mr. Semenov again and made the following points: (1) the principle of inviolability of frontiers should either make explicit reference to possibilities for peaceful change, or be linked to the non-use of force; (2) the Soviet formula on the renunciation of territorial claims tilted the balance firmly away from inviolability and towards virtual recognition of existing frontiers; and (3) where territorial integrity was concerned, the British were happy with the formulation set out in the French draft declaration (letter from Mr. Tickell to Mr. Maxey of 28 November).

No. 57

Mr Elliott (Geneva) to Sir A. Douglas-Home
[*WDW 1/18*]

Confidential

GENEVA, *15 December 1973*

Summary . . .[1]

Sir,

CSCE: The Second Stage So Far

The Conference on Security and Co-operation in Europe (CSCE), the second stage of which opened in Geneva on 18 September, begins its Christmas recess today and will resume work on 15 January.

2. Despite three months of uninterrupted session, there is little progress to report on the substance of the matters under discussion at the Conference. The real negotiation has yet to begin. The chances of forecasting the outcome are indeed hardly better now than they were three months ago. But the initial skirmishes have been fought and the lines of battle drawn up; and we have a somewhat clearer idea of the task facing the West in the pursuit of the aims it has set itself for the CSCE.

Eastern and Western aims

3. It has for many years been a major objective of Soviet policy to bring about a European security conference culminating in a summit meeting. Its purpose for the Soviet Government appears to be to underwrite and consolidate the political *status quo* in Europe and in particular to obtain general acquiescence in the Soviet sphere of influence in the East. A successful conference would also make a major contribution to the atmosphere of *détente* for which the Russians have been working in their bilateral

[1] Not printed.

relations and which would favour the expansion of Soviet influence in Western Europe. The strategy of which it is a part has become identified with Mr. Brezhnev; and there have seemed to be some grounds for the argument (assiduously propagated by the Romanians and other self-appointed interpreters of Soviet views) that just as a satisfactory outcome to the Conference would apparently strengthen his position, so an unsuccessful result would weaken it.

4. The West has succeeded so far in exploiting the leverage which this Soviet posture has given it. Western strategy has been to minimise the undesirable political results of the Conference while forcing the Russians to pay a substantial price for those results in terms of the liberalisation of contacts between the peoples of East and West. We have insisted that a lowering of barriers to the free circulation of people, ideas and information within Europe is at least as important for genuine *détente* as intergovernmental declarations. (We have advocated too some confidence-building measures in the military field as a test of Eastern good intentions.) A normalisation of contacts could help to foster peaceful evolution in Eastern Europe and contribute to conditions which might in the long run increase the freedom of manoeuvre of the East European countries *vis-à-vis* the Soviet Union.

The background

5. The Final Recommendations which emerged in May from the preparatory talks at Helsinki[2] have provided the frame of reference for our discussions in Geneva. The Soviet Union and its Warsaw Pact Allies had intended that the Conference should be brief in time, declaratory in style and narrowly political in content and effect. Instead, they were obliged as a result of the preparatory talks to accept a Conference which would take place over a long period of time in three contingent stages, would set out to achieve practical results and would deal with human contacts, information and military questions as well as with economic and political matters. In particular, Item III of the Recommendations, which reflects Western views on the desirability of the wider dissemination of information and greater movement and contacts among the peoples of the participating countries, was accepted by the Warsaw Pact countries with great reluctance. But the verbal compromises hammered out at Helsinki did not resolve the real issues and the fundamental differences of purpose between East and West remained.

6. The speeches delivered during the first stage of the Conference by Mr. Gromyko and his Warsaw Pact colleagues and the proposals they tabled then left no room for doubt that the East intended, while paying lip-service to the Final Recommendations, to go back on most of the concessions embodied in them.[3] The Eastern Foreign Ministers dwelt on the paramount importance of drawing up a political declaration to guide relations between the participating States, but their references to Item III of the Agenda were cursory and restrictive. Precisely the same was true of the draft declaration of

[2] See No. 37, note 8.

[3] Cf. No. 40.

principles tabled by the Soviet Union under Item I[4] and the three draft declarations on the remaining agenda items which were tabled by other East European States. The declaration of principles, as a means above all of obtaining a clear general commitment to the inviolability of European frontiers, is for the Russians the essential *raison d'être* of the Conference and their draft is skilful and relatively realistic. The East European draft declaration on Item III, however, would involve no genuine commitments on the part of the East in the fields of interest to the West. It is vague and merely declaratory although it echoes some of the compromise phraseology in the Helsinki Recommendations. To the extent that it represents a revision of the result of the Helsinki consultations, it offers indeed a direct challenge to the West.

The Second Stage

7. This was the unpromising background against which the second stage of the CSCE opened. It is not necessary to give a detailed account of the discussions so far. Little need be said in particular of the time which has been devoted to the so-called 'contributions' to the Conference by non-participating States bordering the Mediterranean.[5] Nobody seriously supposed that these countries could contribute usefully to the work of the Conference. Nevertheless a handful of Southern European delegations, led by the Maltese and Yugoslavs but with the active co-operation of Italy and France, have seen fit to come out as champions of supposed Arab interests at the Conference, and have forced us to waste many hours, first arguing about which States should be permitted to make contributions and what arrangements should be made for receiving them, then hearing the representatives of the States in question, and finally debating what should be done with their contributions. I fear we have not yet reached the end of this story.

8. Nor will I attempt to describe the procedural wrangles with which the Conference opened and which have punctuated its proceedings. They have been time-consuming and frustrating and have sometimes seemed an unnecessary deflection of the Conference from its real task. In fact they, perhaps even more than the substantive discussions, have brought out the different conceptions which East and West have of the Conference and its purpose. We may assume that the Warsaw Pact delegations had instructions to bring the Conference to an early conclusion; to ensure that all other aspects were subordinated to the working out of the declaration of principles; to work for conclusions on Item III which would be as insubstantial as possible and would involve no threat to the ideological defences of the East; to obtain whatever they could on trade policy questions while conceding as little as possible on business contacts and information; and to secure the establishment of follow-up machinery which would serve Soviet political aims. They accordingly sought an early beginning to drafting on the basis of the Soviet

[4] See No. 46, note 8.

[5] See Nos. 41, 42, note 11, and 44, notes 4 and 8.

and East European drafts; a generally high tempo of work (partly for the sake of rapid progress but partly too no doubt in order to place a strain on Western co-ordination); a higher frequency of meetings for the Sub-Committee dealing with the Principles than for the others; and an arrangement of work for Item III which would ensure that, whatever concrete commitments the East might be obliged to accept, a preamble would be drafted which would provide justification for a restrictive interpretation of them.

9. The procedural battles thus took place over matters which are in fact of fundamental importance; and it is perhaps not surprising, especially given the fact that our only effective rule of procedure is the principle of consensus, that they were sometimes protracted. In the event the West achieved its main initial objective of postponing the stage of drafting until the matters on the agenda had been discussed in depth in all the working bodies. We also succeeded in moderating the tempo of work generally, although this has been fast enough to impose a heavy burden on most delegations, especially the smaller ones. For various reasons we were unable to avoid a disproportionately high frequency of meetings for the Principles Sub-Committee.[6] On Item III, however, we successfully resisted Eastern attempts to embark on the discussion and drafting of a preambular text as such.[7] We have also managed so far to postpone any detailed discussion of follow-up machinery until we can see what kind of results might emerge from the Sub-Committees.[8]

Item I

10. In the Sub-Committee on Principles our main objective has been to keep the general discussion going for long enough to enable a thorough examination of all aspects of Item III to be completed in the relevant working bodies. Our secondary objective has been to expose the inadequate and prejudicial aspects of the Soviet draft declaration and by contrasting these unfavourably with Western (mainly French) formulations,[9] to exclude language that could be used by the Russians to circumscribe the achievements on Item III. In both respects Western delegates have achieved success, though only through the expenditure of quantities of ingenuity as well as energy. In a special working body set up under Item I, a Swiss proposal for the peaceful settlement of disputes which envisages new machinery based on the principle of compulsory arbitration has been under discussion together *inter alia* with a Romanian draft declaration on the non-use of force.[10] Neither seems likely to survive in any substantial form, the first because the Russians have rejected the principle of compulsory arbitration; and the second because Romanian ideas for a new security system have undesirable implications for the NATO Alliance. In another Sub-Committee discussion of

[6] See No. 49, note 2.

[7] See No. 47.

[8] See No. 53.

[9] See No. 51, note 3.

[10] See No. 48, notes 4 and 5.

Western ideas for confidence-building measures of a political character in the military field (e.g. the prior notification of major military manoeuvres and movements and the exchange of observers) got off to a promising start; but the Russians have since adopted a thoroughly restrictive and defensive attitude and the Americans have got cold feet about the implications for the MBFR negotiations in Vienna.[11] The prospects for useful results in this field do not seem too bright unless we can convince the Russians that some permanent and effective tests of their military intentions are an integral part of a successful Conference.

Item II

11. Discussion of economic and related questions has given rise to a fairly detailed but inconclusive exchange of views. It seemed questionable beforehand whether the CSCE would have anything useful to contribute to existing multilateral and bilateral arrangements for the discussion of East-West economic relations and co-operation in the fields of science and technology and the environment. But the possibility existed that, if the East showed any real desire for some practical progress, the Conference might provide an opportunity to press them in return to make changes in their own commercial and administrative practices which could make life easier for our businessmen and have a beneficial, if marginal, effect on East-West trade. We had nothing of substance to offer, and proposed to argue that such relaxation would be to their benefit as well as ours. So far, the CMEA countries have pressed for a broad interpretation of Most Favoured Nation treatment which in effect would make it impossible for the West to maintain their remaining quantitative restrictions, and have attacked these restrictions as the main obstacle to improved East-West trade; but they have taken pains not to appear as *demandeurs* for Western goods and technology.

12. One of the more interesting developments in Committee II has been the acceptance by the East, after some initial difficulty, of the presence of representatives of the EEC Commission in the delegation of the Danish Presidency. Indeed, for the first time there have been long informal discussions between representatives of the Commission and the Soviet Union. The Item has in general involved particularly intensive co-ordination among the Nine, with the Commission playing an active part. In the early days of the Conference these discussions centred mainly on questions of Community competence.[12] More recently, argument has concentrated on whether the Community should expressly make an offer at the Conference of future

[11] In a minute of 27 December Sir J. Killick, who since November had been Deputy Under-Secretary, recalled that Dr. Kissinger (US Secretary of State since 22 August) had made it clear to him in a private conversation in Brussels that he attached 'no importance whatsoever to the CSCE'. Sir J. Killick noted that they had already seen a change in the US position on CBMs and that it was not inconceivable that other considerations in US-Soviet relations 'may dispose the Americans to want to get CSCE out of the way more quickly and on easier terms than we would'.

[12] See No. 50, notes 4 and 6.

negotiations with the East.[13] This co-ordination has not always gone smoothly but it has had some educative value.

13. The outcome of the discussions on Item II is likely to be, as anticipated, a declaration or series of declarations of little practical import.

Item III

14. The West's tactics during the Conference have been dictated principally by our common interest in achieving results under Item III which would have a practical and discernible effect on the movement of people and information between East and West. It is the extent to which this is achieved that will determine whether the West accepts the outcome of the second stage as justifying the holding of a third and final stage at the level of Heads of State or Government. Our over-riding preoccupation so far has been to involve the East in a substantial and serious discussion of practical measures for expanding and normalising contacts. We wished to avoid drafting until the issues had been debated and the areas of possible agreement thoroughly explored. The West therefore tabled a large number of papers for discussion outlining possible agreements on such matters as the dissemination of printed material, the removal of obstacles to radio broadcasts, improved conditions for foreign journalists, the reunification of divided families, marriages between foreigners, the simplification of administrative procedures for travel, and freer cultural and educational exchanges. Throughout the past three months the Western delegations, working in close concert, and with the active help of the neutrals who have also tabled a number of constructive proposals, have done their best to draw the East into a discussion of these papers.

15. The Eastern delegations for their part have clung to their own vague and non-committal draft declaration and have urged that this should form the basis for the final document on Item III. (They insist that there should be one single document, partly no doubt because this may make it easier for them to keep to generalities but partly because they are anxious to preserve a vehicle for the restrictive preamble to which they attach such importance.) They have not been able to ignore Western proposals completely. But they have kept their direct comments on them to a minimum and, while professing their willingness to be constructive, have emphasised the complex legal and administrative issues which they raise. They have argued too that these problems require to be solved bilaterally and cannot in many cases be usefully discussed at the Conference. They have stressed the differences between Eastern and Western political and social systems and the need for scrupulous observation of the principles of non-intervention and respect for the laws and customs (to which they wish to allude in their preamble). Where the West has talked of the freer dissemination of information, personal contacts and freer circulation, the East has talked about excluding corrupting influences, and of institutional contacts and planned exchanges. There have been a few positive comments, for example on our own proposal for a European magazine,[14] but

[13] Cf. Nos. 50, note 5, and 55.

[14] See No. 46, note 10.

1. Sir Alec Douglas-Home.

2a. Mr. (later Sir) Charles Wiggin.

2b. Mr. (later Sir) Crispin Tickell.

2c. Mr. Anthony Elliott.

2d. Sir David Hildyard.

3a. Sir Terence Garvey.

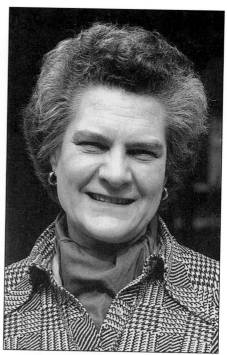

3b. Miss (later Dame) Anne Warburton.

3c. Mr. Peter Maxey.

3d. Mr. (later Sir) Michael Alexander.

4. President G. Ford, Mr. H. Wilson, Dr. H. Kissinger and Mr. L.J. Callaghan at Helsinki on the morning of 30 July 1975.

there has been no meeting of minds. The Warsaw Pact delegations have been saying that compromises cannot be worked out until the stage of drafting is reached. But they have so far given no hint of a genuine readiness to make concessions.

The present situation

16. The position we have now reached is not very different from what we expected. We hoped that more progress might be made in a general discussion on Item III, but we did not suppose we could persuade the Warsaw Pact countries to put their cards on the table before they had to. But the postponement of drafting has served other purposes. It has forced the East to abandon its pressure for an early end to the second stage. The West have demonstrated their determination to hold out until satisfactory results are achieved; and they have shown that they intend to maintain a balance between Items I and III. Our objectives under Item III and the rationale behind them have been set out in detail: the East know[s] what we want and the sort of price we set upon a successful conference. All this is to the good. So, I believe, is the fact that Western delegations have been able to re-establish the sort of good working relations with the neutral and non-aligned delegations which were so important a factor during the Helsinki talks and which will be no less important here during the drafting stage, when middle-men who have so far not played a prominent role, will come into their own.

17. Drafting is likely to start in most Sub-Committees soon after the resumption of work in January. It is then that the crunch will come and that Western unity and tenacity, which are the key to success here as they were at Helsinki, will be tested. Questions of momentum will then loom large. Perhaps the most important benefit for the West of the past three months of preliminary sparring has been that it has provided a training period during which the methods of consultation among the Nine and NATO could be adapted to the circumstances of Geneva. On the whole the opportunity has been put to good use. But mistakes have been made and cohesion needs to be continuously and consciously fostered. The problem of co-ordination between the Nine and the Fifteen has not always been satisfactorily resolved, especially in the context of Item II. So far there have been no mavericks in the Western camp and generally speaking the burdens are being fairly shared, although the Americans are playing a regrettably minor rôle. There are differences of approach. Tension easily builds up between the Dutch and Belgians on the one hand and the French on the other and there has already been one clash in open session. The French have so far fulfilled a valuable and loyal rôle but they like to play out front. They are the preferred interlocutors of the Russians on the Western side and are more inclined than their partners to display a flexible attitude. They could break loose if the issues in question are not thoroughly explored and agreed upon by the Nine, with French views taken fully into account. The Danish Presidency of the Nine has been more effective than we expected but a stronger whip will be needed during the drafting stage. The Germans take over in January and are strongly staffed; but they can be erratic, and their delegation (as always)

seems to be composed of a number of shifting but hostile factions. On most matters we ourselves occupy a central and influential position among the Nine; while in the Conference proceedings we have generally played a prominent rôle in the presentation of the Western case. The Russians have so far treated us with reserve.

The Eastern attitude

18. The Russians have taken to heart the lessons they learned at Helsinki. Both the tactics and the substance of their position have evidently been prepared with great care. Their delegation is three or four times as large as any Western delegation, and its leading members are of high calibre; all of them too (unlike the leaders of many Western delegations) have remained permanently in Geneva. Co-ordination on the Eastern side has been thorough and effective; and due attention has been paid to relations with the neutrals. Above all, the Russians and East Europeans have made anxious efforts to appear as reasonable people with whom (provided that what they regard as the political realities are respected) it is possible to do business. They have even learned that time limits are two-edged weapons; faced with Western determination not to be rushed as well as with a wide range of problematic Western and neutral proposals, they decided in November to stop talking about ending the Conference before Christmas. Not only over the timetable but also on the important question of follow-up machinery their attitude now appears relatively relaxed.

19. This has been a notable change. Considered in combination with the negative stand adopted by the East towards Western proposals under Item III, a certain air of disenchantment on the Eastern side and the coolness which Mr. Gromyko has recently shown in discussing the CSCE, for example during your visit to Moscow,[15] it inevitably prompts some speculation. Have the Russians changed their minds about the value of the Conference? I doubt whether this is so; and I am sure that we have to assume for practical purposes that it is not. No doubt the scope and volume of the proposals tabled on Item III gave the Russians pause. It certainly appears that they took a fresh look at their strategy and tactics for the CSCE some time in November. They may well then have come to the conclusion that the potential benefits and cost to them of the Conference were more finely balanced than they had seemed earlier. But their general attitude is still consistent with a desire to bring about a successful conclusion to the Conference and a readiness to pay the minimum necessary price for it.[16]

[15] Sir A. Douglas-Home held talks with Mr. Gromyko on 3 and 4 December. In a despatch of 11 December Sir T. Garvey, Sir J. Killick's successor as HM Ambassador in Moscow, reported that on Basket III Mr. Gromyko 'was completely negative'. This was, he observed 'because any joint enterprise in such matters [as joint TV programmes or magazine] would amount in the Soviet view to admitting peaceful coexistence in the ideological field' (ENS 3/548/13).

[16] In his minute of 27 December (see note 11 above) Sir J. Killick expressed his general agreement with the views expressed in this paragraph. But he added that there had recently been much less reference in Soviet publicity to a summit-level Stage III, and that he believed

20. Meanwhile, during the last two or three weeks Russian tactics have been directed to arranging that the other participants leave for the recess with the right sort of final impressions. Hence on Item III their discouraging attitude towards most Western proposals, their renewed emphasis on the virtues of the Eastern draft declaration and their constant insistence on a suitable preamble;[17] and their statements in two of the working bodies in Committee I aimed at defining and restricting the area of eventual agreement. They have every tactical reason to put on an appearance of being confident in the merits of their own positions; and, though ready to do business on their own terms, not over-anxious to reach agreement, nor prepared to make major concessions. Nevertheless, some of the leading Russians have recently seemed to show signs of tensions and nervousness. Perhaps the attempts to reconcile a relaxed negotiating attitude with the need to produce results acceptable to hard-liners in Moscow exposes them to a certain amount of strain.

The possible choice for the West

21. Despite the increased sophistication of Soviet tactics, nothing has happened so far to suggest that the West are likely to be out-manoeuvred if they stick firmly to their guns and insist that agreement on the formulation of principles in Item I must be balanced by the acceptance of concrete measures under Item III and some effective confidence-building measures. It must be acknowledged, however, that a successful conclusion of the CSCE according to the criteria by which we have so far been guided may prove unattainable; and Western Governments may be faced with a hard choice between accepting an unsatisfactory result and assuming responsibility for declaring the Conference a failure. In a sense the aims of East and West for the Conference are irreconcilable. The Communist States wish to confirm the political and ideological division of Europe; but the expansion of contacts which we are seeking, whatever our intentions (and they deeply distrust them), could have a directly contrary, and perhaps ultimately greater political effect. In demanding restrictively worded introductory language to whatever agreements may be concluded on Item III, the East is seeking both an assurance from the West that it will not exploit freer contacts for political and ideological ends and a justification for restricting the operation of any agreements. If the East achieve this, any gains for the West in Item III would tend to be reduced and the essential balance between Items I and III could be destroyed. If the East do not get their way on this point, however, the price we are asking in terms of concrete measures on Item III could prove to be too high for them. It is a reasonable assumption that if they came to this

Mr. Brezhnev had been concerned to play down this aspect in order to leave himself the option of a lower level Stage III.

[17] Mr. Hildyard observed in UKMIS Geneva telegram No. 628 of 30 November that the Russians continued 'to attach vital importance to the drafting sooner or later of a preamble to the final document on Item III as a vehicle for reference to be made to the principles'. He thought their concern over this question partly explained their desire to appear constructive in Sub-Committee discussions, and he noted that they continued to emphasise that progress on this point would affect progress on substance in Sub-Committees.

conclusion they would not abandon the negotiation; but merely stick to their position, in the hope that the West's commitment to the promotion of *détente* would be strong enough to force us to make concessions rather than accept responsibility for a breakdown on such an arcane issue. In any circumstances this would face Western Governments with a hard decision. What seems clear now is that one of the tasks of the Western delegations after the recess must be to ensure that, if the crunch comes, the moment is of our choosing; and the circumstances such as to demonstrate where the responsibility for a breakdown truly lies.

22. Yet I do not want to end on a too pessimistic note. Even in Geneva we do not live in a goldfish-bowl and a great deal is bound to depend on the international climate at the time. If during the next three or four months there has been no major deterioration in the general East-West relationship, I would guess that the East will concede the minimum necessary to make it impossible for the West to reject the results of the Conference. About one thing there can be little doubt. Whether or not an acceptable compromise eventually emerges, the delegations to the CSCE are in for a long and tough confrontation next year.[18]

23. I am sending copies of this despatch to Her Majesty's Representatives at Paris, Brussels, Bonn, Rome, The Hague, Copenhagen, Dublin, Luxembourg, Moscow, Washington, Warsaw, Prague, Budapest, Bucharest, Sofia, East Berlin, Ottawa, Oslo, Ankara, Athens, Lisbon, Stockholm, Helsinki, Belgrade, Berne, Vienna, Madrid, Valetta; to Her Majesty's Representatives to NATO, the European Community, the UN in Geneva; and to the Head of the UK Delegation in Vienna (MBFR).

I have, etc.,
T.A.K. Elliott

[18] In a minute to Mr. Tickell of 14 December Mr. Fall observed that there was no public pressure on HMG to reach a rapid conclusion to the CSCE. He added: 'As far as Western public opinion is concerned, I think that the CSCE is now more important as a test of Community and Western ability to stick firmly to certain basic positions, and less important as an indication of our "attitude to *détente*". This puts us in a strong position, which we should try to exploit' (EN 2/23).

No. 58

Minute from Mr. Tickell on CSCE[1]

[*WDW 1/18*]

Confidential   FCO, *20 December 1973*

CSCE

The Second Stage of the CSCE, which opened in Geneva on 18 Septem-

[1] This minute, based on a draft prepared by Mr. Fall and covering Mr. Elliott's despatch at No. 57, was addressed to Mr. Wiggin, Sir J. Killick, Sir T. Brimelow and the Private Secretary.

ber, has now been adjourned until 15 January. During the break the Nine and the Fifteen will be meeting to prepare for the drafting work which lies ahead. No policy decisions are needed before these meetings, but now is a convenient time to take stock.

2. Mr. Elliott's despatch of 15 December,[2] which has been sent for printing as a diplomatic report, provides an excellent basis for this. He argues, I think rightly, that the real negotiation has yet to begin; and that, though it is probable that the Russians continue to attach sufficient importance to the Conference to pay the minimum price necessary for a successful conclusion, we cannot exclude the possibility that the Western participants will be faced with a hard choice between accepting an unsatisfactory result and assuming responsibility (or rather being ready to assume responsibility) for declaring the Conference to be a failure.

3. We shall try during the break to agree with our Community partners and NATO Allies on policies which will give us the best chance of reaching satisfactory results; and at the same time ensure that, if the Conference should fail, it would do so in circumstances in which there would be no doubt that responsibility for the breakdown lay with the East.

4. None of this will be easy, but our basic position is a strong one. The two objectives set out above are happily not in conflict. Western public opinion, even in the Federal Republic, is now relatively free of euphoria about the CSCE, and we are unlikely to be criticised for sticking firmly to certain basic positions.

5. So far as the West is concerned, the main issue remains that of human contacts and information. This is generally regarded by Western Governments and public opinion as the test of a successful Conference. But it will not necessarily prove simple to apply. The Russians could be prepared to accept deceptively attractive texts whose value was in practice nullified by reference to principles such as respect for sovereignty and non-intervention in internal affairs. These principles would be acceptable to us as part of a declaration on principles of relations among states; but the possibilities for their misuse are obvious. In seeking to arrive at conclusions which closed loopholes for evasion, we may have to present our case in terms which seem arcane or unduly suspicious.

6. While keeping the emphasis on Agenda Item III, we must be careful not to neglect other subjects which could contribute to the strength of the Western position. We are rightly sceptical of the value of yet another declaration of principles, but if we are to have one—and I see no escape short of the failure of the Conference—we must make sure that it reflects so far as possible a Western view of the proper basis of relations between states. On confidence-building measures, we should be able to work with the neutrals for useful, if modest, results. This is an area where we can put Soviet good intentions to the test in a way understandable to public opinion. Here

[2] No. 57.

we are unfortunately in some difficulties with the Americans who, in view of the possible overlap between confidence-building measures and MBFR, are going back on their previous positions and are thereby at odds with the other members of the Alliance. Finally, on the economic subjects, we shall want to bring out the importance we attach to practical measures to develop trade, particularly in the field of business contacts and information. In all these areas our approach is more detailed and business like than that of the East; and our public position is correspondingly more attractive then theirs.

7. The West thus remains, on the whole, in the position of advantage in which it emerged from the preparatory talks. But when the Conference resumes, we shall be faced with the need to distinguish the essential from the less important in the many Western proposals tabled in Helsinki and Geneva, and with pressures to conclude the Second Stage before Easter. This is likely to prove a severe test of the cohesion of the Nine and the Fifteen.

8. We have still to decide in the Nine and the Fifteen on the level of the Third Stage and on continuing machinery. For the time being we should continue to argue that both questions must depend on the results of the Second Stage.[3] In fact the prospects for a Third Stage summit are dimming fast. The Secretary of State made his scepticism known at the NATO Ministerial Meeting on 10 December.[4] M. Jobert then also made the good point that whereas the Eastern countries wanted endorsement of the *status quo* of the CSCE they could only give promises of good behaviour in return.[5] In these circumstances it might be wrong to make the Third Stage a summit

[3] Mr. Wiggin minuted on 21 December that he regarded the holding of Stage III as 'more or less inevitable politically', but that he doubted whether anything would in fact emerge from the CSCE which would '*per se* lead to material improvements in any foreseeable time-scale'. On this assumption he trusted that HMG would not 'pay any significant "declaratory" price', that they would not agree to a summit Stage III 'merely for the sake of it', and that they would be wary of lumbering themselves with 'pretentious "permanent" machinery to follow Stage Three'. In his minute of 27 December (see No. 57, note 11) Sir J. Killick expressed his agreement with the substance of Mr. Wiggin's remarks. He had, however, 'one slight reservation' on the subject of permanent machinery, and he wrote: 'it is I think faintly possible that we might one day come to find such machinery of value in order to damp down Soviet-American tendencies to go it alone and take decisions affecting Europe on a bilateral basis. But this time has not yet come, and in any case the mere existence of machinery is unlikely effectively to inhibit such a tendency.'

[4] At this meeting Sir A. Douglas-Home reported on his recent visit to Moscow. He stated that unless there were 'radical changes' in the Soviet attitude Basket III 'would be fairly empty and Phase III of the CSCE would not deserve to be held at summit level' (Brussels telegram No. 592 of 10 December, WDN 21/5).

[5] Whilst Mr. Wiggin was encouraged by M. Jobert's caution with regard to both a summit Stage III and permanent machinery, and recognised that the French had tended to 'cool off towards the CSCE, doubtless owing to their increasing worries about the Russians and about "Superpower Bilateralism"', he thought that HMG could never be sure whether or not they would 'break ranks' (see note 3 above).

meeting as it would make people feel that this was a historic event, whereas the historic event would only lie in putting the promises into effect.[6]

9. On continuing machinery we shall have to take into account the wish of the neutral and non-aligned countries for some follow-up to a Conference which has offered them a place in the sun in European affairs. This may prove harder to resist than an unjustified summit. In practice both the level of the Third Stage and the creation of any follow-up machinery is bound to depend on the general international situation towards the end of the Second Stage.[7]

10. I have written to Mr. Elliott to thank him for his despatch.[8]

C.C.C. TICKELL

[6] In his minute of 27 December (see note 3 above) Sir J. Killick suggested that HMG should still 'be thinking about the possible need to break off the conference without a final result'. He also favoured the UK 'sitting back a little more if it should emerge that the French, for instance, [were] willing to take more of a lead'. Sir T. Brimelow, who in November had been appointed Permanent Under-Secretary, disagreed. He minuted on 3 January 1974: 'I think we might get bad publicity in this country if we were to cease to press for greater freedom of movement of people and ideas. Moreover, if we were to be seen to be behaving cautiously, it is less likely that the French would take the lead in crusading for more freedom of movement than that a number of governments would follow our example. And thirdly, if we do not want a third stage at Summit level, we need an issue on which we can say plausibly that Soviet behaviour does not warrant our going to the Summit. Freedom of movement is such an issue.'

[7] Sir A. Douglas-Home noted on this submission, and with reference to subsequent minuting: 'If it comes to the point we should declare it a failure. A phoney result would be worse than useless. I don't mind a division with the Americans on this. But having said that we must play for a success & if we can't get it, play for a break which is on the popular ground of human rights. Possibly the right answer would be a public adjournment until the Russians are willing to come along with the rest. I agree with Sir Thomas. ADH.'

[8] In an additional minute dated 3 January 1974 Mr. Tickell responded to a query made by Sir T. Brimelow as to what would be the balance of loss and gain if they were to proceed to a Stage III limited only to matters of security. He contended that this 'would represent virtually an unqualified gain for the East and a corresponding loss for the West' since the latter had been trying to use the Soviet desire for a declaration of principles as a lever with which to extract concessions elsewhere. 'On Item I', he concluded, '. . . the main need for the West is to limit the damage and score what points are possible. Our main hopes for gain are in Item III and in the related points in Item II'. On 4 January Sir J. Killick minuted his agreement with this line of argument. On Basket III he observed: 'However limited its practical results, it will contribute to the reinforcement of a rudimentary "public opinion" which will be a certain restraint on Soviet external policies'. But while Sir T. Brimelow thought that the case for standing firm on Basket III was 'well argued', he noted on 7 January that the Warsaw Pact might claim that the West was 'blocking security for the sake of subverting their régimes' and indicated the need to prepare for 'much misleading propaganda'. On this point Mr. Wiggin minuted on 8 January: 'Essentially I regard the whole of the CSCE as a propaganda battle' (WDW 1/5).

No. 59

Sir A. Douglas-Home to Sir E. Peck (UKDEL NATO)
No. 471 Telegraphic [*WDW 1/22*]

Routine. Confidential   FCO, *21 December 1973, 7.15 a.m.*

And Saving to Washington, Bonn, Paris, Rome, Brussels, The Hague, Luxembourg, Copenhagen, Dublin, Oslo, Ottawa, Ankara, Athens, Lisbon, Helsinki, and UKMIS Geneva.

MIPT:[1]

CSCE: Confidence-Building Measures: Future tactics in Geneva

Following is text of British paper. Begins:

Western Objectives

1. The three confidence building measures[2] are a Western idea, and they have so far paid a useful dividend. Our proposals have been supported by the neutrals, and the Russians are on the defensive.

2. We must now look beyond tactics, and consider what we can hope to achieve in substance. Our aim should be to secure agreement to measures which are useful, and which neither harm the military preparedness, operational capability nor defence capacity of any Western state, nor cut across the allied position in the MBFR talks.

3. There are three Western papers on the table in Geneva. Many of the ideas in the earlier British and Norwegian papers[3] are restated in the Belgian paper of 7 December (CSCE/11/C/10).[4] This is a national paper and does not purport to represent an allied consensus. But it has been widely welcomed by the neutrals and non-aligned, we believe that complemented if necessary by other Western national papers, it should help to maintain pressure on the Warsaw Pact and to provide us with a satisfactory basis for the drafting stage.

Soviet Attitude

4. The attitude of the Russians is severely restrictive. The Soviet delegation have shown deep mistrust of Western objectives in promoting discussion of these measures. It seems probable that their present instructions give them little room for manoeuvre. Their main objectives appear to be to limit the amount of Soviet military activity to be included in the CBMs and to leave as many loopholes as possible. They do not want the measures to apply to much if any Soviet territory, and they have also taken minimalist positions on the

---

[1] Telegram No. 470 to UKDEL NATO of 21 December requested Sir E. Peck to circulate this paper and a draft resolution on CBMs (see note 7 below). These, the telegram explained, reflected the approach which HMG wished to promote at the EPC Political Committee on 10 January 1974.

[2] The three CBMs cited in paragraph 23 of the Helsinki Final Recommendations were: (1) prior notification of manoeuvres; (2) exchange of observers at manoeuvres; and (3) prior notification of military movements.

[3] See *Human Rights*, vol. i, pp. 388-90, and vol. iii, pp. 296-8.

[4] *V. ibid.*, vol. iii, pp. 317-22.

size of manoeuvres to be notified and the length of prior notice to be given.

5. The Soviet position may be open to modification in some respects. The Russians have hinted as much in Geneva, and suggested informally that the scope of prior notification might be increased if less binding language were chosen. It is probable, however, that they hope, by offering concessions on length of notice and perhaps the strength of the political commitment, to obtain Western agreement to their very restrictive ideas on the areas of application.

6. The Russians may also be anxious not to prejudice their position in the MBFR discussions in Vienna. If so, they may not be prepared to move significantly from their position in Geneva until they are able to form a clearer picture of what will emerge from Vienna.

Western Tactics

7. The Russians are trying to set aside the Western discussion papers. They have proposed instead an immediate start to drafting on the basis of an 'anonymous' paper of the kind the Soviet delegation circulated during the preparatory talks in Helsinki. They have suggested that the relevant Sub-Committee should begin by tackling some, but not all, of the matters covered by paragraph 23 of the Helsinki Recommendations. They presumably hope to begin with the exchange of observers and go on to the notification of manoeuvres.

8. At present any compromise draft would have to take account of the Soviet and Romanian texts which are the only draft resolutions on the table.[5] These texts are too insubstantial to provide a satisfactory basis for drafting, and the idea of tackling the easy subjects first is clearly intended to help the Russians avoid the more difficult ones altogether.

9. We see no reason for modification of the Western position in present circumstances. As set out in the Belgian paper it is designed to promote common sense and practical arrangements in an area which provides, in a way understandable to public opinion, a test of the goodwill of the Warsaw Pact and of their desire to promote confidence in their military intentions. We should not relax our pressure. Our aim should be to make the Russians recognise that effective confidence-building arrangements are in the Western view an essential ingredient of a successful Conference. Such an approach is likely to be viewed with sympathy by the neutrals and non-aligned.

10. If we are to maintain our present position successfully, three conditions must be fulfilled. First a further effort is required to resolve the outstanding differences in the Alliance on points of detail. This process could be combined with a continuing review of the allied negotiating position.

11. Secondly we must retain the initiative in Geneva. This might best be achieved by the urgent preparation of a draft resolution on confidence-building measures which could be tabled as soon as delegations in Geneva thought tactically appropriate.

[5] *V. ibid.*, pp. 293-4, 299 and 301-2.

12. Thirdly we must agree on our tactics on the prior notification of major military movements. The Alliance has so far agreed (CM(73)79)[6] that it would be tactically advisable to leave it to the Russians to shoot down any reference to movements. This remains the British view, but it is apparent that the Russians will try to avoid assuming this responsibility by postponing discussion of the question. They are already suggesting that the Conference should agree to language indicating no more than readiness to discuss the notification of movements in due course (i.e. after the Conference). We should resist any conclusion of this kind at the present stage, not least because the postponement of difficult questions until an unspecified date after the Conference would have unfortunate implications (e.g. in setting an undesirable precedent for Item III and for follow up machinery).

13. We should therefore maintain a reference to movements in a draft resolution on the lines suggested in para 11 above. If, later, we have to drop it, we should expect concessions in return. The Alliance will need to consider what these concessions might be.

14. The arguments in favour of the early tabling of a comprehensive draft resolution on confidence-building measures can be summarised as follows:

(a) It is clear that the Eastern intention is to record the results of all Committee I discussions in a single declaration dominated by the section on principles. It is however an important element in our strategy that those military aspects of security to whose discussion we are all committed should not be ignored or presented in a way which would suggest that they are of secondary importance. We should therefore work for a separate and self-contained resolution on this subject.

(b) Any move to drafting is likely to be preceded by a period during which the various proposals made in the Sub-Committee would be brought together. It will be important that there is on the table at least one Western draft of equal status to that tabled by the Russians.

(c) Drafting could well take place in an informal working group. In that case it would be essential for the West and the neutrals and non-aligned to have a clear Western text from which to negotiate.

15. The drafting of such a text presents a number of problems:

(a) The nature of the commitment. It is generally agreed that the confidence-building measures will have to be of a voluntary rather than a mandatory nature. It has also been suggested in NATO and in discussion in Geneva that they should have a political and moral force rather than be of a legally binding character. Since, however, it would be more embarrassing for NATO countries than for Warsaw Pact ones to disregard

---

[6] This report by NATO's SPC was submitted to the NAC on 28 September. The SPC felt that, though there was little hope of agreement on the prior notification of movements, the neutrals and non-aligned could be expected to press strongly for this, with the Russians opposing it. The onus for rejection could thus be placed upon the Soviet Union, whilst allied negotiators concentrated upon determining the size and scale of military activities covered by CBMs (WDW 1/22).

their commitments, we shall need to ensure that the strength of the commitment takes account of the importance of the confidence-building measures in question. The Russians have indicated that if their own restrictive proposals were accepted, they would be prepared to consider a political commitment expressed by the word 'will'. They should be held to this form in a more substantial text.

(b) Other confidence-building measures. For tactical reasons it is important that a Western draft should not appear to close the door on measures proposed by neutral or non-aligned countries. We need to reach agreement as soon as possible on what language we could accept to cover such additional CBMs. The British delegation hope to be able to make suggestions at the meeting on 10 January.

(c) The extent to which the draft resolution should cover the subject matter of paras 22 and 24 of the Final Recommendations. It is difficult to say at this stage how discussion of other military aspects will develop, and it would be useful if a separate paper on this problem could be prepared within the Alliance. But it should be possible even now to agree to a draft on CBMs into which additional language on the other aspects could be incorporated if this proves desirable, without at this stage risking antagonising the neutrals by appearing to prejudge the issue.

16. A tentative draft of such a resolution is attached.[7]

Ends.

[7] Telegram No. 472 to UKDEL NATO of 21 December contained the text of this draft resolution. This required participating states to give prior notification of military manoeuvres and movements. Notification was to be given approximately sixty days in advance; it was to apply to any major military manoeuvre or movement comprising activity by the equivalent of a division or more troops; and it was to include provision of information on the name and general designation of the manoeuvre or movement. At a meeting of the NATO delegates at Geneva on 18 January 1974 the British draft resolution was subjected to detailed criticism. The Americans pressed for the omission of any reference to movements, and the Norwegians advocated that some mention be made of 'major independent air and naval manoeuvres' (UKMIS Geneva telegram No. 26 of 19 January, WDW 1/6). The United States also appeared to have difficulties with the amount of information to be provided when prior notification took place and the precision of the language used. A WOD paper of 18 January (WDW 1/6) rejected American claims that a CSCE agreement on the prior notification of movements might prejudice the MBFR negotiations and inhibit allied deployment in a crisis (see No. 53, note 7). It held that the proposed CSCE and MBFR measures were of a very different kind, and that a controversial troop movement of divisional strength or above was only likely in crisis conditions, that it would probably be planned only shortly before it took place, and that it 'would be notified (if at all) at the last moment, perhaps when it had already become known to the press'. Despite American reservations with regard to movements, the Fifteen agreed on 24 January to the tabling of a revised version of the British draft resolution (UKMIS Geneva telegram No. 45 of 26 January, WDW 1/6). See *Human Rights*, vol. iii, pp. 327-9.

No. 60

Sir N. Henderson (Bonn)[1] *to Sir A. Douglas-Home*

No. 44 Telegraphic [*WDW 1/3*]

Immediate. Confidential BONN, *9 January 1974, 7.50 p.m.*

Repeated for information immediate UKDEL NATO, Routine Helsinki, UKREP Brussels, UKMIS Geneva and other Members of the Nine and Washington, Moscow, Vienna and Saving to Oslo, Ankara, Athens, Ottawa, Berne, Stockholm, Madrid, Lisbon, Algiers, Cairo, Tunis, Rabat, Tel Aviv.

Following from Delegation:

Meeting of the Nine: CSCE Sub-Committee[2]

1. The Germans (von Groll) provided brisk and effective chairmanship. They also established the precedent of fielding a separate national delegation (without any harmful effects).[3]

2. The task of the meeting was to co-ordinate positions for the resumed session of Stage II of the CSCE due to open in Geneva on 15 January. In this it was largely successful. The Ad Hoc Group and Committee III experts met in parallel (see MIFTs)[4] and questions of general interest were dealt with in a joint session.

3. Following are main points covered in the Sub-Committee.

Declaration of Principles[5]

4. *Preamble and general provisions.* It was generally agreed that these were of importance to the West and that we should ensure that their drafting was not

---

[1] Mr. Henderson was created KCMG in June 1972, and in the following month became HM Ambassador in Bonn.

[2] The Nine's CSCE Sub-Committee and the Ad Hoc Group met in Bonn from 7-9 January.

[3] These were the first meetings of the Sub-Committee and Ad Hoc Group under Federal German Presidency, and a WOD steering brief of 4 January advised UK delegates 'to encourage the Germans to play an active part in maintaining the cohesion of the Nine at the CSCE, and to subdue any tendency to use their Presidency to impose their more idiosyncratic views on the Nine'. The fielding of a separate national delegation in addition to a Presidency delegation would, the brief explained, 'probably make co-ordination more difficult' (MWP 1/11).

[4] Committee III experts failed to decide on whether or not the Nine should accept some sort of preambular text to the conclusions eventually reached on Item III, but did agree that they should be prepared to proceed with drafting in the Sub-Committees once the remaining Western proposals had been tabled and the general debate completed. Prolonged debate in the Ad Hoc Group about how and when to refer to the possibility of trade negotiations to follow the Conference resulted in the drafting of a paragraph which British delegates considered 'sufficiently hedged to guard against the risks in relation to other committees and to give negotiating elbow-room' (Bonn telegrams Nos. 45 (MTW 10/557/5) and 46 of 9 January).

[5] The WOD steering brief (see note 3 above) made it plain that HMG did not want any wording in the proposed Declaration of Principles which could be construed as implying a legal obligation.

left to the last minute.[6] Drafting would start on the individual principles, but points of importance on which early agreement was not possible should be left in square brackets until a first draft of the preamble and general provisions had been worked out.

5. *Inviolability of Frontiers.* It was agreed that the link between inviolability and peaceful change in the French draft declaration[7] should be maintained. At a later stage some delegations (and in particular the Germans, who are reluctant to press for texts going beyond their Eastern treaties) would be prepared to consider as an alternative a reference to peaceful change elsewhere in the declaration.[8]

6. *Co-operation.* It was agreed that the text in the French draft and a proposed German amendment should be looked at again in the light of the implications for the work of Committees II and III.

Romanian and Swiss proposals (paragraph 21 of the Final Recommendations)

7. *Romanian Proposal.* We introduced a paper which provides material for inclusion in a resolution or in a report of the Special Working Body.[9] It will be considered further by the Nine in Geneva together with a paper to be circulated by the French.

8. *Swiss Proposal.* We suggested that we should continue to support the Swiss proposal so long as it contained the element of compulsory arbitration. If however the Swiss dropped this aspect of their proposal under pressure

[6] On this point the steering brief (*v. ibid.*) stated: 'Given the importance of the preamble in setting the tone of the final document on principles, there is a good case for arguing that it should be drafted first.'

[7] See Nos. 48, note 9 and 51, note 3.

[8] In their steering brief (see notes 3, 5 and 6 above) WOD lamented that the Germans, having 'disowned' their original text on the inviolability of frontiers, had 'been sadly rudderless' on a question where it was difficult for other Western delegations to take the lead. UK delegates were advised to try to persuade the Sub-Committee to agree: (1) that the renunciation of territorial claims included in the Soviet draft was unacceptable because it went 'a long way towards the freezing of existing frontiers'; (2) that for the moment the Nine should 'stick firmly to the explicit reference to peaceful change' which appeared under the inviolability of frontiers in the French text; and (3) that any modification of this line should be submitted to at least the Political Directors for approval. The brief recognised that the placing of peaceful change under the principle relating to national self-determination might prove acceptable to the Russians, the Germans and the Irish. 'Its disadvantage', WOD concluded, 'is that it leaves "inviolability" unqualified and thus open to misinterpretation by the East; and that it requires us to rely on "self-determination of peoples" to cover our concern over European union.'

[9] The Nine's CSCE Sub-Committee had agreed on 6 December 1973 that the British should propose the outline of a possible Western counter-draft to the Romanian proposals on the non-use of force. The resulting paper of 8 January pointed out that if, as seemed likely, the Swiss proposal on the peaceful settlement of disputes remained obstructed by the East's refusal to accept compulsory arbitration, it was difficult to see what the West had to gain from a 'compromise' solution which would duplicate arrangements already available to the West without securing any commitment of substance from the East. It concluded that there might therefore be advantage in dealing with paragraph 21 of the Final Recommendations as a whole in a report of the Special Working Body, rather than producing separate resolutions 'which would be unlikely to be satisfactory' (WDW 1/8).

from the East, we should consider ourselves free to withdraw our support. The French commented that they would in any case welcome the omission of the compulsory element, but considered that we should treat the Swiss proposal with reserve because of its implications for follow-up.

Confidence Building Measures and Military Aspects

9. The Germans introduced the paper which they had circulated in NATO. It emphasises the importance of confidence-building measures and the need to integrate them into our overall strategy at the Conference. It was generally welcomed. We pointed to the significance which public opinion attaches to these measures, which were the only real security element left in the Conference. They were distinguishable from the measures which would be proposed in Vienna, and should be pressed energetically in their own right. The French said that there was a danger of exaggerating the importance of military aspects.

Yugoslav Proposals on Colonialism and National Minorities

10. It was agreed that the Yugoslav text on colonialism went beyond the scope of the Conference and had the particular disadvantage of putting self-determination in a non-European context. Their proposal on national minorities might be better considered under Item III.[10]

Follow-up to the Conference

11. It was agreed that at the meeting of the Co-ordinating Committee on 22 January the Nine should continue to argue that it was premature to discuss the substance of follow-up. But a number of delegations said that if the Western position was to be held, the Nine should work out a common line (albeit a minimal one) as a matter of urgency. It was therefore agreed that we should aim to submit the basis of an agreed position to Ministers at their meeting of 14 February. A special meeting of the Sub-Committee may be arranged immediately before the Political Directors consider the CSCE at their meeting on 5 and 6 February.

12. The French remain negative in their attitude to follow-up (and warned against the possibility that the Americans might be more forthcoming than the Nine). But they are anxious to reach a compromise in the Nine soon, as they are apprehensive about signs of what they see as excessive German flexibility. It may be possible to reach agreement on a fairly modest arrangement for follow-up including provision for putting the promises of the Eastern countries to a kind of probationary test after an interval of time as a condition for further progress.

Mediterranean

13. The Belgians, and to a lesser extent the Germans, had under the influence of the energy crisis[11] decided to take a more forthcoming line on

[10] See *Human Rights*, vol. i, pp. 412-16.

[11] On 6 October 1973 the fourth Arab-Israeli war began with Egyptian and Syrian attacks on Israeli military positions. The United States was instrumental in ensuring that Israel was able to withstand the initial assault and subsequently launch a counter-offensive. In response Arab members of the Organisation of Petroleum-Exporting Countries (OPEC) retaliated by restricting oil supplies to Western states which were perceived as being sympathetic to Israel.

contributions from the Mediterranean non-participants.[12] Agreement was quickly reached on an Italian text, prepared for tabling in Geneva, which would enable the relevant committees of the Conference to seek further clarification from their authors of the papers presented by the non-participants.[13] The question will be considered further by the Political Directors on 10 January.[14]

General Tactics

14. The joint meeting agreed to guidelines introduced by the Presidency on the basis of an informal paper which we had previously passed to them.[15] The guidelines refer to the need for parallelism, and for close co-ordination among the Nine where modifications to the substance of our proposals are concerned. They should enable delegations in Geneva to start drafting on a sound basis without artificial delays in those sub-committees where it seems appropriate.[16]

During the months that followed the price of crude oil was effectively increased by approximately 400%. As a result of this so-called 'energy crisis' manufacturing costs escalated, business confidence was badly shaken, and the global manufacturing economy suffered a severe downturn in business activity.

[12] See No. 44, notes 4 and 8. After its receipt of contributions from Algeria and Tunisia, Committee I agreed on 12 October 1973 to proceed on the assumption that participants would be able 'to take into account and study' the views thus expressed 'when considering the relevant matters in the Sub-Committees' (letter from Mr. Adams to Mr. Burns of 12 October 1973). Telegram No. 388 to UKMIS Geneva of 4 December 1973 confirmed that in HMG's view Israeli, Moroccan, Egyptian and Syrian contributions should be handled in exactly the same way, since any attempt to review the previous decision 'could lead to acrimonious and unproductive debate' (WDW 1/23).

[13] WOD were prepared somewhat reluctantly to agree to additional sessions of Committees I and II at which representatives of the non-participating states could express their views in detail. But, as their steering brief (see notes 3, 5, 6 and 8 above) clearly explained, they were doubtful whether Western interests would be best served by discussing the various energy problems at the CSCE when these would be continually overtaken by events in the world outside.

[14] At its meeting on 10 January the EPC Political Committee approved the Italian proposal (Bonn telegram No. 58 of 10 January).

[15] This paper, misdated 31 January (presumably December) 1973, in addition to making the case for parallelism in the negotiations, stressed the importance of maintaining the support of the neutral and non-aligned countries. This meant giving them effective support on questions in which they had shown an interest, and the West being ready to take them as far as possible into their confidence.

[16] WOD's steering brief (see notes 3, 5, 6, 8 and 13 above) also emphasised that it was essential that the Nine should resolutely oppose any deadlines or even suggested target dates for the completion of Stage II, and that they should 'not allow drafting to start on an "easy points first" basis where this would leave us as the demandeurs at a late stage in the Conference'.

No. 61

Sir A. Douglas-Home to Mr. Hildyard (UKMIS Geneva)
No. 19 Telegraphic [EN 2/557/3]

Immediate. Confidential   FCO, *18 January 1974, 3.50 p.m.*

Info Helsinki, Info saving UKDEL NATO and Moscow.

For UKDEL to CSCE.
Your telegram No. 17:[1]

CSCE: Item III

A certain amount of procedural wrangling and testament of position is to be expected on the resumption of the second stage. Our position is a strong one, since we are prepared to start drafting on the basis of proposals of the kind called for in the Final Recommendations. It is the Russians who are looking for ways to avoid the implications of what they agreed in Helsinki.

2. Our main objective at this stage should be to make it clear to the Eastern and non-aligned participants that we are prepared to fight for the substance of our proposals. It is against this background that procedural suggestions, including Dubinin's ideas, should be judged.

3. Dubinin's reference to the Final Recommendations as a skeleton to which flesh should be added seems designed to provide more justification for a draft along Polish/Bulgarian lines than for the wide range of specific proposals put forward by the West.[2] Maxey spoke well in pointing out that Western delegations would propose the inclusion of the substance of all their proposals. But it is difficult to reconcile Dubinin's acceptance of this with his statement that the East would refuse to draft on the basis of Western texts. A tacit agreement to drop both the present Western proposals and the Polish/Bulgarian text as a basis for drafting would favour the East. We would much rather settle on the basis that both should be drawn upon in the drafting, to the extent that they met the requirements set out in the Final Recommendations.

4. The following are other possible points of difficulty in the Soviet

[1] Mr. Hildyard reported in this telegram of 17 January that the Nine had so far failed to agree on the question of a preamble and possible reference to the principles in the documents on Item III, or 'even to examine the issue realistically'. But, with a view to probing Soviet intentions, UK and West German delegates had met Mr. Dubinin on 16 January and suggested to him that it was in both sides' interest if the continuation of the sterile confrontation in Committee III could be avoided while the Sub-Committees completed their general discussions and tackled problems relating to the transition to drafting (MTW 10/557/6).

[2] During his meeting with the British and German delegates on 16 January (*v. ibid.*) Mr. Dubinin emphasised the Soviet desire to proceed quickly with drafting in Committee III, the importance the East attached to preparing a preamble in the Committee, and their wish that drafting in the Committee and Sub-Committees should proceed in parallel. He presumed that the West would not agree to draft on the basis of the Polish/Bulgarian text (See No. 47, note 2), and, since the East would not agree to draft on the basis of any Western text, he proposed that they use the Helsinki Final Recommendations 'as a skeleton for the drafting process'.

proposals.

(i) The order in which subjects are tackled is not a matter of great importance within each Sub-Committee. But Dubinin's proposal seems designed to bring forward the consideration of a preamble. We should insist on a satisfactory basis for drafting in the Sub-Committee before indicating flexibility on this point.

(ii) The number of final documents is much less important than their content. But if we are to ensure that our proposals are adequately taken into account, it may be necessary to insist on diversity at this stage.

5. You should draw on these points as appropriate in further discussions with our partners and allies, and in conversation with the neutrals. The Nine are perhaps more likely to reach an agreed position when they have had more time to consider the position in Geneva, and we see no reason to rush the question.[3]

---

[3] When Committee III resumed its work on 19 January Mr. Dubinin reiterated the Soviet wish to start drafting, and at the opening meetings of each of the four Sub-Committees the Russians, while showing a readiness to continue the general debate for a short period, pressed for an immediate transition to the drafting stage. Meanwhile, two Western papers, an Italian text on marriage and a Dutch one on personal correspondence (see *Human Rights*, vol. v, pp. 54-6), were tabled in the Human Contacts Sub-Committee, and Western delegates decided that at the Sub-Committee's next meeting they would agree to begin drafting (UKMIS Geneva telegram No. 25 of 19 January, MTW 10/557/6).

No. 62

Minute from Mr. Tickell on CSCE: Brezhnev's Message to the Prime Minister[1]

[WDW 1/4]

Confidential   FCO, *18 January 1974*

The Secretary of State has asked for an analysis of the message from Mr. Brezhnev to the Prime Minister, delivered by the Soviet Ambassador on 11 January.[2] A draft reply is also needed since the Prime Minister promised to set out his views as clearly as the General Secretary had explained his own. Finally there is the question of access for Mr. Lunkov and HM Ambassador, on which the Secretary of State has minuted: 'Unless Mr. Gromyko will see

---

[1] This minute, which was drafted in concert with Mr. Bullard and Mr. Murrell, was addressed to Mr. Wiggin, Sir J. Killick and the Private Secretary.

[2] In his message Mr. Brezhnev warned the Prime Minister that 'unduly prolonging' the Conference could 'only damage trust and common interest existing between the Soviet Union and Great Britain'. Mr. Heath assured Mr. Lunkov 'he had no desire to procrastinate at Geneva: he merely wished to see the best possible result from the CSCE' (record of conversation between the Prime Minister and the Soviet Ambassador, 11 January).

Sir Terence more often we must put a brake on these meetings with the PM and with me'.[3]

2. In his message, Mr. Brezhnev expresses regret at the length of the second stage of the Conference and asks rhetorically whether somebody is trying artificially to impede the work of the Conference or to extract unilateral concessions from the Soviet Union. He goes on to raise two specific questions: the principle of the inviolability of frontiers, and the agenda item on human contacts and information (Basket III). He concludes by expressing the wish that the third stage of the Conference will take place at the highest level.[4]

3. All these points have been made repeatedly in Soviet public statements and by the Soviet delegation in Geneva. Mr. Brezhnev's message does not add to our knowledge of the Soviet position. It seems designed to create an impression of Soviet firmness at the beginning of what we expect to be a period of tough negotiation in Geneva. Mr. Brezhnev evidently hopes to persuade us that if we think the West does not need a successful CSCE we are wrong. At the top of page 2 there is a suggestion that the MBFR talks could be affected, and no doubt this is true.[5]

4. At three places in the message Mr. Brezhnev hints that if the CSCE fails or is unduly prolonged, there will be also damage to Anglo/Soviet relations. The tone of the message at these points is disagreeable and slightly menacing. It reads like the work of Mr. Brezhnev's personal secretariat, with perhaps some touches by the General Secretary himself, rather than that of the Foreign Ministry: it is not unlike the vivid but often ill-judged diplomatic communications of Mr. Krushchev[6] in the early 1960s. Mr. Brezhnev's personality cult is still a long way short of the level of those days, but the built-in Soviet tendency towards one-man rule is clearly reasserting itself.

[3] During his conversation with Mr. Heath (*v. ibid.*) Mr. Lunkov referred to procedural questions which had been raised in connection with his request for an interview with the Prime Minister, adding that the Soviet Government had established direct channels of communication with the US and French Presidents and the German Federal Chancellor, and he would 'not wish there to be any discrimination against the British Prime Minister'. Mr. Heath pointed out that the British Ambassador in Moscow had not the same facilities to meet members of the Politburo, 'the present Ambassador not having yet met Mr. Brezhnev'. There had also, he said, been fewer occasions for Sir T. Garvey to see Mr. Gromyko.

[4] Mr. Brezhnev insisted (see note 2 above) that the principle of the inviolability of frontiers must be 'set forth with crystal clarity and purity' and that to allow anything else 'would mean leaving a loop-hole for those who still live by the spirit of revanchism'. He stated that the 'widening of contacts and of information exchange [was] possible only within the framework of the observation of the principle of non-interference in internal affairs, respect for the sovereignty, laws and customs of each country'. The Soviet Union would, he said, oppose any attempt to use Basket III 'as a means of "whittling away"' at its social system.

[5] Mr. Brezhnev recalled (*v. ibid.*) that it had taken many years of careful preparation to achieve the CSCE. 'How then', he asked, 'can we solve other major international problems that have not been so thoroughly prepared for consideration'?

[6] Mr. N.S. Khrushchev was Chairman of the Council of Ministers of the USSR, 1958-64.

5. The meaning of Mr. Brezhnev's warnings about Anglo/Soviet relations is not clear. He seems to be saying that if the CSCE drags on or ends in failure, we should not expect to go blithely ahead with Anglo/Soviet contacts of the kind envisaged. He is perhaps hoping to chill the Prime Minister's blood with the thought that his projected visit to Moscow may not take place. If so, he has clearly misjudged his man.[7]

6. The message was perhaps written partly for other recipients, some of whom may be more vulnerable than Mr. Heath to threats about their bilateral relations with Moscow. It contains no specifically British points, e.g. a reference to the visit of the Secretary of State or to the prospect of one by the Prime Minister, or even to the recent improvement in Anglo/Soviet relations. On the whole it reads to me like a circular communication. We know little about Mr. Brezhnev's contacts with President Nixon, Chancellor Brandt and President Pompidou[8], but it seems very possible that these three, and perhaps others also, e.g. Mr. Trudeau[9], have been sent similar messages as part of their 'consultative' arrangements with the Soviet Union.[10] Mr. Lunkov represented it as a mark of honour to receive such personal communications from the General Secretary. We should perhaps suspend judgment on this point until we have seen one or two more examples of his style.

7. I submit a draft reply to the message.[11] I have tried to maintain our position on the essentials without offering hostages to fortune on points of detail which are subject to negotiation. A draft covering letter to No. 10 is also attached.[12] It recommends that the reply should be sent through Sir T.

---

[7] In a minute to Mr. M.I. Goulding (Private Secretary to Mr. J. Amery (Minister of State at the FCO)) of 16 January Mr. Bullard observed that it seemed best 'to advise the Prime Minister to maintain an attitude of unruffled calm'. Mr. Amery, who had already commented on the 'threatening tone' of Mr. Brezhnev's message (minute by Mr. Goulding of 15 January, ENS 3/548/2), noted on this: 'I am all for unruffled calm. I have a feeling the weather is getting colder.'

[8] M. G. Pompidou was President of the French Republic.

[9] M. P.E. Trudeau was Prime Minister of Canada.

[10] Mr. Semenov subsequently told Mr. Bullard that Mr. Brezhnev's message had been addressed to a 'short and select list of recipients' (letter from Mr. Bullard to Sir T. Garvey of 25 January, ENS 3/548/2). Both Herr Brandt and M. Pompidou appear to have been amongst the latter.

[11] Not printed. Sir A. Douglas-Home approved Mr. Tickell's draft reply and, after having failed to secure an appointment with Mr. Brezhnev, Sir T. Garvey eventually communicated it to the Soviet leader under cover of a personal letter of 19 February. In his reply Mr. Heath stated that questions under discussion were difficult and complex, that it was not easy to reach agreement by way of consensus amongst thirty-five states, and that he rejected 'both artificial delays and artificial deadlines'. Mr. Heath also agreed that there should be no ambiguity about the inviolability of frontiers and that for this reason reference must be made to the possibility of peaceful change (telegrams Nos. 68, 69 and 105 to Moscow of 31 January and 18 February, and Moscow telegrams Nos. 153 and 178 of 12 and 19 February, ENS 3/548/2).

[12] Not printed.

Garvey;[13] and that it, together with Mr. Brezhnev's message, should be communicated to our partners and Allies.

C.C.C. Tickell

[13] Sir T. Garvey, who did not learn of Mr. Brezhnev's message until 22 January, telegraphed Sir A. Douglas-Home: 'The "new climate" in Anglo-Soviet relations has had the effect of bringing us back within range of Russian arm-twisting from which our previous distance freed us.' He predicted that the Russians would end by showing flexibility in order to achieve an 'historic' Stage III. The present Soviet approach he saw 'mainly as an attempt to bring the heaviest guns to bear as the final period of negotiation is approached' (Moscow telegram No. 81 of 22 January).

No. 63

Mr. Hildyard (UKMIS Geneva) to Sir A. Douglas-Home

No. 68 Telegraphic [EN 2/557/3]

Priority. Confidential   GENEVA, *2 February 1974, 10.05 a.m.*

Repeated for information to Priority UKDEL NATO, and to Saving Helsinki, Moscow, Washington and EEC Posts.

From UKDEL to CSCE.
MIPT.[1]

Committee III

1. During the past week the Swiss, Austrians and Swedes have organised a series of informal meetings with the object of resolving the deadlock over procedure for drafting in Committee III and the resulting paralysis of work in the Sub-Committees.

2. Their proposed compromise was a package comprising three elements:

(i) Committee III should immediately proceed to draft on the basis of any texts which have been or will be tabled relating to paragraphs 42 to 44 of the Helsinki Recommendations.[2]

(ii) The Sub-Committees should begin by drafting the operative passages of their documents and deal with the introductory passages later.

(iii) The final document should consist of several parts, each of which could include the various kinds of texts provided for in paragraph 8 of the final recommendations ('declarations, recommendations, resolutions, or other

[1] In this telegram of 2 February Mr. Hildyard informed the FCO that the East had tried to achieve a tactical advantage by tabling in all four Committee III Sub-Committees, under Bulgarian sponsorship, introductory texts to the Sub-Committees' conclusions. While Eastern delegates argued that these were not preambular but substantive, Western delegates, who blocked the move, argued that discussion should logically begin with concrete proposals, and that it would be improper for the Sub-Committees to prejudge a decision by Committee III as to whether it should itself be responsible for drafting all introductory texts (PW 2/557/1).

[2] See Cmnd. 6932, p. 149.

final documents').

3. The informal consultations culminated in a long meeting during the afternoon and evening of 31 January which was attended by the Austrians, Swiss, Swedes, Russians (Dubinin), Poles, Bulgarians, East Germans, West Germans, French, Italians and ourselves. Discussion began with (iii) above. The East first pressed for its exclusion but after a prolonged exchange of views a broadly acceptable compromise emerged which took account of Western insistence on diversity in the final texts and Eastern insistence on the basic notion of one document and the avoidance of direct reference to paragraph 8 of the Final Recommendations. The resulting text on this point would have read: 'Le document final concernant le 3e point de l'ordre du jour comprendra plusieurs parties, dont les dispositions pourront être de nature et de forme différentes selon les sujets et le degré d'accord realisé.'

4. The other two elements in the package proved intractable. On (i) the Eastern representative insisted that, while the fact need not be stated, all must accept that the Committee's task was to draft a single document which would eventually form the general preamble. They could not agree that introductory passages to the Sub-Committee's documents such as the Bulgarians have recently tabled should be dealt with elsewhere than in the Sub-Committees concerned.

5. The French, who are under firm instructions on this point, took the lead on the Western side in opposing this line and argued that the Committee should draft preambular matter relevant to paragraphs 42 to 44 but that no decision should be taken until a later stage where this matter should eventually be incorporated in the final documents.

6. On (ii) the attitude of the Eastern representatives was that the drafting of introductory texts should not be left until a late stage of the Sub-Committee's works. They could agree that work should begin on substantive texts. But it must be agreed beforehand at what point the introductory paragraphs would be dealt with: and this point must not be far down in the programme of work. The Western representatives argued that substantial progress must first be made on the operative texts in the Sub-Committees and on the drafting of preambular matter in the Committee before the Sub-Committees could come to any useful conclusions as to what should be included in the introductions to their documents.

7. The irreconcilability of Eastern and Western views on the terms on which drafting should begin in the Committee caused the meeting to break up without any conclusion being reached on (ii). It was agreed that in the circumstances the neutrals' proposal was void and that the participants were in no way committed by the discussion on it.

8. In the circumstances it was agreed among the Nine and Fifteen that at the meeting of Committee III yesterday the West should accept the proposal put forward by the Swedish delegation at the meeting on 25 January

(paragraph 2 of my telegram No. 41)[3] on the understanding that the Committee's task should be limited to the drafting of preambular matter relevant to paragraphs 42 to 44 of the Helsinki Recommendations and that the final destination of such preambular matter in the final documents should remain open. The West Germans and we spoke accordingly and rebuffed an attempt by the Poles and other Eastern speakers to persuade the Committee to agree that it should simply take a decision to proceed with drafting. The Russians, Poles and East Germans accused the West of obstructionism and delaying tactics and made it clear that until this problem was resolved there would be no progress in the Sub-Committees. A Swedish proposal that the Committee should meet on Wednesday 6 February in an effort to bring about progress and that the meeting of the Information Sub-Committee scheduled for that day should be transferred to the morning of the Friday was accepted. Meanwhile the neutrals will pursue their efforts to bring about a compromise.

9. There will be stalemate on Item III until an East/West understanding can be reached on the interrelated questions set out in para 2 above: and the only means of reaching such an understanding are the informal consultations conducted by the neutrals. Although there is a certain lack of enthusiasm on the part of some of the Nine for this procedure we propose to continue participating on an informal and exploratory basis provided others on the Western side do so, notably the Germans and French.

10. A compromise on the general basis proposed by the neutrals should not be difficult to work out provided the East do not continue trying to unbalance the package in their favour. The only realistic basis for a deal is Western agreement to draft a preambular text in the Committee against Eastern agreement to give clear priority in the Sub-Committees to the drafting of operative provisions on the basis of our proposals. By their tactics in the Sub-Committees this week and in the discussion on 31 January the East are seeking to ensure that work is done in the early stages on a general preamble and also on preambular texts to the Sub-Committees' documents: and they intend to include restrictive formulae in both. We shall firmly resist this manoeuvre while accepting that introductory texts including the Bulgarian drafts will have to be examined in due course in the Sub-Committees.

11. Although there are differences of approach and emphasis among the Nine, there appears to be a general readiness to consider a deal on the above lines. The Dutch and Italians are now showing much greater flexibility. The Belgians are under instructions not to accept any move to draft in the Committee until the Nine have reached clear agreement on their objectives. But work is proceeding on a Western draft of an introductory text for use in Committee III and agreement on this should satisfy M. Davignon. French

[3] Mr. Hildyard reported in this telegram of 26 January that the Swedes had suggested 'that while Sub-Committees should remain responsible for drafting substantive proposals', preambular matter should be drafted by the Committee. At this same meeting of Committee III the Polish delegate stressed the need for 'parallel progress' between the Committee and its Sub-Committees.

instructions to refuse discussion at this stage of a general preambular text are also a problem. However the French delegation, notably Chazelle,[4] consider the instructions unrealistic and seem likely to get them changed soon.[5]

[4] M. J. Chazelle was a senior member of the French delegation.

[5] As Mr. Hildyard noted in UKMIS telegram No. 41 (see note 3 above), the pattern for drafting was already being set by the Information Sub-Committee. It had established the following ground rules: '(a) all words and phrases accepted in the Sub-Committee for inclusion in the Final Document(s) should be *ad referendum*: (b) the Blue Book [Helsinki Final Recommendations] should be used as the basic framework for drafting: (c) proposals already tabled by delegations and any future proposals could be drawn upon in preparing drafts.'

No. 64

Mr. Hildyard (UKMIS Geneva) to Sir A. Douglas-Home

No. 71 Telegraphic [WDW 1/3]

Immediate. Confidential   GENEVA, *4 February 1974, 2.42 p.m.*

Info priority UKDEL NATO, Bonn, Routine UKREP Brussels, Moscow, Info Saving Vienna, Brussels, Sofia, Ottawa, Nicosia, Prague, Copenhagen, Helsinki, Paris, East Berlin, Athens, Holy See, Reykjavik, Budapest, Dublin, Rome, Luxembourg, Malta, The Hague, Oslo, Warsaw, Lisbon, Bucharest, Madrid, Stockholm, Ankara, Washington, Belgrade.

From UKDEL to CSCE:

CSCE: Meeting of Political Directors of the Nine in Bonn on 6/7 February

1. The following summary of the situation in Geneva may be useful.

General

2. The Conference is edging into the drafting of documents and therefore into the period of real negotiation. There is inevitably an atmosphere of confrontation with East and West holding firmly to their opening positions.

3. On Committee I subjects[1] the Russians are likely to maintain their restrictive interpretation of the principle of inviolability of frontiers and resist any link with the concept of peaceful change. On military aspects they seek to reduce confidence-building measures to optional generalities. In Committee II drafting has begun but procedure is not yet altogether settled and few substantive issues have been taken up. Committee III remains the principal stumbling block. Here the Russians are resisting any progress on the detailed Western proposals in the Sub-Committees until a beginning is made in the main Committee on the drafting of a general preamble (see my tel[egram] No. 67)[2].

[1] Committee I's Principles Sub-Committee decided on 25 January to proceed with the drafting of principles in the order set out in paragraph 19 of the Helsinki Final Recommendations. In consequence, the Sub-Committee began consideration of the first principle, the sovereign equality of states (UKMIS Geneva telegram No. 44 of 26 January, WDW 1/11).

[2] See No. 63, note 1.

4. The Swiss and Austrians have recently taken a robust line with the East over Committee III and we can generally continue to rely on neutral support. But there is a risk of an increasing sense of frustration. If we fail to break the procedural deadlock over Item III satisfactorily and reasonably soon the neutrals could be drawn into making concessions to the East in order to get things moving. (The sort of situation which can arise was illustrated in Committee III on 25 January—my tel[egram] No. 43).[3] Work in other areas is already moving ahead and it may be necessary before long to enforce parallelism between Committees I and III by marking time in the former. As at Helsinki the Russians will have to be made to understand that if we are to give them a certain confirmation of the *status quo* in Europe in the form of a declaration of principles we must see some practical results in freer movement and information.

The Nine and NATO

5. Western co-ordination has been generally satisfactory despite the occasional lapse. Within the Nine the Germans have handled the Presidency with some skill and energy. The main difficulty in Committee III has been Dutch and Italian obstinacy over procedural points. At the same time their value as anchormen is compromised by their apparent inability to follow a consistent line, and their tendency to leave to others the defence in the Conference of the negative positions which they have forced on the Nine.[4] The French continue to be active and loyal. For the time being, their relations with the East are less close. The Fifteen are working well together despite a difficult spell over military aspects: the Turks broke ranks and the Norwegians may be tempted to do so. The Americans are beginning to take a slightly more active interest as the detailed negotiations approach but this seems to spring more from a concern to limit possible damage than from a desire to play a constructive part.

6. In the Ad Hoc Group, while consultation has generally gone well, there have been occasions when some members (especially Belgium) have been too ready to reach private agreements with the neutrals and the East. Consultation within the Fifteen has been more regular since Christmas.

7. Warsaw pact co-ordination continues to be effective. There are some differences of role and emphasis on the Eastern side with the East Germans and Poles taking a more prominent and harder attitude, particularly on Item III. The Russians are anxious to make progress but are not forcing the pace

[3] Mr. Hildyard explained in this telegram of 26 January how on the previous day Western delegations, who had not had time to coordinate their tactics, had been faced by a 'united front' of Eastern and neutral delegations in favour of Committee III's proceeding to the drafting of a preambular text. The West had successfully blocked this move, but was, according to Mr. Hildyard, 'in a weak tactical position for the next round' (WDW 1/13).

[4] In his telegram No. 43 (*v. ibid.*) Mr. Hildyard was particularly critical of the way in which the Dutch and Italians, having been 'adamantly opposed to any move towards drafting in the Committee [III] and to any indication of flexibility on the part of the West', had then left to the British and French advocates of a more flexible policy the task of defending the Western position.

too hard. They continue to assure the West that substantial agreement will be possible on the concrete matters in the mandates under Item III provided that their desiderata as regards preambular matter are met: but they are keeping their cards close to their chest. Eastern representatives have recently shown some readiness in Committee III to criticise Western delegations more harshly and outspokenly for their supposed obstructiveness. But the underlying Soviet wish is clearly to keep the atmosphere of the Conference gentlemanly and relaxed. All the indications here, as apparently elsewhere, are that the Russians' desire for a successful outcome has not diminished.

Outlook

8. The West are now well placed tactically with a multitude of detailed proposals on the table against a thin and unconvincing Eastern contribution. But in standing firm on our proposals we have to avoid giving the appearance of rigidity. Hence the need for a certain flexibility, particularly over procedural matters. If general tactics are discussed at the Bonn meeting it would be useful if this general approach could be endorsed.

9. It would also be helpful if the Political Directors could approve the Sub-Committee's paper on follow-up to the Conference which represents the best compromise attainable at present.[5] It will provide useful guidance to delegations in Geneva who will increasingly have to face up to this problem. The West will however wish to delay substantive discussion of this subject at Geneva for as long as reasonably possible if any leverage is to be gained from it for the final bargaining process. It may well be desirable to remind the enthusiasts for follow-up (the Danes and Germans) of the need for caution in public and in informal contacts.[6]

[5] This CSCE Sub-Committee report was completed at the end of January and enclosed with a letter from Mr. Adams to Mr. Burns of 1 February. It rejected a Czechoslovak proposal, tabled at Stage I, for institutionalising follow-up through the establishment of a Consultative Committee (see *Human Rights*, vol. i, pp. 366-67), but recommended that, after an interim probationary period of three to four years, senior officials should meet to review progress in the implementation of Conference decisions. Further follow-up measures would be considered in the light of this evaluation. At their meeting on 6 February EC Political Directors agreed to submit the Sub-Committee report to the EC Ministerial meeting planned for 14 February (Bonn telegram No. 226 of 7 February).

[6] Throughout the autumn of 1973 the West had taken the line that insufficient progress had been made in the CSCE to justify consideration of the question of follow-up. Denmark, Norway and West Germany tended, like the neutrals and non-aligned, to sympathise with the idea of continuing machinery. But the United States was very negative on the subject, as also, in varying degrees, were the Benelux countries, Italy and France. In a submission of 18 January, in which he reiterated the cases for and against follow-up cited in No. 28, Mr. Tickell indicated that the Nine and the Fifteen were now generally agreed that they should attempt to reach a common position on the issue and he suggested that if the Conference were successful responsibility for following up any work arising from it should be given to the existing Coordinating Committee. Both Mr. Wiggin and Sir T. Brimelow (not least, for reasons of economy) supported this conclusion. So also did Sir A. Douglas-Home. 'But', he noted on the submission, 'we should not concede it unless Stage 3 can show better results than seems likely at present. We can afford to be very sticky indeed over Stage 3 & to say why in public' (WDW 1/19).

No. 65

Mr. Hildyard (UKMIS Geneva) to Sir A. Douglas-Home
No. 78 Telegraphic [EN 2/557/3]

Priority. Confidential   GENEVA, *7 February 1974, 9 a.m.*

Repeated for information to Priority UKDEL NATO and to Saving Moscow, Washington, Helsinki, EEC Posts.

My telegram No. 76:[1] From UKDEL to CSCE:
Committee III

1. After a full day's discussion, much of it informal and some of it heated, Committee III took the formal decision last night to proceed to the drafting stage.

2. The Austrian Chairman read out the neutrals' text (my telegram under reference), which remain unchanged. (Copies were circulated informally.) He then added: 'if there are no objections, my understanding is that point one (of the text) means that the Committee will draft the preamble'.[2] No delegation commented, and the decision to move to drafting was duly registered.

3. The deadlock between preamble in the Committee and substance in the Sub-Committees has thus been broken. Moreover the unity of the Nine and the Fifteen has been maintained although it was necessary at times to exert strong pressure on the Dutch to achieve this.

4. This conclusion came near to being torpedoed in the course of the day by the insistence of Eastern delegations, led by Dubinin and Dobrosielski[3], that the Committee should explicitly acknowledge the fact that it would draft the preamble. This insistence went beyond the agreement reached yesterday (my telegram under reference) and led to allegations of bad faith on both sides. In the event the compromise formula in paragraph 2 above, drafted by the Fifteen, sufficed.

5. It should now be possible to begin drafting 'passages operationnels' in the Sub-Committees, while leaving to later their introductory texts, as prescribed in the neutrals' formula. The Nine and the Fifteen are consulting urgently about a possible text for tabling in the Committee.[4]

[1] This telegram of 6 February contained the text of the neutrals' package proposal, which was provisionally agreed at an informal meeting on 5 February, for resolving the deadlock in Committee III (see No. 63).

[2] Point 1 of the neutrals' text stated that at its next meeting Committee III would begin to draft on the basis of texts relating to paragraphs 42-44 of the Helsinki Final Recommendations. There was, Mr. Hildyard noted, a gentlemen's agreement that for the East this meant that the Committee would draft a general preamble (*v. ibid.*).

[3] Mr. M. Dobrosielski was Polish Head of Delegation.

[4] In UKMIS telegram No. 103 of 16 February Mr. Hildyard observed that the compromise adopted on 6 February had ended the deadlock in Committee III and that work was proceeding on a number of drafts. He added, however, that discussion was frequently interrupted by debates on procedure, and that Eastern delegations, while protesting their desire to press on, were in fact maintaining a restrictive attitude on all matters of substance and appeared to be in no hurry.

No. 66

Letter from Mr. Tickell to Mr. Staples (UKDEL NATO)

[WDW 1/4]

Confidential   FCO, *22 February 1974*

Dear Justin,

The Soviet Union and the CSCE

The question raised by Kastl,[1] reported in your letter of 14 February to Robin McLaren (not copied to all),[2] is an important one, and an exchange of views in the SPC would be useful. I cannot guarantee the freshness of the thoughts which follow, but I hope that they will be of some help.

2. There are many possible outcomes to the Conference, but the main options can be reduced to:

(i) a third stage 'at the highest level', which would serve to confirm the Soviet thesis that the Conference is a historic event of great significance in itself, and would imply also that the participants agreed that it had been a major success;

(ii) a third stage at Foreign Minister level, probably with some provision for further meetings, which would avoid the implications of point (i) above but suggest:

(*a*) that an acceptable bargain had been struck on the subjects dealt with in the final documents; and

(*b*) that the process begun by the CSCE was considered to be worth continuing;

(iii) a failure to agree to a third stage, with or without some provision for a further attempt after a year or so, which would unambiguously make the point that the Final Recommendations of the Helsinki Consultations had not been carried out to the satisfaction of all the participants.

3. The odds at the moment seem against a summit. Our own thinking on the subject was set out most recently in Anthony [*sic*] Acland's letter of 30 January to Tom Bridges, a copy of which I enclose.[3] Nothing that has

[1] Herr J. Kastl was Assistant Secretary-General to NATO.

[2] In this letter Mr. Staples informed Mr. McLaren that Herr Kastl had suggested that, in the light of the recent expulsion of Mr. Solzhenitsyn, consideration should be given to the presentation to Western public opinion of 'the probable lack of concrete achievements in Basket III'. Mr. Staples assumed that, given current progress at Geneva, HMG would think a summit-level Stage III unsuitable.

[3] Not printed. This letter was written in response to a request from Lord Bridges (Private Secretary (Overseas Affairs) to the Prime Minister) for information on the likely level of Stage III. In it Mr. Acland stated that the odds seemed to be somewhat against a summit which, in the FCO's view, it would be wrong to hold if not justified by the results of the Conference (WDW 1/5).

happened in the meantime is likely to modify these conclusions. As far as the Nine are concerned, sub-paragraph 2(*f*) of the conclusions of the Political Directors meeting of 10/11 January is interpreted as a decision that the third stage should be at Ministerial level.[4]

4. The Soviet position on the level of the third stage is I think accurately described in the German speaking note enclosed with your letter:[5] the Russians maintain their line on the 'highest level' (see the recent Fenno/Soviet *communiqué*,[6] and Gromyko's reported remarks to Jobert in Paris telegram No. 231).[7] It is interesting that the reference to the highest level in Brezhnev's message to the Prime Minister[8] is linked to the results of the Conference, and this may indicate some hedging of bets. It is in any case clear that the Russians are anxious for tactical reasons not to appear as the *demandeurs*. A member of the Soviet Embassy in Helsinki (no doubt reflecting the latest guidance) told Roger Beetham that the Russians would not be deeply disappointed if the third stage were not at summit level, and that they were not prepared to make the sort of sacrifices on Item III which seemed to be necessary to persuade the West Europeans to accept a summit.

5. The odds are, I think, against the Conference petering out without a third stage. My guess is that the neutrals would do their utmost to 'save the Conference', and that a solution on the lines of 2(iii) would therefore require a determined effort on the part of the East or the West. The Russians are most unlikely to make such an effort, and it follows that any initiative for breaking off or suspending the Conference would have to come from the West.

6. This seems to me to be the most important question implied in what Kastl has said. I think that it would be generally agreed in the Alliance that we should not take such a step except as a last resort, and for reasons which would be generally understood by Western and neutral public opinion. To meet this condition we would have to distil from our original proposals a short list of important and realistic objectives clearly related to the Final

[4] Bonn telegram No. 58 of 10 January (see No. 60, note 14) reported that EC Political Directors had affirmed that they saw no reason to modify the position assumed by the Nine in their objectives and strategy paper of 13 November (see No. 55, note 4) which foresaw a Stage III at Ministerial level.

[5] See note 2 above. The German delegation's speaking note of 13 February recalled that the Russians continued to criticise the allegedly protracted tempo of the Geneva deliberations, whilst maintaining their demand that the final stage should take place 'at the highest level'.

[6] A *communiqué* issued on 18 February at the end of discussions in Moscow between President Kekkonen and Mr. N.V. Podgorny, the Chairman of the Presidium of the Supreme Soviet, expressed their wish that Stage II should be brought to a successful conclusion and that Stage III should be 'at the highest level' (Helsinki telegram No. 77 of 19 February, WRM 3/303/1).

[7] This telegram of 20 February (WRF 3/303/1) reported that during his recent visit to Paris Mr. Gromyko had told M. Jobert that Stage III should be held at summit level.

[8] See No. 62.

Recommendations; to show that these had been frustrated, in whole or in large part, by the East; and to convince the soft liners that the difficulties were such that they could not be gradually overcome by a low-key conclusion to the Conference followed by continuing efforts through bilateral and multilateral channels.

7. The burden of proof would be a heavy one. The general political situation at the time could make it more or less so. But unless there is a major turn for the worse, I think that we shall find ourselves working towards a solution on the line of point 2(ii) above. So far as public presentation is concerned our main task will be to convince public opinion that this is a sensible middle course.

8. We shall need for this to agree with our partners and Allies a convincing statement of our objectives under Item III. Our general views remain as set out in paragraph 2 of Julian Bullard's letter of 22 November to Peter Maxey (copy attached).[9] A combination of the three points is the most that we can realistically hope to get, and the last is particularly important. We shall want to base our arguments on the texts themselves; and, if they show clearly both the extent and the limits of what has been achieved, the question of presenting the results to Western public opinion should not be too difficult. At the right moment, however, we shall have to define more precisely what we expect.

9. I think that it would be wrong—and dangerous—at this stage to try to define a minimal Western position on the more important questions at present under negotiation in Geneva. It would be difficult to avoid the conflicting dangers of tying our negotiators down to unrealistically rigid positions on detail, and of setting down a list of fall-back positions which would result (with or without leaks) in our moving too quickly into them. If the question is raised in the Alliance, you could argue that what is required at present is that Western delegations in Geneva should continue to fight for the substance of our proposals. The overall assessment of an acceptable final package should be left until the Easter break.

10. I do not think that a more precise line on press briefing will be necessary in the immediate future. The Western press has so far avoided the extremes of optimism and pessimism. Let us hope that it will continue that way.

Yours ever,

C.C.C. Tickell

[9] Not printed. Paragraph 2 of this letter refers specifically to the latest Swiss proposal on information. Mr. Tickell would seem to have had in mind paragraph 5 in which Mr. Bullard stated Western objectives as: '(i) to secure certain bankable improvements; (ii) to give ourselves the means to work for further improvements after the CSCE; (iii) to make it as clear as possible to Western public opinion (a) what has been achieved at the CSCE and (b) whose fault it is that more could not be done.'

No. 67

Mr. Hildyard (UKMIS Geneva) to Sir A. Douglas-Home

No. 145 Telegraphic [MTW 10/557/6]

Immediate. Confidential   GENEVA, *28 February 1974, 5.49 p.m.*

Info Helsinki, UKREP Brussels, UKDEL NATO, UKDEL Vienna, and Saving to Vienna, Brussels, Sofia, Ottawa, Nicosia, Prague, Copenhagen, Helsinki, Paris, East Berlin, Bonn, Athens, Holy See, Budapest, Reykjavik, Dublin, Rome, Luxembourg, Valletta, The Hague, Oslo, Warsaw, Lisbon, Bucharest, Madrid, Stockholm, Berne, Ankara, Moscow, Washington and Belgrade.

From UKDEL to CSCE:
  European Political Cooperation: Ministerial Meeting on 4 March:[1] *CSCE*
  1. The following summary of the present situation may be useful if the CSCE remains on the agenda for the Ministerial meeting on 4 March. MIFT[2] reviews the state of play on the main issues in the various working bodies.
  2. Drafting is now under way in all but the Special Working Body of Committee I.[3] The rate of progress everywhere is slow and in none of the Sub-Committees has negotiation on the issues of major importance to the West been carried to the point where the prospects can be assessed with any confidence.
  3. The Soviet Union and its allies are combining pressure for rapid progress with an unyielding attitude on all matters of substance. There is no reason to doubt that they are anxious to achieve a successful outcome to the Conference in time for Stage III to take place in July. But their determination to pay the minimum price, notably in Committee III, is evident.[4]

[1] This meeting was originally planned for 14 February (see No. 64, note 5), but was postponed because of the political and logistic problems caused by the convening in Washington, on 11 February, of a Conference of the Foreign Ministers of thirteen industrialised nations to discuss the current energy crisis. Much of the discussion centred upon the Middle East and relations between EC countries and the USA (telegram No. 244 to UKREP Brussels of 5 March, MWP 1/3).

[2] See note 3 below.

[3] Mr. Hildyard reported in UKMIS Geneva telegram No. 146 of 28 February: 'In the Special Working Body the Swiss are standing firm on their proposal on the peaceful settlement of disputes, but they seem privately resigned to an anodyne and face-saving resolution at the end of the Conference.' He also noted that most other members of the Nine and Fifteen would be prepared to start drafting on the Romanian proposal on the non-use of force, and that UK delegates would concentrate upon securing agreement to Western amendments. A Soviet proposal on consultations was generally opposed by the West (WDW 1/29).

[4] In Committee III Sub-Committees the Soviet and East European delegations were, in Mr. Hildyard's opinion, 'seeking by every possible means to whittle away at the Western texts and to water them down until they became virtually meaningless' (*v. ibid.*). The East also tried to limit texts on wider contacts and exchanges by restrictive definitions of their purpose. And a procedural wrangle ensued when, on 27 February, Eastern delegates in the Human Contacts

4. On the Western side co-ordination is working well and occasional differences of view on tactics and varying attitudes towards such issues as the form of the final document, follow-up and the Mediterranean have not imposed any serious strain. At Head of Delegation level there is a welcome common determination to stand firm in defence of Western objectives. But this attitude is not consistently reflected in the performance of delegations in all the working bodies. In Committee III the determination and robustness of our partners and allies have not so far been in doubt. In Committee II, however, some of our partners appear unnecessarily eager to seek compromises.[5] And in Committee I (possibly because of an exaggerated sense of the risks likely to result from pressure of time) there is a tendency, on the part for example of the French and Germans, to give away agreed Western positions prematurely.[6]

5. There was near unanimity at the last Co-ordinating Committee meeting that the work of the Conference needs to be intensified. We must take this feeling into account, and avoid giving the impression that it is the West that is delaying progress. Delays would in any case be likely to work to our disadvantage since in the later stages matters of importance to the West will remain outstanding. We need therefore to make as rapid progress in the drafting of the Conference documents as is consistent with the defence of Western interests. There is general agreement among Mr. Elliott's colleagues on this. It is hoped that by Easter a first attempt at drafting (involving a liberal use of square brackets) will have been made on all the major items.

6. It is not possible at this stage to form general conclusions about the possible outcome of the CSCE. If Ministers discuss the Conference on 4 March, the best outcome in our view would be for them to conclude:

(*a*) That the guidelines for Western delegations set out in RM(73)20[7] remain generally valid:

(*b*) That decisions relating to the minimum acceptable outcome, Stage III and follow-up[8] should be left for consideration by the Political Directors

Sub-Committee opposed the placing in square brackets (the method commonly used for the provisional registering of texts under discussion) of a Dutch text on personal correspondence (UKMIS Geneva telegram No. 140 of 28 February, EN 2/557/7).

[5] The major point of East/West confrontation in Committee II related to the application of MFN treatment. The Nine differed on tactics and sometimes on substance.

[6] In UKMIS Geneva telegram No. 146 (see note 3 above) Mr. Hildyard explained that Committee I's Principles Sub-Committee had agreed to register a text on sovereign equality which still contained square brackets, but that the most difficult principles lay ahead and that it would not be easy to ensure that each was given sufficient attention before Easter to isolate the major issues. The Germans and others amongst the Nine and Fifteen were, he added, 'tending (prematurely in our view) to be less than robust in defending passages in their draft for the sake of quick agreement'.

[7] See Nos. 55, note 5 and 66, note 4.

[8] A Working Group on Item IV (follow-up), established by the Coordinating Committee, met for the first time on 28 February.

during the Easter Break with a view to a full review at the Ministerial meeting in mid-May:

(*c*) That Western delegations should meanwhile aim to bring about a rapid first reading of the texts on the table but should make no irrevocable concessions on the substance of Western proposals.

7. We are now discussing with our partners and allies the line we shall take on the next stage of the work programme (from 4 March until the Easter break). We shall need to keep a balance between work on principles and confidence building measures and between principles and Committee III. There is however a widespread feeling that principles need more formal meetings while work on Item III could best be pursued by putting more emphasis on informal groups and less on debate in the Sub-Committees. The delegations of the Nine are conscious of the risks of these informal procedures, and some like the Belgians and Italians are still somewhat hostile. But the majority feel that the risks can be guarded against, and that informal meetings can be successfully exploited by the Nine to provide a generally acceptable basis for drafting in the Sub-Committees.

No. 68

Minute from Mr. Tickell on CSCE: Basket III[1]

[*EN 2/557/3*]

Confidential   FCO, *15 March 1974*

From the beginning the idea of freer movement of people, ideas and information between East and West has been of the first importance in the Western approach to the Conference on Security and Co-operation in Europe. So far as Western (and neutral) Governments are concerned, it has become the point on which the success or failure of the Conference could turn. In these circumstances it may be useful to describe the background, explain where we now stand, and look at the way forward.

Background

2. The Conference was originally a Warsaw Pact idea. Two main items were then proposed for the agenda. The first (or 'security' item in the Soviet sense of the term) was to produce a declaration of principles governing relations between states, through which the Russians hoped further to entrench the *status quo*. They therefore emphasised the inviolability of frontiers, territorial integrity and the non-use of force. The second ('co-

[1] As a result of the General Election on 28 February Mr. Heath's Conservative Government lost its Parliamentary majority, and on 4 March the Labour leader, Mr. H. Wilson, was appointed Prime Minister. On the next day Mr. L.J. Callaghan succeeded Sir A. Douglas-Home as Secretary of State for Foreign and Commonwealth Affairs. This minute, which was addressed to Mr. Wiggin and Mr. Goulding, was drafted to brief new Ministers on developments in the CSCE.

operation' item) was designed to deal with co-operation between states in the economic and technical fields.

3. In the long run-up to the Conference Western countries made it clear that they did not consider that a Conference on Security and Co-operation in Europe could be so restricted. They argued first that the political aspects of security could not be divorced from the military ones; and secondly that both the strengthening of security and the development of co-operation required a lowering of barriers and progress towards freer movement of people, ideas and information.

4. The outcome of over six months' argument at Helsinki was to produce the Final Recommendations which were endorsed by Ministers of Foreign Affairs last July. Briefly it was agreed that the work of the Conference should cover a declaration of principles and some military confidence-building measures (MBFR had meanwhile been hived off), economic and technical co-operation, and a third item under the headings of 'human contacts', 'information' and 'co-operation and exchanges in the fields of culture and education' (i.e. the freer movement complex of ideas expressed in bureaucratic language). The terms of reference for the last group of subjects (usually called Basket III or Commission III) comprise paragraphs 42-52 of the Final Recommendations and may be reckoned a success for the West. The Western and neutral countries followed this up with a variety of specific proposals, none of them provocative in the ideological sense, but together designed to lower barriers in specific ways (each small but collectively important) and to underline the importance of improving contacts between the people of Europe as well as their Governments. I attach at annex the terms of reference for each of the Committees and Sub-Committees in Commission III with a summary of the main Western and neutral proposals.

State of Play in Geneva

5. In Commission III there has so far been little to show for six months' detailed work in Geneva. The Russians and their allies have maintained a restrictive interpretation of the terms of reference, and are trying to avoid both detail and commitment on the points of most interest to the West. The Poles and Bulgarians have tabled a superficial draft declaration which emphasises Government-sponsored exchanges in the cultural field but which on human contacts and information does little more than paraphrase the terms of reference in the Final Recommendations. As for the Western proposals summarised in the annex, the Russians have held up progress by resisting negotiation on a subject by subject basis. They have taken the line that the results of Commission III should be governed by a preamble, in which they want to include wording designed to provide them with an excuse for maintaining their present restrictive practices (and any others they may decide to introduce) and with a pretext for insisting that Western Governments should control the activities of broadcasting authorities, publishers and the like. The Soviet view is that the more detailed are the substantive provisions on human contacts and information, the more explicit must be the restrictive references in the preamble (which they would like to

contain references to 'non-interference' and to 'respect for the sovereignty, laws and customs' of the participating states).

6. Western and neutral delegations have successfully resisted Soviet demands that the preamble should be drafted first. But they have accepted that there should be a preamble covering the results of Commission III, and that drafting work on the preamble and on the substantive provisions should proceed in parallel.

The Prospects

7. Work in Geneva has not yet reached a state where it is possible to predict the outcome. What progress has been made has been on relatively uncontroversial points. The closer we get to substance, the stronger Soviet insistence on escape clauses and restrictive wording. How the issues will be presented for decision should be clearer by the Easter break. We shall then be having detailed discussions with the Nine and the Fifteen (with whom co-operation has been close and effective throughout) about Western strategy at the Conference as a whole. In particular we shall need to consider such points as what leverage we have over the Russians, to what extent we can bargain progress in Commission III against progress in Commission I (the declaration of principles), what the Russians will pay to secure a summit meeting at the third stage, what line we should take on machinery to follow the Conference[2] and—so far as Commission III is concerned—what our minimum requirements should be (we are still some way from any satisfactory definition of them). This should be a good point to consult Ministers and determine the way ahead. In the meantime I attach a copy of the Steering Brief which was prepared for Mr. Elliott (the leader of our Delegation at Geneva) when the second stage began last September.[3]

C.C.C. Tickell

Annex[4]

Summary of Main Western and Neutral Proposals Relating to Basket III

1. *Human Contacts*

Nationals of the participating States should be freely permitted to leave their country for reasons of marriage or family. States should take steps to ensure that no administrative obstacles, such as too expensive travel documents, or unreasonable delays in processing applications, are placed in the way of applicants. Nor should the making of such applications have any adverse effect on the individuals concerned.

Nationals of the participating States should be permitted and encouraged to travel to and within the other countries in Europe.

Where direct personal contact is not possible the exchange of corres-

[2] At a meeting of the NAC on 14 March there was general agreement that the Alliance's attitude towards the level of Stage III and follow-up should be dependent on the concessions made by the Russians during Stage II, especially in Basket III (UKDEL NATO telegram No. 122 of 14 March, MTW 10/557/6).

[3] See No. 46.

[4] The terms of reference of Committee III and its Sub-Committees are not printed.

pondence on a personal basis may provide a reasonable substitute. This correspondence should reach its addressees speedily and should not be the subject of interference by any third party.

Agreements should be concluded on a bilateral or multilateral basis to strengthen contacts between students and young people.

2. *Information*

No obstacles should be placed in the way of the wider dissemination of books and news papers.

A CSCE magazine should be established to promote the exchange of information and to perpetuate the achievements of the CSCE in various fields of cooperation covered by the Conference.

Artificial obstacles to the reception of radio and TV broadcasts should be removed and co-operation between respective broadcasting authorities encouraged.

A series of internationally linked television discussion programmes to be established, concentrating on foreign affairs.

Journalists should be allowed to enter freely and carry out their legitimate professional activities without hindrance in the participating States. They should be permitted to choose their place of work according to the needs of their profession and move and travel within their country of residence. They should not be expelled except in the case of a serious violation and by virtue of a decision based on published law.

International centres for journalists should be established to encourage contact between foreign and host-country journalists.

3. *Co-operation and exchanges in the field of culture*

Works of art should be allowed to circulate freely around the participating States and the public should be allowed free access to these.

Authors should be allowed to publish their works wherever they choose, without restrictions on the subject matter and nationals of the participating States should be allowed free access to these writings.

Artists should be allowed to move freely within the participating States to permit them to improve their professional contacts and to permit them more easily to produce and exhibit their works.

4. *Co-operation and exchanges in the field of education*

An increased number of exchanges between universities and between institutions of higher learning to be encouraged. There should be established on a regular basis an exchange of scholars and research workers and an exchange of scholarly scientific information. Joint seminars should be arranged to study matters of mutual interest in the education field. States should take steps to ensure that visiting scholars are granted access to all necessary archives.

The development and diversification of foreign languages studied in secondary and higher education should be encouraged. More language teachers should be sent to foreign countries and there should be an increased exchange of lecturers, student interpreters and translators of living languages.

No. 69

Miss Warburton (UKMIS Geneva) to Mr. Callaghan

No. 218 Telegraphic [WDW 1/4]

Priority. Confidential   GENEVA, *20 March 1974, 8.55 a.m.*

Info UKREP Brussels, UKDEL NATO, Helsinki, Saving UKDEL Vienna other EEC Posts and Moscow.

From Elliott, UKDEL to CSCE.

General Situation

1. This is not a particularly easy moment to take stock. But we have now been in the drafting stage for just over two months and I think I ought to comment on the situation as I see it at the end of my present visit to Geneva. I am specially concerned about our rate of progress. This problem is not acute but it needs watching very carefully.

2. The analysis of the possible outcomes of the Conference contained in Tickell's letter of 22 February to Staples[1] still seems generally valid. It is clear that the Russians attach major importance to Stage III taking place at the highest level.[2] There have been a number of indications recently that they would like to get the West to tell them our minimum price for agreeing to a summit. In spite of this I share the feeling that on present form the results of our work are unlikely to be impressive enough from the Western point of view to justify holding a third stage at a level higher then that of Foreign Ministers. I believe we now need, however, to think harder about problems of momentum and timing, which will obviously have a major influence on what the West eventually succeeds in achieving at the Conference.

3. All the Sub-Committees are now in the drafting stage.[3] But a formidable amount of work remains to be done. In the Principles Sub-Committee, texts on only two of the ten principles have been registered and even these are larded with square brackets. We are now discussing the inviolability of frontiers but this is the most contentious and difficult issue of all, and by Easter the Sub-Committee may have managed no more than to deal in a preliminary way with four or five of the principles. Several principles of special interest to the West (e.g. human rights) will still be outstanding as well as the

---

[1] See No. 66.

[2] Mr. Fall questioned this assertion. In a minute to Mr. McLaren of 20 March he wrote that he, like Mr. Bullard, was of the opinion that the over-riding Soviet objective was to achieve results which would not affect their vital interests. 'The summit', he observed, 'though important, comes second. The point is one of great importance in planning our strategy.'

[3] The tendency to transfer substantive discussion from Committee III Sub-Committees to informal discussion groups intensified during mid-March. And Mr. Hildyard noted in UKMIS Geneva telegram No. 202 of 16 March that, while the East were not prepared to make substantial concessions, they had moved far enough from their earlier positions to enable partial agreement to be reached on texts important to the West (EN 2/557/7).

preambular and concluding sections of the declaration. In the military Sub-Committee no progress has been made yet in drafting a document on CBMs. In Basket II more ground has been covered but many difficult issues have not been tackled.

4. In Basket III progress is slow. After several weeks of informal discussion not even provisional texts have yet been agreed on any of the important concrete questions on the agenda. The drafting of the introductory paragraphs of the Sub-Committee documents, which is likely to lead to a prolonged wrangle about restrictive provisions desired by the East, is not due to begin until much later. In addition, the question of follow-up (Committee IV) and other peripheral matters like developing countries, national minorities and especially the Mediterranean are likely to take much time.

5. Soviet tactics are not easy to analyse. Their over-riding interest is presumably to achieve a result which soon enough comes and is generally seen to be good enough for a summit Stage III to take place in July. They pay lip-service to the need for rapid progress in all the working bodies but do not always act accordingly. In the Principles Sub-Committee, Mendelevich, who speaks often and at length, does nothing to accelerate progress. On CBMs the thoroughly restrictive Soviet attitude is preventing any move forward. In the Basket II Sub-Committees the East are showing no real give over questions like business contacts and information. In Basket III, the East, while ready for frequent drafting meetings, are resisting the procedure of registering texts recording a measure of disagreement, though this is the only obvious method of achieving a reasonably rapid initial coverage of the agenda. Their attitude may reflect a natural reluctance to make concessions until the latest possible stage as well as a calculation that the June deadline will be tacitly accepted by the Conference as a whole and will work in their favour.

6. The danger is that this calculation may prove to be sound and that unless we plan the use of our time meticulously from now on the pressure of events will impost increasing strains on the endurance and unity of the Nine. I certainly find it hard to see how the work of the Conference can be completed by mid-June unless the pace is much accelerated. Most Western and neutral delegations probably share this view, but the only conclusion which is generally drawn at present is that we should get ahead with drafting as quickly as we can while continuing to press for the acceptance of all our objectives in the fullest detail. A very few, like the Dutch, are inclined to argue that it is pointless now to try to finish our work by the summer and that we should be prepared to demand a summer break and to continue in the autumn. I do not think this either practical or likely to be generally acceptable. There would be a risk of the Conference becoming a permanent gathering and this would serve nobody's interest. Moreover, it is hard to see why extending the period of negotiation should improve our bargaining position. We should lose whatever leverage we possess in the Russian desire

to get the Conference over by the summer. And if transatlantic tensions[4] and divisions among the Nine continue to increase during the summer and autumn we can hardly expect them not to be reflected at our Conference.[5]

7. A number of leading members of EEC delegations are beginning to argue now that a date around mid-June should be treated both in our private conversations and public discussions as a deadline, not necessarily for completing the drafting of the documents but for ending Stage II, whether or not there is a Stage III. Provided that such an attitude could be maintained it would be to the West's advantage, not least in that it would tend to deflect the time pressure from us on to the East. It is a question, however, whether it will be possible indefinitely to hold this line. As Tickell said in his letter under reference, the odds are against the Conference petering out without a third stage. Any initiative for breaking off or suspending it would have to come from the West and the burden of proof that such action was justified would be a heavy one. It may follow that we should firmly make up our minds very soon that our best option is to work for a third stage at Foreign Ministers' level in the summer.[6]

8. If so, we shall need to make the appropriate adjustments in our tactics. What the situation seems to require in any event is a thorough review, certainly no later than the Easter break, of our negotiating posture, and an attempt to select a limited number of major objectives on which we should concentrate in the remaining month and a half. There are risks in such a procedure, as Tickell points out in his letter under reference. But failure now to face up to the problems of our time scale and to work out our priorities

---

[4] During a visit to Washington Mr. Tickell was reminded of differences between the United States and the Nine in their approach to the CSCE. He informed Mr. Wiggin in a minute of 25 March that Mr. Sonnenfeldt had told him on 18 March that the USA regarded the Conference as 'an element in the more important game of US/Soviet relations'. Two days later Mr. E. Streator, Director for European Political Affairs in the State Department, cautioned him that the Americans were 'perhaps a little more inclined to favour the idea of a third stage summit than the Nine', and, Mr. Tickell recorded, 'we should not rely upon the Americans to fight too hard against a summit however meagre the results of the second stage'.

[5] Mr. Fall was not convinced by all the arguments in this paragraph. 'But', he minuted, 'in practice I think it would be unwise for us to work on the assumption that the second stage will go on beyond June' (see note 2 above).

[6] Mr. Fall agreed with this last assertion, as also did Mr. Tickell. However, Mr. Fall felt that what was required was not so much tactical adjustment as 'a firm Western resolve not to concede an unjustified summit'. He reasoned that rather than allowing the Russians to bring the summit into their final negotiating package, which would allow them to square bracket what they might in any case be prepared to accept, the West should state that it was already clear that the results would not justify a summit and that on this basis they agreed to work on texts which fell far short of what they proposed. 'This would not', he concluded, 'deprive us of leverage for the rest of the second stage, as the Russians will press for their Declaration even if it is to be approved by Foreign Ministers. Neither would it necessarily exclude bargaining over a summit, as the Russians many decide to reach further into their bag than I think likely: but in this case, we would be negotiating on firm ground . . . An ill-judged summit would lose us much of what we have gained' (v. *ibid*). In separate minutes Mr. McLaren, Mr. Bullard and Mr. Tickell expressed their sympathy with this view.

accordingly could lead later to the West's making more major concessions under time pressure than is necessary.[7]

[7] In a further minute to Mr. Tickell of 25 March Mr. Fall argued that pressure of work was unlikely to work to the disadvantage of the West if they were prepared to stand firm against a summit. He thought the 'real problems' would only arise if they tried to produce in six weeks results which could be honestly presented as justifying the sort of Stage III the Russians wanted. 'As you know', he wrote, 'I think we have already sold this pass; and if we were to work for a summit we should have to go back on a good deal of what has been tacitly accepted in Geneva.'

No. 70

Mr. Hildyard (UKMIS Geneva) to Mr. Callaghan

No. 247 Telegraphic [*WDW 1/11*]

Immediate. Confidential   GENEVA, *26 March 1974, 1.40 p.m.*

Info Priority UKDEL NATO, Helsinki, Bonn and Saving Washington, Mosow, Copenhagen, Paris, Rome, Luxembourg, UKREP Brussels, The Hague, Dublin.

From UKDEL to CSCE.

Our telegram No. 241.[1]

CSCE: Committee I: Principles

1. The Spanish procedural suggestion reported in our telegram under reference has been subject of much discussion among the Nine and the Fifteen. The Russians are exerting considerable pressure to obtain a solution which will effectively detach the sentence on peaceful change from the principle of inviolability of frontiers. According to Davignon (who has been in Geneva and had a long meeting with Kovalev) the Russians are exceedingly nervous. They apparently have instructions to return home at Easter with a clean text on inviolability of frontiers without any reference to peaceful change and Kovalev made it clear to Davignon that they were prepared to block progress in Committees I and III until Easter if the West did not concede the point.

2. For the present we are taking the line in Western consultations that peaceful change is the one real bargaining counter which the West possesses

[1] In this telegram of 25 March Mr. Hildyard described that day's meeting of Committee I's Principles Sub-Committee and a Spanish attempt to break the deadlock resulting from the East's objections to Western proposals to establish linkage in the third principle between the acceptance of the inviolability of frontiers and provision for peaceful change. The Spaniards, with Swiss backing, proposed that the Sub-Committee should suggest the wording of a text on peaceful change, that the agreed text should be registered on a separate piece of paper, and that its future position in the decalogue should be decided later. The Russians thought the proposal 'very interesting' and that it deserved 'serious attention'. Indeed, Mr. Hildyard suspected that the move had been 'almost certainly encouraged, and perhaps even initiated, by the Russians before the meeting (probably with American, and possibly French and FRG support)', and, as it was likely to attract a good deal of support, he believed that it would prove difficult to resist for any significant length of time.

at this Conference and that we should not give any formal indication of a willingness to separate peaceful change from inviolability of frontiers unless and until:

(*a*) We have secured better formulations of the first three sentences of the principle,[2]
and
(*b*) More importantly, we have obtained a much clearer idea than we have now of possible Soviet counter concessions in Committee III.

We have stressed the views of the Political Directors on this point (Bonn telegram No. 58 to you),[3] and have also argued that, once inviolability and peaceful change are detached, the West will never be able to reattach them. We have urged our partners and allies not to concede an issue of such fundamental importance to the East at this point, when all we shall get in return will be valueless undertakings that progress will follow in Committee III.

3. Ideally this is an issue which the West should keep open until a late point in Stage II, but there are disadvantages to the West's adopting such a tough position. There could be a general deadlock in the work of the Conference which would place Western proposals in Committee III under mounting time pressure in the weeks after the Easter break.

4. Moreover, although the position of the Nine has not yet been entirely eroded, it may prove difficult for us to maintain the support for our views of such delegations as the Dutch, Luxembourgeois, Irish and possibly the Italians plus, perhaps, the Canadians and Turks, in face of the tendency to seek a compromise evident on the part of the French, Germans, Belgians and Americans.

5. The German Presidency have been informed by Bonn that during the Kissinger/Scheel talks there was detailed discussion of the present impasse.[4]

---

[2] The first sentence of the third principle was intended to express participating states' regard for the inviolability of frontiers, and the second sentence related to the renunciation of territorial claims. The Soviet Union wanted an explicit reference to the inviolability of 'existing frontiers', and proposed that participants should promise to 'make no territorial claims upon each other' (enclosure in letter from Mr. J.A. Penney (UKMIS Geneva) to Mr. Adams of 20 March). The Russians also submitted the draft of a third sentence which acknowledged 'that peace in the area can be preserved only if no-one encroaches upon the present frontiers' (UKMIS Geneva telegram No. 239 of 25 March).

[3] See No. 60, note 14. At its meeting on 10 January the EPC Political Committee reaffirmed that 'le principe de l'inviolabilité des frontières ne doit pas être posé sans qu'il soit fait mention, sous une forme ou sous une autre, de la possibilité de changement pacifique, et que le lien direct entre les deux doit être maintenu' (WDW 1/3).

[4] Dr. Kissinger visited Bonn on 24 March for talks with Herr Brandt and Herr Scheel. According to Bonn telegram No. 441 of 25 March, Dr. Kissinger and Herr Scheel were in general agreement on the importance of the inviolability of frontiers, but Dr. Kissinger suggested that the reference to peaceful change should be taken out of the draft Declaration of Principles and put on a separate piece of paper for further consideration of where it should be incorporated. The Germans rejected this, arguing that if it were taken out the West would

Apparently the two Ministers decided that an appropriate solution would be for texts on inviolability of frontiers and peaceful change to be registered together on the same piece of paper but with the sentence on peaceful change asterisked and a footnote indicating that the sentence might be put elsewhere but that a decision on its exact position would be taken later.[5] (This account of the two Ministers' views differs from that given in paragraph 12 of Bonn telegram No. 441.[6] Nor is the robust attitude attributed there to the Germans reflected by their delegation in Geneva.) The FRG delegation here say that their legal advisers in Bonn think that if this procedure is to be adopted, it would be advisable to agree with the Russians beforehand the principle to which peaceful change should be attached.[7] (We have expressed strong reservation on this point). We do not know whether the Germans or Americans (either here or in Moscow) propose to put forward a proposal on these lines, still less whether the Russians would ever accept it.

6. There is little doubt that the Russians and Americans have also been in close touch over all this. We have some reason to believe that the latter may have given the Russians a paper (which has not so far as we know been seen by anyone else on the Western side) on the procedural question. Moreover it seems pretty clear that the Americans have received instructions to the effect that they should try to ensure that this question does not become too contentious and thus possibly sour the atmosphere of Kissinger's visit to Moscow.[8]

7. The Swiss are actively trying to build bridges. Having given public support to the Spanish procedural suggestion, Brunner[9] has now been suggesting that the passages on inviolability and peaceful change should be

be the demandeurs in trying to have it reinserted, whereas the Russians were presently the demandeurs in trying to change it. Finally, Dr. Kissinger agreed, but he suggested that the best course might be both to leave peaceful change where it was in brackets and to put it on a separate piece of paper in order to see where it might be included (WRG 3/304/1).

[5] After two meetings of the Nine at Geneva on 27 March and subsequent discussions between the Belgians and the Russians this variant of the Spanish proposal (see note 1 above) seemed to emerge as an acceptable compromise. But the Russians ended by rejecting the idea of a footnote, and the West opposed their alternative, a statement by the Chair when the texts were registered (UKMIS Geneva telegrams Nos. 257 and 263 of 28 and 29 March).

[6] See note 4 above. Sir N. Henderson reported in Bonn telegram No. 450 of 28 March that the German Foreign Ministry were in some doubt about what had been agreed between Dr. Kissinger and Herr Scheel because there was no authoritative record of their discussion.

[7] According to Sir N. Henderson (*v. ibid.*), the German Foreign Ministry were insisting that instructions to their delegates at Geneva contained no authority to agree to any compromise involving a footnote about peaceful change; the German position was to oppose any proposal at this stage to separate peaceful change from the principle of the inviolability of frontiers. Sir N. Henderson thought, however, that the Foreign Ministry might be prepared to contemplate the attachment of peaceful change to the principle of the sovereign equality of states, provided the interdependence of all principles was clearly established.

[8] Dr. Kissinger visited Moscow during 24-27 March in an unsuccessful attempt to break the deadlock on SALT negotiations and for discussions on the Middle East.

[9] M. E. Brunner was a senior official in the Swiss Federal Political Department.

drafted on two separate pieces of paper and then put aside unregistered until a later stage of the Conference. But the Russians seem unlikely to agree to this. From our point of view this proposal shares with the Spanish and Kissinger/Scheel suggestions the major disadvantage of detaching peaceful change from inviolability without any significant *quid pro quo*.

8. It is regrettable that some of our more important partners and allies seem to have sold the pass to the Russians. We might on present indications find ourselves faced with the choice whether or not to stand out in virtual isolation, against a compromise with the Russians in the near future. To do so would have obvious effects on our own relations with them. But, on the other hand, the Russians will have won a major psychological victory if they can succeed so quickly in persuading the Conference to give them what they most want without any *quid pro quo*. In view of the importance of this question in overall context of the Conference, we should be glad to know whether you believe that Political Directors should be consulted again before any final decision is taken.[10]

9. Meanwhile, unless instructed to the contrary, we shall continue to argue along the lines set out in paragraph 2 above, but may have to seek your authority to agree to a procedural compromise.

[10] Mr. Callaghan replied in telegram No. 119 to UKMIS Geneva of 27 March that the question of the inviolability of frontiers was one on which the UK 'should keep in line' with its allies and partners and British delegates were instructed not to stand out against a generally acceptable compromise. The FCO recognised the force of the tactical considerations advanced by Mr. Hildyard, but, if the text on inviolability did not contain implications of immutability and the East agreed to a satisfactory reference to peaceful change elsewhere in the declaration, they saw no reason for withholding agreement to a formula on the lines discussed by Dr. Kissinger and Herr Scheel.

No. 71

Sir T. Garvey (Moscow) to Mr. Callaghan

No. 337 Telegraphic [MTW 10/557/6]

Priority. Confidential   MOSCOW, *29 March 1974, 1.00 p.m.*

Info Routine UKMIS Geneva, UKDEL NATO, UKREP Brussels and Helsinki and Info Saving EEC Posts and UKDEL Vienna.

UKMIS Geneva tel[egram] No. 218.[1]

CSCE: Soviet Tactics

1. As seen from here Soviet tactics appear to be following consistent even 'traditional' pattern.

2. It was always expected that they would use Stage II to try to claw back concessions made in the preparatory talks. By Christmas they must have realised that Western unity and aims in Basket III remained unshaken. Early

[1] See No. 69.

this year a major diplomatic exercise was launched—letters from Brezhnev to Heads of State/Government;[2] Gromyko and others to Western capitals; use of high-level visits (Bahr,[3] Pompidou, Bratteli,[4] Kissinger to USSR) to stress Soviet desire for speedy conclusion at summit level approving satisfactory declaration of principles and minimum content in Basket III. It would have been uncharacteristic to have given ground in Geneva while this exercise was in progress. As Mr. Elliott points out last-minute trade-offs are a Soviet hall-mark (SALT I, Berlin Agreement, etc).

3. Soviet interest in a Western minimum position fits into this picture. They too probably wish to assess the results of their tactics and present state of play over the Easter break before moving (hopefully) into the final negotiating phase. A clear idea of the Western minimum position would greatly assist them.

4. I agree that to work for a third stage at Foreign Ministers' level in the summer would now be our best negotiating tactic. It would deflect the time pressure from us on to the East and put the burden on them to come up to our level of requirements for a summit Stage III. A Foreign Ministers' Stage III would be interpreted in Moscow as a Conference that had failed. Indeed, given Brezhnev's emphatic personal commitment to a Stage III 'at the highest level', I am not at all sure that the Soviet Union would agree to such an important Conference, as they have regarded it, being signed off by the Foreign Ministers. If the final documents are signed at less than summit level, the Conference will not have that 'historic significance' which is now the main prize that they hope to gain from it. The pressure on the Russians to make some concessions in the final stage of negotiations will be very strong.[5]

5. I note that the Russians and the Poles are now hinting that formulae might be found to meet Western requirements over the possibility of peaceful change of frontiers (UKMIS tel[egram] No. 204[6] para 5 and Warsaw

---

[2] See No. 62.

[3] Herr E. Bahr was Minister without Portfolio attached to the West German Chancellor's Office.

[4] Herr T.M. Bratteli was Prime Minister of Norway.

[5] Already in a despatch to Sir A. Douglas-Home of 12 February, *Soviet Détente Policy—The Internal Background*, Sir T. Garvey had emphasised the political significance for Mr. Brezhnev of a summit-level Stage III. He reasoned that in his international behaviour Mr. Brezhnev was 'promoting the political security of his régime no less than the strategic security or strategic ambitions of his country', and that his presence at a Stage III summit was important in so far as it made it 'the more difficult for his rivals in the Party ever to relegate him to the dustbin of history'. '*Détente* abroad', Sir T. Garvey concluded, 'is a highly convenient counterpoint to discipline and control at home. The two things together enable Brezhnev to occupy that invaluable middle ground of politics where he can appeal on the one hand to the conservative forces who want to keep the familiar Soviet-style law and order and not stray too far from traditional ideology; and on the other to the more progressive or radical forces, especially among the scientific intelligentsia, who seek a greater opening to the outside world. In 19th-century terms he can appeal both to the Slavophile and to the Westerner' (ENS 1/3).

[6] In this telegram of 18 March, in which he summarised general points so far made in discussion of the principle of inviolability of frontiers, Mr. Hildyard reported that, while the

tel[egram] No. 111)[7]. See also Brezhnev to Kissinger (para. 6(*c*) of my tel[egram] No. 332).[8] The document that comes out of Basket III will perhaps not expose the Soviet people appreciably more to Western influence but it could at least make any Eastern retrogression in this respect in the future more difficult.

Russians had stressed that this principle was the 'very core of peace in Europe', Mr. Mendelevich had said that the Soviet Union did not exclude 'any possibilities of integration' that may lead to the disappearance of frontiers and that frontiers in Europe would not necessarily be the same in fifty years' time (WDW 1/11).

[7] Mr. T.F. Brenchley, HM Ambassador in Warsaw, reported in this telegram of 26 March on a conversation with the Polish Deputy Foreign Minister, Professor J. Bisztyga, regarding the inviolability of frontiers. When Mr. Brenchley pointed out that in Northern Ireland and Gibraltar HMG considered the inhabitants' wishes to be paramount and that it could not therefore exclude the possibility of the peaceful change of frontiers, Professor Bisztyga said that the East had decided to disregard these cases as peripheral. He added that the East 'now recognised the need to accommodate the possibility of peaceful change and had just begun a study on how to do this without undermining the principle of inviolability' (WDW 1/11).

[8] In Moscow telegram No. 332 of 28 March Sir T. Garvey informed Mr. Callaghan of the US Ambassador's account of Dr. Kissinger's recent talks with Mr. Brezhnev (see No. 70, note 8). The latter had said with regard to the CSCE that 'if inviolability of frontiers were made "crystal clear", peaceful change could be mentioned separately elsewhere'. Mr. Brezhnev also engaged in 'Customary fulminations about Basket III' (ENS 3/304/1).

No. 72

Minute from Mr. Tickell on CSCE: Inviolability of Frontiers[1]

[WDW 1/11]

Confidential   FCO, *4 April 1974*

You will see from UKMIS Geneva telegram No. 278[2] that the Delegation have asked for urgent instructions (by 4 pm today) on a text on inviolability which they think might possibly be acceptable to everybody. The price for

[1] This minute was addressed to Mr. Wiggin and Sir J. Killick. Mr. Tickell subsequently noted on it: '*Mr. Adams*. The S. of S. accepted this recommendation & I informed Mr. Elliott that he cd. accept the package provided (*a*) the 9 & 15 remained clearly in favour & (*b*) it was understood we might have editorial changes to suggest. Pl. now dft. telegram to confirm. C.C.C.T., 4/iv.' The substance of the minute was conveyed to UKMIS Geneva in telegram No. 128 of 4 April.

[2] In this telegram of 4 April Mr. Hildyard reported that as a result of extensive private discussions between the Russians and various members of the Nine it now seemed 'just possible' that the Russians might be prepared to accept the following formulation of the third principle: 'The participating states regard as inviolable all one another's frontiers (as well as all frontiers in Europe) and therefore they will refrain now and in the future from assaulting these frontiers. Accordingly they will also refrain from any demand or act aimed at seizure and usurpation of part or all of the territory of any participating state.' Mr. Hildyard further explained that there was to be an extra meeting of Committee I's Principles Sub-Committee that afternoon when agreement on a text would have to be reached if it were to be registered before the Easter break.

Russian acceptance of this text is that the West should drop the reference, originally advanced in the French draft, to frontiers being regarded as inviolable 'irrespective of the legal status which, in their opinion, they possess'.[3]

2. You will recall that this principle is the one to which the Russians attach the most importance. A clear and unqualified statement on inviolability is what they most wish to take home from the Conference because it would clearly confirm the *status quo* in Europe. The Western objective, having agreed at the Helsinki talks to drop an explicit link between inviolability and the use of force, has been to ensure that the formulation does not in any way imply immutability. For this reason we originally pressed for the inclusion of a reference to the possibility that frontiers might be changed by peaceful means in this context. Our own attitude throughout has been to leave the running on the Western side to those most immediately affected by this principle.

3. Agreement is now close on a satisfactory formulation of the idea of peaceful change but the Eastern countries are insisting on its separation from the inviolability of frontiers. A rather patchy compromise has been agreed whereby both texts would be registered on separate pieces of paper and the one on peaceful change would be accompanied by a statement by the Chairman to the effect that its exact positioning among the principles in the Declaration of Principles had yet to be agreed.[4] The Western wish to see peaceful change tacked on to inviolability would thereby be technically protected but in practice it would be difficult to claim it back.

4. Although the English of the proposed text on inviolability reflects the butchery of several weeks bargaining over language, I think it is just satisfactory. It puts inviolability clearly in the context of the use of force. Words like 'seizure' and 'usurpation' make the point very clearly and, although 'assaulting' is used in the wrong context, the text could not in any way be read as endorsing the concept of immutability of frontiers. The loss of the reference to 'irrespective of their legal status' is a pity, but as the Germans, Americans and French are prepared to accept it I do not think it is for us to resist it. The Legal Advisers and the Departments concerned have confirmed that neither text presents us with any problems *vis-à-vis* Ireland,

---

[3] According to Mr. Hildyard (*v. ibid.*) the Russians had stated 'in blunt terms' that the retention of this phrase was politically unacceptable to them, and that if the West continued to insist upon it, this would prevent even the provisional registration of any text before Easter, the West's responsibility for such a situation would be clear to all, and the Soviet position would not change when work resumed.

[4] At its meeting on 2 April the Principles Sub-Committee settled on a text covering peaceful change. This asserted that the participating states considered that frontiers could 'be changed only in accordance with international law through peaceful means and by agreement'. The Fifteen and the Russians subsequently agreed to the registering of this text and a text on the inviolability of frontiers on separate pieces of paper, without any footnotes, but accompanied by a statement from the Chairman that it was his understanding that the Sub-Committee agreed 'that the decision on a generally acceptable place, in one of the principles for the sentence on peaceful change of frontiers [would] be taken later' (UKMIS Geneva telegrams Nos. 276 and 279 of 3 and 4 April).

Gibraltar, Malta, Cyprus, Iceland or Quadripartite Rights and Responsibilities in regard to Berlin.

5. We are now being pressed with indecent haste to agree to wording on one of the most important areas of the Conference. I would have preferred to have left the question in suspense until after the Easter break when we could have studied it more closely and conceivably used it as a bargaining counter for when the Conference resumed. But I understand from our Delegation in Geneva that the other members of the Nine and the Fifteen, in varying degrees of enthusiasm are in favour of agreeing quickly on texts which they consider meet their needs. They maintain that the point on peaceful change has in effect been given away already, and that nothing would be gained by withholding our agreement to the sort of package proposed, particularly since the Soviet leadership appear to attach such significance to settling this before the Easter break. They see this gesture as a carrot which might make the Russian donkey more amenable over Item III after Easter. If therefore we withhold our agreement, we could be effectively isolated on the Western side, and might incur the wrath of the Russians on a subject which is of less intrinsic importance to us than to our Allies.

6. In these circumstances, although it goes against the grain, I think the right course is to tell our Delegation to accept the proposed package provided that the Nine and the Fifteen remain clearly in favour of such a course. We might add that the English of the text is unbeautiful and that we therefore reserve our right to propose editorial changes later.[5]

C.C.C. TICKELL

[5] The texts on the inviolability of frontiers and their peaceful change were provisionally registered on 5 April. But negotiations were complicated at the last minute when the West German delegation unexpectedly received fresh instructions which required them to set new conditions for the acceptance of the text on the inviolability of frontiers, including the bracketing of the words 'demand or' and 'aimed at' (see note 2 above). After severe criticism from their allies and partners, who thought it too late to set such conditions, and in face of Soviet opposition to the registration of a bracketed text, the Germans were eventually persuaded to accept the following amended text: 'Accordingly, they will also refrain from any demand for or act of seizure and usurpation of part or all of the territory of any participating State' (see *Human Rights*, vol. iii, pp. 166-67). Mr. Hildyard thought the result 'as good as could have been obtained in the circumstances', and that when the time came to decide the principle to which the provision for peaceful change was to be attached the West might still have some leverage for use as appropriate in Baskets I or III (minute from Mr. McLaren to Mr. Wiggin of 5 April; UKMIS Geneva telegrams Nos. 294-97 of 8 April).

No. 73

Mr. Hildyard (UKMIS Geneva) to Mr. Callaghan

No. 288 Telegraphic [WDW 1/4]

Priority. Confidential   GENEVA, *6 April 1974, 12.15 p.m.*

Repeated for information to UKDEL NATO, Saving to EEC and NATO Posts, Helsinki and Moscow.

From Elliott, UKDEL to CSCE.

My telegram No. 218:[1]

General Situation

1. The Conference adjourned yesterday evening until 22 April. Most Western and neutral delegates will be returning to capitals disappointed by the lack of progress and with reduced expectations about the practical significance of what the Conference will ultimately achieve. I suspect that the Soviet and East European delegations for their part are not dissatisfied with the way things have gone, despite the slow rate of progress and the deadlock over the drafting of the preamble in Committee III. They are no doubt gratified by having secured the registration before Easter of a satisfactory provisional text on the principle of inviolability of frontiers.[2]

Progress

2. Drafting has advanced little in the two weeks since my telegram under reference. In the Principles Sub-Committee seven of the ten principles as well as the preambular and concluding sections of the Declaration of Principles remain to be drafted, and much will have to be done before the three principles which have been dealt with are finally agreed. The placing of the sentence on the peaceful change of frontiers could prove contentious and time-consuming. In the Military Sub-Committee there has been no movement by the East towards acceptance of Western and neutral idea on confidence-building measures, nor has much progress been made on the other, for us less important, military aspects of the mandate, although the prospects here are better. In the Basket II Sub-Committees too the pace has been slow and the East continue to resist drafting on certain issues of importance to the West, notably business contacts.[3]

3. In the Basket III Sub-Committees texts have been registered on family meetings, the dissemination of printed information, contacts between academic institutions and information in the field of culture. But by far the greater part of the mandates of these Sub-Committees has not been touched on. Most of the questions over which the East are sensitive and on which

---

[1] See No. 69.

[2] See No. 72, note 5.

[3] In a letter to Mr. Kay of 5 April, in which she reported the Ad Hoc Group's pre-Easter assessment of work in Committee II, Miss Warburton noted: 'It was accepted that prospects after Easter depend quite largely on developments on the Third Principle in Committee I, since the East seem determined to block progress elsewhere until satisfied on that.'

satisfactory texts are essential for the West lie ahead.[4] In Committee III itself no part of the text of the preamble has yet been even provisionally agreed.[5] Much remains to be done too on the question of follow-up and the nature of the final document, and on such peripheral but always time-wasting questions as the Mediterranean, developing countries and national minorities.

Warsaw Pact

4. There has been no significant change in the tactics of the Warsaw Pact delegations since my telegram under reference. They continue to advocate more rapid progress but withhold the concessions needed to produce it. In the drafting of the principles they are fighting every inch of the way. Over CBMs they are on the defensive but adamantly negative. In Basket III their attitude has if anything hardened recently as far as the Information and Contacts Sub-Committees are concerned. It is possible that this has been merely a temporary manoeuvre designed to put pressure on the West over the drafting on inviolability of frontiers in Basket I. If so, the East may show a greater readiness to do business after Easter. But they will probably continue even at that stage to hold up progress on the sensitive issues (unless the West are prepared to accept emasculated texts) until they see what we are willing to concede in the way of a restrictive reference to the principles in the preamble. This tactic, together with the normal Soviet reluctance to make concessions until the latest possible stage is likely to mean that the crucial negotiation will be crammed into the last few weeks. Even then we should not expect to find much give on the Eastern side. They will no doubt continue to maintain the outwardly bland and cool negotiating posture which has proved so rewarding to them during this Stage.

The Neutrals and Non-aligned

5. The neutrals have been active in promoting informal contacts and have supported the West on the substance of most issues. But they are generally in favour of an early conclusion to the Conference and are inclined to look to follow-up machinery to carry forward its aims. They are eager for progress and disappointed by the lack of it. They have therefore been ready sometimes to make greater concessions in the interests of speed than we would wish. The Yugoslavs and Romanians ride their usual hobby-horses, the former more prominently than the latter, who (elsewhere than in Committee

---

[4] Mr. Hildyard suggested in UKMIS Geneva telegram No. 290 of 6 April that the East's 'relative eagerness' to improve the momentum of work in areas of less sensitivity to themselves in the Culture and Education Sub-Committees might well be designed to substantiate a claim that 'satisfactory progress' was being made in Basket III. He added: 'If this trend continues, we shall need to consider carefully our possible reaction, including slowing down progress in these Sub-Committees' (EN 2/557/3).

[5] In UKMIS Geneva telegram No. 289 of 6 April Mr. Hildyard described how the last meeting of Committee III had ended in 'a long and sterile wrangle with both sides seeking to blame the other for the deadlock'. Mr. Dubinin blamed the West for 'refusing to put into effect the 6 February compromise', and the East German delegate, Dr. Bock, 'denied that square brackets could be used where important matters such as basic aims were involved, and voiced dark hints about the Committee's failure having repercussions elsewhere' (EN 2/557/3).

II) have generally kept their heads down and been less troublesome than might have been expected.

The West

6. The cohesion of the Nine has stood up reasonably well to the strains of the past three months of negotiation. But there have sometimes been serious differences of view on tactics. Taken with the scope and complexity of the negotiations and the absence of a common view of the broad strategy and timing these have meant that the Nine have tended to react slowly to developments and have on occasion got out of step. The Germans have in the event proved weak and disorganised in the Presidency. All this has given an impression of greater disunity than has in fact existed and has exposed the Nine to accusations of causing delay. Their general credibility and influence on the neutrals have suffered in consequence and so have relations between the Nine and the other NATO delegations. (Under the bureaucratic German Chairmanship the Nine have too often presented draft resolutions and papers to the rest of the Fifteen as *faits accomplis* to which no amendments are permissible). The Americans, who returned after the Christmas break with instructions to be more active, have shown an anxiety to speed up progress which has intensified in recent weeks. But, although clearly eager to get the Conference out of the way, they have not thrown their weight around.

The Next Phase

7. This situation is a matter for disquiet. In particular there is a risk in the face of these tough but skilful Soviet tactics and mounting time pressure the West may find it difficult to maintain their cohesion and to achieve the best possible outcome to the negotiations. What seems essential is that at the meetings during the Easter break of the Nine in Bonn and of NATO the situation here should be assessed realistically and decisions taken on the vital strategic questions. The Presidency have prepared a paper listing the outstanding points that need decision.[6] This is useful but not all the questions are of equal importance or urgency. I hope we can ensure that the Political Directors will not be sidetracked but will concentrate on establishing the broad strategy for the final stage of the negotiations which delegations here at present lack.

8. The essential points are in my view:

(*a*) *Timing.* My views are as in my telegram under reference. Later developments have underlined the urgency of the problem. Unless a June/July deadline can be avoided—and it continues to be the working hypothesis of most delegations here—the greater part of the CSCE negotiations will have to be squeezed into a couple of months. However undesirable this may be, I continue to believe that we must accept the situation and adjust our tactics and fix our priorities accordingly. But while seeking to achieve our main objectives within this period and exploiting the

---

[6] Not printed.

Soviet desire for a Stage III in the summer to this end, we should recognise that it may now not prove feasible and that Western Governments may be faced at a very late stage with a choice between accepting much less than they have hoped and insisting on a postponement of Stage III until later in the year.

(b) *Level of Stage III.* A clear decision at Geneva on the level of Stage III will not be possible unless Western Governments agree to a summit. I continue to think that the results will not justify this. In any case this is one of the few levers we retain for putting pressure on the Russians to accept our demands on CBMs and Basket III. We need therefore to proceed on the assumption that Stage III will be at Foreign Minister level and to let it be generally known that only large-scale Eastern concessions in the areas of interest to the West could change this view.

(c) *Strategy and Tactics.* We have few other bargaining counters left. Although they have made concessions to achieve it, the Russians have now got a registered text on inviolability which is reasonably satisfactory to them and we have little leverage left in the field of principles. Indeed on a number of the remaining principles we are 'demandeurs'. In these circumstances the West and Nine in particular will need to be united and tenacious on the main issues in order to turn the time factor to their advantage. Having established our priorities we must be prepared to hold out for them until what may seem a dangerously late stage. An eagerness on our part to make early progress would be more likely than not to lead to concessions.[7] We may have problems as a result with the neutrals and the Americans as well as the East. We must be flexible in our use of the Sub-Committees and informal drafting methods in order to cover the ground and stake out the issues but not give up any of our main desiderata, at least until the final crunch. To this end we must force the East to accept a liberal use of square brackets in Basket III and ensure that any resistance on their part to this is generally seen as the reason for the lack of progress. And the West should be ready to refuse consensus on particular principles or the Declaration as [a] whole until we obtain satisfaction in other areas. A directive by the Political Directors in this sense (preferably endorsed by NATO) would be the most useful result their meeting could have.[8]

[7] Mr. McLaren explained in a minute of 8 April covering the transmission of this telegram to the Private Secretary that this last sentence was open to some ambiguity. 'As drafted', he observed, 'this could be read as meaning that Western pressure for early results could produce concessions on the part of the Russians; whereas Mr. Elliott clearly intended to say that eagerness to make progress would be more likely than not to lead to *Western* concessions.'

[8] Cf. No. 75.

No. 74

Mr. Hildyard (UKMIS Geneva) to Mr. Callaghan

No. 293 Telegraphic [WDW 1/6]

Priority. Confidential   GENEVA, *8 April 1974, 7.46 a.m.*

Repeated information UKDEL NATO, UKDEL Vienna, Saving Washington, Bonn, Paris, Rome, Helsinki, The Hague, Luxembourg, Brussels, Dublin, Ottawa, Rabat.

From UKDEL to CSCE.

CSCE: Military Aspects of Security

1. Sub-Committee 2 has now virtually completed a first round of drafting on the main texts relevant to paragraphs 22, 23 and 24 of the Helsinki Recommendations.[1] But although there has been some discussion of preambular language at the request of the Western and neutral/non-aligned delegations who want at least one separate document on the military aspects of security there is no understanding yet of how the various texts under discussion might be combined.

2. The NATO delegations are working well together. Their present good negotiating position could be usefully strengthened by a productive discussion in the NATO Political Committee in Brussels after Easter of the various points of difficulty on the agenda they have proposed for that meeting (our tel[egram] No. 285—not to all).[2]

Confidence Building Measures

3. The Warsaw Pact delegations have been kept on the defensive throughout this session of work.[3] Fortified by useful discussions in NATO in the Christmas break the West tabled first a German explanatory document[4] which tackled some of the Eastern arguments against anything more than minimal CBMs. Shortly thereafter (and after a rather difficult exchange with the Americans on movements) we were able to put forward a British draft resolution on CBMs[5] which maintained the pressure on the East, was well received by the neutrals/non-aligned and helped to focus discussion on the specific provisions of CBMs. This draft resolution was thereafter completed by another one tabled by six neutral/non-aligned delegations led by Yugoslavia.[6] Although this second draft conceded a number of unnecessary

---

[1] See Cmnd. 6932, p. 146.

[2] Not printed.

[3] Mr. Adams minuted on 20 March that the Russians seemed 'to be making almost as much of a meal of CBMs as they [were] of Committee III subjects'. He said reasons for this might be: (1) the Russians thought they might suffer military disadvantage even from the prior notification of major military manoeuvres; (2) the East were 'truly isolated over CBMs and . . . unable to provide convincing arguments for their restrictive position'; and (3) they had realised that CBMs would be a 'clearer test of their sincerity . . . than most other areas of the Conference'. Mr. Adams thus concluded 'that, despite all our difficulties in NATO, we have the Russians on the run over confidence building measures and should keep them there as long as possible'.

[4] See No. 59, note 7 and *Human Rights*, vol. iii, pp. 322-7.

[5] *V. ibid.*, pp. 327-9.

[6] *V. ibid.*, pp. 329-32.

points to the East it was sufficiently ambitious in content to make our own draft look [the] reasonably moderate middle of the road proposal which it is.

4. Drafting started quite quickly thereafter, despite Eastern reluctance because most other delegations thought that this was the best way of keeping up the pressure and ensuring that work in the Military Sub Committee which was lagging behind was not separated completely from the rest of the Conference. Nonetheless the start of drafting did not mean that there was any meeting of minds on the fundamental points of detail. In the event therefore (and in total contrast with some of the Committee III Sub Committees) the Sub Committee has contented itself with registering provisionally a mosaic of alternative proposals whose numerous square brackets can only be resolved when the Warsaw Pact show a political willingness to make sizeable concessions.

5. Present Soviet proposals on manoeuvres show virtually no advance from September. They are proposing notification not less than five days in advance, to neighbours only of manoeuvres of army corps size in certain narrow frontier zones only. Given this position it is inevitable that their position on the exchange of observers is also so restrictive as to mark a retreat from the Helsinki recommendations. They have (apparently for MBFR as well as security reasons) ruled out completely any agreement to notify major military movements—a position which the West should try not to disguise in the final document. And they are resisting other fairly simple proposals suggested by the Spanish and Swedish delegations for military exchanges and more open presentation of military budgets.

6. The East are in an exposed and untenable position. They will be obliged to make concessions if they are not to call in question their own commitment to *détente*. But the Russians are clearly operating under tight instructions from Moscow and although in mid-session they were indicating fall-back positions (e.g. notification up to 500 kilometres from their western borders)[7] which would be quite a satisfactory achievement for the West they are keeping a close eye on developments in Vienna and have not recently indicated any such flexibility.

7. We ourselves are playing an unexpectedly prominent role in the CBM discussions though our position may be damaged if we cannot go some way to meet the concerns of some of our flank allies and of the neutrals and non-aligned by showing some flexibility on the question of notification of independent air and naval manoeuvres and of lower level activity in certain areas round Europe.[8]

[7] In a letter of 8 February Mr. Adams, who was then with UKMIS Geneva, informed Mr. Burns that he had learned from the French that Mr. Mendelevich had suggested that the Russians 'might be able to accept a line into Soviet territory from the frontier equivalent to the radius of the largest other European country'. This, according to French calculations would produce a line about 500 kilometres within the USSR.

[8] Mr. Burns, who had replaced Mr. Adams in Geneva, wrote to the latter on 19 March that British delegates looked like becoming isolated on the notification of separate air and naval manoeuvres, and that the Americans had recently spoken very strongly in favour of notification.

8. The outlook for the West is good so long as nerves hold and the temptation is resisted to settle prematurely for less than the Warsaw Pact might concede in the final trade-off at the end of the Conference. There seems no good reason why with persistance CBMs should not be one of the real Western successes at this Conference with the Russians conceding the right to the West to go on pressing in future for more assurances about the Western part of the Soviet Union.

MBFR and Disarmament

9. There is less to say on the drafting of texts to cover paragraphs 22 and 24 of the Helsinki Recommendations. The neutral and non-aligned delegations have moderated their earlier demands to link the CSCE and MBFR negotiations and as a result have tabled a draft resolution which has proved an acceptable basis for drafting.

10. The Russians and East Europeans are clearly concerned to limit the kind of guidelines which the CSCE might lay down for future negotiations elsewhere. The Americans without instructions are silent but anxious. The French also without fresh instructions question the need for any text at all on the grounds that all that the Final Recommendations require is an exchange of views. Having reserved their position however they are active in seeking language which does not imply any approval of MBFR but could be acceptable to the rest of the Conference.[9] NATO delegations are giving them active and sympathetic support in this effort.

[9] The French particularly disliked references in the neutral/non-aligned text to disarmament 'in Europe'. This, they argued, was a concept of regional disarmament unacceptable to NATO (letter from Mr. Burns to Mr. Adams of 6 April).

No. 75

Mr. Callaghan to Sir E. Peck (UKDEL NATO)

No. 80 Telegraphic [WDW 1/3]

Immediate. Confidential   FCO, *19 April 1974, 5.30 p.m.*

Repeated for information to immediate UKMIS Geneva (CSCE Delegation), Routine EEC Posts, Washington, Moscow, Vienna, Info saving Helsinki, Oslo, Ankara, Athens, Ottawa, Berne, Stockholm, Madrid, Lisbon, Algiers, Cairo, Tunis, Rabat, Tel Aviv.

Following from Delegation.

European Political Co-operation: CSCE: Meeting of the Political Committee on 18 and 19 April[1]

1. The Political Committee discussed the CSCE on 18 April on the basis of reports from the Presidents of the Sub-Committee and Ad Hoc Group following meetings on 17 April. There was discussion of most of the main problems, but, as so often, tactical questions and drafting points took precedence

[1] The Nine's CSCE Sub-Committee and the Ad Hoc Group met in Bonn on 17-18 April, and the EPC Political Committee met there on 18-19 April.

over strategy. Most Political Directors seemed discouraged by the way the second stage had so far gone and took a gloomy view of future prospects. Only the Dane seemed fairly optimistic, but he put this down, at least in part, to his relatively low expectations of the CSCE from the beginning. But if there was staleness and a sense of fatigue among some representatives from delegations at Geneva, there was also a disposition to see things through and insist on progress on matters of importance to the West (in particular in Committee III) as a condition for further progress elsewhere.

Report of the Sub-Committee

2. The Directors had before them a report which incorporated extensive amendments to an earlier paper (CSCE/74/101 P)[2] agreed at the meeting of the Sub-Committee on 17 April. Subject to a few further amendments this report was approved. It is a sensible document which should provide useful guidance to the delegations of the Nine in Geneva. Copy follows by bag (not to all).[3]

3. The main result of the meeting will be clear from the document and the conclusions of the Political Committee.[3] They should be read in the light of the following comments.

(a) *Nature and form of final documents.* After discussion of the various alternatives the Committee expressed a preference for signature of a fairly substantial looking document on the lines of the Dutch paper already tabled in Geneva.[4] Within the framework of the Final Act there should be a multiplicity of resolutions and other texts in conformity with our understanding of the procedural compromise already arrived at in Geneva on 6 February.[5] As always this subject engendered considerable heat and the result was hard-won.[6]

(b) *Inviolability of frontiers.* The problem here was to decide to what principle we should aim to attach the agreed text on peaceful change of frontiers in the declaration. After discussion of the possibilities (in which the Germans seemed to change their views over again), the Committee agreed to our suggestion that it was too early yet to decide.[7]

(c) *Confidence-building measures.* It was agreed that there would be tactical advantage in maintaining our position on the prior notification of military

---

[2] This paper of 3 April summarised outstanding problems in the CSCE and endeavoured to refine the objectives of the Nine. In a letter of 6 April covering its despatch Mr. Maxey advised Mr. Tickell: 'We need a clear political steer from the Political Directors so that we can maintain the point of importance to us in the gadarene rush to the end of Stage II.'

[3] Not printed.

[4] See *Human Rights*, vol. iii, pp. 37-40.

[5] See No. 65.

[6] In his letter of 6 April (see note 2 above) Mr. Maxey reported that the French had 'taken up a strong position against including the texts of the various documents within the overall final act to be signed by Ministers'.

[7] Mr. Maxey thought that the 'best way of stopping the Nine surrendering precipitately what [was] left of this bargaining counter [would] be to prevent any early decision being taken on the exact alternative place for the sentence on peaceful change'.

movements until the final trade-offs in Geneva and that the eight NATO members would seek to persuade the Americans of this when the question was discussed within the Alliance.[8] The Irish argued on the merits rather than on the tactics of the case, and the resulting reference in the report and conclusions of the meeting is therefore less clear than it might have been.

(*d*) *Committee III.* This is perhaps the most useful part of the report. It sets out the priorities for the West without entering into a degree of detail which might otherwise have prejudiced our bargaining position in Geneva. We said that we thought our principal effort should be directed in the first instance to getting the Russians and their allies to agree to the use of square brackets to speed up the drafting of texts in the way that has already been done in the other Committees.[9]

(*e*) *Follow-up.* It was agreed that there would be advantage in tabling a Western resolution on the resumption of work in Geneva. The Danes had earlier volunteered to do this and produced an improved version of their earlier draft.[10] The main question discussed was whether we should stick to the idea of a meeting of senior officials in 1977 previously considered by Ministers of the Nine, or take a cautious step forward by proposing a committee on follow up to meet in 1976. The Danes, with our support, expressed a strong preference for the more forthcoming alternative. But the other members of the Committee, recognising that we should in any case be obliged to make concessions when the drafting began in Geneva, were strongly inclined to caution. In the end we agreed to the text annexed to the report *ad referendum*.[11] Given the tactical situation its early tabling in Geneva should be regarded as a modest step forward on the part of the Nine. This is also about as far as we understand the Americans are likely to go in present circumstances.

(*f*) *Mediterranean.* The question was discussed by Political Directors over lunch. A satisfactory procedural compromise was reached which confirms the preference of the Nine for a separate document but directs the Presidency to have further discussions with the Americans.[12] Further

---

[8] See No. 59, note 7.

[9] This was very much in line with the course recommended by Mr. Maxey on 6 April. 'What we shall need from the Political Directors', he wrote, 'is firm support for a show-down with the Russians on the question of the slowness of progress in the sub-committees on Human Contacts and Information if this continues after Easter.'

[10] The Danish draft resolution, annexed to the CSCE Sub-Committee report of 3 April and dated 26 February, foresaw the convening in 1977 of a meeting of high officials to evaluate the implementation of CSCE decisions and the state of the international political situation. They were also to make proposals on measures to pursue Conference aims, further meetings and a new conference.

[11] Not printed.

[12] Already on 16 April Mr. James of the US Embassy in London had called on Mr. Wiggin to register his Government's objections to an Italian draft CSCE declaration of 19 March which expressed, *inter alia*, the intention of participants to promote good-neighbourly relations in the Mediterranean region and to contribute to the elimination of tension there. Mr. James

soundings will be taken among the Mediterranean countries, this time including Israel.

(g) *Level of the third stage.* It was agreed that the possibility of a third stage at summit level could not be excluded. But the majority clearly thought that the results of the Conference, insofar as they could now be predicted, would not be of sufficient importance to justify a summit (although we should of course take care not to present the Conference as a failure). A third stage at Foreign Minister level would best reflect the idea of a step in the continuous process towards *détente* if the results of the Conference turned out to be relatively small.

Part II: Report of the Ad Hoc Group

4. The Political Directors took note of the oral report of the Chairman of the Ad Hoc Group. The Ad Hoc Group had reached agreement on the tactics to be followed in dealing with the Eastern pressure for an endorsement of the principle of most favoured nation treatment, and the Political Directors were not therefore required to consider this subject. Instead they spent much time on the less important question of how far we should go to meet the Romanians and others in their wish for an acknowledgement that there were developing countries in Europe. A compromise text was eventually agreed for proposal in Geneva. This may not go far enough to satisfy the special interests of the countries concerned, but the Belgians in particular thought that to go further would cause us difficulty, e.g. over generalised preferences.[13] It was agreed that any proposed amendments to the text should be referred to capitals for decision.

said that the US Government disliked the very idea of a comprehensive declaration which, they feared, would merely serve to open up the CSCE to contentious Middle Eastern questions, and that they wanted to see the issue broken up and dealt with as appropriate in Baskets I and II. In a letter to Mr. Sykes of 29 April Mr. Wiggin remarked that he felt the American attitude to be much influenced by their suspicion that this was a further venture by the Nine into the 'stormy waters' of the Arab-Israeli dispute (MWP 1/11).

[13] Paragraph 4 of a draft preamble to Item II, tabled by the Yugoslavs on 15 November 1973, declared participants' interest in promoting economic and social development in developing countries. On 19 March the Romanians tabled a further draft provision which made specific reference to the 'needs of the developing countries of Europe' (see *Human Rights*, vol. iv, pp. 7-8 and 11). This the Belgians were reluctant to accept, especially since it seemed likely to profit Romania. But other members of the Ad Hoc Group, including the UK, saw tactical advantage in using the provision to secure the support of the 'more moderate "developing" members of the Conference' on issues of importance to the West, such as reciprocity (main brief for the meeting of the Ad Hoc Group at Bonn on 17 April, MTW 10/557/5).

No. 76

Mr. Burns (UKMIS Geneva) to Mr. Callaghan

No. 334 Telegraphic [EN 2/557/6]

Priority. Confidential   GENEVA, *27 April 1974, 11.40 a.m.*

Repeated for information to Saving Moscow, Washington, Helsinki, UKDEL NATO, EEC Posts.

From UKDEL to CSCE.

Committee III: Sub-Committees

1. The disparity between progress in the Sub-Committees on human contacts and information on the one hand, and those on culture and education on the other, has grown more pronounced this week. While the latter continued to move slowly forward, the deadlock reached in the former before the Easter break showed no sign of being resolved. There has been no hint on the Eastern side that, having achieved an agreed text on inviolability of frontiers, or for any other reason, they are now prepared to make concessions in the sensitive areas of contacts and information. If anything, their position there has hardened.

2. The chief reason for this intransigence probably remains the East's anxiety to see what sort of restrictions they can incorporate in the preamble before allowing substantive drafting to proceed in the more sensitive Sub-Committees.[1] The decisive move over the drafting of the preamble which has been agreed on by the Nine (my tel[egram] No. 330)[2] is partly designed to put Eastern intentions in this area to the test. The position may thus become

---

[1] Mr. Burns maintained in UKMIS Geneva telegram No. 317 of 24 April (MTW 10/557/6) that as a result of informal discussions with Eastern delegations it had become apparent that satisfactory progress in Committee III Sub-Committees on issues to which the West attached importance was unlikely until the East had a clearer picture how the preamble, especially the reference to principles, would be drafted. He thought the West had 'nothing to gain by playing it long' and he favoured more Western flexibility in the drafting of the preamble. But, while Mr. Callaghan agreed that it was in the Western interest to secure an early agreement on a preamble, he insisted in telegram No. 148 to UKMIS Geneva of 25 April that this depended on 'satisfactory formulation on the question of state competence' (EN 2/557/3).

[2] UKMIS Geneva telegrams Nos. 330 and 331 of 27 April reported that the Nine had agreed that Western delegations should now express readiness to accept a Finnish draft preamble to Basket III. This had not yet been tabled in full (see *Human Rights*, vol. v, pp. 15-16), and an additional fourth paragraph referred to participants 'bearing in mind the principles guiding relations among the participating states, adopted by this Conference'—a non-committal statement whose acceptance by the East Mr. Burns thought would represent a major gain for the West (EN 2/557/3). But Western tactics were defeated when, on 1 May, the Finns declined to table the new paragraph, and other neutrals and the non-aligned refused to back the initiative. The Nine decided to await developments in Committee III, to test the readiness of the East to use square brackets, and to insist, if there was continued resistance to this, that the preamble be considered as a whole (UKMIS Geneva telegram No. 350 of 2 May, MTW 10/557/6).

clearer in the course of the next two weeks.

3. Despite three meetings this week the Human Contacts Sub-Committee failed to register agreement on any part of a text on family reunification. In informal discussions the Russians made it clear that they were not ready to move any further towards the Western position. The resulting gap between the two sides was discussed at length at the last meeting of the Sub-Committee, a process which was clearly disagreeable to Eastern delegations. The effect was slightly marred by an unhelpful intervention from the Swedish delegate who, by trying to reconcile the irreconcilable, enabled the East to avoid bearing full responsibility for the deadlock.

4. Informal discussions on access to printed information proved equally fruitless. The subject was therefore referred back to the Sub-Committee, where in the course of a useful discussion Western speakers again sought to pin the blame on Eastern intransigence. There can be little doubt that the Russians and East Germans in particular dislike having to defend their hard-line positions in the Sub-Committee. There is general agreement among the [W]estern delegations that the continuation of such debates, even if they are unproductive in the short term, may have a useful effect. For the present informal meetings on both contacts and information have lapsed.

5. In marked contrast the Russians have in the Sub-Committees on culture and education shown the same willingness to push ahead as they did in the last weeks before Easter. The French proposals on information in the cultural field (K/124)[3] have now been provisionally disposed of with the registration of a new paragraph in place of one previously in square brackets: and a Yugoslav proposal on cultural amenities for migrant workers (K/109)[4], suitably amended by ourselves, is likely to be adopted at the next meeting of the Sub-Committee (texts to follow by bag). However, there has so far been no reaction from the Russians to the French proposals on access to cultural works (K/125—text by bag)[5], the references in these to the dissemination of literature may well delay further progress in the Sub-Committees for some time.

6. In Education, the Russians seem to have accepted the idea of including a separate text on scientific cooperation (based on the French proposals in L/115—copy by bag),[6] but they are resisting an introductory passage put forward by the Germans[7] which would have the effect of detaching the French proposals from previously registered texts under paragraph 51(B) and giving them a special status among the final documents of the Sub-Committee.

[3] See *Human Rights*, vol. v, pp. 229-31.

[4] *V. ibid.*, p. 220.

[5] *V. ibid.*, pp. 231-32.

[6] *V. ibid.*, pp. 325-27.

[7] *V. ibid.*, p. 331.

No. 77

Minute from Mr. Tickell to Private Secretary
[*WDW 1/5*]

Confidential   FCO, *30 April 1974*

Dr. Kissinger's Message on the CSCE[1]

A draft reply to Dr. Kissinger's message to the Secretary of State is submitted. It follows the line set out by the Secretary of State at his office meeting this afternoon.[2]

2. One or two points may be worth bringing out. First Dr. Kissinger is clearly anxious to reach an agreed position within the Alliance. To that effect he has made it clear that the Americans have made no commitment to the Russians. But I doubt if he is fully aware of the extent to which the Alliance (and in particular the Eight out of the Nine) have already co-ordinated their positions on this point at meetings at official level during the Easter break.[3] It was then agreed that while we should not exclude the possibility of a third stage meeting at the summit (and this would be an essentially political decision for our Heads of State or Government themselves), the results of the second stage, so far as we could then assess them, were unlikely to justify it. As you know Western co-ordination at the CSCE has so far been extremely effective, but all are, I think, anxious lest anyone should now decide to cut and run. The Americans, who have always taken less interest in the CSCE

---

[1] In this message, transmitted in Washington telegram No. 1506 of 29 April (AMU 18/6), Dr. Kissinger informed Mr. Callaghan that during a meeting with Mr. Gromyko at Geneva on 28-29 April the Soviet Foreign Minister had 'raised rather forcefully the question of winding up the CSCE Conference and particularly the desirability of making an early decision about making the final stage occur at the summit level'. Dr. Kissinger was 'very concerned' that this question should not be allowed to become 'another cause for a squabble' between the United States and its allies under Soviet pressure, and, he asserted, he was 'particularly concerned' that he and Mr. Callaghan should be 'together on this matter'.

[2] Mr. Fall prepared this draft reply, an amended version of which was conveyed to Washington in telegram No. 976 of 2 May. In this Mr. Callaghan stated that his first impression was that, on the basis of results to date, there must be some doubt as to whether a final stage at summit level was warranted. He further explained that, although this assessment would change if real progress were made in May and June, the Russians had pocketed Western concessions on the inviolability of frontiers, but shown 'little sign of their promised flexibility over human contacts, information and military confidence building measures'. Until the West knew what the Russians were prepared to pay for a summit, he thought they should keep an open mind about Stage III and that the NATO Ministerial meeting in June would perhaps offer the right opportunity for taking such decisions. Mr. Callaghan added that he would be very happy to discuss all this with Dr. Kissinger and that he should let him know when he could 'stop off in London'.

[3] See No. 75. At a special meeting of the NAC on 22 April it was generally agreed that it would be 'reasonable' for NATO delegations to aim for mid-July as the end of Stage II, so that Stage III could take place in September or early October. It was also agreed that the most appropriate level of Stage III was likely to be Foreign Ministers (UKDEL NATO telegram No. 173 of 23 April, WDW 1/4).

than the others, have long been suspect.[4] The main danger of anyone breaking ranks is of course that others will do so too.

3. The Soviet proposal for a third stage 'at the highest level' was restated at the recent meeting of the Consultative Committee of the Warsaw Pact, which was attended by Mr. Brezhnev and his opposite numbers.[5] It is not surprising that Mr. Gromyko should have made a major issue of this in his talks with Dr. Kissinger. The Russians may hope that President Nixon will be the first Western leader to come out in favour of a summit, and that this would persuade others to follow suit. The Polish Vice-Minister for Foreign Affairs recently told HM Ambassador in Warsaw that it was now clear that President Nixon would attend the final stage, and that it seemed unlikely that other Western leaders would exclude themselves from a Conference attended by Mr. Brezhnev and President Nixon.[6] Our own thinking on the level of the third stage remains as set out in your letter of 8 April to Lord Bridges.[7]

4. In the last few months the Russians have made it clear that agreement on the point of most interest to them—inviolability of frontiers—in Committee I would lead them to be more accommodating on the points of most interest to the West in Committee III. Provisional agreement on inviolability of frontiers was reached before Easter; but since the resumption of the talks afterwards, the Russians and their allies have shown no signs of flexibility on Committee III. In these circumstances to give any indications in favour of a summit now would imply that we were satisfied with what had been achieved in Geneva and would deprive us of tactical leverage in the final phase of the negotiations.

5. Dr. Kissinger mentioned in his message that he had also written to Herr Scheel on the matter. We have no reason to believe that Herr Scheel would reply in any sense different from that suggested by the Secretary of State, but I think it would be wise of us to let the Germans have a copy of the Secretary

---

[4] In a letter of 18 April Mr. Beetham, HM Embassy in Helsinki, informed Mr. Fall that he had questioned Mr. M.N. Streltsov, Soviet Minister there, on an AFP report which headlined in the Finnish press and claimed that Dr. Kissinger and Mr. Brezhnev had agreed a summit-level Stage III. Mr. Streltsov had no confirmation of the news from Moscow, but said that 'it was quite likely to be true since he expected that to be Nixon's position for various reasons'.

[5] The Warsaw Pact's Political Consultative Committee met in Warsaw on 17-18 April: see Cmnd. 6932, pp. 176-8. On 23 April Mr. Bullard minuted to Sir J. Killick that while the British press interpreted the Consultative Committee's *communiqué* as a renewed commitment to *détente*, he feared that *détente* was 'becoming one of those words which are used so often that they cease to have much meaning'. He added: 'The paragraphs on the CSCE are dressed up to look like a positive contribution, but a close reading shows that all progress in Basket III is made dependent on the definition and application of principles of relations between states. This is only the Warsaw Pact position at Geneva in somewhat more cosmetic terms' (WDW 1/4).

[6] This discussion occurred on 3 April (Warsaw telegram No. 126 of 3 April, WDW 1/319/1).

[7] This was drafted in reply to Mr. Wilson's query on prospects for a Stage III summit. It explained that a summit would risk giving the public an impression that the major questions of security, cooperation and freer movement in Europe had been settled, and that 'we could now afford to relax our efforts, particularly in the field of defence'. Mr. Acland noted there was 'no particular advantage' to be had from a Stage III summit, but concluded that equally nothing was to be gained from holding out against one if it were favoured by the UK's major allies.

of State's reply as soon as possible after its despatch.[8] Herr Scheel, as current President of the Nine, will have to decide on the thorny problem of whether or not to tell the others about the present correspondence. As Dr. Kissinger has said that he has asked the US Permanent Representative to NATO to 'initiate' a discussion of this problem with his colleagues,[9] I think it would be as well to send copies of Dr. Kissinger's message and the Secretary of State's reply[10] to our Permanent Representative to NATO as soon as possible.

C.C.C. TICKELL

[8] On 1 May Mr. Callaghan noted on this minute: 'I told the German Ambassador at Windsor last night the line I was taking.' Mr. Tickell subsequently gave Dr. E. von Schmidt-Pauli of the German Embassy the gist of the Kissinger-Callaghan exchange, and received the English text of a somewhat less flexible West German response to Dr. Kissinger's initiative (telegram No. 307 to Bonn of 3 May).

[9] According to UKDEL NATO telegram No. 190 of 6 May the US delegation had not so far done anything to begin new discussion in the Council on the level of Stage III and had said they were in no rush to do so. They also indicated the 'US would not press for allied agreement to Stage III at a summit level in connection with President Nixon's plans to visit Moscow in June, despite Soviet pressure to juxtapose the two events'. During a NATO Permanent Reps'. lunch on 9 May the Netherlands proposed that Council should have a special meeting in early June (reinforced by experts from capitals) to discuss '(a) what constituted a satisfactory outcome to Stage II and (b) the level of Stage III' (UKDEL NATO telegram No. 201 of 10 May).

[10] On 2 May Sir P. Ramsbotham, the newly-appointed British Ambassador in Washington, delivered Mr. Callaghan's reply to Mr. Sonnenfeldt, now Counsellor in the State Department. Mr. Sonnenfeldt said that Dr. Kissinger 'harboured the suspicion' that several countries had already given the Soviet Union a strong hint of their readiness to agree to a summit. The US, he observed, 'did not wish to be the last to agree to a summit: but equally they did not wish to push others towards it unwillingly'. He added that Dr. Kissinger took the view that 'we all knew pretty well what would emerge from the CSCE. So to say that we could not decide on the level of the third stage until we had a better idea of the final outcome was rather disingenuous' (Washington telegram No. 1573 of 2 May).

No. 78

Mr. Callaghan to Sir P. Ramsbotham (Washington)

No. 1035 Telegraphic [*WDW 1/6*]

Immediate. Confidential   FCO, *8 May 1974, 4.50 p.m.*

Repeated for information priority Helsinki, UKDEL NATO, UKMIS Geneva.

Your tel[egram] No. 1580.[1]

CSCE: Confidence Building Measures

1. We welcome Sonnenfeldt's proposal that we should discuss possible fall-

[1] In this telegram of 2 May Sir P. Ramsbotham reported that Mr. Sonnenfeldt had told him that, in the light of discussions with Mr. Gromyko at Geneva (see No. 77, note 1), Dr. Kissinger would like to ask Mr. Callaghan to take another look at the British draft resolution on CBMs (see No. 74, note 5). Dr. Kissinger thought 'it would be a mistake to hold up successful completion of a CSCE on what were relatively minor points'.

back positions on CBMs. We see advantage in this being done in Washington (at whatever level you think appropriate) since the American delegations in Geneva and at NATO do not seem to be given much flexibility in their instructions.[2]

2. There has already been more discussion in the Alliance than Sonnenfeldt appears to realise. The background is set out in UKDEL NATO tel[egram] No. 1 to UKMIS Geneva (copied to you)[3] and the detailed record of the last meeting of the NATO Political Committee on 23 April (Burns' letter to Adams of 26 April copied to your Chancery).[4]

3. We hope that you will have an opportunity to assure Sonnenfeldt that we have no intention of being inflexible in our approach. But we regard the main CBM issues as more than 'relatively minor points'. We believe that most Western and neutral delegations would share this view and would like to see an agreement on CBMs which (apart from the special question of the prior notification of movements) was substantially along the lines of what we had proposed.

4. The British draft no longer constitutes the basis for work in Geneva, since its language and ideas have now been incorporated into provisionally registered texts which set out in logical sequence the alternatives under discussion. We are ready to adapt our language in an effort to meet neutral and non-aligned concerns as well as to show flexibility towards the East. But we must bear in mind that our draft resolution was discussed at length in NATO and represents a hard fought balance between those in the Alliance who wanted more and those (in particular the Americans) who wanted less. The American delegation in Geneva have often been the least ready to alter

---

[2] Already, during a discussion with Mr. Callaghan in London on 28 April Dr. Kissinger had said that the British draft resolution 'provided a good basis for agreement'. But, as Mr. Callaghan recorded in telegram No. 944 to Washington of 29 April, given the Soviet stance, there was clearly no prospect of achieving agreement on the notification of major military movements, and at this stage he could see no point in making a further attempt to modify the American position on the substance of this measure. Drawing on this information, Sir P. Ramsbotham told Mr. Sonnenfeldt (*v. ibid.*) that HMG was now ready to drop reference to the notification of military movements 'at the right moment'. He also stated that the attitude of the US delegation in Geneva had been 'rather lame', and that he hoped they could be instructed to be more active in support of the UK.

[3] In this telegram of 23 April Sir E. Peck informed the British delegation to the CSCE that he and his colleagues had argued in the NATO Political Committee that day that the Alliance 'should resist the temptation to settle prematurely for less than the Warsaw Pact might concede in the final trade-off at the end of Stage II'; that the most important requirement was for the West to obtain a satisfactory definition of the amount of Soviet and East European territory to be involved in CBMs; and that it would be important to handle carefully the neutral delegations who would be seriously disillusioned if the West were unable to maintain a firm position on CBMs. He further reported that there had been 'useful support' both for the British point of view and for a Canadian suggestion that NATO should show the East that they were ready to negotiate constructively if they showed a real willingness to 'discuss realistic and effective arrangements for CBMs'.

[4] Not printed.

the text for fear of re-opening arguments in Washington.[5]

5. Although we think it would be wrong for the Alliance to settle prematurely for less than might be obtained with persistence later in Stage II, we agree with the conclusions of the NATO Political Committee Meeting that we should be ready to show selective flexibility in order to keep work moving in Geneva. It will be for delegations there to decide on tactics. But experience (e.g. over inviolability of frontiers) suggests that concessions to the Russians which are not reciprocated at the time are unlikely to encourage any greater Soviet flexibility.[6]

6. Please see my immediately following telegram for guidance on the specific points raised by Sonnenfeldt.[7]

[5] Mr. Burns minuted Mr. Tickell on 8 May: 'The American delegations in Brussels and Geneva do not have much flexibility in their instructions primarily because it has proved very difficult for them to extract effective instructions from the Washington machine where the Pentagon in particular takes a very dim view of confidence building measures.' However, Mr. G.L. Warren, a member of the US delegation at Geneva, told Mr. Hildyard on 20 May that the Pentagon were in favour of the prior notification of military movements, and that 'opposition lay only with the White House' (UKMIS Geneva telegram No. 453 of 21 May).

[6] Sir E. Peck noted in UKDEL NATO telegram No. 1 to UKMIS Geneva (see note 3 above) that the NATO Political Committee had agreed that the timing of any Western concessions on CBMs would have to be coordinated in Geneva, and that 'initially we should make it plain to the Russians that we expected some considerable movement on their part in response to the constructive Western gesture on inviolability of frontiers'.

[7] This telegram of 8 May made the following points: (1) there was scope for flexibility on period of notification, although most NATO delegations felt that the 30 days proposed by the neutrals was the lowest that could be accepted; (2) that HMG still thought that where numbers were concerned the division threshold made the most sense; (3) that if only contiguous countries were to be notified this would 'let the Russians off the hook', since they would usually only need to notify their allies of manoeuvres held on Soviet territory; and (4) that on area most 'if not all our allies consider it of fundamental importance that the CBMs should apply in principle to the whole of Europe, whatever particular exceptions may be agreed'.

No. 79

Mr. Hildyard (UKMIS Geneva) to Mr. Callaghan

No. 404 Telegraphic [WDW 1/4]

Priority. Confidential   GENEVA, *11 May 1974, 9.54 a.m.*

Repeated for information UKDEL NATO, Moscow, Washington, Bonn, Saving Helsinki, UKREP Brussels, EEC and NATO Posts.

From Elliott, UKDEL to CSCE.

CSCE: General Situation

1. Progress in drafting continues to be slow where it is occurring at all. In most of the areas of interest to the West there has been a virtual impasse since Easter.

2. This situation is of Soviet making. During the past week or ten days the Russians have made little effort to hide their delaying tactics. As regards CBMs their attitude has continued to be uncompromisingly negative. In the Sub-Committees on contacts, information and culture, where some of the most sensitive issues are under consideration they have wasted time and in the informal working groups concerned they have blocked progress by intransigence and even on occasion by reverting to earlier positions.[1] In discussion of the preamble to Item III also they have accepted if not caused a standstill. They have thus totally failed to give the West the *quid pro quo* in Basket III which was implicitly part of the deal over inviolability of frontiers.

3. In Basket III the Russians have combined their delaying tactics on current questions with pressure in the Sub-Committees and in informal contacts for early discussion of the subsequent items in the mandates and suggestions for global discussion at a higher level of contentious questions. This manoeuvre is being resisted by the West and will I hope continue to be resisted. It may be based on the calculation that, if they can succeed in stalling on the difficult issues now and in pushing ahead with discussion and drafting on the others, the Russians may be able in the final crunch to get away with fewer concessions.[2] There is speculation here too that current political developments in France, Germany and the US may have led the Soviet Government to re-examine their CSCE strategy.[3] Again, one or two

[1] One of the main sticking points in the Sub-Committee on culture was a French paper on access to cultural achievements (see No. 76, note 5). Although it received solid support from the Nine, the Canadians and the Austrians, it was comprehensively rejected by the Russians. However, those parts in the French paper dealing with reading-rooms and cinemas were also criticised by the Finns and the Swedes as too far-reaching, and the latter privately expressed fears about over-exposure to Soviet influence should these projects ever be implemented on a reciprocal basis (UKMIS Geneva telegrams Nos. 369 and 405 of 4 and 11 May, MTW 10/557/6).

[2] In UKMIS Geneva telegram No. 363 of 3 May Mr. Hildyard had already argued that such a broad discussion of Basket III issues would be premature since it was clear that 'one of the East's objectives would be to elicit a statement of Western priorities and therefore an indication of the expendable elements in Western proposals'. They also, he suggested, had an interest in 'inveigling the West into accepting the earliest possible trade-off of contentious elements' no doubt wishing to 'avoid being pushed up against a final deadline when they might have to concede more than they wished to the West in order not to wreck their preferred timetable' (MTW 10/557/6).

[3] President Pompidou of France died on 2 April and in the first ballot of presidential elections on 5 May the socialist candidate, M. F. Mitterand, emerged as the leading contender with over 43 per cent of the popular vote. The second ballot on 19 May was narrowly won by M. V. Giscard d'Estaing. Meanwhile, in West Germany, on 6 May, Herr Brandt resigned as Chancellor after the arrest of a Chancellery aide on spying charges, and in the United States, on 9 May, the House of Representatives judiciary committee formally opened its hearings on whether there were grounds to impeach President Nixon in connexion with the Watergate scandal. Mr. Elliott was also under the impression that the Russians might have concluded that political uncertainties in Washington and Western Europe made any concessions on their part premature (minute of 10 May from Mr. Tickell to the Private Secretary).

of my colleagues have detected what they consider to be signs of difference of attitude between Moscow and the Soviet delegation here. The imposition of a halt on progress would be consistent with a dialogue between the two on tactics for the next phase.

4. It is significant that Dobrosielski, the Head of the Polish delegation, made no attempt when I spoke to him about this situation yesterday to deny that the Russians have been preventing progress: and claimed to have no better idea than we what their motives are. But he confirmed that it remained the objective of the Warsaw Pact countries to enable Stage II[I] to be held in July:[4] and agreed that recent Soviet tactics were putting this timetable in jeopardy. (It is not however out of the question that Soviet ideas on timing could change. A recent remark made by Mendelevich to my Portuguese colleague suggested that the Russians might be prepared to contemplate an autumn Stage II[I] and even a resumption of Stage II in the autumn.)[5]

5. The situation I have described may perhaps be about to change: during the last two days there have been indications that the Russians may have decided that the time has come to get things moving in Basket III. They have made no concessions but there appears to be a greater readiness on their part to do serious business in the informal working groups.[6] But unless this change of attitude becomes plain in the next week or two and leads to steady progress throughout Basket II[I], the possibility of Stage III in July, which is already open to question will disappear. We and our partners are losing no opportunity of pointing this out to Eastern representatives here. It seems important too that the blame for the lack of progress should be seen by public opinion to lie with the East and that the press should be briefed accordingly. We and other Western delegations are doing what we can here in this sense.

[4] During his conversation with the Prime Minister on 7 May Mr. Lunkov suggested that Stage III could take place at summit level 'as soon as the second stage had been completed, which should be possible in June'. Subsequently, at a meeting with Mr. Callaghan which took place three days later, Mr. Lunkov spoke in similar terms (records of conversations between Mr. Wilson and Mr. Lunkov on 7 May, and between Mr. Callaghan and Mr. Lunkov on 10 May, ENS 3/548/2).

[5] In his minute to the Private Secretary (see note 3 above) Mr. Tickell recorded that on 10 May Mr. Elliott had informed him that the Russians 'had been careful not to commit themselves openly to such a proposal, which would of course represent a reversal of their previous stand on the timetable'.

[6] UKMIS Geneva telegram No. 405 of 11 May (see note 1 above) confirmed a greater willingness by the East to prepare in informal discussion texts which would be for subsequent tabling in the Sub-Committees. However, continuing disagreement on almost all issues of substance had required the wide-scale use of square brackets and it was still not clear whether the East were now prepared to accept registration of these texts complete with square brackets.

No. 80

Mr. Callaghan to Sir. P. Ramsbotham (Washington)

No. 1126 Telegraphic [WDW 1/19]

Immediate. Confidential   FCO, *17 May 1974, 4.50 p.m.*

Repeated for information to Priority UKMIS Geneva, UKDEL NATO, Moscow, and to Routine all EEC and other NATO Posts, and to information saving Helsinki.

CSCE: Follow-Up

1. I have been giving thought to the kind of arrangements which might be established to follow up the work of the CSCE provided that the Conference reaches a successful conclusion.

2. We are at present associated with the Danish draft resolution which was tabled in Geneva on 29 April with the general support of Western delegations.[1] Its main points are that no decision should be taken on new machinery until a meeting of Senior Officials in 1977: and that the interim period should be used to assess the achievements of the Conference and the extent to which its decisions have been implemented. This approach reflects both the caution of some of our Community partners (among whom the French have been particularly negative) and the general feeling among Western delegations that it would be a mistake to go too far on follow-up until we have a clearer idea of what the Conference will achieve. We have made it clear in the Nine and the Fifteen that out position on the Danish draft is a tactical one, and that we would like to go further. But we have not so far been very specific about our ideas.

3. I should like now to explain our position in more detail to our partners and allies, and to encourage them to be more forthcoming. But before doing so I should like to know how the Americans would react to the ideas I have in mind. I know that their attitude to follow-up has so far been restrictive, and it would obviously be bad for Western Europe and for the Alliance as a whole if they failed to participate effectively in whatever arrangements were made.[2] But I do not think it either realistic or in the Western interest to take a negative line on proposals designed to continue the dialogue without an unnecessary amount of bureaucracy. I am encouraged by the record of Mr. Hattersley's recent conversation with Sonnenfeldt to think that the Americans would be open to persuasion.[3]

---

[1] See *Human Rights*, vol. iii, pp. 24-25, and No. 75, note 10.

[2] This point was raised again Mr. Tickell in a submission of 10 May, on which Sir J. Killick noted: 'We *must* avoid driving the Americans into further "bilateralism" with the Russians'.

[3] During their meeting at the State Department on 13 May, Mr. R. Hattersley, Minister of State for Foreign and Commonwealth Affairs, asked Mr. Sonnenfeldt for his views on 'the creation of some permanent follow-up machinery'. Mr. Sonnenfeldt replied that 'the Americans would go along with the general consensus in the Alliance but the US was not keen to see any elaborate machinery' (record of conversation, WDW 1/4).

4. I should like you to take an early opportunity to explain to the Americans at whatever level you judge appropriate the main points I have in mind, which are as follows:

(*a*) Although it is too early to forecast the results of the CSCE, a useful multilateral dialogue has begun which should be continued in one form or another after the third stage. This should be distinct from the purely technical arrangements which will anyway be necessary to put the Conference decisions into effect.

(*b*) There is no need for elaborate machinery or a new bureaucracy to enable the dialogue to take place.

(*c*) I see virtue in the Romanian proposal that future East/West meetings should not be confined to one place, but should rotate among the capitals of the participating states.

(*d*) I support the idea of a probationary period after the Conference to enable the Western countries to see whether Conference decisions are properly respected. This in itself should act as an inducement to those who would probably prefer the results of the Conference to be declaratory rather than practical.

(*e*) The period of two or three years suggested in the Danish draft is, however, too long.

5. If we were to proceed on these lines I believe that a meeting of Ambassadors or senior officials—whether described as such or as a Conference Committee—could take place about a year after the Conference to review the situation and consider proposals for future meetings and further work. This would help to ensure that the momentum of the dialogue was maintained without any commitment to the sort of machinery which might be exploited by the Russians to our disadvantage.

6. The CSCE will be discussed by the Political Directors of the Nine in Bonn on 27/28 May. It would be useful to have at least a preliminary American reaction to my ideas before then.[4] Meanwhile other recipients of

---

[4] The State Department reacted cautiously to British views on follow-up, and on 22 May, during a meeting in Washington with Mr. Sonnenfeldt and Mr. A. Hartman (Assistant Secretary of State for European Affairs), Mr. Callaghan received a short paper which stated that any continuation of the multilateral dialogue begun in the CSCE must 'depend heavily on how the various declarations and resolutions [were] carried out in practice'. The State Department was of the opinion that the West should continue to advocate a probationary period of about three years, and that since the Russians would probably seek as short a delay as possible between the conclusion of Stage III and any subsequent follow-up it would be better to hold the suggestion of one year in reserve in order to gain future leverage on other issues at Geneva. They also wanted to 'keep Moscow in the role of *demandeur* on this point', and therefore preferred not to begin early discussion of the British idea in any NATO forum for fear lest there be a leak and the East be encouraged to assume that the West were willing to make any concessions in this area (Washington telegrams Nos. 1813 and 1857 of 20 and 22 May).

this telegram should regard it as for their own information only.[5]

[5] Mr. Elliott, while welcoming instructions for 'smoking the Americans out' on follow-up, reminded Mr. Tickell in letter of 21 May that at the last NATO Heads of Delegation meeting it had been agreed that until there was a substantial advance in the general Soviet position at the Conference as little as possible should be said at meetings of the CSCE Working Group on Item IV. Follow-up was, in his opinion, the one major issue on which a Western position of reserve had been maintained intact and on which the West still had 'bargaining power', and, he added, 'a policy of go-slow in the Working Group [was] as striking and effective a means' as they had of advertising their dissatisfaction about Russian blocking tactics without contributing to a slow-down of work. This had worked well at the Working Group's meeting on 21 May, and Mr. Elliott thought it advisable that HMG should make it clear that they would not be pressing the Nine or the Fifteen to take a more flexible attitude in public until the Russians had shown some sign of being in earnest about the basic matters under negotiation.

No. 81

Minute from Mr. Tickell on CSCE[1]

[WDW 1/4]

Confidential   FCO, *20 May 1974*

I spent 16 and 17 May in Geneva with our Delegation to the CSCE. During this time I attended meetings of the Co-ordinating Committee (of the 35 participants), the Alliance Group (the Fifteen), and the Sub-Committee and Ad Hoc Group (the Community Nine). It may be worth recording one or two general impressions.

2. It is hard to exaggerate the sense of frustration which is universally felt. This emerged in the open at the meeting of the Co-ordinating Committee when the Maltese, supported by the other neutral countries, complained about the prodigious waste of time, effort and resources which the Conference now represented.[2] This was, he said, even worse for the small countries than for the big ones. In any case it was profoundly damaging to the cause for which the Conference had been assembled.[3] The Polish representative, who clearly felt the same way as the Maltese, expressed it well when he said that in the past people tried to see how many angels could

[1] This minute was addressed to Mr. Wiggin and Sir J. Killick. On 23 May Sir J. Killick minuted on it to Mr. Acland: 'I have had a word with Mr. Wright & Mr. Tickell about the level of Stage III, & of course there will be no question of agreeing to break off without consultation. But you should be aware of this very unpromising background.'

[2] On a copy of this minute Mr. Braithwaite sidelined and marked these last two sentences with an 'X'. He noted: 'I have no sympathy *at all* about X: this situation was entirely predictable & predicted by the FCO' (MWP 1/11).

[3] At this meeting of the Coordinating Committee on 16 May neutral and non-aligned delegates concentrated particularly upon the poor results achieved by the Sub-Committee responsible for CBMs which, Mr. Hildyard reported, 'they said would represent an indispensable element in the final results of the Conference' (UKMIS Geneva telegram No. 439 of 16 May, WDW 1/24).

be balanced on the point of a pin, but now they wanted to see how many square brackets could be inserted into a sentence.[4] No-one to whom I spoke had any doubt that it was the Russians who were holding up progress for reasons which were not clear (perhaps not even to the Soviet Delegation itself).

3. This atmosphere is not easy to work in. Our own Delegation remains amazingly cheerful and balanced. But others, particularly at lower levels, seem to be losing their sense of perspective. This was very clear in the present dispute between the Belgians and the other Community Eight about a reference to 'developing countries in Europe' in Committee II;[5] and in the argument between the Italians and the Americans about the idea of a separate Mediterranean declaration.[6] The mixture of general frustration and—in both cases mentioned above—personal vanity among those concerned breeds a kind of self-righteous bloody-mindedness.

4. On the big points at issue there is also some lack of perspective. The CSCE obviously looms largest for those on the spot but I noticed, particularly among the smaller countries in the Nine, a tendency to forget the real world outside. There is not much we can do about this, but Mr. Elliott is, I know, doing his best to underline the broad political factors, and make his colleagues realise that the CSCE is only one of the games on the East/West board.

5. As for the other side I had the chance of a brief talk with Mr. Mendelevich (Soviet Union). He was very affable, and spoke of the good co-operation between our Delegations. He said that Mr. Gromyko took a keen personal interest in the Conference and had been over all the main points during the Easter recess.[7] We should, Mr. Mendelevich said, set ourselves the target date of 30 June to end the second stage. This was 'perfectly possible' but 'I won't say it will happen'. Some Delegations were showing too much legalism in drafting the declaration of principles, which was not, after all,

---

[4] The Polish delegate also called for a 'new attitude' towards the work of the Conference and suggested 14 June as the target date for the end of Stage II. He added: 'If such progress were not made there was a risk that the Conference might be "overtaken by events outside it". The Conference could either be an accelerator of *détente* or a brake upon it' (*v. ibid.*).

[5] See No. 75, note 13.

[6] *V. ibid.*, note 13. On 2 May Mr. James (US Embassy in London) told Mr. Tickell, with regard to the US attitude towards a Mediterranean Declaration, that he feared that 'Dr. Kissinger had got personally involved', and that 'he probably saw it as mixed up in some way with the Euro-Arab dialogue and had given instructions to oppose it. 'As so often happened on these occasions', Mr. James added, 'no one felt inclined to pursue Dr. Kissinger on the matter and so his instructions to the US Delegation remained as they were' (minute from Mr. Tickell to Mr. Wiggin of 3 May, WS 2/557/1).

[7] On 14 May Mr. Gromyko told Sir T. Garvey that 'if HMG were looking for an "arena" of positive action, Geneva was a good place'. He said that the Soviet Government were not satisfied with progress there, that HMG had been 'more receptive of ideas of slowness', and that 'too many small matters had been magnified ten times or a hundred times out of their proportion'. With regard to Basket III, he confessed that he 'sometimes wished that he could cut the bottom out of the Basket and let all the accumulated details in it fall out' (Moscow telegram No. 499 of 14 May).

supposed to be a legal document. Here the British and Russians should work together. He was very ready to negotiate—'but only realistically'—over military confidence-building measures. Incidentally I hear that Mr. Mendelevich has let it be known that when this Conference is over his next job will be to run an Asian Security Conference, presumably to erect another verbal glacis, this time on the Eastern frontiers of the Soviet Union.

6. We also saw the Polish representative. He went so far as to say that he agreed with us all the way in Basket III except over 'subscriptions' to Western periodicals which, he said, would never be acceptable to the Russians. We had to understand their problems.

7. In his speech to the Co-ordinating Committee on 16 May (UKMIS Geneva telegram No. 439)[8] Mr. Elliott made the point that if the present deadlock was not broken in the next couple of weeks, there would be little chance of our ending the Conference this summer. I gather that this speech—and those from the neutral representatives in the middle of which it fell—made a considerable impact, not least on the Eastern delegations. The ball is now in their court.

C.C.C. TICKELL

[8] See notes 3 and 4 above.

No. 82

Mr. Hildyard (UKMIS Geneva) to Mr. Callaghan

No. 458 Telegraphic [WDW 1/4]

Immediate. Confidential   GENEVA, *22 May 1974, 9.28 a.m.*

Repeated for information to Priority UKDEL NATO, Moscow, Washington, Bonn, and to Saving other EEC and NATO Posts, Helsinki, UKREP Brussels, Stockholm.

From Elliott UKDEL to CSCE.

CSCE: General Situation: Political Directors Meeting in Bonn 27-28 May

1. The assessment in our telegrams numbers 404[1] and 432[2] remains generally valid. In the areas of interest to the West (confidence building measures and Basket III) the Russians continue to drag their feet. In Basket III their intransigence has if anything increased and there is a total standstill. Only in the drafting of the principles, where Eastern countries are individually canvassing texts on the remaining principles, and in Basket II, is there any sign of willingness to make progress.

2. Soviet motives remain obscure. Whether for reasons related to a major foreign policy reappraisal or for purely CSCE tactical consideration (or

[1] No. 79.
[2] In this telegram of 15 May, Mr. Elliott pointed out that, although it was still uncertain as to whether the Conference would be able to produce an agreed final document, the Russians seemed to have abandoned their delaying tactics and to be adopting a 'more businesslike approach' while remaining 'extremely tough on substance' (WDW 1/5).

both),[3] the Russians appear ready to risk losing Stage III in July. In the CSCE context they may hope to wrap up the principles and Item II subjects before the crunch on CBMs and Item III and then bring heavy pressure on the West and neutrals to accept last-minute and doubtless inadequate concessions in those fields. But I suspect that there is more behind the Soviet attitude than mere tactical considerations. It is noteworthy for example that the East European delegations appear to be in the dark about the reasons for it and to be feeling some irritation.

3. Warsaw Pact cohesion remains close but in some Sub-Committees there is now a tendency for the East Europeans to leave it to the Russians to fight their own battles. Western co-ordination is good and there is a growing determination among the Nine to resist any premature concessions. The Americans wobble occasionally in private but compensate for this by playing a robust role in difficult Sub-Committees.

4. The neutral position is less satisfactory with the Finns responding to Eastern pressure and the Swedes (and to a lesser extent the Austrians) showing signs of weakening. My Swedish colleague has told me that Mr. Palme[4] is worried about the internal political repercussions for his Government of a failure to end Stage II reasonably soon and that he is conducting a major review of policy in time for discussion in a Parliamentary Committee at the beginning of June. As at Helsinki we must accept that there will be an increasing tendency for certain neutrals to lose their nerve. The Swiss however continue to be tough and the Yugoslavs plough their own furrow.

5. In the face of Soviet intransigence the West really have no choice but to sit it out.[5] It does not appear that new working methods are necessary or desirable. The problems are political and the Sub-Committees have already developed sufficient flexibility of procedure where this is required. On the other hand it is becoming increasingly easy to expose the Soviet position for

[3] Mr. Elliott postulated in telegram No. 432 (*v. ibid.*) that the Russians might have concluded that the maintenance of a slow rate of progress in Basket III and elsewhere was compatible with a policy reappraisal which Sir T. Garvey had recently suggested was either in course or contemplated, in Moscow (Moscow telegrams Nos. 476-9 of 10 May, ENS 2/1). Mr. Murrell doubted this, though he conceded that there might well have been a 'pause for reconnaissance' whilst the Soviet leaders sized up the effects of leadership changes in the West. He considered it more probable that the Russians thought they could win the CSCE battle outside Geneva 'by persuading Western leaders to override their obstinate officials and bring Stage 2 to an early and "successful" conclusion' (minute to Mr. Fall of 22 May).

[4] Herr O.J. Palme was Swedish Prime Minister.

[5] Mr. Elliott was not, however, at all sure that it was in the West's interest to encourage the Russians in the impression that they could 'with impunity dictate the timing of the later stages of the Conference'. As he explained in telegram No. 432 (see notes 2 and 3 above), there was a 'substantial risk' that if the Conference were prolonged the West would lose interest and cohesion. The Russians, he opined, 'are probably better equipped (both administratively and psychologically) to survive a long haul in the Conference than the Nine or the Fifteen: and if we were to find in the autumn e.g. that M. Mitterand was in power in France and the CDU in Germany, the difficulties of maintaining a united Western line could become very great indeed'.

what it is on CBMs and Item III subjects and we are seeking every opportunity to do so. Our best line will no doubt be to stick to the substance of our position but, in order to promote progress and conciliate the neutrals, to show the maximum of flexibility over language and a readiness to drop fringe proposals. We can also hint in debate at areas of compromise without in any way implying a readiness to move unless the East show greater flexibility. At the same time we should speak our minds to the Russians in private and warn them that their present attitude is imperilling the whole Conference.

6. The West needs to appear reasonable but firm and unwilling to sacrifice basic objectives for the sake of an early end to the Conference. It would be helpful if articles in the Western press on these lines could be encouraged.

7. At the same time it is obviously essential for us to cling on to what bargaining counters we have (the provisional nature of our agreement on inviolability, the level of the third stage and follow-up).[6] Though individually of doubtful value, their collective weight should not be underestimated. And it remains in our interest to keep the Russians' mind in doubt about all three points until the shape of the final package is reasonably clear.

8. On timing my views are unchanged. I do not believe that a Stage II which lasted beyond late July would be in the interests of the West. Quite apart from anything else we have no grounds for thinking that we shall receive from the Russians in September what they fail to give in July. I believe therefore that the West should let it be known that if we have not agreed a satisfactory Final Act by late July we will have reluctantly to accept an indefinite recess until the climate improves.[7]

9. It would be helpful for delegations if Political Directors could confirm this broad approach. Indications here are that the Nine are generally ready to think on these lines.[8]

[6] In his minute (note 3 above) Mr. Murrell pointed out that these bargaining counters were not of equal weight: 'The Russians think they have already won on inviolability and in my view are not much concerned about follow up. The Summit finale is what is really important to them now and they may think that counter will slip from our fingers if they hold on.'

[7] Mr. Elliott had already made it clear in telegram No. 432 (see notes 2, 3 and 5 above) that, while he thought it almost impossible to complete Stage II in June, there was a 'reasonable chance' of completing in July, with Stage III in the autumn, if the Russians allowed steady progress to be made. 'But that', he added, 'does not mean that we would then have no alternative to meek acquiescence in a policy of resuming Stage II in the autumn and negotiating until the cows come home.'

[8] Feelings of frustration and exasperation were evident during the meeting of EC Political Directors on 27-28 May when progress in the CSCE was discussed, but, as reported in telegram No. 187 to UKMIS Geneva of 29 May (MWP 1/11), these 'were not uppermost, and no-one favoured an early crisis or attempt at a showdown'. It was agreed that patience was still the best policy; no-one objected to views expressed by the Danes, Luxembourgers and, less specifically, the Germans that the Nine should be ready to continue Stage II in September; and it was agreed that they should try to keep their options open at meetings on the future work programme in Geneva. It was also settled that if the deadlock continued it might be useful for the nine Foreign Ministers at their meeting on 10-11 June to make public their dissatisfaction. See Cmnd. 6932, pp. 178-9 for extracts of the press statement released in Bonn on 10 June.

No. 83

Mr. Hildyard (UKMIS Geneva) to Mr. Callaghan

No. 500 Telegraphic [MTW 10/557/6]

Priority. Confidential   GENEVA, *31 May 1974, 6.30 p.m.*

Repeated for information to Saving Moscow, Washington, Helsinki, UKDEL NATO, EEC Posts.

From UKDEL to CSCE.

Basket III Sub-Committees

1. There has been little change this week in the overall situation as reported in our telegram No. 472.[1] Deadlock persists in the Sub-Committees on human contacts and information. The East continue to urge parallel drafting, in informal discussions and in the Sub-Committees, on different issues: the West continue to resist this scheme. In culture, some semblance of progress is now being made in discussions in the Sub-Committee, while in education drafting has begun again.

2. In human contacts, discussion continued in the Sub-Committee on marriage between nationals of different states: both sides stuck to their respective positions.[2] Informal discussions to resolve the stalemate on family reunification revealed no readiness on the Eastern side to make the further concessions necessary.

3. In information, the Sub-Committee concentrated its debate on the new Eastern text on broadcasting (para 3 of our tel[egram] under reference).[3] Although Eastern speakers seemed prepared to be flexible on some of the less important issues, they continued to insist on a reference to agreements and contracts as governing the dissemination of broadcast information. They remained adamant that governments should undertake the responsibility for ensuring that all broadcasts from their territory met Eastern desiderata. Informal discussions on access to printed information are to be resumed next week, in yet another attempt to break a deadlock for which the East have been energetic in blaming the West.[4]

[1] In this telegram of 25 May Mr. Hildyard reported signs of a 'slight easing' of the Eastern attitude, no doubt, he thought, because the Russians wished 'to avoid a total deadlock throughout Basket III and to compensate to some extent for their intransigence in the Committee and the other two Sub-Committees'.

[2] See *Human Rights*, vol. v, pp. 67-8.

[3] *V. ibid.*, p. 141 for the Bulgarian/GDR text on broadcasting. Mr. Hildyard's telegram No. 472 recorded that Western speakers had made clear their opposition to its requirement that participating states assume responsibility for ensuring that all broadcasts from their territory did 'not prejudice the easing of tension', were of 'a sympathetic character', and served 'the interests of peaceful cooperation between peoples and states'.

[4] So tedious was the work of the Information Sub-Committee that during one session, on 30 May, the Canadian delegate read aloud the account in George Orwell's *Nineteen Eighty-Four* of the collective drafting in the Ministry of Truth of an interim report on the eleventh edition of the 'Newspeak Dictionary'. The passage, with its description of days when 'the argument as to

4. In culture, the Czechs tabled a 'compromise' text including references to some of the French and other Western proposals on access to cultural achievements, while omitting those dealing with cinemas, libraries and sales outlets, which the Russians continue to refuse to discuss even informally.[5] The French fiercely criticised the paper and ridiculed the Soviet representative for answering questions addressed to his Czech colleague. But at the end of the week the atmosphere was calmer, with both sides hinting at the possibility of a compromise on most of the proposals now on the table. The French are contemplating a new text in which their proposals on cinemas, etc., would be presented as a series of bilateral options.

5. In education, the Russians proved anxious to get the ball rolling again. This resulted in provisional agreement by the Sub-Committee of virtually the same text dealing with exchanges of scientific information which the Russians had suddenly held up two weeks ago. But the acid test of Soviet willingness to make further progress in this Sub-Committee will come next week when informal discussions begin on direct contacts among scientists.

what they were supposedly arguing about grew extraordinarily involved and abstruse, with subtle hagglings over definitions, enormous digressions, quarrels—threats, even, to appeal to higher authority', could easily have been mistaken for a parody of the Sub-Committee's proceedings (letter from Mr. Miller to Mr. D.J. Young (EESD) of 31 May, EN 2/557/3). Cf. G. Orwell, *Nineteen Eighty-Four* (London: Penguin, 1989), pp. 307-8.

[5] See *Human Rights*, vol. v, pp. 236-8 for the Czechoslovak text. In a letter to Mr. Young of 22 May Mr. Miller noted that French and Austrian proposals dealing with sales outlets for foreign books, the setting up of libraries, reading rooms and cinemas, as well as access to film archives had 'stuck in the Russians' craw'. France's representative, he observed, repeatedly emphasised that the French regarded the question of access to cultural achievements as being crucial to the success not only of the Sub-Committee's work but of the Conference as a whole and that they would 'stick to their proposals until the bitter end ("nous sommes partis pour la gloire")' (EN 2/557/4).

No. 84

Minute from Mr. Fall to Mr. Tickell

[*WDW 1/5*]

Confidential   FCO, *4 June 1974*

CSCE: Timing of Stage III

1. Mr. Burns has reported in yesterday's bag an Italian story that Mendelevich has said that the Russians have told the Finns to work on the basis that Stage II will end in the first days of July and Stage III will take place at the end of that month. Other delegations in Geneva however (including the Romanians in conversation with Mr. Burns) consider that the Russians have decided privately that their interests would best be served by spinning out Stage II in the expectation that the longer it lasts the less they

will need to concede.[1]

2. My own guess is that the Russians are more interested in the level of Stage III than in its timing. They may well have concluded that it is now very late in the day to get a summit laid on for any time before the summer holidays; and that the concessions required to get everyone moving quickly in the right direction would have to be large. They may feel that Western leaders would be more inclined to see the wider arguments for a summit in the autumn at the beginning of a new diplomatic year; and that nothing very spectacular by way of concessions at the CSCE will be required to achieve their object. Brezhnev will get his picture in the papers at the end of June in any case, during President Nixon's visit to Moscow,[2] and he may be prepared to wait for the next round.

3. Mr. Elliott, who, in your absence spoke to me on the telephone from Helsinki yesterday morning, continues to think that extending the Second Stage into the autumn would be to the disadvantage of the West. He was therefore rather annoyed by the line taken by von Groll at the meeting of the Coordinating Committee on 30 May (Geneva telegram No. 499 attached).[3]

4. I agree that it is annoying to appear in the position of allowing the Russians to pick their own timing. But I do not think we have much choice. It is clearly not to our advantage to make ourselves the demandeur for a Third Stage in July; and I do not think that an attempt to put pressure on the Russians by threatening to break off the Conference at the end of July is politically realistic. Our partners and Allies appear to share this view. We should perhaps therefore concentrate on how to make the best out of a resumed session in the autumn. I see no reason why the Russians should get it all their own way—especially if any new Western representatives are given firm instructions that, if in any doubt as to the state of the negotiations before the summer break, they should turn to the Final Recommendations and the original Western proposals rather than to explanations from "experienced

[1] In a letter to Mr. Adams of 30 May, in which he speculated on Soviet intentions, Mr. Burns recalled that Mr. Mendelevich had twice insisted in the Principles Sub-Committee that conditions existed for completing Stage II in mid-July.

[2] President Nixon was in Moscow from 27 June until 3 July.

[3] Not printed. This telegram of 31 May reported that, by prior arrangement among the Nine, Freiherr von Groll had made a statement designed to reflect the conclusions of the Political Directors (see No. 82, note 8) and to prepare the ground for possible public statements after the forthcoming meetings of EC and NATO Foreign Ministers. After having complained about the situation in Committee III and the discussion of CBMs, he had said that his Government was prepared to go on working for the success of the CSCE 'even if, as now seemed only too possible, this meant resuming Stage II in the autumn after a summer break' (MTW 10/557/15). But in a minute to Mr. Tickell of 4 June Mr. Adams argued that despite the 'pass selling' by Freiherr von Groll, it was 'surely possible and advantageous for the West to leave this question a little blurred'. The West could hint that if the Conference was still blocked at the end of July, they might opt for an indefinite recess and, since he did not believe that the Russians could 'stomach a break-down', this should encourage them to make their concessions in early to mid July 'in the hope that we will swallow them quickly and allow Stage II to end then'. Mr. Tickell agreed. 'We have', he noted, 'to leave things blurred.'

Delegates".

5. A question which is, however, worth considering further is whether in agreeing to a resumed session in the autumn we should place some limit to its length. My own view is that we shall by then have reached a stage when the arguments against deadlines will have lost much of their force. If delegations in Geneva work throughout June and most of July they will surely have reached the stage where a six-week session in September/October will either finish the job or lead to the conclusion that it cannot be finished. I would see some advantage in making this clear before agreeing to a summer break.[4]

6. You may wish to consider at your meeting this morning whether we should offer some views on this question (or others) to guide the delegation to the NATO meeting on 7 June. I understand that Mr. Elliott will be attending.[5]

B.J.P. FALL

[4] After discussing this with Mr. Fall, Mr. Tickell minuted: 'On para 5, I think it is too early to fix deadlines, & we shd tell Mr. Elliott so.'

[5] Telegram No. 127 to UKDEL NATO of 5 June informed Sir E. Peck that while it should still be possible 'to get a satisfactory conclusion' of the CSCE before the summer, if it proved necessary to resume work in the autumn HMG would 'continue to work patiently and constructively' to put the Helsinki Final Recommendations into effect. 'It is possible', Mr. Callaghan concluded, 'that disappointment at the lack of progress in Geneva will be used by some of our allies to argue for public pressure on the East in the form of a threat to break off or suspend the work of the Conference. We doubt if this sort of line would be helpful, and it might easily boomerang.' Mr. Tickell noted in a minute covering the final draft of this telegram that, like others at Geneva, Mr. Elliott had 'a slight tendency to favour strong-arm tactics with the Russians: hence the corrective in the last paragraph which represents the Secretary of State's views'.

No. 85

Sir T. Garvey (Moscow) to Mr. Callaghan

No. 627 Telegraphic [*WDW 1/4*]

Priority. Confidential   MOSCOW, *7 June 1974, 3.43 p.m.*

Repeated for information to Routine Washington, Bonn, Paris, Helsinki, UKDEL NATO, UKMIS Geneva.

MIPT.[1]

Call on Gromyko: CSCE

1. Gromyko said that Soviet Government was not fully satisfied with present situation. Too much time was being spent on trivia and some people were

[1] In this telegram of 7 June Sir T. Garvey briefly described his meeting that afternoon with Mr. Gromyko. Sir T. Garvey had called on Mr. Gromyko to deliver a message from Mr. Callaghan in response to his conversation with Mr. Lunkov on 10 May (see No. 79, note 4). Mr. Callaghan expressed his disappointment that there was 'so far so little to show for all the months of hard work in Geneva', adding that he had hoped to see Stage III held before the end of July, but that it was quite clear this would be impossible unless a great deal more progress could be made very soon (telegram No. 350 to Moscow of 3 June, ENS 3/548/2).

interested in creating artificial obstacles. Britain could do a lot more than she had done to contribute to success of Conference. The attention being devoted to Item 3 was 100 times greater than one item deserved, in proportion to other items. 'An ant is being turned into an elephant.' The same was true of CBMs, on which the FRG and UK proposals in particular were quite unrealistic. The area of the Soviet Union of which full account had to be given was enormous, stretching to the Urals: 'we have other things to do.' The UK was fully capable of a realistic approach when it wished to reach an understanding: an understanding on these aspects of CSCE would be a considerable success and confirmation of the opportunities which existed for cooperation between us.

2. Foregoing formed part of Gromyko's long recital. When at the end I got a brief innings I said that Gromyko's views on UK's role at Geneva seemed to have evolved since I last saw him. Then, he was 'not sure' that the UK was doing its bit.[2] He now thought that we were devoting too much attention to trifles. HMG's view was that since the recess, despite inch-by-inch progress on Items 1 and 2 there had on Item 3 been no use of the normal negotiating process. Eastern delegations had adopted a maximalist position on a number of substantial points. We were puzzled by the combination of this with apparent importance attached by Soviet Government to a timetable which would produce Stage III in July. If there was to be any chance of this, real progress had to come soon. I reminded Gromyko of imminent and relevant meetings of Ministers of the Nine and the Fifteen[3] and told him that if one stated Soviet target was to be met we were, if only for practical reasons, running into a period in which the timing would be very tight. I reminded him of what I had said at our last meeting about public opinion in the UK, to which HMG had to be responsive; and emphasised that you and the Prime Minister entertained great goodwill towards the Soviet Union and were long-standing advocates of good relations with the Soviet Government and people. Gromyko did not respond.

3. The interest of this exchange lay primarily in the absence of any reference on Gromyko's part to either level or timing of Stage III. While repeating the usual complaints about time-wasting, he displayed no sense of urgency.[4]

---

[2] Cf. No. 81, note 7.

[3] The Nine were to meet in Bonn on 10-11 June, and the Fifteen in Ottawa on 18-19 June.

[4] On 10 June Mr. Lunkov handed the Prime Minister a message from Mr. Brezhnev, confiding that similar ones had been addressed to the German Chancellor, the French President and President Nixon. The message concluded: 'Objective possibilities exist for bringing the Conference to a successful conclusion in a short space of time' and urged that they should be 'fully utilised'. The Ambassador said that 'the position of the two sides in Geneva was now close on many questions, that time was being wasted, and that some matters would have to be left over until a later stage'. Mr. Wilson responded that HMG also hoped to see a successful final stage and that the proposal in the message to step up the level of representation would be considered with Mr. Callaghan. A draft reply to Mr. Brezhnev's message, prepared by WOD, was, however, deemed 'pretty dry' by Mr. Callaghan, who preferred to 'test out ideas' at the forthcoming NATO Ministerial meeting before relaying it to No. 10. Agreement was finally reached with No. 10 that no reply would be sent (minutes by Mr. Tickell of 12 June and 1 August).

No. 86

Minute from Mr. Fall to Mr. Tickell
[WDW 1/4]

Confidential   FCO, *17 June 1974*
CSCE

1. I understand from Mr. Alexander that the Secretary of State would find useful a short note on the remaining points of difference between East and West.[1] It is not easy to present a clear picture. We are faced not with a handful of well-defined major issues but with a large number of points of detail the solutions to which will mark the difference between a better and a less good result.

2. The following are the main points.

(i) *Declaration of Principles*
    (a) *Inviolability of frontiers/peaceful change*
    The compromise reached before Easter comprised the provisional registration of texts on inviolability and on peaceful change but with the place of the reference to peaceful change deliberately left open. The West Germans would clearly prefer it to be attached to the principle of inviolability and the point has from the strictly formal point of view not been given away. But the general understanding of the compromise is that the reference to peaceful change will be placed somewhere else. The new team in the West German Foreign Ministry[2] clearly feel that their delegation in Geneva have given away too much and are seeking the support of their allies (and in particular the three Powers) for a tougher line.[3] It is unlikely that they will insist on the reference to peaceful change appearing under inviolability; and if we were to insist on this we would have to do so in the knowledge that it might lead the Russian to break off the Conference. It is possible to get a satisfactory reference to peaceful change elsewhere in the declaration, though the better the formulation from the Western point of view the harder it will be to get Soviet agreement.

[1] Mr. Callaghan had requested a 'note of the *outstanding differences*' at the CSCE to take with him to Ottawa (see No. 85, note 3).

[2] Following Herr Brandt's resignation (see No. 79, note 3) a new Social Democrat/Free Democrat coalition Government was formed in Bonn under the Chancellorship of Herr Schmidt. Herr H.-D. Genscher was appointed Foreign Minister.

[3] During a discussion at Dorneywood on 15 June, Herr Genscher told the Secretary of State that the Germans attached considerable importance to the principle of the peaceful change of frontiers and to maintenance of existing treaties. He added that 'this was not a German problem alone: Four-Power responsibilities for Germany as a whole and Berlin could also be involved. It was important that the CSCE should not result in an erosion of the position in favour of the GDR.' Mr. Callaghan replied that the British would try to be helpful on this issue (telegram No. 421 to Bonn of 19 June, MTW 10/557/5).

(*b*) *Principle of Non-intervention*

The Russians would like the principle of non-intervention to include references to 'hostile propaganda' and to 'respect for the cultural foundations of states' in order to make it easier for them to restrict what is agreed to in Basket III. We shall wish to confine the definition of non-intervention to what has been generally accepted in previous international definitions.

(*c*) *Principles of respect for human rights and fundamental freedoms and of self-determination*

The Russians will want these principles defined as narrowly as possible. We hope to get texts which will make clear the importance of these subjects to a genuine *détente*.

(*d*) *Brezhnev doctrine*

The doctrine depends in theory on the argument that relations between socialist countries are based on different principles than relations between countries having different political systems. We shall wish in the preamble to the declaration to make clear that the principles must be applied by each participant towards each, irrespective of their political systems.

(ii) *Confidence-building measures*

There is no chance of getting Soviet agreement to the prior notification of movements. The East remain extremely negative on the prior notification of manoeuvres which they would like to confine to manoeuvres at the level of an army or army corps (not defined but probably about five divisions) held near frontiers. (The Russians have recently suggested 100 kilometres zone.)[4] These manoeuvres to be notified only to neighbouring countries and then only five days or so before the manoeuvre is carried out. The Western proposals are that manoeuvres of one division and above should be notified to all participants approximately sixty days before they take place if they are carried out anywhere in Europe, including the European territory of the Soviet Union.

(iii) *Peaceful settlement of disputes*

The Russians have effectively vetoed the Swiss proposal which is based on the principles of compulsory arbitration and judicial settlement.[5] But they will now seek for presentational reasons to provide for further work on this subject after the Conference without taking any commitment on compulsory arbitration and judicial settlement.

[4] At an informal meeting of Heads of Delegation on 12 June to discuss the lack of progress at the CSCE, Mr. Kovalev offered to extend from 50 to 100 kilometres the size of the border zones to which prior notification of manoeuvres would apply. This, as Mr. Hildyard pointed out, maintained the concept of border zones to which NATO was firmly opposed and had the particular disadvantage of covering virtually all the UK while imposing no comparable obligation on any of the other major European states (UKMIS Geneva telegram No. 546 of 13 June).

[5] See No. 53, note 8.

(iv) *Economic Questions*

The work of the Economic Committee could be brought to an end if it were not for the Soviet insistence [*sic*] on some commitment to most favoured nation treatment. They hope thereby to gain trade policy advantages from the Americans over tariffs and from the Europeans over quantitative restrictions without making any commitment to effective reciprocity. This could be ensured only in detailed trade negotiations through the appropriate bilateral or multilateral channels and the Russians must know that they will not gain their point at the CSCE. They may feel, however, that it is worth keeping it alive until the final package is negotiated. Our own interest in the Second Committee has been concentrated on facilities for businessmen, business contacts and information. It is probable that we shall get results confirming the best of existing East/West practice but it is unlikely that we shall get any real improvements.

(v) *Basket III*

This continues to be the main problem. The Russians have slowed up the negotiations by refusing to apply the normal practice of placing disagreed sections in square brackets and then moving on. As a result a number of important subjects have yet to be dealt with on a first reading in the drafting groups. Where the Russians have agreed to put Western proposals in square brackets they have sought to balance this 'concession' by tabling at the last minute highly restrictive proposals of their own which they know will be unacceptable.[6] The following are the main detailed points.

(a) *Preamble*

The Russians are maintaining their insistence on restrictive clauses in the preamble, but they may be able to accept the present Finnish proposal[7] if the principle of non-intervention in Committee I[8] is defined in

---

[6] A WOD paper of 30 May, which chronicled the basic issues in Basket III, noted that little progress had been made and that it was difficult to form a truely clear picture of the situation. It pointed out that a working paper on family re-unification, which although only a page and a half long, contained no less than thirty passages surrounded by square brackets (PW 2/557/1).

[7] See No. 76, note 2 and *Human Rights*, vol. v, pp. 15-17. Paragraph 4 of the Basket III preamble was intended to refer to the principles agreed in Basket I. But at an informal meeting of Committee III on 18 June no progress was made on this issue as the Eastern delegations continued to insist on adding references to matters such as non-intervention, sovereignty and laws and customs to the latest Finnish text, which referred only to cooperation taking place 'in full respect for the principles defined in the document on the principles guiding relations among the participating States' (UKMIS Geneva telegram No. 566 of 20 June, EN 2/557/3).

[8] On 4 June the Finns tabled in the Principles Sub-Committee a new draft proposal on non-intervention in internal affairs, the fourth sentence of which provided that participants would 'respect the political, economic and cultural foundations of other participating States as well as their right to determine their own legislative and regulatory systems' (*Human Rights*, vol. iii, p. 171). In the opinion of Mr. Hildyard, the Russians were 'the manifest inspirers of the Finnish text'. Nevertheless, despite Western reservations about the content and context of the formula,

a way satisfactory to them.

(*b*) *Human contacts*

Western countries have already accepted that we will not be able to get from the Conference a clear endorsement of the right to leave one's country without qualifications which would make it meaningless.[9] We are therefore concentrating on resolutions which would embody a precise political commitment to ease restrictions on travel in general and on travel for family re-unification and marriage in particular. The drafts being considered are still far from being agreed and the Soviet attitude remains very negative. The Russians are trying in particular by combining discussion of the right to leave one's country with proposals of their own on visa requirements and other restrictions on entry to produce a general watering down of the Western proposals.[10]

(*c*) *Information*

Some progress has been made on printed information, although the drafts under discussion are unlikely to lead to very much in practice.[11] On broadcast information the East are continuing to insist on restrictions concerning the type of information to be broadcast and are trying to get from Western governments undertakings which would involve them in exercising censorship over broadcasts originating from their territory.

B.J.P. FALL

at a NATO caucus on 18 June the Americans and West Germans 'urged the need to reach early agreement with the Russians on some package deal covering language on this point in both the Declaration of Principles and the preamble in Basket III' (UKMIS Geneva telegrams Nos. 564 and 565 of 19 June, WDW 1/11).

[9] According to the WOD paper (see note 6 above) the East had so far been prepared only to 'consider under mutually acceptable conditions', rather than 'deal expeditiously with', requests for family reunification.

[10] Evidently with a view to exploiting difficulties faced by the British with regard to Commonwealth immigration, the East were insisting that resolutions should deal with entry as well as exit procedures, and equating exit permits with entry visas. And whilst the East accepted that persons leaving to be reunited with their families might take their household and personal effects with them 'in accordance with existing regulations', they flatly opposed any reference to the transfer of savings and the disposal of property. They were also evasive about the legal rights of those applying to emigrate (WOD paper of 30 May, see notes 6 and 9 above).

[11] As Mr. Hildyard reported in UKMIS Geneva telegram No. 551 of 15 June, there was a 'chance of progress' on this subject after Soviet agreement to accept a reference to subscriptions (EN 2/557/3).

No. 87

Mr. Hildyard (UKMIS Geneva) to Mr. Callaghan

No. 583 Telegraphic [*WDW 1/11*]

Immediate. Confidential   GENEVA, *24 June 1974,* 6.45 *p.m.*

Repeated for information to Immediate Helsinki, Priority UKDEL NATO, Saving to Washington, Moscow, EEC Posts.

From UKDEL to CSCE: Your telegram Number 222:[1]

Non Intervention in Internal Affairs

1. At the meeting this morning 24 June of Sub Committee I, Western and neutral delegations declined to start drafting on the fourth sentence of the Finnish proposal. Mendelevich protested. He said that the Russians would not meanwhile be willing to move to discussion of the next principle. The Finns then suggested an adjournment to enable informal consultations to take place.

2. Although among Western delegations and the neutrals there are still many differences of detail over the best way to handle the Finnish 'package deal', two main schools of thought have emerged:

(*a*) The great majority of the Nine are in favour of playing it long or refusing to negotiate on the Finnish sentence until such time as the Eastern side have given reasonably firm indications of concessions to the Western point of view elsewhere. For early negotiation on the Finnish text could pose a dilemma: either the West would obtain satisfactory wording on it in the Declaration of Principles (which would remove the inducement for the Eastern side to make concessions elsewhere): or the West would concede unsatisfactory language (which would invalidate or at least prejudice concessions in the context of Basket III).

(*b*) The neutrals wish to try to negotiate a package fairly soon: the Swiss and the Austrians, who have been keenest to elicit the maximum concessions from the East, took part in a neutral and non aligned caucus this afternoon attended by the Finns, at which they succeeded in securing agreement to support the package outlined in MIFT.[2]

[1] In this telegram of 20 June, which responded to reports of the latest discussions on Finnish proposals regarding non-intervention in internal affairs (see No. 86, note 8), Mr. Callaghan signalled HMG's strong opposition to the West making concessions in the Declaration of Principles in exchange for vague assurances of Eastern willingness to compromise in other areas. 'In our view', Mr. Callaghan stated, 'even precise drafting concessions by the East on the substance of Basket III will be of little value until it is clear that the preamble and any texts referred to in it are not such as to deprive the agreed texts of their practical effect or to present an obstacle to further progress after the Conference.'

[2] The new neutral package outlined in this telegram of 24 June comprised: (1) negotiation of a text based on the Finnish proposal for the fourth sentence of the principle on non-intervention; (2) a proposal that the sentence should be included in the principle relating to the sovereign equality of states; (3) the redrafting of the whole of the preamble for Item III; (4) the drafting of mini-preambles for Item III containing no safeguard clauses, or references to principles or 'laws and regulations'; and (5) the simultaneous registration of these texts.

3. Brunner of the Swiss delegation has explained to us that the neutral group have drafted texts both for the preamble and mini-preamble as a whole,[3] which they will present on a take-it-or-leave-it basis, leaving the text of a fourth sentence of the Finnish proposal for the principle of non intervention to be negotiated in Sub Committee I. The idea is that the Finns who become Chairmen of the Co-ordinating Committee on 27 June will soon thereafter convene an informal meeting of Heads of delegation and put the package to them.[4]

4. There is to be a meeting of NATO Heads of Delegation on 27 June to consider the neutrals' proposals, preceded by a similar meeting *à neuf*. Subject to your views and to those of Mr. Elliott at Helsinki, we propose to say that it might be worth our allowing the neutral package a fair run for its money, while remaining ready to fall back on some variant of paragraph 2 (*a*) above should the need arise. We shall need of course to be satisfied that the proposed texts for preamble and mini-preambles of Basket III are satisfactory and that the neutrals would not accept any changes proposed by the other side. We must also be alive to the likelihood that it will be harder to negotiate such a deal with the Russians than Brunner appears to think and that such negotiation could in any case take some time.[5] (This will be the inevitable result of the requirement that all three sets of texts mentioned in points 1, 3 and 4 of the package should be registered simultaneously, taken in conjunction with the decision of 6 February that mini-preambles in Basket III should not be registered until substantial progress had been made on the contents of that Basket.)

---

[3] It subsequently emerged at a meeting of Heads of Delegation of the Nine on 25 June that these drafts were not yet ready (UKMIS Geneva telegram No. 585 of 25 June).

[4] See No. 90, note 2.

[5] Mr. Callaghan informed Mr. Hildyard in telegram No. 231 of 25 June that the FCO would be content for him to speak on the lines of paragraph 4.

No. 88

Minute from Mr. J.C. Cloake[1] to Mr. Marshall[2]

[*MWP 1/11*]

Confidential   FCO, *3 July 1974*

CSCE: Committee II

Although there is still no clear indication of the timing of the completion of Stage II of the CSCE, there is a reasonable chance that the conference will go into summer recess in mid-July, reconvening in Geneva in September.

---

[1] Head of TRED.

[2] On 4 July Mr. Marshall noted to Sir D. Maitland (Deputy Under-Secretary of State) on this minute: 'You ought perhaps to look at this useful survey. 2. It remains to be seen whether Dr. Kissinger has queered the pitch in the recent talks with the Russians.' See No. 89, note 2.

Since the Easter recess there has been little sign of the movement in the Soviet position that would have been needed to achieve their declared aim of terminating Stage II in the summer. Meanwhile the work of the sub-committees has proceeded at differing speeds and a number of texts have been registered, liberally sprinkled with square brackets. Certain aspects of Basket II (exchanges, contacts and information) are based on the same philosophy as in Basket III; we have pressed these in the Economic Committee as hard as in Basket III but although the East have generally accepted Wesern drafts as the basis of negotiation, actual progress has been made only where there was no conflict with the restrictive Eastern objections in Basket III.

2. In the various Sub-Committees the position is as follows:

(a) Sub-Committee D—Commercial Exchanges
Pressure from the West on business contacts and information has faced the same negative attitude displayed by the East in Basket III. The texts now registered on information are reasonably satisfactory but they have been reached only by the insistence of the Irish and UK Delegations. Many of our partners in the Nine would have been content to accept Eastern proposals which did no more than acknowledge the present level of information provided by the Warsaw Pact countries.

Discussions on business contacts is now in progress and the East have raised the delicate Basket III topic of 'national legislation' (i.e. that any agreed measures should be subject to the domestic laws and regulations of the individual countries). Apart from this there has been useful negotiation and reasonably acceptable texts appear to be emerging. We have framed mention of MFN treatment in the Western draft resolution on commercial exchanges[3] to reflect the concept of effective reciprocity and to acknowledge that any juridical award of MFN would have to follow the CSCE in separated negotiations. It was agreed at the ad hoc meeting in Bonn during the Easter recess that we should move towards a reference to MFN treatment in the operative part of the resolution only after we had tabled a draft paragraph on the offer of subsequent negotiations.[4] The 'offer' paragraph was frostily received and the enthusiasm of the Nine for moving on to the second part of the operation has dimmed. It is clear that there will be continuing pressure from the East for wording on MFN that will provide them with at least optical satisfaction.[5]

[3] See *Human Rights*, vol. iv, pp. 27-28.

[4] See No. 75.

[5] On 16 July Mr. Marsden minuted that the interesting point for EID was paragraph 2 (*a*): 'I think it is of some importance that the East Europeans should be prevented from using the CSCE apparatus—pan-European as it is—for avoiding negotiations with the Community. Therefore the Nine must stick to their guns and insist that negotiations on matters like MFN which are within the competence of the Community should be separate from the CSCE discussions.' Mr. Fall disagreed. 'There is', he noted on 18 July, 'no reason to keep matters out of the CSCE just because they are within the competence of the Community: that, after all, is why we have insisted on Commission representation in Geneva.' He added that the reason for keeping the substance of MFN out of the CSCE was that they did not want to give

(b) Sub-Committee E—Industrial Cooperation and Projects of Common Interest

Texts have been registered but little real progress has been made. Discussions continue on what, or what should not, be defined as potential projects and there is confusion among delegations on where real interests lie. We are a long way from solving these problems. We have pressed for recognition that, in free market economies, it is for companies not governments to make the decision on the viability of projects.

(c) Sub-Committee F—Science and Technology

The East have been just as obstructive in this sub-committee on questions of exchanges, visits and direct contacts as in Basket III.

(d) Sub-Committee G—Environment

The sub-committee has now completed its provisional drafting work but has left open its future. We have avoided taking any action which would imply the sub-committee was no longer in existence, thus keeping our options open. The result of this committee's work is considered satisfactory and meets all our preoccupations.

(e) Sub-Committee H—Other Areas

Tourism, transport, training and migrant labour provide the substance for this committee's work and we have limited our commitment by including 'escape clause' wording. The work of this sub-committee has thrown up few problems and the only major point of contention at present is the Swiss objections to the Turkish draft resolution on migrant labour.[6] The Swiss amendments to this are now causing difficulty within the Nine because of references to 'national legislation' and 'demographic structure of society'.

3. In these last three sub-committees we have had some success in steering future work on these topics in the direction of existing international organisations, notably the ECE. This concept, which should help to avoid duplication and simplify 'follow-up', has also been accepted in the draft text of the 'Basket II' part of the Final Document.

4. The question of MFN treatment is clearly the principal one for the Soviet Bloc but it is one on which the West can give away nothing of substance at the CSCE. There is however a tendency towards a weaker attitude on the part of some of the Nine, notably Belgium. The Commission can be relied upon to help maintain a firm position. In Helsinki the Russians insisted that MFN treatment should be discussed and there must therefore be some mention of it in the Final Document. We could accept wording acknowledging that MFN can be a good thing when granted under suitable conditions, including effective reciprocity, but which does not commit participating states to accept any obligation to grant it. The wording in paragraph 7 of the Western draft was designed to achieve this formula, but with a little negotiating fat. The sting seems to have left the Soviet attack on

concessions without reciprocity, and because such reciprocity could only 'be negotiated in GATT or in some form of Community/CMEA or Community/East European country arrangement'.

[6] See *Human Rights*, vol. iv, pp. 230-31.

MFN questions recently and they no doubt recognise that CSCE will not provide them with any satisfaction on this question. Nevertheless it has been made clear to us in informal contacts with Eastern delegations that some form of cosmetic wording on MFN will have to be reached so that the Russian delegation can justify the 'concessions' made in Basket II. The Russians probably feel that it is worth keeping the question of MFN treatment alive until any final package is negotiated, in the hope that they might be able to win some last-minute concession from the West as part of such a package. We must continue to make it clear to them how little room we have for manoeuvre on this question.

5. Apart from the MFN point, negotiations on Basket II have reached a position where we could wind them up very quickly if there were general agreement to do so. But we cannot close this basket without a move in the Soviet position on MFN

6. It is difficult to draw up a score card for progress achieved so far in Geneva but in the face of the Eastern blocking tactics our delegation has performed well. Admittedly we have gained little but we have lost nothing. The registered texts in Basket II are all 'acceptable' to us; the prospects of achieving anything better, unless the Russians suddenly change their line on business contacts and information (which are essentially Basket III topics) are virtually nil.

J.C. CLOAKE

No. 89

Sir E. Peck (UKDEL NATO) to Mr. Callaghan
No. 350 Telegraphic [WDW 1/4]

Flash. Confidential   BRUSSELS, *4 July 1974, 2.30 p.m.*

Repeated for information to Priority Washington, Bonn, UKMIS Geneva, Routine Paris, Rome, The Hague, Oslo, Copenhagen, Ottawa, Moscow and Saving Athens, Ankara, Luxembourg, Brussels, UKREP Brussels, Lisbon, Reykjavik and Helsinki.

My tel[egram] No. 348.[1]

Kissinger Briefing: CSCE

1. Kissinger said that during the Moscow visit the Americans had been pressed very hard by the Russians on CSCE, especially on the slow rate of progress in Geneva and the level of Phase III.[2] He wished to repeat to the

---

[1] This telegram of 4 July reported that Dr. Kissinger had briefed the NAC that morning on the results of his and President Nixon's visit to Moscow during 27 June-3 July. Dr. Kissinger said: 'the basic problem remained of the USSR wanting *détente* on the cheap, or rather the appearance of *détente* without any content. It was up to the West to ensure that there was some content.' Soviet bellicosity was, he thought, 'now effectively restrained by the degree of practical cooperation that had been built up' (WDN 26/304/2).

[2] The joint *communiqué* issued on 3 July, at the end of the meeting of the American and Soviet leaders, affirmed their conviction that the successful completion of the CSCE would be

Council the questions which he had put to the Ottawa Ministerial meeting:[3] was there any CSCE result now foreseeable which would justify Stage III at the summit level? And if so, what was it? He could say emphatically that the United States did not have an agreement with the USSR on holding Stage III at summit level. It was however necessary for the Alliance to answer the specific questions he had put. The US was prepared to consider these jointly within the Alliance: we should stop talking in general terms and get down to drawing up a list of aims—perhaps 8 or 10—that were to be reckoned as attainable. The US would not press the other Allies to adopt any position against their will, nor did they wish to be pressed themselves.

2. Van Elslande,[4] Belgian Foreign Minister, admitted that he had been unhappy about the passage in the Moscow *communiqué* about the CSCE:[5] he was happier now that he had heard Kissinger's comment on it, and could see it in the context of the Ottawa *communiqué*.[6] He asked whether in Kissinger's view the Geneva talks could be adjourned fairly soon until early September, and whether in that case we could take advantage of the break for allied consultation.

3. Kissinger replied that the US position on the CSCE was as he had outlined it, in whatever way the Moscow *communiqué* might be interpreted. He believed that allied consultation on the lines he had suggested should start in the very near future. He did not think the CSCE could finish by July, and would recommend that a recess should be arranged for the Geneva talks in the most unostentatious way possible (i.e. as a normal August holiday). At the same time he felt that the present negotiating process in Geneva had become over-bureaucratic, with each individual country promoting its own

'an outstanding event in the interests of establishing a lasting peace'. And, proceeding from this assumption, they 'expressed themselves in favour of the final stage of the Conference taking place at an early date', and of the Conference being 'concluded at the highest level, which would correspond to the historic significance of the Conference for the future of Europe and lend greater authority to the importance of the Conference's decisions' (see *Public Papers of the Presidents of the United States. Richard Nixon, 1974* (Washington: GPO, 1975), pp. 571-2).

[3] During the NATO Ministerial meeting at Ottawa on 18 and 19 June, Dr. Kissinger denied that the United States either wished, perhaps as the result of a bilateral agreement with the Soviet Union, to accelerate progress at Geneva, or had decided that Stage III should be held at summit level. 'The Americans', he said, 'had never wanted the CSCE and regarded it as a mistake. They had gone along with the Conference at the prompting of the Europeans and in order not to be isolated. Against this background the US expected only modest benefits for the West from the CSCE.' But, Dr. Kissinger also remarked that the United States wished to avoid an outcome which would advance the Soviet purpose of setting up a new security system in Europe to replace NATO and the Warsaw Pact, and that for these reasons they would prefer an early end to Stage II. He urged NATO to consider what results would justify a Stage III summit and to define 'what would in fact be attainable' (Ottawa telegram No. 426 of 19 June, WDN 21/4).

[4] M. R. van Elslande had been Belgian Foreign Minister since 1973.

[5] Mr. McLaren minuted to Mr. Tickell on 3 July regarding an advance copy of the *communiqué*: 'At first glance the section on the CSCE reads like a Soviet draft' (WDN 27/14).

[6] See Cmnd. 6932, pp. 182-4 for extracts from the Ottawa *communiqué*.

shopping-list of measures especially under Basket III.[7] We should consider in more fundamental terms what was the essential aim of Basket III, and what we could hope to achieve. The Geneva talks were in danger of turning into nothing but a drafting exercise: we should not give the Russians the impression that we were being purely obstructive.[8]

4. In summing up, Luns said that he would urge member Governments to take up Kissinger's suggestion for very early consultation here on the lines proposed.[9]

[7] Mr. Tickell refuted this indictment of Western conduct. In a submission of 5 July he contended that the negotiating strategy worked out among the Nine and the Fifteen covered all aspects of the CSCE and had stood the test of time remarkably well, and that now to 'compose a list of precise minimum requirements, or requirements to justify a summit, would, on the assumption that such a list would soon leak to the other side, risk producing two effects: first the abandonment of all requirements not included in the list; and secondly failure to achieve even our minimum requirements (as the Russians would certainly regard these as the starting rather than the ending point for subsequent negotiation)'. He, nevertheless, considered it worthwhile preparing, with Mr. Fall's assistance: (1) a list in general terms of Western objectives which were reckoned attainable (even if this did not 'frighten the other side', he believed it might 'hearten ours'); and (2) a more detailed but 'safely unspecific' list of what might be done in respect of Basket III. Meanwhile, he thought it best to leave the level of Stage III to be decided nearer the time and in the light of the political conditions then prevailing. 'The criteria for attendance at a summit must', he noted, 'be subjective. But if greater security and co-operation in Europe are to mean anything, we must get more than a declaration of principles to justify the *status quo*. Such an outcome could lessen our security by creating a misleading impression of euphoria and deprive us of our first real chance since the War of achieving the conditions for [a] more civilised relationship between the peoples as well as governments of East and West.'

[8] At the Ottawa NATO meeting (see note 3 above) Dr. Kissinger had said that there was a risk that the Russians would return to a harder line on East/West relations if they were given to believe that this would bring them greater benefits, and that the West should therefore concentrate on what was essential and not pick arguments with them on minor issues. And while he agreed with promoting Western values in Basket III, he reminded the Allies that the Soviet system had survived for fifty years and 'would not be changed if Western newspapers were put on sale in a few kiosks in Moscow'.

[9] Mr. Callaghan and Dr. Kissinger agreed, at a meeting on 8 July, that the review exercise should go ahead (undated record of meeting between Mr. Callaghan and Dr. Kissinger on 8 July). But telegram No. 163 to UKDEL NATO of 9 July instructed Sir E. Peck that, if the proposal were discussed in general terms prior to the planned Council examination of it on 17 July, he should say that the review should 'seek to establish "the conditions for a satisfactory outcome" rather than what we would consider a fair price for the Russians to pay in return for Western agreement to go to a summit'. The results of Stage II were not, Mr. Callaghan maintained, the only factor in deciding whether there should be a summit, and other considerations, including the development of East/West relations, must be taken into account.

No. 90

Mr. Hildyard (UKMIS Geneva) to Mr. Callaghan

No. 617 Telegraphic [MWP 1/11]

Immediate. Confidential   GENEVA, *6 July 1974, 11.36 a.m.*

Repeated for information to UKDEL NATO, UKREP Brussels, Washington, Helsinki, Paris, Bonn Saving Moscow, other NATO Posts and Dublin.

From UKDEL to CSCE.

Meeting of Political Directors 11 July: CSCE: General Situation

1. At the beginning of this week the paralysis which Soviet obduracy had inflicted on Basket III and the discussion of CBMs for some weeks and which was affecting the few sensitive issues in Basket II became virtually total with the deadlock in the Principles Sub-Committee.[1] This deadlock in the area of greatest interest to the Russians has now been resolved, at least temporarily by their agreement that four meetings of the Sub-Committee should be devoted to the seventh principle (human rights) before the unfinished discussion on non-intervention is resumed. But elsewhere there is little sign of movement and the Russians have clearly reconciled themselves to a much longer haul. The question at the present stage is whether their evident desire to achieve tangible progress in certain fields before a summer break will outweigh their reluctance to make the sort of concessions on which the West and the neutrals are insisting. It also remains to be seen whether the discussions during Mr. Nixon's visit to Moscow will have affected their attitude and if so in what way. Agreement on the package deal proposed by the neutral and non-aligned delegations which links certain elements in the principles and the preambular sections of Basket III would constitute a big step forward: but it would not directly affect most of the issues of substance which are preventing progress, notably in Basket III.[2]

---

[1] Proceedings in the Principles Sub-Committee were deadlocked when, on 2 July, the Russians insisted that, without substantive debate of the fourth sentence of the Finnish proposal on non-intervention in the internal affairs of states, there could be no official discussion of the next principle. Meanwhile, the West were adamant that, pending the outcome of negotiations amongst the neutrals and the non-aligned on their proposed package deal, the Sub-Committee must progress to the examination of the principle relating to human rights (UKMIS Geneva telegrams No. 605 and 607 of 2 and 3 July, WDW 1/11; see also No. 87).

[2] *V. ibid.* The package deal, whose exact status was somewhat questionable, since not all the neutral and non-aligned states were happy with its contents, was distributed to delegations at the beginning of July. It proposed the incorporation in Principle 1 (sovereign equality) of a commitment on the part of participants to 'respect each other's right to choose its political, economic and cultural systems as well as its own laws and regulations', and the inclusion in Principle 10 (fulfilment of obligations under international law) of a provision requiring participating states 'in exercising their sovereign rights', to pay 'due regard to their international obligations and commitments' assumed in virtue of this document. The package also proposed a new Basket III preamble which referred to cooperation amongst participants 'irrespective of their political, economic and social systems', and in 'full respect for the

2. The Principles Sub-Committee after some five months of work is now just over halfway through the first reading of the ten principles i.e. much less than halfway towards completing its work. The Russians are anxious to press on but the scope for accelerating the present pace of work is limited. There are many conflicting interests to be reconciled in the formulation of the principles and the process of drafting is inevitably long and laborious. In the Sub-Committee dealing with CBMs the second reading continues of the text on the notification of manoeuvres but little real progress is being made or seems likely in the near future. The Russians having made two small concessions as regards the area and timing of notification are taking the line that they have gone as far as they can to meet Western demands, that their present position marks a departure from previous Soviet attitudes in the security field which is of great political significance and that no comparable gesture is involved as far as the West are concerned.

3. In Basket II steady progress has been made and two Sub-Committees (environment and science and technology) have finished or nearly finished drafting. There has been no progress for some considerable time on the major trade policy issues: but informal talks with the East suggest that they may eventually settle in a final package deal for a satisfactory paragraph on reciprocity and a relatively mild mention of MFN.[3]

4. In Basket III the impasse over the preamble seems likely to be resolved sooner or later in the context of a package deal of the kind advocated by the neutrals and non-aligned. In the Sub-Committees discussion has continued on successive points in the mandates and further Western drafts have been tabled. But the process of drafting which is taking place in informal groups remains generally deadlocked on certain key issues (access to printed information, reunification of families and access to cultural achievements) and for important tactical reasons the West are refusing to draft on subsequent items until texts are registered on these. In the Education Sub-Committee few problems remain but in the other three most of the big hurdles are still ahead.

5. The Working Group on the Mediterranean has started work. The East are prepared to accept the idea of a separate declaration and to take the Italian draft as the basis for compromise.[4] As regard follow-up the last five

principles guiding relations among participating states', and introductory passages for each of the texts in preparation in Committee III's Sub-Committees. There was general agreement amongst NATO Heads of Delegation on 4 July that they 'must not appear to reject the neutrals' suggestions out of hand and should try at any rate for the time being to keep the idea afloat' (UKMIS Geneva telegrams Nos. 611, 612 and 613 of 4 July, WDW 1/11).

[3] See No. 88.

[4] At a meeting on 11 June Herr Genscher succeeded in persuading Dr. Kissinger to lift the US reserve on the tabling of an Italian draft declaration on the Mediterranean (see No. 75, note 12, and No. 81, note 6). This freed the way for the Coordinating Committee to establish on 20 June a Special Working Group on the Mediterranean. It met for the first time on 1 July (UKMIS Geneva telegrams Nos. 542 and 567 of 13 and 20 June; letter from Mr. Burns to Mr. Adams of 2 July, with enclosure; WDW 1/28). In addition to the Italian draft declaration,

meetings of the Working Group have adjourned without any discussion. It is generally accepted that this is not an appropriate time to try to reach decisions on this item.

6. The neutrals and non-aligned have not yet completed their preliminary sounding of Western and Eastern reactions to their idea for a package deal which would satisfy the Western desire to avoid restrictive formulations in the preambular sections of Basket III while providing the Soviet Union and the East European States with some reassurance in the Declaration of Principles that the West will respect their internal order (our telegram number 613).[5] Some deal on these general lines must sooner or later form part of the trade-off which will produce a generally acceptable outcome to the Conference. But opinion on the Western side continues to be divided as to whether this is the time to try to conclude such a deal, particularly in view of the imminence of the summer break and the undesirability of negotiating under time pressure: and as to whether the contents of the package as now proposed are favourable or unfavourable to Western interests.[6] Our own view is that a package on the lines now being discussed is acceptable subject to one or two drafting changes. But the situation is fluid: the neutral delegations are not unanimous: none of them is committed to the present proposal and it is likely to be amended. In the circumstances this is not an issue on which the Political Directors can usefully take a decision. Western delegations should be left to deal with it as the situation develops in consultation with capitals.

7. As regards the timetable, the Russians are continuing to reject the idea of a summer break. It is clear from informal discussions with Eastern delegations that this attitude is a temporary and tactical one. In particular the Russians no doubt see advantage in keeping the Conference in session for as long as there is a chance of achieving some tangible results. But recent remarks by Mendelevich suggest that they may try to trade agreement on a break (on 19 or more likely 26 July) against informal agreement on a target date for completing Stage II.[7] There are obvious reasons why we should not

tabled on 13 July, the Group had to consider a counter-draft put forward by Malta, Yugoslavia and Cyprus. See *Human Rights*, vol. iii, pp. 42-45.

[5] See note 2 above.

[6] At the NATO Heads of Delegation meeting on 4 July the Italians, Belgians, Canadians and Luxembourgers expressed the strongest doubts about whether the proposed package deal would be in Western interests. The Norwegians spoke strongly in favour, and most other delegations stated that they hoped something useful might emerge (*v. ibid*).

[7] The Russians had previously been reluctant to accept the notion of a summer adjournment, and Mr. Beetham informed Mr. Elliott in Helsinki telegram No. 18 to UKMIS Geneva of 3 July (WDW 1/4) that Mr. Y.S. Deryabin of the Soviet Embassy had told him at lunch that day that it would 'be very difficult for the Russians later to make the sort of concessions they knew [the West] wanted if there were a summer break in Stage 2'. At a meeting of the Coordinating Committee on 11 July the Russians finally agreed to a five week break, beginning on 29 July, but only on condition that delegations committed themselves to keeping one or two officials available for contacts in Geneva. 'It is', Mr. Hildyard noted, 'a mystery why the Russians should have been ready to generate such bad blood by standing out

agree to a firm deadline: but we have presumably no more interest than the Russians in accepting an indefinite continuation of the negotiations. It will be clear from the foregoing review of the state of play that it would be difficult to complete Stage II before the end of the year.

8. In all the circumstances and particularly since in many working bodies the first reading of proposals on the table is far from complete, this does not seem to be the moment for a general reappraisal of Western strategy. This could more appropriately take place in September before the resumption. Western policy now should be to continue to stand firm on the important issues and to work patiently for substantial results on the points of interest to the West. We should not cause unnecessary delays but nor should we allow ourselves to be bullied by pressure or threats from the Russians (e.g. Lunkov's recent statement)[8] or by US concern to bring the Conference to an early conclusion. It would no doubt be useful for the Nine and the Fifteen to reassess our negotiating priorities in general terms, bearing in mind that such a process has a limited value, since the real problem is not to decide what points are essential but to negotiate formulations in the Final Document which give effective expression to our desiderata. It would be useful too for delegations here to be reminded that they should not get entrenched in relatively unimportant detail (a situation which obtains in the discussion on family reunification, largely as a result of German stubbornness).[9] But whatever work is done towards defining our basic objectives it is important that it should not become a prelude to a hurried global negotiation such as the Russians would dearly like to bring about. We should on the contrary continue drafting on the successive points in the agenda. All the indications are that the Russians continue to attach great political importance to a successful outcome however long it may be postponed and are ready to pay a good price. Despite the frustrations and wear and tear of a continuous session since Easter, Western delegations here are in good heart are working well together and favour the maintenance of a robust negotiating posture.

against a break for so long' (UKMIS Geneva telegrams Nos. 646 and 647 of 12 July, WDW 1/4).

[8] During a lunchtime address to the Diplomatic and Commonwealth Writers' Association on 2 July, Mr. Lunkov referred to the danger of a 'new cold war, or even hot war' if the CSCE broke down. This off the cuff remark was omitted from the text of the address circulated afterwards, and Mr. J. Dickie, *The Daily Mail*'s diplomatic correspondent and Chairman of the Association, was subsequently tackled by a Soviet diplomat in an unsuccessful attempt to claw back the unscripted portion of the speech. On the next day Mr. Lunkov's warning made the headlines in several national newspapers (letter from Mr. T.C. Wood (WOD) to Mr. A.D.S. Goodall (UKDEL Vienna) of 5 July, WDW 1/4).

[9] In letter to Mr. Young of 11 July Mr. M.A. Pakenham (UKDEL CSCE) explained that the informal discussions on family reunification had become a dialogue between the Russians and the West Germans. The latter among the Western delegations had the greatest interest in the issue, and it was hoped by some in the West that exposure to the Russians would force them to give up their 'less reasonable demands'. Nevertheless, the West were, Mr. Pakenham added, 'ensuring that no ghost of Rapallo should walk this particular corridor' (EN 2/557/7).

No. 91

Mr. Callaghan to Sir E. Tomkins (Paris)

No. 310 Telegraphic [WDW 1/3]

Priority. Confidential   FCO, *12 July 1974, 4.25 p.m.*

Information Priority UKDEL NATO, UKMIS Geneva, Routine other EEC posts, Washington, Moscow, Vienna, Helsinki, Information Saving Oslo, Ankara, Athens, Ottawa, Berne, Stockholm, Lisbon.

European Political Cooperation: Meeting of the Political Committee on 11 July: CSCE[1] Following from Delegation.

1. The Political Committee discussed the CSCE against the background of President Nixon's visit to Moscow, Dr. Kissinger's proposal for a review of Western negotiating priorities,[2] and the elaboration of this proposal by the American representative in NATO on 10 July (UKDEL NATO tel[egram] No. 362, not to all).[3]

2. It was clear that the American performance in Moscow had had a dispiriting effect on the members of the Nine,[4] particularly those who have been most concerned in the past to maintain close coordination with the Alliance and to restrain the enthusiasm of the French and the Italians for going ahead *à neuf*. The point is one which may cause difficulty in the future. On this occasion we were able to persuade the Political Directors to adopt an approach on the review exercise which should go a long way to meet the Americans and should avoid upsetting their susceptibilities. Much will depend on how far they in turn are prepared to take into account the views of their allies in working out the details of the review.

3. Three main criticisms were made of the ideas put forward by the

[1] The EPC Political Committee met in Paris.

[2] See No. 89.

[3] In this telegram of 10 July Sir E. Peck reported that during that day's meeting of the NAC Mr. W.B. Prendergast, the United States representative, had repeated Dr. Kissinger's proposal that NATO consultations should concentrate on determining (1) whether any foreseeable CSCE result justified a summit, and (2) if so, what that result would be. Mr. Prendergast also said that he hoped that, after substantive discussion on 17 July, the Council would instruct the SPC to undertake a study defining major allied goals regarding principles, outlining an acceptable compromise on CBMs, and selecting priority issues in Basket III. The Count Tricornot de Rose, France's Permanent Representative, replied that the aim of consultations in Brussels should be 'agreement on general guidelines for action at the Conference', and warned the Council against 'any over-precise formulation' of the results NATO wished to obtain. Sir E. Peck, basing himself on Mr. Callaghan's instructions (see No. 89, note 9), spoke on similar lines (WDW 1/4).

[4] Mr. Hildyard also reported in UKMIS Geneva telegram No. 641 of 11 July that initial reactions amongst NATO Heads of Delegation to the proposed review of objectives was 'fairly hostile'. The Dutch strongly opposed the idea, arguing that the West had spent two years formulating their positions in NATO and that the documents produced were still valid. But opposition to the proposal was subsequently muted and there was general agreement that some kind of review might be useful (WDW 1/4).

Americans in NATO:

(i) They looked too much like a bloc to bloc trade off with the Russians, and failed to take account of the interests and feelings of the neutral and non-aligned participants:

(ii) They failed to recognise the difficulties of producing an overall statement of priorities at the time when, largely because of procedural obstruction on the Eastern side, we had no means of assessing the Soviet position on a number of important proposals which had not yet been considered by the drafting group: and

(iii) They did not give sufficient weight to the agreed Western objectives in Basket III.

4. The Political Directors had before them a report by the President of the Sub-Committee (CSCE/74/140 P Rev. 1)[5] which comprised first a general evaluation of the state of play and the questions still to be resolved, and secondly a 'provisional evaluation' of Western priorities for the final phase of the negotiations. It was agreed that the first part of the paper was generally on the right lines. A number of delegations (including ourselves) indicated that they would have minor amendments to propose, and a revised version will be produced for incorporation in the report to be submitted to the Ministerial meeting of the Nine on 16 September. The second part of the paper will be circulated by the French within the Alliance as a contribution to the further discussion of the review which is to take place on 17 July.[6]

5. The question of where the review should be conducted gave rise to a complicated debate. It was generally agreed that the Nine and the Fifteen would be able to work together most effectively in Geneva, and that as much as possible should be done there before the break. We were careful to leave open the possibility of further work in the Alliance during the summer, but any suggestion of a 'NATO take-over' would be firmly opposed by the French and Italians (and for obvious reasons by the Irish).

6. It was recognised that the debate in the North Atlantic Council on 17 July would require tactful handling. The French Permanent Representative, who will make a statement to introduce the provisional evaluation of the Nine, will call a meeting of the Eight beforehand. It was agreed that we should draw on the useful elements of the American paper, and emphasise the provisional nature of our own ideas, we should also avoid giving an impression of rigidity.

[5] Not printed.

[6] The second part of the paper maintained that it was important that the Nine should continue to insist on the first reading in detail of all the Conference texts, and that they must hold back the possibility of any 'marchandage final' until this had been completed. 'C'est seulement après ce marchandage', it stated, 'que, faisant un bilan d'ensemble, les gouvernements porteront un jugement sur le passage à la troisième phase et sur le niveau de celle-ci: un tel jugement ne peut être émis en fonction d'un "paquet minimum" défini à l'avance. Il se fondera sur une appréciation synthétique de la valeur politique des résultats dans leur ensemble' (CSCE (74)140P Rev. 1 of 10 July, MWP 1/11).

7. MIFT[7] contains the relevant sections of the draft conclusions of the Political Committee.

[7] Not printed.

No. 92

Mr. Hildyard (UKMIS Geneva) to Mr. Callaghan
No. 692 Telegraphic [WDW 1/4]

Priority. Confidential   GENEVA, *24 July 1974, 7.10 a.m.*

Repeated for information to Priority UKDEL NATO, Routine Paris, Washington, Bonn, Helsinki, Rome, The Hague, Brussels and Saving UKREP Brussels.

From UKDEL to CSCE.

UKDEL telegram No. 383.[1]

US Policy towards CSCE

1. At today's (23 July) meeting of NATO Heads of Delegation[2] the US Ambassador Sherer made a statement on instructions (copy by bag).[3] We are given to understand in confidence that he queried the instructions but that Washington insisted he go ahead.

2. Sherer began by saying that the US were pleased that discussions in the NATO Council had demonstrated 'a certain convergence of views with regard to the preparation of a paper setting out agreed allied essential requirements in CSCE'. The US wished to pursue this exercise so that agreement could be reached on the choices which would need to be made especially with regard to Basket III and CBMs. NATO delegations in Geneva should prepare a study which clearly identified the issues in Basket III and fleshes out the principal allied objectives The US were prepared

[1] This telegram of 19 July reported that day's discussion in the NAC of the proposed review of allied objectives in the CSCE (see note 2 below). The Council's consideration of an American and an EC paper on the subject had begun on 17 July. According to Mr. D.A. Logan (UK Deputy Permanent Representative to§ NATO), the Americans had then 'seemed to go a little further towards a direct trade off', proposing that, in order to give the Russians a clear view of NATO goals, the West should 'decide what their basic requirements [were], define them in some detail and agree on a method of conveying them to the Soviet Union so that Moscow [would] have a better sense of the range of concessions required of them to achieve Stage III'. But when the French representative introduced the Nine's paper, he stressed that the first reading of all agenda items should be completed before any trade-off so as to isolate the points on which Eastern resistance was strongest and avoid giving the East the opportunity to press for a conclusion of Stage II on the basis of what had been achieved; and that the West's position on trade-off should not be communicated to the East since if they mentioned only essential points other matters of interest would be neglected (UKDEL NATO telegram No. 373 of 17 July).

[2] The NAC agreed on 19 July that, except for CBMs which would be considered further in Brussels, the examination of Alliance aims in the CSCE should be taken further by NATO delegations at Geneva on the basis of the papers prepared by the Americans and the Nine.

[3] Not printed. Mr. A.W. Sherer had succeeded Mr. Boster as US Head of Delegation.

generally to accept the section of the paper of the Nine of 10 July on Basket I.[4] They assumed that the SPC in Brussels would develop the section on CBMs. The Basket III texts should be discussed and the operative elements of each text set out succinctly for subsequent review by the NATO Council. Brackets should where necessary be included to indicate differing national positions. And a rough order of priority should be established with a view to an eventual narrowing of the number to six or eight.[5]

3. As their contribution the US delegation were now circulating drafts on a few selected issues: working conditions for journalists, broadcast information, travel and access to literary works.[6] These texts had been moderated to make them more realistic in terms of their acceptability to the Russians. On the question of marriage the US considered the current Norwegian draft satisfactory. As regards broadcast information the British text called for the removal of all artificial obstacles, whereas the Bulgarian draft required the acceptance of an obligation to control the content of broadcasts. The best approach therefore [would appear] to be a minimal text based on the UK draft. The US were convinced that the Russians would resist existing Western proposals on the establishment of libraries and reading rooms and therefore urged that a more realistic formula should be considered as a fall-back position. Sherer concluded by suggesting a programme of work by expert groups which would result in the completion of a paper on the principles [of] Basket II and Basket III by the end of this week.

4. Discussion of the American statement was curtailed by the imminence of a meeting of all Heads of Delegation to discuss the neutral package deal. The French, Dutch, Danes and we however expressed surprise at the tone and content of the statement, questioned the need and desirability of precipitate action and pointed out that the proposals now made by the Americans went far beyond the conclusions of the recent NAC discussions as summarised by de Staercke.[7] It was agreed that discussion of the US

---

[4] See No. 91.

[5] *Ibid.* On 23 July Mr. Streator informed HM Embassy in Washington that the United States had difficulty in accepting the Nine's paper 'which so far as Basket III was concerned amounted to little more than a check list of items'. He said that it was 'not the US purpose to short-circuit a stage of hard bargaining with the East', but that the Americans feared the allies might be in disarray when the moment for such bargaining came if they had not carried through this exercise in good time. He emphasised that his Government attached 'a good deal of importance to their proposal' for a review of Western objectives, and he rejected the French argument that no order of priorities should be established until the first reading of all texts had been made (Washington telegram No. 2489 of 23 July).

[6] Not printed.

[7] At the end of the Council meeting on 19 July (notes 1 and 2 above) M. de Staercke stated that the main divergence of view between the Americans and the Nine seemed to be essentially one of timing: 'It was', he continued, 'agreed that delegations in Geneva would discuss the two papers with the ultimate idea of defining priorities but there was no consensus in favour of an early report from Geneva. Indeed human considerations might make this impossible by August. Our experts need some leave. CBMs could be considered here in more

statement should be continued at a meeting of Heads of Delegation tomorrow afternoon.

5. The US statement is astonishingly tactless. It totally disregards the views of the Nine as expressed at Brussels and here, and shows no understanding at all of the character of the CSCE and the role and susceptibilities of the neutrals. The proposed timetable of work is unrealistic. The texts circulated by the Americans are reasonable enough as fall-back positions but embody significant and premature concessions to the East. The statement represents moreover a blatant attempt to by-pass the NAC by putting pressure on delegations here to work out at high speed a minimum statement of Western desiderata for presentation to the Russians. There will undoubtedly be much opposition at tomorrow's meeting to any further action this week of the kind proposed by the Americans.[8]

detail with a view to a report to the Council but it would be dangerous to reach over-rigid conclusions. Discussions must remain confidential.'

[8] At the resumed NATO Heads of Delegation meeting on 24 July it was agreed that there should be an exchange of views on the American paper and that the Chair (Denmark) should subsequently draft a report summarising the salient points raised, and that this should serve as the basis for discussions in Brussels during the recess. UKMIS Geneva telegram No. 699 of 24 July reported that Mr. Sherer, after welcoming this proposal, 'made the point that unless Heads of Delegation in Geneva took some positive action in response to the US request someone (unspecified) might "pull the rug out" from under their feet'.

No. 93

Mr. Hildyard (UKMIS Geneva) to Mr. Callaghan

No. 730 Telegraphic [*EN 2/557/3*]

Priority. Confidential   GENEVA, *27 July 1974, 12.42 p.m.*

Repeated for information to Moscow, Helsinki, UKDEL NATO, Washington, EEC Posts.

From UKDEL to CSCE.

Basket III Sub-Committees

1. The final week before the summer break has seen a last-minute effort by the East to give the impression of progress in Basket III, and some slight readiness on their part to make concessions. In the end agreement within the neutral package on the Basket III preamble (our telegram No. 725)[1] and of a

[1] This telegram of 27 July (WDW 1/11) reported that on 26 July, after three days of intensive discussions and more than a month of consultations, the Coordinating Committee had at last reached a consensus on a revised neutral package deal (see No. 87). The package, which Mr. Hildyard considered a 'satisfactory result' balancing effectively the interests of East and West, was similar to that outlined in No. 90, note 2, but Principle 10 now also required participating states, 'in exercising their sovereign rights', to comply with 'their legal obligations under international law', and to 'pay due regard to and implement' the provisions of the final document(s). Moreover, introductory passages for Basket III items were left to be drafted by Committee III Sub-Committees in accordance with the procedure agreed upon on 6 February

text on scientific co-operation in the Education Sub-Committee were the only results.

2. The deadlock on the texts under discussion in human contacts and information thus remains unbroken, despite a total of four months work on them, and extra meetings of the Sub-Committees demanded by the East.

3. In human contacts the wrangle over 'mutually acceptable conditions' (our telegram No. 685)[2] continued, both in the Sub-Committee and in informal discussions. Throughout the week Eastern delegations, under a strong Soviet lead, insisted that the details of the family reunification text could not be discussed further until an opening paragraph incorporating these words had been agreed, even if the paragraph were then inserted elsewhere in the Sub-Committee's texts. At the last moment the Russians agreed to drop this pre-condition. The result was the 'mental registration' by the Sub-Committee of a sentence which had already been agreed informally a month ago. But the Russians indicated that they will return to the question of 'mutually acceptable conditions' early in the next session.

4. In information, Soviet attempts to register a text on access to printed information were even more strenuous. They went so far as to agree that a reference to 'access by the public' should be included in the text. But they insisted on a Russian translation of this phrase which would have had restrictive implications. No agreement was therefore possible.

5. In the Culture Sub-Committee, the Russians also declared their wish to register parts of a text on access to cultural works, or at least to register them 'mentally' if no formal agreement was possible. But despite intensive unofficial negotiations at the end of the week, no agreed elements of a text emerged and the last meeting of the Sub-Committee ended on a particularly sour note.[3]

(UKMIS Geneva telegrams Nos. 644, 645 and 691 of 12 and 23 July, MTW 10/557/6). The agreed preamble did not, as the East had wished, contain any reference to respect for law and customs. An unsigned FCO paper of 27 July, summarising developments in Committee III, commented on this outcome: 'With the acceptance of the neutral package, the West can fairly claim to have come out ahead in Committee III. It must however be recognised that a Western "victory" on the preamble must lead to greater Eastern pressure for restrictions in the substantive texts of the Sub-Committees' (PW 2/557/1).

[2] Mr. Hildyard explained in this telegram of 20 July that during informal discussions on family reunification the Russians had adopted, apparently on Polish insistence, a new tack and demanded reference at the beginning of the text to 'mutually acceptable conditions' (later abbreviated to MAC). The phrase had figured in paragraph 46 of the Final Recommendations, but while the West held that it had been intended to apply merely to agreements to be reached at the Conference, Eastern delegations interpreted it as meaning that bilateral agreements must be reached after the Conference before any CSCE declaration on family reunification could be implemented.

[3] *V. ibid.* According to Mr. Hildyard, most delegations were inhibited from trying to draft the details of this text by the continuing lack of agreement, as in information, on a formula qualifying access itself. At the end of June the Russians even went so far as to demand that 'knowledge' be substituted for 'access' in the introductory paragraph of the text on cultural achievements (letter from Mr. Miller to Mr. Young of 12 July, EN 2/557/4). Mr. Hildyard also noted that the East showed great reluctance to discuss the question of the jamming of

6. In education, all delegations except the East Germans were anxious to register before the break a lengthy text on scientific co-operation (incorporating the much watered-down West German 'scientific forum' proposal) which had been under negotiation ever since Easter.[4] But the discovery of a deliberate distortion in the Russian text (on a point of relatively little significance) delayed registration while the Russians opposed the necessary amendment. This clearly reflected the situation in the Co-ordinating Committee where the Russians were sticking to their inaccurate translation of part of the neutrals' package text. It was not until they had climbed down over the latter (albeit unrelated) point that an extra meeting of the Education Sub-Committee was arranged at which the Russian version of the science text was amended and registration took place.

broadcasts. He added: 'All indications are that any text acceptable to them on this subject would need to condone, at least by implication, their continued jamming of Radio Free Europe and Radio Liberty.'

[4] The West Germans had first proposed the establishment of a Scientific Forum during Stage I, and on 6 December 1973 they submitted an explanatory note to the Conference detailing the tasks for which it might be responsible. See *Human Rights*, vol. v, pp. 299-300 and 336-43.

No. 94

Mr. Elliott (Helsinki) to Mr. Callaghan

[*WDW 1/4*]

Confidential   GENEVA, *29 July 1974*

Summary . . .[1]

Sir,

CSCE: The Long Haul

1. No early end to the long saga of the Conference on Security and Co-operation in Europe (CSCE), which began with the opening of the preparatory talks in Helsinki in November 1972, is in sight. The second stage opened here in Geneva in September of last year. I concluded my despatch of 15 December,[2] reporting on the general debate which occupied its first three months, by saying that delegations would be in for a long and tough confrontation when they began to draft the documents for the final Ministerial stage of the Conference. Experience might have taught me what to expect; but I hardly imagined then that the confrontation would last throughout 1974. Now, as the Conference adjourns for a six-week summer recess, the Second Stage hardly seems likely to conclude before the end of the year. I shall argue in this despatch that a much earlier ending is unlikely

[1] Not printed.

[2] No. 57.

to suit Western interests.

Delaying factors

2. There are two main reasons why progress has been so slow. The first derives from the composition of the CSCE and its procedures. The countries represented are all the states of Europe (with the exception of Albania but including Liechtenstein, San Marino and the Holy See), and in addition the United States and Canada—a total of 35. Agreement among them has to be reached by consensus.[3] Each has an equal right to submit proposals and to make its views known; and each has the power to prevent agreement. Thus the Conference has the unusual merit of providing smaller states with an unrestricted opportunity to speak out on matters of general European concern. They jealously defend the principle of equal status and the rules of procedure which enshrine it; and they react strongly to anything which they interpret as a move by the Eastern and Western blocs towards imposing solutions on the participants as a whole. Malta has no less capacity than the United States to hold up the progress of the Conference; the only difference is that she sees more reason to use it. A Conference so constituted, which has these procedures, and which, moreover, has to fulfil the specific and elaborate tasks agreed by Ministers in Helsinki can hardly help being slow moving. There sometimes seems no reason why it should move at all.

3. The second main reason for the Conference's slow progress is the determination of the Soviet Union and its East European allies to keep to a minimum the concessions they must make in order to persuade the West to proceed to the Third Stage at summit level; and their patience in establishing what that minimum is. The genesis of the Conference was the Soviet hope that it might be a vehicle for bringing the states of Europe and North America, notably by means of a declaration of principles governing the relations between states, to acknowledge the political and territorial *status quo* in Europe and thus to acquiesce in the Soviet sphere of influence in Eastern Europe. At the same time a successful Conference would promote *détente* in East/West relations in the limited sense in which the Russians conceive of it. In the Helsinki preparatory talks, however, the Russians found themselves faced by the insistence of a united and tenacious West on an enlargement of the notion of *détente* to include a gradual liberalisation of contacts between peoples. When it became clear that this would be the price of a successful Conference, the East indicated in principle their readiness to pay it. But since the opening of the first stage they have been fighting hard to bring down the price. Because the West have stood firm on their demands, the bargaining has been protracted, and it is still far from complete.

[3] In a minute of 5 August covering the submission of this despatch Mr. Tickell agreed that the CSCE was 'not as other conferences are' and that Mr. Elliott had rightly brought out the effects of the consensus rule. But Mr. Tickell added that he would give equal weight to the importance of the Helsinki Recommendations since they provided 'a charter for the Conference's work which delegations ignore at their peril'. 'It is', he concluded, 'as if the 35 participants had invented, wound up and set in motion a machine which has now got a life and pace of its own that is very hard to control.'

Course of Negotiations so far

4. These six months of negotiation of the final texts for Stage III have therefore been tedious and slow. I attach a short annex summarising the course of the negotiations so far,[4] but I will highlight a few salient events and indicate our scanty achievements.

Agenda Item I (Declaration of Principles and Military Aspects of Security)

5. The formulation of a code of international conduct raises subtle and complex issues which keenly concern all thirty-five participants. The declaration of principles must simultaneously harmonise with existing international law and yet mark progress upon it; and drafting takes place in formal sub-committee meetings at a speed which, given Conference procedures, cannot be much accelerated. It thus seems likely that this single paper (rather than the negotiation over human contacts and information) will determine the timetable of the Conference. Certainly the declaration of principles is not yet half complete.[5]

6. For the Russians and their allies this declaration is the *raison d'être* of the Conference: and the idea of the inviolability of frontiers is its essence. This principle, together with that of non-intervention in internal affairs, provides the clearest way for them to commit the participants to respect the *status quo* in Europe. The crucial issues here came to a crunch shortly before Easter. The West then agreed under strong Soviet pressure to separate from the statement that frontiers cannot be changed by force any reference to the acceptability of peaceful frontier changes under international law.[6] This confrontation provided a test of the unity and effectiveness of the West from which we did not emerge well. Admittedly the Russians, who had previously insisted that the concept of peaceful change should not figure anywhere in the declaration, acquiesced in a compromise which will ensure that the idea does ultimately find a place there. Admittedly, too, the West has obtained a definition of inviolability of frontiers which is not in itself unsatisfactory. On the other hand, the East are undoubtedly pleased to have achieved agreement on this vital point without being obliged to concede progress in other areas of the Conference of particular interest to the West. They are already interpreting the new text as meaning that European frontiers cannot be changed.[7]

[4] Not printed.

[5] Mr. Elliott pointed out in the annex to this despatch that six of the ten principles to be included in the declaration had now been provisionally drafted and that the seventh was under discussion. But, he reminded Mr. Callaghan, the provisional drafts were replete with square brackets, and the process of removing these on the second reading would be arduous, while the drafting of the introductory and concluding sections of the declaration would 'be far from straightforward'.

[6] See No. 72.

[7] On 26 July, at the last meeting of the Principles Sub-Committee before the summer break, the Americans, with West German agreement, tabled a revised formula on peaceful change for inclusion in Principle 1. It stated: 'In accordance with international law, the participating States consider that their frontiers can be changed through peaceful means and by

7. In the Sub-Committee dealing with military aspects of security, the Russians have shown a deep suspicion that confidence-building measures of the kind proposed by the British delegation on behalf of NATO are designed to provide other states with an unwarranted insight into the workings of the Soviet military apparatus. They argue that, for the Warsaw Pact, secrecy on matters which are open knowledge in the West is an essential element in the balance of power in Europe. Hence they have refused to contemplate at this stage the prior notification of major military movements and are intent on confining confidence-building measures to the notification to a limited number of states of major manoeuvres conducted in border areas.[8] They are not likely to concede satisfactory results even in this last limited field until the final stages of the Conference.

Agenda Item II (Commercial Exchanges, Industrial Co-operation, Projects of Common Interest, Science and Technology, Environment etc).

8. There has been steady progress in this relatively uncontroversial area.[9] The outstanding points mainly relate to questions of general trade policy, in particular MFN treatment and reciprocity in trade relations, and ways and means of improving business contacts and the flow of economic information. The remaining work here could be concluded in a matter of weeks, but this will probably not happen until agreement on the major issues in other fields of the Conference is in sight.

Agenda Item III (Human Contacts, Information, and Co-operation in Culture, and in Education)

9. The basic aim of the West is to secure clear commitments by the Soviet Union and its allies to promote freer movement of people and information between East and West. Given the profound political and ideological implications for Communist régimes of any expansion in the movement of people and the flow of information, the East have worked tirelessly to emasculate our texts and to introduce limitative formulations which would rob them of much of their practical significance. Eastern tactics have been doggedly aimed also at the early drafting of preambular language which would form an 'umbrella' or protective screen over the individual agreements reached on substance, by committing the participants to respect the political and ideological *status quo* in Europe. The aim has been to introduce into the preamble to Item III restrictive provisions—for example an undertaking by the participants to respect each others 'sovereignty, laws and customs'—which could be exploited to deprive the substantive measures of most of their practical significance. Mr. Gromyko expressed this idea with vivid cynicism when he told M. Sauvagnargues recently in Moscow that the bottom of Basket III must be cut away so that all the splendid things the West

agreement' (enclosure in letter from Mr. P.M. Laver (UKDEL to CSCE in Geneva) to Mr. Adams of 30 July, WDW 1/11). This formulation had the virtue, from the West German point of view, that it did not appear to make 'international law' a third condition for frontier change as did that of 5 April. See *Human Rights*, vol. iii, p. 137.

[8] See No. 86, note 4.

[9] See No. 88.

insisted on putting into it could fall through.[10]

10. The West's answer to these Soviet tactics has been to insist on the sub-committees working patiently through the subjects laid down in the mandates agreed at Helsinki. Although there has been some progress in drafting, little of real value has been achieved. In June, however, the Finnish Delegation, joined later by the other neutrals and non-aligned, put forward a compromise proposal.[11] This provided for the inclusion in the preamble to Item III of a general reference to the declaration of principles instead of the restrictive formulae for which the East argued; and guaranteed the East in return that the declaration would contain an assurance that all countries would respect the rights of others to determine their own internal order. This package, which represents a reasonable balance between the interests of East and West, was finally agreed after a protracted discussion on the last day before the summer recess. The autumn will show whether we have achieved a break-through or have merely transferred the battle on this central issue to other ground.

Agenda IV (Follow-up to the Conference)

11. A variety of proposals for establishing some means of continuing the work of the Conference have been given the equivalent of a first reading.[12] When it became clear, during the summer, however, that Stage II was likely to drag on into the autumn the subject lost its appeal to most delegations. The neutrals and non-aligned remain nevertheless determined that effective arrangements for 'follow-up' should eventually be agreed; and interest will certainly quicken when the Conference reassembles.

Soviet Tactics

12. During the past six months there has inevitably been speculation about the motives for Soviet tactics. The spectrum of their policies in this period has included apparent anxiety to make rapid progress as well as the apparent desire to block any progress at all. At various times they have seemed simply to be waiting for something to turn up. I suspect that it would be wrong to suppose that the Russians have been following a consistent strategic line. We may, however, have underestimated their patience and their preparedness from the start to accept a long haul. It has always been clear that the CSCE represents a central element in Soviet policy in Europe and that the Russians would like to bring it to the earliest possible conclusion. But for them the level of the Third Stage is more important than the timing; and they have chosen to pursue a policy of prolonged attrition in order not to pay a higher price in the field of human contacts and military confidence-building measures than is

[10] Cf. No. 81, note 7. According to a report to the Nine by M. Andréani, who had accompanied M. J.V. Sauvagnargues, French Foreign Minister since May, Mr. Gromyko had said that 'either Basket III should be "filled with mushrooms" or else it should be filled with what the West wanted but should then have its "bottom cut out so that everything fell through"' (letter from Mr. Burns to Mr. Fall of 16 July). Mr. Gromyko insisted that what the West were asking for 'amounted to interference in internal affairs'.

[11] See No. 87.

[12] See No. 80, note 1.

necessary in order to ensure that it takes place at summit-level. They may reasonably have calculated that they are better equipped psychologically than the West to stand up to a long confrontation, and that the longer it lasts the more Western determination and cohesion will suffer. They may indeed, and again probably with reason, have judged that the concern of Mr. Nixon's administration (particularly under the pressure of Watergate) to develop the Soviet American relationship offers then an excellent means in the not too long term of inducing a compliant attitude on the Western side.

13. What must be said is that the Russians and their allies have never made a sustained effort in Geneva to bring about quick progress. But they have done all they can to press the West to abandon their demands for clear commitments to the freer movement of people and information across frontiers, as well as to the notification of major military manoeuvres and movements. In messages to Western Governments, conversations with Western Ministers at home and in Moscow and a steady barrage of press comment, the Russians have demanded more rapid progress at Geneva, complained of the bureaucratic and dilatory attitude of Western delegations, and argued that Western proposals imply interference in the internal affairs of the Eastern bloc. They have suggested, more subtly, that the West can afford to be more 'realistic' in their demands in the knowledge that the Soviet Government is committed to *détente*, and that the restrictions on contact with the West will gradually be relaxed. Their East European allies have told us in innumerable private conversations that although the balance of internal forces within the Soviet Union limits the speed of their progress in the direction we require, such progress is inevitable. And they have reminded us that if we are interested in the continuation of *détente*, Mr. Brezhnev is the best Soviet leader we have and an early conclusion to the Conference at summit-level the best possible option. All this has been a fascinating demonstration of the diplomatic methods of the Eastern bloc.

Western Tactics and Problems

14. The cohesion and determination of the West to achieve a satisfactory result from the Conference have stood up well during most of these six months of negotiation; but there have been increasing signs of strain during recent weeks. There are two main problems. The first is to maintain the unity of the Nine, on which success depends. The NATO delegations on the whole rally willingly to a lead from the EEC caucus. The French delegation are now discharging the responsibilities of the Presidency with an efficiency, firmness and impartiality that contrast with the sloppiness and ineffectiveness of their German predecessors. Our other partners, despite undue rigidity on the part of some (notably and familiarly the Dutch) have generally subordinated their views in the end to those of the majority. But the German delegation has presented an increasing problem. The instructions they have received on the political side during the past four months have concentrated overwhelmingly on the promotion of special German interests *vis-à-vis* the East; and they have far too often involved sudden changes of direction, including sometimes the public abandonment without warning of agreed

positions of the Nine, in order to suit German domestic political contingencies.[13]

15. Though these strains have been serious, the structure of EEC co-ordination will no doubt survive. It was predictable that during the present stage of the Conference, when drafting was taking place on concrete issues and national interests were at stake, particular Western delegations would be tempted to take independent action to defend them. The Germans' geographical problems, the division of their country and their resulting close interest in a number of the political and humanitarian questions which are central to these negotiations, were bound to make them feel in a special position. They are, moreover, traditionally and acutely sensitive to the repercussions on their national interests of the relations between the two super-powers. The way in which they have trimmed their sails during recent stages of the negotiations has no doubt reflected the development in the official US thinking about the Conference.

16. This shift in US policy has been the second and major problem facing the West in the last few months. It has been an obvious Soviet ploy to exploit the Nixon Administration's heightened interest in its relations with the Soviet Government in order to promote their CSCE objectives. As seen from here, they have not been at all unsuccessful. As many predicted when the Nixon-Brezhnev summit was first mooted, it was swiftly followed by efforts on the part of Dr. Kissinger to persuade his NATO allies to adopt precipitately what he judges to be a more realistic stance in the CSCE negotiations. Dr. Kissinger's interest in the CSCE has notoriously never been great, though in the days of the preparatory talks this was merely reflected in the adoption of a very low profile by the US delegation. In recent months, however, it appears that he has come to see the Conference as a positive obstacle to his task of developing Soviet-American co-operation and carrying through his negotiations with the Russians to reduce the dangers and costs of the strategic balance. His fears may have been fed by the recurrent hints in Eastern capitals that slow Russian progress at least on MBFR and possibly on SALT are in some way related to the delays in completing the CSCE. At any rate, he had made it very clear that he concurs with the Soviet view that the Western negotiators in Geneva have become too stubbornly immersed in unnecessary detail; and that they need firm guidance from a higher level with the object of bringing the Conference to an early end.

17. It would be rash to suggest that Dr. Kissinger is wrong on all counts. In certain fields Western delegations here have fought too long over peripheral points, and it is essential to retain a sense of what we can realistically hope to achieve. Reviews of Western negotiating priorities and tactics with such

---

[13] In his covering minute of 5 August (see note 3 above) Mr. Tickell noted with regard to Western cohesion: 'Inevitably the Nine are under strain. From within the main problem arises from the German performance. The Germans have more to lose or gain from the Conference than most other European countries, and it is not, I suppose, surprising that they have been weaving about in a manner embarrassing to their allies now that some of the more delicate points for the Federal Republic are under negotiation.'

considerations in mind are needed, and soon. But the recent US suggestion that Western demands should be reduced to a minimum of essential points and presented to the Russians with a view to a rapid global negotiation shows a misunderstanding of the nature of the CSCE and of Western interests. Naturally the US, as a fellow super-power, is more interested in developing bilateral than multilateral relations with the Soviet Union. Smaller powers who cannot look the Russians in the face may take a different view. Thus blatant US pressure to end the negotiations may be disastrously divisive. It will inevitably be seen as an attempt by the two super-powers to impose their views on the other 33 states. It will be thought to ignore the views and interests of the Nine and the effort they have devoted to working out a common position and defending it for so long in the negotiations. It is a fact in any case that under the Helsinki Recommendations the working bodies of the conference are committed to a point-by-point examination of proposals on the items in their mandates. To by-pass this procedure would offend the susceptibilities of the neutral and non-aligned participants, who are determined to defend the principle that no participant is more equal than another, and who if provoked have the power to block the further work of the Conference.

18. It sometimes seems that Dr. Kissinger misunderstands the significance of the CSCE to the West. He often gives the impression that *détente* is primarily a matter of inter-governmental accommodation and that the human aspect is secondary. Painful discussions in Geneva about increasing the number of kiosks at which foreign newspapers will be sold in the Soviet Union are no doubt insignificant by comparison with the issues of the strategic balance. But there is more to it than that. One thing the Conference has already achieved: to get it accepted for the first time by the Communist states that relations between peoples—and therefore the attitudes of Governments towards their own citizens—should be the subject of multilateral discussion. Three questions follow. Should the West not take advantage of this opportunity? Is it possible that, by exercising quiet pressure through the Conference, they may eventually be able to get the Soviet Union to lower, even a little, the barriers to human contacts and to the flow of information and ideas between East and West? And unless that happens, will it be possible to create a lasting *détente*?

19. Dr. Kissinger would perhaps regard these questions as naive. To him it is axiomatic that more liberal practices in the Eastern bloc cannot be induced by direct pressure, but will come about as a natural concomitant of the process of *détente* in inter-Governmental relations. He has made it clear that he shares the view (which has been often enough expounded to me by my East European colleagues) that Western demands for relaxations in the Soviet Government's control over its citizens are bound to be counter-productive, and may very well endanger this process.[14] It is not within my

---

[14] Mr. Tickell was particularly impressed by Mr. Elliott's analysis of the American position. He reflected in his minute of 5 August (*v. ibid.*) that Dr. Kissinger tended to see the Conference in super-power terms and sometimes. on the basis of inadequate information,

competence to argue at length about such fundamental issues in East-West relations. It seems a starry-eyed assumption, however, that accommodation in the field of nuclear weapons and armaments will automatically entail relaxations in the restrictions imposed by Communist régimes on the contacts of their ordinary citizens with the outside world. Yet without a progressive relaxation of this kind it is hard to see how *détente* will have any real meaning or will last. In any case, the Russians themselves apparently expect to have to make concessions in this vital field as part of a general adjustment in East-West relations: their attitude throughout the CSCE negotiations confirms that they are prepared to make a move in this direction, albeit a minimal one. It is plain that the West has not been demanding, as apologists for the East often contend, that the Russians should make fundamental changes in their political system. The suggestion is merely that the Russians and their more illiberal satellites should undertake an initial move in a direction which has already been followed, tentatively enough, by the Poles and the Hungarians without endangering the existence of their régimes. In short, the West has not been asking for a break-through, but the beginning of a continuing process of normalising human relations in Europe.

20. If it is accepted that this is a valuable objective, two conclusions follow about the work of the Conference. First, the West may well have as great an interest as any other group of participants in ensuring that arrangements are made for following up the results of the Conference in future years. The neutral and non-aligned countries are attached to this idea largely because they see the CSCE as a forum which will give them an effective say in European questions. The East have seen in it a possible means of increasing their capacity to interfere in the affairs of Western Europe. For the West the attraction of follow-up machinery would be that it could provide the means of maintaining pressure on the Soviet Union and the East European countries to give effect to their commitments in Basket III and in the field of confidence-building measures. Of course there are risks in the idea. The East will certainly insist that provision should be made in any continuation to the Conference for discussion of all aspects of the present agenda. But in any case the idea of a follow-up will not just go away. What seems essential is that we should start thinking hard about the implications now; and work out how we can best ensure that the West is the net gainer from whatever arrangements are made.

21. The second conclusion is a simple one. There is no alternative for the West under present circumstances but to follow the tactics we have followed

allowed his impatience to get the better of his judgement. 'In particular', he wrote, 'I do not think he understands the genuinely idealistic element in the European approach but rather, in the manner of his hero Metternich, wants stability and *détente* (in the Russian sense of the word) for their own sakes.' He, nevertheless, thought that Dr. Kissinger's initiative for a review of Western objectives could 'do little but good', provided that the West remained faithful to the Helsinki Recommendations. On 6 August Sir J. Killick noted his agreement with Mr. Tickell's views, 'save only for some apprehension that we may yet find ourselves in difficulty with Dr. Kissinger over the "review of objectives"'.

so far: the tenacious defence of reasonable Western proposals during a point-by-point discussion of the items in the mandates of the various working bodies. It is a rational procedure, one which is generally accepted by the participants and gives them all a chance to have their say, and one which enables us to maintain a steady pressure on the East to accept clear commitments to relax their existing restrictions. The detail of the texts we are drafting is important: the attention which the East pay to every word and phrase and the energy they expend on achieving the least attenuation of the texts demonstrate this. The better and more precise the texts, the greater use they will be later as levers for moving the East in the direction of a gradual normalisation of contacts. We cannot therefore and should not seek to avoid a continuation of the detailed negotiation, though the process may be a long one.

22. My conclusion is simply that this Conference is worth understanding and worth taking seriously. During the 22 months that I have been concerned with its work it has sometimes been hard to sustain this conviction; and to be sure that we were not simply arguing about how many angels could balance on the point of a pin. But I am immensely grateful to the members of the British delegation for having maintained during these often tedious months not only their cheerful good humour, but also their contact with reality. Mr. Maxey, who had to act as leader of the Delegation during my absences in Finland, has borne the brunt of the negotiation with imperturbable logic and determination. The Delegation as a whole have displayed an ingenuity and an ability which has been widely admired and envied throughout the Conference. I wish them the best of luck for the crucial round of negotiations in the autumn.[15]

I have etc.,
T.A.K. ELLIOTT

[15] Mr. Tickell thought the results of the Western review exercise unlikely to be 'as specific as the Americans first wanted' and he doubted if there would be much inclination to hand over a paper to the Russians when the Conference resumed in September. The best result, he minuted (*v. ibid.*), would be 'a paper which would give new definition to our objectives, based on negotiating experience over more than a year and tempered with a necessary measure of realism', and which could be 'a sort of revised negotiating brief to take us through the last most slippery stretch of the Conference'. Mr. Callaghan agreed with this prescription, provided they worked to achieve a paper that both the Nine and the US could agree to for the autumn session. 'By all means', he noted, 'stick to Basket III at present. Pressure from US for a Summit will presumably be less now, but we should still be ready for one (and for continuing machinery)' (minute from Mr. P.J. Weston (Assistant Private Secretary) to Mr. Tickell of 27 August). Mr. Hildyard formally succeeded Mr. Elliott as Head of Delegation after the summer recess.

CHAPTER III
Concluding Stage II
20 August 1974 - 28 July 1975

No. 95

Letter from Sir T. Garvey (Moscow) to Mr. Tickell

[*WDW 1/4*]

Confidential

MOSCOW, *20 August 1974*

Dear Crispin,

CSCE

1. I have read with interest the views on Soviet negotiating tactics expressed by Anthony Elliott in his despatch of 29 July.[1] In particular, the question whether there is any point in continuing to negotiate at length about various minutiae in Basket III is one to which we naturally give some attention. On the one hand, I think that few Western diplomats who have spent any time in Moscow would expect any documents signed in Geneva significantly to improve the access of ordinary Russians to the West, Western people or information in the short term. The machinery of control on the Soviet side is too strong, and our means of enforcing the precepts of such documents too limited; so the Russians must be expected to circumvent the original intentions of anything we may induce them to sign.[2] And I agree with Elliott's contention (paragraph 19) that it would be starry-eyed to assume that military accommodations will entail relaxations in the restrictions on contacts between the populations of communist countries and the outside world. Indeed, the reverse may prove true: the process of *détente* has so far been accompanied in the Soviet Union by regular calls for internal vigilance, by harsh treatment of those who dissent from the official view of life, and by stultifying cultural orthodoxy. Theologically, there is every reason why this pattern should continue, for as is known, ideological convergence is specifically

---

[1] No. 94.

[2] In a letter to Mr. Tickell of 3 September, Mr. Elliott expressed his agreement with this assessment of the intentions of the Soviet authorities. 'On the other hand', he argued, 'if they thought that they would be able to circumvent them completely, it would hardly have been necessary for them to devote so much time and care to criticising our textual formulas; they could simply have accepted texts (and thus moved towards their aim of bringing the Conference to an early end) without having any intention of doing anything about them.'

excluded from the Soviet concept of *détente*.

2. On the other hand, like Elliott, I do not believe that it is a waste of time hammering away at the East in Geneva on the points which are proving so sticky. First, I do not think it does the UK, the West, or the citizens of Russia any harm. The Russians have frequently hinted to us that our attitude at Geneva provides a yardstick of our sincerity in developing relations with them; quite rightly, we have not fallen for this one. Obduracy over, say, MBFR or Berlin has failed to do measurable damage to the recent development of Franco/Soviet or FRG/Soviet relations. Likewise if the Russians are seriously interested in progress in SALT or MBFR, they will not be deterred by lack of it in Basket III; conversely we should not expect concessions in CSCE to lead to advances in other theatres, unless directly linked.

3. Secondly, there is a parallel with Basket I here; the Soviet Union is as concerned as ever to legalise its tenure of positions already held. They are not fighting against measures for the freer movement of peoples and ideas because they lack confidence in their ability to negate these measures, but because they would prefer their right, under existing legal provisions, to control or prevent the circulation of Western publications to remain unimpaired. What we are presumably fighting for is a *locus standi* for those, both within the socialist countries and outside them, who are trying to promote a more normal flow. If we are successful we shall not see immediate results, but we will have improved the position of those involved. Acquiescence in the Soviet line would be a grave blow to them.[3]

5. [*sic*] A further benefit of the campaign to obtain freer exchange (which CSCE has brought into focus) is that in opposing it the Soviet Government has exposed a lot of surface to its own people.[4] To take one small example, in the last month an illustrated 500-page critique of bourgeois culture, covering the whole spectrum, has appeared on the bookstalls and been eagerly snapped up. Its detailed exposé of our art, cinema, music etc. contains much that will be new to the general Soviet reader, not all of which will be unattractive to the younger generation. The steady pressure to which Elliott refers in paragraph 21 will continue to provoke this sort of defensive reaction, which in turn will surely raise certain questions in the minds of the more intelligent Russians. This is not a quantifiable process, and its benefits, if any, will not be apparent for a long time to come.

6. From the above it follows that I agree with both of Elliott's conclusions. For all its disadvantages, follow-up machinery will enable us to keep the implementation of Basket III commitments in the public eye; though we must bear in mind that, as these commitments are liable to be circumvented or

[3] Mr. Elliott made the point in his letter of 3 September (see note 2 above) that the texts agreed at the CSCE would provide a *locus standi* for 'liberal' Communists in Western parties who were habitually critical of the rigidity of Soviet practice.

[4] In his letter of 3 September Mr. Elliott also noted that this had interesting implications. 'How far', he asked, 'would it be possible for the Soviet government, at any rate in the long run, to conceal from the Soviet public the texts of whatever document may eventually be signed—as now appears likely, at "a very high level"—during Stage III?'

distorted by the East, the follow-up to CSCE may well turn out to be a continuing source of friction between East and West. With regard to future tactics, if we accept that the fine print of the final documents will be of use to protect those who stand up for freer movement and exchanges, then the Western case would seem likely to suffer as the result of an overall trade-off. Since the beginning of the summer break the Russians have been pushing the line that the major part of Stage II has been completed, and that there is now no reason why the resumed Conference should not move quickly towards its conclusion (as reported in Moscow Savingram 13 of 21 July).[5] They claim that a number of Western leaders are sympathetic to this view. However there is as yet no evidence that this presages concessions on their part, but rather that it is yet another attempt to get the bandwagon rolling. Assuming that we do not all jump on it, there must be a further long haul in prospect.

7. At a number of points in his despatch Elliott raises the question of the meaning of *détente* (with which my despatch of 29 January was concerned).[6] As he points out in paragraph 4, within the context of CSCE the East has been forced to accept an interpretation of it which includes contacts between peoples. Nevertheless I do not think that it follows (paragraph 19) that *détente* cannot last without freer contacts. To the Russians, *détente is* all about inter-governmental and inter-system accommodation, and has worked quite well so far without freer contacts. Admittedly this has led to strains, notably with the United States over Jewish emigration; but I do not think this poses an insuperable obstacle to the continuation of *détente*. Anything the West can squeeze out of it on the human aspect is by way of a bonus rather than a fundamental prerequisite.

8. Finally, a question on the genesis of the Finnish/neutral package. This has, at a convenient moment got the Russians off the hook. Do we know to what extent, if any, they may have had a hand in initiating the package proposal?[7] And is there any likelihood that similar manoeuvres may be undertaken as a face-saving way of giving ground when the time comes to do so?

Yours,

TERENCE GARVEY

[5] Not traced.

[6] Sir T. Garvey enclosed with this despatch a note by his Head of Chancery, Mr. B.G. Cartledge, which explained the relationship in Soviet eyes between *détente* and ideological struggle. 'The Soviet leadership', Mr. Cartledge concluded, 'clearly expect the contradictory dynamics of *détente* to produce in due course a "qualitative shift" in the world balance of forces as between the socialist and capitalist systems, in favour of the former' (ENS 2/1).

[7] In a letter to Sir T. Garvey of 4 September, Mr. McLaren replied that though the origins of the package were obscure, the Finns were unlikely to have acted as they did without being reasonably certain that the Russians would not object. 'But', he added, 'we have been told that it was in fact the American delegation who initially suggested to the Finns that they should promote a compromise. This interpretation of the American role is supported by the performance of the West Germans, whose early commitment to the Finnish idea (which embarrassed their delegation in Geneva) apparently resulted from a conversation between Dr. Kissinger and Herr Genscher at which the latter was unbriefed and the former particularly persuasive.'

No. 96

Mr. Callaghan to Sir P. Ramsbotham (Washington)

No. 1842 Telegraphic [WDW 1/4]

Immediate. Confidential FCO, *5 September 1974, 3.25 p.m.*

Repeated for Information immediate Paris, Priority UKDEL NATO, UKMIS Geneva, Bonn, Info Saving Helsinki.

MIPT.[1]

CSCE

1. Following is text of reply.[2]

Begins.

I was glad to have your message of Sept 1 about the CSCE. This is another subject on which I hope we can keep closely in touch in the weeks ahead. I am looking forward to having a talk with you when I come over later this month:[3] the CSCE should certainly be on our agenda. By that time the series of Western co-ordination meetings which are due to take place in Paris and Brussels in the next 10 days will have been completed.[4] We shall be able to consider their results in the light of Eastern and neutral attitudes at the opening of the resumed session of the Conference in Geneva. As you know, I believe we must, in our own interests, give due weight to the reactions of the neutrals in all this. I agree that we should now concentrate on defining a realistic position on confidence building measures and Basket III. The paper on confidence building measures on which NATO is working should serve as a brief for Western delegations in Geneva.[5] The Nine are

---

[1] This telegram of 5 September transmitted the text of a message from Dr. Kissinger to Mr. Callaghan, dated 1 September. In it Dr. Kissinger stated that the Americans continued to attach importance to the allies reaching an early agreement on acceptable results for Stage II. He said that he regretted that allied Governments did not share the American desire that they should further refine their CSCE positions in order to present them when the Conference resumed after its summer break. If they could state clearly their objectives so that the East could 'consider the concessions they would need to make to meet allied concerns', he thought it would significantly improve their negotiating stance. Accordingly, Dr. Kissinger asked Mr. Callaghan to consider specific steps to carry forward allied efforts in this direction, particularly with regard to Basket III and CBMs.

[2] In telegram No. 1840 to Washington of 5 September Mr. Callaghan asked Sir P. Ramsbotham to arrange for the delivery of his reply as soon as possible.

[3] Mr. Callaghan was due to visit New York for the opening of the autumn session of the UN General Assembly.

[4] Mr. McLaren, who prepared the first draft of Mr. Callaghan's reply to Dr. Kissinger, forecast in a covering minute of 3 September that the more cautious members of NATO were more likely to agree to a 'realistic assessment of Western negotiating priorities if we do not try at the same time to commit them to an early statement of these objectives at the Conference itself'.

[5] On 19 July the NAC had instructed NATO's Political Committee to consider outstanding issues relating to CBMs. Amongst the specific objectives decided upon at a meeting of the

working on similar papers for Basket III which will, I hope, incorporate the essence of the very useful texts circulated by Ambassador Sherer among NATO Heads of Delegation in Geneva on 23 July.[6] I am optimistic that these co-ordination meetings will make a helpful contribution to the refinement of Western objectives at the Conference.[7] There are still some difficulties to be sorted out, but it is my impression that they mostly concern tactics rather than substance. Most of our allies would agree that the Basket III texts which you have circulated—or something like them—offer a reasonable basis for compromise;[8] but some of them will certainly argue that, if we table these texts—or even show them informally to the Russians—too soon after the resump-tion, they will simply be taken by the East as the point of departure for the final stage of the negotiations; and that we may as a result end up with less than we would achieve by a more measured approach. You will also be aware of the strong feeling among some Western and

Committee on 5 September was an agreement on prior notification of land and combined manoeuvres, which would involve all participants in notifying all other participants of politically and militarily significant national or multinational manoeuvres taking place in Europe. In the case of the USSR the area of application would be limited to a 'significant band of territory' (UKDEL NATO telegram No. 462 of 7 September, WDW 1/6). The Committee subsequently agreed that NATO's initial fall-back position on this area of application would be territory within 700 kilometres of the USSR's western frontiers; and their minimum fall-back should be 500 kilometres (letter from Mr. W.B. Sinton (UKDEL NATO) to Mr. A.St.J. Figgis (WOD) of 16 September, WDW 1/6).

[6] See No. 92, note 6. The four revised texts which the Americans circulated amongst their allies at Geneva dealt with working conditions for journalists, the right to travel, broadcast and filmed information, and access to reading rooms. They were, according to Dr. Kissinger (see note 1 above), intended to reflect Western efforts to balance basic allied objectives against the 'limitations on Soviet flexibility in these matters'.

[7] When the Nine's CSCE Sub-Committee and Basket III experts met in Paris on 3 and 4 September agreement was reached on a report to the EPC Political Committee which made clear the need to define points of major interest to the West. But the general view of delegates was that it would be a tactical mistake to present the East with a list of minimum demands soon after the CSCE's resumption. They considered it difficult to define the minimum when a number of subjects covered by the Final Recommendations had yet to be examined by drafting groups, and when it seemed likely that the East would simply treat such a list as a point of departure for the final phase of the negotiations. The French were in any case under the impression that the Russians were in no particular hurry to end Stage II and were hoping to exploit signs of impatience in the West. UK delegates suggested that they should agree that 'Christmas was a reasonable target date' for the end of the substantive work of Stage II, but, while this went unchallenged, a majority of the Nine thought it unwise to write it into the report because it might become known to the East and be exploited by them in the negotiations. The Sub-Committee's report was susequently approved by the EPC Political Committee at its meeting on 11 September and by EC Ministers at their meeting on 16 September (telegrams Nos. 458, 459, 475 and 498 to Paris of 5, 11 and 17 September, WDW 1/3).

[8] At their Paris meeting on 3-4 September (*v. ibid.*) representatives of the Nine 'generally recognised' that Eastern acceptance of the US texts 'would represent a fair degree of success for the West in Basket III', but they thought it tactically better not to table them at this stage.

neutral delegations that there should be at least a first reading of all the subjects covered in the recommendations which were agreed in Helsinki before we embark on the final bargaining about the questions of most importance. I am in broad agreement with your views on all this. The maintenance of Western solidarity is going to be more than ever necessary if we are to get a successful conclusion to the Conference in a reasonable timescale. You asked for my views about how we might proceed with the review of Western objectives. I would suggest something on the following lines:

(i) We should seek informal agreement in the Western group to work for a successful conclusion to the second stage of the Conference before the end of the year.

(ii) We should prepare texts which will demonstrate Western willingness to a compromise, but which (as we agreed when we met here in July) still contain some negotiating fat;[9]

(iii) We should leave it to our delegations on the spot to decide when to table part or all of these texts, in the light of the negotiating situation and of the target date suggested above; and

(iv) We should encourage our allies to take a realistic view of Western priorities. But we must accept that the Final Recommendations will have to be covered in some way or other in their entirety if all participants in the Conference, including the important neutrals, are to be satisfied with its outcome.[10] I hope that you will agree generally with this approach, and that we can discuss it in more detail when we meet. We have a lot to talk about, as we have been out of direct contact for too long.

Ends.

[9] Cf. No. 88, para. 4. At their discussion on 8 July (see No. 89, note 9) Mr. Callaghan and Dr. Kissinger agreed that any paper produced from a review within NATO of what would constitute realistic and acceptable results from the Conference 'should contain a sufficient measure of negotiating fat'.

[10] When on 13 September M. Andréani explained the main features of the Nine's report to the NAC (see note 7 above) he suggested that the allies agree to cooperate in preparing the 'essential points' which would be involved in the final negotiations, and that they should begin by pressing in Geneva for a first reading covering all the points in the Final Recommendations. The Americans were willing to accept that there was a consensus within the Alliance in favour of the report, but according to Sir E. Peck, continued to think 'that we should seek to reach early agreement within the Alliance on texts which most would regard as too near the minimum at this stage in the negotiations' (UKDEL NATO telegram No. 482 of 13 September).

No. 97

Mr. Hildyard (UKMIS Geneva) to Mr. Callaghan
No. 894 Telegraphic [WDW 1/4]

Priority. Confidential   GENEVA, *20 September 1974, 6.38 p.m.*

Repeated for information to Priority UKMIS New York, Routine UKDEL NATO, UKDEL Vienna, Moscow, Washington, Paris, Rome, Stockholm, Berne, Helsinki, and Saving to Dublin, other NATO Posts, Vienna, Belgrade, UKREP Brussels, Warsaw, Prague, Bucharest, Budapest, East Berlin, Valletta, and Nicosia.

Our tel[egram] No. 872.[1]

CSCE: State of Play

1. The outlook at the end of two weeks is not encouraging. Whether or not we shall be able to avoid more set-piece debates on Cyprus, the Cypriots and Greeks have given clear warning of their intention to re-open some of the provisionally agreed texts on principles and to refuse to give their consensus to the final documents and to Stage III unless a solution to the Cyprus problem has been agreed or perhaps is in sight (our tel[egram] No. 891).[2]

2. The Principles Sub-Committee continues at its previous slow pace. But, despite private hints of some flexibility, there has been no progress at all on points of interest to the West elsewhere, i.e. confidence building measures[3]

[1] Mr. Hildyard observed in this telegram dated 12 September that the Russians were being very careful not to give the impression that they were under any time pressure. 'There is', he added, 'a widespread hope but no general expectation that Stage II will be completed by Christmas.'

[2] On 15 July Greek-officered units of the Cyprus National Guard overthrew the Government of President Makarios of Cyprus. Turkey, which together with Greece and the UK was a guarantor of the 1960 Cyprus Constitution, reacted strongly to this *coup d'état* and, on 20 July, Turkish forces invaded the northern coast of the island. Tripartite talks amongst Greece, Turkey and the UK opened at Geneva on 25 July, and a ceasefire declaration was accepted and signed on 30 July. But when subsequent talks on Cyprus's future collapsed, Turkish forces resumed their advance with the result that by the end of August they had established the *de facto* division of Cyprus along the so-called 'Attila Line'. UKMIS Geneva telegram No. 891 of 19 September described that day's debate in the Coordinating Committee on the Cyprus question. In the course of this debate both the Greek and Cypriot delegates had threatened to withhold their assent to documents agreed in Stage II if the Turkish occupation continued (WDW 1/33).

[3] In UKMIS Geneva telegram No. 872 (see note 1 above) Mr. Hildyard reported that, while the Principles Sub-Committee had resumed discussion of the human rights principle in a businesslike fashion, the Russians had been less encouraging with regard to CBMs. Mr. Mendelevich was calling for 'greater realism about what was possible and acceptable in terms of national security, and suggesting that the small steps which were all that could be achieved now should be supplemented by bilateral arrangements and further discussion in the framework of the follow-up'. There had, according to Mr. Hildyard, been hints that the Russians would like to settle prior notification of manoeuvres at a political level.

and Committee III. Western initiatives to facilitate work in these areas have met no response.[4] On confidence building measures, the Russians maintain that they cannot improve upon their present offer, and in Basket III flatly refuse to use square brackets for Western texts with which they disagree fundamentally. Although they are among those who called for an early start to draft-ing on follow-up and make occasional calls for an acceleration of work, they continue to give the impression that they are not under any time pressure.

3. The impression of the Nine is that, encouraged by Western initiatives to accelerate work and the widely known efforts by the Americans to persuade the West to set their sights lower and 'more realistically', the East are now concentrating on testing the unity and determination of the West. The East also appear to be hoping to take advantage of the feelings of frustration which are likely to build up among the neutral and non-aligned delegations if the lack of progress continues. The Swedish delegation has already received instructions that as there is no hope of obtaining anything on confidence building measures they should now concentrate on follow-up. During a visit to Berne last week the Swedish Foreign Minister seems to have encouraged the Swiss to think of more radical initiatives. We know that Brunner (Switzerland) is already toying with the idea of a package deal with Basket III and follow-up and the Swiss are also beginning to talk about the possibility of the neutral and non-aligned delegations submitting radically different proposals in order to try to obtain more rapid progress.

4. Swedish (and Finnish) weakening may be having some influence on the Norwegians and Danes but the NATO and Community delegations continue to maintain a united front. The US delegation appear to welcome the willingness of the Nine to continue the exchange of views on Conference tactics and are considering with us alternative ways of getting round the blockages in Basket III and CBMs. Scherer [*sic*] tells me that Kissinger has been briefed to urge on Gromyko at their meeting today the need for a full first reading in Basket III as an essential step for further progress.[5]

---

[4] On 11 September M. Chazelle took the initiative on behalf of the Nine in Committee III, and, with a view to accelerating its pace of work, he proposed increased informal contacts between delegations and indicated that within the next few days the West would be setting out their *desiderata*. He also called for a rapid 'first reading' of Basket III proposals (UKMIS Geneva telegram No. 871 of 12 September, EN 2/557/3).

[5] Dr. Kissinger met Mr. Gromyko during his visit to New York for the opening of the UN General Assembly (see No. 98, note 3).

No. 98

Mr. Callaghan to Mr. Hildyard (UKMIS Geneva)

No. 398 Telegraphic [WDW 1/4]

Immediate. Confidential   FCO, *30 September 1974, 4.58 p.m.*

Repeated for information to Routine Moscow, Washington, Paris, Bonn, Berne, Stockholm, Vienna, Helsinki.

Your telegram No. 908.[1]

CSCE

1. We share your two main concerns: we want to make American support for the Western position more visible and to persuade the neutrals to continue to hold firm.

2. As regards the Americans, our aim is to build on the wide measure of agreement reached at the Western coordination meeting during the recess. We naturally hope that the Americans will make clear in the Coordination Committee on 3 October their support for the policy of pressing for a first reading.[2] But it is still more important that they should take every opportunity to give public support to the substance of the Western position on the main points at issue. The sooner the Russians can be disabused of the idea the Americans are pressing their allies to make unrequited concessions, the better the prospects for an early conclusion to the Conference on acceptable terms.[3]

3. We welcome American interest in continuing work in the Western group on common drafts. A good start has been made on Basket III (your tel[egram] No. 904) and we would be happy to extend these procedures to

---

[1] In this telegram of 27 September Mr. Hildyard argued that the UK delegation's two main concerns were 'to maintain effective American support for the position of the rest of the Alliance', and to ensure, by keeping them sufficiently abreast of Western thinking, that the neutrals did not, through impatience, weaken pressure upon the Russians.

[2] Mr. Hildyard reported (*v. ibid.*) that on 27 September Mr. Sherer had assured M. Andréani and himself that, if they were prepared to try to produce common drafts with the Americans which were closer to American ideas, he would seek authority to say in the Coordinating Committee on 3 October that the United States fully supported the policy of pressing for a first reading.

[3] At a breakfast meeting with Mr. Callaghan in New York on 26 September Dr. Kissinger said that he thought the right course for the Western powers was to work out a common position and present it to the Russians. 'He did not', he maintained, 'want accusations from the Europeans that they were being "raped" by the Americans.' Dr. Kissinger had had talks with Mr. Gromyko on 20 and 24 September and had, he added, gained the impression that he 'was not pressing things either' (minute from Mr. Acland to Mr. Tickell of 26 September). Nevertheless, at a subsequent meeting in New York of the Nine's Political Directors Herr van Well claimed that he had evidence that the Russians were attempting to undermine allied unity and that Mr. Gromyko's version of recent discussions at Bonn differed from those the West Germans had given the Americans (UKMIS New York telegram No. 1191 of 26 September).

other areas subject to the provisos suggested by Sherer.[4]

4. A clear demonstration of Western cohesion over the next few week[s] should have a salutary effect on the neutrals,[5] but in any event we want to ensure that neutral initiatives are steered in the right direction. A clear distinction should be made between neutral compromise proposals on questions of substance, and ideas (such as the Swedes appear to have in mind on confidence building measures) designed to remit difficult questions to follow-up machinery or future conferences.

5. On the first we recognise that it will be necessary to make further concessions on confidence building measures and on aspects of Basket III. There is no reason why the neutrals should not play a helpful role, whether by making proposals of their own or by floating ideas which it might be tactically undesirable for a Western delegation to table at this stage. We naturally hope that the neutrals will keep us fully informed of any initiatives they have in mind, and that they will continue to take our views into account.[6] For their part, Western delegations should keep in close touch with the neutrals and take them as far as possible into their confidence.

6. But neutral proposals to remit difficult questions to follow-up machinery or future conferences are a different matter. As you know we see merit in continuing the multilateral dialogue which the Conference has initiated and we recognise that continuing machinery could be used to monitor progress in the areas to which we attach most importance. In so thinking we are ahead of most of our Western partners but once it had been accepted that one contentious problem should be postponed until after the Conference, there would almost certainly be a gadarene rush to deal similarly with other difficult questions and the Western countries would lose most of their negotiating leverage, the chances of securing good results on substantive issues would be

[4] Mr. Hildyard reported in UKMIS Geneva telegram No. 904 of 27 September that it now seemed that the firmness of the Nine, supported by the Alliance (including the Americans), might be having some effect upon the Russians who appeared to be 'reconciling themselves to a less partisan use of square brackets'. He further explained that the Nine had formally replied to Mr. Sherer commenting on the four American texts on Basket III subjects, circulated in July (see No. 96, note 6), and that this had been designed to bring out the fact that there were 'no major differences of substance between the Americans and [the Nine] and that the misunderstandings of July [had] been largely overcome'.

[5] Discussions amongst NATO delegates at Geneva soon resulted in agreement on the need for concerted pressure from all delegations for a first reading of all texts, and when the Coordinating Committee met on 3 October the British, Dutch, French, West Germans and Norwegians all, with American backing, emphasised the urgent need for a clear picture of all outstanding topics. 'Altogether', Mr. Hildyard commented, 'it was quite an impressive display of Western resolve' (UKMIS Geneva telegram No. 923 of 5 October, EN 2/557/3).

[6] Mr. J.R. Wraight, HM Ambassador in Berne, reported in Berne telegram No. 124 of 1 October that he had learned from the Swiss Federal Political Department that during the summer the Russians had sought to persuade the Austrians, Swedes and Swiss to press for agreement on small issues at the CSCE in order to break the deadlock. Whilst neither the Austrian nor Swedish responses had given the Swiss any cause to think that the Russian overtures had been successful, both the Austrian and Swedish Foreign Ministers had seemed, during visits to Switzerland, to be weakening under Soviet pressure.

radically diminished, and it would be much harder to reach an agreement on follow-up acceptable both to the neutrals and to the majority of Western participants. The situation would be made still more difficult if the neutrals and non-aligned were to use the precedent of the discussion of Cyprus at the Conference[7] to press for continuing machinery designed to play a part in crisis management. We think it may be wise to put these points squarely to the neutrals as soon as possible. Given their strongly held views on follow up, the Americans and the French might be best placed to do the job.

7. Please take an early opportunity to discuss these ideas with your Western colleagues. If it were generally felt useful to approach certain neutrals in capitals we would be willing to play our part.

[7] See No. 97, note 2.

No. 99

Minute from Mr. Bullard to Sir J. Killick

[*EN 2/2*]

Confidential   FCO, *1 October 1974*
The CSCE and the Conference of European Communist Parties

1. Mr. Gaspari[1] of the Yugoslav Embassy asked me today for my impressions of how things stood at the CSCE. I said that during the summer holidays we had reviewed the situation nationally and with the Nine and the Fifteen. We were quite convinced that it was not our fault that the Conference had not made faster progress. But we had resolved to make it even more impossible, from September onwards, for anybody to make this accusation. We had punctiliously prepared papers to support all our initiatives. To our surprise, the Soviet and East European delegations appeared to have reversed their positions. They were now behaving as if they thought there was no urgency about the business. As an example I described the Soviet attitude to the use of square brackets.[2]

2. Gaspari, who seemed none too well informed for once, asked what motive the Soviet Union might have for delaying. I said I could think of 3. The Russians might believe that Western delegations would come under time pressure as a result of internal affairs in their own countries; or they might have reason to suppose that the neutrals would lose patience and suggest settling for what has been achieved already, leaving disagreed points to be reverted to at some unspecified time in the future; or the Russians might be seeking to establish a link between the CSCE and MBFR, and calculating that Western eagerness for results in the second would make us ready for concessions in the first.

[1] Mr. D. Gaspari was Minister-Counsellor at the Yugoslav Embassy in London.
[2] See No. 97.

3. Gaspari asked whether I did not see a connection between the CSCE and the proposed Conference of European Communist Parties. According to his information, the Russians were in favour of holding this Conference before Stage III of the CSCE.[3] The Yugoslav view was the opposite. Yugoslavia had agreed to take part in the preliminary consultations, due to be held in Warsaw in mid-October, for an eventual Conference of European Parties. They had taken this decision because they detected some progress in recent years towards recognition of the rights of individual Parties and the principle of equality between them. They had made it clear how they would expect the Warsaw consultations to be conducted. These must be open to the public, and democratic; there must be no criticism or condemnation of any Communist Party; and all Parties must recognise the right of any other to refuse to accept any document that might be formulated. Gaspari said that this position was similar to that of Romania (see today's 'Financial Times')[4] and certain Western Communist Parties. He understood that altogether 31 Parties had been invited, of whom 28 or 29 had accepted. (He could not say whether Albania was one of those to send a negative answer, or who the others might be.) The exiled Greek Communist Party in Moscow had been invited, but Yugoslavia had proposed that the Party actually in Greece should be invited also, preferably forming a joint delegation with the other. In any case, said Gaspari, Yugoslavia had maintained that this forthcoming Conference, if it took place, should not be regarded as having any link with that held at Karlovy Vary.[5] And their participation in the Warsaw meeting did not prejudice their position as regards future consultations or the Conference itself.

4. Gaspari produced his theory about the connection between the CSCE and the other Conference as if it were generally accepted. I am not quite clear how the Russians think that their hand in Geneva would be strengthened by even the most conclusive unanimous vote at a Conference of European Parties.[6] There must surely be a risk of discordant voices giving a

[3] A consultative meeting of European Communist Parties assembled in Warsaw during 16-18 October in order to prepare for the summoning of a European Conference of Communist Parties. The twenty-eight participating delegations initially agreed that such a gathering would be convened no later than mid-1975. But a further preparatory Conference, which met in Budapest during 19-21 December, apparently decided that the projected Conference would be summoned to meet in Berlin after the conclusion of CSCE Stage III.

[4] The *Financial Times* reported that coordination meetings between Romania and Yugoslavia on tactics for the preparation of a meeting of European Communist Parties had taken place during the previous week.

[5] The Conference of European Communist Parties which met at Karlovy Vary (Karlsbad) during 24-26 April 1967 focused upon European security. As a result, Bulgaria, Czechoslovakia and Hungary agreed not to open full diplomatic relations with the FRG. Neither Romania, which had established diplomatic relations with Bonn, nor Yugoslavia were represented at this gathering.

[6] In a letter to Mr. D.I. Lewty (EESD) of 24 October Mr. B.P. Noble (HM Embassy in Warsaw) speculated upon the possible connexion between the proposed Conference and CSCE. 'What is not certain', he observed, 'is whether the Soviets wish to use a successful

handle to Western negotiatiors at Geneva. In general I am struck by the serenity of the Soviet attitude to the outside world at the moment. There is a piece on this in today's 'Financial Times' also, but the mood comes most clearly out of Gromyko's speech at the UN. It would be in keeping with this mood, I think, for the Russians to mark time at Geneva. But I would plump for the link with the MBFR as the most convincing explanation of all.

J.L. BULLARD

Conference as a weapon of strength in CSCE negotiations (i.e. a Conference before the end of CSCE) or whether they hope to seal the culmination of *détente* as represented by a successful conclusion to the CSCE by a European Communist party jamboree.' He added that as the timing of the Conference was then clearly intended for May 1975, this seemed to put a 'limitation on the more relaxed Soviet attitude to the speed of CSCE progress'.

No. 100

Minute from Mr. Fall to Sir O. Wright[1]

[*WDN 27/14*]

Confidential   PARIS, *18 October 1974*
CSCE/MBFR Link

1. During the discussion of the CSCE in the Political Committee this morning your Danish colleague suggested that there should be an exchange of views on the possibility of making a link between progress at the CSCE and progress in MBFR. He was supported by the Italians, and it was agreed that there would be a discussion of the question at your dinner this evening.[2]

2. The subject has a long history. A procedural link was established at the outset when Dr. Kissinger, during a visit to Moscow, secured Soviet agreement to the opening of preliminary talks on MBFR as a condition for American agreement to the opening of the multilateral preparatory talks for the CSCE.[3] Subsequently, when the CSCE preparatory talks were seen to be making faster progress than the MBFR talks, the suggestion that Western Delegations should go slow in Helsinki unless the East were more forthcoming in Vienna was advanced informally on a number of occasions. In each case it was decided that it would be wrong to try to introduce such a link. The main arguments were:-

(i) That the West had its own reasons for wanting a successful outcome to the CSCE and that we therefore had no reason to obstruct progress provided that it was in the right direction in CSCE terms;

[1] Mr. J.O. Wright was created KCMG in 1974. Both Sir O. Wright (Political Director) and Mr. Fall attended the meeting of the EPC Political Committee in Paris on 18 October.

[2] Mr. Tickell informed Mr. Logan in a letter of 22 October that there had been no time to prepare for a proper exchange of views on the CSCE/MBFR link either at the Political Committee meeting or the subsequent Political Directors' dinner.

[3] See No. 13.

(ii) that the French, who do not participate in MBFR, would be adamantly opposed to any such link and that its introduction would thus prove divisive;
(iii) that to introduce a link would antagonise the neutrals, who attach great importance to the CSCE, but do not participate in MBFR, and whose support for the Western position at the CSCE had proved a factor of considerable importance at the multilateral preparatory talks.[4]

These arguments are regarded by most Western countries as retaining their validity, and there has until recently been no suggestion that a link should be established between the negotiations in Vienna and the CSCE proper.

3. The most recent development is that the Russians—who have consistently opposed any link between CSCE and MBFR—have indicated on a number of occasions (including in a conversation between Gromyko and Kissinger in New York last month) that the prospects for MBFR would be improved by a satisfactory conclusion to the CSCE.[5] The Americans have concluded that the Russians are considering the idea of establishing a link; and they have suggested in NATO that the North Atlantic Council should consider the idea of reversing this link (i.e. by arguing that it will not be possible to reach a satisfactory conclusion to the CSCE unless Warsaw Pact Delegations in Vienna are prepared to move from their present rigid positions).[6] There has already been a preliminary exchange of views in NATO; but the debate in the North Atlantic Council has not yet taken place. We think that NATO is the most appropriate forum for the debate; and if the Political Directors are to discuss the matter this evening, it would be best to preserve a high degree of informality.[7]

[4] These arguments against linkage were advanced by Mr. Tickell in a minute to Sir J. Killick of 19 August. But Mr. Tickell also contended that the timings of the two sets of negotiation did not fit and that, even at its present pace, the CSCE would be over long before the MBFR talks: there would then be no effective means, in terms of linkage, with which to hold the Russians to any bargain struck. Furthermore, he felt that if priority were to be given to progress in the MBFR process the West would 'in effect be admitting a major reverse in the CSCE, damaging to their other relationships in Europe and acknowledging a measure of super-power dominance which the other CSCE participants have hitherto strongly resisted'.

[5] See No. 98, note 3. Already in his minute of 19 August (*v. ibid.*) Mr. Tickell had noted that the Russians had 'clearly not abandoned their hope of using the American desire to make progress in MBFR to persuade the all-too-easily persuadable Dr. Kissinger that the CSCE is best concluded as soon as possible'.

[6] On 2 October Mr. V.E. McAuliffe (US Deputy Chief of Mission to NATO) informed the NAC that Mr. Gromyko had told Dr. Kissinger in New York that a successful conclusion of the CSCE would improve conditions for the MBFR talks, and that the USA considered that the Russians were seeking to establish a link between the two negotiations. 'The Alliance', he said, 'should consider if there was any advantage to the West in exploiting this Soviet move, for example by making progress in CSCE contingent on Soviet movement in MBFR' (UKDEL NATO telegram No. 524 of 2 October, WDN 27/304/1).

[7] The SPC discussed the US proposal on 3 October. The Canadian representative then argued, with Dutch support, that any such linkage should be considered only after a general

4. On the substance of the question, it seems clear that any attempt to establish a 'reverse link' would be highly unwelcome to the Russians. It could therefore only hope to succeed if the Americans were to take the lead and put their full authority behind the idea. Even then, the arguments about the French and the neutrals summarised in para. 2 above would remain valid if the Americans were to propose blocking consensus on individual points on the agenda of the CSCE until further progress had been made in MBFR. There would be a grave risk both of dividing the West and of weakening our position at the CSCE.

5. There is however one way in which the Americans could seek to establish a link without producing such difficulties. If they were to make it known to the Russians that President Ford[8] would be unwilling to attend the third stage of the CSCE unless there had been some progress in MBFR, the Americans could present their action not as blocking the negotiations in Geneva, but merely as indicating a position on the as yet undecided issue of the level of the third stage.[9] They could in these circumstances count on the sympathy and support of a number of West European countries; and the French, who remain categorically opposed to a CSCE/MBFR link, but who have always been very sceptical about the idea of a Summit might be relied upon at least not to oppose the American proposal. The neutrals, many of whom see attraction in a third stage at Summit level, might not like the idea; but they could not very well dispute the fact that it is for each participant at the CSCE to decide in what circumstances their Heads of State or Government would be prepared to attend a Summit.

6. Even if the Americans were prepared to do this, I doubt whether they would get from the Russians any concessions in MBFR which they were not prepared to make in any case. But they might well succeed in getting these concessions made sooner, and this in itself might present some advantage. It would also mean that Western representatives at a CSCE Summit would be able in their speeches to justify the occasion, not only with reference to the documents produced by the CSCE but by pointing to a degree of progress in the rather more important negotiations in Vienna.

7. Ideally therefore the message which we would like the Americans to get from the debate in the North Atlantic Council is that:-

(i) No reverse link will succeed unless they are prepared to take the lead;

reassessment of *détente*, since it would amount to 'making Western objectives in CSCE (especially Basket III) secondary to MBFR' (UKDEL NATO telegram No. 530 of 3 October).

[8] Mr. G.R. Ford became US President on 9 August, following the resignation of President Nixon.

[9] Mr. Tickell suspected that in the last resort Soviet willingness to make progress in either negotiation in the way HMG desired would depend on the Soviet assessment of United States support for allied objectives (see note 4 above). 'The one major asset we have', he reasoned, 'is the Soviet interest in the development of the US/Soviet relationship.' Nevertheless, as he admitted in a letter to Sir E. Peck of 30 September, 'whether the Americans would be ready thus to turn one hundred and eighty degrees and put their *détente* policy in some measure of risk' was a question only they could answer.

(ii) a link with the substance of the CSCE agenda is likely to prove counter-productive in CSCE terms; but

(iii) it might be worth considering a link with the level of the third stage of the CSCE.

The difficulty of course is that the question of the Summit is a political one and few, if any, Western officials would feel able to recommend such a linkage without consulting their Ministers. They in turn might well feel hesitant about associating themselves with a negative-sounding idea which the Americans might well choose not to implement. The probability therefore is that the debate in the North Atlantic Council will be conducted in such a way that the Americans will be able to say that, after being criticised by their allies for going too quickly at the CSCE, they suggested a tough position but found that it was rejected by their allies.[10]

Line to Take

8. We should not strive officiously to keep the American idea alive. Equally, there is no reason why the Nine should show too much zeal in trying to kill it.[11] There might be advantage in maintaining the issue as a subject for debate by concentrating not so much on the recognised disadvantages of a link between MBFR and the substance of CSCE but on the extent to which these disadvantages might be reduced if the link were to be established with the level of the third stage. At the least, it would do no harm if it became known to the other side that the subject was under discussion in the Alliance and that progress in MBFR might increase the chances of a Summit.

B.J.P. Fall

[10] The proposed MBFR/CSCE link was discussed in the SPC on 18 and 31 October (UKDEL NATO telegrams Nos. 561 and 593 of 19 and 31 October), and work began on the preparation of a paper analysing options for linkage. When, however, this was eventually considered by the NAC on 27 November delegates accepted its implied conclusion that an attempt at linkage would not be desirable in present circumstances. Indeed, Mr. McAuliffe stated that 'Washington had no predisposition in favour of any form of reverse linkage'. Ms. A.J.K. Bailes (UKDEL NATO) thought the outcome suited HMG well. Some issues had been clarified and, she observed in a letter to Mr. Lever (now in WOD) of 27 November, the 'tone had been constructive enough to avoid any too blatant "overkill" of the US initiative, and should demonstrate to Washington that the Allies [were] prepared to take American suggestions for strategic innovation seriously (perhaps more so than they [did] themselves?)'.

[11] In his letter to Mr. Logan of 22 October (see note 2 above) Mr. Tickell wrote: 'We naturally wish to avoid encouraging the Americans in a direction which would prove counter-productive at the CSCE, both in terms of Western cohesion and of neutral support. But we should not show ourselves too anxious to choke off an initiative which it might be possible to steer into more desirable channels.'

No. 101

Mr. Hildyard (UKMIS Geneva) to Mr. Callaghan

No. 945 Telegraphic [EN 2/557/6]

Priority. Confidential   GENEVA, *19 October 1974, 9.35 a.m.*

Repeated for Information saving Moscow, Washington, Helsinki, UKDEL NATO, EEC Posts.

From UKDEL to CSCE.

Basket III Sub-Committees

1. In our tel[egram] No. 936,[1] summing up the progress made last week,[2] we cautioned that the Russians might shortly lower the boom again. This has happened even sooner than might have been expected. Having taken three paces forward last week, the Russians took two smart paces backward at the beginning of this week. The overall picture remains confused, but it would appear that either they were only seeking to give a short term impression of flexibility and movement and are satisfied that they have done so: or that someone felt the pace was accelerating unduly and decided to put the brake on. Their very abrupt and somewhat disorganised change of direction is perhaps more consistent with the second thesis.

2. In human contacts, the Russians are now adopting an extremely hard line, amounting to a virtual standstill on all five issues now under discussion, presumably in the hope of winning further concessions from the West on the key issue of 'mutually acceptable conditions'. Drafted in a certain (Russian) way, the section of the text including these words would effectively negate all the following texts of substance in human contacts.[3]

[1] In this telegram of 12 October Mr. Hildyard reported that as the result of an effort by Eastern delegations to advance work in Basket III, particularly on human contacts and information, 'some substantive progress has been made in these fields for the first time for several months'.

[2] Already, during the first week of October, Western and Eastern delegations had agreed to draft in parallel on five Basket III subjects: family reunification, marriage, travel, the mini-preamble and MAC (UKMIS Geneva telegram, No. 924 of 5 October; see No. 93, note 2). During the following week some progress was made on family reunification and marriage, and while on the surface the East's attitude towards the introductory passages, including MAC, remained very negative, there were, according to UKMIS Geneva telegram No. 936 (*v. ibid.*), indications that the Russians might be prepared to be more flexible. Meanwhile, the preparation of a neutral package deal incorporating all five elements of human contacts was moving ahead, and the information Sub-Committee had registered its first text since the end of March, albeit only by agreeing to disagree on the central issue of whether, and if so how, access to information should be qualified.

[3] Mr. M. Alexander (recently appointed Head of Chancery in UKMIS Geneva) warned Mr. Fall in a letter of 18 October that it had long been clear that for the Russians the MAC text was the 'key one in Human Contacts' and that it was very likely they would be prepared to deadlock discussion on all other issues until a solution to the MAC problem was in sight. Mr. Alexander thought it likely that Russian tactics would be 'to continue to conceal their

3. To increase the pressure on the West, the Russians reneged on an agreement reached two months earlier, by demanding changes in part of a text on family reunification, already mentally registered by the Sub-Committee.[4] There have been no further developments on the neutral package deal, but the mere fact of its existence is an influential factor in the course of the present negotiations. It encourages both sides, since they know the compromise will be drawn roughly midway between their position, to adopt maximalist attitudes.[5]

4. In information, the Russians also reneged on an agreed text. This time it was a formula on the publication of the final texts of the Conference which they had accepted last week (my tel[egram] No. 946, paragraph 3),[6] but now refused to register unless it was altered in several major respects. The Soviet change of front, to which other Eastern delegations gave half-hearted support, led to some outspoken discussion in the Sub-Committee, during which the Russians in particular were soundly castigated by the West and the neutrals for their behaviour. No progress was made on the other information issues under discussion.

5. In culture, a French compromise text, negotiated bilaterally with the Russians on access to books has been held back from informal discussions for further discussion among the Fifteen. (The text involves the abandonment for this round, and probably for good, of the proposal on reading rooms.) Subsequently and unexpectedly the Russians have blocked progress on other aspects of cultural access hitherto regarded as uncontroversial. This may simply be retaliation or it may be part of a broader pattern (paragraph 1 above).

6. In education, slow progress continues on language teaching. The neutrals, encouraged by the Russians, are canvassing Western support for a compromise draft mini-preamble. There is general agreement among the Nine to discourage the neutrals from pursuing this compromise at present.

restrictive intentions concerning MAC with at least a semi-decident [*sic*] veil of ambiguity' (EN 2/557/7).

[4] *Ibid.* The amendment required by the Russians involved the substitution of 'favourable' for 'positive' in the first paragraph of the mentally registered text on family reunification. See *Human Rights*, vol. v, p. 69.

[5] See note 2 above. Mr. Alexander remarked in his letter to Mr. Fall of 18 October (see note 3 above) that the knowledge that the neutral package existed and at some point would be produced naturally had 'an effect on the present negotiations, with both sides jockeying for a better position when it is revealed'.

[6] This is evidently a reference to UKMIS Geneva telegram No. 936 (see note 1 above). Mr. Hildyard reported in this telegram that 'informal agreement' had been reached on a text referring to the publication of the CSCE's final documents and that this would probably be registered in the Sub-Committee during the coming week.

No. 102

Mr. Hildyard (UKMIS Geneva) to Mr. Callaghan

No. 964 Telegraphic [WDW 1/4]

Priority. Confidential   GENEVA, *2 November 1974, 9.28 a.m.*

Repeated for Information UKDEL NATO, UKDEL Vienna, Washington, Moscow and Bonn, and Saving to EEC Posts and Helsinki.

From UKDEL To CSCE.
Our tel[egram] No. 954.[1]

CSCE: State of Play

1. There has been little progress to report, but the atmosphere is one of hesitation rather than impasse. This basically reflects the uncertainty of Western and neutral delegations about the willingness of the East to move. Such evidence as there is suggests that the Russians are looking for a way forward, but have not made up their minds how to proceed.[2]

2. In Basket I, Mendelevich has been active in trying to overcome the remaining obstacles to the registration of a complete text on human rights[3] and there have been informal indications that the Warsaw Pact are considering new ideas on confidence building measures.[4] But in Basket III Dubinin has remained aloof from the informal groups which have been discussing human contacts and information, and has given the impression that

---

[1] Mr. Hildyard reported in this telegram of 26 October: 'No new patterns have emerged during the week. Both the Russians and the neutral/non-aligned group seem uncertain about how best to proceed' (EN 2/557/2).

[2] Although the Russians had appeared to be under more time pressure, Mr. Hildyard was uncertain as to whether Mr. Mendelevich's talk of timetables was anything more than 'another tactical ploy' (*v. ibid.*).

[3] Discussion of the human rights principle was at this stage deadlocked very largely as the result of disagreement over a Yugoslav proposal for the inclusion of a text guaranteeing respect for the rights and interests of national minorities. The French were only prepared to accept a text referring to individuals belonging to national minorities, and both the Belgians and the Spaniards opposed anything which might imply that national minorities, as distinct from persons belonging to them, enjoyed rights (UKMIS Geneva telegram Nos. 955 and 965 of 26 October and 2 November, WDW 1/11).

[4] In a letter to Mr. Burns of 1 November Mr. Figgis reported from Geneva that information gathered from East German and Romanian sources seemed to suggest that Warsaw Pact delegations were engaged in a serious study of the modalities of prior notification. 'One wonders', he remarked, 'whether, behind the fortifications they have erected in the Sub-Committee, the East may perhaps indeed be working on ideas for compromise.' The Russians had, however, so far been reluctant to concede anything more than the application of prior notification 'to the territory of every participating state within a distance of up to 100 kms from frontiers'. This fell short of Western objectives, defined by Mr. Hildyard as: (1) to commit the Soviet Union to notification in a substantial part of its territory; (2) to wean the Warsaw Pact away from any attempt to exclude large areas of Poland and the GDR from prior notification; and (3) to ensure that the area of Soviet territory covered was measured from coastlines as well as land frontiers (UKMIS Geneva telegram No. 932 of 11 October, WDW 1/6).

he is still hoping to play off individual delegations against each other. He has now come out definitely against any neutral package on human contacts at this stage, but he has been at pains not to appear too negative and to reassure the neutrals about the importance which the Russians attach to their role.[5]

3. The Nine and the Fifteen have spent more time comparing notes about the possible intentions of the other side than discussing their own strategy. But we have finally reached agreement in principle on two points of potential importance. First, that we should voluntarily restrict our participation in the informal groups in order to encourage more forthcoming and constructive changes. Secondly that we should make further efforts amongst ourselves to refine our position on the substance of the subjects in Basket III which are most likely to yield to a determined effort to reach agreement in the weeks before the anticipated Christmas break.[6] This would be followed by a 'deepening of contacts' with the neutrals. Our main job in the Western group in the next week or two will be to translate this agreement into practice. It will not be easy to persuade some of our partners that in Basket III the technique of sitting tight is not in all cases the best.

4. My colleagues in the Nine have yet to focus effectively on what might be discussed at the meeting of the Political Committee on 7 November. We shall be meeting again on Tuesday afternoon and a clearer picture may then emerge. As things stand at present, I see no reason to depart from the guidelines approved by Ministers in September or to modify the conclusions reached by the Political Committee in October. It would, however, be useful if the Political Committee were to take note of the possibility that negotiations will enter a more active phase in the next few weeks. There are a number of questions (e.g. the family issues in human contacts and outstanding problems in Basket II) which could well be settled before Christmas, and on balance I believe it will be in our interest to clear the decks whenever there is a chance to do so on satisfactory terms. Later will not necessarily mean better.

5. The performance of the German delegation remains erratic. There is a clear need both for more effective leadership and for a more convincing demonstration of willingness to cooperate with the Nine and the Fifteen. I had started to work on Brunner but he will be leaving very shortly to replace Dahrendorf[7] in the EEC Commission. I hope that Blech,[8] when he arrives,

---

[5] In a letter to Mr. Young of 1 November Mr. M. Alexander recorded that Mr. Dubinin had said on one occasion that if the West had concessions to make 'let them make them direct to the Russians'. The Russians had also indicated that they would like talks between themselves and one or two Western plenipotentiaries on the most contentious issues (EN 2/557/7).

[6] 'This', Mr. Alexander explained, 'in effect means working out in more detail than was done in September the points which we wish to see retained and those which we could if necessary negotiate away' (*v. ibid.*).

[7] Professor R.G. Dahrendorf was EC Commissioner for Science and Education, 1970-4.

[8] Dr. K. Blech replaced Herr Brunner as Federal German Head of Delegation in November.

will be active on both fronts: and it would be helpful if Killick could tell van Well on 4 November that I look forward to working closely with Blech when he takes over his new responsibilities. (In this connexion please see also my tel[egram] No. 965[9] not to all.)

[9] In this telegram (see note 3 above) Mr. Hildyard suggested that Sir J. Killick might raise with Herr van Well, whom he was due to meet on 4 November, the possibility of the West German delegates waiving their objections to the 'mental registration' in a human rights text of a phrase confirming the 'right of the individual to know and act upon his rights and duties in this field' (UKMIS Geneva telegram No. 966 of 2 November, WDW 1/11). Herr G. Dahlhoff, the West German representative on the Principles Sub-Committee, argued that basic human rights should 'not be trammelled by corresponding duties'.

No. 103

Minute from Mr. Fall to Mr. Tickell

[*WDW 1/4*]

Confidential   FCO, *11 November 1974*
            CSCE: A View From the Residence Amat[1]

1. A fortnight in Geneva is not enough to give one a delegate's view of the second stage. But it does afford a perspective rather different to that of a two-day visit tied to a co-ordination meeting of the Nine. The main conclusion which I have drawn from my stay is that, while the meetings of the Nine and the Fifteen which are being planned for the end of the Christmas break will be important, it would be wrong to look at them in terms of a major re-appraisal of Western policy.

2. Our present policy is to work for a conclusion of the Conference in terms which are satisfactory in the light of the objectives re-defined by Ministers of the Nine in September.[2] We have always recognised that these objectives would have to be kept under review as the negotiations proceeded; but the idea of a major re-appraisal suggests something more than this. It is therefore worth considering what fundamental changes might be proposed.

3. I can think of two 'radical alternatives' to our present policy. The first would be to propose interruption of the second stage until 'conditions improved'. The second would be to try to get it over with as quickly as possible on terms which would be readily acceptable to the East. The most important point about these extreme solutions (and my excuse for stating them in bald terms) is that they both rest on the same assumption: that it is already clear from the negotiations in Geneva that to pursue them on

[1] The Hotel Amat-Carlton was used to accommodate UK delegates to Stage II of the CSCE. Mr. Fall stayed there when he visited Geneva during the last week of October. His minute, and another of 8 November from Mr. Burns were forwarded by Mr. Tickell to Mr. H.T. Morgan (Assistant Under-Secretary of State) and Sir J. Killick under a covering minute of 12 November.

[2] See No. 96, notes 7, 8 and 10.

present lines would not lead to a solution acceptable to the West within a reasonable time.[3]

4. Two lines of argument are put forward to justify this assumption. To caricature both, there is:

(i) a 'hard line' argument, that the Conference has never offered much to the West; and that, if we continue on present lines, we shall give the East what they want (multilateral endorsement of the *status quo*, a diplomatic triumph, and the embryo of a 'new security system' for Europe with the scales tilted in their favour) without anything in exchange; and

(ii) a 'soft' argument that the balance of forces has altered in favour of the hawks in the Kremlin over the last two years (the energy crisis, disarray in the West) and that we are likely to lose rather than gain if the Conference is protracted.

5. Both sets of arguments seem to me to be wrong. The hard-liners apply double standards to the texts which are likely to emerge from the Conference: those which could be developed to favour the East are judged on the basis of what might happen later; while those which could be developed to our advantage are criticised for not providing cash on the nail. The soft-liners, for their part, appear to assume that, if there are hawks and doves in the Kremlin, Western agreement to a conclusion to the CSCE on the terms favoured by the former would be likely to strengthen the latter.

6. There is obviously much more which could be said on both sides, but I want to return to the view from the Résidence Amat. During my two weeks in Geneva, I was able to talk to a number of Western and neutral delegates who have been involved in the Conference since the preparatory talks; to participate in the informal negotiating groups on Basket III; and to get a first hand impression of Eastern thinking from a long *tête à tête* dinner to which I was invited by the head of the East German delegation and from a bilateral lunch which Mr. Laver and I gave to Mendelevich in response to a clear hint that he would find it useful. The general conclusion which I would draw is that we should stick to the main lines of our present policy.

7. The fact of the matter is that we are not in a situation where the West can be convincingly represented as holding up the conclusion of the second stage. If agreement were reached on the Declaration of Principles, and the only major questions still outstanding were confidence building measures, the most difficult issues in human contacts and information, and the nature of follow-up, it might be relatively easy for the East to persuade some of the neutrals and non-aligned that the West were asking too much and (in the

---

[3] FCO estimates as to when the Conference might be expected to finish its work varied. Mr. Burns minuted on 8 November (see note 1 above) that he could see little prospect of its being over by Easter 1975 and a much greater one that, like the MPT, it would linger on for several weeks after, 'allowing a bare four weeks or so before a summit in early July'. But Mr. Tickell recalled in his covering minute that Mr. Callaghan had recently indicated that Western negotiators should aim to conclude the CSCE by Easter. Mr. Tickell considered this a 'very reasonable target date'.

case of follow-up) granting too little. We shall have to be ready to deal with the problem if it arises.

8. At the moment, however, there are three principles (and the preamble and final paragraphs of the Declaration) which have still to be considered in detail by the drafting group. This is not the fault of the West. Of the fifty meetings which have been devoted to [the] principle of respect for human rights and fundamental freedoms, only a minority have been concerned with issues which could have been dealt with on a purely East/West basis. The main difficulty has arisen over a proposal on national minorities put forward by the Yugoslavs.[4] A similar situation may arise in the next principle, self-determination. It would be a relatively easy matter to reach agreement between East and West on the basis of a Hungarian proposal and the corresponding section of the draft declaration tabled by the French. But, once Spain, Romania and, perhaps, Cyprus have had their say on questions of concern to them, the Conference may be faced with major problems —including that of reconciling the views of the FRG and the GDR on the question of national unity. More problems will arise when we get to Principle 10. Recent Western discussion of quadripartite rights and the enemy states clauses of the Charter has so far led to only one conclusion: that there is no longer general agreement in the Nine to the proposed text of this principle which the French put forward with our support at the beginning of the Conference.[5] Our first job must therefore be to re-establish a common

[4] See No. 102, note 3. On 8 November the Principles Sub-Committee mentally registered a Yugoslav text on national minorities. This committed participants to 'respect the right of persons belonging to such minorities to equality before the law' and to afford them 'the full opportunity for the actual enjoyment of human rights and fundamental freedoms' (UKMIS Geneva telegrams Nos. 972 and 973 of 8 November, WDW 1/11).

[5] The West, and more especially the West Germans, were anxious that nothing emerging from the CSCE should be seen as constituting a permanent peace settlement in Europe, and for this reason considered it important to protect such arrangements as left open the German question and demonstrated that quadripartite rights and responsibilities (QRR) in Germany remained unaffected. But in seeking to safeguard QRR, the West also wanted to avoid the use of language which either referred specifically to Germany, or which could be interpreted as condoning the Brezhnev doctrine of limited sovereignty. Discussion within the Bonn Group during August and September eventually produced a formula for inclusion in the text of the tenth principle, and the French agreed to sponsor it in the Principles Sub-Committee. The draft principle, which required participating states to recognise that obligations assumed towards one another in conformity with international law were binding and must be fulfilled in good faith, would thus also indicate that the Declaration of Principles would not 'affect the rights held by participating states or the bilateral or multilateral treaties, agreements and arrangements in accordance with international law, which [had] been entered into by participating states or which [concerned] them'. In addition, participants were to note that nothing in the Declaration would be 'interpreted in a manner conflicting with a provision of the Charter of the United Nations'. It soon emerged, however, that both the Germans and the Italians were averse to mention of the UN Charter since this could be regarded as endorsing Articles 53 and 107, which referred explicitly to possible action against enemy states of the Second World War (letter from Mr. Tickell to Mr. Hibbert of 2 August; UKMIS Geneva telegrams Nos. 952 and 953 of 26 October; Bonn telegram No. 1215 of 30 October; WRE 2/4).

Western position. But we shall then have to sell it not only to the Russians but to the 35 (including the Romanians, who are likely to have views both on 'enemy states' and on the idea of rights not deriving from agreements).

9. It is of course possible that the difficulties which I have referred to—and others which I have left out—will be dealt with more quickly than the Yugoslav proposal on national minorities: it may serve as a warning rather than as a precedent. But Mendelevich made it clear that he was worried; and he invited us to interpret in the light of these difficulties with maverick delegations a reference to the responsibility of the participating states in a speech made by Gromyko on 6 November. At this stage, I think that it would be fair to conclude that the pace of work in the sub-committee on principles is susceptible to influence, but not to control, by the major Eastern and Western delegations; that the Soviet delegation is not expecting very rapid progress; and that, if the situation described in paragraph 7 above arises at all, we shall receive timely warning from our representatives in the sub-committee on principles.

10. Given the time at our disposal, I see no reason why the West should at this stage make any major changes to its policy on Basket III. Our main aim should be to make it clear to the East that we are prepared to modify our proposals in order to reach agreement; but that the necessary changes can be brought about only through a process of genuine negotiation, and not as a result of stone-walling on the Eastern side.

11. A lot has already been done in Geneva to this end, but it may be possible through more aggressive tactics to do even more. It should be possible, by more active use of the machinery for Western consultations and by showing a greater readiness to take the initiative, to put the East in a position where they are consistently under pressure to state their objections to specific texts on a wide range of the subjects under discussion, and to react to counter proposals from the West. The British delegation is well placed to play a leading role in this field. There has been a favourable reaction in the Nine and the Fifteen to our suggestion of more intensive group consultations, which we hope will serve to both increase the authority of Western representatives in the informal negotiating groups and to ensure that any speeding up of the negotiations does not take place at the expense of effective co-ordination. It is too early to say whether we shall be successful, but the fact that both the French and the Irish have attended in our Mission supplementary co-ordination meetings *à seize* is in itself an encouraging feature.

12. It is less easy to see how the time which is available could be used to best effect in the sub-committee dealing with confidence building measures. There have been some indications that the East are giving thought to new proposals, but the official line—emphasised to me by the East German—is that confidence building measures will be settled only 'on the last night'. This may be fair enough where a last-minute compromise on the crucial figures is concerned, but we shall need time to establish the main lines of the resolution. I would see advantage in our tabling, just before or immediately after Christmas, a revised draft resolution, which would take into account as

many as possible of the points which have been made and aim to provide a generally acceptable basis for the final negotiations. Even if we were to leave out the contentious figures, the tabling of such a text would serve to maintain the initiative in Western hands and to emphasize the constructive approach of the British delegation to this subject.

13. In conclusion, I should like to say a more general word about the British role at the Conference. We have a number of important assets: an effective delegation; a reputation for talking sense in the Nine and the Fifteen; a reputation for not promising more than we can deliver in discussions with the East; and the freedom to look at the Conference as a whole without the commitment to particular hobby horses which distorts the perspective of many other participants. These assets are likely to come increasingly into play over the next few months, and we should be able to make an important contribution to the final negotiations. We have no reason to despair of the prospects for the Conference, or to look for short cuts; the present machinery is cumbersome, but workable, and I think that we are in a good position to encourage it to produce results.

B.J.P. FALL

No. 104

Paper by the FCO on the CSCE[1]

[WDW 1/4]

Confidential   FCO, *27 November 1974*

It is now inevitable that the second stage of the CSCE will continue into the New Year. There will be an opportunity during the Christmas break for the Nine and the Fifteen to review the progress made in the autumn session, and to concert their position on the points which remain outstanding. It may nevertheless be useful before the Ministerial Meeting of the North Atlantic Council on 12/13 December to review the state of play and the prospects; and to consider the implications for British policy at the Conference.

State of Play

Basket I

Declaration of Principles

2. Provisional texts have been registered for seven of the ten principles, although a number of points have been left in brackets for the second reading. The main difficulty over the next principle, self-determination, is likely to come from those delegations (Spain, Romania, Cyprus and perhaps

---

[1] This paper, which was prepared by WOD and EESD in consultation with TRED, was intended to bring Mr. Callaghan up to date on the Conference and to serve as background for an Office meeting to which he had agreed. Although originally scheduled for 4 December, the meeting had to be postponed until the evening of the 5th. The paper was submitted by Mr. Tickell to Mr. Morgan and the Private Secretary under cover of a minute of 27 November.

Ireland) who wish to include a reference to political or national unity in this context. This will cause major problems for the Germans (East as well as West), and it is not possible to predict how long the negotiations will take. The tenth principle (fulfilment of . . . obligations under international law) will also be difficult; and recent Western discussion of some of the points involved (including the protection of quadripartite rights and responsibilities over Germany,[2] and the conflicting interests of the three states primarily interested in Cyprus) has shown how difficult it will be to establish a common negotiating position which is likely to hold up in Geneva.

3. Once the first reading of the principles is completed, attention will have to be given to the preamble and the final paragraphs of the Declaration. The relevant sections of the French draft[3] contain two points of major importance to the West: wording designed to make it clear that we do not accept the so-called Brezhnev doctrine of 'limited sovereignty'; and a phrase on the relationship between the principles designed to guard against a selective interpretation of the Declaration which could cause us trouble in seeing that agreements are properly respected, especially in Basket III.

Peaceful Settlement of Disputes

4. Eastern delegations have made it clear that they will not accept the principle of compulsory arbitration which (rightly, in our view) underlies the Swiss proposal to establish new machinery for the peaceful settlement of disputes. But the terms of reference provide that the Conference 'shall . . . undertake the elaboration of a method for the peaceful settlement of disputes among participating states', and the Swiss remain concerned that their initiative should not be lost sight of.

Romanian Proposal on the Non-Use of Force

5. An acceptable solution will also have to be found to the problems raised (now more for the East than for the West) by an over-ambitious Romanian proposal designed to 'give effect' to the principle—which will appear in the Declaration—of refraining from the threat or use of force.[4]

Confidence-Building Measures

6. Agreement has been reached on the simplest of the three measures specifically referred to in the Final Recommendations: the *exchange of observers* at military manoeuvres.[5] The most far-reaching of the three—the prior notification of major military *movements*—has run into strong opposition from the East. As the Americans are also unhappy about the original Western proposal (they wanted it dropped but reluctantly accepted the tactical arguments for maintaining it), it is clear that nothing of substance will emerge. But a formula will have to be found to cover the requirement in the Final

---

[2] See No. 103, note 5.

[3] *Ibid.*

[4] See *Human Rights*, vol. iii, pp. 266-68 and 280.

[5] The text on the exchange of observers, as it appears in the Final Act (but without verbs expressing the nature of the commitment), was 'mentally registered' at the last meeting of the CBMs Sub-Committee before the summer recess (UKMIS Geneva telegram No. 712 of 26 July, WDW 1/6).

Recommendations that the Conference should submit its conclusions on this point.

7. The main question now before the Committee is the prior notification of *manoeuvres*, where Western and neutral delegations are working for an agreement with sufficient content to make a practical contribution to the building of confidence. The Warsaw Pact countries affect to be suspicious of Western motives and have so far taken a very restrictive line. The threshold they have proposed is so high that only a few exceptionally large exercises would qualify; and they would like to confine notification as far as possible to neighbouring states and to manoeuvres taking place near frontiers.[6] The question has been further complicated by the position of the Turks, who are insisting on the exclusion from the scheme of large parts of Central Anatolia (and thus making it harder for the West to put pressure on the Russians to include a substantial portion of the European part of the Soviet Union).[7]

Basket II

8. Some useful texts have been agreed on economic and technical co-operation, and Committee II is near to completing its work. The main points which remain are in the areas which touch on trade policy, and work is now concentrated on a number of inter-related questions which will probably have to be settled as a package. Eastern delegations appear to have accepted that it will not be possible at this Conference (which is not designed to serve as a forum for trade negotiations) to advance their case for most-favoured-nation treatment beyond what has previously been agreed; but they would still like to get a text to help them in future negotiations. The situation has been complicated by the efforts of some delegations (Romania, Yugoslavia and—to a lesser extent—Turkey) to get recognition of their developing or less-developed status; and the problem is therefore not only one of getting agreement on an East-West basis.

Basket III

Human Contacts

9. A satisfactory text on family re-unification is on the point of agreement; and it should then prove easier to make progress on marriages, where a

---

[6] 'We have', Mr. Burns later confessed, 'made no progress anywhere in Sub-Committee 2 since the summer' (letter to Mr. Figgis of 21 December, WDW 1/6).

[7] As Mr. Burns explained in a letter to Mr. Figgis of 11 October, it was 'quite understandable' and, he thought, 'generally acceptable' in NATO, that Asia Minor would have to be in some sense an exception from the normal run of prior notification: not only did the Turks have borders with non-participating states and a non-European border with the Soviet Union, 'but it would have been unreasonable to expect the Turks to notify manoeuvres throughout their territory if the Russians were going to be so parsimonious over theirs'. Nevertheless, Mr. Burns thought it regrettable that the Turks wanted to have excluded that part of the coast from which they had invaded Cyprus; that they were trying to make notification along their Aegean and Mediterranean coastline dependent upon Soviet agreement to notify along the northern shore of the Black Sea; and that in determining the depth of the coastal strip, in which they might be prepared to make notification, they were insisting on a depth proportional to what the Russians would give and then defined by 'some fairly arbitrary co-ordinates' (WDW 1/6).

number of the same issues are involved (but where the East Germans are taking a particularly negative line). Proposals on travel outside the 'humanitarian' field may prove more difficult, as the range of potential beneficiaries of the Western proposals as they now stand is much wider; and it is probable that we shall have to water our wine. A major difficulty is the Eastern insistence on a phrase which would make the implementation of the decisions of the Conference in this field subject to 'mutually acceptable conditions'. It should be possible to make some mention of this phrase without depriving the substantive texts of their effect, but the negotiations are likely to prove difficult.

Information

10. The basic position of the Eastern countries can be simply stated: either Western governments should act to ensure that the information and ideas which are published in and broadcast from their territories conform to the requirements of Communist governments, or the latter should be left to control matters in their traditional way. Western delegations have naturally resisted attempts to cast their governments in the role of censor, and have refused to accept qualifications on the nature of the information to be disseminated which would appear to condone Eastern censorship. But they have had as a result to pitch their demands of the East at a more modest level, and to concentrate on securing texts which—if carried out in good faith—would lead to some improvement in the accessibility and range of information received from abroad within the bounds of the present system. Texts on access to printed information have already been agreed and, given the situation described above, are reasonably satisfactory. The negotiations are now dealing with broadcast information, and will turn next to working conditions for journalists.

Culture and Education

11. These subjects, which are traditionally the subject of government-sponsored exchanges between Eastern and Western countries, are less controversial than the others in Basket III, and the negotiations were expected to be easier. Even so, attempts by Western negotiators to put the emphasis on non-governmental contacts and exchanges have met with opposition from the East. But some useful texts have been agreed, more particularly in the field of scientific exchanges, where the Russians have a real interest.

Prospects

Timing

12. It is difficult to predict how long the second stage will take.[8] The best guide may be the rate of progress on the Declaration of Principles, which the Russians consider to be the most important and which they have tried to

---

[8] In his covering minute (see note 1 above) Mr. Tickell noted: 'An East/West grand slam or package deal is unlikely. At a Conference of 35 states, where the neutral and non-aligned states play an important—and generally helpful—role, we have to proceed carefully across a broad front registering agreements where possible and working on the principle of the coral reef rather than the prefabricated house.'

move forward even when they were stonewalling for tactical reasons on other subjects. Despite their efforts, it has recently taken 56 half-day meetings to complete the first reading of the principle of respect for human rights—not because Western delegations were holding out for too much, but because the Yugoslavs (and to a lesser extent the Swiss) put forward proposals which cut across East/West lines. The same sort of cross-currents are likely to arise in the principles of self-determination and the fulfilment of international obligations; and they may therefore take a lot of time even though it should be possible to deal fairly easily with the basic East/West issues which are involved. A further incalculable factor is the attitude which the Greeks and Cypriots will take during the second reading of those Principles (refraining from the threat or use of force, inviolability of frontiers, territorial integrity, peaceful settlement of disputes) which have an obvious relevance to the Cyprus question. Both delegations have already said that they may wish to re-open provisionally registered texts.

13. In brief, a large number of delegations (and more especially the neutrals and non-aligned) have particular interests to promote or defend in the Declaration of Principles; and a lot of work remains to be done. It is reasonable to hope that it will be over by Easter; but it is not a foregone conclusion. The amount of work still to be done on confidence-building measures and on Basket III is no more than that in the Sub-Committee dealing with principles; and there is no reason why it should take longer unless the Eastern delegations decide to stonewall.

Substance

14. What the Conference is likely to achieve is more important than how long it is going to last. But it is no easier to predict. The following may be reasonable guesses on the more important subjects, though in each case it is important to note that the texts which are approved will not have legal force, and that the extent to which they are put into effect will become clear only after the Conference.

(i) *Principles.* The major issues which remain from the Western point of view are the precise wording of the text on peaceful change of frontiers; the handling of the Brezhnev doctrine; and the relationship between the principles. It should be possible to reach an acceptable solution on each of these points, and the resulting Declaration should provide a code of conduct to which Western countries can subscribe without reservation, and which it would be difficult to improve upon in subsequent negotiations with the East.

(ii) *Confidence-Building Measures.* The most important agreement we can hope for is an agreed scheme for the prior notification of manoeuvres. This will be a practical recognition of the fact, to which the neutral countries attach as much importance as the West, that a Conference on European Security should not ignore its military aspects. There have been some indications that the Russians may be prepared to move from their present very restricted position, though perhaps only at the last moment.[9] Various Soviet leaders, including Mr. Brezhnev, have criticised the Western proposals in conversation with their Western counterparts, but it is noteworthy that they have always described an extreme caricature of what they were purporting to attack. It may be therefore that the Russians can be brought to agree to something acceptable to the West if pressure is maintained in Geneva (with neutral support) and reinforced at a higher level.

(iii) *Trade Policy Issues.* Provided that the package on MFN and reciprocity is settled on acceptable terms—and there is no reason why this should not be possible—the results in Committee II should be useful from the Western point of view, mainly reflecting our attitude on how co-operation should be developed.

(iv) *Business Contacts and Economic Information.* The texts already agreed represent no breakthrough but do embody Eastern recognition—for the first time in a multilateral forum—of the importance of continued improvement in this area. Detailed provisions should be of some help to our businessmen in Eastern Europe.

(v) *Human Contacts.* The texts on family reunification and on marriage will not change the rules in force in Eastern Europe. But they may lead to their more flexible application; and they should provide a useful point of leverage for Western governments wishing to take up personal cases. The texts on travel will be vaguer, but should (together with the relevant part of the preamble) reflect some degree of endorsement of the objective of freer movement.

(vi) *Information.* This is the most difficult area to assess. The texts which are likely to be approved will not deal with radio jamming, or make all the Western press accessible to Soviet readers. But they may provide opportunities in the information field, if private institutions in the West (e.g. publishers and broadcasters) in a position to do so are prepared to make the running. If they are, Western governments will be in a better position than before the CSCE to intervene on their behalf with the Eastern governments concerned.

(vii) *Basket III: General.* At the multilateral preparatory talks the West succeeded (with neutral support) in placing on the agenda of the Conference subjects which the East had never previously accepted as proper subjects for negotiation. This in itself was something of an achievement. The texts eventually agreed, though less substantial than we

---

[9] Mr. Burns wrote to Mr. Figgis on 19 December with regard to the prior notification of manoeuvres: 'Our objective is to find a text which incorporates the two unknowns (the distance in kilometres and the controversial reference to the particular situation of States whose territory extends beyond Europe) in such a way that a decision on the unknowns can remain unresolved until a late point in Stage II without damage to the Western position; that is to say a text in which it will not matter if the Russians plump for a low number of kilometres with a specific reference to themselves, or a high number of kilometres to be generally applied in Europe' (WDW 1/6).

would have wanted, should bring some benefits and should also provide a basis on which further progress can be sought. In this respect the most important requirement of the texts is that they should not give multilateral endorsement to the sort of blanket qualifications ('respect for sovereignty, laws and customs') which would not only deprive them of their present value but constitute an obstacle to progress in the future.

(viii) *Publication of Final Texts.* We hope to get agreement that the texts approved by the Conference will be published in each participating country and disseminated as widely as possible. If the East pay more than lipservice to such a provision, it could have a significant impact.

(ix) *Follow-Up.* Agreement is unlikely to be reached until later in the second stage. There will have to be some advance on the Danish draft resolution (which embodies the lowest common multiple of Western views) if general agreement is to be reached. We may be well placed to promote a compromise when the time comes. Some form of continuing multilateral dialogue seems likely to result.

General Assessment

15. Results of the kind suggested above will fall short of a major breakthrough in East/West relations. The Russians will not accept a system of peaceful settlement of disputes based in the last resort on compulsory arbitration; they will not give prior notification of military movements; and they will maintain in the field of human contacts and information controls which are far more strict than those which are considered in the West to be compatible with the rights of the individual and with the objectives of the Conference.

16. This does not mean that the Conference should be regarded as a failure. Before it started it was widely regarded by Western governments as an exercise in damage limitation. In the event the Nine and the Fifteen have succeeded not only in maintaining their cohesion, but in focussing the attention of the Conference (and thereby of public opinion) on the issues which both the Western and neutral participants would regard as the important factors in *détente*. The results will fall short of original Western requirements but they are also well beyond our most sanguine expectations of a few years ago. They should provide a basis on which to build in the future.

Implications for British Policy

17. In the light of this assessment, it may be possible to draw some conclusions about the line we should take at the NATO Ministerial Meeting; in the Western co-ordination meetings during the Christmas break; at the resumption of the Conference in January; and during the visit of the Prime Minister and the Secretary of State to Moscow.[10] The main one might be that there is no reason to make radical changes in the policy which we have pursued with some success since the Conference resumed in September.

[10] Mr. Wilson and Mr. Callaghan were due to visit Moscow during 13-17 February 1975. Cf. No. 112.

18. In meetings of the Nine and the Fifteen we should encourage a realistic assessment of the prospects for the Conference and of Western objectives. The case for a major re-appraisal of Western policy has not been made out; but we must be ready to interpret our present policy flexibly. On timing, we should work to complete the work of the second stage before Easter, without setting a formal deadline or trying to short-cut the time-consuming but democratic procedures to which the neutral and non-aligned delegations attach particular importance. On substance we should be prepared to modify our proposals to the extent required by the negotiations; but we should make it clear to the other side that we expect a similar willingness to negotiate on their part. Finally, we should seek to persuade our partners and Allies that they should be ready at the appropriate time to take the steps necessary to reach a generally acceptable compromise on follow-up.

19. At the Conference itself, we should play an active part in working for acceptable compromises. We have a major asset in that we are free from the commitment to individual hobby horses which distorts the perspective of a number of participants; and we are therefore able to take the overall view. This is recognised both in the Western group and in the Conference as a whole. Our delegation are already actively involved in the negotiations on the points of major importance, and are well placed to influence the final stages.

20. It is too early to predict how things will stand when the Prime Minister and the Secretary of State visit Moscow; and there is in any case a limit to what can be done in bilateral talks on questions where the interests of 35 states are involved and where our policies are closely co-ordinated with our partners and Allies. There may however be an opportunity to influence the decisions which it seems clear that the Russians will be prepared to take only at the highest level; and the outstanding issues on confidence-building measures might usefully be discussed with this in mind.

No. 105

Letter from Mr. Hildyard (UKMIS Geneva) to Sir J. Killick
[*WDW 1/4*]

Confidential   GENEVA, *29 November 1974*

Dear John,
CSCE

1. In advance of next week's office meeting on the CSCE and in parallel with the Department's Submission (which I have not seen)[1] you may like a note on how the prospects look from Geneva.

2. In my recent telegrams I have referred to the atmosphere of movement

---

[1] No. 104.

here.[2] The Russians like to give the impression, no doubt for tactical reasons, that the 26 July package[3] was not a very good one from their point of view. I think that in fact they consider that it provided adequate assurances for them to move out from their entrenched positions. When the Conference resumed they seem to have hoped for substantive negotiations between plenipotentiaries rather then exploratory discussions in which they would feel that they were being lured forward all the time without any guarantees that concessions on their part would achieve agreements. But when they saw the Americans joining the Nine in pressing for a first reading, in the sense of a first drafting in each sector, they appear to have concluded that they would have to go along with this procedure. They then had to decide how and when to move. Over the last few weeks they have been sounding out practically all the Western and neutral delegations in order to chart major national interests, and to obtain a picture of the likely timetable for the future.

3. There is now no doubt that, in certain areas at least they are trying to press ahead even at the expense of surrendering points of some substance to them. At heart they are extremely cavalier about the interests and views of the smaller countries, and they may have reached more optimistic conclusions than would we in regard to the extent and importance of these countries' problems. We have all been fascinated to see Soviet representatives trying to go ahead on more than one occasion regardless of the views of one of the East Europeans. Nevertheless they have not always succeeded. I think that they used to find it difficult to believe that the leading members of the Nine (and the US) could not get their way with their allies on issues of real importance. Increasingly they are accepting, however, that on both sides the need for consensus is very real. As regards timing, I have little doubt that they have reached the conclusion, as we, the French and the Americans have done, that the Conference can move no faster than the drafting of the Declaration of Principles, and that while there is a general wish to conclude the work of Stage II by Easter, the number and nature of the problems which remain to be resolved in the first Basket ensure that it will not be easy to meet such a deadline.

4. The recent preliminary agreement to a good text on Human Rights, the 7th Principle, leads me to hope that we may be able at least to start work on the 9th Principle, Co-operation, before Christmas. We are making a determined effort to this end together with the French, the Americans and insofar as they can, the West Germans. Debate on the intervening Principle of Self-Determination, however, has shown that it may be difficult to reach a quick conclusion in the light of the diametrically opposed interests of several

[2] UKMIS Geneva telegrams Nos. 989 and 998 of 15 and 22 November both reported on the quickening pace of negotiations and the evident desire of the Russians for more rapid progress. After the registration on 14 November of the Basket I text on human rights the Russians began pressing for the speedier drafting of the next principle on self-determination. 'Mendelevich', Mr. Hildyard recalled, 'only half-jokingly, suggested that no more than a week would be needed.'

[3] See No. 93, note 1.

delegations, particularly over the problems of the two Germanies and Cyprus. In Basket II there are relatively few problems remaining. In Basket III we have reached informal agreement this week, after eight months' argument, on a text on Family Reunification, a subject of major importance to a number of delegations. Negotiations on Marriage and Travel are well advanced though not yet in their final stages. Discussions on Education and Culture are making good progress. Important problems in Basket III will inevitably remain to be solved after Christmas—notably perhaps in regard to Information—but I am hopeful that as on previous occasions we can make significant progress just before the break.[4] If we can agree, or at least begin to see the shape of an agreement, on Mutually Acceptable Conditions, this will be a big step forward.

5. This general impression of movement is of course still not reflected in the work on Confidence Building Measures where the East continue to maintain that they cannot advance on positions which are patently unacceptable to everyone else. (I assume that the Alliance will remain solid on the need for a satisfactory provisions for the Notification of Manoeuvres.) The drafting on Follow-Up will also soon run into the sand pending the emergence of a clearer consensus on the substance of follow-up arrangements, i.e. in the final phase of Stage II.

6. There is a general desire among my colleagues of the Nine to complete as soon as possible the agreement of common Western positions on outstanding aspects of the Conference.[5] The French have done a checklist (copy enclosed)[6] which shows that there are a number of issues still to be resolved. Some of the questions raised have been in the deep freeze since they were last considered by the Nine in the spring and will not be easy to settle. The paper will form the basis of discussions between the experts in the various Baskets, and then for a meeting of the Sub-Committee of the Nine in Geneva on 17 December from which the draft of a report to Political Directors will emerge. This should enable the meetings of the Nine in Dublin in January to focus effectively upon all aspects of Western strategy for the next, and hopefully the final, stage of the detailed negotiations.

7. We are playing an active role in all the major discussions here and are

---

[4] In UKMIS Geneva telegram No. 989 (see note 2 above) Mr. Hildyard drew attention to the fact that in Basket III the Russians had for the first time begun to put forward their own negotiating texts. 'The main complications', he observed, 'have in fact been on the Western side arising partly from amour propre or poor organisation within some delegations, and partly from a failure to take sufficient account of the views of the neutrals.'

[5] Mr. Hildyard reported on 22 November (see note 2 above) that the French shared the British wish to speed up progress. 'We hope', he added, 'that our two delegations, as the most coherent and co-ordinated of the Nine, can form a private ginger group, even if overt joint pressure on our colleagues would be likely to be resented and counter-productive.' In general he thought most of the Fifteen now in favour of more rapid movement, with the Dutch and Italians still 'hard liners'. Dr. Blech, who had taken over leadership of the West German delegation, appeared to bear out reports that he was inclined to be inflexible, but seemed more likely to be 'more reliable (and available) than Brunner'.

[6] Not printed.

endeavouring to ensure that the momentum generated recently is sustained and, if possible, increased. But we cannot, of course, ourselves decide the pace of work. There are too many sensitive issues of deep interest to other delegations still to be solved. If, however, we and the rest of the Nine, with the encouragement of NATO Foreign Ministers, could resolve the main outstanding problems amongst ourselves before we resume in Geneva next January, we should be well placed to make a major effort to reach overall agreement on a basis satisfactory to us by the spring. With two months or so for negotiating the structure of the final document, cleaning up texts and translations (*toilette*), and printing the documents in their final form, this would mean Stage III in Helsinki in the summer.

Yours ever,

D.H.T. Hildyard

No. 106

Minute from Mr. Fall to Mr. Tickell

[*WDW 1/34*]

Confidential   FCO, *20 December 1974*

CSCE: Follow Up[1]

1. The paper which we have circulated in the Nine and shown to some of our other Allies is rightly directed to the negotiating situation which will face us in Geneva after the Christmas break.[2] I think that it strikes a proper balance. Earlier papers of the Nine have tended to exaggerate the dangers of continuing machinery, and to take insufficient account of the political facts

---

[1] Mr. Tickell sent this minute and the attached annex to Mr. Morgan and Sir J. Killick under cover of a minute of 31 December. The Irish Republic was about to assume the EC Presidency and Mr. Tickell thought it would be useful to outline at the forthcoming meetings of the Political Committee and CSCE Sub-Committee in Dublin what HMG regarded as the scope of the follow-up problem, and suggest what specific aspects should be shared out amongst the Nine. Concerned lest, without a strong Presidential lead, the results be 'tardy, mutually inconsistent and (given the views of some of our partners on the subject) unhelpful', he suggested that it might not be a bad idea if, as with the preparations for the Conference as a whole, the NATO Secretariat were brought into the process at an early point.

[2] Not printed. This paper, the first draft of which was prepared by Mr. Figgis, was discussed at the Office meeting on 5 December (see No. 104, note 1) and, after receiving Ministerial approval, was sent to Mr. Burns on 12 December for tabling at a meeting of the Nine's CSCE Sub-Committee at Geneva on 17 December. It rejected as exaggerated fears that follow-up machinery would provide the Soviet Union with the means to interfere in the affairs of Western Europe. Arrangements for continuing the dialogue were, the paper argued, more likely to cause problems for the closed societies of the East than for the open societies of the West, and it went on to recommend meetings of senior officials at fixed intervals and rotating from one capital to another: a system which would avoid the emergence of a self-generating bureaucracy and the means to justify interference on the part of those who might be tempted to abuse Conference decisions. It further proposed a one year probationary period after Stage III before the first review meeting at ambassadorial or senior official level.

of life. Provided that we temper our optimism with a clear recognition of the necessary safeguards (among which I would emphasise American participation,[3] the 'principle of rotation' and the desirability of having meetings at fixed intervals rather than at the request of individual participants), I do not think that we will lose by a more flexible approach to the negotiations on Basket IV.

2. We should, however, be on our guard against an uncritical acceptance of the thesis that, because the Conference has on the whole been a success for the West, future meetings of the 35 will be so too. Western achievements at the Conference are the fruit not only of patience and much hard work, but of the particular situation in which we found ourselves at the multilateral preparatory talks: the East were sufficiently keen to have a Conference to accept one very much on the terms proposed by the West. Once the Conference has been successfully concluded, and some form of continuing machinery established, the negotiating position may prove rather different; and the West may find itself more on the defensive.

3. Perhaps the only conclusion which can safely be drawn at this stage is that we should beware of general assessments which are not founded on a detailed examination of what the continuing machinery is likely to do. I attach, by way of illustration of what will be needed, an annex[4] which is neither comprehensive nor exhaustive. At the most, it seeks to suggest the sort of points which will require further study in the Nine and the Fifteen if we are to enter the era of follow up with a common assessment of the opportunities and difficulties which future meetings will present.

4. I think that it emerges from this preliminary analysis that the question 'where do we go next' is easier to answer in institutional than in substantive terms. The results of the Conference will represent a high common factor agreement among the 35, and it may be some time before further progress can be made. What is true of the 35 is to some extent also true of the Western group. We were remarkably successful in agreeing with our partners and Allies what we should ask for at the Conference, and what we should concede in order to reach a consensus. It will be more difficult to establish a common position on new initiatives, on our reaction to the initiatives of others,

[3] Sir J. Killick minuted on 8 January 1975 with reference to this minute: 'There is no reason to suppose that Washington will have the slightest enthusiasm for follow-up, even if the Americans reluctantly agree to it. We must expect any real dynamism to come from the 9. But it is most important to keep the Americans engaged if we can.'

[4] Not printed. In this annex Mr. Fall examined in detail some of the Basket I and Basket III issues which might be raised in follow-up meetings. He accepted that a major argument in favour of follow-up was that it would allow the West to maintain the *locus standi* they had gained in the field of human contacts and information, but insisted that there was also a need for a thorough discussion amongst the Nine and the Fifteen of how individual items might be handled. In this context he proposed that Western Governments should attempt to maintain a common position by instructing their embassies in the Soviet Union and elsewhere in Eastern Europe to exchange information and to adopt a common monitoring system.

and on the best way to ensure the implementation of the decisions of the Conference.[5]

5. It may be that I have given too much emphasis to the difficulties, and not enough thought to the opportunities. It was not my intention to sound defeatist. But if the West is to make a success of the follow-up, it seems to me essential that we should approach it not as the tail end of one campaign, but as the start of a new one which will be at least equally important.

6. The main lesson of the CSCE is that effective Western co-ordination depends not on exhortations from the Political Committee and the North Atlantic Council, but on preparatory work intensive enough to produce a common position in sufficient detail to hold up under the strain of the subsequent negotiations. The sub-committee of the Nine will no doubt feel that they have earned a rest after Stage II. But I hope that they will be re-convened shortly thereafter to begin work on the substance of follow up. As a first step, it might be useful to commission papers on the various points suggested in the Annex to this minute and on others which will no doubt occur to us and to our partners; and to specify a degree of informality in the early stages in order to encourage some original thinking.

B.J.P. FALL

[5] In a minute of 6 January 1975 Mr. Morgan pointed out that there were three kinds of follow-up activity: '(*a*) to give effect to the final agreements of the present Conference; (*b*) to assess how far these were being carried out; (*c*) to seek new agreements which might include clarification and refinement of the original ones'. He considered that initial implementation 'and our experience with it in practice, must largely influence our eventual attitude to the other two types of follow-up'.

No. 107

Letter from Mr. Hildyard[1] *(UKMIS Geneva) to Sir J. Killick*

[*WDW 1/4*]

Confidential   GENEVA, *24 December 1974*

Dear John,

CSCE

1. In my telegram number 1048 of 21 December I gave a brief account of the Session which has been ended.[2] Those in charge of the various Baskets or sectors have now reported in detail on what has been achieved, and outlined what remains to be done. As you know I do not think there is any need to reconsider the broad lines of our strategy or the directives which were given to us. This letter is to bring you some general impressions of the way things

[1] Mr. Hildyard was appointed KCMG in January 1975.

[2] The autumn session of the Conference ended on 20 December and in his telegram No. 1048 Mr. Hildyard explained how, after a slow start, progress had quickened considerably, particularly in Basket III, only to falter again in the final stages.

are going, of the attitudes of the main participants and groups, and of the part which we can hope to play in helping to bring about an early and satisfactory conclusion of Stage II, bearing in mind particularly the visit by the Prime Minister and the Secretary of State to Moscow in mid-February.[3]

2. The last week or so before the break was disappointing, especially the poor results of the French 'coups' when they were in a particularly favourable position to take initiatives which could have been valuable.[4] Nevertheless we have made a good deal of progress, the Russians are clearly anxious for an early conclusion, and even if the going will be hard I think that M. Van der Stoel[5] was right in saying that the negotiations have now built up a momentum of their own. Quite apart from the increasing desire of almost all concerned to get Stage II over, moreover, there are the Summit Conference of the European Communist Parties which it is planned to hold as soon as the Conference is finished,[6] and the elections in North Rhine Westphalia which could lead to a government in Bonn with considerably tougher *Ostpolitik*.[7] We can hope therefore that April and May will see agreement on the outstanding issues particularly the important cluster of problems in the Principles Sub-Committee.[8]

3. The Russians are very tough negotiators, but even when they have decided to move they often find it difficult to know how best to do so. They

---

[3] See No. 104, note 10.

[4] Mr. M. Alexander reviewed recent French conduct in a letter to Mr. Young of 21 December (EN 2/557/7). The French had, apparently, in the margins of a visit by Mr. Brezhnev to Paris (2-7 December), settled secretly with the Russians on the terms of a mini-preamble for the human contacts section of Basket III. On 13 December this text, which included provision for MAC, was 'negotiated' in the presence of the Austrian delegate, Herr H. Liedermann, and other neutral representatives. Herr Liedermann disliked the draft, but was persuaded to table it in his capacity as coordinator of the Human Contacts Sub-Committee. 'He was', Mr. Alexander recalled, 'prepared to go this far only because the French repeatedly, and mendaciously, told him over the weekend [14-15 December] that the Nine wished him to table it. At this time the Nine had not seen the text.' The reaction of France's partners to this initiative was extremely cool and, as the Russians resisted amendments, the Sub-Committee ended the session in deadlock. 'French tactics and the failure to reach agreement', Mr. Hildyard observed, 'have led to a good deal of resentment and renewed mistrust. Altogether a disappointing end to the French Presidency' (UKMIS Geneva telegram No. 1047 of 20 December, EN 2/557/3).

[5] Heer M. van der Stoel was Netherlands Foreign Minister.

[6] See No. 99.

[7] A trend against the governing SPD had been apparent during the closing months of Herr Brandt's Chancellorship. But in the Land elections in North Rhine-Westphalia in May 1975 the SPD lost only 1 per cent of the popular vote, and its coalition partner, the FDP, increased its poll by 3 per cent.

[8] Mr. Hildyard noted in UKMIS Geneva telegram No. 1048 (see note 2 above) that a good text had been registered on human rights and, he added, 'another good text on the principle of equal rights and self-determination, which avoids "anti-colonialist" language, is ripe for registration after the Conference resumes'.

are constantly looking for *interlocuteurs valables* on the Western side.[9] For a time they had high hopes of being able to work out the framework of a limited agreement with the help of the Americans who themselves were trying to concentrate and speed up the negotiations. The Americans, however, soon realised that this would not be generally acceptable. They have now agreed a common line with the rest of the Fifteen, and seem to be under instructions to adopt a low profile at least for the time being.

4. Soviet relations with the West Germans have always fallen into a rather special category; the Conference after all is more about the German question than anything else. The East Germans also have remarkable close contacts with the FRG delegation. Nevertheless, the West Germans are not good interlocuteurs. It is true of course that they believe themselves to have more important interests at stake than others on the Western side, but they have not kept their allies fully informed of their thinking and as they so often play their own game as well as change their minds frequently, they are seldom if ever in a position to bring along their partners. Coordination in and with Bonn still leaves much to be desired particularly where legal advisers are concerned. These German lawyers, said Mendelevich to us the other day not without some justification, they react so slowly and then hold everyone up.

5. The French seemed very promising particularly with Brezhnev's visit to Paris in early December. They have always been the central figures in the Western side on Culture, and longed to play a leading part on the main stage. The Franco-Soviet arrangements, however, came badly unstuck.[10] Maybe the French will make a great effort to salvage their credibility when the session resumes. They have had a large, able, and articulate delegation, and they can be clear thinking and effective operators. Nevertheless they are unlikely to be too ambitious for a time, and now that they are no longer in the presidency they may decide that an effort on the scale deployed during this Session is no longer justified.

6. A major problem for both the Russians and the West is the strong resistance among the smaller countries to attempts by the major powers to push through their own preferred solutions (para. 3 of my letter of 29 November).[11] The Romanians may go much further than anyone else in their determination to safe-guard their own independence by querying and

[9] Mr. Hildyard commented on the Soviet delegates (see note 2 above): 'After showing substantially greater flexibility and willingness to move on to a number of issues . . . they proved as difficult as ever on the major points. Their preference for trying to make deals with the delegations which they consider the most receptive and influential made the smaller countries even more determined to have their say.'

[10] See note 4 above. In UKMIS Geneva telegram No. 1047 Mr. Hildyard pointed out that in the Culture Sub-Committee the Russians were refusing to negotiate on the establishment of foreign reading rooms. The French had not seemed able to exploit Mr. Brezhnev's visit to advance matters on this or the other main policy problems in the Sub-Committee, and it seemed possible that negotiations on cultural issues may yet prove the most protracted in Basket III.

[11] No. 105.

usually insisting on changing in some way any agreement reached without their participation. A number of other smaller countries, however, have also shown that they are prepared to fight for points which they consider of importance against the opposition or lack of enthusiasm of members of NATO and the Warsaw Pact combined. We need to bear their reactions in mind both in our calculations about the duration of the Conference and also in any initiatives which we may consider taking ourselves.

7. Apart from the French attempts during the last week to build a special position for themselves the Nine and the Fifteen have shown an impressive solidarity. In the Nine the Germans can be secretive and unreliable on issues of special concern to them, the Italians erratic, suddenly changing their minds or losing interest after having insisted on extreme positions, the Danes feeble and the Belgians touchy and anxious to score personal successes (everyone suffers a little from this I fear). In general, however, great and continuous efforts are made to co-ordinate effectively and all the East Europeans constantly tell us how impressed they are by the Nine's solidarity. Now that our fences have been mended with the Americans the Fifteen are working well together, the Canadians being particularly helpful. After the yelps of the first few days, the Greeks and Turks have settled down and cooperate reasonably cheerfully.

8. On the Soviet side I have been impressed by the increasing willingness of the East Europeans to allow their differences with the Soviet Union to emerge publically, and indeed what appear to be their hopes of building on their experiences during the Conference to press for a growing measure of consideration and thus for independence of view in the future. This movement could well eventually prove one of the most satisfactory results of the Conference.

9. This brings me to the role of our own delegation. All those in charge of the various Baskets or sectors, Patrick Laver, Andrew Burns, Anne Warburton and Michael Alexander have proved excellent operators, who have gained respect and influence in both camps. Their skill and imagination in finding acceptable formulations or compromises have enabled them often to be helpful to the Russians without any disloyalty to our partners and allies. So far we have not proposed major new initiatives or full texts covering as they usually do a package of some kind. Our influence in the Sub-Committees, the fact that the Irish will be in the Presidency of the Nine and to be frank do not carry much weight, the problems of other major Western powers as interlocuteurs, and the visit to Moscow in mid-February, all combine to make it possible that the Russians may turn increasingly to us. We should have to be very careful and to avoid the mistakes made by others, but we have a good position, we have not lost credibility and there certainly should be opportunities.

10. We should not have much room for manoeuvre. On the cluster of problems in the Principles Sub-Committee we can only help devise realistic and acceptable positions. On CBMs the Russians might be prepared to tie to the visit the movement which they are likely to have to make fairly soon. In

Basket II we could find ourselves isolated even in the Nine on most favoured nation treatment; we are in a rather different position from our partners and there is no easy way out, but you may think it worth considering whether there is any scope for being more forthcoming if circumstances make some movement on our side highly desirable. In Basket III our new position as *chef de file* in the Information Sub-Committee would make it appropriate for us to negotiate with the Russians provided that we cleared our lines adequately with our partners and allies. And subject to the same proviso we might be able, together with the Russians, to find some formulation on Mutually Acceptable Conditions which could bridge the gap after the French failure; it must be bridged fairly soon after the resumption. In Basket IV our initiative among the Nine may start things moving in Geneva for which we might be able to gain credit in Moscow.

11. I think that we could at least try out the ground in all these sectors. It might for instance be possible in some cases to agree with the Russians to leave a little fat on both sides so that each camp could then happily remove the bits favouring the other. After the experiences of the past, particularly with the French, we should have to expect a good deal of suspicion and mistrust but if we were considerably more frank and willing to take the views of others into account we might be able to make a substantial and constructive contribution. If you agree in principle we should need to sound out the Russians very soon after the session resumed. If they were receptive, as I believe they would be, we should need to start working on texts at once so that briefs could be prepared as early as possible in February. I think that it would be better not to bring these possibilities up ourselves in Dublin so as not to arouse mistrust while we have no very clear ideas to explain. In any case everything would depend on Soviet reactions; if asked in Dublin what we had in mind, we could say that we should be exchanging views with the Russians before the visit, and undertake to keep our partners as fully in the picture as possible.[12]

Yours ever,

D.H.T. HILDYARD

---

[12] This proposal for a bilateral action with the Russians was poorly received in the FCO. Sir J. Killick thought it would be unwise for HMG to take any initiative in sounding out the Russians on CSCE matters before the Prime Minister's forthcoming Moscow visit. In a letter to Sir D. Hildyard of 3 January 1975 he contended that the Russians could use such an approach 'to divisive effect in Geneva' and that they would probably judge the UK 'a potential soft touch, and raise their price accordingly'. In any case Sir J. Killick considered the Soviet desire to complete the Conference greater than the British: 'If they want to approach us, well and good; if they do not, no harm will be done' (MTW 10/557/6).

No. 108

Mr. Callaghan to Sir A. Galsworthy[1] (Dublin)
No. 24 Telegraphic [WDW 1/24]

Immediate. Confidential   FCO, *17 January 1975, 10.29 p.m.*

Info immediate Dublin, UKMIS Geneva, Priority UKDEL NATO, Info EEC Posts, UKREP Brussels and Moscow, Info Saving Helsinki, UKDEL Vienna, Washington, Ottawa, Oslo, Sofia, Bucharest, Belgrade, Budapest, Warsaw, Prague, Berlin and Berne.

European Political Co-operation: CSCE: Sub-Committee

Following from Delegation.

1. The Sub-Committee of the Nine met on 16 and 17 January to prepare a report for the meeting of the Political Committee on 23 January on outstanding problems in the CSCE. As completed, the report (copies—not to all—by bag)[2] shows how matters stand at Geneva, gives general guidance to delegations for the resumption of work on 20 January, picks out a number of areas for further work among the Nine, and directs the attention of Political Directors to points on which they might focus on 23 January in particular:

(i) Military confidence-building measures:
(ii) Follow-up:
(iii) Duration of the Conference, including the possibility of setting a target date for its completion.

Basket I
(a) Principles

2. It was agreed to stick for the present to the American formula of 26 July[3] on peaceful change of frontiers and to language on the value and inter-relationship of the principles on the lines set out in the French draft declaration[4] and the Declaration on Friendly Relations.[5] While the Italians, Belgians and Dutch continued to express some doubts about the text on QRR, the Sub-Committee agreed that the best plan for any text of this kind would be in the final clauses of the Declaration of Principles rather than in any specific principles.[6]

[1] HM Ambassador in Dublin.

[2] Not printed.

[3] See No. 94, note 7. The EPC Political Committee agreed at its Dublin meeting on 23-24 January that the Nine should make a real effort to persuade the Russians to draft on the basis of this American text, and that if the Russians insisted on returning to the formula of 5 April (see No. 72, notes 4 and 5) the Nine should insist that that text could only figure in the third principle (telegram No. 18 to UKMIS Geneva of 27 January).

[4] See *Human Rights*, vol. iii, pp. 105-8.

[5] See No. 27, note 8. Article 2 of the *UN Declaration Concerning Friendly Relations Among States* stated that the principles of the Declaration were 'interrelated and each principle should be construed in the context of the other principles'.

[6] See No. 103, note 5.

3. A French formula designed to bring together in one place the various references to the Charter of the United Nations found a cautious welcome but will require further study in Geneva. We pointed out that as such a formula would deal only with the interpretation of the principles in case of doubt other language in the declaration would be required to safeguard those cases where the use of force was legitimate, and proposed a text to cover this point.

(b) Confidence-building measures

4. The text on CBMs in the draft report is designed to prompt Political Directors to reaffirm the importance of satisfactory measures in this field and consider how their negotiation should be fitted into the strategy of the Nine in the weeks ahead.[7] The Germans and Dutch expressed their determination to obtain firmer guidance for delegations in Geneva. The Dutch have since told us that they are thinking of forming an action group of those particularly concerned at Geneva to push things forward.

Basket II

5. The Report of the Ad Hoc Group has already been reported separately from Dublin.[8]

Basket III

6. There was a welcome absence of recrimination about events at the end of the last session in Geneva. The report recognises the persisting differences among the Nine on the human contacts mini-preamble (the question of 'mutually acceptable conditions')[9] but leaves delegations in Geneva room for manoeuvre. Problems caused by the relatively slow rate of progress in the Sub-Committee on culture are also acknowledged: the French appear to be willing to drop a number of secondary objectives.

Follow-Up

7. As usual this subject generated a good deal of heat. We spoke on the lines of our recent paper[10] to recommend a continuing multilateral dialogue

[7] EC Political Directors reaffirmed at their Dublin meeting (see note 3 above) the importance of CBMs and concluded that: (1) the outline of an acceptable text on CBMs should be clear before the first reading of the Declaration of Principles had been completed; and (2) CBMs should apply to the whole of Europe, and that while the Nine could accept exceptions for parts of the territories of the USSR and Turkey, it was necessary to ensure that there were no other special zones (telegram No. 19 to UKMIS Geneva of 27 January, WDW 1/24). Cf. No. 109.

[8] The main conclusions of the Ad Hoc Group were reported in Dublin telegram No. 33 of 16 January. As Mr. P.J. Popplewell (TRED) explained, in a minute to Mr. Cloake of 21 January, the meeting 'marked a useful move forward on the most difficult problem in Committee II, MFN treatment'. Thus, the report stated that the EC wished to ensure that the projected agreement on MFN could not be interpreted either as constituting in itself a grant of MFN treatment, or as applying to non-tariff matters: a formula which seemed to avoid gratuitously conceding in CSCE a bargaining counter which could be used by the East in future trade discussions, or which might enable them to claim that MFN treatment should be automatically extended to them on the basis of existing agreements.

[9] See No. 107, note 4.

[10] See No. 106, note 2.

after the Conference as distinct from but linked with the process of putting its eventual decisions into effect. In particular we emphasized the need for the Western countries to stop jumping at shadows and be more confident of their ability to turn continuing machinery to their advantage: to exercise some modest constraint thereby on the Russians and help the East Europeans and neutrals: and to maintain and build on what we hoped to achieve at the Conference through multilateral means. In so arguing we had full support from the Danes, and some from the Belgians and Italians. The Germans said that we should work within the framework of the existing Danish resolution[11] on the subject which gave us the flexibility we needed. But the Dutch and still more the French flatly opposed our ideas on the grounds that this would open the way to direct Soviet interference in our affairs, lend support to Eastern ideas of a security system, and damage the development of political unity among the Nine.[12]

8. After considerable discussion we suggested that the subject should be taken by the Political Directors on the basis of a text we circulated to draw attention to four main points: how the decisions of the Conference should be put into effect: how, and after how long an interval, there should be an assessment of how its decisions were being respected: whether and how the multilateral dialogue should be continued, and what content it might have: and the implications of such a dialogue for European unity. This was eventually agreed together with a recommendation that the Political Directors should instruct the Sub-Committee to prepare a paper on the subject to deal with the considerations which should guide the Nine, and examine the possibilities and options open to them.[13]

Timetable

9. This also generated heat. We supported a French proposal that the Political Directors should be asked to consider the possibility of setting a target date for the completion of Stage II, and indicated our own preference for completion by the end of March. We argued in particular for a real effort to finish while the going was good and to set perfectionism aside. Although the Germans, Italians and Benelux countries eventually agreed with much reluctance that this question should be discussed by the Political Directors, they were strongly critical of the wisdom of setting of target dates or showing

[11] See No. 80, note 1.

[12] M. C.V.M. Arnaud, the Assistant Political Director of the French Foreign Ministry, repeated this last contention at the meeting of EC Political Directors on 23-24 January (see note 3 above), and he was then supported by Sig. R. Ducci, the Director-General of the Italian Foreign Ministry. 'The idea of an interim period long enough to ensure that Conference decisions had been properly put into effect was', M. Arnaud added, 'our one real lever over the Russians. A one year interim period was not enough to allow for a proper assessment of what had been achieved by the CSCE' (telegram No. 20 to UKMIS Geneva of 27 January).

[13] The Political Directors agreed (*v. ibid.*) to a British suggestion that the EC Presidency should circulate an account of views expressed on follow-up so that the CSCE Sub-Committee could produce a report for subsequent Political Committee meetings.

ourselves to be in any haste.[14]

Structure of the Final Document

10. The Germans introduced their new ideas for the form of the final Conference document. We and others expressed interest. Delegations in Geneva are asked to consider this problem in the near future in the light of an illustrative draft which the Germans will prepare at our request.

General

11. There was also some discussion, reflected in the report for the Political Directors, on the problems raised at the Conference by the Mediterranean Declaration,[15] the Maltese initiative for a Euro-Arab Federation,[16] and the Cyprus Question.[17] The Irish provided effective chairmanship. For the first time at such meetings the proceedings were largely in English.

[14] During the Political Committee's meeting (see note 3 above), no agreement was reached on the French idea of setting a target date for the end of Stage II, but there was general acceptance of the need to hold Stage III by the summer.

[15] See No. 90, note 4.

[16] On 11 September 1974 the Maltese had tabled a paper on Mediterranean security (see *Human Rights*, vol. iii, pp. 45-7), which proposed the formation of a federation of European and Arab States, including Iran and the countries of the Persian Gulf; the establishment of a monitoring Committee to watch over its formation; and the progressive withdrawal from the Mediterranean of the US and the Soviet Union.

[17] See No. 97, note 2.

No. 109

Minute from Mr. Tickell to the Private Secretary

[WDW 1/4]

Confidential   FCO, *24 January 1975*

CSCE: Confidence-Building Measures[1]

The Secretary of State has commented on paragraph 2(*e*) of Moscow telegram No. 100[2] (the point about confidence-building measures in the latest *Pravda* article on the CSCE):

'Can I have an up-to-date account of this? You remember Lunkov complained about it.'

2. During his conversation with the Secretary of State on 22 January Mr.

[1] Mr. Callaghan noted on this submission: 'Hildyard to follow up in Geneva conversations. Let us give up "movements" & concentrate on a reasonable formula on "manoeuvres" & see how far we get before Moscow. LJC. 27/1.'

[2] This telegram of 21 January reported an article in that day's *Pravda* which described CBMs as one part of the CSCE negotiations on which it was difficult to describe progress 'even as minimal'. The fault, it maintained, lay with those countries which insisted on maximal positions, 'in the first place those belonging to NATO' (WDW 1/303/1). The CSCE reconvened at Geneva on 20 January.

Lunkov, apparently acting on instructions from Mr. Gromyko, accused the British delegation in Geneva of seeking to impose controls on the armed forces of other states and implied that the delegation was out of line with the Secretary of State's own views.[3] Since then we have received a private approach from the Soviet delegation in Geneva suggesting that, in the light of the Prime Minister's forthcoming visit to Moscow, bilateral discussions on confidence-building measures would be useful.[4]

3. At the CSCE least progress has been made on the section of the agenda dealing with the military aspects of security. Agreement was reached in July on the least contentious of the three confidence-building measures specifically mentioned in the Helsinki Recommendations: the *exchange of observers* at military manoeuvres. The most far-reaching of the three, the *prior notification of major military movements*, has run into strong opposition from the East (and from the Americans, who developed cold feet after the agenda had been agreed but who have refrained from making known their doubts in public). The notification of movements is still supported by the rest of NATO and by the neutrals and by the non-aligned, but it is already privately accepted by most of our Allies that no decision of substance will be taken.

4. The chief remaining issue is the third measure: the *prior notification of major military manoeuvres*. Western, neutral and non-aligned delegations are working together for an agreement with sufficient supporting detail to make a practical contribution to the building of confidence (the only remaining security element in what is after all a Security Conference). Briefly their objective is to provide for the notification of all major manoeuvres which take place anywhere in Europe, including a reasonable amount of Soviet territory. Throughout the Warsaw Pact countries have tried to wriggle out of their commitment at Helsinki. They have for example proposed a threshold so high that only a few exceptionally large manoeuvres would qualify; and they would

---

[3] Mr. Lunkov called on Mr. Callaghan on the evening of 22 January and said, 'on instructions', that Mr. Gromyko understood Mr. Callaghan's attitude with regard to the CSCE to be 'roughly the same' as that of the USA, France and the FRG, but that HMG had 'been maintaining official silence on the subject and that the British delegation in Geneva was out of line with [his] views'. This, Mr. Lunkov added, applied especially to CBMs. Mr. Callaghan denied that the British were trying to impose anything on others that they would not accept themselves, and stated that, while he would be glad to discuss the whole subject in Moscow, he would not be willing to 'run ahead' of the UK's allies or 'appear to be currying favour with the Soviet Union' (telegram No. 89 to Moscow of 22 January, ENS 3/548/2).

[4] After approaching Sir D. Hildyard on 23 January, Mr. Dubinin arranged to lunch with Mr. M. Alexander on the 24th. He told Mr. Alexander that the CSCE was regarded in Moscow as being, at present, 'the most important single element in the process of *détente*', and he suggested that, by way of preparation for Mr. Wilson's forthcoming visit to Moscow, the two delegations work together in seeking to resolve differences over: (1) the location of the reference to peaceful change of frontiers in Basket I; (2) CBMs; and (3) the education and information items in Basket III. It was agreed that Mr. Laver and Mr. Figgis would explore further (1) and (2) with Mr. Mendelevich. But Sir D. Hildyard, who favoured continuing this dialogue, thought it clear that the Russians wished to exploit Mr. Wilson's visit to 'enlist our assistance in accelerating progress at the Conference' (UKMIS Geneva telegrams Nos. 20 and 21 of 24 January, WDW 1/303/2).

like to restrict notification to neighbouring states and to manoeuvres taking place near frontiers (in effect ruling out notification of Soviet manoeuvres to the West). But they have agreed to include some of their territory, including some Soviet territory, within the arrangements.

5. It is no surprise that the Russians should wish to pursue the question with us in the context of the Prime Minister's visit to Moscow. We ourselves have recognised that this is one area of continuing contention in Geneva where we can hope to push matters forward in Moscow. With this in mind we have been trying recently to obtain a clearer understanding of the importance which our partners and allies attach to obtaining better arrangements than the Russians have so far been prepared to offer. Although we and the Germans have played a leading part in the debate at the Conference on confidence-building measures, the Western position is the fruit of lengthy Alliance discussion and we have, as the Secretary of State pointed out to Mr. Lunkov, taken great care to remain in step with the Nine and the Fifteen at all stages.

6. Yesterday's discussion at the Political Committee of the Nine in Dublin[5] clearly showed that, some French reticence apart, all our partners attach very great importance indeed to obtaining some practical acknowledgement that a conference on security cannot ignore the military aspects of security. The Belgians, Dutch and Danes indicated that satisfactory measures were essential in the context of their domestic efforts to maintain public support for an adequate level of defence spending. The Germans said that they continued to attach primary importance to obtaining arrangements which would show that the Soviet Union and its Warsaw Pact allies were in principle ready to be included in arrangements in the military field. For domestic political reasons they needed arrangements which would, without discrimination, cover all the participating states in Europe as a counter-balance to the concentration in MBFR upon a particular part of Central Europe.

7. Our Allies have similar preoccupations. The Canadians, Norwegians and Americans give us good support, as do the neutral and non-aligned delegations, including Romania, who are particularly interested in avoiding discriminatory arrangements. We ourselves, contrary to what the Russians have said, have frequently made it plain in Parliament that we see confidence-building measures as an essential part of a conference which we hope will produce results of sufficient content and value to justify a summit Stage III. Mr. Hattersley reaffirmed Her Majesty's Government's commitment in the House of Commons on 18 December:

'The major security element in the Conference now is the confidence-building aspect of it, and the notification of manoeuvres is an essential part of that. The British Government, as part of the Western co-ordinated attitude on these matters, will continue to press for satisfactory answers in that area.'[6]

[5] See No. 108, note 7.

[6] *Parl. Debs.*, 5th ser., H. of C., vol. 883, col. 1564.

8. The Russians are in a fix. They have admitted privately that they made a mistake in agreeing at Helsinki to draw up detailed confidence-building measures at all, even though this was an essential element in the bargain at the time. They have tried on every possible occasion to discredit Western motives. They have exaggerated the impact of the measures, which we and our Allies believe to be modest and voluntary in character, and political rather than military in effect. They have suggested too that the Allies are hiding behind the smaller neutral and non-aligned countries. The last high-level exchange on this point was between Mr. Brezhnev and Chancellor Schmidt in October when the latter replied robustly for the West.

9. We do not believe that the Russians have said their last word. Their negotiators in Geneva have privately indicated as much. Yet they are clearly under strict instructions from their military advisers in Moscow to give away as little as possible. It seems probable that they will not make the necessary hard decisions until they are forced to recognise that they will have to come to terms sooner or later in Stage II.

C.C.C. Tickell

No. 110

Minute from Mr. T.J. Alexander[1] to Mr. Popplewell

[*MTW 10/557/1*]

Confidential   FCO, *5 February 1975*

CSCE Basket II

1. You asked for my thoughts on Miss Warburton's letter of 31 January on the situation in Geneva in the aftermath of the Dublin meeting.[2]

2. It has long been our view that if Basket II can be completed with satisfactory texts in advance of other baskets, this is to be encouraged. This would avoid the economic issues being thrown into the final bargaining session which will inevitably come in the closing stages of the Conference. The lack of urgency now demonstrated by the East is clearly an indication that they consider that the issues in Basket II have been narrowed down to 'the 3'[3] and that little is to be gained from dispassionate debate in the committees. I am not convinced that the Russian attitude can be wholly credited to the renunciation of the Trade Bill. I would have thought that it was too early for them to have formulated a considered position as far as the CSCE is

---

[1] First Secretary in TRED.

[2] In her letter to Mr. Popplewell, Miss Warburton reflected on the timing, substance and modalities of progress towards a final package in Basket II. She pointed out that the East were no longer showing any urgency in seeking to complete work in the Basket, and that the EC Commission seemed more interested in negotiating bilaterally with the CMEA than with developments in the Committee. Cf. No. 108, note 8.

[3] Reciprocity, MFN treatment and reference to developing countries.

concerned.[4] The previous indications were that they were taken aback at the Western and in particular US press reaction to their decision.

3. One of our cardinal tenets is that the CSCE should not produce wording that would prejudice the actions of the Commission in its discussions with the CMEA and we shall have to play this by ear. It will be necessary to await the result of the Moscow meeting (though I doubt if this first session will produce anything significant).[5] Our 'wait and see' line will continue to prevail in the meantime.[6]

4. On the question of substance, I do not think it is illogical in negotiations of this type to set a minimalist position on an issue (MFN) where the East are *démandeurs* and likewise to set a maximalist position of [*sic*] reciprocity which *we* seek. The compromise which will inevitably emerge will amend both these positions. (It is interesting to note that the East have now come down hard against the link between MFN and reciprocity. The previous indications that they might accept a weak link appear to have dissipated.) Provided that there are movements from the East on MFN I think we shall be pushed into watering down our reciprocity wording and I incline to agree with Miss Warburton and Dr. Fielder that the barest mention of MFN and reciprocity would be acceptable to us in the last resort.[7]

5. The EEC/East contacts are clearly not going well. Miss Warburton's report of 29 January of the meeting on the previous day does little to provide encouragement that these meetings are providing a real stimulus to the negotiations.[8] Clearly we need a strong EEC team, but for the sake of

[4] Miss Warburton offered two possible explanations for apparent Soviet efforts to slow down progress in Basket II: (1) that the Russians were reacting to the activities of Senator H. Jackson, who had only lifted his opposition to the passage through Congress of a Trade Reform Bill, permitting MFN status for the Soviet Union, on the assumption that the Russians were going to grant large numbers of exit visas each year to Jewish emigrants; and (2) because the East wanted to keep the main economic questions open for the final round of negotiations at Geneva.

In January the Russians abrogated the Soviet-US trade agreement when Congress insisted on imposing a low ceiling on Export-Import Bank credits to the Soviet Union and required the Soviet Government to increase the issue of exit visas to Jews (cf. *The Times*, 15 January 1975).

[5] EC Commission staff held what proved to be inconclusive talks with the CMEA Secretariat in Moscow during 4-7 February. Miss Warburton reported in her letter of 31 January that M. Kawan was concerned lest any formula adopted at Geneva prejudice the negotiating position of the EC with Eastern countries.

[6] At the EC Political Directors meeting in Dublin on 23-24 January (see No. 108, note 3) Mr. Morgan had made clear HMG's reluctance to reopen old arguments over a suitable formula for agreement on MFN before it was clear how the situation in Geneva had been affected by the Soviet rejection of the American Trade Bill and the Commission-CMEA talks in Moscow. This Miss Warburton described in her letter of 31 January as 'the "wait and see" line" taken by Hugh Morgan' (see note 2 above).

[7] Miss Warburton stated in her letter (*v. ibid.*) that both she and Dr. Fielder believed that the West 'could tolerate omitting all but the barest mention of both MFN and reciprocity'.

[8] The Nine, represented by the French and Irish delegations accompanied by a representative of the Commission, had made tentative approaches to the Eastern countries, represented by the Soviet, Hungarian and East German delegations, during December 1974. Their purpose was to enable progress in the negotiations on the questions of reciprocity and

Committee solidarity I think we shall have to abide by the rotation principle. While the team that included the Belgians on one side of the Commission and ourselves on the other would provide a good negotiating basis, the differences between ourselves and M. Ernemann[9] would inevitably emerge. Our own bilateral discussions with the East have been useful but it seems likely that the Russians would use these to cement areas in which we were not as distant from them as other members of the Nine (the absence of any reference to MFN by the Russians in the last session is perhaps an indication of this).

6. It is difficult at this stage to offer Miss Warburton any firm advice. Our 'wait and see' attitude, shared by the Ad Hoc Group, serves our purpose for the moment. Once the Prime Minister's visit to Moscow is over and there are clearer indications of the course of the EEC/CMEA negotiations we shall have a firmer plank on which to tread. By then too, there may be a more coherent Eastern approach resulting from a considered assessment of the consequences of the renunciation of the Trade Bill.

MFN (report of the CSCE Sub-Committee and the CSCE Ad Hoc Group to the Political Committee of 16/17 January 1975, WDW 1/24). At the first post-Christmas meeting the Eastern representatives had asked to have re-read to them the formulae on MFN and reciprocity, which they subsequently described as 'unacceptable and dead' (letter from Miss Warburton to Mr. Popplewell of 29 January, MTW 10/557/5).

[9] M. A. Ernemann was a leading figure in the Belgian delegation to the CSCE. During the meeting of the Ad Hoc Group in Dublin on 15 January (see No. 108, note 8) he sought, much to the irritation of the UK delegates, to re-open the debate on the agreed EC text relating to MFN treatment with the view to adopting a more conciliatory approach towards the East.

No. 111

Sir E. Peck (UKDEL NATO) to Mr. Callaghan

No. 73 Telegraphic [MTW 10/557/15]

Immediate. Confidential   BRUSSELS, *8 February 1975, 9 a.m.*

Info immediate UKMIS Geneva, Info Priority Moscow, Washington, Bonn and Paris. Saving to Dublin, Helsinki, UKDEL Vienna, Ottawa, Oslo, The Hague, Brussels, Luxembourg, Rome, Ankara, Athens, Lisbon and Copenhagen.

North Atlantic Council: CSCE

1. The North Atlantic Council, attended by Heads of Delegation from Geneva and officials from capitals, met on 7 February to review progress at the CSCE. You may like the following impression of allied views on the present state of play in Geneva, and on the problem of follow-up arrangements since the meeting fell rather appropriately just before your forthcoming visit to Moscow with the Prime Minister. MIFT[1] summarises the other main points in the discussion.

2. There was widespread agreement among our allies with the views of the

[1] UKDEL NATO telegram No. 74 of 8 February reported that the NAC had also discussed timing, CBMs, Baskets II and III and legal questions.

Nine expressed at the recent meetings of the CSCE Sub-Committee and Political Committee of the Nine in Dublin (Dublin tel[egram] No. 33[2] to you and your tel[egram] Nos. 18 to 20 to UKMIS Geneva),[3] business was continuing as usual in Geneva but a number of our allies detected a slight slackening of momentum by comparison with the pace of work before Christmas. It was agreed that this was only to be expected so soon after the resumption of work given that the Conference was now reaching the hard-core of difficult political problems. There was general agreement with the American assessment that the Soviet repudiation of the Soviet-American Trade Agreement (and any associated events in Moscow) had not had any impact on the Conference so far.[4] There was also agreement that Stage III would be unlikely to take place before the summer.

3. The two issues of particular concern to the meeting were the persisting lack of progress on confidence building measures (CBMs) and the problem of how best to follow up the work of the Conference.

4. On the former, there was complete agreement on the need to continue firmly in pursuit of existing NATO objectives. We said that we hoped to try to find some common ground on this question in Moscow,[5] urging the Russians to act now before attitudes hardened on Geneva. Blech (FRG) said that the Germans attached great importance to achieving arrangements for the prior notification of manoeuvres on the lines laid down in the conclusions of the Political Committee of the Nine of 23/24 January (Your tel[egram] No. 19 to UKMIS Geneva).[6] We supported suggestions that the Alliance in Geneva and Brussels should continue to study alternative ways and means of achieving these same objectives. The Americans reaffirmed their opposition to notification of movements and to any public statements at present linking better progress on CBMs with further progress elsewhere in other areas of the Conference. Such forcible methods were best kept for a future occasion, but they would be prepared to support an allied consensus at a later stage either for an Alliance demarche to the Russians or for a further discussion of CBMs in the Coordinating Committee in Geneva.

5. As regards follow up, most of our non-Community allies expressed broad support for the ideas in the British paper.[7] With the exception of the French, all our allies reaffirmed the importance of continuing the multi-lateral dialogue, but they placed emphasis upon the need first to ensure adequate implementation of the results of the Conference, through an adequately long interim period. The Norwegians supported our idea of one year or so, while the Germans cautioned against allowing the interim period to become even

[2] See No. 108, note 8.

[3] See No. 108, notes 3, 7 and 12.

[4] See No. 110, note 4. Mr. Sherer told the NAC (see note 1 above) that the Russians had said their attitude would not be affected by their repudiation of the trade agreement and their interest in the Conference 'did not stem from Brezhnev's personal interest alone'.

[5] See No. 112.

[6] See No. 108, note 7.

[7] See No. 106, note 2.

shorter without any effective concessions from the East.

6. We explained that the British paper (which has been distributed in the Alliance on a bilateral basis only at the [*sic*] Stage) was intended to provoke further thought on an important subject. We believed that the kind of balanced agenda which the West had obtained for the CSCE provided a good framework through which to continue the multi-lateral dialogue. We thought that the West should show more confidence in its ability to counter the dangers inherent in follow up and try to see the advantages as well as the disadvantages. We emphasised that effective Western coordination among the Nine and the Fifteen had always been the secret of Western success and must provide the basis of our approach to follow up. For the present we must support the Danish draft resolution.[8] Further studies were needed, among them particular problems presented by the implementation of the results of the Conference, a subject which could usefully be pursued in NATO.

7. The French (and Turks) joined the rest of the Alliance in support of the Danish draft proposal on follow up, but repeated that they saw no reason to go beyond what already represented for them a difficult compromise. Regular meetings implied the possibility of an '*entente régionale*' or an identity of views on the future of Europe. The Italians suggested that recent experience in Geneva in fact indicated that the Russians were much less interested now than before in permanent machinery of the kind proposed by the Czechs:[9] they were content to continue supporting that proposal, which they knew was unacceptable to the Conference as a whole, while working instead for agreement to a future conference, which could then be postponed indefinitely.

[8] See No. 80, note 1.
[9] See No. 64, note 5.

No. 112

Note of a meeting between Mr. Callaghan and Mr. Gromyko at the Kremlin on the afternoon of 14 February 1975[1]

[*WDW 1/2*]

Confidential   FCO, *15 February 1975*

In the course of Mr. Callaghan's meeting with Mr. Gromyko at the Kremlin on 14 February (which was mainly a drafting session devoted to

[1] This note was sent to the Private Secretary under cover of a minute from Mr. Tickell of 19 February. Mr. Tickell, who accompanied Mr. Wilson and Mr. Callaghan on their visit to Moscow, explained that 'some very delicate points' had been discussed between Mr. Callaghan and Mr. Gromyko, the most important being Mr. Callaghan's 'indications that perhaps the solution to the problem over Peaceful Change of Frontiers lay in Principle Four, and his suggestions about how to make progress over prior notification of military manoeuvres in the field of confidence-building measures'.

eliminating difficulties in the draft texts)[2] a number of CSCE points were discussed.

CSCE Summit

2. The first was over the reference to the level and timing of the third stage of the CSCE in the joint statement. This problem was resolved the following morning and the detail is not worth recording. It is sufficient to say that Mr. Gromyko seemed more concerned about the language covering the timing of the third stage than about the qualifications in our language agreeing to go to a summit meeting.[3] During a long argument Mr. Gromyko tried on two or three occasions to browbeat Mr. Callaghan, and prevent the elaboration of alternative texts. British officials eventually withdrew and produced the text which was the basis of the agreement reached next day.

Peaceful Change of Frontiers

3. Mr. Gromyko reverted to the earlier discussion between Mr. Brezhnev and Mr. Wilson about Peaceful Change of Frontiers.[4] He said that the Soviet Union was ready to express the provisionally agreed formula of 5 April[5] in positive rather than negative terms. He then read out a text, which Mr. Callaghan pointed out was word for word the text to which we had already given provisional agreement on 5 April. In the course of discussions it emerged that the Russians had been working on the French text where the formulation 'ne . . . que' was used.[6]

4. Mr. Callaghan explained the British position. We had provisionally accepted the formula of 5 April, and believed the right place for it was in the Third Principle on Inviolability of Frontiers. He understood that the Russians could not agree to put this formula in the Third Principle but wanted it to go into the First Principle. Our view was that if it went into any Principle other

---

[2] Extracts of the final documents resulting from this visit are printed in Cmnd. 6932, pp. 194-200.

[3] At their first meeting with Mr. Brezhnev and Mr. Gromyko on 13 February, the Prime Minister said that he and Mr. Callaghan were keen to have a CSCE summit Conference later in the year, and thought that 'if it was possible to make enough progress, in coming weeks, it should be possible to hold the conference in the summer, and thus combine a meeting which would improve security of all the peoples of Europe with opportunities for the leaders of the conference to acquire a healthy sun tan' (record of a meeting between Mr. Wilson and Mr. Brezhnev in the Kremlin on 13 February at 6.00 p.m., ENS 3/548/2).

[4] When this issue was raised during his meeting with Mr. Brezhnev that morning, Mr. Wilson said: 'So far as he knew, there was no difference between us on the form of words, only on where the phrase should go in the Declaration.' He then went on to ask 'why we could not include the phrase both in the place where the Soviet Union wanted it and where others wanted it also'? After Mr. Gromyko had replied at length, Mr. Wilson claimed 'that he was an amateur on these matters, and that the discussions had been very educational for him' (record of a meeting between Mr. Wilson and Mr. Brezhnev in the Kremlin on 14 February at 11.00 a.m., ENS 3/548/2).

[5] See *Human Rights*, vol. iii, p. 167.

[6] This is evidently a reference to the French translation of the phrase 'frontiers can be changed only in accordance with international law through peaceful means and by agreement' (*v. ibid.*).

than the Third Principle it would require adaptation. He had heard that the Soviet Government had already rejected the formula of 26 July[7] which had been designed to adapt the formula of 5 April to fit into the First Principle. If Mr. Gromyko did not like this formula perhaps he could suggest another one which could be fitted into the First Principle or perhaps the Fourth Principle. Mr. Callaghan emphasised the great importance of this issue for the Federal Republic. The Federal Government had to be able to defend whatever formulation was agreed to an anxious public opinion, and show that it did nothing to prejudice the German position on the wider question underlying this issue. Did Mr. Gromyko wish to render the SPD vulnerable to attack from the CDU?

5. Mr. Gromyko said that the whole argument was unnecessary. The Principle of Inviolability did not need a qualifying phrase on Peaceful Change: inviolability of a frontier did not mean it could not be changed by peaceful means. He was interested to hear Mr. Callaghan's reference to Principle Four. Did Mr. Callaghan think that the Germans would agree to put the formula of 5 April into Principle Four?

6. Mr. Callaghan said that he was sure they would not agree unless the formula was suitably adapted. The problem was how to do so. Did Mr. Gromyko have any ideas? Mr. Gromyko said that he had no other formulations in mind. So far as the Soviet Government was concerned only the formula of 5 April was acceptable.

7. After some further exchanges, Mr. Tickell said that the competition between formulae and where to put them could easily be solved if there were agreement on the problem of substance. So far as the British Government was concerned we had accepted the 5 April formula because the ways in which it was there stated that frontiers could be changed were—in lawyers' language—disjunctive and hence alternatives. Was this also the Soviet position or did the Russians maintain that frontiers could not be changed until three conditions had been satisfied: conformity with international law, through peaceful means, and by agreement? Mr. Gromyko said that all three had to be satisfied. Mr. Callaghan said that in that case he saw no possibility of moving forward. The formula of 5 April was ambiguous and so open to both interpretations. He suggested that the Russians should have another look at the whole problem and see whether they could not produce a formula which could fit into Principle Four.

Inter-Relationships of the Principles

8. Mr. Gromyko raised the question of the inter-relationship of the Principles and set out the classic Soviet case. Mr. Callaghan said that so far as we were concerned the language set out in paragraphs 11 and 12 of the

[7] See No. 108, note 3. During their earlier discussions (see note 4 above) Mr. Gromyko had explained how the American formula of 26 July, which he claimed was inspired by West Germany, differed from that of 5 April. 'The accent', he contended, 'had now shifted to imply that it was almost a basic function of international law to bring about changes in international frontiers.'

original French draft Declaration of Principles of October 1973[8] was about right.

9. This language seemed new to Mr. Gromyko. One of his assistants borrowed Mr. Tickell's text and translated it into Russian. Mr. Gromyko then said with a show of annoyance that as we must well know this text was unacceptable to the Soviet Union and we had wasted his time by referring to it and obliging them to translate it. Mr. Callaghan said that that was our position and we were sticking to it.

Confidence-Building Measures

10. Mr. Gromyko made a number of rambling complaints about the Western proposals on confidence-building measures. They were unnecessary and went too far. The two Ministers agreed to concentrate on prior notification of military manoeuvres and to leave the question of prior notification of military movements. Mr. Gromyko said that the Western countries were asking for the inclusion of too much Soviet territory. Mr. Callaghan said that he agreed that we had perhaps asked for too much. He had no authority to negotiate for anyone else but speaking personally he thought that the basic element in an eventual agreement should be the inclusion of all Europe with exceptions for Turkey and the Soviet Union. A band of Soviet territory 400 kms deep should be sufficient for the purpose. He reminded Mr. Gromyko that the problem was much more political than military. One of the main reasons for the whole CSCE was to permit participating countries to gain greater confidence about each others' intentions: prior notification of military manoeuvres would be very important in that respect. Other participants would have the whole of their territory included. This would be a real demonstration of confidence. We were proposing an exception for the Soviet Union because we recognised that the Soviet Union was in a special position as only some of Soviet territory could be described as European. He thought the suggestion he had made was a generous one. He asked what size of manoeuvre—in short how many troops—the Russians thought should qualify for prior notification.

11. Mr. Gromyko said he was attracted by Mr. Callaghan's statement that the problem was more political than military. This was the right way to look at it. What was wrong with the Soviet proposal that the zone to be covered should be 100 kms from the frontiers of participating states? Mr. Callaghan said that this idea was laughable. He did not see how it could possibly create confidence in the way which was required. Besides this idea resurrected the problem of frontiers which he had no wish to go into again. It was more important to agree on all Europe with a band for the Soviet Union of 100 km or whatever size was right than to argue about how much should be counted from frontiers. Mr. Gromyko said that the idea of 35 participating states notifying each other of military manoeuvres would create a lot of unnecessary work and make necessary a bureaucratic machine. Mr. Callaghan said that he did not see how. Agreement on a satisfactory arrangement covering

[8] See *Human Rights*, vol. iii, p. 108.

military manoeuvres would have a big impact on public opinion and would certainly count as one of the achievements of the Conference. Mr. Gromyko would of course know that no-one was suggesting that the Soviet Union or anyone else should enter into a legal obligation to notify. Whatever agreement was reached would be essentially voluntary in character. Mr. Gromyko made no answer and there the conversation on this point effectively ended.

12. We noticed that the Soviet record takers took down three of Mr. Callaghan's points verbatim: first his suggestion that the zone of Soviet territory might be fixed at 400 kms; secondly when he said that it was more important to agree on all Europe with a band for the Soviet Union 'of 100 kms or whatever size was right' than argue over how much should be counted from frontiers; and thirdly his reference to the voluntary character of any agreement. Later Mr. Vasev[9] (Second European Department) mentioned to Mr. Tickell that Mr. Callaghan's points on CBMs had been very carefully noted in Moscow, and in particular the importance he had attached to reaching an agreement.

[9] Mr. V.M. Vasev was Deputy Chief in the Second European Department of the Soviet Ministry of Foreign Affairs.

No. 113

Minute from Mr. Tickell to Sir J. Killick

[WDW 1/21]

Confidential   FCO, *21 February 1975*

CSCE: Visit to Geneva

As you know I visited Geneva yesterday to brief the Delegations of the Nine on the CSCE points which arose during the Prime Minister's and the Secretary of State's visit to Moscow; and to discuss with Ambassador Mendelevich of the Soviet Delegation how Anglo/Soviet co-operation at the Conference should be followed up. The Delegation are preparing records of these meetings but you may like to have a brief account of what happened.

2. The briefing of the Delegations of the Nine seemed to go well. Most Delegations had already received an account of what you told their Ambassadors in Moscow on 17 February, but were glad to have the opportunity of pursuing points of detail. M. André (for France) seemed particularly interested in the inter-relationship of the Principles, M. van der Valk[1] (Netherlands) in the timing of the third stage, and M. Blech (FRG) in the discussion in Moscow on Peaceful Change of Frontiers. I expressed the general view that the Russians seemed in more of a hurry to complete the CSCE than they generally liked to admit, and the next few months might be less of a slogging match and more of a war of movement than people now seemed to expect. In these circumstances we should be ready to show

[1] Heer J. van der Valk was Netherlands Head of Delegation.

flexibility, follow up opportunities, and generally make the most of circumstances which might not recur. Although I repeated most of what the Secretary of State had said about Principle Four in the argument over Peaceful Change of Frontiers, I avoided any reference to the figures in describing the discussion in Moscow on prior notification of military manoeuvres. I was asked about the Kissinger/Gromyko conversations in Geneva,[2] and Dr. Kissinger's subsequent visit to London,[3] but I pleaded ignorance. I also took the opportunity to convey something of the atmosphere of the visit, and Mr. Brezhnev's general approach to international problems.

3. I had almost an hour and a half with Mr. Mendelevich. He had clearly received no detailed account of the Moscow visit but had of course seen Mr. Gromyko on 17 February. I told him about the exchange between the Prime Minister and Mr. Brezhnev in Moscow that day, and emphasised his wish to continue the Anglo/Soviet co-operation which had begun on account of the visit.[4] I added that I hoped that this time we could deal with fundamental as well as textual problems. We then discussed five main points:

(a) *Peaceful Change of Frontiers.* Here we went round the course several times. If Mr. Mendelevich had any new information he did not reveal it. I referred to the Secretary of State's indication to Mr. Gromyko that maybe we should make progress by looking at the possibilities of including a suitably adapted formula on Peaceful Change of Frontiers in Principle Four.

(b) *Confidence-building Measures.* Again we went round the course. I emphasised the Secretary of State's view that CBMs were essentially a political measure in the military field rather than a matter of military significance in itself; and suggested he should study carefully the record of

[2] During a visit to Washington on 28 February Mr. Tickell learned from Mr. Hartman that during a meeting between Dr. Kissinger and Mr. Gromyko in Geneva on 16 February the latter had 'agreed without commitment' to look at a formula for the peaceful change of frontiers, which had been worked out with the West Germans, and which stated: 'The participating states consider that their frontiers can be changed in accordance with international law by peaceful means and through agreement.' Mr. Gromyko had said that he did not think that Principle 4 'was a bad place to put whatever was eventually agreed', but the West Germans had subsequently indicated that they preferred the clause to go into Principle 1, and had asked for commas to be placed around the words 'in accordance with international law' (minute from Mr. Tickell to Sir J. Killick of 3 March, WDW 1/2). See also No. 94, note 7.

[3] Dr. Kissinger dined with Mr. Wilson and Mr. Callaghan in London on 17 February. Mr. Callaghan told Dr. Kissinger, with regard to the visit he and Mr. Wilson had recently made to Moscow, that the Soviet intention 'seemed to have been to bring Britain into line with the position of other Western countries. We had hitherto been behind them' (record of conversation, 17 February, AMU 3/548/12).

[4] During his conversation with Mr. Wilson on 17 February, Mr. Brezhnev said that 'he had noted with satisfaction that the British and Soviet Delegations at Geneva had been working closely together during the last few weeks, and might well have been able by quiet diplomacy to push matters forward on some difficult points in Basket 3' (record of meeting between Mr. Wilson and Mr. Brezhnev on 17 February, ENS 3/548/2).

Mr. Callaghan's discussion with Mr. Gromyko of 15 February.[5] The time had come for all concerned in this problem to stop striking attitudes and indulging in rhetoric, and to get on with finding practical solutions to problems of great importance to the success of the Conference. Mr. Mendelevich warmly agreed. It was, he said, time for the matter to be passed to 'the professionals' (he showed he is well aware of the way Mr. Brezhnev misrepresents the Allied position). What we now had to do, he said, was to find a basis for negotiation. I agreed; and picking up some earlier remarks he had made, said that we might at least be able to agree on certain criteria for CBMs. To judge from what he had said we could probably agree on at least three: the need for them to fulfil a useful purpose, their sufficiency in doing so, and the undiminished security of the participating states. Mr. Mendelevich said that if we could propose something like that in the Sub-Committee there could be a breakthrough. I said that I would gladly consider something of this kind. The trouble about discussion of such matters as criteria was that it risked delaying rather than advancing the debate. At the same time if Mr. Mendelevich thought that it could get a real negotiation going we would gladly see what could be done. In the meantime I repeated that he should study the record of the conversation between the Secretary of State and Mr. Gromyko.

(c) *QRR.* Mr. Mendelevich said that the Russians liked the text which had been produced on this subject by us among others, and regretted that it should now have run into difficulties with the neutrals.[6] He thought that the Four Powers should firmly defend it, and repeated to me the arguments he had already used with the neutrals. (Unfortunately these arguments seemed to have scared rather than mollified them). We agreed that the right place for the text was after the Declaration but that if need be we could put it into Principle Ten.

(d) *Principle Nine on Co-operation.* Mr. Mendelevich said that the British and Soviet Delegations more or less saw eye to eye on this question. The trouble was that certain Delegations were trying to make the Russians go further than they ever would on co-operation between individuals. As we well knew there were limits in this respect beyond which the Soviet Government could and would not go. He therefore appealed for our help in instilling 'a pragmatic spirit' into the minds of the idealists. If this matter

[5] No. 112.

[6] See No. 103, note 5, and *Human Rights*, vol. iii, p. 138. On 29 January a caucus of neutral and non-aligned Heads of Mission (Switzerland, Sweden, Finland, Austria, Yugoslavia, Malta and Cyprus) unanimously agreed to oppose inclusion of the formula anywhere in the Declaration of Principles. It was condemned for being 'bad in law (e.g. it wrongly implied that there could be treaties not in conformity with international law) and bad politically for condoning the Brezhnev doctrine'. The Cypriots were particularly concerned about their appearing to endorse language implying that they fully accepted international arrangements made in the wake of the Turkish invasion of Cyprus (UKMIS Geneva telegram No. 33 of 31 January, WDW 1/2).

dragged on he feared it might become a bigger issue than it deserved.

(*e*) *Square Brackets*. Mr. Mendelevich said that the text of the Declaration of Principles was littered with square brackets. We should try to get these out as soon as possible: a lot of them were due to arguments between the Yugoslavs and 'certain' Western Delegations, not, he added, the British. These could cause a lot of trouble later on, and he hoped we could cooperate with the Soviet Delegation in persuading others quietly to drop them.

4. This was a very amiable conversation. Mr. Mendelevich is of course an able and companiable colleague. He was speaking without instructions, and it would be unwise to read very much into what he said. But he seemed pleased by my initiative in coming to see him, and promised he would make a full report on it. I think we have now done our bit, and the next move (if there is to be one) should come from the Russians.[7]

C.C.C. TICKELL

[7] On 24 February Sir J. Killick noted on this minute: 'Very useful. I agree that the ball is in general in the Soviet court. But I wonder if a Western initiative on "criteria" in para 3b. would not be a good idea. We do not want a time-wasting discussion on criteria, but a Western paper on the subject might give the Russians a background against which to move.'

No. 114

Sir D. Hildyard (UKMIS Geneva) to Mr. Callaghan

No. 132 Telegraphic [*WDW 1/22*]

Immediate. Confidential　　　　　　　　　　GENEVA, *28 February 1975, 5 p.m.*

Info immediate Washington, Moscow, UKDEL NATO, Saving EEC Posts, Helsinki, Berne.

CSCE: General State of Play

1. The Russians remain tough and anxious to give the impression that they are under no time pressure, but behind this I think that they still much want to bring the Conference to an end as soon as possible. Kovalev was recalled to Moscow last night at very short notice, which may herald a reappraisal of Soviet tactics. I am due to lunch with him on 4 March when I may discover more.[1]

2. In the areas in which the Soviet delegation had had some flexibility we have made a little progress (the Romanian Paper in Basket I,[2] developing countries in Basket II, and some Basket III issues). As against this the Russians have been tightening up on individual contacts in all sectors, and appear

[1] When Mr. Kovalev returned to Geneva he claimed to have no new instructions except on peaceful change of frontiers (see note 4 below). Nevertheless, Sir D. Hildyard reported in UKMIS Geneva telegram No. 161 of 7 March, the Russians 'appear to be trying to find ways of moving forward in both Baskets II and III, though they seem not only uncertain but also divided as to how best to proceed so that they have to concede as little as possible'.

[2] See *Human Rights*, vol. iii, p. 280.

385

indeed to be preparing to back-track on some provisionally registered formulations. As regards the major issues on which they have been inflexible there has been no movement on CBMs, but some progress on peaceful change of frontiers (see paragraph 4 below).

3. The Americans tell us that they are under instructions to avoid confrontations with the Russians. The French have regarded themselves as having something of a special relationship encouraged by the Rambouillet meeting.[3] The Germans seem to be trying to build up contacts on a number of issues. We have been working increasingly closely with the Soviet delegation before and after the Moscow visit. The Russians may consider, therefore, that the danger of a united front against them, with far-reaching demands, has been much reduced. This does not mean that the West will not obtain reasonably satisfactory results, but the Russians may calculate that they will not have to go very far.

Basket I

4. (a) *Peaceful Change of Frontiers (PCF)*. We understand in strict confidence from the FRG delegation (please protect) that the Russians are contemplating a significant concession in that they are prepared to envisage the insertion of a text in Principle I reading: 'The participating States consider that their frontiers can be changed in accordance with international law, by peaceful means and through agreement'. Bonn, it seems are holding out for the insertion of a comma after 'changed'. Van Well may say something to us about this privately in Dublin.[4]

(b) *Quadripartite Rights and Responsibilities (QRR)*. Discussions are continuing between Bonn Group delegations and the neutral and non-aligned. Neither side has changed its position. The Americans, FRG and ourselves are willing to envisage minor changes in the QRR text tabled by the French but the latter are not. The neutrals and non-aligned are content for the time being not to raise their difficulties publicly, although they have told us that they hope that Bonn Group delegations will be ready to make some move after Easter.[5]

(c) There have been no discussions of the interrelationship between the principles recently with the East.

Basket II

5. The East remain very tough on the main outstanding issues of MFN and reciprocity while conveying through private contacts the impression that the

---

[3] See No. 107, note 4. On 5 December 1974 Mr. Brezhnev was received by President Giscard d'Estaing at the Château of Rambouillet for three days of talks.

[4] At a meeting of the EPC Political Committee on 3 March Herr van Well confirmed that the Americans had obtained Soviet agreement to this text with the comma inserted. Since, however, the Poles and the East Germans had refused to accept the placing of this formula in Principle 4, it was to be included in Principle 1 (UKREP Brussels telegram No. 1223 of 4 March, MTW 10/557/5). Sir D. Hildyard regarded this as a 'very major advance' and further evidence that the Russians were 'extremely concerned to bring the Conference to an end as soon as possible' (see note 1 above).

[5] See No. 113, note 6.

time for final solutions to these issues is approaching.[6] Meanwhile progress is slowly being made on other outstanding points, particularly developing countries, but in the science and technology Sub-Committee the Russians are trying to reopen some important paragraphs, including those related to direct and individual contacts.

Basket III

6. Progress continued on working conditions for journalists though the registration of what are supposed to be agreed texts has been attended by various difficulties caused by extreme Russian caution and suspiciousness (and also on occasion incompetence). Serious multilateral work on the information mini-preamble is now getting under way. In human contacts a minor text on youth exchanges is nearing completion but the main problems, the mini-preamble and travel, remain virtually deadlocked. In education the Russians are preventing agreement on the final text, and have hinted at reservations about references to 'contacts' in text already negotiated. In culture, they have said there will be no further progress until the 'issues of substance' (in particular, presumably, reading rooms) are cleared out of the way.

---

[6] During a conversation with M. Kawan on 26 February, Mr. T. Jodko (Polish delegation) had said that he did not want reciprocity and MFN to be dealt with at the last minute because he feared that at that stage he would have rigid instructions which would not allow him to accept anything, thus making any compromise impossible (minute from Miss Warburton to Dr. Fielder of 27 February, WDW 1/6).

No. 115

Sir D. Hildyard (UKMIS Geneva) to Mr. Callaghan

No. 172 Telegraphic [*WDW 1/22*]

Priority. Confidential   GENEVA, *14 March 1975, 6.25 p.m.*

Info Washington, Moscow, UKDEL NATO, Saving EEC Posts, Helsinki, Berne.

CSCE: State of Play

1. The Russians have now moved on the two issues which have been generally considered the most important and difficult, CBMs and peaceful change of frontiers. We have only just started to move again on CBMs[1] and

---

[1] Sir D. Hildyard reported in UKMIS Geneva telegram No. 168 of 13 March (WDW 1/4) that Mr. Kovalev had, at a Coordinating Committee meeting that day, appeared to suggest three elements of an agreement on the prior notification of manoeuvres: 'notification should be to all participating states; it should cover both national and multinational manoeuvres; and it should be on a voluntary basis'. In response to a request from the UK delegation for guidance on the notion of 'voluntary' notification, telegram No. 90 to UKMIS Geneva of 17 March (WDW 1/4) expressed the FCO's preference for 'a firm political commitment (tacitly qualified by considerations of national security) by which the parties would be expected to give notification in most circumstances'. This, the telegram added, 'would not involve any legal obligation or military constraint, and would therefore be voluntary: but it would involve a clear moral obligation'. When, on 18 March, Mr. Kovalev repeated the Soviet proposals in the

we have still a good way to go on PCF (see paragraph 4 below). The Russian toughening on individual contacts (my telegram No. 132),[2] however, and the indications that they may now be regarding the other main outstanding issues, particularly in Basket III, as interdependent, give the impression that they are preparing for the final bargaining phase. We must be prepared, therefore, for increased linking of issues as well as the usual hard bargaining on each.

2. As regards timing I very much agree that it would be unwise to set a definite deadline.[3] I also agree about the amount of purely mechanical work which still remains to be done (paragraph 5 of your telegram No. 86).[4] Even if fairly rapid progress could be achieved on the major issues, the removal of brackets during the second reading seems likely to be a slow business, and agreements on translations could be just as difficult. In recent months agreement on texts in all the various languages has been reached before registration in Basket III, but even in this Basket there is still a backlog of language discrepancies from the past.

Basket I

Principles

3. Progress on Principle IX (Co-operation) is slow. The Yugoslavs are being difficult, and the Eastern delegations and the rest generally are deadlocked over the 'role of the individual'. On this latter point, the Russians have today hinted that the second paragraph of the recent *communiqué* of the Heads of Government of the Nine (Dublin telegram No. 156 to the FCO)[5]

Coordinating Committee NATO delegations, while making no substantive response, welcomed this evidence of Soviet flexibility. But the neutrals and non-aligned made clear their disappointment at the Russian rejection of obligatory notification (UKMIS Geneva telegram No. 176 of 19 March, WDW 1/4).

[2] No. 114.

[3] Mr. Brezhnev wrote to Mr. Wilson on 8 March proposing that the 'final stage of the Conference at the highest level' should open in Helsinki on 30 June. Similar messages were sent to President Ford, President Giscard d'Estaing, Herr Schmidt and Sig. Moro. The Soviet initiative was discussed at the European Council meeting on 10-11 March and in the NAC on 17 March, and on 19 March Mr. Wilson replied to Mr. Brezhnev that he expected that it would be possible to obtain 'balanced and satisfactory results on all the subjects on the agenda', which would permit them to reach Stage III, and that, while he considered it too soon to fix an exact date, he still thought they should aim to have the final stage that summer (telegram No. 79 to UKMIS Geneva of 11 March; telegram No. 100 to UKDEL NATO of 14 March; UKDEL NATO telegram No. 132 of 17 March; telegram No. 333 to Moscow of 19 March; WDW 1/23).

[4] Paragraph 5 of this telegram of 13 March reported doubts expressed by M. Davignon at an informal meeting of the Political Directors on 10 March about meeting a 30 June or mid-July deadline given the amount of mechanical work which needed to be done (WDW 1/23).

[5] The *communiqué* contained in this telegram of 11 March expressed the hope of EC Heads of Government that their policy of *détente* and cooperation in Europe would encourage ever-increasing understanding and trust among peoples. 'This objective', it affirmed, 'will find particular expression in the development of relations between states and peoples in which an important part should be played by the individual' (WDW 1/24). The European Council meeting in Dublin on 10-11 March was the first occasion on which EC Heads of Government considered a subject submitted by the EPC (Davignon) machinery of the Nine.

suggests a possible solution to the problem (i.e. they could accept a reference to 'persons' provided it was not associated with a mention of 'contacts'). But they do not want to rush matters. In an abrupt reversal of their previous position, they have now indicated readiness to start discussing Principle X (Fulfilment in Good Faith of Obligations under International Law) before completing the first reading of Principle IX.

Peaceful Change of Frontiers (PCF)

4. The Americans told the Fifteen today that, on Monday, they would formally be tabling the PCF text which they have agreed with the Russians (paragraph 9 of UKREP Brussels telegram No. 1223).[6] They are under instructions to seek its provisional registration in Principle I (Sovereign Equality) before the Easter break, the precise placing to be determined later. This they will not get. The Romanians object both to the wording and the proposed placing. The Italians have now accepted the wording, but consider that if it is to go in Principle I, the rest of the principle may need modification. The French have made it known that they have instructions to withhold consent to provisional registration pending agreement on texts safeguarding Quadripartite Rights and Responsibilities (QRR) and on interrelationship between the principles (the French have all along insisted on linking the PCF and QRR texts, making their support for the FRG position on the former dependent on FRG support for their position on the latter). The Russians, who want to see the new text registered soon, in case the FRG change their minds, are not at all pleased with the French. (As I have reported separately they also had a row over the Easter break.)[7]

Quadripartite Rights and Responsibilities (QRR)

5. All four Bonn Group delegations are agreed that, for the time being, we should continue to defend the text tabled by the French before Christmas.[8] This week's meeting *à quatre* discussed tactics. Yesterday, I addressed the neutral and non-aligned group on the subject (the latter have already had 'presentations' from the French, the Russians and the Americans) and am to have a further meeting with them on Monday. The Yugoslavs (and the Romanians) remain opposed to accepting any QRR formula, anywhere in the final documents, which is couched in general terms and does not refer

[6] See No. 114, note 4.

[7] In a letter to Mr. Tickell of 11 March Sir D. Hildyard described Soviet efforts to 'steamroller' other delegations into accepting only a short Easter break. This was opposed by neutral and non-aligned delegations, who wanted a week's break, and an attempt by Mr. Kovalev to win M. André's support 'ended angrily as well as unsuccessfully'. Evidently impressed by M. André's attitude, Sir D. Hildyard, who had for some time been wanting to work more closely with the French, took up with M. André the idea of establishing a 'ginger/troubleshooting group' (cf. No. 105, note 5). This, he informed Mr. Tickell in a further letter of 19 March, would include the West Germans and would allow the three delegations to let each other know of their preoccupations and of Soviet attempts to drive wedges between them. Mr. Tickell had, however, doubts about this initiative. 'I don't mind ginger', he noted on 20 March, 'but I wonder how far it shd. go into yet new groups. The fairy godmothers not invited will soon hear & arrive on broomsticks' (WDW 1/22).

[8] See No. 113, note 6.

solely to Germany. But I think that most of the neutral and non-aligned now accept that some general formula is needed, even if they still wish to see some amendments made to the present text.

Basket III

6. No developments of major interest this week. A further paragraph in journalists text and a text on youth have been agreed but not yet registered.

No. 116

Minute from Mr. Burns to Mr. Tickell

[*WDW 1/14*]

Confidential   FCO, *26 March 1975*

CSCE: Follow-Up[1]

1. I attach the latest version of the '*rapport circonstancié*' of the Nine on follow-up.[2] It is a considerable improvement upon its predecessor.[3] Mr. Carter has done well in getting so many of our comments accepted. The paper will be reviewed in the meeting of the Sub-Committee on 3 April in Geneva. There are a number of changes which we should still seek, (as indicated on the attached copy), especially as regards paragraphs 18 and 28.[4] But I think we shall then have carried the study as far as is tactically wise at this stage or indeed possible at the present level. The paper provides a good

---

[1] Mr. Tickell marked up this minute to Mr. Morgan, who subsequently noted his qualified approval of its recommendations as modified by Mr. Tickell (see note 12 below).

[2] Not printed. This detailed report was prepared by the Nine's CSCE Sub-Committee as the result of a heated debate generated by consideration of the latest British paper on follow-up (see No. 106, note 2) in the EPC Political Committee at its meeting on 23-24 January. Both the French and the Italians opposed British views on the grounds that that institutionalised follow-up could have a dangerous effect on the process of European political cooperation. M. Arnaud also claimed that a longer interim period was required between the end of Stage III and a review conference in order to ensure the implementation of measures agreed in the CSCE. The Committee finally agreed to a British suggestion that its CSCE Sub-Committee should draft a report on follow-up for further examination at ministerial level (telegram No. 20 to UKMIS Geneva of 27 January, WDW 1/24).

[3] Not printed. The first draft of the report, dated 26 February, was judged 'not very satisfactory' by Mr. Burns, a fault which he attributed in part to its 'multiple parentage' and 'surfeit of Cartesian logic' (minute to Mr. Tickell of 11 March). Nevertheless, he informed Mr. A. Carter (UKMIS Geneva) in a letter of 10 March that, 'with improvements', it should be possible to have a paper which would 'represent a useful shift in the thinking of the Nine, not so much about the form which follow-up should take in the short term, but on the potential value of the CSCE process to the West'. The FCO wanted the paper to recognise the positive advantages of follow-up as well as its risks, to accept 1977 as the date for a review conference, and to back the idea of future regular meetings as a genuine option.

[4] Paragraph 18 stated that the interim period between Stage III and the review conference should be sufficiently long to allow for an evaluation of the manner in which Conference decisions were being implemented; and paragraph 28 stipulated that there should be no automaticity about future CSCE meetings (CSCE(75)14P Rev. 2 of 20 March).

basis for discussion by Political Directors on 8/9 April, when I dare say the French will show themselves more negative than has seemed the case so far.

2. We shall need at some stage to submit the paper to Mr. Hattersley and Mr. McNally.[5] I am accordingly preparing an English translation, but I imagine a submission can wait until after the meeting of Political Directors.

3. I shall attend the meeting of the Sub-Committee on 3 April and subsequently prepare the briefing for the meeting of Political Directors. I should welcome your views of the following points:

(*a*) *The interim period.* 1977 is the date proposed for the review conference of officials in the Danish draft[6] and the date mentioned to Dr. Kissinger by the Secretary of State.[7] It is the date favoured by our partners in the Nine, though it could be altered and must be made more precise in the course of negotiation. We need to balance:

(i) our desire to maintain the momentum of the CSCE and;

(ii) to keep up the pressure on the Russians to implement the Conference decisions; against

(i) our need for sufficient breathing-space to demonstrate a comparable performance on our own part in the implementation of the results; and

(ii) our desire to hold the review conference not so soon that effective decisions on follow up cannot be taken, but rather at a moment when there is a wide-spread willingness to do more than has been agreed so far. In the circumstances we can agree firmly to 1977, though we must strongly argue for a date in the first not the second half of the year. But we can agree to leave a decision on the precise date to a later moment since it will be a valuable bargaining counter.[8]

(*b*) *Continuity.* This is the big problem. We want to ensure continuity in the long term; this could be done by agreement in principle at the Conference to regular meetings in future, though a firm decision need not be taken until the review meeting. On the other hand, our partners are strongly opposed to tieing their hands in this way. I think they are wrong, if only because the Russians seem to be having cold feet about such regular meetings of officials. And we must therefore at least seek to make paragraph 28 consistent with paragraph 35 of the rapport.[9] But I suggest

---

[5] Mr. T. McNally was Political Adviser to Mr. Callaghan.

[6] See No 80, note 1.

[7] During a conversation with Dr. Kissinger at the State Department on 30 January Mr. Callaghan suggested that officials might meet in 1977 to assess how CSCE decisions had been put into effect. Dr. Kissinger indicated that he could 'go along' with British ideas on follow-up (record of conversation, 30 January, NFX 2/598/1).

[8] On 2 April Mr. Morgan minuted to Mr. Burns (see note 1 above) that he saw no point in pressing for a decision on when in 1977 to hold the follow-up meeting: 'life', he added, 'will take charge of this question & there is no point in expending any negotiating capital on it now. We can express a preference for the first half, resist any move to choose the second half, but agree to leave it open.'

[9] See note 4 above. Paragraph 35 stated that following a positive evaluation of the implementation of Conference decisions a number of options were possible, including additional

that, providing the paper of the Nine does not prejudge the question, we can probably allow the course of the negotiations themselves to force our partners to concede this point.

(*c*) *Review Conference*. Much more work needs to be done on the best arrangements for the Review Conference, since it could well be unwise to leave all decisions until 1977. Paragraph 36 raises a number of relevant points. We shall need to consider:

(i) *Place*. Modified rotation will be best. Choice by lot might hit upon Moscow or London, but the Romanians will resist leaving the privilege to one of the standard neutrals. We should let a choice emerge by consensus as a result of corridor discussion, and the Nine may be able to exploit this issue to their tactical advantage. In any case, my preference is for Belgrade.

(ii) *Rules of Procedure*. We wish to preserve the rule of consensus, and a decision to maintain the present rules of procedure, including paragraphs 54 and 58 of the Helsinki Recommendations,[10] could provide the necessary compromise with the Maltese on the question of associating the non-participating Mediterranean states with the follow-up. But the Commission may well try to convince the Community that they should have a more formal role in the follow-up if not at Stage III; this is something to which the Political Directors must address themselves in the context of paragraph 32, particularly if Coreper is not to pre-empt the position at their meeting on 10 April.

(iii) *Length of the Review Meeting*. This question too is raised in the follow-up paper. Provided that we avoid landing ourselves with a never-ending and thus permanent institution (which the French see as the danger of an open-ended discussion), we should not try to impose a deadline now to discussions in 1977, but rather look to a meeting conducted on the lines of the multilateral preparatory talks.

4. In reading the report I have been particularly struck by two things:

(*a*) that we have not substantially altered the lines of the Danish draft or discussed amendments which we could accept in the course of the negotiations (though some of these may be inherent). What we have done is at last bring all our partners to the point of giving firm and vigorous support to that draft. This is a considerable achievement given the luke-warm support it has had in the past.[11]

meetings of experts, a meeting of senior officials, and meetings of senior officials held periodically by rotation in the various capitals.

[10] See Cmnd. 6932, p. 152.

[11] At its meeting on 8-9 April the Political Committee focused on two main questions with regard to follow-up: (1) the precise date of the proposed review conference; and (2) the idea that the Nine should accept as an option a series of meetings held at regular intervals and that this should be explicitly stated at the Conference. Both issues were left to the attention of Ministers. Meanwhile, the Committee reaffirmed the Nine's support for the Danish draft (telegrams Nos. 124 and 125 of 10 April, WDW 1/24).

(*b*) The vast majority of the decisions of the Conference require implementation on a unilateral or bilateral basis. There is very little demand for multilateral implementation. Any follow-up will thus be primarily concerned with multilateral assessments of where we have got to and multilateral discussions of where we might go next, but not with multilateral efforts to do anything together. This reinforces our argument that the West should not be afraid of follow-up.

R.A. BURNS[12]

[12] On 28 March Mr. Tickell minuted to Mr. Morgan on this document: 'The latest version of the report is a great improvement, and needs only one or two small changes. On the points raised above by Mr. Burns: (*a*) the interim period: I agree with his conclusion. (*b*) I am not sure whether it would be wise to press for agreement in principle at the Conference to regular meetings in future. On para. 28 of the report, I think I prefer it in its original form, less the phrase *cas par cas* which gives too ad hoc an implication. I suggest we leave things as they are in our discussion among the Nine, and allow other CSCE participants to make the running on this point when the time comes. (*c*) review conference: I agree with Mr. Burns on place and length of meeting, but doubt if the Political Directors will be in a position to reach any conclusion on the Community aspect at their meeting on 8/9 April. After all we shall be writing the briefs for you and Sir M. Palliser [UK Permanent Representative to the EC, Brussels] (for his meeting on 10 April) and will make sure they are consistent. 2. I still feel that much more work is required on the simple practical problem of how the results of the Conference are to be put into effect. Mr. Burns could perhaps raise this at the Sub. Cttee. on 3 April, and repeat our previous suggestion that this is the sort of nuts-and bolts problem on which the NATO Secretariat could make a very useful contribution.'

No. 117

Minute from Mr. Tickell on CSCE: Easter Break[1]

[*WDW 1/22*]

Confidential   FCO, *27 March 1975*

Sir David Hildyard's telegrams Nos. 187[2] and 188[3] provide a useful statement of the state of play in Geneva as the participants in Stage II of the CSCE take a short break for Easter. I add the following comments.

[1] This minute was addressed to Mr. Morgan, Sir J. Killick and the Private Secretary. The CSCE took a long weekend from 27 March to 1 April, rather than the usual week's break.

[2] This telegram of 22 March examined the tactical situation at Geneva. Sir D. Hildyard explained that the Soviet delegation appeared 'to be searching rather desperately for ways of moving while making minimum concessions', that Mr. Kovalev was in 'a highly nervous state', and that bilaterally he and Mr. Dubinin were 'exerting maximum pressure, often disagreeably' wherever they thought it might be effective. He concluded that the pattern of recent weeks seemed to confirm that only patience and firmness over long periods achieved reasonably satisfactory results for the West, though he added that where Basket III was concerned, the Russians had vowed so often that they could 'never consent' that 'if they reach any genuinely final positions while we are still hoping for more it may not be easy for us to distinguish the signals'.

[3] This telegram of 22 March reviewed the situation in the individual Baskets on the eve of the Easter break.

2. The Western and neutral countries are not in a bad bargaining position. By suggesting 30 June as the date for beginning the third stage, Mr. Brezhnev has once again put his delegation in the invidious position of working against a self-imposed deadline. Moreover the Russians have attracted much criticism for having sought to impose a deadline in top-level communications with a few of the major Powers without respect for the wishes of the smaller ones.[4] On the spot the Soviet delegation has contrived to offend almost all other delegations (and on the Western side particularly the French) by its handling of the programme of future work. Neutral and Western delegations are by contrast in better heart. They see the beginnings of a Soviet retreat, and in my judgment the difficulty will be as much to persuade them not to press the Russians too hard as to find the necessary compromises. The next round of meetings of the Nine takes place early next month: the CSCE Sub-Committee in Geneva on 3 April and the Political Directors in Dublin on 8 and 9 April. We shall then do our best to encourage the others to demonstrate the flexible behaviour asked of them by their Heads of Government earlier this month.[5]

3. Substantial progress has been recorded on three major issues. Agreement to the text of peaceful change of frontiers is not yet complete, and haggling is continuing over precisely where the text should go into Principle One; but by and large it should now be possible to concentrate on the other oustanding issues in the Declaration of Principles, especially the search for a good text on the inter-relationship between them.[6] The Russians have at last conceded that in the Ninth Principle on Co-operation between States there should be a clear reference to the role of the individual. After nine months of sterile discussion the Russians seem ready to talk sensibly about arrangements for the prior notification of manoeuvres: in this respect we are doing our best to persuade our Allies and the neutrals (some of whom are standing out for a more binding obligation than we think the Russians will

---

[4] See No. 115, note 3.

[5] At the Dublin summit of 10-11 March EC Heads of Government pronounced themselves in favour of 'as rapid a conclusion as possible' of the work of the CSCE. 'To this end', their *communiqué* stated, 'they intend to continue and intensify their efforts to seek, in an open and constructive spirit, positive solutions to the problems which are still under discussion or outstanding' (see No. 115, note 5). The meeting of Political Directors on 8-9 April made little progress on outstanding CSCE points. They did, however, discuss inconclusively the Sub-Committee's report on follow-up (see No. 116), focusing upon the precise date for a review meeting and the extent to which the Nine should acknowledge that the holding of regular meetings remained an option. They also affirmed their support for the Danish draft resolution (telegrams Nos. 123 and 124 to UKMIS Geneva of 10 April, WDW 1/24).

[6] The French, as Sir D. Hildyard explained in his telegram No. 188 (see note 3 above), were withholding their assent to the registration of the latest text on the peaceful change until agreement had been reached on texts covering quadripartite rights and responsibilities and the inter-relationship between principles. Meanwhile, neutral and non-aligned countries continued to object to the French formula on QRR and, while some seemed ready to accept the necessity of such a text, they evidently resented the idea of yielding to a big-power *Diktat* on the subject.

even accept) to seize the opportunities now presented.[7]

4. It is a pity that these signs of movement in Basket I have no clear parallel in Basket III where the Russians seem to be having renewed difficulty in agreeing with their allies on how best to reflect Western and neutral demands for clear commitments to improve the lot of the individual in the field of human contacts and information. In some cases the Russians have gone back on provisional agreements previously registered.[8] By contrast the outstanding issues in Basket II—largely over language to govern MFN and reciprocity —seem unlikely to present serious problems: it is generally accepted that the CSCE is not the place to negotiate any major changes in trade policy.[9]

5. I think Sir David Hildyard is right to be cautious about the likely duration of Stage II.[10] All Western delegations are working to complete the work of the Conference to permit the holding of the third stage in the summer, and our own Delegation has assumed an increasingly active and central role in negotiating texts with the Russians on behalf of the West. But even if the Russians continue to show flexibility in Basket I and, as we hope, extend it to Basket III, the remaining work will still take much time and effort. Many of the issues cut across traditional East/West lines, and neutral dislike of Great Power pressure has been well demonstrated by the resistance they have put up to the formula agreed between the French, British, Americans, Germans and Russians to safeguard Quadripartite Rights and Responsibilities.[11] Moreover there are such other problems as the Turkish refusal to recognise the credentials of the Cyprus Government,[12] the

---

[7] See No. 115, note 1.

[8] But Sir D. Hildyard admitted (see note 3 above) that only in the Culture Sub-Committee was the situation clearly unsatisfactory. 'Whereas in the other three Sub-Committees negotiations could', he wrote, 'given one or two Soviet concessions, be wound up rather rapidly, in Culture the discussions are still in a confused state and the sides far apart.'

[9] An attached summary of outstanding issues (see note 15 below) pointed out that the East were trying to obtain a text which would strengthen their claim to *de jure* MFN treatment on all aspects of trade by extending the definition to embrace not merely the tariffs covered by GATT but also quota restrictions. The Nine, on the other hand, wished to reserve the grant of *de jure* MFN treatment and any widening of its scope as bargaining counters in the negotiations which they hoped would ultimately take place between the EC and CMEA. At the same time the Nine wished to extract a clear statement on the need for, and scope of, reciprocity in the conduct of trade. Matters were further complicated by the demands of the Romanians and Turks that the CSCE take account of the interests of developing countries.

[10] In his telegram No. 187 (see note 2 above) Sir D. Hildyard noted that it was still possible that Stage II could be concluded in time for Stage III at the end of June or in early July. But he thought the end of July a more realistic date.

[11] See No. 113, note 6.

[12] The Turks had recently circulated a letter to all participants in the CSCE warning them that 'serious complications' would arise if Cyprus were represented at Stage III by Greek Cypriots. British officials assumed that this was probably designed to counter statements made by Greeks and Cypriots in the autumn of 1974 to the effect that they would not be prepared to agree to Stage III if there had been no progress towards a solution of the Cyprus question (UKMIS Geneva telegrams Nos. 191 and 200 of 24 and 26 March; letter from Mr. Figgis to Mr. Laver of 2 April; WDW 1/13). See No. 97, note 2.

intransigence of the Maltese in defence of Mr. Mintoff's proposal for a Euro/Arab federation,[13] and the shadow now cast by the crisis in Portugal.[14]

6. I attach a summary statement of the issues which remain to be resolved.[15] A clear review of how matters stand may not be available until the middle of next month.

7. At the Heads of Government meeting of the Nine in Dublin and more recently to Dr. Kissinger, the Secretary of State proposed that the level of the forthcoming NATO Foreign Ministers' Meeting might be raised to that of Heads of Government. It is not of course certain that Stage II will be finished by the end of May although, if there is to be a CSCE Summit in July, it must be within sight of completion. If, contrary to our hopes and expectations, things were to go wrong in Geneva and got bogged down for whatever reason, then we would presumably have to think again about the value of a NATO summit. Hence we should, I think, continue to keep all discussion of the possibility confidential: a public reference or commitment to it could impale us on the same sort of hook as that on which Mr. Brezhnev has now impaled the Russians. This is a question which might be profitably discussed when the Foreign Ministers of the Nine next meet in April.

C.C.C. Tickell

[13] See No. 108, note 16. At the initiative of the Nine good progress had been made in preparing a declaration dealing with the interests of non-participating Mediterranean states (cf. No. 90, note 4), but, as the attached summary of outstanding issues indicated (see note 15 below), no-one was sure that Mr. Mintoff would be satisfied with its 'fairly minimal character'.

[14] Revolutionary developments in Portugal, which began with the overthrow of the authoritarian administration of Dr. M. Caetano in the spring of 1974, brought to power a Government in which Socialists and Communists were strongly represented. Subsequent Government measures aimed at excluding centre and right-wing parties from the political process raised fears in the West of possible Soviet involvement. The FRG even suggested that the West should make it clear to the Russians that if Portuguese politics continued to move in this direction, Stage III would be called into question.

[15] Not printed. This summary also recorded that a working group had been set up to consider arrangements for Stage III.

No. 118

Sir D. Hildyard (UKMIS Geneva) to Mr. Callaghan

No. 262 Telegraphic [WDW 1/22]

Priority. Confidential GENEVA, *19 April 1975, 8.50 a.m.*

Repeated for Information to Washington, Moscow, UKDEL NATO and UKDEL Strasbourg and Saving to EEC Posts, Helsinki and Berne.

CSCE: State of Play

General

1. Although there has been substantial movement during the last few weeks on a few major issues, we have not been able to make any progress on the

remaining important points. After some difficulties, the discussions on CBMs are now going ahead reasonably satisfactorily,[1] but this week there has again been no substantive advance on Principle 10 or in Baskets II or III. The Russians, however, are clearly still in a great hurry to finish off the Conference, and we have agreed on a number of contacts next week to see how we can push things on.

2. In the Co-ordinating Committee on 17 April Kovalev drew attention to what he described as the important reference to CSCE in Gromyko's report to the CPSU Central Committee Plenum (Moscow tel[egram] No. 599).[2] In the course of a talk on Thursday evening he asked me how long I thought agreement on CBMs would take, and what the chances were of finishing Stage II by the end of May. I said that given goodwill on both sides, CBMs need not take too long, but QRR looked like being difficult,[3] and there were a number of total impasses in Basket III.[4] He said that the Soviet move on CBMs seemed to have been a mistake as it had only led to increased pressure in Basket III. I said that, on the contrary, it had improved the atmosphere, and made the negotiations in Basket III easier. Pressure was bound to build up on everyone as we moved into the final stages.[5] He

[1] The Soviet proposal for a 'voluntary system with middle of the road parameters' for the prior notification of manoeuvres (see No. 115, note 1) proved, despite some inflexibility on the part of the Dutch, generally acceptable to the Fifteen. Indeed, the crumbling of initial neutral resistance to a voluntary system encouraged the Russians to press hard for its acceptance before the discussion of parameters (UKMIS Geneva telegrams Nos. 188 and 240 of 22 March and 12 April). Finally, on 11 April, it was agreed that the relevant Sub-Committee should deal in parallel with both the voluntary concept and parameters (UKDEL NATO telegram No. 152 of 26 March and UKMIS Geneva telegrams Nos. 220 and 241 of 5 and 12 April, WDW 1/4).

[2] According to this telegram of 17 April Mr. Gromyko's report, which was delivered that day, referred to the special significance of the early and successful conclusion of the CSCE in giving the *détente* process 'an irreversible character'. Mr. Gromyko added that 'the imperialist policy of the Cold War [was] suffering a defeat', but that 'the forces of war, reaction and aggression' had not stopped their efforts to disrupt 'positive processes' (ENS 1/1).

[3] The French remained reluctant to consider even minor modifications to the text on QRR which they had tabled in December (see *Human Rights*, vol. iii, p. 138). But Sir D. Hildyard thought the neutrals and non-aligned to be moving towards accepting the need for some general formula on the lines of the French draft. There was also the problem of the location of the text, but UKMIS Geneva telegram No. 240 (see note 1 above) reported growing support for the idea of placing it in the final clauses rather than in Principle 10.

[4] A WOD 'State of Play' paper of 18 April instanced the case of the Information Sub-Committee where the main issues were the West's concern for a clear preambular reference to the desirability of the dissemination of, and access to, information, and the right of individuals to be informed. The East, by contrast, was concerned to refer to the content of information covered by the text and to the responsibility for it of states (WDW 1/23).

[5] In a minute to the Private Secretary of 18 April Mr. Tickell observed: 'Soviet tactics at this point fit into a classic pattern. The Russians are seeking to generate irresistible momentum towards an early summit Stage III while reducing the number of outstanding issues to which they attach real importance. In this way they may hope to force a showdown in which it is the Western and neutral countries, with most points of importance then outstanding in particular in Basket III, which have to sacrifice essential objectives' (WDW 1/23).

expressed some resentment on the belated US interest and pressure, especially on conditions for journalists,[6] and suggested that Dubinin and Alexander should meet again early next week to explore the possibilities again in Basket III.[7] Dubinin then joined us, and expressed some doubts. Eventually we all agreed they should resume exploratory talks keeping in close touch with the Americans. I had the impression that Kovalev was casting around for ways of moving ahead and hoping to use us, while Dubinin thought (as does Alexander) that the Americans were likely to play the major role at least on journalists.

3. By agreement with Scherer [*sic*] and myself, André (France) saw Kovalev yesterday morning on QRR. André said Paris had come to the conclusion that the present text was not negotiable and had authorised him to discuss with the other three Powers concerned the possibility of some qualification of the word 'responsibilities'. As expected, Kovalev was unforthcoming but he suggested that he, André, Scherer [*sic*] and myself should meet to review the position. As André is in a hotel, I have suggested that we should all dine in my house with one adviser each on 25 April, when we could try to run through the main outstanding issues.[8] I think that the Russians have hoisted in that if they want to make progress they must move on further points as they have done already on PCF and CBMs. We have implied that we will do our best to respond.

See MIFT for state of individual baskets.[9]

[6] Discussions on working conditions for journalists in the Information Sub-Committee were proceeding on the basis of a Swiss (though, according to Mr. M. Alexander, largely Soviet inspired) text tabled on 19 December 1974 (see *Human Rights*, vol. v, pp. 154-5). US delegates had recently begun to take an increasingly tough line on this issue, seeking amendments intended to cover contacts between journalists and individuals, the time factor, technical staff and expulsion. Mr. Alexander predicted that this firmer American stance would 'certainly serve to make the negotiations more difficult and prolonged but may also enable us to get a somewhat better text in the end' (letter to Mr. Burns of 11 April, EN 2/557/5).

[7] A subsequent meeting between Sir D. Hildyard, Mr. M. Alexander and Mr. Dubinin which was held on 24 April proved singularly inconclusive (UKMIS Geneva telegram No. 295 of 26 April).

[8] The four-power dinner on 25 April concentrated entirely on QRR. The three Western participants argued that some minimal modification of the French text should now be considered in order to overcome neutral and non-aligned opposition. The Russians, according to Sir D. Hildyard, initially favoured the 'big stick', but eventually agreed to report to Moscow, without commitment, the Western view that some qualification for the word 'responsibilities' would be needed to make the text negotiable (UKMIS Geneva telegram No. 296 of 26 April, WDW 1/2). In telegram No. 159 to UKMIS Geneva of 30 April Mr. Callaghan informed Sir D. Hildyard that in the FCO's view the time had come for the Bonn Group countries in Geneva to try to agree upon a modified text which had a better chance of success with the neutrals and non-aligned. The Russian desire to press ahead in Basket I could, he noted, 'make them receptive to a formula which commanded greater support in the rest of the Conference' (WDW 1/2).

[9] Not printed.

No. 119

Letter from Mr. M. Alexander (UKMIS Geneva) to Mr. Burns

[*EN 2/557/5*]

Confidential   GENEVA, *25 April 1975*

Dear Andrew,

Basket III: Human Contacts and Information

1. As far as East/West discussions are concerned, this has been an uneventful week. No new texts have been tabled and, with one exception, no agreements have been reached. If anything positions on both sides have tended to harden.

2. In large part this has been because the Russians, while continuing to evince anxiety about the rate of progress, have shown no readiness to make the concessions which, as they well know, will alone make progress possible.[1] However, the stalemate this week has also been in part the result of the hard line being taken by the West on all the texts under discussion. I have been encouraging this latter trend, which has its origin in the American attitude on the journalist's text[2] because, I believe, the moment is approaching when we should offer the Russians the option of a global solution to the outstanding problems in I and J[3] and because, prior to any such initiative, we should adopt a rather hard attitude.

3. My analysis starts from the fact that the attitude of the Russians, at least in Basket III, suggest they are still hoping to adhere to Brezhnev's time table.[4] If so they must realise that time is getting very short. As long as there is a chance of having a Summit in July they may be prepared to pay a relatively significant price for major progress in that direction. (At the point when they abandon hope of meeting Brezhnev's deadline, their attitude may of course harden significantly.) The completion of work in I and J (as well as L)[5], would represent major progress by any standard.

4. I am therefore working to persuade my colleagues, and have made good progress in doing so, that we should give to Dubinin at the end of next

---

[1] Sir D. Hildyard reported in telegram No. 295 of 26 April (see No. 118, note 7) that the Russians still could not bring themselves to make substantive concessions for fear, they implied, that these would 'merely be swallowed up by the West and base lines shifted against them'. He thought that they were also concerned lest a move in one sector, by casting doubt on their resolve, increase pressure in others. 'The main Western powers', he added, 'are agreed that we should let them stew for a little longer, but that at the same time we should prepare to make moves ourselves which would be conditional on satisfactory responses from them.'

[2] See No. 118, note 6.

[3] Sub-Committees I and J dealt respectively with Human Contacts and Information. See Appendix I.

[4] In the FCO it was assumed that the main motive of the Russians was to hold things up on Basket III issues and military CBMs until they achieved what they wanted on the Declaration of Principles (telegram No. 160 to UKMIS Geneva of 30 April, WDW 1/22).

[5] The Education Sub-Committee.

week or the beginning of the following week a single document containing all texts on Human Contacts and Information. This would include the chapter headings and sub-titles and would have no square brackets in it. On the outstanding texts I would envisage compromise language on the Human Contacts mini-preamble (text enclosed already discussed with French, Germans and Americans);[6] a compromise text on travel (text next week); a new text on the Information mini-preamble (copy enclosed already discussed with French, Germans and Americans);[6] a completed text on radio and TV incorporating the new American language (text enclosed)[6] and a tough text on journalists (copy enclosed).[6] I would envisage telling Dubinin that this document was a response to his repeated (and disengenuous [*sic*]) requests for a clear statement and what the West wanted. We would be grateful if he could study it for 24 hours and tell us what difficulties he saw in it. We would be prepared to consider a reasonable number of amendments but if his demands struck us as excessive we would withdraw the global text and continue with the negotiations on the basis of our existing well-known positions. If, following its withdrawal, Dubinin referred to our compromise texts at multilateral meetings, we would respond by tabling 'maximalist', statements of Western positions. If, on the other hand, Dubinin's response was moderate, we would hope to be able to negotiate to a rapid conclusion on the basis of the global approach.

5. An approach on these lines, while not without risks, would, I believe, place Dubinin in a difficult position. He would have to choose between in effect placing the July Summit in considerable jeopardy (assuming the Russians still want it then) or making some real gesture towards the West and thereby bringing the July Summit markedly closer to realisation. In either case it would be more difficult for him thereafter to lay the blame for lack of progress in Basket III on the Western side.

6. I would be grateful for very early warning if you see any difficulties in this approach.[7] It may fail, before or after the meeting with Dubinin, for all sorts of obvious reasons, but I think it is worth having a go. The Ambassador agrees.

Tourism

7. The only agreement of the week was the mental registration of the text

---

[6] Not printed.

[7] Telegram No. 160 to UKMIS Geneva (see note 4 above) informed Sir D. Hildyard that the FCO agreed to the idea of putting together some of the outstanding issues in Basket III and suggesting a 'package solution'. But it also pointed out that the West would have to avoid giving ground for neutral or Romanian complaints about a bloc-to-bloc arrangement and take particular care about timing. 'From here', the telegram stated, 'it seems best to wait until progress begins on the present cluster of problems in the Declaration of Principles, but you are the best judge of the tactical opportunities.'

on tourism (my letter of 26 March refers).[8] This was made possible after the Italians, under 'intense' Soviet pressure here (and, I infer, in Rome) agreed to registration with an oral reservation linking their final agreement to the solution of the problem of titles and sub-titles. The Italians, I fear, had only themselves to blame for the position in which they found themselves.

Yours ever,

M.O'D.B. ALEXANDER

PS: Since dictating the above I have seen your valuable letter of 24 April on the journalist's text.[9] I will of course take this into account in developing our position, and the journalist's text in particular, next week.

[8] Mr. Alexander enclosed with this letter a text committing participants to the promotion of the development of tourism on an individual or collective basis. Registration of the text was delayed largely because of Italian demands that it refer to improving 'human contacts' rather than just 'contacts' (EN 2/557/7).

[9] In this letter Mr. Burns expressed his regret that the Swiss text (see No. 118, note 6) had had the effect of distracting attention from the key British objective of ensuring that journalists should not be liable to expulsion for reasons arising specifically from their legitimate professional activity. And he wondered whether Mr. Alexander's 'best tack' might not now be to exploit Soviet resistance to adequate language on expulsion and technical staff in order to obtain recognition of the right of journalists to go about their legitimate business without fear of their writing or journalistic activities being used against them. Mr. Burns added that the FCO continued to believe that a reference to 'technical staff' was more important than one to 'expulsion', on the principle that it was 'more important to get people in than to stop them being expelled'.

No. 120

Minute from Mr. Burns to Mr. Tickell

[*WDW 1/22*]

Confidential   FCO, *29 April 1975*

CSCE State of Play[1]

1. The news from Geneva is not good at the moment and the weekend's crop of telegrams require us to send the delegation some guidance on:

(*a*) Basket III

(*b*) QRR

(*c*) Confidence Building Measures

2. I attach a draft telegram dealing with Basket III and CBMs[2] and a

[1] Mr. Tickell marked-up this paper to Mr. Morgan and Sir J. Killick. He noted: 'You should see this useful analysis with which I agree. The telegrams have gone off: copies of the final versions are within. At some point we should consider whether the time is not coming for the S. of S. to call in the Soviet Ambassador & read him the riot act. On this we are consulting the Delegation in Geneva. Crispin Tickell 30/iv.'

[2] This was despatched as telegram No. 160 to UKMIS Geneva (see No. 119, notes 4 and 7).

second draft telegram dealing with QRR.[3]

3. It may however be useful to set out in broad terms the present negotiations position in Geneva.

4. First, the *facts*. In Basket III not a single word has been registered since the Easter break and attitudes have hardened on all sides. The main outstanding issues are the politically sensitive ones of working conditions for journalists, access to information, freer travel and the general objectives for human contacts and information. The Delegation's efforts to find common ground have not recently been successful; the Russians show no inclination to negotiate and some tendency to argue that the information issues can best be solved in bilateral discussions between them and the Americans.

5. In the Declaration of Principles, a number of the most important issues are interlinked: PCF, the inter-relationship of principles, a text on QRR, the texts of Principles X and I and the introductory language of commitment will not be resolved independently but only as part of a composite (probably messy) package compromise. At the moment the most intractable problem is QRR. The Russians are showing great keenness to settle the QRR language, but are not willing to show the necessary flexibility in the drafting of a text. Mr. Laver says that there is no question of there being agreement to a quadripartite interpretative statement as an alternative solution, but it is hard indeed to see how, without accepting seriously insufficient language, we can square the circle of:

(*a*) protecting the continuing validity of QRRs without referring to them specifically, and

(*b*) avoiding any implication that we condone the Brezhnev doctrine of limited sovereignty.

6. In Confidence Building Measures, the Russians are insistent that they will not be specific about the concessions which they profess to be ready to make on the parameters without a clear Western statement that we are willing to accept notification 'on a voluntary basis'. The West has tabled a text which explains in clear and tight terms what we mean by a 'voluntary' basis (without using that word)[4] and has subsequently indicated its willingness in principle to continue the discussion in due course on the basis of a Yugoslav amendment which does include a specific reference to the voluntary basis.[5] Nevertheless, the Russians and their allies are still maintaining that this is not sufficient.

[3] This was despatched as telegram No. 159 to UKMIS Geneva (see No. 118, note 8).

[4] One problem raised by the Americans with regard to the use of the term 'voluntary' in the context of CBMs was that it implied that participants must have intended commitments not so described to be other than voluntary. The Western text, which the Italians proposed on 21 April, recognised 'the individual responsibility of each state in the realisation of their common objectives of strengthening confidence through prior notification of major military manoeuvres' (note for the record, Sub-Committee 2, 21 April; letter from Mr. Burns to Mr. Carter of 24 April; WDW 1/4).

[5] On 22 April the Yugoslav representative on Sub-Committee 2 indicated that he was prepared to see the 'magic words' included, 'but on condition that the commitment to notify

7. In Basket II the Commission is engaged in sounding out with the Russians possible language for MFN and reciprocity. The negotiations which are going painfully slowly appear to reflect a Soviet assessment that time is in their favour.

8. The discussion on follow-up is virtually stalemated. Delegations are discussing the operative part of a resolution dealing with the precise arrangements for follow-up, but there is no sign yet of any common ground or of any hurry to find a solution.

9. Now, Soviet *motives*. I continue to feel that the main Soviet motive is to mark time in Basket III until they have won what they need in the Declaration of Principles.[6] They have always seen Basket III in the context of the Declaration of Principles, but have never sought to make concessions in the Declaration contingent on Basket III concessions by the West. Their present tactic would reflect not only their desire not to make important concessions in Basket III until they have achieved their primary objectives in the Declaration; but also their plan, once the Declaration of Principles had been got out of the way, to force the West into sacrificing some of its Basket III objectives in an effort to conclude the Conference quickly. Soviet tactics towards follow-up are consistent with this in that they seem to be avoiding any showdown there both because they realise the strength of Western opposition to their ideas for permanent machinery and thus do not wish to prolong the Conference with an unproductive debate; and because they do not wish to give the West an excuse for further delay by provoking a confrontation on follow-up.

10. I believe that the Russians share our desire that the work of the Military Sub-Committee should not be left until the last moment. Unlike the Basket III texts, which are more diffuse in character, the language in the Military Sub-Committee is tight and precise; the scope for fudging the issues at the last moment is therefore very much less than in the other contentious parts of the Conference. It must be admitted however that present Soviet tactics in the Military Sub-Committee are consistent with a desire to entice the West on to ever weaker ground with the intention of forcing us to negotiate the details at the eleventh hour. The Russians are well on their way to obtaining Western agreement to a voluntary basis to prior notification at the expense of unconfirmed professions of flexibility and the concession (always inevitable) of notification to all participating states.

11. *How should we react?* I believe that we are right to do what we can to push the negotiation forward in each area where it is deadlocked. Not in order to reassure the Russians of our willingness to negotiate (the Russian line

was firm and unambiguous, and that the voluntary basis meant only that States entered into this firm commitment of their own free will'. Three days later, the UK delegates stated that they could accept a Yugoslav text which referred explicitly to notification on a 'voluntary basis' (letter from Mr. Carter to Mr. Figgis of 23 April; UKMIS Geneva telegram No. 294 of 26 April; WDW 1/4).

[6] Mr. Tickell sidelined this sentence and noted in the margin: 'I agree'.

recorded in paragraph 1 of UKMIS Geneva tel[egram] No. 295[7] seems to me thoroughly disingenuous), but in order to seize the initiative. I think this is particularly true in Confidence Building Measures where there is in my view the prospect of a break-through provided that the Russians are prepared to recognise the need for balanced progress. The instructions in our telegram No. 148[8] were designed to maintain the momentum by seizing the initiative at little cost to ourselves in the negotiation of the parameters. We may have to re-think them if the Russians go back on their agreement to negotiate the 'voluntary basis' and the parameters side by side.

12. We have also for some time been trying to push matters forward on QRR. We have at least and at last got the French to recognise the need for flexibility and I hope that the West can now agree upon a revised draft, in the light of our tel[egram] No. 151[9] and subsequent telephone conversations.

13. I agree with the Delegation that it is worth adopting a similarly forward approach in Basket III. Mr. Alexander tells me that the strategy outlined in UKMIS Geneva tel[egram] No. 295 and his letter to me of 25 April[10] has not won immediate acceptance amongst Western delegations, but that before addressing the tactics the Nine and the Fifteen are trying to agree upon the kind of texts which might appear in a package deal.[11] This is right since not all the texts Mr. Alexander has sent us match up to the need to provide some tangible concessions while preserving room for subsequent manoeuvre. It is to be noted however that the Basket III negotiations are

[7] See No. 119, note 1.

[8] This telegram of 24 April considered the time right for the West to make a 'limited but meaningful' step towards the middle ground of the parameters of notification, suggesting the following concessions: '(a) Timing: a substantial move, e.g. to 30 days. (b) Threshold: a move calculated to promote eventual consensus on 20,000 men, e.g. a reinforced division or 15,000 troops, with a clear statement that notification would be required when either threshold was reached. (c) Area: a substantial public move which stays within the NATO guidelines but leaves room for further bilateral negotiation, e.g. 500 kms from the European frontiers of the USSR, provided that all the rest of Europe was included (though we would envisage special arrangements for Turkey). We should be prepared to go to 400 kms if our allies preferred'. It was hoped that this would keep Mr. Mendelevich 'in play' and oblige him to explain the specific concessions he had in mind (WDW 1/4).

[9] This telegram of 25 April discussed the various modifications which had been proposed to the French tabled-text on QRR (see No. 118, note 3). The FCO's preferred amendment was to omit from this 'responsibilities' and 'or which concern them' (WDW 1/2).

[10] See No. 119.

[11] Mr. M. Alexander discussed his letter of 25 April with Mr. Burns over the telephone. In a subsequent letter of 29 April he told Mr. Burns that he had found a meeting of the Nine on 28 April more difficult than he had expected. He had been under the impression that he had secured the agreement of Heer van der Valk to the global approach, but at the meeting of the Nine the Dutch delegate had repeated his country's familiar view that the West should 'stonewall' the Russians with a view to outbargaining them in the *'marchandage final'*. Mr. Alexander added that, as so often happened on these occasions, Heer van der Valk's 'general approach did not get much support, but in discussion of the actual texts, individual delegations in effect supported his attitude by their extreme reluctance to give up individual points to which they attach[ed] importance' (EN 2/557/7).

deadlocked. There is no momentum at present and it is far from certain that a take it or leave it package deal will suffice to get matters moving again.

14. We should recognise that it is probably the Russian strategy to refuse to make effective concessions in Basket III, and perhaps also on CBMs, until the outstanding pieces of the Declaration of Principles have begun to fall into place. We should recognise too that it will not be easy to persuade our partners and allies to take the kind of bold step advocated in our tel[egram] No. 148[12] on CBMs and Mr. Alexander's letter to me of 25 April.

15. There may be little alternative therefore but to sit out the confrontation, making painfully slow progress, but underlining again and again to the East that if they do not adopt a more flexible and constructive approach fairly quickly, the NATO summit[13] will be faced with a pretty lamentable state of affairs in Geneva; and that this could risk provoking a Western decision that the Russians were not serious in their wish to bring the Conference to an end this summer on terms which the West could accept.[14] It would follow from any such decision that Stage III could not be held until the autumn at the earliest.[15]

R.A. BURNS

[12] See note 8 above.

[13] The NAC met at Heads of Government level on 29-30 May. See Cmnd. 6932, pp. 203-4.

[14] In his letter to Mr. Burns of 29 April (see note 11 above) Mr. M. Alexander speculated that since, at a working level, the Russian line was tougher than ever, the West may already have missed the chance to make a major breakthrough, and the Russians might be preparing to sit the Conference out to the 'bitter end, even at the expense of postponing the summit until the autumn'. But he thought that it might still make sense to adopt the global approach as a means of demonstrating where the blame lay for the lack of progress.

[15] In UKMIS telegram No. 312 of 2 May Sir D. Hildyard seemed far less pessimistic. He was of the opinion that Russians 'would like to press ahead in all Baskets'. 'Their tough line in Basket III', he observed, 'probably reflects a wish to demonstrate that they are not under time pressure combined with an inability to see how to move forward without making unilateral concessions rather than a desire to hold things up until they get what they want on principles.' He pointed out that the West had firmed up their demands on journalists and the Russians had as usual responded by taking a step backward. On the other hand, Mr. Kovalev had been anxious to get Mr. Dubinin and Mr. Alexander talking again, and at lunch on 1 May had asked how they could quicken the tempo in Baskets II and III.

No. 121

Sir D. Hildyard (UKMIS Geneva) to Mr. Callaghan

No. 330 Telegraphic [WDW 1/22]

Priority. Confidential   GENEVA, *8 May 1975, 6 p.m.*

Repeated for Information to Washington, Moscow, UKDEL NATO, Bonn, Paris, and Saving to other EEC Posts, Helsinki, Berne.

CSCE: State of Play

1. Mendelevich returned to Moscow briefly last weekend and saw

Gromyko. He called on me this morning primarily to discuss CBMs and told me that he had been given a certain amount of additional flexibility. He pointed to the inter-relationship between the principles (para. 4 of MIFT)[1] and said he could move further on CBMs when there had been more progress on the voluntary concept (my letter of 8 May to Figgis).[2] He also implied that the Russians could be flexible in regard to the French document.[3]

2. After the Co-ordinating Committee yesterday Kovalev spoke to a number of Heads of Western delegations including myself with great optimism about the chances of reaching early agreement: he told some that the Soviet Government had decided to make a great effort to finish the Conference by the first or second week in June, Stage III following in Helsinki in July. The Eastern delegations seem to be in a state of near euphoria and Kovalev himself is a different man. The Russians are tough and slippery negotiators but so far they have shown themselves bad actors. The delegation may be relieved because they think that the fear of criticism from Moscow (for the recent lack of movement) has been lifted, but I have the impression that they really believe that they can now go far enough to meet us to make feasible an early conclusion of the Conference.[4] The end of Stage II at the end of June or early in July now seems much more than a possibility, although there are still plenty of problems ahead from the neutrals and non-aligned as well as from the Eastern side. The next two weeks will be critical. The NATO meeting will come at a good moment.[5] The Russians are likely to try to ensure that substantial progress has been made before it. We have argued that this is a powerful reason for pressing ahead with our initiative in

[1] Sir D. Hildyard reported in this telegram of 8 May that the Russians had made a 'major concession' in accepting a French tabled-text on the inter-relationship and equality of principles. But in a letter to Mr. Burns of 23 May Mr. Alexander observed that it looked increasingly 'as though the euphoria being displayed by Mendelevich after his visit to Moscow ... owed more to the boost given to his personal position (as the man who knows how to deal with the West) than to anything specific he brought back' (EN 2/557/7).

[2] In this letter Sir D. Hildyard noted that Mr. Mendelevich had repeated that additional Soviet flexibility on CBM parameters 'depended on a further step by the West towards acceptance, even if conditional, of the voluntary concept' (WDW 1/4).

[3] This line was subsequently amended by UKMIS Geneva telegram No. 332 of 9 May to read 'in regard to the final (repeat final) document'. The form and structure of the final document became increasingly important as Stage II entered its concluding phase. Western delegations wished to ensure that all of the Conference documents were given a comparable status (i.e. that the Declaration of Principles should not have a preeminent status) and that they were political and not juridical in character.

[4] In a letter to Mr. Burns of 2 May, in which he speculated on Soviet motives, Mr. M. Alexander stated that he still believed the global approach, 'correctly and *firmly* handled', provided 'the best way of smoking the Russians out'. It would also have the incidental advantage of making it easier for officials to present to Ministers Basket III problems in a clear and comprehensive manner (EN 2/557/7).

[5] See No. 120, note 13.

Basket III (para. 8 of MIFT).[6]

3. This afternoon the Nine discussed and agreed the oral report which the Irish Presidency will submit to the Political Committee. This will be circulated by Coreu[7] on 9 May. It will contain a reference to the general situation followed by sections on follow-up, the Final Act, the Maltese proposal and the organisation of the third Stage.

4. I am reporting separately the discussion on follow-up.[8] Decisions are now becoming urgent in the light of the likely acceleration of the negotiations.

5. The present position in regard to the Final Act is described in my tel[egram] No. 323.[9] As regards the Maltese proposal the French and Italians accepted our two amendments (as reported telephonically to Burns).[10] Other delegations were without instructions and could not agree that the paper should be submitted on behalf of all the Nine in Geneva: rather than suggest that we should become the third co-author, I said that we would indicate in the Political Committee our agreement to the paper with the two amendments. The organisation of the third Stage is likely to be raised informally at dinner. The Finns are suggesting opening on the Monday

[6] This telegram (see note 1 above) reported that little real progress had been made in the Basket III Sub-Committees that week, and that Soviet representatives, particularly in the information discussions, were in effect 'filibustering'. 'Speaking in private', Sir D. Hildyard observed, 'Dubinin continues to show signs of concern about the slow rate of progress overall and has asked more or less openly for Western help in getting the Soviet delegation out of the impasse into which they have got themselves.' In these circumstances Sir D. Hildyard thought it a pity that the attitude of one or two Western delegations, 'notably the Dutch', had made the process of agreeing on a global approach to human contacts and information (see No. 119) so protracted.

[7] EC telegraphic correspondence.

[8] Sir D. Hildyard reported in UKMIS Geneva telegram No. 334 of 9 May that after prolonged discussion on 7 and 8 May the Nine had agreed that the Presidency should report to the Political Committee two amendments to the Danish draft resolution on follow-up which many, if not all, of the neutrals favoured. These were: (1) that continuity after the 1977 meeting of senior officials should be ensured by the insertion of a reference to further such meetings; and (2) that the 1977 meeting should be preceded by a preparatory meeting to settle the agenda and timing (WDW 1/14).

[9] This telegram of 8 May (WDW 1/15) reported that the Dutch, with the consent of the Fifteen, had tabled the latest version of their draft cover note for the final document (see note 3 above). Already on 19 February the Dutch had tabled a draft final document which envisaged each of the participants signing a statement of what had happened at the CSCE, with all other resolutions and documents attached in an annex. See *Human Rights*, vol. iii, pp. 37-41.

[10] The Nine's CSCE Sub-Committee agreed on 23 April that the French and Italians should jointly produce a paper for the Political Committee setting out the various options for dealing with the Maltese proposal for a Euro-Arab federation (see No. 117, note 13). Mr. Figgis, who dubbed the resulting paper 'a monstrosity, with potential to waste even more time than the Maltese paper itself', subsequently suggested two amendments aimed at making it clear that the Nine shared US opposition to many of the ideas contained in the Maltese paper and that the Nine would consult fully with other Western delegations in dealing with the subject (UKMIS Geneva telegram No. 279 of 24 April; letter from Mr. B.E. Cleghorn (UKMIS Geneva) to Mr. Figgis of 30 April; letter from Mr. Figgis to Mr. Cleghorn of 6 May; WDW 1/13).

afternoon and continuing until the Friday evening, leaving three days at least for speeches, and a full morning or afternoon for the signature ceremony. The Dutch have given notice that they may also raise informally the question of translations.

6. MIFT reports the latest position in the various Baskets.[11]

[11] Not printed (see notes 1 and 6 above).

No. 122

Minute from Mr. Tickell on CSCE: Basket III[1]

[*EN 2/557/5*]

Confidential   FCO, *16 May 1975*

You will have seen from UKMIS Geneva telegram No. 343[2] that our Delegation in Geneva has at last presented the Russians with a package deal of texts on human contacts and information.[3] It has taken since Easter to persuade all our friends and allies that such a package deal, although itself within the limits of policies agreed by Ministers at successive meetings, was right and timely; but, although the Dutch professed still to be unhappy during the meeting of Political Directors in Dublin on 12 May,[4] the package deal now has the support of all Community and Western delegations and the leading neutrals.[5] With Sir J. Killick I today commended its terms to Mr. Semenov of the Soviet Embassy as a further effort on our part to bring the Conference to an early and satisfactory conclusion, and asked him so to report to his government. I gather that the US delegation in Geneva is

[1] This minute was addressed to Mr. Morgan, Sir J. Killick and the Private Secretary.

[2] In this telegram of 15 May, Sir D. Hildyard reported that the proposal for a 'global approach' to the outstanding issues in the Human Contacts and Information Sub-Committees (see No. 119) had been put to the Russians, and the latter had undertaken to respond in due course. Sir D. Hildyard added that he and other Western Heads of Mission would be trying to bring home to the Soviet delegation that this was a serious initiative and that, while there were other equally important issues outstanding, their response would have a substantial effect on their chances of achieving a summit before the summer break.

[3] The texts were handed to Mr. Dubinin on 15 May by a Western team lead by Mr. M. Alexander and his Danish colleague, Herr N. Helskov (letter from Mr. Alexander to Mr. Burns of 16 May).

[4] During the meeting of EC Political Directors at Dublin on 12-13 May Mr. Morgan asserted that a good opportunity had arisen for Western initiatives in Basket III and on CBMs and that he hoped it would not be missed. But Heer C. Rutten, Director-General for Political Affairs in the Dutch Foreign Ministry, said that he saw no need for a further show of flexibility from the Western side and that he had reservations about the proposed initiative in Basket III. Both Sig. Ducci and Viscount Davignon endorsed his remarks (Dublin telegram No. 257 of 13 May, WDW 1/24).

[5] Already in a letter of 13 May, Mr. M. Alexander had informed Mr. Burns that 'after further long hours of discussion, Western delegations, at expert level, [were] now agreed that the global approach should be tried'.

recommending that Dr. Kissinger should speak in its support when he sees Mr. Gromyko on 19 May.[6]

2. The Russians, who have been aware that this package deal has been under preparation, have not yet made any substantive comment. I imagine that there is some chance that they will wish to respond positively before the state of play at the Conference is reviewed by NATO Heads of Government at the end of the month.[7]

3. Recent reports indicate that the Russians are still very keen on concluding Stage II in time to hold Stage III before the summer holidays. Throughout the CSCE however they have shown themselves to be extremely sensitive about Western demands in the fields of human contacts and information, whose potential impact upon their form of society could be far reaching. They will naturally object to a number of the points contained within the package deal, but I think that they will welcome its global approach because it will enable them to see the full range of Western requirements in this area of the Conference agenda.

4. The package deal would present a good and satisfactory outcome for the West.[8] Its contents do not of course match up to all the hopes and ambitions which were expressed at the beginning of the Conference. The Russians have fought tenaciously to qualify the reference to freer movement, and the wider spread of information and the commitments to improve administrative practices in individual fields, such as visas or access to information, are somewhat less clear-cut than we should have liked. We must recognise however that in these fields Western Governments themselves have real problems of competence. For most countries in the West matters of information are not within the ordinary power of Governments, and in matters relating to travel in and out of our countries we and many of our allies have administrative requirements which would not be easy to relax.

5. Provided that the Russians do not exact too many changes in the attached texts[9]—and provided too that comparable results are achieved

[6] Dr. Kissinger and Mr. Gromyko met in Vienna on 19-20 May to discuss SALT, the Middle East and the CSCE.

[7] See No. 120, note 13.

[8] On 16 May Mr. Morgan noted on this minute: 'Our Delegation in Geneva is to be congratulated on its part in getting this package proposal agreed & tabled by the Western group. Not only the Dutch but the Belgian Political Director was scornful of the idea in Dublin last Monday [see note 4 above] & both assured me that our initiative had been stillborn for lack of Western support! Both Davignon & Rutten admit that their Ministers are considerably more positive in their view of CSCE than they are themselves—hence the apparent contradictions of Dutch & Belgian policy. It means that discussion in the Political Directors' Ctee. is often of doubtful value.' Sir J. Killick added that he had had 'the Czech and the East German' calling that afternoon (16 May), and that he had informed them in general terms of this development, 'underlining that it was a serious attempt to make progress and referring to the desirability of being able to demonstrate solid progress by the time of the NATO Summit'.

[9] Not printed. The texts, which were enclosed with Mr. Alexander's letter of 13 May (see note 5 above), included the titles, sub-titles and solutions for all square bracketed provisions of the human contacts and information items of Basket III. In addition, Mr. M. Alexander

elsewhere in the agenda of the Conference—I believe that the end results should provide a reasonable basis for a Western decision to go to a Summit Stage III.[10] I doubt whether it would yet be right for the Foreign Ministers of the Nine on 26 May or NATO Heads of Government on 29/30 May to make a firm judgment. But what is already clear is that the Western ability to obtain from the Conference some real changes in European relationships will depend upon the vigour with which we pursue the various decisions in following up the Conference.

C.C.C. TICKELL

prepared, at the request of the Fifteen, speaking notes for use when presenting the texts to the Russians. These explained that, for purposes of the experiment, the West were making many concessions. Texts relating to personal correspondence and bilateral mixed commissions were omitted; there was a reduced degree of engagement in the travel text; and there was no reference to individuals, people, access, or the value of information as such, in the revised mini-preamble on information. But the text on journalists contained few concessions to the East and, in a footnote, extended the definition of journalist to include persons 'regularly and professionally engaged as reporters, photographers, camera men or technicians of the press, radio, television or cinema in any participating State'.

[10] Mr. Callaghan wrote on this minute: 'Good. Pl. let me know the response.'

No. 123

Letter from Mr. M. Alexander (UKMIS Geneva) to Mr. Burns

[*EN 2/557/7*]

Confidential   GENEVA, *30 May 1975*

Basket III: Human Contacts and Information

1. The Russians, to continue the metaphor in last week's letter to you (paragraph 12),[1] now seem to be firmly on the hook. As reported in our telegram Number 369 of 28 May,[2] they have withdrawn a considerable

[1] In this letter of 23 May Mr. Alexander informed Mr. Burns that the Russians had replied to the West's 'global approach' on 21 and 22 May; that they had largely accepted the Western mini-preamble on human contacts with it emphasis on 'humanitarian' considerations; that they had adopted a much more negative approach to the text on travel; and that, where journalists' rights were concerned, they had rejected their extension to technical staff, provision for access to individual sources and Western language on expulsion. Mr. Alexander further explained that, while he had not discouraged his colleagues' initial verdict that the Soviet response was 'highly unsatisfactory', he personally felt that it contained 'evidence of a real effort on [the Russians'] part to move', and that the West needed to 'keep the heat on the Russians' who might well make further concessions if the West could 'sustain a united display of disappointment'. 'We need', he concluded, 'to try to get the Russians to impale themselves on the hook a good deal more firmly without provoking them to break the line or allowing our more hot-headed colleagues to cut it.'

[2] Sir D. Hildyard reported in this telegram that the Russians had substantially qualified their 'earlier and unsatisfactory response' to the Western initiative. They had, he stated, now agreed to accept: (1) all Western proposals for the structure, titles and sub-titles of the documents, with one negotiable exception; (2) almost the entire Western text on travel; and (3)

number of their original requests for amendments to the Western text of 15 May. I enclose a full list of the Soviet concessions.[3]

2. The circumstances of the Soviet climb-down were not without an element of drama. The Ambassador and Patrick Laver were due to have a QRR lunch with the Russians, French and Americans on Wednesday.[4] The Ambassador was told by Mendelevich in the course of the morning that the Russians were expecting new instructions and that Dubinin's appearance at the lunch would be a signal that the instructions had been received. Mendelevich asked the Ambassador that Patrick Laver[5] should attend so that there should be no sign that we had had any advance warning. In the event, Dubinin did appear but the conversation did not turn to Basket III matters at once. It was only after Kovalev had received a telephone call, followed by Kondrashev's[6] appearance with a telegram, that the Russians showed their hand. Dubinin was then given what must have been for him the galling task of reading out the list of points on which the Russians are now prepared to accept the language of 15 May text.[7]

3. We can of course only guess at the Russian motives in acting as they did. They must presumably have been impressed by the united front maintained by the West (with the partial exception of the French) in expressing their disappointment at the initial Soviet response.[8] The energetic but fruitless activities of the neutrals may also have been some help in so far as they helped to demonstrate conclusively that the West was not prepared to move. However, the extreme haste and evident disorder with which the Russians acted on Wednesday must, I think, be linked with the NATO Summit which, we have always assumed, must have loomed large in the Soviet thinking from the moment that it was announced My own view is that at the end the Russians were concerned rather to avoid a really bad *communiqué* than to get a good one, much as they would have liked the latter.[9] I base this on the fact that the Russians while eager to begin negotiations yesterday, which gave

the whole of the Western proposal on the expulsion of journalists These concessions did not, he thought, permit the West to say that a satisfactory result had been achieved or was in sight, but they did 'reduce the number of outstanding questions on human contacts and on information to manageable proportions'.

[3] Not printed.

[4] i.e. 28 May.

[5] Mr. Laver was mainly responsible for handling negotiations in the Principles Sub-Committee.

[6] Mr. S.A. Kondrashev [Kondrachev] was a member of the Soviet delegation.

[7] Mr. Alexander had reported in his letter of 23 May (see note 1 above) how on 20 May the Russians had made a 'major blunder', leaving it to junior officials to read out 'long lists of trivial (and occasionally absurd) amendments' to the West's human contacts proposals. 'Dubinin', he added, 'tried to score minor procedural points and had a couple of brisk exchanges with me as a result.'

[8] Mr. M. Alexander thought the Russians had been 'struck by the consistency of the message which [had] been coming through'. He understood from the US delegation that the speaking notes he had prepared for use with Mr. Dubinin (see No. 122, note 9) had served as the basis of what Dr. Kissinger had recently said to the Russians about the CSCE (*v. ibid.*).

[9] See No. 120, note 13.

them an opportunity to prove their good faith, did not press for prolonged negotiations or for a resumption today.

4. The role of Mendelevich in all this has been of some interest. I referred in last week's letter (paragraph 9)[10] to his evident disagreements with other members of his Delegation. I also mentioned speculation that his position might have been strengthened as a result of his recent visits to Moscow and Vienna. (I should have made it clear that this is Conference speculation and that more than one interpretation can be put on the outcome of his visit to Moscow). Talking to the Ambassador yesterday, Mendelevich asked Sir David whether he had not been a good prophet and went on to say that he had 'been more than a good prophet'. It is hard not to think that Dubinin's reputation in Moscow will have taken something of a knock as a result of the events of the last fortnight.

5. Even after Wednesday's concessions, there was at least one Western delegation, the Dutch, which remained doubtful about entering into negotiations on the basis of the 'global approach' However, once they were convinced that the Russians had in fact withdrawn rather over a third of their proposed amendments, they raised their objections. The first negotiating session therefore took place yesterday afternoon in the presence of a number of Heads of Mission. (The Western team is made up of the 'experts' from the Danish, Irish, UK and US delegations i.e. the same team which handed over the global approach and took delivery of Soviet response.) As a result of three hours' negotiation, we solved the outstanding problem in the mini-preamble on Human Contacts, and two of the translation problems in the text dealing with meetings on the basis of family ties (details enclosed).[11] This first session also served to confirm that the Russians are willing to negotiate seriously on the outstanding points (i.e. that they are not expecting us simply to accept their proposed amendments) but that, as we had always assumed, everything would have to be negotiated and that the distinction between major and minor points is largely illusory.

6. The position in summary is now as follows:

Mini-Preamble on Human Contacts
Bar any last minute problems in the texts other than English and Russian, and assuming that our Allies accept the compromise negotiated yesterday in the English language text, the mini-preamble is now finished. (The translation problem relating to 'further efforts' referred to in last week's letter[12] has been dealt with.)

[10] In his letter of 23 May (see notes 1, 7 and 8 above) Mr. M. Alexander drew attention to the evident 'disagreements and rivalries' within the Soviet delegation. He reported that, according to Mr. Mendelevich, Mr. Gromyko had been 'very appreciative' of the Western initiative and had said 'that the experts, who were "emotionally" involved, had got it wrong'.

[11] Not printed.

[12] The third paragraph of the Western draft mini-preamble on human contacts had referred to the desire of participating states to develop 'further efforts to achieve continuing progress in this field'.

Travel Text

Barring the Vatican problem[13] and the Romanian text on Consular agreements (which poses major difficulties for the Germans which they will be taking up in Bucharest)[14] this text is also finished.

Mini-Preamble on Information

There is no change from the position in last week's letter. Our exchange with the Russians yesterday merely served to emphasise again that this problem will be difficult to deal with but that the Russians are prepared to negotiate on the changes they have proposed.

Journalists

We did not reach this subject in yesterday's negotiations but the Soviet acceptance of our language on expulsion is, of course, a major advance. There may be considerable difficulties with the Romanians on the expulsion question. We shall be making it clear to the Russians that this is something for coping with which they will be primarily responsible.

Titles

The Russians have accepted our structure and our titles *in toto* with the exception of the general sub-title on the dissemination of information, which they have said is negotiable.

Yours ever,
M.O'D.B. Alexander

[13] The Vatican wanted this text, which expressed the intention of participating states to facilitate wider travel by their citizens, to make specific reference to its provisions applying to members and representatives of religious communities. See *Human Rights*, vol. v, pp. 26-7.

[14] The West Germans considered the language on Consular agreements, of which the Romanians were the main proponents, to have undesirable implications for intra-German relations.

No. 124

Sir D. Hildyard (UKMIS Geneva) to Mr. Callaghan

No. 392 Telegraphic [*WDW 1/22*]

Priority. Confidential   GENEVA, *7 June 1975, 11 a.m.*

Repeated for Information to Priority UKDEL NATO, Routine to EEC Posts, Washington, Moscow, Helsinki, UKDEL Strasbourg, UKREP Brussels, Berne.

CSCE: State of Play

1. An encouraging week with remarkable progress in Basket III (in which Alexander has played the leading part)[1] and agreements on various points

[1] 'In the last phase of the negotiations on technical staff', Mr. M. Alexander subsequently recalled, 'Kovalev, Dubinin and Kondrachev sat at one end of the hall . . . the Western Caucus sat at the other end and I oscillated between the two groups: the rest of the Warsaw Pact countries were nowhere in sight' (letter to Mr. Burns of 6 June, EN 2/557/5).

which were better than the West had expected (see my two IFTs not to all)[2]: also improved prospects for a satisfactory agreement on CBMs which Kovalev now describes as the most important issue outstanding (my third IFT).[3] We remain stuck, however, on QRR and are making only slow progress on Principles (my fourth and fifth IFTs).[4]

2. The Russians have now abandoned the pretence that they are not under time pressure and urge on all possible occasions that the tempo of work be further speeded up. The discussions both in Basket III and on CBMs seem to indicate that they need to report substantial progress to Moscow after every negotiation. Soviet tactics appear to be to make a major effort to finish in Basket III and on CBMs during the next week of so, to start serious negotiations again in Basket II in the middle of next week (Pojarsky[5] (USSR) mentioned 11 June as a key date to Kawan (EEC Commission)) and then to concentrate on Principles where the main work remains: they seem to have concluded that follow-up and the final document need not cause them serious problems. As soon as Baskets II, III and CBMs are settled we must be prepared for a large-scale Soviet campaign to try to put pressure on the West to reach rapid solutions, on the basis that the Western countries have achieved what they said they wanted and only minor points remain outstanding.

3. There continues to be some differences among the Nine and Fifteen about the tactics which the West should follow. Some delegations still incline to want to sit back on the basis that the Russians will be forced to come to us.[6]

[2] These telegrams reported that agreement had been reached *ad referendum* on the mini-preamble for the text on information (EN 2/557/5). See *Human Rights*, vol. v, pp. 159-60.

[3] UKMIS Geneva telegram No. 395 of 7 June (WDW 1/4) reported that during a Sub-Committee discussion of CBMs on 6 June, Mr. Kovalev had produced three 'combinations', previously mentioned to him by Mr. Sherer, all of which provided for a twenty-one day notification of Soviet military manoeuvres, but with related threshold and area parameters of 20,000 to 30,000 men within 200 to 330 kilometres of the USSR's European frontiers. Mr. Kovalev 'implied that that although all three in their existing form were quite unacceptable, some combination between them might lead to a solution'. In reply, Sir D. Hildyard repeated that 300 kilometres was the 'minimum for the West', and that they could not go beyond a threshold of 20-22,000. 'This', he noted in parenthesis, 'is of course a considerable advance on our previous figure but we are now coming up to the crunch and I think that we must be prepared to be flexible.'

[4] UKMIS Geneva telegrams Nos. 396 and 397 of 7 June reported on the protracted debate in the Principles Sub-Committee on the general paragraphs preceding the Principles (WDW 1/2).

[5] Also referred to as Mr. Pozharski. See No. 36, note 2.

[6] In his letter to Mr. Burns of 6 June (see note 1 above) Mr. Alexander reasoned that Western persistence was not a sufficient explanation of Soviet readiness to compromise. He found it 'hard to believe that anything other than an almost desperate Russian wish to have the Summit in July would have led them to make such abrupt concessions on, for instance, the question of technical staff', which until recently they had attempted to prevent the West raising in any way. 'Mr. Brezhnev's health is', he added, 'prima facie, the obvious explanation: the Soviet delegation's instructions give every sign of originating with the "old man in a hurry" mentioned by Dr. Kissinger to the Prime Minister and the Secretary of State.' According to

Others, amongst whom we have been prominent, believe that there is a limit to the extent that the Russians can be forced to swallow their words, and that we shall obtain the best results by making concessions easier for them. The success of the initiative in Basket III, to which the hard-liners were initially reluctant to subscribe, has strengthened the moderates' hand, but we may still have sporadic difficulties particularly with the Dutch.

4. The Finns appealed in the Coordinating Committee on 5 June for notification in good time of this 'very important peaceful manoeuvre' (Stage III). Privately they have been stimulating discussion of the possibility of opening on 28 July. Although the Russians clearly want a July Summit several of the East Europeans are still talking of the autumn, perhaps in an outdated attempt to show that they are not really under time pressure. The West continue to take the line that it is too early to fix even tentative dates and that results are more important than speed. One obstacle is the series of difficulties being raised by the Romanians almost across the board, much to the irritation of the Russians as well as of the West. Privately the Romanians are now giving the impression that their real interest is in follow-up and that the other points are mainly bargaining counters.

the British record of a White House meeting on 7 May, amongst Mr. Wilson, Mr. Callaghan, President Ford and Dr. Kissinger, it was Mr. Wilson who had said that he 'had been impressed by the fact that Brezhnev gave the appearance of an old man in a hurry. We should turn this to our advantage' (NFX 3/304/1).

No. 125

Minute from Mr. Burns to Mr. Tickell

[*EN 2/557/7*]

Confidential   FCO, *12 June 1975*

Basket III: Human Contacts and Information

1. Since I shall be in Dublin on 13 and 16 June[1] and since the texts on human contacts and information are rapidly nearing completion in Geneva, you may like to have the following statement on how matters stand.

2. After some initial confusion, the Russians accepted most of the package deal which we gave them in the middle of May. The negotiations have concentrated on a few particularly sensitive subjects and agreement has now been reached on almost all the points in these two sub-committees. I attach the text of the package deal amended to show how matters stand at present.[2] There is I fear still some uncertainty about the exact language which has been agreed since the Russian texts do not always accord with the English version. I am pursuing these translation points separately with Mr. Alexander on the advice of Research Department.

[1] The EPC Political Committee met in Dublin on 16 June.
[2] Not printed.

Human Contacts

3. The two remaining issues concern the text on travel, where the Romanians have had a problem about the reference to consular conventions and the Holy See has had difficulty in negotiating a text making explicit reference to religious communities. UKMIS Geneva telegram No. 408[3] indicates the compromises which have been reached on these two issues. I am consulting Mr. Burrows[4] about the consular conventions text and am reasonably confident that we can agree to the text. The text on religious communities, however, presents us with much greater problems. I attach a copy of my minute of 12 June to Mr. Burrows and hope for a positive response before the end of the day.[5]

Information

4. The most difficult points in the information text concern the working conditions for journalists and the mini-preamble setting out the objective of wider dissemination of information:

(i) *Working Conditions for Journalists.* I have told Mr. Alexander that the text which has been negotiated is acceptable to us but that we should prefer greater clarity about the provisions of the text to which the footnote on technical staff refers.[6] Mr. Alexander says that there is no chance of the Russians agreeing to extend the footnote to cover the texts on transmission of material or expulsion of journalists. He also says that, although it is his understanding that the footnote refers to all the other seven sub-paragraphs of the journalists' text, the Russians are refusing to make this plainer in the text. I believe that we should seek to eliminate the ambiguity

---

[3] This telegram of 11 June transmitted the texts of two paragraphs agreed *ad referendum* for insertion in the Basket III sections relating to personal and professional travel. The first asserted the need to improve arrangements to provide consular services; and the second confirmed that 'religious institutions, organisations and faiths, active within the constitutional framework of the participating states, and their representatives, [could] have meeting [*sic*] and contact among themselves within the field of their activity'. Cf. No. 123, note 13.

[4] Mr. F. Burrows was FCO Legal Counsellor.

[5] In this minute, Mr. Burns, whilst recognising the validity of doubts expressed by Mr. Burrows about the phrase 'active within the constitutional framework of the participating states', argued in favour of HMG's approval of the paragraph on contacts amongst religious institutions. The UK delegation was subsequently advised to accept its adoption.

[6] See *Human Rights*, vol. v, pp. 162-3. Negotiations on this text were completed *ad referendum* on 4 June. As a result of Soviet objections, the footnote relating to technical staff which had featured in the Western package deal (see No. 122, note 9) had been replaced by another asterisked on the sub-paragraph granting journalists the right to import technical equipment necessary for the exercise of their profession. This simply extended to technical staff from other participating states the provisions of the preceding sub-paragraphs. In Mr. Burns's opinion this was the 'least satisfactory point' in a text which he otherwise regarded as better than almost all the Western delegations had expected to achieve, and he told Mr. M. Alexander that if the text were reopened 'our priority objective would be to apply the footnote to the final two sub-paragraphs dealing with the transmission of material and expulsion' (UKMIS Geneva telegrams Nos. 388 and 389 of 5 June; minute from Mr. Burns to Mr. Tickell of 6 June; EN 2/557/5).

on this point since this will be a text which will be put into practice by those who have no experience of the CSCE negotiation itself. I have suggested that an asterisk should be inserted after each of the first sub-paragraphs. Mr. Alexander is trying to find an acceptable solution.

(ii) *Mini-Preamble*. In UKMIS Geneva telegram No. 393 the delegation explain the background to the mini-preamble text.[7] I believe that the text is acceptable to us in its present form, despite the omission 'within their countries' from the first paragraph. GIPD,[8] IRD, News Department and Research Department, together with Mr. Burrows, concur in this judgement.

5. This leaves two main sources of difficulty. First, the Holy See would like a reference to 'religious information' to parallel the reference to 'religious communities' in the human contacts text. I fully share Mr. Alexander's opposition to such a text. One of the most important features of the information document is that it nowhere defines information. This is a signal achievement and one we should protect. The Russians will resist any effort to say explicitly that information includes 'religious information' and if they were to agree to any compromise it would constitute a definition and thus a limitation of religious information.

6. Secondly, radio broadcasting. The main purpose of a text on broadcasting should be to obtain a clear statement that jamming is impermissible. The Russians have stoutly resisted this except on the condition that it should be paralleled by a text stating the responsibility of Governments for the content of such broadcasting. Such a proviso is, of course, unacceptable to the West and is particularly unacceptable to HMG, given the uniquely free position of the BBC external services.

7. For reasons which are spelled out in UKMIS Geneva tel[egram] No. 403,[9] the Americans have now decided that they need a text which deals with radio broadcasting and they have exploited a British idea of making a reference to the recent improvement in the jamming situation (which in practice means that jamming has ceased on all broadcasts to Eastern Europe, except for Radio Free Europe and Radio Liberty). The text the Americans have agreed reads as follows:

'The participating states note the expansion in the dissemination of information broadcast by radio, and express the hope for the continuation of this process, so as to meet the interest of mutual understanding among peoples and the aims of this Conference.'

[7] See No. 124, note 2.

[8] Guidance and Information Policy Department.

[9] This telegram of 10 June reported that the Americans needed a text to use 'in forthcoming discussions with members of Congress on the financing of R[adio] F[ree] E[urope] and V[oice] O[f] A[merica] to demonstrate that the existence and continued activity of these stations is not inconsistent with the policy of *détente*' (EN 2/557/3).

8. The reasons for our dislike of this text were set out in my letter of 6 June and the minute from the head of IRD which it enclosed.[10] The Russians rejected Mr. Barker's proposed revised text but in UKMIS Geneva tel[egram] No. 403 Mr. Alexander proposed a new formula.[11] The Russians will only accept this formula from the Americans and the American delegation are not prepared to put it forward without the approval of Washington which they are seeking.

9. This question of radio broadcasting is an important one. It would be necessary in my view to submit the matter to Ministers before we accepted the text of the kind agreed by the Russians and Americans. This view is I believe shared by the heads of EESD, IRD and GIPD.

10. Finally you will be aware from UKMIS Geneva tel[egram] No. 405 that the Romanians are having difficulty with the texts on journalists.[12] It is quite possible that these difficulties stem not from tactical considerations, but from the nature of Romanians' [*sic*] domestic regime.

11. I am sending a copy of this minute and its enclosures to Mr. Alexander in Geneva by tonight's bag both because it provides some additional advice on the points raised in recent telegrams and because it would be helpful to know from him that our understanding of the present form of the texts is as set out in the first enclosure to this minute.

R.A. Burns

[10] In this letter to Mr. M. Alexander, Mr. Burns pointed out that the use of the word 'expansion' seemed to indicate an increase in hours allotted to broadcasting rather than a broadening of the area receiving broadcasts. He also considered it bad in such a text 'to specify radio and not TV'. Mr. T.C. Barker, Head of IRD, believed that the text was 'dishonest', and that the words 'so as to' after 'process' had been deliberately 'chosen so as to obscure the persistent, and unresolved, disagreement whether governments [were] expected to control the content of broadcasts according to their interpretations of what [was] good for "mutual understanding among peoples" and what [was] consistent with "the aims of this conference"' (EN 2/557/5).

[11] The text proposed by Mr. Barker, after noting the expansion in the dissemination of broadcast information, expressed the hopes of participating states that this would continue, 'thus helping to meet the interest of mutual understanding among peoples' (*v. ibid.*). That transmitted in UKMIS Geneva telegram No. 403 (see note 9 above) was similar to the American formula, but the final clause read: '. . . express their hope for the continuation of this process, and expect it to contribute to the growth of confidence between peoples'.

[12] This telegram of 11 June had reported that the Romanians could not accept the paragraph in the journalists text on expulsion in its existing form and would wish to renegotiate it. They had also asked for the inclusion in the Information mini-preamble of 'a reference to the "political and moral responsibility" of journalists'. Both proposals were unacceptable to the Fifteen and the neutrals. And since the Russians appeared ready to stand firm on the negotiated text, it seemed likely that at some stage the Romanians would 'have to be forced to accept the existing language' (WDW 1/330/1).

No. 126

Mr. Callaghan to Sir D. Hildyard (UKMIS Geneva)

No. 214 Telegraphic [*WDW 1/4*]

Immediate. Confidential   FCO, *19 June 1975, 12.55 p.m.*

Repeated for Information to Immediate Moscow, Washington, Helsinki and to Priority Bonn, Paris, The Hague, UKDEL NATO and to Routine Rome, Copenhagen, Ottawa, Oslo, UKDEL Vienna, Brussels, Luxembourg, Dublin and UKREP Brussels.

CSCE: CBMs and Stage III

1. The Soviet Ambassador called at his own request on me on 18 June. He said that he had fully reported to Moscow what had been said at his meetings with me and the Prime Minister on 3[1] and 16 June[2] respectively. He noted that we had said we would do our best to find solutions to the outstanding problems in Geneva but he wished to say that he had received alarming reports from Geneva which indicated that the British delegation was playing a far from constructive role and seemed to be delaying a conclusion to Stage II.

2. Lunkov had CBMs particularly in mind. The Soviet authorities had fully explained their position but were very puzzled that the British delegation in Geneva seemed now to be going back on what they had said and that you had yourself expressed doubt about establishing prior notification of manoeuvres on a voluntary basis.[3] While you were continuing to insist on 300 kms, 20/22,000 men and 21 days, the Soviet Union knew that certain Western countries supported their proposal for 250 kms, 30,000 men and 18 days.[4] Lunkov said that his authorities in Moscow could not but take note of

---

[1] During their meeting at the FCO on 3 June Mr. Callaghan told Mr. Lunkov that NATO was still ready for a July summit, but that if there were to be one outstanding problems would have to be settled soon. 'If, he said, 'July were missed he was not sure that we would get the Summit this year. People would come back from their holidays refreshed for further argument' (record of meeting on 3 June, ENS 3/548/1).

[2] The main purpose of Mr. Lunkov's call on Mr. Wilson was to deliver a message from Mr. Brezhnev proposing 22 July as the date for Stage III. The gist of the message was that the Russians had reached their limit as far as any further concessions were concerned and that the time had come for Western Governments to decide that Stage III should be held in July (minute by Mr. Burns of 17 June, WDW 1/23).

[3] Cf. No. 124, note 3. On 16 June Mr. Gromyko complained to Sir T. Garvey about the hardening of the position of the British delegates at Geneva on the subject of CBMs. But Mr. I.J. Sutherland, HM Minister, Moscow, reminded the FCO that it was a 'standard Soviet tactic in conference diplomacy to make a fuss bilaterally on issues where they [were] not getting their way multilaterally', and he suggested that they need not take Mr. Gromyko's tirade 'too seriously' (Moscow telegrams Nos. 908 and 919 of 16 and 17 June, WDW 1/23).

[4] On 9 June Sir D. Hildyard was 'amazed and horrified' to learn from Mr. Sherer that Dr. Kissinger had told Mr. Dobrynin that he found these parameters acceptable. As Sir D. Hildyard pointed out in UKMIS Geneva telegram No. 400 of 9 June, it had been agreed on the Western side that the UK should take the lead in the CBMs negotiations, and having managed to persuade the Fifteen, the neutrals and the non-aligned to accept the voluntary

these actions which had a serious and important character since our behaviour at Geneva was the touchstone of the effectiveness of the documents which had been signed in Moscow in February.[5] In Moscow's view the time had come for joint efforts to conclude Stage II and they hoped that I would take all necessary steps, including contacts with my Western colleagues to work for holding Stage III in July.

3. I replied that what Lunkov had said about our own role was complete rubbish. We were not acting as plenipotentiaries in Geneva. We had to carry our friends and allies with us and could not order the Germans or the Dutch to do what we wanted—the Soviet Government could perhaps treat its friends in this way but we could not. We had been asked by our allies to take the lead in the negotiations. This we were doing but we could not impose a solution.

4. I pointed out that it was in fact Dobrynin who had crossed wires in Washington by seeking to establish agreement with Kissinger on parameters (including 250 kms) which did not command general acceptance in Geneva. My own relations with Kissinger were close and I did not mind the bilateral discussion on this subject in Washington. But others had been very upset and it was these irritations behind the scene which often led people to be more stubborn than was necessary. I was glad to see that the negotiations were now being conducted again on the right rails, but 2 or 3 days had been lost unnecessarily.[6]

5. As far as voluntary basis of negotiation was concerned, we had been working hard on one particular ally who did not like this concept. We could only exercise persuasion but I thought that probably they would come round in the end.[7] This showed however that the difficulties in Geneva did not

basis for notification, they had been hoping to do the same on parameters. 'Now', he complained, 'the Americans had cut the ground from under our feet'. Mr. Callaghan minuted on this telegram: 'I understand Hildyard's reactions—but it is the reality of power I suppose.' And although Mr. Hartman denied American acceptance of the Soviet proposal, on 9 June Dr. Kissinger wrote to Mr. Callaghan and the French and German Foreign Ministers suggesting that they settle on the Soviet parameters (Washington telegram No. 1981 of 9 June).

[5] See No. 112, note 2.

[6] Already in a minute of 9 June Mr. Tickell, who personally considered an area parameter of 250 kilometres to be 'a pretty good result', had expressed doubts about whether this would be acceptable to the West Germans who had 'recently come down somewhat reluctantly to 300 kms'. But Mr. Callaghan commented on this minute that he had gathered from quadripartite discussions in Paris, in which Herr Genscher and Dr. Kissinger participated, 'that we should all accept something below 300 kms, and that we should therefore accept the 250 kms' (minute from Mr. Weston to Mr. Tickell of 10 June). In his reply to Dr. Kissinger (see note 4 above) Mr. Callaghan stated that he thought 250 kilometres 'not unacceptable', but that, if others found it 'difficult to swallow', he would be ready 'to have another go at the Soviets'. He added that he considered 30,000 too high a threshold, especially as few NATO manoeuvres would then qualify for notification, and as the Warsaw Pact would then derive most of the credit from what had been a Western proposal (telegram No. 1268 to Washington of 13 June).

[7] On 16 June Sir D. Hildyard reported that the Dutch had 'bolted', and had made it clear in one of the NATO coordination meetings that they could not be counted upon to go along

necessarily come from the British side. We certainly had not gone back on our words, and if the Russians wanted to move matters forward more quickly they had better speak to some of the other countries who had more difficulties at this stage of the negotiations than we did.

6. I reminded Lunkov that we wanted to have the Conference finished in July. I had sent a telegram to my colleagues in the Nine suggesting that we should talk about this when we met in Luxembourg on 24 June.[8] There was no point in demanding that one or the other side gave way. In our thankless role on CBMs—thankless if it was to result in this kind of accusation from the Soviet Union—we had got to find a middle way. I was sure that the Soviet delegation in Geneva understood our problems and we welcomed our close working relationship with them. It would be a great pity if Moscow got it wrong and our activities in Geneva clouded our bilateral relations. I doubted whether it was in the Soviet interest for us to resign our lead on CBMs and leave the Russians to deal with all our allies individually.

7. Nevertheless, I was worried about the threshold of 30,000 men. If the Russians insisted on such a figure no doubt we could live with it but if the threshold was set so high only Soviet manoeuvres would qualify. I supposed that it might be possible to settle for such a high figure but I doubted whether it was in the Soviet interest that no manoeuvres should qualify on the Western side. It would therefore be better to settle the threshold at a lower level. As for the question of the difference between 300 and 250 kms, it was a fact that this was a matter of vital importance to some delegations, even if we did not all share their view.[9]

8. In conclusion, I stressed that we were not going back on our words. Negotiations in Geneva had reached a difficult phase when we must all use what influence we had to move matters along in a way which would be acceptable to all delegations. I noted that some subjects like follow-up were lagging behind. I then handed over the Prime Minister's reply (text in

with the voluntary basis. Sir D. Hildyard hoped that, with the assistance of other Western delegates, he would be able to 'push and cajole them back into line', but he informed Mr. Kovalev that British efforts to 'shepherd the Allliance along the road to a generally acceptable solution had broken down'. Sir D. Hildyard thought the Dutch 'probably the most determined of all to squeeze everything possible out of the Russians' (UKMIS Geneva telegram No. 420).

[8] At the Luxembourg Foreign Ministers meeting the British, French and Danes favoured seizing the opportunity offered by recent developments at Geneva to bring the CSCE to an early conclusion, whilst the Dutch and Belgians considered it unwise to be committed to a date for Stage III before satisfactory results had been achieved on all outstanding issues. Agreement was eventually reached on the basis of a compromise supported by the Germans, Italians and Luxembourgers by which the Nine would accept July as a 'working hypothesis' but make it clear that there were still questions which needed to be settled (Luxembourg telegram No. 147 of 24 June, WDW 1/23). See also Cmnd. 6932, p. 205.

[9] Parameters were discussed by NATO Heads of Delegation in Geneva on 18 June. 'It is generally hoped', Sir D. Hildyard reported, 'that we can obtain 300 kilometers, 21 days and something better than 25,000 for the threshold, but if necessary I am sure that 25,000 would be acceptable' (UKMIS Geneva telegram No. 425 of 18 June).

MIFT)[10] to Mr. Brezhnev's message (my tel[egram]s Nos. 623 and 624 to Moscow)[11] emphasizing that we shared the Soviet desire to conclude the Conference in July.[12]

9. Washington only. Please pass advance copy to Tickell.

[10] In his reply the Prime Minister confirmed that the British also believed that the Conference 'can and should be concluded by the end of July', but he thought it only realistic to note that there were a few issues important to many delegations that were still outstanding and to which generally acceptable solutions had to be found. He agreed to consider the date proposed by Mr. Brezhnev, but stressed that there was 'absolutely no question of [HMG] lending support to any artificial attempts to obstruct the course of the negotiations' (telegram No. 215 to UKMIS Geneva of 19 June, WDW 1/23).

[11] Not printed. See note 2 above.

[12] Mr. Callaghan subsequently informed Sir D. Hildyard that, while he thought Mr. Lunkov's complaints might well be part of a 'clumsy effort' to put pressure on HMG, they also indicated that the Soviet delegation in Geneva was not conveying back to Moscow the same impression of good working relations with UKDEL that the FCO had received. He further noted that the FCO would not want British efforts 'to nurse our allies towards an acceptable solution on CBMs . . . to be misinterpreted in Moscow in such a way that they cloud our bilateral relations' (telegram No. 216 of 19 June, WDW 1/23).

No. 127

Mr. Callaghan to Mr. J.C.A. Roper (Luxembourg)[1]
No. 30 Telegraphic [WDW 1/4]

Flash. Confidential   FCO, *24 June 1975, 12.05 p.m.*

Repeated for Information to Immediate UKMIS Geneva, and to Priority Mosow, Washington, Helsinki, UKDEL NATO.

Following for Weston[2] from Tickell.

CSCE: CBMs[3]

1. You will have seen from UKMIS Geneva tel[egram] Nos. 448 and 449 that the new package which the Russians seem to be offering in Geneva involves a series of improvements.[4] They are now prepared to accept a

[1] HM Ambassador in Luxembourg.

[2] Mr. Weston accompanied Mr. Callaghan to the meeting of EC Foreign Ministers in Luxembourg on 24 June. See No. 126, note 8.

[3] At a meeting of the CBMs Sub-Committee on 20 June neutral and non-aligned delegates proposed as main parameters: threshold, 25,000; area, 300 kilometers; and time, three weeks. Sir D. Hildyard gathered from a conversation that evening with Mr. Kovalev that the outline of a compromise package incorporating these figures was visible (UKMIS Geneva telegram No. 444 of 21 June).

[4] These telegrams of 23 June reported: (1) further discussions between Sir D. Hildyard, Mr. Kovalev and Mr. Mendelevich, during which the Russians indicated their readiness to accept an area parameter of 250 kilometers; and (2) the cautious reaction of the NATO caucus at Geneva to the latest Soviet proposals on CBMs. At a meeting of the caucus on 23 June Sir D. Hildyard argued strongly in favour of their acceptance 'asking only for 300 kms instead of 250'.

compromise definition of the voluntary basis and figures of 25,000 for the threshold, 21 days for the timing and 250 kms for the area of Soviet territory defined along lines proposed by the Swedes with Western support. The Swedish proposal is that the measurements should be taken not merely from those frontiers which the Russians share with other participating states, but also from those which face other states: in short those parts of Soviet territory which face other participating states across the Baltic or Black Sea would be included up to 250 km from the coast.

2. We think that a package deal on these lines would be a good result, although Sir D. Hildyard may well be right in thinking that a slightly higher number of kilometres may be necessary to satisfy the neutrals and some of our allies. The time seems now to have come for Western delegations in Geneva to discuss these figures within the framework of the whole military document (draft copy with you).[5] There are a number of other elements in the arrangement (e.g. discretionary notification of smaller-scale manoeuvres and references to amphibious and airborne troops)[6] which need to be taken into account before full consensus can be obtained. We still have a problem with the Turks over how much of Turkey should be included,[7] and there are some other military points of concern to the neutrals (e.g. the principles of military security) which are still outstanding.

[5] This framework document, which omitted specific parameter figures, was handed to the Soviet delegation at Geneva on 26 June (UKMIS Geneva telegram No. 454 of 26 June).

[6] The neutrals and non-aligned had proposed a sub-threshold of 12,000 men for amphibious and airborne manoeuvres (see note 3 above).

[7] See No. 104, note 7. On 3 June the Turks proposed to other NATO delegations that in their case prior notification should only apply within 100 kilometres of their frontiers with participating states (UKMIS Geneva telegram No. 383 of 3 June). This seemed likely to damage Western chances of securing a 'respectable width of Soviet territory agreed by the Russians', and the Turks were, for the moment, dissuaded from proceeding with their formula (letter from Mr. Figgis to Mr. Reeve of 9 June).

No. 128

Minute from Mr. Tickell on CSCE: Committee III: Broadcasting[1]

[EN 2/557/5]

Confidential   FCO, *25 June 1975*

The Basket III negotiations in Geneva have nearly reached the point when complete texts, in all six languages, for human contacts, information, culture and education can be provisionally registered. This is an important step after which it will be virtually impossible to change the language which has been agreed, except to make any adaptations which may be necessary to fit the texts into the Final Act of the Conference as a whole.

[1] This minute was addressed to Mr. Morgan, Sir J. Killick and Mr. R. Westbrook, Private Secretary to Mr. Hattersley.

2. The only outstanding issue in the information texts, and one of the few remaining issues in Basket III as a whole concerns the text on radio broadcasting. For reference purposes, I attach the complete text on information;[2] but the relevant section on radio broadcasting reads as follows:

'(iii) *Film and Broadcast Information*
—To promote the improvement of the dissemination of ('sposobstvovat uluchshenie rasprostranenia') film and broadcast information.
To this end:
—they will encourage the wider showing and broadcasting of a greater variety of recorded and filmed information from the other participating states, illustrating the various aspects of life in their countries and received on the basis of such agreements or arrangements as may be necessary between the organisations and firms directly concerned;
—they will facilitate the import by competent organisations and firms of recorded audio-visual material from the other participating states.
—The participating states note the expansion in the dissemination of information broadcast by radio, and express the hope for the continuation of this process, so as to meet the interest of mutual understanding among peoples and the aims of this Conference.'

3. The problem is as follows. The last paragraph of the above text reflects efforts to find a balance between Western demands that the Conference should recognise that the jamming of radio broadcasts is incompatible with *détente*, and the Soviet position that Western governments should be responsible for the content of broadcasting. We do not like the text, and have argued strongly against it. The BBC have made it clear to us that they would prefer no text at all to one which, like the last sentence of the present one, carries the implication that Governments should accept some degree of responsibility for the content of broadcasts. The BBC are of course anxious to protect their unique tradition of independence from Government control.

4. The last paragraph of the disputed text was negotiated by the Russians and Americans. Although the Americans recognise that it is not wholly satisfactory, they attach great importance to having a text on this subject which they can use in their efforts to persuade Congress that the continuing financing of Radio Free Europe and Voice of America is not incompatible with *détente*.

5. In view of the Soviet attitude, we should ideally have preferred no text at all. Given the American position, however, we have sought instead to improve the language which the Americans have negotiated. I was asked to take this subject up in Washington during Mr. Hattersley's visit and found the Americans sympathetic to our point of view.[3] We have therefore concentrated on three main issues:

---

[2] Not printed.
[3] Mr. Tickell accompanied Mr. Hattersley on a visit to Washington during 18-20 June.

(*a*) to retain at the beginning of the text on 'film and broadcast information' an introductory phrase which underlines the importance of film and broadcast information. This has been achieved;

(*b*) to amend the words 'so as to' in the middle of the last paragraph in such a way that we can more successfully argue that they do not mean (as the proposed Russian translation clearly implies) that the continued dissemination of information by radio should be dependent upon the content promoting mutual understanding;

(*c*) to eliminate or redraft the reference to the 'aims of this Conference' which, since they are nowhere defined, are vague, and will lend themselves to propaganda use by the East.

6. The Russians have turned down the second and third of our proposals out of hand. The advice we have been given by the delegation (UKMIS Geneva telegram No. 451)[4] is that we are unlikely to obtain any significant improvement to the text, and that neither the Americans nor the Germans feel strongly about the changes we have proposed. The delegation recommend that we should accept the present ambiguous formulation (with or without an improvement to the final phrase) and use our acquiescence to extract a slightly better deal on some other issue elsewhere.

7. We are thus faced with a choice, on which I should be grateful for Ministerial guidance:

(*a*) We could insist that changes in the text must be made if there were to be a text at all. In this event we should not enjoy full support from our partners and Allies, and would probably be accused by the Russians of delaying tactics. Moreover there would be a risk that the result would be no text at all which would, as explained above, be unwelcome to the Americans.

(*b*) We could acquiesce in a text which we regard as unsatisfactory, and render ourselves vulnerable to Soviet or Eastern pressure in the future to exert some measure of control over broadcasting in 'the interest and mutual understanding among peoples'. I do not have to say what trouble we might have if this point were picked up in Parliament or by the press.

The importance that the Russians have attached to agreement on the existing text is an indication in itself of the uses they might well try to make of it. My own view is that we should have another go at improving the text, using, if need be, the line I suggested in Washington as a fallback position: in other words that the English text should read 'in order to' in place of 'so as

---

[4] In this telegram of 24 June Mr. M. Alexander reported to Mr. Burns that Mr. Dubinin had described the text on broadcasting 'as being for his Government the most sensitive, apart from that dealing with the inviolability of frontiers, of all those appearing in the documents of the Conference'! Mr. Alexander added that neither the Americans nor the Germans were enthusiastic about the change in the link phrase for which the British had been pressing, and he recommended accepting the original US-Soviet version of the text. 'It would', he observed, 'be a pity, after all that has happened in the last six weeks, if we were to find ourselves alone with the Romanians in preventing the completion of work in Basket III.'

to' leaving the Russian text as it is. In such circumstances we would be much less vulnerable to pressure. I cannot say from here whether the Russians would in the end agree to change the text. The Delegation are clearly despairing. But I think we ought to try. It would not be worth doing so and running the risks outlined above if we did not have Ministerial authority for doing so.[5]

C.C.C. Tickell

[5] On 26 June Mr. Morgan noted on this paper: 'No ordinary man, in my view, could readily suppose that the phrases in question meant anything much one way or the other. The passion they have aroused on both the Soviet side and our own seem to me characteristic of people living a good deal too close to their subject. How they can be interpreted to require Govt. control of radio, I altogether fail to see. If the Russians were to object to any broadcast one would just blandly say: "We consider this to be entirely in the interest of mutual understanding etc. etc.", and who is to prove it otherwise? 2. By opposing the language, we have of course shown that we do give it a particular significance, so that if we eventually accept it we lose a point. But there are no records of the bargaining in Phase II & my instinct would be to let the text be accepted now, rather than build more significance on it by further opposition, which seems unlikely to be successful.' Sir J. Killick added 'we must proceed from the fundamental consideration that HMG should not appear to be holding up the conclusion of Stage II over a rather "angels on a pin" point on which we have no support', and he advocated 'cutting our losses' and letting the text go through. This view was endorsed by Mr. Hattersley on 27 June. 'I could', he observed, 'defend the objectivity of the BBC as being in the "interests of mutual understanding etc etc . . ."'

No. 129

Minute from Mr. Tickell to Mr. Weston

[*WDW 1/22*]

Confidential   FCO, *3 July 1975*

CSCE: State of Play: 3 July 1975

The Secretary of State has asked for a short account of the latest state of play in Geneva.

2. Progress in the last few days has not been wholly encouraging. The Russians have been exerting constant pressure on individual delegations to fall in line and have insisted on daily time-consuming meetings of the Co-ordinating Committee in an effort to force the Conference to make a decision about the date of Stage III. There is a widespread desire at the Conference to complete work this summer, though the Finns, who claim to need at least four weeks' prior notice, are beginning to suggest that 4 August rather than 28 July may have to be the date for Stage III.

3. When the Finnish Ambassador called yesterday, Mr. Hattersley said that we thought there was still a good prospect of completing Stage II in time for a July Stage III, and that although the organisation was a matter for the Finns themselves it might be wise for them to work on that assumption. There is little doubt that the Finns are already planning on this basis but Western

delegations in Geneva and a number of neutral and non-aligned governments are continuing to say that they cannot take a firm decision on a date for Stage III until a number of outstanding issues have been settled. There should be a Co-ordinating Committee meeting this morning at which the question of a date will again be discussed but I do not expect any firm decision to emerge.

4. The remaining questions fall into two main categories: East/West issues and issues affecting individual delegations. In brief they are as follows:

East/West Issues

(*a*) A satisfactory text safeguarding quadripartite rights and responsibilities. We, the Germans and the Americans have at last persuaded the French and Russians to accept a shorter text on this point, but the language which the French have now tabled is still causing difficulty to a number of neutral and Western delegations (including the Italians).[1] Until this issue is settled, a number of questions elsewhere in the Declaration, particularly concerning the conditions governing the non-use or threat of use of force, cannot fall into place.

(*b*) Preambular language of a political character. It has always been a primary Soviet objective to dress up the results of the Conference, particularly the principles, as a *de facto* peace treaty and as committing the West to the present *status quo* in Europe. Despite their efforts to complete the Conference quickly, the Russians are continuing to try to obtain political language in the preamble to the Declaration of Principles and in the Final Act of the Conference which is unacceptable to most Western governments. Our aim, in which we should succeed, is to achieve a non-controversial text without prejudice to the issues covered in the Declaration.

(*c*) Confidence-building measures. Good progress has been made on confidence-building measures on the basis of a British draft paper at the end of last week.[2] The main outstanding issues boil down to two:

[1] On 27 June the French tabled the following text in the Principles Sub-Committee: 'The participating States note that the present (title of document) cannot and will not affect their rights or obligations, nor the corresponding treaties, agreements and arrangements.' This had already been circulated amongst EC Heads of Delegation and NATO experts, and the omission of the qualifying phrase 'in conformity with international law' (cf. *Human Rights*, vol. iii, p. 138) had been criticised by the Canadians, Greeks, Italians and Dutch, who feared that 'it would give the Russians an excuse for not implementing Conference decisions they disliked'. When the formula was discussed in the Principles Sub-Committee the Swedes, Spaniards and Romanians argued that it should cover only 'existing' rights or obligations 'in conformity with international law'. The Russians, who had previously discussed the text with the British, French and American delegations, stated that they could accept it as a compromise, but deplored the omission of any reference to 'responsibilities'. For them 'it represented the "outer limit" of acceptability' (UKMIS Geneva telegrams Nos. 443 and 474 of 21 and 28 June, WDW 1/2).

[2] See No. 127, note 5. This draft paper was tabled at an informal meeting of the CBMs Sub-Committee on 28 June. When, on 1 July, the Sub-Committee began examining its preambular paragraphs discussion focused upon the statement that the prior notification of

(i) A Soviet refusal to move above 250 kms and a Federal German refusal to go below 275 kms.[3]

(ii) Turkish refusal to include within the scope of prior notification most of Central Turkey. In my judgment this is the main problem and it may be necessary for representations to be made in Ankara. The Turks have no support in Geneva.[4]

Basket II

(*d*) At their meeting in Luxembourg on 24 June, Foreign Ministers of the Nine reaffirmed the importance they attached to obtaining an adequate text on effective reciprocity in conditions of trade.[5] The Russians are showing no sign yet of movement on this question.

(*e*) *Follow-up.* Despite intensive drafting work no agreement has been reached on the fundamental question of whether it should be decided now or in 1977 whether to set up a pattern of regular meetings of senior officials or Ministers to carry on a multilateral dialogue. All the neutral and non-

manoeuvres 'derives from political decision and therefore rests upon a voluntary basis'. The Romanian, Dutch and Turkish delegations argued against acceptance of the voluntary principle, and Mr. Mendelevich insisted that its omission would lead to the withdrawal of all Soviet proposals on parameters. He also proposed the deletion of the word 'therefore', but indicated his readiness to accept a rephrasing of the paragraph to read 'this measure, deriving from political decision rests upon a voluntary basis' (UKMIS Geneva telegrams Nos. 473 and 485 of 28 June and 2 July on WDW 1/4).

[3] It had been clear for some time that other NATO members would be prepared to accept an area parameter of 250 kilometres, if and when the FRG did so, and on 3 July Herr Blech informed Sir D. Hildyard that his Government agreed to this figure. At a subsequent meeting with Mr. Kovalev and Mr. Mendelevich, Sir D. Hildyard confirmed that the West would accept parameters of 250 kilometres, 25,000 men (including amphibious and airborne troops), and twenty-one days' notice. On 4 July Mr. Kovalev confirmed Moscow's acceptance of both these figures and the revised reference to the voluntary basis of CBMs (UKMIS Geneva telegrams Nos. 490 and 502 of 3 and 5 July, WDW 1/4).

[4] The British framework document (see note 2 above) included a sentence on lines similar to the text proposed by the Turks on 3 June (see No. 127, note 7), but without any mention of a specific area parameter figure. This was criticised by the Spanish, Greek and Cypriot delegations who, while accepting that Turkey would require some exception covering its borders with non-participating states, could see no reason why it should require special parameters for its European frontiers. Moreover, other countries, including the Soviet Union, opposed the Turkish demand for special treatment and an area parameter of only 100 kilometres. But, as Sir D. Hildyard reported in UKMIS Geneva telegram No. 486 of 2 July (WDW 1/4) it was clear from private soundings that a formulation excluding notification of manoeuvres 'close to' frontiers with non-participating states could be generally acceptable even to the Greeks and Cypriots. This would have excluded supply bases for Cyprus and was thus a considerable move to meet Turkish preoccupations. The issue nevertheless, continued to exercise Turkey's allies. UKDEL, like other Western delegations, was reluctant to appear to take the lead in applying pressure on Turkey and eventually, at the suggestion of Sir D. Hildyard, a contact group drawn from the EC and NATO was established to liaise on representations to Ankara (UKMIS Geneva telegram No. 499 of 4 July, WDW 1/4). 'The Turkish problem', Sir D. Hildyard predicted in UKMIS Geneva telegram No. 498 of 4 July, 'could well hold us up for a very inconveniently long time'.

[5] See No. 117, note 9.

aligned delegations are insisting that a commitment to regular meetings should be made at this Conference. Most Western delegations are prepared to go along with this but the French are resisting tooth and nail. The East are seeking to obtain instead agreement to hold another full-scale Conference within the next two or three years. There is also disagreement about how many meetings should be held in the period before 1977.[6]

(f) *Structure of the Final Act.* Agreement is close on this question, but the Nine have not yet proposed to the Russians their formula for associating the European Communities with the results of the Conference.[7]

Other Issues

(a) In addition to their lone battle to limit the application of CBMs on their territory, the Turks are continuing to threaten serious difficulties if President Makarios goes to Stage III.[8]

(b) Mr. Mintoff repeated to Mr. Hattersley yesterday his view that the Conference had not adequately dealt with the problems of the Mediterranean (see FCO telegram No. 225 to Geneva attached).[9] He continues to insist upon his proposals for a Euro/Arab Federation and the withdrawal of Soviet and American fleets from the Mediterranean. Mr. Gromyko's recent attempts to bully him into submission have only made him more determined. We have put some compromise ideas to him which he has not rejected, and might eventually accept.[10]

[6] See further No. 131.

[7] On 4 July the Brussels CSCE Ad Hoc Group finally agreed on the text of a declaration to be made by the President of the EC Council at the time of the signing of the Final Act (UKREP Brussels telegram No. 3248 of 4 July, WDW 1/15).

[8] See No. 117, note 12.

[9] Not printed. This telegram of 2 July (WDW 1/13) recorded that Mr. Mintoff had told Mr. Hattersley that he could not attend Stage III and 'hypocritically applaud this "success for European security" if steps were not taken to ensure immediate follow-up that would help avert the coming war in the Middle East'. Mr. Hattersley and his officials sought to disabuse Mr. Mintoff of his illusions about CSCE, insisting that it was a 'tender plant' which 'could not cope with the problems of the Middle East'. Already, on 26 May, the Maltese had tabled for inclusion in the Mediterranean Declaration (see No. 117, note 13) a text encapsulating some of the ideas expressed in the Maltese paper on a Euro-Arab federation (see No. 108, note 16, and *Human Rights*, vol. iii, p. 19). Both the Americans and the Russians were irritated by Maltese conduct and, on 27 June, after discussions amongst the Nine and the Fifteen, Mr. Cleghorn indicated to Mr. V.J. Gauci, the Maltese Ambassador at Geneva, that, if the Maltese would drop their proposed addition to the Mediterranean Declaration and agree not to reopen the question at Stage III, the West would seek: (1) to include in the Declaration a paragraph committing participating states to 'promote the development of good neighbourly relations with the non-participating Mediterranean states in connection with the multilateral process initiated by the Conference'; and (2) to make provision in the follow-up resolution for contributions by non-participating Mediterranean states (UKMIS Geneva telegrams Nos. 464 and 465 of 27 June, WDW 1/13).

[10] *V. ibid.* During his conversation with Mr. Hattersley on 2 July Mr. Mintoff remarked 'that he hoped we did not think he was trying to sabotage the Conference. He was running into accusations from the Russians which he much resented. Gromyko had been insufferably rude.'

(*c*) The Romanians are standing out on a number of issues throughout the Conference, probably in order to ensure that their own proposal for a declaration on the non-use of force does not founder under Soviet and German opposition.

5. This is a formidable list at such a late moment in Stage II. The Delegation believe it unlikely that Stage II can be brought to a completion before the end of next week. Much will depend upon the speed with which the Declaration of Principles can be completed. The Turkish problems are particularly intractable.

C.C.C. TICKELL

No. 130

Sir D. Hildyard (UKMIS Geneva) to Mr. Callaghan
No. 504 Telegraphic [WDW 1/22]

Immediate. Confidential   GENEVA, *6 July 1975, 12.20 p.m.*

Repeated for Information to Immediate Rome (for Morgan and Burns), and to Priority UKDEL NATO, All NATO posts, Moscow, Helsinki, UKDEL Strasbourg, UKREP Brussels, Berne.

My telegram Number 498.[1]
CSCE: State of Play
1. We achieved remarkable progress yesterday even if not all that Kovalev had predicted (my telegram number 503).[2]

(*a*) The sentence on quadripartite rights has now generally accepted *ad referendum* (but see my telegram number 506).[3]

[1] In his telegram of 4 July (see No. 129, note 4) Sir D. Hildyard reported that, although the Principles Sub-Committee was 'still moving slowly', there had been 'a very considerable speed-up in almost all other sectors particularly in the last few days'. A Working Group of Heads of Delegation and experts had also been established to accelerate progress on principles. It met for the first time on 5 July.

[2] 'The Russians', Sir D. Hildyard observed in this telegram of 5 July, 'are in a highly nervous state and are exerting maximum pressure for a conditional agreement tonight on holding Stage III before the end of July.' Mr. Kovalev had told him that the Soviet Union could not accept a date after July and that he believed agreement could be reached that day 'on QRR, PCF, the Berlin sentence [see note 5 below] and follow-up' (WDW 1/4).

[3] This telegram of 6 July reported that after a two-day debate in the Principles Sub-Committee, delegates had achieved a compromise on QRR involving: (1) the revision of the first sentence of Principle 10 so that it referred to participants fulfilling in good faith 'both those obligations arising from the generally recognised principles and rules of international law and those obligations arising from treaties or other agreements in conformity with international law'; and (2) the inclusion in the final clauses of the Declaration of a provision which, whilst making specific reference to this sentence, asserted that the Declaration did not affect participants' 'rights and obligations, nor the corresponding treaties and other agreements and arrangements' (WDW 1/2). See *Human Rights*, vol. iii, p. 182.

(*b*) Peaceful change of frontiers is agreed by all except Romania and Malta whose reserves are almost certainly tactical.

(*c*) We are practically through on follow-up and the texts should be finally agreed at the beginning of next week (my telegram numbers 508, 509).[4]

(*d*) The Berlin sentence has been agreed by the Russians and can be expected to be generally accepted early next week.[5]

2. There seems no reason why the outstanding issues, apart from the Maltese proposal and CBMs, should not be resolved in the course of next week. There is still a good deal of work to be done on principles, but we have now made contingency plans for two groups to work in parallel if necessary. The final document and Basket II should be capable of solution within the same time scale and I cannot see the Russians making real trouble on the double signature.[6] Kovalev assured me that the Romanians would not go to the brink: he had spoken to Moscow on the telephone after their discussions with Macovescu.[7]

3. We are putting forward a revised formulation on the Maltese proposal. It may take a few days to obtain general agreement on this and Mintoff's approval or acquiescence, but it does not look as if he would go so far as to refuse consensus.[8]

4. The main outstanding problems are thus the Turkish case on CBMs and perhaps Cyprus representation. No-one here has yet received any information about representations in Ankara to appeal for the cooperation on the part of the Turks which is needed if Stage III is to be held in July, if not to

---

[4] These telegrams of 6 July reported on the drafting of the text of the second operative paragraph of the proposed resolution on follow-up. This provided for the continuation of the multilateral process, beginning with a meeting of senior officials (WDW 1/14).

[5] The West Germans wanted the three Western occupying powers to make it clear at Stage III that the CSCE documents applied also in Berlin, and in discussions with the Russians at Geneva the Germans floated the idea of inserting in the *chapeau* of the Declaration of Principles a sentence to which such an allied statement might be linked (Bonn telegrams Nos. 506 and 524 of 21 and 26 June, WDW 1/2). This, the so-called 'Berlin sentence', which was negotiated by the French with the Russians during the first week of July, read: 'Guided by their intention to provide, throughout Europe and among themselves, the opportunity for the enjoyment of the benefits of the process of *détente* which have found expression in the results of the Conference' (telegram No. 233 to UKMIS Geneva of 9 July, WDW 1/24).

[6] During the meeting of the EPC Political Committee in Rome on 8 July the Italians reported that they had warned Mr. Kovalev in Geneva of the necessity to associate the EC with the final document (telegram No. 233 to UKMIS Geneva, *v. ibid.*).

[7] The Romanians alone had stood out against accepting the latest compromise on QRR. Mr. G. Macovescu was Romanian Foreign Minister.

[8] See No. 129, note 9. UKMIS Geneva telegram No. 510 of 6 July reported that recent discussions with the Maltese had indicated that for presentational reasons it would be easier for them to accept a compromise on their proposal for an addition to the operative section of the Mediterranean Declaration if this took the form of a separate paragraph, rather than an addition to an existing one (WDW 1/13)

prevent a breakdown.[9] Time is now running out very fast.

Timing

5. There had been much talk in the corridors to the effect that the meetings of the Coordinating Committee yesterday would be decisive: either a decision, definite or conditional, would be taken to fix a date at the end of July for Stage III, or July would be impossible and we should have to envisage some time in August or later. In the event although there could be no agreement to fix a date, the possibility of July remains open.

6. At the meeting of the Nine during the afternoon the majority considered that even a conditional agreement was not acceptable until the final outstanding points had been resolved. The French (in the absence of André who is in Helsinki) then broke ranks, and said that they would propose a conditional agreement. The Danes supported them in the light of the fact that this was what all the other Nordic countries wanted. Appeals for solidarity among the Nine had no effect (I understand that Fourcade[10] is negotiating contracts in Moscow).

7. Before the Coordinating Committee, which has been successively adjourned until 21.30, Kovalev, Blech (FRG), Maresca (US)[11] and I together with Farace (Italy)[12] who not only holds the Presidency of the Nine but who was also Chairman of the Committee for the day, worked out a scenario: (1) we would all speak positively and non-polemically: (2) we would all agree that very great progress had been made, and that there was good reason to expect an early conclusion to the negotiations: (3) while some would press for agreement on a date, others would bring out that there was no consensus for this: (4) we would underline our hope or desire for Stage III to be held by the end of July: (5) some would add that it was to be hoped that the Finns would keep open this possibility. The Italian Chairman would then sum up on the lines of (4) and (5).

8. All went approximately according to plan though the French made their proposal and obtained a certain amount of support from the Nordics and neutrals. The Turks, Maltese and a few others came out strongly against a decision of any kind. I spoke as agreed, bringing out that although no consensus on a decision was yet in sight, there were good reasons to hope that we could all be able to agree to reach agreement if not next week then

---

[9] Cf. No. 129, note 4. The West German authorities had, according to Herr Blech, learnt that Mr. O. Benler, the Turkish delegate, was having to follow the line of the military in Ankara, to which the majority of Government Ministers were opposed. The Turkish Chief of Staff visited Bonn on 7 July, and it was thought that after his return to Turkey his Government would adopt a more flexible approach (UKMIS Geneva telegram No. 503, see note 2 above). On 8 July, at a meeting of the NAC, the Turks indicated their readiness to increase their desired area parameter to 150 kilometres, but Mr. Logan sought to persuade his Turkish colleague that the simultaneous discussion of the matter in Brussels and Geneva was 'bound to cause confusion and delay' (UKDEL NATO telegrams Nos. 320 and 321 of 8 July, WDW 1/4).

[10] M. J-P. Fourcade was French Minister of Economics and Finance.

[11] Mr. J.J. Maresca was a senior member of the US delegation.

[12] Sig. A. Farace di Villaforesta was the Italian Head of Delegation.

by the middle of the month. The FRG made the point about the Finns keeping open the possibility of July. The Chairman then summed up, concentrating on this latter point rather than both (4) and (5) in paragraph 7 above in spite of the clear draft which we had given him. To satisfy the Russians he proposed that his summing up should be recorded in the journal, but he dropped this when it was opposed by the Maltese and Dutch. The Russians seemed content: they can report that there was a constructive and optimistic debate. Neither the Finns nor the others seem over concerned. According to the present programme the Coordinating Committee will meet at mid-day each day next week to monitor progress.[13]

[13] On 7 July the French formally proposed to the Coordinating Committee that they should agree to a date for Stage III at the end of July on condition that all problems were resolved by 12 July (UKMIS Geneva telegram No. 511 of 7 July, WDW 1/15). Belgian and Dutch representatives to the EPC Political Committee, then meeting in Rome, complained that the French had thereby broken the solidarity of the Nine. But British, Danish and German representatives favoured maintaining the momentum of the negotiations and, on 8 July, a compromise text was prepared which endorsed the desirability of completing the Conference's work in July, and called on the Coordinating Committee to hold a review meeting on 15 July to determine whether sufficient agreement had been reached on outstanding questions for a decision to be reached on the date of Stage III (telegrams Nos. 233 and 234 to UKMIS Geneva of 9 July, WDW 1/24). This, however, was subsequently rejected by the East (UKMIS Geneva telegram No. 519 of 9 July, WDW 1/15).

No. 131

Sir D. Hildyard (UKMIS Geneva) to Mr. Callaghan

No. 529 Telegraphic [WDW 1/14]

Immediate. Confidential   GENEVA, *9 July 1975, 8.20 p.m.*
For Figgis.
My tel[egram] No. 518.[1]

CSCE: Follow-up

1. After a long, and occasionally heated, discussion in the informal drafting group this afternoon the text in MIFT[2] was put in note-books in its French language version by the official Working Group: we shall be resuming discussion at 11 pm this evening when the text may be provisionally registered. Only two delegations have major reservations on the text and, although it is far from satisfactory, it represents a compromise which it would be extremely difficult for Western delegations to reopen.

2. The text for paragraph 2(*b*) evolved in negotiations between Chazelle

[1] This telegram of 8 July reported on discussion in the informal drafting group of paragraph 2 of the follow-up text (see No. 130 note 4), and an unsuccessful Belgian attempt to reduce the commitment to the holding of further meetings after the proposed 1977 review Conference.

[2] Not printed. See *Human Rights*, vol. iii, pp. 72-3 for the text registered by the Coordinating Committee on 16 July. This differs only slightly and insignificantly from the text transmitted in UKMIS Geneva telegram No. 530 of 9 July in the wording of the first sentence of paragraph 4.

(France), the Belgians and Lipatti[3] (Romania) this morning. In the NATO caucus this afternoon we and others pointed out that the phrase 'define the appropriate modalities for the holding of other meetings' goes much further towards those who want a commitment to the holding of further meetings than our own phrase 'submit appropriate proposals for the holding of other meetings' and that this is not compensated for by the inclusion of 'could' which follows. However, since the amended texts and the reference to 'the first of the meetings' in paragraph 3 were acceptable to the Belgians, French, Italians and Dutch we felt that we could not object. The French were as unable to explain the logic of their text as were the others to justify their change of position[4] (though no doubt Kovalev's recent exchange with Davignon played its part).[5]

3. The Maltese placed a reservation on the reference to *détente* in paragraph 2(*a*). (In the corridors they have made it plain that their objection to this reference is linked to their position on the QRR text. No doubt it is also tied in with their position on the Mediterranean Declaration.) They have also placed a general reservation on paragraph 2(*b*), and though they did not specify their difficulties may well attempt to amend it. The Yugoslav insisted that the final phrase of paragraph 2(*b*) should read 'which would include further similar meetings etc.' rather than 'could include etc.'. The Nine and the Fifteen have made it clear that this is unacceptable. This point, which stems from the failure of the French to clarify the meaning of their text when negotiating with the Romanians, may cause difficulties tomorrow.

4. Paragraphs 3 and 4, when presented by the Swedish Chairman, were liberally sprinkled with the verb 'shall': we insisted on the use of 'will'.

5. The Swedish Chairman also suggested that the preparatory meeting for the meeting of high officials should be held on 1 June 1977. This appeared acceptable to all, with the exception of the French who proposed 1 July 1977. Eventually all agreed on 15 June 1977.

6. In discussion of paragraph 4 we attempted to obtain a text which made

[3] Mr. V. Lipatti was the Romanian Head of Delegation. Mr. Cleghorn observed in an analytical paper, enclosed with a letter to Mr. Figgis of 18 July, that, throughout Stage II, 'the Romanians' vocal and insistent advoc[ac]y of an institutionalised follow-up, with frequent periodic meetings of all kinds, distinguished them clearly from their Warsaw Pact partners, with whom they did not appear to co-ordinate'. But Mr. Cleghorn added that the extravagance of their demands had weakened their credibility, and in the final stages of the negotiations, when they had come under considerable Russian pressure, they had displayed 'unexpected moderation'.

[4] Mr. Cleghorn insisted in his paper (*v. ibid.*) that the West's major objective had been to ensure the effective implementation of Conference decisions, and that they had therefore sought to make this a condition of follow-up by postponing any decision on future meetings until after an interim period. 'In the final stage of negotiations', he recalled, 'the lack of realism, failure to identify objectives precisely, and tactical ineptitude of the West's laggards, the Dutch, the Belgians and above all the French, denied the Alliance a final result which would have been more satisfactory than the compromise which actually emerged.'

[5] Viscount Davignon appears to have stopped off at Geneva on his way to the EC Political Directors meeting in Rome on 7-8 July.

it clear that the expenses of expert meetings during the interim period provided for under paragraph 1(*c*) would only be borne by the States actually taking part. The Roumanians tabled a satisfactory text drafted in consultation with us. However this encountered fierce resistance from the Swiss, who alleged that such a provision would jeopardize the agreements in the Special Working Body on the financing for the expert meeting on the Swiss proposal on the peaceful settlement of disputes. We received no support from the Canadians and others who shared our reservations on the original text. Under pressure from all the other delegations (and the clock) we finally agreed to accept the compromise in MIFT.

7. There was no discussion of the venue for the 1977 preparatory meeting. In the NATO caucus no strong preferences were expressed though a number of delegations mentioned Belgrade.

8. The Working Group tomorrow will register the text either tonight or tomorrow. If you see any insurmountable problems in it, we would be grateful for very urgent advice. At this stage it is very unlikely that we could obtain substantial improvement. The solution to this problem is inextricably entangled with the question of setting a date for Phase III and it is essential therefore that a solution should be found swiftly.

No. 132

Sir D. Hildyard (UKMIS Geneva) to Mr. Callaghan

No. 540 Telegraphic [*WDW 1/13*]

Immediate. Confidential   GENEVA, *11 July 1975, 11 a.m.*

Repeated for Information to Immediate Helsinki, Priority UKDEL NATO, Valletta and Rome.

For Tickell, WOD.
My telegram No. 536.[1]

Timing of Stage III and Malta

1. Mintoff is still refusing consensus to the Canadian proposal for a conditional agreement on the date for Stage III.[2] He has undertaken to let

---

[1] This telegram of 10 July reported that Mr. J.A. Kingswell (Maltese diplomat multiply-accredited to Western capitals) had just rejected as inadequate an offer made to him by the Yugoslavs on behalf of the Nine, NATO and the Warsaw Pact, with a view to overcoming Maltese objections to the agreed texts of the Mediterranean Declaration and the Follow-up Resolution. The offer included the insertion as a final paragraph in the Mediterranean Declaration of a text expressing the intention of participants to maintain and amplify the contacts and dialogue initiated by the CSCE with non-participating Mediterranean states 'with the purpose of contributing to peace, strengthening security, lessening tension in the area, and widening the scope of cooperation'. See No. 130, note 8.

[2] Under pressure from the Finns, who had contracts to confirm if conference arrangements were to be settled within three weeks, the Coordinating Committee worked throughout 9 and 10 July to secure agreement on the end of July as a date for Stage III. On 9 July the Canadians, with the backing of the Fifteen, proposed that the Committee should set 30 July as

[me] have a considered reply by 1100 this morning and the Co-ordinating Committee is due to meet at 1200.

2. During the afternoon of 10 July the Romanians proposed an additional sentence to the text in paragraph 2 of my telegram under reference. The revised offer is set out in my telegram No. 539.[3] It was quickly cleared by all groups, Mendelevich (USSR) and Alexander jointly chairing the Western meeting (without reciprocity from the Warsaw Pact). The Maltese delegation gave the impression of being prepared to recommend acceptance.

3. According to the Finns, Mintoff, in his telephone conversation with their Foreign Minister, expressed full understanding of Finnish difficulties but said that he was not yet in a position to give his consensus. All the other delegations then continued to sit around in increasing rage and humiliation until about 2200 when Kingswell appeared with Mintoff's reply. This was to the effect that he would not be able to consider the offer and reply definitively before 1100 on 11 July: meanwhile Malta could not agree to the Canadian proposal. Kingswell added that Mintoff was in bed with a slight fever, and could not discuss the question until he had had further consultations with his advisers in the morning.

4. Kovalev was by then threatening to tear down the building with his bare hands and Iloniemi[4] (Finland) only just managed to restrain himself from hitting the Maltese Ambassador. When Kingswell arrived Kovalev had been telling Sherer (US) and myself that we had been placed in an intolerable position. He suggested that we should now all (i.e. all except Malta) consider whether we could not (i) express formally to the Finns our support for the Canadian proposal, (ii) ask them whether bilateral undertakings to share responsibilities, given outside the formal framework of the Conference, would be sufficient for them to go ahead, and (iii) if so, agree to give these undertakings as soon as possible. Kovalev also told us that he had sent Gromyko a draft of an extremely strong letter to Mintoff. Sherer then arranged for a draft to be prepared for Kissinger who was spending the evening in discussions with Gromyko at the Soviet Mission. I said that Mintoff knew that the consensus rule was considered of crucial importance by many, if not all, of the participants. We should be very careful not to give the

the target date, aim to complete Stage II business on 15 July, and ask Finland to proceed with the necessary arrangements on the understanding that the political and financial responsibilities for any other course would be shared by participants. Only the Maltese offered any resistance to this formula. They had already blocked progress by refusing to lift their reserve on the follow-up text until they received satisfaction on the Mediterranean Declaration, and without agreement on follow-up neither the Romanians nor the Swiss were prepared to accept the QRR provision (see No. 130, notes 3 and 7) upon which the West Germans were insisting (UKMIS Geneva telegrams Nos. 532 and 533 of 10 July, WDW 1/23).

[3] The additional sentence transmitted in this telegram of 11 July declared that participants 'would seek, in the framwork of their multilateral efforts, to encourage progress and appropriate initiatives and to proceed to an exchange of views on the attainment' of the purposes of the Declaration.

[4] Mr. J. Iloniemi was Head of the Political Department of the Finnish Foreign Ministry.

impression that any of us wanted to undermine it otherwise many others might rally to Malta's support. Sherer agreed, and said that we should not dramatise the situation.

5. After Kingswell's statement Kovalev expanded his ideas to a number of others. It was agreed to consider the situation in our usual groups. The Fifteen had a long discussion in which I argued that of the three elements, the date, resistance to blackmail and consensus, we could only remain firm on two which should be the last two. Eventually it was agreed that we could do no more at that stage than express our support for the Canadian proposal, to encourage the Finns rather than in the hope of influencing the Maltese, and wait for Mintoff's considered reply. Meanwhile Kovalev and Sherer went to see Gromyko and Kissinger. According to Sherer, Kovalev made a tough statement with the references to irresponsibility, blackmail and betrayal that the Warsaw Pact countries have been repeating at every meeting. He then put forward the ideas mentioned in paragraph 4 above. Gromyko asked what Kissinger thought. After consulting Sherer Kissinger said that he did not believe that any such plan would command sufficient support. Gromyko accepted this and they then discussed the draft letters: also the possibility of asking the Italians to appeal to Mintoff. They agreed that the letters would have little effect and might indeed be counter-productive. Sherer consulted Farace (Italy) who declined to ask Rome to make an appeal: Sherer believes, however, that the US and USSR may make direct representations in Rome.

6. In the Co-ordinating Committee 26 delegations spoke in support of the Canadian proposal including those, such as ourselves, who had spoken yesterday. The Finns made another restrained statement and appealed again to the Committee to put them out of their agony. The Committee was then adjourned until 1200 on 11 July.[5]

7. In retrospect I think that the main features of this miserable day were:

(i) The widespread and genuine indignation at Mintoff's tactics. No doubt he intends us all to pay for not having given sufficient consideration to his proposals at an earlier stage, as well [as] achieving what he wants in the conclusions. The Maltese have certainly made themselves quite exception-

---

[5] When the Committee resumed, the Maltese proposed to insert into the Mediterranean Declaration the words 'reducing the armed forces in the region' after the phrase 'lessening tensions in the area' (see note 1 above). But while the US and Soviet delegates seemed ready to accept this amendment, Turkey and France were not (UKMIS Geneva telegrams Nos. 541 and 542 of 11 July). Sir D. Hildyard reported that the Americans hoped to have more influence over the Turks once Congress had agreed that military aid should be resumed, and that the next few days were 'likely to be spent in US-led probing of the Maltese and Turkish positions', whilst others continued to narrow the range of the remaining problems. Meanwhile, the Finns, who had decided to make greater use of their armed forces in preparing for a summit, were evidently reassured by the massive support for the Canadian proposal, 'which', Sir D. Hildyard observed, 'implied that some padding of bills for Stage III to compensate for their present difficulties would not lead to an outcry'. They would, Sir D. Hildyard thought, be prepared to see the final decision put off until about 18 July (UKMIS Geneva telegram No. 543 of 12 July).

ally unpopular, and Kovalev at least is vowing revenge.

(ii) The concern of the smaller countries especially the NNAs[6] and Romania at the possibility that the consensus principle may be undermined. Hence the Romanian efforts to find solutions. The Yugoslav Prime Minister also telephoned an appeal during the afternoon.

(iii) The impotence of the other 34 when faced by the determined opposition of any country which is relatively invulnerable to bilateral pressure, as long as the consensus rule is maintained. We were all in the Conference building until 2 a.m., Kissinger and Gromyko were in the Soviet Mission a few hundred yards away, and no-one could do anything.

FCO please pass advance copies to Figgis, WOD and Burns, EESD.

[6] Neutral and non-aligned.

No. 133

Sir D. Hildyard (UKMIS Geneva) to Mr. Callaghan
No. 554 Telegraphic [WDW 1/23]

Immediate. Confidential   GENEVA, *14 July 1975, 3 p.m.*

Repeated for information to Priority Washington, Helsinki, UKDEL NATO, Valletta, Moscow, Bonn, Paris, and to Saving all other NATO Posts.

For Tickell, WOD.
My tel[egram] No. 551.[1]

CSCE: Timing of Stage III and State of Play

1. The scenario outlined in my T[elegram]U[nder]R[eference] was followed this morning. Although there were some complications the texts of the Mediterranean Declaration, follow-up and QRR were agreed and noted or registered, and the Canadian proposal was adopted with one small amendment.

2. When Dubinin (USSR) was informed of NATO agreement to the last Maltese amendment he pressed strongly for the Canadian proposal to be revised to make the date of 30 July final, and to put off the review date of 15 July for a few more days. He said that the Soviet delegation attached great importance to these amendments. Representatives of the Fifteen and the neutrals told Kovalev that the package deal with the Maltese had been conditional on no amendments of any kind, and he climbed down within a matter of minutes.

[1] This telegram reported that at the NATO Heads of Delegation meeting on the afternoon of 12 July all the Fifteen, including Turkey, had expressed willingness to accept the new Maltese amendment (see No. 132 note 5). As the East and the neutral and non-aligned states had indicated that they would follow NATO, the way was clear for the Mediterranean Declaration to be agreed on the morning of 14 July, and subsequently follow-up, QRR and the Canadian proposal. It also seemed likely that the latter would be amended to make 18 July the date for the completion of Stage II work (WDW 1/13).

3. The Mediterranean Declaration with the Maltese amendment and a short reference to the friendly relations declaration (drafted rapidly by ourselves) was then registered (new texts in MIFT)[2] the French version of follow-up was agreed[3] accompanied by statements from the Soviet delegation and ourselves to the effect that we regarded the Russian and English versions as a true reflection of the French. (The Yugoslavs have a problem with the English translation which we hope to clear up this afternoon.) Sub-Committee A[4] then adopted the QRR sentence. Somewhat surprisingly there were five reservations (Sweden, Spain, Romania, Cyprus and Portugal), on which I shall be reporting separately.[5] Thereafter the Coordinating Committee adopted the Canadian proposal with an amendment, originally proposed by the Romanians, removing the direct reference to financial responsibility (text in MIFT).[6]

4. Both after the adoption of the text on the Mediterranean and of that on follow-up, the Belgian representative made a short statement in regard to the abuse of the consensus rule to which we had all been subjected. When the Canadian proposal had been safely adopted André (France) made a much stronger statement, attacking the Maltese for the way they had treated the other 34 delegations, their abuse of the consensus rule and their lack of the sense of responsibility which should animate all delegations at international conferences. André added a reference to the French attitude to MBFR and, without entering a reservation, said that France would have to return to this question in due course.[7] Farace (Italy) speaking only for the Italian delegation followed with a reference to the Maltese action which gave by the end an impression more of sympathy than of criticism. We will forward texts of these two statements as soon as we can obtain them. Mallia[8] (Malta) replied

---

[2] UKMIS Geneva telegram No. 555 (WDW 1/13) of 14 July transmitted the text of the final operative paragraphs of the Mediterranean Declaration. See *Human Rights*, vol. iii, pp. 74-5 for the full text registered by the Coordinating Committee.

[3] See No. 131, note 2.

[4] The Principles Sub-Committee.

[5] The interpretative statements of Sweden, Spain and Romania, with which Cyprus and Portugal associated themselves, each stressed that the 'rights and obligations . . . corresponding treaties and other agreements and arrangements' referred to in the QRR text in Principle 10 were those which were valid in, or in conformity with, international law (CSCE Journal No. 332 attached to minute from Mr. Burns to Miss S.J. Lambert (WED) of 16 July, WDW 1/2).

[6] See note 2 above. This amendment simply requested the Finns to make the necessary Conference arrangements on the understanding that all participating states accepted fully 'their joint responsibility for the achievement of this goal' (cf. No. 132, note 2).

[7] UKMIS Geneva telegram No. 551 (note 1 above) reported that, although the Maltese had had an 'outstanding diplomatic triumph', having 'obtained a substantial reflection of their original proposals', they had aroused 'quite extraordinary resentment and bitterness'. Mr. Kovalev told Sir D. Hildyard that 'large animals like elephants and the Soviet Union had remarkable memories, and never forgot insults or injuries'. And the French were 'furious' at having to accept tacitly a reference in the Mediterranean Declaration to the kind of MBFR with which they would not be associated on the European continent.

[8] Mr. C.J. Mallia was Maltese Ambassador to Switzerland.

not very impressively.

5. We have thus made a very big step forward. There are still a certain number of relatively important issues outstanding but the prospects of agreement on one of the most difficult, the Turkish case on CBMs, appear now to have improved considerably.[9] No mention has been made recently of the question of Cyprus representation but this remains of course a potential time bomb.

[9] During an informal meeting of the CBMs Sub-Committee on 16 July a text on amphibious and airborne manoeuvres was agreed (see *Human Rights*, vol. iii, pp. 357-8), on the basis of which the Turkish delegation were seeking approval from Ankara for their acceptance of a 250 kilometre area parameter (UKMIS Geneva telegram No. 568 of 17 July, WDW 1/4).

No. 134

Sir D. Hildyard (UKMIS Geneva) to Mr. Callaghan

No. 586 Telegraphic [*WDW 1/22*]

Immediate. Confidential GENEVA, *19 July 1975, 12.50 p.m.*

Repeated for information to Priority UKREP Brussels, Helsinki, Moscow, UKDEL NATO, UKDEL Strasbourg, Washington, Bonn, The Hague, Brussels, Luxembourg, Copenhagen, Paris, Dublin, Rome and to Saving Ankara, Athens, Oslo, Ottawa, Lisbon, Reykjavik.

CSCE: Agreement on outstanding issues and confirmation on the date of 30 July for Stage III

1. At 0240 this morning, but still formally on 18 July as the clock had been stopped at 2350, the Co-ordinating Committee adopted the Final Act (to be telegraphed later) and then confirmed the date of 30 July for the opening of Stage III in Helsinki in an atmosphere of rather artificial bonhomie and general exhaustion.

2. At the beginning of the evening's negotiation five main problems remained unresolved:-

  (*a*) The Turkish area exception in the CBM paper;
  (*b*) The reference to the 'irreversibility' of *détente* in the Final Act;[1]
  (*c*) Double signature;[2]
  (*d*) A group of translation problems in the principles;
  (*e*) The site of the 1977 meetings.

[1] The Russians had made their acceptance of the 'Berlin sentence' (see No. 130, note 5), then under discussion in an informal drafting group, dependent upon Western agreement to insert a reference to the 'irreversibility of *détente*' in the Final Act (telegram No. 384 to Bonn of 16 July, WDW 1/2).

[2] COREPER agreed on 11 July that EC delegations in Geneva should be informed that the Committee's position was, as agreed by Foreign Ministers in Luxembourg on 24 June, that the Italian Prime Minister must sign the Final Act in his dual capacity as President of the Council of Ministers of Italy and President of the Council of the EC (UKREP Brussels telegram No. 3374 of 11 July, WDW 1/15).

It was clear that at least the first three of these problems, and preferably all of them, would have to be resolved before the final decision could be taken.

3. The first and most difficult of the East-West problems was that of the reference to irreversibility. The Russians had been insisting that the inclusion of this word in the Final Act was essential for them. I had had a signal from Mendelevich several days ago that if the Fifteen made clear to Kovalev that the reference was unacceptable, it would probably be possible eventually to find some other solution. Unfortunately, the anxiety of the Germans about the so-called European clause[3] with which the Russians had linked the reference to irreversibility, led them to give the impression that they might be induced to put increasing pressure on all the rest of us to accept it.[4] This combined with the fact that agreement on the last few issues, particularly CBMs, had still not been reached, encouraged the Russians to remain very tough longer than might otherwise have been the case. After further futile discussions early in the evening, however, by which time it was clear that CBMs were the only remaining problem to be solved, they finally gave in and proposed a new Russian word which we have translated into English by 'continuing' (full text follows).[5] Mendelevich told me later that they hoped that by clearing this issue out of the way, they would build up pressure on the Turks and Cypriots.

4. A solution on the double signature, based on unilateral notification to the Secretariat by the participating states on 28 July of the form and style of their signature (by which time it will be too late for anyone to contest the double signature or the Turks whatever Cyprus may decide), had been put forward two days ago and apparently accepted by the Russians. Early yesterday evening, however, Kovalev told Farace that nothing had happened to change the views of his Government on their unwillingness to recognise the Community in this way. Delegations here were consequently faced with the difficult decision as to whether or not to insist on explicit Soviet acceptance now of double signature.[6] It was generally agreed, however, that Kovalev's

---

[3] i.e. the 'Berlin sentence'.

[4] In a minute to Sir J. Killick of 18 July Mr. Tickell explained that the West Germans were the 'principal wobblers on the Western side' since they had already indicated their readiness to accept reference to the irreversibility of *détente* in exchange for the Russian agreement to the 'Berlin sentence'. But, as Mr. Tickell warned Dr. van Well in a telephone conversation that morning, Mr. Callaghan 'was not prepared to subscribe to nonsense in a document of this kind' (WDW 1/15).

[5] The 'Berlin sentence' with its accompanying commitment 'to broaden, deepen and make continuing and lasting the process of *détente*' emerged as the fifth sub-paragraph of the preamble to the Final Act. See Cmnd. 6932, p. 226.

[6] Cf. No. 130, note 6. On 17 July Mr. Tickell informed the delegation in Geneva that Mr. Callaghan did not think the question of a Community signature should be regarded as a breaking point in the negotiations. He was ready to go along with his colleagues in pressing for something to go into the Final Act to establish that the Italian Prime Minister was signing in his capacity as EC President as well as representative of Italy (see note 2 above), but in the last resort he did not see why Sig. Moro could not make the point perfectly clear in his speech

remarks had probably been made for the record. Since he did not object to the procedure (details follow)[7] and since it would seem inconceivable for the Soviet Government to place the Conference at risk by raising objections in Helsinki, it was considered unnecessary to insist on clarification in Geneva.

5. The translation problems in Basket A [*sic*] relate largely, though not entirely, to the Russian language version of the agreed English texts. In my talks with both Kovalev and Mendelevich last night (para. 7 below) I said that if the other outstanding issues were resolved, we would not attempt to hold up the final decision on the basis of translation problems alone, but that they must help us over these. Laver made clear that we regarded the difficulties, particularly those in the seventh principle, as serious and if a mutually acceptable solution could not be found we would insist on making and having recorded a formal complaint. Mendelevich indicated that he took this seriously and that his delegation would co-operate in seeking a solution today.

6. Following a *coup de théâtre* engineered by the Romanian, Yugoslav and French delegations (without informing let alone consulting either the Nine or the Fifteen (in André's absence in Paris)), Belgrade's candidature to be host for the 1977 meetings was launched at a meeting of the Co-ordinating Committee early in the evening.[8] The Finns and their supporters, who were taken completely by surprise, failed to get Helsinki into the lists at all. However, the Soviet delegation, who were generally considered to be behind the Finnish candidature, made it clear in the corridors that they were not prepared to give up so easily. It was therefore evident that no decision on this would be possible during the evening without a major public confrontation. By common accord the problem was postponed until the next meeting of the Co-ordinating Committee today at 1800 hours. Although the Romanians are making difficulties and insisting that both the preparatory meeting and the main meeting should take place in one city, Belgrade, most of the Fifteen had come to support the compromise solution of the preliminary meeting in Helsinki and the main meeting in Belgrade (para. 3 of my tel[egram] No.

at Stage III (telegram No. 249 to UKMIS Geneva of 17 July, WDW 1/15). See Cmnd. 6932, pp. 222-3 for extracts from Sig. Moro's speech on 30 July.

[7] UKMIS Geneva telegram No. 590 of 20 July transmitted to the FCO the text of a statement to be made by the Executive Secretary of the Coordinating Committee before proceeding to register the text of the draft Final Act. It explained that the names of participating states would have to be inserted at the bottom of the text, along with the 'names and functions of their high representatives', and that that this information should be supplied to the Secretariat on 28 July (WDW 1/15).

[8] According to UKMIS Geneva telegram No. 569 of 17 July, the Yugoslavs had already made it plain that it might suit them very well to have a major international meeting in Belgrade in 1977. Western delegations were inclined to sympathise with this view, and were doubtful about the other contender, Helsinki, because there was a risk of appearing to make it the permanent headquarters for pursuit of the CSCE process. Eastern delegations, despite having previously given the Yugoslavs an undertaking that they would support Belgrade, now seemed to be supporting Helsinki.

582),[9] and the Eastern delegations have now come out informally in favour of this. While administratively much less satisfactory, it now seems likely to be the only politically acceptable arrangement.

7. By 1130 last night, therefore, the only problem unresolved was that of the Turkish area exception on CBMs. The Russians began to panic as badly as they had in the Maltese case, and to submit us to their usual mixture of intense pressure and desperate appeals. Kovalev told me that his position in Moscow was becoming impossible as he had made concessions especially on irreversibility which were only considered justified if we could confirm the date that day. I said that we were helping as much as possible (see para. 5 above). During the whole day we, the Canadians, and Norwegians continued to try to narrow the gap between the Turks and Cypriots, (see MIFT)[10] and as time passed both came under increasing emotional and political pressure. The Turks, who spent a great deal of time arguing among themselves, moved a little but then dug in and met all further approaches with long, impassionate [*sic*] and mainly incoherent defences of their policies. The small Cypriot delegation wandered around by themselves for over an hour in an agony of indecision. Eventually the Greek Ambassador who both as a Greek, and as an ex-Ambassador in Cyprus has wanted to maintain a low profile while playing a generally helpful part, plucked at my sleeve, and told me that he thought that a solution might be possible on the basis that the Cypriots would protest but not block consensus. The Cyprus Ambassador then confirmed this to me and we were through. There was a further moment of suspense when he and the Turk had a heated exchange in Sub-Committee C, but all was well. We must now expect further very tough statements at the last meeting of the Co-ordinating Committee, but there is no reason to fear any serious upset.

[9] In this telegram of 18 July Sir D. Hildyard suggested that the 'only way to avoid a potentially embarrassing disagreement may be to have the preparatory meeting in one capital (? Helsinki) and the main meeting in the other (? Belgrade)'.

[10] This telegram of 19 July reported that, after a marathon 15-hour negotiation, the problem of the Turkish area exception had been settled, and a 'fragile' text agreed in the CBMs Sub-Committee for registration. This asserted, with regard to the prior notification of manoeuvres, that a participating state whose territory extended beyond Europe need not 'give notification in cases in which that area [was] also contiguous to the participating state's frontier facing or shared with a non-European non-participating state'. The Cypriot delegation did not withhold consensus to the text, but read a statement of interpretation into the Journal (see *Human Rights*, vol. iii, pp. 358-9), which said that the new phrase was not only 'merely unnecessary but also detrimental to confidence building in a sensitive part of the world'. It further pointed to the discretionary nature of the commitment and expressed the hope that there would be no abuse of this provision. The Turkish delegation then insisted on inserting a further statement in the Journal to the effect that more than one participating state was covered by the provisions of this paragraph. Although the Turkish delegate had said that he would withdraw consensus to the agreed CBMs text if the Cypriots did not withdraw their statement, Sir D. Hildyard was confident that 'wiser counsel' would prevail that morning (19 July) enabling the Sub-Committee to proceed to registration in the afternoon (WDW 1/4).

No. 135

Letter from Dr. Fielder (UKMIS Geneva) to Mr. T. Alexander
[*WDW 1/5*]

Confidential   GENEVA, *21 July 1975*

Dear Tom,

CSCE: Economic Committee: The Closing Stages

1. It might be useful to you to have a record of the last days of the debate on MFN and reciprocity. The first signs of a possible pattern for a future solution came on 10 July when the Swiss delegate, Mr. Lugon,[1] presented a formula which included the suggestion that reciprocity should permit an equitable/balanced sharing of advantages and obligations. The East argued that they preferred the word 'equitable' and that they could not accept 'balanced' whereas the Nine argued the reverse. This formula on 'sharing', or 'distribution' as it later became, was to dominate the discussion in the closing days of the debate. The main problem, however, was that the Swiss formula was clearly much too weak for the Community and was not suitable to form the basis of a possible compromise. The days following were marked by rather bad-tempered discussions and attempts by both sides to manipulate the Swiss formula to their own advantage. During this phase the East consistently refused any other form of working other than the large open groups, although the Nine favoured a small representative group. This phase was brought to a head when, at an afternoon session on Saturday 12 July, the Federal Republic and myself both made very strong statements condemning the Eastern philibustering and pointing out that unless we had a more constructive attitude from the Eastern countries we could end up with no mention of either MFN or reciprocity.

2. These interventions apparently unnerved the Soviet delegation, who started to worry about whether they would be able to obtain any mention of MFN in the final document. This enabled Kawan (Commission) to arrange an impromptu dinner party on that evening, at which the East, neutrals and Nine were represented. The most positive element to come out of this dinner party was that the Swede, Ekholm,[2] who had until that time been fairly silent, surfaced as a possible middle man in the negotiations. His sensible ideas dominated the group, where the Nine were represented by the Italian Presidency and Kawan, and on Monday,[3] when discussions restarted, it was clearer that there might be some possibility of a compromise. It was on that day that Ekholm, with some help from myself on the English language, produced a text which was in fact to serve as a basis for the future compromise. This text was discussed on that Monday evening and I attach a

---

[1] M. J. Lugon was a member of the Swiss delegation.

[2] Herr G. Ekholm was a member of the Swedish delegation.

[3] i.e. 14 July.

copy for the record.[4] For the first time the Soviet delegation appeared to be rattled and their performance that evening suggested that it would be difficult to persuade them to agree to any text at all, but when on the following morning Ekholm produced a second text, which I also attach,[5] the possibilities improved.

3. During 15 July the Soviet Union reverted to a very negative attitude. They refused to discuss anything and said that they had instructions from Moscow to stop negotiations on the question of reciprocity. However, a number of us felt that this was simply their traditional stance of appearing particularly negative prior to giving in.

4. In retrospect, it looks as though the East had decided to give in at about this time, but had not decided exactly how to do it. As it turned out, they invited the French delegate, de Soye,[6] to their Mission that evening and kept him there most of the night, negotiating on the basis of the second Swedish text. During this all-night discussion the Russians, led apparently by Dubinin, made it clear to de Soye that they were prepared to qualify reciprocity in some way. They told him that they could accept 'an equitably balanced distribution of advantages and obligations'. However, de Soye apparently retired to bed at 6.00 a.m. and, under the effects of the Soviet hospitality, slept through most of the morning without informing his Ambassador, André, who attended a meeting of the Heads of Delegation of the Nine that morning at 10.00 a.m. oblivious of these discussions. At this meeting, the Nine's Ambassadors decided that André should make a *démarche* to the Soviet Union explaining the importance which the Community put on a satisfactory solution of the question of reciprocity. A text using the words 'comparable scale' which I also attach,[7] was agreed at this meeting for André to use as a negotiating

---

[4] Not printed. This text reaffirmed in its preamble participants' will to intensify economic cooperation, irrespective of their economic and social systems, in order 'to achieve mutual satisfaction, arising from equality and reciprocity, permitting on the whole, a balanced and equitable distribution of advantages and obligations'. Its trade chapter expressed their resolve 'to promote on the basis of reciprocity, and under conditions stipulated in bilateral and multilateral agreements, the expansion of their mutual trade', and recognised the beneficial effects of MFN treatment.

[5] Not printed. This differed from the previous Swedish text insofar as it made explicit reference in its preamble to economic cooperation 'with due regard for the different levels of economic development', and to this 'permitting, on the whole, a distribution of advantages and obligations of comparable scale, in observance of bilateral and multilateral agreements'. The trade chapter omitted any reference to reciprocity, stated participants' resolve to promote 'on the basis of the modalities of their economic cooperation' the expansion of their mutual trade, and again recognised the value of MFN treatment.

[6] M. de Soye was a member of the French delegation.

[7] Not printed. The structure of the text agreed by the Heads of the Nine on 16 July was much the same as the previous Swedish one (*v. ibid.*), but it recognised that economic cooperation could be developed 'on the basis of equality and mutual satisfaction of the partners, and of reciprocity permitting, as a whole, a distribution of advantages and obligations of comparable scale and in an equitable way; with due regard for bilateral and multilateral agreements'.

basis.

5. The rest of the events of 16 July are shrouded in mystery, but it is clear that, although de Soye was aware later that his Ambassador was to approach the Russians, he himself hoped that the text he had negotiated with them during the previous night might serve as a basis for future compromise. Both he and the Russians tried very hard to jump Committee II into agreeing on a text at its session that afternoon. But neither the Nine, nor members of the Fifteen, had given their approval to the text which de Soye had negotiated and in fact the Americans were very angry that negotiations of which they were unaware had taken place. Although de Soye was persuaded not to put his text forward, the US delegation were particularly angry that the Nine had implicitly suggested to the Russians that they were willing to drop any link between MFN and reciprocity in exchange for a relatively strong definition of reciprocity.

6. The French delegation eventually managed to uncross their wires and negotiations continued between them and the Russians into Thursday 17 July. Meanwhile, the US delegation opened up their own bilateral negotiations with the Soviet Union on the question of the link between reciprocity and MFN. Rather surprisingly, but possibly because of the increasing time pressure on everybody concerned, a compromise was reached on both these questions during Thursday. Things moved rapidly on the Thursday afternoon and I was able to report to you by telegram that evening (our tel[egrams] Nos. 578 and 579)[8] that a text had been provisionally registered concerning reciprocity in the preamble to Committee II and MFN in the operative part of the Commercial Exchanges section.

7. That evening the Committee met to discuss all outstanding questions and, although I eventually had to withdraw our proposal that the economic information paper should include a reference to information on balance of payments, it was possible for the Committee to agree on a structure for the whole of the Committee II text, based on a proposal which I had made at an informal meeting the day before. For once we were able to use the Russians' self-imposed deadline and obtained compromises from them, that we had not anticipated, concerning the sub-titling of the Environment and Science and Technology texts.

8. Other outstanding points and the actual wording of the titles and sub-titles were cleared up on the Friday morning, but it was soon apparent that the Secretariat would take some time before they would be able to produce a completed document which Committee II could pass to the Co-ordinating Committee. This did not deter the Soviet Union, aided by a biased Czech Chairman, from insisting during the Friday afternoon that it was not lack of documentation from the Secretariat that was preventing us from putting our document to the Co-ordinating Committee, but that the Western delegations

---

[8] The text reported in these telegrams of 17 July was virtually the same as the second Swedish text of 15 July (see note 5 above), but included in the general provisions of its trade chapter the phrase: '. . . bearing in mind that the provisions contained in the general preamble apply in particular to this sector'.

lacked the political will to complete their work. When it became transparently clear that this was nonsense, the Soviet delegate transferred his anger onto the Secretariat, who were staunchly defended by delegations from the Nine. After a rather stormy session that evening it was agreed that it was useless for the Committee to meet throughout the night simply to receive the documents from the Secretariat in dribs and drabs and the Czech Chairman was forced into accepting my proposal, seconded by the US, that we should meet early on the Saturday morning.

9. In the event the Committee met on the morning of Saturday 19 July and approved all the texts for Committee II in all six languages in a much improved atmosphere. They were adopted by the Co-ordinating Committee that evening. I attach a copy of the English, French and Russian versions of the agreed text.[9]

Yours ever,

M.L. FIELDER[10]

[9] Not printed. See Cmnd. 6932, pp. 237-57 and *Human Rights*, vol. vi, pp. 197-218 for those parts of the Final Act relating to cooperation in the field of economics, of science and technology and of the environment (Committee II).

[10] In a letter to Mr. Preston of 12 August, in which he paid tribute to the contribution of Dr. Fielder to the Basket III negotiations, Sir J. Killick recalled that a Home Civil Servant would not normally be expected to be separated from his wife and family for such a long period. He added: 'From this point of view (if not others) there was perhaps something to be said for the Cold War! Indeed, it remains to be seen whether it is over, or has only taken new shape. It will, I am afraid, still involve a great deal of time and effort on the part of a number of Whitehall Departments, including your own, before we find out.' (MTW 10/557/11).

No. 136

Sir D. Hildyard (UKMIS Geneva) to Mr. Callaghan

[*WDW1/22*]

Confidential GENEVA, *25 July 1975*

Summary . . .[1]

Sir,

CSCE: The Conclusion of Stage II

As I reported in my telegram No. 594 of 21 July,[2] Stage II of the Conference on Security and Co-operation in Europe was concluded in the

[1] Not printed.

[2] This described the final meeting of the Coordinating Committee, which ended at 03.40 a.m. on 21 July, and the decision then taken, after a prolonged debate, to convene the 1977 follow-up Conference in Belgrade. Completion of the Committee's work was further delayed by: (1) a clash between the Turkish and Cyprus representatives over the composition of the Cyprus delegation to Stage III; and (2) an undignified argument between Mr. Lipatti and Mr. Mendelevich over the motion of thanks to be addressed to the Governments of Finland, Switzerland and Yugoslavia. 'By the time that this wrangle was finished', Sir D. Hildyard

early hours of the morning of that day, after 22 months of extremely tough negotiations.

2. In his despatch of 29 July, 1974, which he called 'The Long Haul'[3] my predecessor set out the background to the Conference, the different interests in play, and the tactics and procedures which had developed. I do not propose in this despatch to describe these again in any detail. Nor to analyse either the lengthy and tortuous course of the negotiations, which I hope has been sufficiently covered in telegrams and letters, or the conclusions set out in the 115 pages of Declarations, Resolutions and Recommendations which are contained in what will no doubt come to be known as the Green Book, to distinguish it from the Blue Book of the Helsinki Recommendations which constituted the mandate for Stage II. (A summary of the various sectors is attached at Annex I.)[4] The results of Stage II, and their implications for all the participants, are now being subjected to careful and detailed studies which will form a separate and voluminous series. I shall confine myself to trying to highlight what seem to me to be the most important or interesting aspects of the Conference, and to offering some comments on the objectives, methods and reactions of the main delegations and groups.

Eastern objectives and policies

3. For many years the Soviet Union had wanted the West formally to accept, in Mr. Gromyko's words, 'the political and territorial realities' resulting from the Second World War, and at the same time to subscribe to East-West *détente* in the limited sense which the Russians conceived of it. The Helsinki preparatory talks showed that the price of the West's agreement would be the broadening of the concept of *détente* to include a gradual liberalisation of contacts between people and in the fields of information and ideas. The Soviet Union was clearly anxious to limit this price as much as possible when the concrete details came to be worked out during Stage II.

4. The Soviet delegation was large (almost 100), very active and well briefed, and quick to use any bargaining weapon or to exploit any opening whether in bilateral or multilateral relations. I attach at Annex II some notes on their personalities and tactics together with those of other main delegations,[5]

concluded, 'everyone had had enough and the Conference ended abruptly without any of the gestures of friendship or the plethora of congratulatory speeches which we had all expected.'

[3] No. 94.

[4] Not printed.

[5] Not printed. In this summary Sir D. Hildyard described Mr. Kovalev as 'extremely tough, even if inclined to get into a great state of nerves when things looked like going wrong for him', and temperamentally inclined 'to use the big stick wherever he could'. Mr. Dubinin, he noted, 'gave the impression that he himself would have much preferred to stare us out, if necessary for years'; and Mr. Mendelevich he considered 'an old hand at multilateral diplomacy and a wily old fox'. Sir D. Hildyard also thought Mr. Mendelevich much more sensitive to the attitude of others and to the 'political realities' than his colleagues. 'He and Ambassador Dubinin', he added, 'were clearly at daggers drawn and, as regards tactics at least, he appeared to have no great respect for Kovalev. On several occasions he asked us in strict confidence to help him put across a more moderate line within his own delegation. Some of this may have been carefully staged, but in fact the moderate line proved successful in almost every case.'

which may be of some interest in the context of future discussions. The Soviet delegation's difficulty was that in the Conference as a whole they were the *demandeurs*, and that after negotiating extremely toughly for a long period they were put by the Soviet leadership under a time pressure which became intense in the latter stages. Strategically they would have done better to have shown more flexibility much earlier, rather than stand firm for so long only to have to make very substantial concessions towards the end in order to ensure that Stage III could be held at the end of July.[6] Tactically also the rigidity of their system created problems for them; they wasted a good deal of time and bargaining strength on points which realistically they could not hope to obtain, or which were of only secondary importance, apparently because they had high-level instructions, issued some time ago in very different circumstances, which were very difficult for them to change.

5. The Soviet leadership have achieved political, though not legal, recognition of the *status quo*; the results of the Conference are not legally binding. Also a summit meeting in July from which they will try to extract every possible propaganda advantage. No doubt Mr. Brezhnev needed this badly for his own time-table. I believe, however, that they have paid quite a high price, particularly in Basket III. It may be that they intend to take advantage of all the escape clauses which they succeeded in having included, and to pay little more than lip-service to the agreements reached. In this case they will, if the West remains determined, come under great and increasing pressure in the years to come, and may be put almost permanently on the defensive. Alternatively they may calculate that movement in the direction of greater liberalisation is inevitable, and that the conclusions of the Conference will still permit them to control the rate of evolution in order to ensure that it constitutes no serious threat in the foreseeable future. This is the official line of the professional diplomats in the Soviet delegation. Speculations in these fields are more for Her Majesty's Ambassador at Moscow than for the delegation in Geneva,[7] but it is clear that the Conference took a very different course from that which the Soviet Union had originally expected, and that the Soviet authorities were thankful when at last they could extricate themselves from it.

Co-ordination among the Warsaw Pact States

6. The Warsaw Pact delegations co-ordinated as a group in the same way as did those of the Nine and Fifteen (NATO). I have already reported on various occasions about the divergencies within the Warsaw Pact. The Roman-

[6] In a retrospective paper of 30 September, 'Negotiating with the Russians: a personal view based on experience during Stage II of the CSCE', Mr. Alexander analysed the weaknesses exhibited by Soviet diplomacy at the Conference. Amongst the Soviet negotiating errors he listed were: (1) their underestimation of the scope for obduracy and obstruction on the part of participants who were able to shelter behind others when their own special interests were at stake; (2) their underestimation of the patience of Western public opinion and Western Ministers; (3) their tying of Mr. Brezhnev's own prestige to the achievement of a summit by a given date; (4) their 'self-defeating inflexibility' in Basket IV; and (5) tactics which alienated most other delegations and emphasised the 'we/they character of the negotiations' (ENZ 3/303/1).

[7] See No. 141.

ian delegation, who were both able and highly articulate, pursued very much their own policies and interests, to the great irritation of the Russians (and of the West in Basket III), until near the end of the negotiations. They then became far more moderate and co-operative over a wide range of issues on which they had previously been very tough; apparently as the result of Soviet pressure and Romania's growing economic difficulties. Even so the Romanians obtained a satisfactory document on the non-use of force which they regard as strengthening still further their hand against the Russians.

7. The other Warsaw Pact members all toed the line obediently, at least on major issues. Several times the Russians negotiated away points which one or other considered of great importance without informing let alone consulting them. This was particularly the case with the East Germans (Peaceful Change of Frontiers, Irreversibility of *Détente*, etc.) who may, however, have played up to the West Germans their resentment at the way in which they had been treated. On a few occasions one or more of the East Europeans differed from the Russians on a not very significant issue, almost always in the direction of greater inflexibility, and on minor matters such as the Easter break (which the Russians none the less made into a major political question) several were prepared to come out publicly against them. At this stage the conclusion can only be that the Russians can still crack the whip on any matter of importance and do not hesitate to do so. The Conference together with its follow-up, however, and above all the consensus rule, should gradually have an influence on relationships. And even if the Russians themselves only pay lip-service to the results in Basket III, they will find it very difficult to oppose movement towards greater liberalisation in any other Warsaw Pact country which is prepared to allow it.

Western objectives and policies

8. The main Western interests were on the one hand to avoid any commitments which could imply eventual acceptance of a pan-European security system or condonation of the Brezhnev Doctrine, or which could prejudice the reunification of Germany, the development of the European Communities, or the complicated position in Berlin; on the other to reduce to the maximum extent possible the barriers of suspicion and mistrust between East and West (paragraph 3 above). Their view on the latter issue was well summarised by President Kekkonen at the opening of Stage I when he described security as a matter of opening gates rather than erecting fences.[8] Certain US journalists like to talk in terms of winners and losers in the protracted negotiations, but in practice it was clear from the early stages that the result would be a series of compromises. The West protected its position in the political sector, with the references in the Principles to Self-Determination and to the possibility of Peaceful Change balancing that to the Inviolability of Frontiers to which the Russians attach such importance. And the references to Human Rights together with the conclusions of Basket III have ensured that these questions are now accepted as legitimate matters for

[8] See *Human Rights*, vol. i, p. 36.

international concern; a whole series of agreements have been reached and commitments, even if very often qualified, accepted.

9. It is difficult to assess from Geneva the importance of the Confidence Building Measures for which the UK delegation in particular worked so hard. Their value was always political, in reducing the huge barriers of secrecy within which the Russians, and above all the Soviet State, have always operated. I believe the Soviet negotiators when they say that although the commitment is on a voluntary basis, it will not be possible for the Soviet Union not to comply with it. There are indeed many pointers to Soviet desire to complement political with military *détente* in due course in order to reduce their crippling armaments bill. The results of the Conference could be a very useful first step, and an encouragement to progress in the talks in Vienna.

10. Nor is it easy to evaluate here the result of the second (Economic) Basket. The conclusions on Business Contacts and Facilities and on Economic and Commercial Information should be useful. The great battles on Most-Favoured-Nation treatment and Reciprocity ended in a draw but slightly to the advantage of the West. Possibly the most important result of all was the *de facto* recognition of the European Economic Community by the Warsaw Pact countries (see also paragraph 12 below).

11. The Conference could only be a stage in the process of *détente*, and a great deal will depend on the way in which the implementation of its results can be assessed and reviewed; thus on the continuing cohesion and determination of the West. Nevertheless, starting from the premise that the West had no practical alternative to the recognition of the *status quo* and that the *Ost-Verträge* had already taken a large step in this direction,[9] I believe that we can conclude that a satisfactory price was extracted for this recognition, while the potentially awkward consequences were avoided.

Co-ordination among the Nine and the Fifteen (NATO)

12. Co-ordination among the Nine was both one of the major successes of the Conference, and a major contribution to the achievement of satisfactory results. Some heads of delegation of the Nine while intelligent and good negotiators in their own right, could be extraordinarily verbose and finicky. Both the French[10] and the Germans[11] in their different ways caused compli-

[9] See No. 1, note 8 and Cmnd. 6201, pp. 221-2, 226-7 and 268-70 for treaties between the FRG and Soviet Union (August 1970), Poland (December 1970) and Czechoslovakia (June 1973).

[10] In Annex II (see note 5 above) Sir D. Hildyard was particularly scathing in his criticism of the 'unpredictable' conduct of the French and their endeavours to negotiate separately with the Russians. 'Though tightly controlled from Paris, the French delegation', he wrote, 'contained individuals who appeared incapable of refraining from highly personal operations and intrigues. The official mainly responsible never seemed to learn from experience, and after every failure was quickly to be seen again whispering in corners in the same conspiratorial way (thereby adding a new word to a number of languages—to "chazzle", meaning to intrigue unsuccessfully).'

[11] One of the main problems of the West Germans, in Sir D. Hildyard's opinion, 'was that they were divided both in Geneva and in Bonn, and consequently they acted at times both individually and with unco-ordinated instructions'.

cations. So on a much lesser scale did at times the Dutch[12] (see also Annex II). Co-ordination consequently absorbed an immense amount of time which many delegations hoped to devote to other work. Nevertheless the repeated failures of those who tried to go it alone, and the effectiveness of the Nine when acting together, must, I believe, have had their effect, including on many, although alas not all, of the French. There was a general feeling that the success of our co-ordination had given a considerable fillip to the development of political co-operation in the future. At the same time the European Commission considered that it had emerged with increased status and influence *vis-à-vis* the State trading countries.

13. Co-ordination among the Fifteen NATO members was very good on the whole although there were moments when the Nine took so long to reach a common position that they appeared to be giving the others far too little time for adequate consideration and consultations. There were also moments when the Scandinavians felt that they had special interests, e.g. where Finland was concerned. Fortunately the Cyprus question caused very little trouble within the Alliance or indeed within the Conference at large; even the last-minute flurries over the Confidence Building Measures and representation at Stage III did not hold us up long.

14. The US deserve a special mention. Dr. Kissinger had given instructions that the US delegation should keep in line with the Nine, indeed 'half a step behind' if this were logically possible. On certain issues the US negotiated directly and effectively with the Soviet Union, e.g. at the behest of the Federal Republic of Germany over Peaceful Change [of] Frontiers. On others their influence and support was extremely helpful, for instance over the package deal in Basket III, and in particular on Working Conditions for Journalists. As against this Dr. Kissinger's discussions on Confidence Building Measures were widely considered unhelpful, and may indeed have led to the West obtaining rather less than they could have expected on Prior Notification of Military Manoeuvres. In most sectors, however, the Americans were faithful but lack-lustre allies, determined not to allow themselves to be inveigled by the Russians into Super Power negotiations which could have been very unpopular with all the other Europeans.

Neutral and non-aligned objectives and policies

15. The neutral and non-aligned delegations stood together on many issues as the best way to ensure that their interests were taken into account. They had, of course, only a certain amount in common. They all felt to some extent out in the cold outside the main military alliances, and welcomed a conference in which they could participate as equals. They all attached crucial importance to the consensus rule. They all wanted definite arrangements for continuing the multilateral dialogue, and indeed most would have liked to see some form of institutionalisation. On this as on many

[12] 'The Dutch', Sir D. Hildyard remarked in Annex II, 'were never sure that the Conference was a good thing from the Western point of view, and for most of the negotiations remained stubbornly determined to press a little harder than anyone else.'

questions the Romanians behaved more as a non-aligned country than as a member of the Warsaw Pact. On other issues some of the neutrals, particularly the Swedes and the Swiss, were clearly Western in outlook. And in Basket III the Russians said quite rightly that there were no neutrals. Unfortunately at times personalities counted more than policies with usually unhelpful results. In general, however, both neutrals and non-aligned were of considerable assistance to the West, and it remained a cardinal point of Western policy to ensure close and continued consultations with them.

Malta and the Mediterranean States

16. I shall not recount again in this despatch Malta's efforts to extend the scope of the Conference to include the non-participating Mediterranean States, and her success in extracting general agreement at the last moment, both to the continuation and amplification of the dialogue with these States, and to the inclusion in the document on the Mediterranean of a reference to lessening tension and to reducing armed forces in the region. This operation was certainly important as an illustration of the use or misuse which can be made of the consensus rule. It remains to be seen how successful it will prove in practice. Also, what effect Malta's behaviour will have on the other participating States and their attitude to future meetings.

The follow-up to the Conference

17. After a battle in the corridors it was decided that both the preparatory meeting and the meeting of the representatives of Foreign Ministers in 1977 should take place in Belgrade rather than in Helsinki as the Russians wished, or one meeting in each capital as was suggested at one time. Politically this could be a very interesting and important time for Yugoslavia. If there is to be a satisfactory review of the implementation of the results of the Conference, preparatory work will have to be well co-ordinated and begun in good time. Consideration is now being given both by delegations and in capitals to the most effective procedures.

The UK contribution

18. I have left until last the contribution which the UK delegation was able to make. In recent years at least we have been apt to be more modest than other countries about our achievements. There is no doubt, however, that particularly in the later phases of the Conference, the delegation played a considerable role in almost every sector.

19. We played a major role in the drafting of the Final Act proper. In Basket I we were tough on Principles but ready with helpful suggestions and compromises, while on Confidence Building Measures we had the leading part throughout. In Basket II (Economic) we were prominent in paving the way for agreement, and were specially thanked by the representatives of the European Commission for the support and assistance which we had given them. In Basket IV (Follow-up) we also helped considerably towards the achievement of a compromise solution. It was in Basket III, however, that we made the biggest impact with our initiative for a package deal which led to a breakthrough after many months of impasse. Our concept of exploiting the time pressure on the Russians to confront them with a choice between

making rapid and substantial concessions, but with an assurance that these represented the outer limit of the commitments which they would be called on to accept, or indefinite delay with no assurance that better terms would eventually be forthcoming, proved highly successful, and had a significant influence on the negotiations in all other sectors.

20. One should not exaggerate the part which any Western delegation could play either in achieving results or in speeding up the work of the Conference. As I have emphasised in paragraph 12 above, by far the most important factors were the unity and determination of the Nine and the Fifteen. Nevertheless I am sure that the relatively satisfactory results of the Conference, and the fact that it was terminated in time for Stage III to take place in July, were due at least as much to us as to any other Western participant. I should like to pay warm tribute to all who participated in the work of the delegation in the course of the three long years since the early days at Dipoli, and particularly to the skill, imagination and endurance of those who formed part of it during the last gruelling months.

21. I am sending copies of this despatch to Her Majesty's Representatives in all participating States and to Her Majesty's Permanent Representatives to NATO, to the European Communities, to the UN and to the Council of Europe.

I have, etc.,

DAVID HILDYARD

No. 137

Mr. Callaghan to HM Representatives Overseas

Guidance No. 120 Telegraphic [MTW 10/557/6]

Confidential   FCO, *28 July 1975*

Conference on Security and Co-operation (CSCE)

My telegram Guidance No. 117.[1]

Instructions for Use

1. The following commentary is for your own information only.

Commentary on Points of the Final Act

General

2. Throughout the negotiations it was a common Western aim to ensure that the documents comprised in the Final Act of the Conference[2] should not have legal status. This was partly because we did not want to set up what would have amounted to a regional system of international law; partly because the matters dealt with were in many cases beyond the competence

---

[1] This telegram of 24 July instructed HM Representatives overseas to be guided in any general discussion of the CSCE by the opening speech made by Mr. Hattersley in the House of Commons on 15 July. See Cmnd. 6932, pp. 205-14 for extracts.

[2] For the text of the Final Act *v.ibid.*, pp. 225-82 and *Human Rights*, vol. vi, pp. 185-250.

of individual Western governments and in other cases might have required enabling domestic legislation; and partly because agreement on a document with status in international law would probably have required many years of negotiation (the UN Declaration on Friendly Relations took just short of seven years).

3. It was also our aim to ensure that the documents comprised in the Final Act had an internal balance and should be regarded as having equal value. The Russians and their allies, whose interest was mainly in the Declaration of Principles, wanted to give the Declaration pride of place. For their part the Western countries and the neutrals insisted that the contents of the documents dealing with confidence-building measures, economic co-operation, and humanitarian, information, cultural and educational matters had equal importance, and in many ways embodied the practical Western rather than the political Eastern view of *détente*. In our judgment the structure, language and balance of the Final Act fully meet our requirements. The fact that the Final Act has been drawn up on the basis of consensus and will have been approved at the highest level will of course give all the documents strong moral authority.

4. All the participating governments are committed to publication of the Final Act in their own countries and to its wide dissemination therein.[3] The original of the Final Act will be kept in Finland, and a copy will go to the Secretary-General of the United Nations and each participating state.

Questions Relating to Security in Europe
Preamble

5. This involves a statement of the relationship between the political and military aspects of security.

Declaration of Principles

6. The Declaration of Principles guiding relations between the participating states conforms with the Charter of the United Nations and the United Nations Declaration on Friendly Relations. It amounts to a political code of good behaviour, drafted with an eye to Europe but applicable throughout the world. Each of the principles is to be interpreted in terms of the others and applied unreservedly to all participating states, irrespective of political, economic and social differences between them. This in itself is an implicit repudiation of the Brezhnev doctrine of limited sovereignty. The Declaration does not consecrate the political or territorial *status quo* in Europe. Quadripartite rights and responsibilities in Germany as a whole are safeguarded.

7. The main novelty in the Declaration is a principle to define the inviolability of frontiers. Agreement on this principle was one of the main Soviet objectives at the Conference, and to judge from Soviet propaganda

---

[3] Mr. Sutherland attached particular importance to the publication of CSCE documents in the USSR. In a letter to Sir J. Killick of 16 July he argued: 'Any efforts we make in the Soviet Union to ensure that the provisions of Basket III regarding improved exchanges of information etc. are carried out in practice will be much more difficult if Soviet organisations can claim ignorance of the text' (PBE 9/507/1).

the Russians may well try to present 'inviolability of frontiers' as meaning 'immutability of frontiers'. It was equally important to the other participating states, and in particular the Federal Republic, that means should be stated in the Declaration by which frontiers could be changed. The result of a prolonged and sometimes bitter negotiation was the inclusion of a phrase in the principle dealing with sovereign rights to the effect that frontiers could be changed 'in accordance with international law, by peaceful means, and by agreement'.

8. There are good definitions of those principles which deal with mutual respect among states, such as sovereign equality and non-intervention in the internal affairs of other states. The principle of the non threat or use of force is a constant theme of the Conference texts.

9. The emphasis on the rights of the individual throughout the Declaration was the result of hard-fought negotiation. We welcome the emphasis in this respect in the principles on self-determination of peoples, human rights and fundamental freedoms, including freedom of thought, conscience, religion or belief; and co-operation. The participants confirm the right of the individual to know and act upon his rights and duties in the field of human rights.

Application of the Principles

10. We gave strong support to the Swiss draft convention for the peaceful settlement of disputes. So far as we were concerned the essential new element in it was mandatory provisions. This aroused opposition not only amongst the Eastern countries but in some Western ones as well, and it was not possible to make real progress. The proposal will be taken up again after 1977. We are not interested in any non-mandatory system which would risk duplicating existing arrangements.

11. The Romanians laid particular emphasis on the principle of the non use of force and insisted on its treatment outside as well as inside the Declaration of Principles. Not surprisingly they ran into strong Soviet opposition, but the Western countries gave them the best help which they could. The resulting document is harmless and may go some way to giving the Romanians the help they think they need.

Confidence-building Measures and Certain Aspects of Security and Disarmament

12. Despite its title the Conference has not dealt with the problems of European security in any real sense of the word. Some countries tried to link discussions under this heading with the force reductions talks in Vienna but others as strenuously resisted any connexion. A not very satisfactory compromise can be found in the four principles of military security drafted at Yugoslav and neutral demand.

13. The confidence-building measures eventually agreed have political rather than military significance, and rest on a voluntary basis. But they bring the member countries of the Warsaw Pact into a system of obligations in the military field which would have seemed inconceivable before the Conference began. The British played a major part in promoting the original proposals for confidence-building measures and in drafting the agreements eventually reached.

14. The most important agreement relates to the prior notification of military manoeuvres. The participating states decided to give 21 days' prior notification to all other participants (not just their neighbours) of the main details of their major military manoeuvres involving more than 25,000 ground, amphibious or airborne troops. These arrangements will be applicable throughout Europe but in the case of the Soviet Union and Turkey only within the area up to 250 kilometres from their European frontiers. On a still more discretionary basis the participating states may notify smaller-scale manoeuvres and military movements, exchange observers at manoeuvres, and arrange visits by military staff. In spite of British—and Allied—efforts no comparable arrangements were possible for prior notification of military movements. The Americans developed strong misgivings and the Russians and their allies firmly resisted any real agreement in this respect. But prior notification of military movements may be notified on a discretionary basis. The whole idea will be further studied at a later date.

Co-operation in the Field of Economics, of Science and Technology and of the Environment

15. The texts in this field provided for deep and far-reaching co-operation in a wide range of subjects. They should provide a stimulus to the work of the Economic Commission for Europe while preparing the ground for wider co-operation on the major world economic problems. The arrangements for economic, commercial, environmental, scientific, technological and industrial co-operation should make a modest contribution to overcoming the differences between economic systems. They will also facilitate direct contacts between businessmen, scientists etc. They provide for improvements in the availability of commercial and economic information, access to end-users, and better facilities and working conditions for individual firms and business representatives.

16. Although the European Commission did not participate as such at the Conference, its representatives played an active role and were in practice recognised by the members of the CMEA as having both competence and the confidence of the Nine. The provisions for effective reciprocity in conditions of trade should be of particular importance for future relations between the EEC and the CMEA.

17. The text on co-operation in the field of the environment usefully associates the Russians and East Europeans with the work set in train by the Stockholm Declaration on the Human Environment. Other texts deal with particular matters such as transport, tourism, migrant labour, training, arbitration etc, which should be helpful to many of the participants, with particular problems in these fields.

The Mediterranean Declaration

18. The elaboration of this declaration caused great difficulties during the negotiations.

The final text recognises the inter-relationship between European and Mediterranean security and the interest which a number of non-participating Mediterranean states have shown in the Conference from its beginning. The non-participants are promised that what is done in Europe is not designed to prejudice security in the Mediterranean and told of the willingness of the participants to promote co-operation in so far as this is consistent with the aims of the Conference. The document avoids implying any willingness to extend confidence-building measures into the Mediterranean, something which a number of CSCE participants are at present unwilling to do. When Mediterranean problems are reconsidered at future meetings to follow up the Conference, it should be possible to deal with them without—as the Maltese still seem to want—bringing in the Middle East dispute. The reference to reducing armed forces in the region, though weak, is a subject of potential discord in future.

Co-operation in Humanitarian and Other Fields (i.e. Basket III)

Preamble

19. The preamble to the whole of this section is important. It recognises that the broad aims of co-operation, contacts and the broader dissemination of information, are important elements in the process of strengthening security and developing co-operation, and should be put into effect in full respect for the principles set out in the Declaration of Principles. This means that while co-operation in these fields should not damage the sovereign rights of individual states or constitute intervention in the internal affairs of other states, it must take place in full respect for the principles of self-determination, human rights and fundamental freedoms.

Human Contacts

20. The texts in this field constitute a clear commitment on participating states to facilitate freer movement inside and outside their countries, in order to promote contacts and regular meetings on the basis of family ties, the reunification of separated families, marriage between citizens of different states, and increased possibilities for travel for personal, professional or tourist reasons. The Russians sought to make these improvements subject to mutually acceptable conditions which would have made progress dependant [*sic*] on subsequent negotiations. The provisions tackle, with some success, the administrative hindrances which face applicants for visas, licences etc. and should help to reduce the chances of a person being penalised for trying to travel abroad.

Information

21. The texts in this field set out practical ways, accepted by all participants, for facilitating the freer and wider dissemination of oral, printed, filmed and broadcast information of all kinds (including religious information) together with improved access to this information for the ordinary man in the street. The provisions deal for example with practical ways for increasing the availability of foreign newspapers (through libraries, subscriptions, kiosks etc.).

22. The text on radio broadcasting was the scene of a long argument, in which the Russians made any reference to the end of radio jamming dependant [*sic*] upon the notion of governmental responsibility for the content of broadcasting. This notion was unacceptable to us, but in deference to American wishes we acquiesced in a text which hopes that recent

improvements in the field of broadcasting (the end of jamming for all except Radio Free Europe and Radio Liberty) will be continued but does not compromise our position on the question of content.

23. The provisions for the improvement of working conditions for journalists are particularly useful in their references to visa and travel applications, access to sources, the right of journalists to transmit their reports home completely, normally and rapidly and their right not to be penalised or expelled for the legitimate pursuit of their profession. Most of these provisions are extended to technical staff as well as the journalists themselves.

Culture Co-operation

24. The lengthy texts on culture—something of particular interest to the French—provide for wide-ranging co-operation and expanded cultural relations designed to develop mutual knowledge of all forms of cultural activity, improve the facilities for their exchange and for public knowledge of and access to all kinds of works of art. The practical proposals in this field are many and should provide a sound basis for promoting direct contacts between specialists and artists and for easing the task of the British Council and similar bodies abroad.

Educational Co-operation

25. The texts on education again provide a good and practical basis for co-operation by promoting direct contacts between educators, scientists, facilitating the exchange of information among these people, improving teaching methods and knowledge of foreign languages and civilisations.

Follow-up Arrangements

26. The question of the best arrangements for following up the work of the Conference caused long and anxious debate, in the West as well as at the Conference. We and the Danes argued strongly in favour of continuing the multilateral dialogue begun at the Conference which we thought would give us a valuable device for monitoring Soviet performance. But a number of Western countries, particularly the French, Italians and Benelux countries, feared that arrangements for regular meetings or permanent machinery would give the Russians an opportunity to interfere in Western affairs and inhibit the development of the European Community.

27. In the event the Russians turned cool on the idea which they had originally proposed through the Czechs for permanent political machinery, evidently fearing the use to which it would be put by the West, and preferring instead the idea of a second Conference in the indefinite future. The Romanians, supported in varying degrees by all the neutrals, advocated an elaborate system of meetings of committees and expert groups in which they could continue to play an active role. In the face of strong Western opposition to such a flow of regular meetings, the neutrals and non-aligned settled for the present arrangements which contain the seeds of what they want but make any firm decision hinge on what happens between now and 1977.

28. The resolution on follow-up emphasises the need for all states to put into practice the decisions of the Conference but fairly clearly indicates that, provided this is done, the multilateral process will continue with further

meetings. The first requirement is for action unilaterally, bilaterally and multilaterally (by meetings of experts or through the ECE and UNESCO) to respect and put into effect what has been decided. Senior officials will meet in Belgrade in 1977 (after a short preliminary meeting there on 15 June that year) to assess how far the decisions of the Conference have been put into effect, to consider the state of their mutual relations and the course of *détente*.[4] On this basis they will consider the form and agenda of future meetings, including the possibility of another Conference.

[4] See Appendix III.

CHAPTER IV

Stage III
2 August - 9 September 1975

No. 138

Mr. Callaghan to Sir. T. Garvey (Moscow)

No. 725 Telegraphic [WDW 1/23]

Confidential. Priority   FCO, 2 August 1975, 8.30 p.m.

Repeated for Information to Washington, Paris, Bonn, UKDEL NATO, UKREP Brussels and for Information Saving to Warsaw, Prague, East Berlin, Budapest, Bucharest, Sofia, Belgrade, Peking and Lisbon.

CSCE: Anglo-Soviet Bilateral Meeting[1]

1. The Prime Minister and I had twenty minutes with Brezhnev and Gromyko on 1 August. Originally intended to last for an hour, the meeting was shortened by the Soviet request to hold it immediately before the signing ceremony rather than after it as planned. As a result, it was not possible to cover some issues, including Portugal,[2] as fully as we would have wished.

2. After the presentation to Brezhnev of his inscribed red box, the Prime Minister opened the proceedings by saying that he and the General Secretary could both take great satisfaction from this meeting in Helsinki. Both the Soviet and the British Governments had worked very hard to bring it about. His own speech to the Conference,[3] the first, had reflected the

---

[1] Stage III of the CSCE opened at Helsinki on 30 July. See No. 139.

[2] See No. 117, note 14. Revolutionary developments in Portugal continued to worry Western observers, and in mid-July the British Ambassador at Lisbon warned the FCO of reports of an impending seizure of power by the Communists in alliance with left-wing officers (Lisbon telegrams Nos. 445, 450 and 453 of 22 and 23 July, WSP 1/1). Meanwhile, from Moscow Mr. Sutherland reported that, although it could be taken for granted that the Russians were financing the Portuguese Communist Party and that they could influence both the Party and elements within the Portuguese Armed Forces Movement, he knew of no evidence that could prove this incontrovertibly. He added that the Russians 'must all the time be weighing the balance of advantage between achieving a Communist bridgehead in Western Europe, with all its strategic and political implications, and the risk of preventing further successes for their détente· policy' (Moscow telegram No. 1026 of 18 July, WSP 1/1).

[3] See Cmnd. 6932, pp. 216-25 for the text of Mr. Wilson's speech and extracts from Mr. Brezhnev's.

aspirations which he and Brezhnev had expressed in Moscow in February.[4] He had drawn encouragement from being able to refer to peaceful coexistence in the terms which he had used in the Kremlin then and to quote the definition which Brezhnev had given it on the same occasion.[5] What had been signed in Moscow had produced good results, especially in the field of trade: he had been glad to hear Gvishiani say, during his recent visit to London,[6] that expectations in this sphere had even been exceeded.

3. Brezhnev replied that this was only the beginning. The fact that he and Mr. Wilson were here together in Helsinki for the final stage of the Conference gave him and all his colleagues great satisfaction. The final stage attested to the fact that both the Soviet Union and Britain had crowned the efforts which they had made. While it was true, as many speakers at the Conference had pointed out, that not every problem had been solved, there were still questions which should be elaborated and discussed further: but a very good beginning had been made. The final declaration was a strong political and moral document. He was sure that both the Soviet and the British peoples would be happy when they read it. It was now up to the leaders to implement it. Mr. Wilson's visit to Moscow had been an important landmark along the road. The document which they were both about to sign instilled conviction that grounds existed for better developments in European relationships than ever before. Mr. Wilson's visit to Moscow had not been merely a protocol occasion or one on which both sides had been looking over their shoulders: even then, the Soviet side had felt that Anglo-Soviet relations were moving towards *détente*. There were now grounds to hope that the two countries could move forward in a bold way, and talk in a still more frank and friendly manner—certainly there were things which needed to be sorted out further and talked about more.

4. Brezhnev said that his own speech had spelt out the Soviet attitude to cooperation between states with different social systems (the Prime Minister remarked that his had also referred to this).[7] Brezhnev believed that a lot of what had piled up in the past would be cleared away after the Conference. In particular, as he had said in his speech, exchanges of information and human contacts could assume different forms: they could either promote favourable trends or they could poison the atmosphere. The Soviet side would do all it could to ensure that its propaganda did everything to promote closer ties with Britain and other countries.

5. The Prime Minister agreed that the meetings in Moscow had been a turning point. In a special sense, he and Brezhnev were custodians of *détente*, as defined in the documents which they had signed.

6. The Prime Minister then said that there was one problem which he

[4] See No. 112.

[5] See Cmnd. 6932, p. 217.

[6] Mr. J.M. Gvishiani was co-chairman of the USA-USSR Trade and Economics Council's Sub-Committee for Science and Technology.

[7] See note 3 above.

wished to mention specially and about which he felt anxiety. One test of *détente* was the position of Portugal. The United Kingdom was greatly disturbed about it and he hoped that Brezhnev would use all his influence to ensure that the situation was resolved in a way which accorded with the wishes of the Portuguese people.[8] He had seen President Costa Gomes[9] earlier in the day.[10] But since time for discussion was so short, he would like to send Brezhnev a memorandum about the question (see Helsinki tel[egram] Nos. 16 and 17 to Moscow, not to all).[11]

7. Brezhnev replied that he would just like to say two words. Portugal was an independent state. The Soviet Union was in no way involved in the situation. They were not sending arms to Portugal. But the situation was complicated. Gromyko interjected that this was an internal affair of the Portuguese people. Brezhnev continued that many countries had approached him during the Conference at Helsinki: he and his colleagues would think the matter over when they returned to Moscow to see what could be done. The Soviet Union had not started the revolution. The Prime Minister concluded by saying that he should make it clear that the British Government had welcomed the revolution in Portugal. In opposition the Labour Party had opposed Caetano's visit to London and he had been crucified for it in Parliament.[12] He was sure that everybody should use all their influence to help the situation.

8. The atmosphere of our conversation was good. As in his speech to the Conference, Brezhnev spoke in moderate and positive terms. His energy and command of the situation seemed undiminished by comparison with his performance in February.

[8] At the European Council meeting on 16-17 July Mr. Wilson and President Giscard d'Estaing agreed to take the lead in a joint approach to Mr. Brezhnev at Helsinki on the situation in Portugal. But Mr. Callaghan rejected a request from Sr. M. Soares, the Portuguese Socialist leader and former Foreign Minister, that the West make Stage III dependent upon the Russians desisting from encouraging a Communist takeover in Portugal. Mr. Callaghan thought that such a course would anger the Russians and that the West would risk losing the opportunity to constrain them (Lisbon telegram No. 453 at note 2 above and telegram No. 337 to Lisbon of 25 July, WSP 1/1).

[9] Gen. F. da Costa Gomes was President of Portugal.

[10] During this meeting Mr. Wilson expressed HMG's grave concern over recent events in Portugal. Gen. da Costa Gomes illustrated with his hands the two parallel lines of Portugal's political evolution, the electoral and the revolutionary. 'The question', Mr. Wilson asked, 'was which hand would ultimately be round the people's throats?' (record of meeting on 1 August, WSP 2/5).

[11] In this memorandum of 1 August Mr. Wilson stated his belief that the actions of the Portuguese Communist Party would, 'rightly or wrongly, be regarded by many as reflecting a view of ideological struggle' inconsistent with the principles to which participants in the CSCE had just subscribed (WSP 2/5).

[12] Dr. Caetano's official visit to London, during 15-19 July 1973, had given rise to considerable political controversy and led to demonstrations by those critical of his régime and its policies in Portugal's African territories.

9. The Prime Minister was able to hand to Gromyko, as we broke up, a list of Soviet Jews whose circumstances had given rise to Parliamentary concern,[13] explaining that it was the list he had intended to give to Kosygin[14] in February.

[13] Not printed.

[14] Mr. A.N. Kosygin was Chairman of the Council of Ministers of the USSR.

No. 139

Mr. Elliott (Helsinki) to Mr. Callaghan
[*WDW1/23*]

Confidential   HELSINKI, *12 August 1975*

Summary . . .[1]

Sir,

The CSCE Summit: Finland's Place in the Sun

The Third Stage of the Conference on Security and Co-operation in Europe took place in Helsinki from 30 July to 1 August. Of the 35 European States only Albania and Andorra were not represented. The Conference was attended by the Prime Minister and yourself, the Presidents of eight participating countries, the Prime Ministers or Heads of Government of 17 countries, and the Party Secretaries of six more, as well as the Secretary of the Council of Public Affairs of The Holy See, the Deputy Prime Minister of Malta and the Foreign Ministers of almost all 35, including San Marino. The only notable absentee, to no one's regret, was the bane of Stage I, Mr. Dom Mintoff, Prime Minister of Malta.

2. It is not for me to draw up the balance sheet of the three years of negotiations on Security and Co-operation in Europe, which started here in Helsinki on 22 November, 1972, and culminated in the only European Summit Conference of this century. Sir David Hildyard's despatch of 25 July[2] summarises with clarity and perception the long and arduous work of Stage II and its likely meaning for the future. In comparison the three days of Stage III may best be described as a happening, of impressive symbolic significance, illuminated by brilliant sunshine and the elegant architecture of Alvar Aalto's Finlandia Hall, and only partially obscured by the activities of some 3,000 supporting delegates, journalists and security police.

3. Since all the documents before the Conference had been agreed during Stage II, the sessions in the hall itself were inevitably in the nature of a set piece. The opening address of President Kekkonen was followed, as during Stage I in 1973, by speeches from the representatives of each of the 34 other

[1] Not printed.

[2] No. 136.

countries, this time at the level of Heads of Government rather than Foreign Ministers.[3] On both occasions the proceedings (appropriately enough in Finland) bore some resemblance to a marathon. But there was a difference this year. In 1973 the Foreign Ministers had been obliged to talk about the immediate and often pedestrian problems before the Conference. In 1975 the Heads of Government were free to talk about the future.

4. The tone was set by the Prime Minister who (as the fortune of the ballot decreed) made the first speech and also took the chair at the last working session. His speech brought home the basic point that the success of the Conference would depend upon the extent to which its moral commitments were carried out in practice, in particular in relation to such sensitive issues as the status of Berlin, the MBFR negotiations in Vienna, and the possibility of future multilateral negotiations in the field of nuclear disarmament. He emphasised too, in a passage which has already been widely quoted, the extent to which the Conference would be judged by the effect it had on the lives of ordinary people in Europe; 'there is no reason why in 1975 Europeans should not be allowed to marry whom they want; hear and read what they want, travel abroad where and when they want, and meet whom they want'.

5. Inevitably succeeding speeches by other Western leaders were variations on the same basic themes. Herr Schmidt spoke of the significance of *détente* to the Federal Republic and again underlined the significance of Berlin and the negotiations in Vienna. President Giscard d'Estaing, in a speech of great elegance, also spoke of Berlin, though his approach to the question of disarmament was notably distinct from that of his two colleagues. President Ford urged on the Conference, with notable firmness and force, the 'decent respect for the opinions of mankind' prescribed in the Declaration of Independence, and reminded his audience succinctly that history would judge them 'not by what we say today but what we do tomorrow; not by the promises we make but by the promises we keep'.

6. On the Eastern side there were (possibly orchestrated) indications of a rather wider range of views. Mr. Honecker[4] of the German Democratic Republic and Dr. Husak[5] of Czechoslovakia both took a hard line, emphasising the basic importance of the Declaration of Principles and in particular the inviolability of frontiers; while referring only perfunctorily (and in the context of official initiatives) to the need for the development of human contacts. Mr. Brezhnev, however, in marked contrast to them (as well as to Mr. Gromyko during Stage I two years ago) made a thoughtful and positive speech. He stressed the need for 'a further development of military *détente*', and called for 'further headway along the lines mapped out by the Conference', making none of the reservations that might have been expected

[3] For the verbatim records of Stage III see *Human Rights*, vol. vi, pp. 5-181.

[4] Herr E. Honecker was the First Secretary of the Central Committee of the Socialist Unity Party of the GDR.

[5] Dr. G. Husak was the President of Czechoslovakia.

about further work on confidence-building measures or in Basket III. He also attempted a redefinition of the idea of non-interference in the internal affairs of other States. Controversy will continue about his precise meaning; but the Prime Minister at his Press conference the same day was able neatly to turn the Soviet leader's words to suggest that if he had made that pronouncement in 1967 the fate of Czechoslovakia might have been different.

7. Since the total time available for the meeting was limited, its prospects of success depended on there being no major dispute in the Conference Hall. In Mr. Mintoff's absence the most likely cause of conflict was the Cyprus question. The Turkish delegation (clumsily) walked out during Archbishop Makarios' speech, and subsequently circulated a formal reservation denying the applicability of the Final Act to Turkish relations with a Cyprus Government headed by the Archbishop. The move, which was not unexpected, at least diminished the likelihood of the Turks' refusing to sign the documents or of any requests for rights of reply, for which the agreed arrangements for Stage III had made no provision. It also unwarily provided the Cyprus Delegation with the opportunity to circulate, 10 minutes before the close of the final working session, a consummately timed and thus devastating reply to the Turkish note which gave Cyprus a victory on points and prevented any disruption of the arrangements for the signature of the Final Act immediately afterwards. The prospect of protracted argument on the issue was averted to the vast relief of most Delegations; and no one chose further to comment on the fact that reservations were being made to the Final Act even before its formal signature.

8. The formal proceedings of the Conference thus concluded without a hitch in the time allotted for them. The speeches of Heads of Delegations will of course provide those who are fully versed in the intricacies of Stage II—as well as the historians of the future—with a great quarry of material for study and analysis. On the face of it, what went on in the corridors outside the hall may have been of as much immediate significance. The Conference provided unique opportunities for bilateral meetings. In addition to acting as host at a luncheon in the Embassy for his American, West German and French colleagues, the Prime Minister took part in a Community lunch given by the Italian Prime Minister, had breakfast with President Ford, and other bilateral meetings with Secretary Brezhnev, President Kekkonen, Marshal Tito[6] of Yugoslavia, and Messrs. Demirel[7] of Turkey, Karamanlis[8] of Greece, Gierek[9] of Poland, Husak of Czechoslovakia, Cosgrave[10] of Ireland and Costa Gomes of Portugal. You yourself, Sir, in addition to accompanying the Prime

[6] Marshal J.B. Tito was the President of Yugoslavia.

[7] Mr. S. Demirel was the Prime Minister of Turkey.

[8] Mr. C. Karamanlis was the Prime Minister of Greece.

[9] Mr. E. Gierek was the First Secretary of the Central Committee of the Polish United Workers' Party.

[10] Mr. L. Cosgrave was the Prime Minister of the Irish Republic.

Minister at his meetings, held bilateral talks with Foreign Ministers of Cyprus and Bulgaria.

9. It was obvious to those who were present in Helsinki, as well as to the millions who watched the proceedings on television, that this was by any standard a remarkable gathering. Its organisation presented a formidable challenge for which the Finnish Government had long been preparing. Even their high level of organising skill was taxed by the fact that they received from Geneva less than three weeks' notice of the final date; while their difficulties were compounded by what they judged to be the need to take security measures on a scale unprecedented in Finland. The Government brought rather more than half of the whole police force of the country to Helsinki (at some risk to international understanding, since most of the rural police spoke only Finnish); and acquiesced in suggestions that helicopters and MiG aircraft should circle the city whenever President Ford and Mr. Brezhnev were at large outside their respective Embassy premises. Yet (although there was one fatal accident involving a Finnish boatman who approached too near to a cocktail party attended by Heads of Delegations[11]) there were no untoward incidents directly affecting delegates or the Press; and the lavish nature of the facilities provided for the latter did something to correct the cynicism with which many of them had at first approached the Conference.

10. All this could hardly have happened in any other Western European capital. Helsinki is still a small town by European standards, and its life was disrupted by the CSCE. All hotels were commandeered by the Government, all traffic diverted or brought to a standstill simply to allow delegates to move between hotels and the Conference Hall; and all this occurred without a murmur of protest from the population. On the contrary, they lined the streets for three days, applauding the Heads of Government (especially the Western ones) in their restrained Finnish manner; and showing every sign of realising that this was the most remarkable political event in their country during their 60 years of independence.

11. The fact is that the ordinary Finns have been and have felt more involved in the CSCE than the citizens of other participating states. For, as the Finnish public have come to understand, Finland stood to gain from the process of the Conference almost irrespective of its results. In promoting it the Finnish Government acted not (as some impercipient Western critics have suggested) as advocates of a stock Soviet cause; but out of pure self-interest. It is hardly true that, as has rather too often been said (by Mr. Brezhnev among others), there have been no winners or losers in this Conference. The main Helsinki newspaper was nearer the mark when on 27 July it carried the headline 'Finland the only winner of the CSCE'.

12. The six-year process that ended here last week was thus a triumph for

[11] A Finnish boatman died on 1 August when his fibreglass motorboat was blown up by a warning flare fired by security forces.

President Kekkonen. It was in May 1969, in the aftermath of the invasion of Czechoslovakia, (an event that had both alarmed and angered the Finns), that he had had the prescience to offer Helsinki as the site for the Conference. Even at that time he had realised how it could serve his twin aims of improving Finnish security and enhancing Finnish neutrality. A country like Finland in an exposed position on the Soviet borders has most to fear from tension between the great powers; and little to lose from the sort of understanding between Super-Powers that is criticised by many as Great-Power hegemony. Its interest is quite simply to reduce the risk of the sort of power game in which it itself can be used as a pawn by one side against the other. So Finland is bound to work for *détente* and to welcome any manifestations that will serve to persuade its Eastern neighbour that *détente* is becoming a reality.

13. President Kekkonen also had a more elaborate aim in mind; to try to use the development of *détente* to gain international recognition of the genuine 'neutrality' of Finnish policy (a concept that the Soviet Union declines explicitly to acknowledge) and to increase Finland's freedom of manoeuvre in the international field. He was involved at the time in attempts (not all of which were successful) to gain for Finland membership of the Security Council, as well as the Secretary-Generalship of the UN, and to make Helsinki a centre for major international conferences, starting with SALT. But it was from the CSCE that in his calculation there was most to gain. Not only would the Conference itself deepen the process of *détente*; but the fact that it was held in Helsinki would serve as proof of the confidence of the participating countries in the reality of Finnish neutrality; while the presence of 35 Heads of Government on Finnish soil might serve to create a new interest in their part in the preservation of Finnish independence.

14. These arguments were always more enthusiastic than logical, and it seems doubtful if all the President's aims will be achieved. They always contained an element of contradiction. The Finnish Delegation played their hand with skill throughout the Conference; and succeeded often enough in acting as 'honest broker' while contriving to conceal their anxiety lest Western insistence on getting 'results' from the negotiations should jeopardise their outcome and perhaps also European hopes for *détente*. But Finnish enthusiasm for the idea of the Conference was sometimes misunderstood in the West as eagerness to play the Soviet game; and the misunderstanding did not help to promote belief in the genuineness of Finnish neutrality. Again, Finland's freedom of manoeuvre in international policy has not perceptibly increased during the three years of negotiation; Finnish Governments look over their shoulders to study Soviet reactions to their policies as anxiously today as they did during the opening year of the Conference when they were obliged by Soviet pressure to defer for many months the signature of their trade agreement with the EEC. And although Helsinki is now firmly on the map as an international meeting point, its geographical position is always

likely to militate against its becoming a second Geneva or Vienna.

15. President Kekkonen, however, would be justified in claiming the success of the Conference as a success for Finland. The people of his country, who have long felt themselves an almost forgotten nation in an isolated corner of Europe, have for a short time had the sensation that they had been in the centre of the world. They have profited from the promotion of something which may become known as the 'Helsinki spirit'—to be defined as the readiness to argue and negotiate over issues which in the past were considered too dangerous for discussion in international conferences in Europe. President Kekkonen has some cause for self-satisfaction when he recalls his words of 1967: 'Today we can say we have been on the right road. We have taken upon ourselves the often thankless task . . . of a bridge-builder. Our example has been followed.'

16. I have written at length about Finland's attitude to the Conference because I am bound to approach the remarkable events of the last week in Helsinki from that angle. But there is perhaps a general point to remember. Many of those in the West who have criticised the Conference have done so because of their calculations about its supposed effect on the relationship between the big Powers. What seems certain is only that that effect will be very difficult to estimate; and that no complete assessment can be reached before years have passed. There are points that the East can exploit in the Declaration of Principles; and points in Basket III which the West would be foolish to fail to exploit. But it must also be remembered that, not least because of the rule of consensus, the CSCE was a small nations' Conference. It obliged the big Powers to argue out and to justify their policies in front of the representatives of smaller Powers—in the case of the Soviet Union in front of the representatives of countries who have long unhappily considered themselves as its satellites. And it is precisely those nations who think themselves most threatened by the Soviet Union—besides Finland, Yugoslavia and Romania are the obvious examples—who have been most enthusiastic about the Conference, and most anxious that there should be some real follow-up to it in 1977. If the Conference has indeed contributed anything towards building up the self-respect and the security of the smaller European States, it will truly, to quote the words of the Prime Minister, Mr. Wilson, when he closed the last working session, have been an historic event.

17. I am sending copies of this despatch to Her Majesty's Representatives in Stockholm, Oslo, Copenhagen, Moscow, Bonn, Paris, Washington, Bucharest, Belgrade and UK Mission Geneva.

I have, etc.,
T.A.K. Elliott

No. 140

Major-General D.W. Scott-Barrett[1] (British Military Government Berlin) to Mr. Bullard[2] (Bonn)

[*WRL 2/3*]

Confidential   BERLIN, *15 August 1975*

Summary . . .[3]

Sir,

The Implications for Berlin of the CSCE

In his speech at the Helsinki Summit the Prime Minister said that 'since the war the fate of Berlin has been, as it is and will continue to be, a touchstone of the state of relations in Europe'.[4] Following reference to the Eastern Treaties[5] and to the Quadripartite Agreement[6] he added that 'these benefits must continue to be developed further after this conference has been concluded'. The purpose of this despatch is to attempt to explore what if any benefits the CSCE may bring to Berlin and what dangers may lie in wait from those closely argued texts.

2. There are three principal areas where the CSCE touches Berlin. The first concerns short-term Soviet tactics over Berlin now that the CSCE is in the bag, the second the immediate impact of the final act[7] and the third the long-term implications for Berlin of post-CSCE Europe and of the follow-up arrangements.

Short-term Soviet tactics over Berlin

3. It has been feared both in the Federal Republic and in Berlin that once the constraints of the negotiating process of the CSCE were lifted the Russians would feel free to revert to their earlier pressure tactics over Berlin. Soviet signature of the Quadripartite Agreement was anyway a Western condition for agreeing to attend the preliminary talks for the CSCE and the Russians might well now feel that, with their objective achieved, they could work more openly against those parts of the Quadripartite Agreement which they disliked.

4. I doubt this thesis and would on the contrary concur with recent assessments to the effect that no dramatic change in Soviet policy is to be expected. The CSCE is after all merely one manifestation of *détente* and the imperatives for *détente* from the Russian side would seem to remain and, if anything, to be enhanced. Above all, the overriding Soviet concern for

---

[1] General Officer Commanding, Berlin.

[2] In June 1975 Mr. Bullard was appointed HM Minister in Bonn.

[3] Not printed.

[4] See No. 138, note 4.

[5] See No. 136, note 9.

[6] See No. 10, note 8 and Cmnd. 6201, pp. 236-42.

[7] See No. 137, note 2.

continuing good relations with the US makes excessive pressure on Berlin unthinkable so long as the American guarantee is seriously maintained and such pressure would inevitably create friction between the two countries. In addition, the Russians wish to present the CSCE as a new departure in peace and co-operation in Europe, and Mr. Brezhnev's personal prestige is very closely linked to this. Artificially contrived crises in Berlin would swiftly destroy this impression. Indeed because Berlin remains a symbol of the cold war and of confrontation, it is in the Soviet view best excluded from the limelight. The Russians certainly played it down at the CSCE. It is also noticeable that in our day-to-day contact with Soviet diplomats here they underline the importance of avoiding tension over Berlin. The atmosphere can, they say, only continue to improve as a result of the successful conclusion of the Conference.

5. Thus, in Soviet eyes it would seem that Berlin's role in the current strategy of *détente* is essentially passive. It must not act as too effective a reminder of the threat from the East and of the harsh difference between the ideologies of East and West. But it must also be said that there are conflicting forces which militate against this strategy. For all its subtle mechanisms, Berlin remains a trouble spot which cannot always be contained within the tight framework of Marxist theory. There are 12,000 armed East German guards who surround West Berlin to guard the wall and to prevent East Germans escaping. The opportunity for an ugly incident which can quickly inflame West Berlin public opinion and lead to a slanging match is ever present. An East German escapee bleeding to death at the wall or a child drowned in the boundary waters with East German guards unwilling to help are examples which spring to mind. There are the air corridors where Allied planes cross the heavily congested air space of the GDR and where a collision, due perhaps to negligence by Soviet or East German military aircraft, is always possible. Very recently there was a near miss where serious loss of life was only just avoided. In addition to the ever-present risk of such incidents, Berlin also remains a tempting lever for the Russians to use against the FRG in their bilateral relations or against one or all of the Allies. The local vulnerability of the West in Berlin must remain a constant invitation. There is also the understandable tendency for the FRG and the Berlin Senate to interpret the clause in the Quadripartite Agreement on developing the ties between them in a dynamic and somewhat provocative way. In such situations the East feel constrained to act against them. There is also the GDR, a not always exemplary Soviet client, despite the degree of Soviet control, which is sometimes faced with distasteful and humiliating situations and may feel compelled to take public issue with West Berlin for reasons of internal policy. The conflict in the GDR between newly recognised sovereignty and the limitations which Berlin and Allied rights impose on it is not easily resolved. As Herr Honecker has just stressed, sensitivity over the sovereignty issue is paramount in his mind. Thus for a number of different reasons trouble can and will arise in Berlin and life will never be entirely straightforward and easy. However, for the foreseeable future it will be in no one's interest to work the levers too hard or to allow the situation over Berlin

seriously to endanger East/West relations. Friction should thus be contained provided of course that the current foreign policy imperatives of the main protagonists remain unaltered.

The immediate impact of the final act of the CSCE

6. Despite earlier Federal Government concern, the conclusion must be that the final act applies to Berlin and Western statements at Helsinki have confirmed this.[8] It would be difficult indeed for the Russians or East Germans to claim that Berlin was not a part of Europe or that by extension it was not a participant, and there has been no sign of their seeking to do so.

7. It is the declaration of principles that Berliners will have read with the greatest concentration. In particular the principle of the inviolability of frontiers and the determination with which the East fought for its inclusion have inevitable implications for the division of Germany and for the role of Berlin as the future capital of a reunited Germany. The GDR have predictably been at pains to interpret this principle as having particular significance. For Berliners this all seems to confirm the unsavoury truth implied by the Eastern Treaties that the division of Germany is here to stay for a very long time. Non-Germans will claim that this is obvious to all but the most obtuse. It is also true that the West, by successfully inserting a reference in the declaration to the peaceful change of frontiers, has kept the options open and that the declaration anyway lacks legal force. However, these points do not provide full reassurance. Thirty years at painfully close quarters with the East has made Berliners wary and they tend to interpret the results of the Conference as confirming, despite all the determined Western attempts to prevent it, Soviet hegemony over Eastern Europe. This is a daunting prospect for a city locked in the middle of the Soviet sphere of influence.

8. Shortly before the Declaration of Principles was completed, certain Germans in Berlin and in the Federal Republic, mainly of a CDU complexion, became concerned that the text would in some way compromise Berlin's status, the rights of the Allies and the Quadripartite Agreement. This had, of course, long been an Allied preoccupation and our negotiators at the Conference had obtained the necessary safeguards. This now seems to have been accepted by all except the most intransigent members of the CDU and the firm Western statements at Helsinki on the status of Berlin and on Allied rights have provided some necessary reassurance. Herr Honecker's subsequent words in support of the Quadripartite Agreement have also been noted.

9. On the military aspects of security, the focus now moves to Vienna. Berlin, surrounded by perhaps the most formidable concentration of troops and weaponry in the world, is bound to be interested in the progress of MBFR and the possibility of troop reductions. The voluntary agreement at the CSCE on confidence building measures will be of only marginal interest although if and when the Russians do begin to notify their not infrequent large-scale manoeuvres in the region of their city, Berliners may waken to the significance of this unprecedented breach of Soviet military secrecy.

[8] See Cmnd. 6932, p. 218.

10. The effect on Berlin of the so-called Basket III undertakings, on the free movement of people, ideas and information in Europe must be somewhat paradoxical. Through the visits arrangements negotiated between the Berlin Senate and the GDR Government under the umbrella of the Quadripartite Agreement in 1971, very real improvements were achieved in freedom of movement from West Berlin into East Berlin and the GDR. There is also the very considerable penetration of Western information media into the GDR from Berlin radio and television stations. There is thus an existing measure of exchange at least from West to East, both licit and illicit, which in some ways goes beyond the Basket III provisions and Herr Honecker has not been slow to point this out, in his own inimitable way. At the same time the most savage manifestation of the Eastern resistance to these Western pressures for movement in the opposite direction is present in Berlin in the form of the Berlin Wall.

11. It is difficult to assess at this stage what use the CSCE texts can be put to in the Berlin context. The GDR have certainly made it abundantly clear that they will have to be forced every step of the way over Basket III subjects and will doubtless continue to seek financial compensation for every concession. Nevertheless the texts, for all their imperfections, stand and can be appealed to in future negotiations. They will also provide a court of appeal in the event of retrogressive action by the GDR such as their 1973 decision to double the minimum exchange requirements for tourists.

Long-term implications of continuing machinery

12. A city in Berlin's anomalous situation must have a sense of purpose if it is not to wither into provincial obscurity. As I have mentioned earlier, Berlin's traditional role has been to stand ready as the capital of a reunited Germany. With the recognition of the GDR this role has necessarily become much more distant and illusory and the Governing Mayor has sought to develop the more nebulous concept of the city as a 'Mittelpunkt' (middle point) for Germans from both States, a reminder and symbol of common German nationality. Berlin has of course also traditionally stood for Western freedom and democracy. In the era of *détente* this image has lost something of its brilliance but recent events in Portugal and elsewhere have perhaps done something to restore it.

13. The CSCE has significance for both roles. In so far as the division of Germany is considered to have been further confirmed by the CSCE, so the role of 'Mittelpunkt', a shadowy reminder of Germany's past unity, becomes a more plausible alternative for Berlin. But it is a hard pill to swallow, so Berlin's role even as a 'Mittelpunkt' must ring hollow. Secondly, Berlin as the symbol of democracy would have little meaning if the Conference had ended in an atmosphere of euphoria and mistaken optimism over the nature of *détente*. In reality neither of these things has happened, but there will nevertheless be a tendency for Berliners to suspect that something has been given away and that Berlin's future role is yet more uncertain.

14. The more informed in Berlin are also highly suspicious of any follow-up mechanism to the Conference, however insubstantial this may at present be.

For some of them Berlin is a highly complex mechanism which is paradoxically a stabilising factor in East/West relations. Pressures can be brought and predictable responses practised; the city thus makes a serious contribution to the maintenance of Western security. If some form of permanent machinery was eventually to be set up, Berlin would be relegated to a secondary role and the subtle quadripartite mechanism would be eclipsed by a much less predictable and wayward forum of 35 nations. This is a thesis which should not be altogether discarded. There is nevertheless no reason why the modest arrangements now envisaged should in any way harm Berlin's particular contribution. More powerful machinery might however eventually hold some danger for the Allied position in Berlin.

Conclusion

15. These comments and conclusions must necessarily be tentative. What seems certain is that the CSCE is unlikely ever to make the same impact on Berlin's consciousness as the four key moments in her post-war history: the 1948 attempt by Stalin[9] to strangle the city; the 1958 Khrushchev ultimatum; the building of the Berlin Wall,[10] and the Quadripartite Agreement. This does not mean, however, that the effects of the Conference on the city will necessarily be negligible The proof of the CSCE pudding will, for Berlin as elsewhere, be in the eating. Only perhaps in 10 years' time will we be able to assess the balance sheet for the city.

16. I am sending a copy of this despatch to Her Majesty's Principal Secretary of State for Foreign and Commonwealth Affairs, to Her Majesty's Ambassadors in Moscow, Washington, Paris and East Berlin, and to the Secretariat, Commanders-in-Chief Committee, Germany.

I have, etc.,

DAVID SCOTT-BARRETT,

Major-General

[9] Generalissimo J.V. Stalin was the President of the Soviet Council of Ministers, 1946-53.

[10] See *Selected Documents on Germany and the Question of Berlin 1944-1961*, Cmnd. 1552 (London: HMSO, 1961).

No. 141

Sir T. Garvey (Moscow) to Mr. Callaghan

[*ENZ 3/303/1*]

Confidential   MOSCOW, *9 September 1975*

Summary . . .[1]

Sir,

CSCE and Soviet Westpolitik

The conclusion on 1 August of the Conference on Security and Co-

[1] Not printed.

operation in Europe (CSCE) has been claimed by the Russians as a great diplomatic success and a major landmark in post-war history. This satisfaction is not surprising. The Russians had been calling for 20 years for a conference on security, and its achievement was one of the most important of the 'six concrete tasks' in the 'peace policy' adopted by the 24th Congress of the CPSU in 1971.[2]

2. 'Security in Europe' has meant for the Soviet Government the consolidation and perpetuation of the new territorial and political order in Eastern Europe established by Soviet arms, diplomacy and skulduggery [*sic*] in the years following 1944. The facts of Soviet achievement were not in doubt—Soviet territorial gains, the creation of a *glacis* proof against conventional attack, the division of Germany—indeed no one since Dulles[3] had seriously considered trying to reverse them: and the principal loser, the German Federal Republic, had already assented, in its bilateral treaties with the USSR, Poland and the GDR,[4] to most of the more unpalatable consequences. But the Russians, baulked of a peace treaty, still looked for reassurance, legitimacy, recognition, both for their own sake and as a springboard from which the 'peace policy' could be launched to further successes. For them, the key importance of the Final Act of Helsinki[5] lies in the multilateral acceptance of frontiers and of the political *status quo*. The non-binding character of the Final Act, and the reservation on peaceful change of frontiers, will not prevent the Soviet Union from interpreting Western signatures as confirmation that NATO will not try to set back the map of Europe. Moscow intends that note should be taken of this in Eastern Europe, in case anyone there had hoped for change.

3. Nevertheless, the document signed on 1 August is greatly different from the straight security proposal put forward by Molotov in 1954[6] and from the Prague Declaration of Warsaw Pact Foreign Ministers in 1969,[7] which added to discussion of security the second conference agenda point of expansion of commercial, economic and scientific ties. Having campaigned for many years for a conference, the Russians got one but without the Peace Treaty they really wanted and in return for a double price. One instalment of the price was agreement to start the Vienna negotiations on mutual reduction of forces in Central Europe. The other was the widening of the CSCE agenda, proposed by NATO in May 1970, to include many questions of human contacts and the flow of information which the USSR found potentially dangerous and had previously insisted on regarding as nobody's business but its own.

4. How will the Russians assess the balance sheet? I think they will see these

[2] See Volume I, pp. 325-7 and Cmnd. 6932, pp. 95-6.

[3] Mr. J.F. Dulles was US Secretary of State, 1953-9.

[4] See No. 136, note 9 and Cmnd. 6201, pp. 261-4.

[5] See No. 137, note 2.

[6] See Cmnd. 6932, p. 2. Mr. V.M. Molotov was Soviet Foreign Minister, 1953-6.

[7] See Volume I, pp. 196-7 and Cmnd. 6932, pp. 61-2.

gains:

(*a*) They have got the multilateral endorsement, which they wanted, of the post-war *status quo* in Europe, and will claim, whatever the documents say, not to have abandoned their right, under the special type of relations existing between Socialist States, to intervene if necessary in Eastern Europe under the so-called Brezhnev doctrine. Although the text on European frontiers contains some unwelcome reservations, the Russians will impute legal validity to it.

(*b*) The Soviet Union has gained international status, and a success useful in internal propaganda, by bringing off a conference for which it had campaigned for many years.

(*c*) The principles in Basket I of CSCE, being above all about peaceful behaviour, should help to spread an impression in the West that the Soviet Union presents no threat to security or peace. The Russians may now seek to reinforce this tendency by propaganda and intensified contacts, official and non-official.

(*d*) The Russians have secured, in the Final Act, a quarry of texts to use against those whom they class as 'enemies of *détente*' in the West, which means the people who express public scepticism of Soviet objectives.

(*e*) The Helsinki document may provide a basis from which to give new impetus to the Soviet attack on the division of Europe, caused as they claim by NATO in the political and military fields and the European Community in the economic field. We shall hear more about the benefits of all-European security and all-European co-operation: on the former there may be suggestions of a binding European security system, and, on the latter, ideas for Europe-wide collaboration in energy and other fields.

(*f*) Although persuaded to negotiate about MBFR, the Russians have retained after CSCE their freedom to resist in the Vienna talks any agreement which would diminish their considerable superiority in conventional weapons.

(*g*) The Russians will be able to represent CSCE as an example to other areas of the world. Their scribes are already busy applying the CSCE principles to the Asian scene, so as to further the Soviet idea of a collective security system in Asia.

5. The Russians ran some risks in engaging in CSCE. One or more of the East European delegations might have got off the lead, but they managed very largely to prevent this. In the Final Act itself some blemishes mar the Basket I principles, notably the Western flavour of Principle 7 about respect for human rights. The Russians have had to break with past practice by agreeing to notify major military manoeuvres and they may even be persuaded to invite foreign observers to some manoeuvres.

6. The main debit, however, is in Basket III. It was a major setback even to have to discuss some of the humanitarian subjects. The Russians managed to attenuate the language in many instances. But there are still dangers for them in the agreed text. Brezhnev drew attention at the Helsinki Summit to

the dangers of misuse of information, which 'can spread the poison of discord between countries and peoples'.[8] Since then, 'Agitator', the journal of guidance to party activists, has warned that 'in contemporary conditions it is particularly important to instruct the Soviet people in political vigilance against the intrigues and traps of imperialist propaganda'.

7. The Basket III provisions on reunification of families and freedom of travel will pose problems. Brezhnev and others in the Politburo talked tough to visiting US Senators and Congressmen this summer about the inadmissibility of trying to tell the Soviet Union how to apply its emigration laws. The Press has warned against interference in Soviet internal affairs. Soviet officials concerned with exit visas to Soviet citizens were nonplussed when a visiting Boston Irish priest demanded to know why a fee was required for each visa application when the Final Act said clearly that a fee was payable only when the visa was granted. The embarrassed Soviet officials confessed that in the past they had charged for repeated applications and would have now to review this practice.

8. The Russians have managed so far to avoid internal repercussions from *détente* and will try to make use of the small print in the Final Act, and its voluntary character, to minimise the action they need take under Basket III. Where the language is unclear—what, for instance, is a 'moderate' fee for a visa?—their interpretation will be as restrictive as possible. Where the Final Act allows for bilateral agreements to implement specific points, the Russians will probably play for time: seeking, in ensuing negotiations, to water down the relevant commitment in the Final Act. Their initial approach is exemplified by failure so far to respond to the US offer to grant reciprocal multiple entry/exit visas for journalists.

9. The growing Soviet concern about the likely difficulties from Basket III probably lay behind the evaporation, some time back in the Geneva stage of CSCE, of Soviet support for the Czechoslovak proposal of a permanent follow-up body.[9] Such a body had been proposed by the Warsaw Pact as a whole in June 1970.[10] It would have been a useful court for pillorying the West on Basket I and for using Basket II to criticise the EEC; but the risk of the West pillorying the Russians on Basket III could not be tolerated. Nevertheless, the Russians had no chance of avoiding follow-up activity altogether. From their point of view, one of the most unfortunate results of CSCE is that the meeting in 1977 will almost inevitably focus on Baskets II and III. The Russians will try to concentrate attention on the principles in Basket I; they will accuse us of violating certain principles, as they are already doing over Portugal. But they must fear that the main business of the 1977 meeting will be Western, and indeed neutral, pestering about Soviet and East European fulfilment of humanitarian and other provisions in Basket III.

10. The recently increased economic dependence of the East Europeans

[8] See No. 138, note 3.

[9] See No. 46, note 8.

[10] See Volume I, p. 239 and Cmnd. 6932, pp. 77-9.

on the USSR will probably inhibit their freedom of action in implementing the Final Act. But the implementation of Basket III may nevertheless cause strain between Moscow and its allies, whose treatment of foreign journalists, access to information, etc., is, for the most part, less restrictive. The Russians cannot easily bring the Eastern Europeans back to the Soviet line; but they will no doubt insist that any innovations flowing from the CSCE should be co-ordinated and introduced gradually so as not to make the existing gap more obvious.

11. On the question of further Western action I am writing separately to the Department with suggestions on priorities and tactics for raising specific points in the Final Act with the Soviet Union between now and 1977. The general approach, I suggest, should be to move quite soon on points where current Soviet practice is clearly incompatible with the Final Act. We might start with those where, because of this incompatibility, British citizens are not accorded the treatment here which we would accord Soviet citizens in Britain. If we proceed, in concert with our partners in EEC and NATO, to raise practical cases with the Russians, firmly, patiently, and without publicity, we may gain more than through public moves engaging Soviet prestige. We should not overrate the prospects of securing improvements; but Helsinki offers us a locus for trying, and there is unlikely to be much change unless we make the attempt. The Russians for their part can be relied upon to take us to task wherever they can claim that our performance does not accord with the Final Act.

12. Brezhnev at Helsinki was at pains to propound that CSCE gave a square deal to all parties: there was [*sic*] no losers, only gainers. He added that it was not an end, but a beginning. So, certainly, the Russians plan it. The next chapter, to quote again Brezhnev's synopsis, is to be the 'materialisation' of *détente*, which means the extension to the military behaviour of both sides of the relaxation of tension achieved in generalised political terms at Helsinki. It is the same thought as underlies the passage in the Anglo-Soviet Joint Statement of 17 February about 'complementing measures of political *détente* with those of military *détente*'.[11] This is an area in which the UK and its allies need to walk with caution. On the assumption that the 'peace policy' continues to unfold on these lines (and, despite occasional warnings by Moscow commentators that it is not the USSR's only option, we should expect it to do so), we and our friends must bring to the next phase all the clearness of head and strength of will that we possess. For the Russians will come to it armed with two alternative theses for Western public opinion: that the Soviet Union is not dangerous; or that, given Soviet strength, resistance to Soviet designs is anyhow futile. In MBFR, which touches us most directly, we should look not for new Soviet flexibility but for intensified propaganda calling for Western flexibility.

13. To predict this is not to suggest that *détente* is a fraud or that Helsinki was a stage on the road to ruin. The CSCE has given the Russians something

---

[11] See No. 112, note 2.

that they had long wanted very much, perhaps even come to over-value. But the Western Governments have gained also—in limiting and qualifying their endorsement of a situation they do not intend to change, in forcing the Russians to do battle on ground hitherto taboo and, not least, in cohesion and the practice of co-operation. Elsewhere too—in the Quadripartite Agreement on Berlin[12] and in the development of Western exports to CMEA countries—the Soviet peace policy has been shown to carry advantages for the West as well. Mishandled by the West, the pursuit of *détente* could lead to a Soviet walkover in Europe. But if Western countries continue, negotiation by negotiation, to stick together, to keep their guard up and to settle for nothing less than a fair balance of concrete advantage, they need not shrink from it. *Détente* of that kind would differ widely from the Soviet prospectus. And, in the longer perspective, the practice of *détente* may foster developments in Soviet policies which ultimately make the USSR a less intractable, even a more reliable, partner.

14. I am sending copies of this despatch to Her Majesty's Representatives at NATO, the UN in Geneva, and the European Communities: and at Helsinki, Washington, Paris, Bonn, Rome, Belgrade, East Berlin, Warsaw, Prague, Budapest, Bucharest and Sofia.

I have, etc.,
T. GARVEY

[12] See No. 117, note 6.

APPENDIX I

ORGANISATIONAL STRUCTURE FOR STAGE II OF THE CSCE (1973-75)

Co-ordinating Committee

Committee I
Questions relating to security in Europe (13-24)

A. *Sub-Committee 1*
Principles (17-20)

B. *Special Working Body*
Swiss proposal on the peaceful settlement of disputes (21)

C. *Sub-Committee 2*
Confidence-building measures (22-24)

Committee II
Cooperation in the fields of economics, science and technology and environment (25-41)

D. *Sub-Committee 3*
Commercial exchanges (31-32)

E. *Sub-Committee 4*
Industrial cooperation and projects of common interest (33-36)

F. *Sub-Committee 5*
Science and technology (37-38)

G. *Sub-Committee 6*
Environment (39-40)

H. *Sub-Committee 7*
Cooperation in other areas (41)

Committee III
Cooperation in humanitarian and other fields (42-52)

I. *Sub-Committee 8*
Human Contacts (45-46)

J. *Sub-Committee 9*
Information (47)

K. *Sub-Committee 10*
Cooperation and exchanges in the field of culture (48-50)

L. *Sub-Committee 11*
Cooperation and exchanges in the field of education (51-52)

Working Group on the Mediterranean

Working Group on Follow-Up

Working Group on Stage III

Working Group on technical aspects of the Final Act

Working Group on financial questions

The numbers in brackets refer to the paragraphs of the Helsinki Final Recommendations with which respective bodies were concerned.

APPENDIX II

Letter from Mr. M. A. Pakenham[1] (UKMIS Geneva) to Mr. Fall

[EN 2/557/3]

Personal and Confidential   GENEVA, 26 July 1974

Dear Brian,

CSCE: BASKET III

1. We who toil in the Third Basket often feel that our negotiations are so little understood by the general public, because the language we use in them is so esoteric. We also wonder whether the impact on the negotiations of the various personalities is fully appreciated.

2. David Miller and I have therefore prepared the enclosed report, which we hope will lead to a greater understanding of the current state of play and the progress we have made since Christmas. It is drafted, as you will see, in rather more common-place language, using terms more readily comprehensible to 'the man on the terraces'. Needless to say, it is not intended to replace the more detailed and official report, which we are sending at the same time to the Department.

Yours ever,
M.A. PAKENHAM

ENCLOSURE

Warsaw Park 1(1), Brussels Casuals 0(0)
Teams as per programme: See Annex A

Geneva, July 26: Today's narrow victory for Warsaw Park in this second-leg tie of the European Cup left them level with their old rivals from Brussels. The earlier meeting in Helsinki between these two evenly-matched sides ended with Casuals one ahead. Thus, the future position in Division III is no clearer and some observers close to the game are indeed wondering whether the replay will be worth the entrance money.

As soon as the teams were announced, it was obvious that the selectors had created problems for themselves. Warsaw Park had chosen an elderly, defensive side (average age—59). The successful Soviet team was well-represented and the elegant sweeping of Dubinin was bound to be a major factor. Nevertheless, some of his colleagues seemed short of match practice. Another feature was the presence of Ernst (they shall not pass) Krabatsch[2] in goal, whose nickname 'the Berlin wall' was not earned lightly. From the make-up of the team, it was clear that Warsaw would rely on their well-proven tactics of obdurate and intransigent defence, hoping to sneak a victory by the odd goal in a break-away.

The Brussels selectors had greater talent to draw upon, but their eventual choice caused a collective sinking of the heart among experienced commentators. Shenstone[3]

---

[1] UK delegation to the CSCE.

[2] Herr E. Krabatsch was a member of the East German delegation.

[3] Mr. M. Shenstone was Canadian Head of Delegation.

in goal was known to be lacking in decisiveness within the 6-yard area. The back four, while individually talented, could not be said to be well-paired: Maes[4] playing alongside Chazelle would produce an uneven rhythm, and it had to be hoped that the uncompromising Maxey would be able to protect Foley,[5] whose slowness on the turn was well-known. The linking of Ersun[6] and Evangelidis[7] was an ill-judged move which would, and did, cause trouble later. A lack of pace in mid-field might make some regret the absence of former schemer and pocket general Fall (Brentford). Finally, the aristocratic Huydecoper, for all the silkiness of a Talleyrand, would hardly have the necessary distributive skills to act as the central striker. In addition to these difficulties, the side caused themselves further problems by indulging in so many pre-game team-talks that they neglected their basic training.

The Administration of both teams gave the cognoscenti much cause for reflection. Warsaw were being managed by 'Iron-Hand' Kovalev, an old campaigner in the international field, but previously better known for his skill at the Kremlin Wall Game. Brussels at first were run on the democratic principle of collective irresponsibility. In the middle of the game, however, greater control was imposed by the appointment as coach of Henry 'Golden Wonder' Kissinger, famed adviser at White House Lane.

The presence of the influential Brunner (Zurich Young-fellows) in the stands added to the confusion. Unable to decide which team to support, he cheered for each in turn.

As the match opened in a sultry haze traditional to the fog-bound cauldron they call Geneva, the clouds released a few drops of rain, perhaps symbolic of the at times spotty play to come. With these unhappy portents the game began. The stadium was disappointingly empty of spectators, although the Warsaw substitutes' bench, packed with a solid phalanx of 'advisers', presented a diverting sight. The opening minutes set the tone for the whole match. Apart from several preambular attacks, during which they won a couple of corners, Warsaw were content to rely on their legendary *catennacio* defence. Anyone who had expected them to play an open, free-running game, so alien to their usual style, was quickly disappointed. Dubinin had clearly adapted well to a more sophisticated role behind the back four, although his lack of forward movement disqualified him from the title of 'libero'. Behind him Krabatsch, recently transferred from Rückwärts Rostock, was as solid as a rock, once tipping over a searing volley from Maxey, striding forward in a move codenamed 'oral information'. These forays upfield by the muscular Brussels centre-back were an early feature of the game, causing considerable excitement among the sparse crowd but failing to disrupt the almost Chekhovian calm of Park's Stakhanovite defence. Fifteen minutes into the first half, Huydecoper eluded a clumsy tackle by Misha 'Wooden-Leg' Kharlamov[8], only to be bracketed from behind and felled with a scything tackle by Dubinin. This incident caused a degree of ill-feeling between these two star players, which further niggling encounters did nothing to diminish.

[4] M. F. Maes was a member of the Belgian delegation.

[5] Mr. Foley was a member of the Irish delegation.

[6] Mr. O. Ersun was a member of the Turkish delegation.

[7] Mr. L. Evangelidis was a member of the Greek delegation.

[8] Mr. M.A. Kharlamov was a member of the Soviet delegation.

Both sides were playing cultured, educated and scientific football, but there was too little contact for the liking of the spectators. They were not helped by an absence of information, owing to Park's insistence on jamming the public address system. The Brussels defence (among whom Maes calling for the ball could be heard on the back terracing) had settled down well; Chazelle, disdainfully laying off the ball with the outside of his foot, and swatting it either to Maxey or to Maes, was already showing signs of the authority he was increasingly to exert as the game wore on. Although Stefan[9] had tended to blow hot and cold, and the dribbling of Ferraris proved more confusing to friend than foe, Casuals had dominated mid-field. But one could have wished for more bite in the tackle (lack of experience telling here?) and less evident reluctance to go for the 50/50 ball 'for fear of spoiling the atmosphere', as one Brussels player later put it.

The real trouble lay with the attack, where Evangelidis appeared content to delay his blind-side runs until the Greek Kalends. Casuals refused to exploit the reluctance of Krabatsch, known to be suspect to anything over his head, to deal with the high cross. The odd bicycle-kick from Huydecoper proved fruitless, though one could not but admire the courage in his willingness to take on the whole Park defence in head-on confrontation. Marking was tight; and while Witte[10] was quick with his subtle one-twos to exploit the gap left by the youngster Afanasevsky[11] dropping back to play alongside Dubinin, Brussels were given very little freedom of movement. The side in fact cried out for a schemer to negotiate a way round the road-block erected at the edge of the Warsaw area.

On the stroke of half time came the first real chance of the day, and tragedy for Brussels. Casuals defence suddenly seemed to have sworn a vow of non-interference as a Warsaw attack down the middle developed on expected lines. Slipping past the retreating figure of Witte, Sedlak[12] rifled over a strong cross-shot. No real danger threatened however, until a leg suddenly emerged from a ruck of Casuals players to steer the ball unerringly between the Brussels posts. Net-minder Shenstone was left speechless, gesturing at the empty air.

One down after forty-five minutes, Brussels had given few signs of being the same team that had brought back such a good result last year from the first leg in Helsinki. The uncompromising Park defence had evidently upset their rhythm, and team spirit suffered accordingly. A certain edginess had crept into their play by half-time.

The start of the second half showed no change in either side's tactics. Brussels continued to hold sway in mid-field, producing some interesting ideas and dainty footwork. But in front of goal they were sadly lacking in penetration, and any sort of access to the Park net remained barred. After ten minutes, while the gentle ebb and flow was only interrupted by a glancing header from Maxey which grazed Krabatsch's left-hand post, Henze[13] came on to replace his West German colleague. Witte's insistence on holding the ball for too long had revealed a lack of tactical judgement.

[9] Mr. G. Stefan was a member of the US delegation.

[10] Herr B. Witte was a member of the West German delegation.

[11] Mr. N.N. Afanasevsky was a member of the Soviet delegation.

[12] Mr. J. Sedlak was a member of the Czechoslovakian delegation.

[13] Herr G. Henze was a member of the West German delegation.

His departure from the field caused no great regret, even though Henze with his first kick almost conceded an own goal, which would have reunited him with his family in Munich without delay. Thereafter he limped along the wing as a virtual passanger [*sic*].

For Warsaw, the promised combination-play of Nowak[14] and Sava[15] had so far failed to materialise. The former's jinking runs through the middle had provided welcome entertainment for the sorely starved spectators, but he had never looked dangerous; while the latter had sulked for much of the game on his wing. It was therefore no surprise when Nowak was replaced by his fellow-countryman Rotfeld[16], an event which caused the momentary reappearance on the field of the legendary Park trainer Mendelevich (Serbsky Medics).

By mid-way through the second half, a lethargy unusual in such an important game appeared to have settled on the players. It was hard to resist the impression that some had even stopped trying. No shots on goal had been seen for some time and the traditional cries from the Park supporters of "Ron-knee" had become muted.

But as time ran out and Liedermann began to study his watch, drama suddenly erupted. First a nasty incident off the ball involving Evangelidis and Ersun led to the collapse, for reasons not immediately apparent, of the left-hand lines-man, Georgiades[17] (Famagusta Freebooters). Liedermann was quick to enter the names of both players in his little Blue Book, and they were later reprimanded by their manager; but Warsaw demands that they be sent off the field were not upheld. Seconds later, while the stadium still seethed with unaccustomed excitement, Maes overlapped on the left and crossed a cunning ball to the far post. Once again the heads went up, the grey-streaked quiff of the over-immaculate Dubinin being clearly visible. His failure to clear the ball cleanly, however, gave Casuals their final chance of access to the printed score-sheet. A melee ensued and in the confusion the ball was seen trickling past Krabatsch as he went the other way. At that moment the whistle blew for full time. In the confusion the result was not immediately clear. It was, however, later established that in the view of the referee the ball had not crossed the line; Casuals claims to the contrary were unavailing.

A hard match had thus brought no conclusive result. The outcome of the replay is imponderable, although rumours already are circulating that the Casuals manager has been keeping strange company behind the main Stand. No credence can be given at this stage to unsubstantial gossip about throw-weights. There is, however, little doubt that Brussels will need to show greater determination and cohesion if they are to progress successfully to the next round (tentatively slated for the end of the year in Helsinki).[18]

[14] Mr. J. Nowak was a member of the Polish delegation.

[15] Mr. M. Sava (Sawa) was a member of the Romanian delegation.

[16] Mr. A.D. Rotfeld was a member of the Polish delegation.

[17] Mr. A. Georgiades was a member of the Cypriot delegation.

[18] Other members of the Warsaw Park team were Mr. S.A. Shumovsky, Mr. H. Milatinov, Mr. E.N. Nassinovsky and Mr. G. Zagor.

Warsaw Park

Krabatsch
(Erfurt Kickers)

Sub
Rotfeld
(Gornik Streakers)

Dubinin
(Dynamo Dzerzhinsk)

Shumovsky
(Kronstadt Academicals)

Afanasevsky
(Lubyanaka Ravens)

Milatinov
(Sofia Sycos)

Nassinovsky
(Kiev Old Chekists)

Nowak
(Bydgoszcz Ulans)

Kharlamov
(All-Union Agitators)

Zagor
(Budapest Bygones)

Sawa
(Ploesti Oilworkers)

Sedlak
(Prague End Vipers)

Referee Liedermann (Vienna 1848)

Witte
(Jusos '53)

Huydecoper
(Nee Eintracht)

Evangelidis
(Panathanaikos)

Ferraris
(Juventus Aeterna)

Stefan
(Washington Jets)

Ersun
(Trebizond Towers)

Foley
(Shamrock Rovers)

Maxey
(Croydon Amateurs)

Chazelle
(Racing Club)

Maes
(Waterloo)

Sub
Henze
(Tennis Borussia)

Shenstone
(Winnipeg Haverers)

Brussels Casuals

APPENDIX III

Mr. R.E. Parsons[1] *(Budapest) to Dr. D.A.L. Owen*[2]

[ENZ 441/1]

Confidential   BUDAPEST, *13 March 1978*

Sir,

The Belgrade CSCE Follow-up Meeting

A full report is being prepared separately on the Belgrade Meeting of Representatives of the participating States of the Conference on Security and Co-operation in Europe, at which I had the honour to lead the British delegation. In this despatch I shall limit myself to some general comments and reflexions.

2. The story of what actually happened at Belgrade from October 1977, to March 1978, can be briefly told. The Helsinki Final Act signed at Head of Government level in August 1975, contained an ambitious charter for the development of security and co-operation in the political, military, economic, humanitarian and other fields. It was obvious that implementation on so extensive a scale would be neither easy nor rapid. At Helsinki the Western representatives pressed successfully for continuing the multilateral process by organising meetings to exchange views on the implementation of the provisions of the Final Act and the deepening of their mutual relations. Belgrade, only two short years later, was the first of these follow-up meetings.

3. The position of the nine countries of the European Community was carefully prepared in advance. It was agreed to conduct a frank and extensive review but to phrase our comments in non-polemical terms in the hope that, at the end of the review of implementation, the way would be clear to negotiate with the Soviet Union and their allies proposals for improving implementation in the future. The course of the Conference went somewhat differently in the event. The American delegation, under Mr. Justice Goldberg,[3] adopted a high-profile position and did not hesitate to criticise named Eastern European countries for their treatment of individuals. A further complication was the introduction from a wide variety of sources of over ninety proposals which, even in the best circumstances, would have been difficult to digest. The Western negotiators were realistic enough to understand that the concluding document could not be expected to take account of proposals on so extensive a scale. What we aimed for in particular was recognition of the right of the individual to assist in the implementation of the CSCE process; some progress on human contacts and confidence-building measures; and realistic language on implementation taking account of the shortcomings still existing in certain countries. A reference in the concluding document to the principle of respect for human rights and fundamental freedoms was added to our aims early in the meeting at American suggestion. The doubts of the Nine on this last point related simply to the prospects of obtaining Eastern agreement

[1] HM Ambassador in Budapest, 1976-80.

[2] Secretary of State for Foreign and Commonwealth Affairs, 1977-79.

[3] Mr. Justice A.J. Goldberg was US Head of Delegation.

to such a proposal in a meeting governed by the consensus principle. By the time that the meeting went into its Christmas recess, these positions had been firmly staked out.

4. When the Conference resumed in January the leader of the Soviet delegation, Ambassador Vorontsov,[4] made it clear that the rulers of the Soviet Union were not prepared to make even minimal concessions on these essential points. This fundamental decision by one single Government was responsible for the comparative failure of the whole meeting. It was perhaps just as well, however, that the Russians did not attempt to split the unity of the West by making an offer which some, but not others, could have accepted. Instead they offered us a long but largely insubstantial draft for the concluding document which would have contained flowery language on *détente* and disarmament but nothing on our own requirements. It also contained a number of proposals of interest to the East, such as the 'special consultations' in the military field which we could not possibly have accepted. Dismayed by the impasse which resulted, the Neutral and Non-aligned delegations got together and offered language which, although a watering down of our original proposals, would have satisfied us on the essential points indicated above. This, too, the Russians and their allies rejected. The host Government, Yugoslavia, fearing that the meeting would appear to end in failure, then offered a different form of apparent compromise, less controversial than the Russian text but equally deficient in references to the essential Western requirements as regards human rights and the individual. The Western negotiators felt obliged to reject this. We were well aware of the danger of misleading our public opinion by accepting a text implying that there had been substantial agreement on essential points which was far from being the case. We thought it better to produce a short and largely factual concluding document which would at least be realistic and not misleading. In the final stage of the meeting such a document was negotiated primarily by the Danish Chairman of the Nine in conjunction with the representatives of the two other Superpowers, US and the Soviet Union. The Neutral and Non-aligned delegations regretted vociferously this method of proceeding but eventually had no option but to give their consensus. The outcome represents the Lowest Common Denominator available rather than the Highest Common Factor.

5. The concluding document is certainly a disappointment, though perhaps not surprisingly so as the product of a meeting of 35 sovereign States each one of which had the right to refuse consensus to any proposal. The document itself at least has certain positive merits. As indicated above, it is not misleading. It includes a reaffirmation of the resolve of Governments to implement fully all the provisions of the Final Act (including by implication the human rights aspect). It says frankly that different views were expressed as to the degree of implementation of the Final Act reached so far and recognises that this exchange of views was in itself valuable. Finally, it fixes precise dates in the autumn of 1980 for the next Belgrade-type meeting to be held in Madrid, thus ensuring the continuity of the process. Having said this, one must recognise that the West unfortunately failed at Belgrade to obtain Soviet and Eastern Europe [*sic*] agreement to precise proposals designed to make life easier for the individual in Eastern Europe and for those caught in the so-called 'interface' between the two political systems.

[4] Mr. Y.M. Vorontsov was Soviet Head of Delegation.

6. Nevertheless, I am glad that you felt able to take the view that the meeting as a whole had not been without value. The Helsinki Final Act is really a blueprint for Utopia. A Europe entirely governed by its provisions would be something of an earthly paradise. One should therefore not take too tragically the undoubted fact that its implementation is so far incomplete. The Belgrade follow-up meeting must be seen essentially as part of a process and as the first checkpoint along a lengthy and weary road. The meeting itself concentrated the attention of governments and of public opinion on this process, thus assisting the Western aim of keeping the Soviet Union and their allies firmly committed to what they undertook at Helsinki. The preparations for the meeting were in themselves valuable since there is no doubt that the Soviet Union and her allies felt obliged to do some spring-cleaning in order to reduce their vulnerability to criticism at Belgrade. The meeting may be compared to a kit inspection in an army barrack room. This is not an inspiring activity but a barrack room which was never inspected would be an unattractive place. We have positive proof of the value of these preparations in practical terms. The UK, for example, has solved two-thirds of its personal cases with the Soviet Union and the countries of Eastern Europe in the years since Helsinki. There is no doubt that the CSCE process played a part in this. The review of implementation at Belgrade was useful even though it was not held in public and even though the Eastern side were reluctant to enter into a meaningful dialogue. The review firmly established the right of all participating States to criticise frankly the implementation record of other CSCE States. What we said about this will have filtered through to a wide readership in Eastern Europe. From the Western standpoint this was really more important than the proposals for improved implementation which achieved so little success. Moreover, the Soviet Union and their allies made no attempt to wriggle out of their Helsinki obligations. They subscribed to the above-mentioned reaffirmation of the provisions of the Final Act while their acceptance of a meeting in Madrid provided for the continuity of the process. This is important to the West and the Neutral countries since the CSCE process was the price paid by the Eastern side at Helsinki for the European security settlement to which Mr. Brezhnev attached so much importance in 1975. His subsequent illness and the resulting power vacuum in Moscow may have caused the Russian negotiators to be more cautious this time.

7. The Belgrade follow-up meeting and its limitations must be seen in perspective. It is a comparatively short time since Helsinki and it would not have been reasonable to expect sensational progress in so wide a field. In fact there is no doubt that some progress has been made in the implementation of the Final Act, in the essential humanitarian field as well as others. One problem at the beginning of the Belgrade meeting was the exaggerated interest of the Western Press who, somewhat naïvely, seemed to expect that there might be a complete breakthrough there on 'human rights'. In view of the exchange of signals about human rights between the rulers of the Soviet Union and the US which had taken place earlier in 1977, it was never likely that the Soviet Union would concede to Western representatives at Belgrade points on which they had clashed publicly with the President of the US. The Eastern side had exacerbated the atmosphere by harassment of Charter 77 signatories in Czechoslovakia and members of Monitoring Groups in the Soviet Union. The reaction in the West had been understandably strong. The effect of all this was to raise the political temperature

at Belgrade, to the chagrin of some CSCE experts who continually harked back with nostalgia to the calmer and more club-like atmosphere existing in the Geneva and Helsinki days. Several of them persisted throughout the Belgrade meeting in their inability to understand quite what had hit them.

8. It can be argued that some of the Western and the Non-aligned delegations laid undue emphasis throughout the meeting on the concluding document. The need for such a document is not in fact mentioned in the Helsinki Final Act. Special attention was devoted to it at the preparatory meeting last summer as a device for dealing with the Soviet wish to fix a definite term to the main Belgrade follow-up meeting. Fearing that this would permit the Eastern delegations to impose time pressure and obstruct proceedings, the Western delegates at the preparatory meeting insisted on obtaining in the Decisions of the preparatory meeting a reference to the need for the main meeting to end by adopting its concluding document. This position snowballed to the extent of leading some Press commentators, particularly in the Federal Republic of Germany, to believe wrongly that the whole purpose of the Belgrade meeting was to obtain some new written concessions from the Soviet Union. In fact the Helsinki Final Act is so far-reaching that it is much more important to have the Act itself properly implemented than to obtain new written assurances. In the considered view of the Nine therefore the key part of the Belgrade meeting was the review of implementation. But some Governments, particularly the Germans, tended to over-estimate the importance and chances of obtaining Soviet acceptance of new proposals.

9. It has been argued that the high posture adopted by Ambassador Goldberg during the review of implementation led to a regrettable souring of the atmosphere with the results summarised above. I do not myself attach much importance to this argument. If anyone really 'provoked' the Soviet Union on the human rights issue, it was much less Ambassador Goldberg at Belgrade in October 1977 than President Carter[5] at the beginning of that year. There could be something in Vorontsov's argument that but for the so-called orchestrated Western campaign on human rights, the Soviet Union would have been prepared to give some further assurances on this point which, after all, is something they have themselves accepted in Principle VII of the Final Act. But the argument should not be pressed too far. No doubt President Carter's own view would be that his decision to raise the human rights issues on a world-wide basis as the moral foundation of American policy, a point on which he received full support from Her Majesty's Government, was much more important than obtaining fresh scraps of paper at Belgrade. Quite apart from this, some people in the West may have been over-optimistic in their assessment of the willingness of the Soviet Union and their allies to listen calmly to criticisms of their implementation record if couched in non-polemical terms. I have myself found in Budapest that it is possible to conduct such a review in a dispassionate atmosphere on a bilateral basis. But we recognised from the start that a multilateral operation of this kind, with States rallying to the support of their allies, is almost bound to be a tension-provoking exercise in the present state of Europe.

10. It would never have been politically or morally desirable for the US or her allies to fail to raise the human rights issue at Belgrade. Recognising this, the Nine had prepared a proposal designed to safeguard the rights of individuals in implementing the

[5] Mr. J. Carter was President of the US, 1977-81.

CSCE process as indicated above. It was only when the meeting had actually begun that, on an American initiative, we joined in co-sponsoring a separate text specifically reaffirming the principle of human rights. This latter decision was recognised in the Nine at the time as diplomatically far from ideal since it involved us in putting forward a provocative non-starter. But it would have been politically quite impossible for the Governments of the Nine, including Her Majesty's Government, to refuse to support a human rights proposal of this kind. I doubt whether this had a decisive effect on the Soviet attitude. We did succeed in dissuading the Belgians and Americans from proposing the establishment of a CSCE Committee on Human Rights which, however attractive in the abstract, would have been another non-starter in practice. In the event, these ideas were submerged in the huge and indigestible mass of new proposals. Even if the political will to negotiate had existed, these would have absorbed the attention of any meeting for a great many months.

11. The relationship between the Superpowers at Belgrade was particularly interesting and even entertaining. Ambassadors Vorontsov and Goldberg had clearly elected themselves from the beginning as the stars of the meeting, each determined to cap the other's speeches. They enjoyed proceeding around the Sava Centre at majestic pace, flanked by scurrying acolytes. They affected to have a warm personal relationship while privately each cordially disliked the other. The Soviet rôle was predictable, with Vorontsov playing a rather more inflexible part than previous Russian negotiators in the CSCE process. The American position was more spectacular. It had become traditional in the CSCE for the Americans to adopt a helpful, but modest, supporting position, leaving most of the work to their European allies on the grounds that the process mainly concerned Europe. But Ambassador Goldberg, a former Secretary of Labour, Supreme Court Justice and Ambassador to the UN, and an engaging and entertaining personality, has not been cast by nature for supporting rôles. His imperious and sometimes insensitive manner certainly incensed many of the Neutral and Non-aligned delegations. His final accommodation with Vorontsov seemed to many to be in the worst traditions of Superpower diplomacy. President Carter may feel pleased with Ambassador Goldberg's undoubted flair for public relations and his ability to blow the trumpet of human rights without doing any real damage to the relationship between Moscow and Washington. But, on the whole, it has not been a good meeting for America's reputation within Europe.

12. Nevertheless, it must be conceded that Ambassador Goldberg was a loyal ally, willing to stick to consensus within the Alliance. The unity of the Nine was particularly good and it was a heartening experience to see just how effective the delegations of the Nine can be at a large multilateral meeting so long as they stick together and do their homework. This has been one of the most lasting and useful results of the Belgrade follow-up meeting. We had our difficulties with the French whose Gallic logic prevented them, as usual, from feeling the rhythm of a meeting which was bound to take its pace from some of the slower members. Their own unilateral initiative in producing a compromise draft towards the end of the meeting was particularly irritating. It came on the day after you and other Foreign Ministers had just spent several days in person with the French Foreign Minister in New York and Copenhagen without his making French intentions clear. The Nine certainly regretted this as an unfortunate example of French duplicity and unreliability. Nevertheless, their ill-prepared solo effort

did no great harm and indeed it helped to show how adamant the Soviet Union were in refusing to negotiate on our essential points. Another important though tricky ally was the delegation of the Federal Republic of Germany. Their position was fundamentally different from ours since, for good reasons, they attached immense importance to obtaining improvements in human contacts even at the expense of other points we considered more important. But they stuck by their partners. The Belgian Presidency was competent and the Danish Presidency splendid.

13. A word must be said about the Neutral and Non-aligned delegations who played a disappointing rôle in this meeting as indicated above. They failed either to agree on a combined strategy or to leave each other free for individual initiatives. On all the real issues connected with human rights and human contacts most of the Neutrals were firmly, though somewhat ineffectively, on the Western side, with Yugoslavia and Finland playing a more equivocal rôle. It was therefore irritating of some of the Neutrals towards the end of the meeting to use tactics which had the effect of making the West appear to be denying consensus to a more substantial document. The Yugoslav delegation, in particular, went somewhat beyond the latitude normally accorded to a host Government in pursuing their own aims. This could be an unfortunate precedent for Madrid and one which the UK needs to watch, in view of the Gibraltar issue.

14. The problems of dealing with some Neutral and Non-aligned countries were further highlighted at the very end of the meeting when Malta alone threatened to deny consensus if its particular Mediterranean preoccupations were not met in the concluding document. The Maltese delegation were able to hold up proceedings for nearly five days in an eleventh-hour bid to include the subject of Mediterranean security in the mandate of a proposed experts meeting in Valletta in early 1979. The Nine had agreed to such a meeting (the only new experts meeting to be established at Belgrade apart from those already envisaged in the Final Act itself) only on the condition that its mandate be restricted to economic, cultural and scientific fields. In the event the Maltese finally climbed down by accepting a largely, if not entirely, face-saving clause to the effect that security in the Mediterranean would be discussed at Madrid. But this was not until after the nerves of some had been badly frayed and many delegates had begun to talk openly of the possible collapse of the meeting. The Maltese performance throughout CSCE has gone some way towards discrediting the whole principle of consensus. Somebody ought to get a grip on them!

15. Having now lived through five months of this meeting during a depressing winter in one of the least attractive capitals of Europe, I still retain some degree of enthusiasm for the CSCE process. It certainly has its limitations, which we must never forget. There is an air of unreality about the proceedings. It is a group of 35 independent and equal nations. But some are more independent and ·equal than the rest. Nor can the existence of blocs be gainsaid in the real world. The presence of Neutral and Non-aligned countries in an unwieldy framework and a club-like atmosphere allows the Russians to make play with propaganda gestures. It is therefore not a suitable forum for negotiating subjects of major importance with the Soviet Union such as substantial disarmament questions. The latter are clearly more important to the real development of *détente* than anything which can be expected of the CSCE in the short term. In the long term the 'human dimension' of *détente* emphasised in CSCE could be at least equally important. On balance the whole process does seem to have

real value. It is particularly appreciated by the Neutral and Non-aligned countries and by those countries of Eastern Europe, such as Romania, Poland and my clients here in Hungary who overtly or covertly, are seeking to obtain more liberty of manoeuvre for themselves. CSCE provides an umbrella under which such countries can extend their contacts with the West. Nor must we forget the effect even on the hard-line countries such as the Soviet Union, Czechoslovakia, Bulgaria and even the GDR. I believe that in all these countries there do exist people within the official hierarchy who are prepared to see some loosening up of the system and correspondingly greater toleration for individuals. It is these people that we need to encourage discreetly in order to weaken the Soviet grip on Eastern Europe and the aggressive dynamic of international Communism. CSCE is one of the tools we have available for this purpose.

16. In a separate despatch, designed to be read with this one, I am submitting ideas for improving the CSCE process between now and the Madrid follow-up meeting.[6]

17. I am sending copies of this despatch to Her Majesty's Representatives in all European posts and at Washington and Ottawa, and to the UK Permanent Representatives at NATO, CCD & MBFR, the European Economic Communities, the Council of Europe and the UN.

I have, etc.,

R.E. PARSONS

[6] This follow-up meeting took place from February to July 1983 with a Foreign Ministers concluding session from 79 September 1983.

Index of Main Subjects and Persons

This straightforward index is designed to be used in conjunction with the Chapter Summaries. In a departure from previous *DBPO* practice, references in this index are to page, rather than document numbers.

Aalto, A. 464

Aaron, D. 60

Acland, A.A. 43, 57, 163, 245, 278, 286, 335

Adams, C.C.W. 85, 95, 99, 153, 163, 180, 191, 211, 233, 243, 258, 262, 269-71, 280, 293, 308, 320

Agenda Items
see Baskets I, II, III and IV

Albania 167, 318, 338, 464

Alexander, M.O'D.B. 43, 163, 296, 343-4, 346, 364, 366, 372, 398-9, 401, 404-6, 408-18, 425, 436

Alexander, T.J. 374, 444

Algeria 93, 139, 156, 160-3, 165, 167, 173, 175, 233
Algiers non-aligned conference (1973) 174

Allan, J.N. 19, 40

Amalrik, A.A. 177

Amery, J. 237

Ananichev, K.V. 174

Andorra 464

André, G. 98, 382, 389, 398, 432, 439, 442, 445

Andréani, J. 129, 191, 196, 321, 332, 335

Andreotti, G. 71

Andropov, Y. 178

Angliya 54

Anglo-Soviet Consultative Committee 52

Arnaud, C.V.M. 370, 390

Associated Press (AP) 176

Audland, C.J. 90

Australia 56

Austria 11-12, 59, 77, 89, 93, 120, 141, 143, 174, 183, 238-9, 242, 282, 289, 292, 300, 336, 364, 384

Bahr, E. 261

Bailes, Miss A.J.K. 342

Baker, R.H. 83

Barder, B.L. 53

Barker, T.C. 418

Basket I 155, 158, 169, 171, 175, 178, 180, 188, 191-2, 202-3, 210, 215-16, 219, 221, 225, 228, 233, 241-2, 248-9, 252, 257, 262, 264-6, 274, 278, 298, 301, 314, 319, 328, 345, 351, 362, 368, 372, 385-6, 388, 395, 398, 442, 453, 455, 476-7
see also Principles, Confidence Building Measures and Peaceful settlement of disputes
colonialism 232
national minorities 232, 255, 266, 345, 349-50

Basket II 116-17, 125, 129, 133-4, 136, 158, 171, 175, 180, 189, 192-4, 197-8, 201-3, 206, 208, 217-19, 225, 231, 233, 241, 249, 255, 265, 267, 274, 283, 287-9, 298, 301-4, 307-8, 314, 320, 346, 353, 356, 360, 367, 369, 374-6, 385-6, 397, 403, 405, 414, 428, 431, 444, 446-7, 451, 453, 455, 477
see also Commercial exchanges, Industrial coöperation, Science and technology and Environment
Quantitative Restrictions (QRs) 208, 217
reciprocity 13, 93, 117, 134-5, 139, 207-8, 274, 298, 302-3, 308, 320, 356, 374-6, 386-7, 395, 403, 428, 436, 444-6, 451, 457

Basket III 77, 81-3, 93, 97, 116-18, 120, 122-3, 126-9, 135, 143, 147-8, 150,

Basket III cont'd

158, 171, 178-80, 183, 186-7, 189, 191-2, 197-201, 203-6, 214-16, 218-21, 223-5, 228, 230-2, 234-6, 238-52, 254-5, 257-8, 260, 262, 264-6, 268-70, 272-3, 275, 278, 282-3, 287-91, 295, 297-304, 306-9, 311-16, 320-1, 325-8, 330-1, 334-6, 341, 343, 345-6, 348, 350, 352-6, 360, 362-5, 367, 369, 372, 376, 385, 387-8, 390, 393, 395, 397, 399-411, 413-16, 423-5, 449-50, 452-3, 455, 458, 466, 469, 473, 476-8

see also Human contacts, Information, Culture and education

Basket IV

permanent/follow-up machinery 1, 3, 15, 19-20, 25, 29, 61-2, 70-2, 78, 82, 89, 91, 94, 97, 99, 108-13, 117-18, 120, 124, 129-30, 158, 169, 181, 183, 201, 204-5, 215-16, 220, 224-5, 228, 232, 243, 249, 252, 255, 266, 273-4, 284-6, 290, 303, 308, 321, 325-6, 328, 333-4, 336, 348, 357-8, 360-3, 367-70, 376, 378, 390-4, 403, 407, 414, 428, 430-1, 433-5, 438-40, 442, 447, 450, 453, 459, 469-70, 473, 477

Beetham, R.C. 94-5, 146, 246, 278, 309

Beith, Sir J. 104, 120, 123, 152, 203

Belgium 16, 42, 64, 147, 153, 155, 157, 186, 203, 207, 209, 212, 219, 226-7, 232, 240, 242, 250, 258-9, 274, 287, 303, 309, 345, 366, 368, 370, 373, 376, 409, 421, 433-4, 439

Bellamy, B.E. 1

Benler, O. 432

Berlin 2, 4, 8, 17, 22-3, 25, 36, 40-1, 43, 47, 56, 149, 261, 264, 296, 328, 430-1, 440-1, 450, 465, 470-3

Final Protocol (1972) 261

senate 471, 473

wall 159, 473-4

Bindschedler, R.L. 192, 197, 200

Bishop, K.A. 106, 180

Bisztyga, Prof. J. 262

Blech, Dr. K. 346-7, 360, 377, 382, 428, 432

Bochet, G. 116

Bock, Dr. S. 143, 266

Bondarenko, A.B. 72

Bonn Group 8, 63, 349, 386, 389, 398

Boster, D.E. 199

Braithwaite, R.Q. 8, 15, 19-20, 34-6, 39-40, 43, 46, 50, 286

Brandt, W. 99, 129, 157, 237, 258, 282, 296, 364

Bratteli, T.M. 261

Brenchley, T.F. 262

Bretton Woods 64

Brezhnev Doctrine 1, 6-7, 27, 29, 73, 101, 108, 122, 138, 144, 148, 185, 297, 349, 352, 355, 384, 402, 450, 455, 476

Brezhnev, L.I. 6, 58, 61, 102, 106, 129, 138, 147-50, 159, 167-8, 177-8, 180, 214, 221, 235-8, 246, 261-2, 278, 293, 295, 322-3, 356, 364-5, 374, 377, 379, 383-4, 386, 388, 394, 396, 399, 414, 419, 422, 449, 461-3, 465-7, 471, 476-8

meeting with M. Giscard d'Estaing at Rambouillet (1974) 386

message to Mr. Heath (1972) 235

Bridges, Lord 245, 278

Brimelow, Sir T. 1, 18-19, 21, 34-7, 43, 45, 48, 56-7, 60-2, 72, 84, 87, 96, 99-100, 102-3, 108, 110, 113-14, 158, 163, 222, 225, 243

British Broadcasting Corporation (BBC) 54, 121, 417, 424, 426

British Council 52-3, 459

Brooke, G. 55

Brown, Miss G.G. 48

Brown, R.H. 59, 81-2, 84, 106, 108

Brunner, E. 259, 301, 334

Brunner, G. 131-2, 196, 346, 360

Brussels Assembly of Representatives of Public Opinion for Security and Cooperation in Europe (1972) 53

Bulgaria 13, 26, 31, 55, 76-7, 99, 118, 142, 158, 187, 190, 234, 238-40, 251, 291, 314, 338, 467

Bullard, J.L. 1, 25, 33, 50, 59, 101-2, 104, 106, 113, 147, 157, 159, 162-4, 177, 183, 235, 237, 247, 256, 278, 337, 339, 470

Burner, E.A. 96

Burns, R.A. 96-7, 99, 101, 107, 160, 172, 180, 191, 194, 233, 243, 270-1, 275, 280-1, 292-3, 308, 321, 345, 348, 353, 356, 361, 366, 390-1, 393, 398-9, 401-2, 404-8, 410, 413-6, 418-9, 425, 430, 438-9

Burrows, F. 416-7

Butler, M.D. 34

Cable, J. 1

Caetano, Dr. M. 396, 463

Callaghan, L.J. 250, 254, 257, 260, 262, 265, 269, 271, 275, 277, 279-81, 283-5, 288, 291, 294-6, 300-1, 304, 306-7, 311, 313, 315, 317, 319, 326, 330, 333, 335, 343, 345, 348, 351, 357, 368, 371-2, 376, 378-85, 387, 391, 396, 398, 405, 410, 413, 415, 419-20, 422, 426, 430, 433, 435, 438, 440-1, 447, 454, 461, 463-4, 474
    visit to Moscow (1975) 357, 364, 376, 378, 382

Camp David 90, 99

Canada 8, 24, 42, 56, 65-6, 109, 111, 161-2, 174, 196, 212, 258, 280, 282, 291, 309, 318, 340, 366, 373, 435-9, 443

Carter, A. 390, 402-3

Cartledge, B.G. 329

Ceausescu, N. 153

Chazelle, J. 241, 334, 433

China 5, 25, 39, 64, 181
    Nixon-Chou *communiqué* (1972) 39

Chnoupek, B. 159

Chou En-lai 39

Cleghorn, B.E. 407, 429, 434

Cloake, J.C. 301, 304, 369

Collings, Miss J.J. d'A. 50

Commercial exchanges 194-5, 202, 207-8, 302, 320, 446, 451
    business contacts 203, 208-9, 215, 224, 255, 265, 298, 304, 320, 356, 451

Committees (Commissions) I, II, and III
    see Baskets I, II, and III

Conference on Security and Cooperation in Europe (CSCE/CES)
    site of 127

Conference of European Communist Parties 337-8, 364

Confidence Building Measures (CBMs) 38-9, 43, 45, 48, 61, 76, 92-3, 96, 105, 110, 113, 128, 185, 189-91, 202, 214, 217, 221, 223, 226-9, 232, 241, 250, 255, 265-6, 268-72, 277, 279-82, 286, 288-90, 293, 295, 297, 307-8, 311, 313-14, 320-1, 325, 330, 333-4, 336, 345, 348, 350, 352, 355, 360, 366, 368-9, 371-4, 376-8, 381-3, 386-7, 397-9, 401-2, 404-6, 408, 414, 419, 421-2, 427-9, 431, 440-1, 443, 451-3, 455-6, 466, 472
    disarmament 76, 183, 189, 271, 456
    exchange of observers 217, 226-7, 270, 352, 372
    military aspects of security 184, 202, 228-9, 232, 241-2, 265, 269, 319-20, 355, 372-3
    prior notification of manoeuvres 217, 226-9, 269-70, 280, 297, 308, 320, 322, 331, 333, 345, 352-3, 355-7, 360, 372-3, 377-8, 381-2, 387, 394, 397, 402-4, 414, 419-20, 423, 427-8, 452, 457, 476

Conservative Women's Association of Lytham St. Anne's 164

Coordinating Committee 156, 168-73, 175, 180, 182-3, 187-9, 191-2, 199-200, 205, 232, 243, 249, 286, 288, 293, 301, 308-9, 315, 317, 333, 335-6, 377, 387, 397, 406, 415, 426-7, 432-3, 435-7, 439-40, 442-3, 446-7
Cosgrave, L. 466
Costa Gomes, Gen. F. da 463, 466
Council for Mutual Economic Assistance (CMEA/COMECON) 13, 29, 31, 93, 149, 194, 208, 217, 303, 374-6, 395, 457, 479
Cradock, P. 60
Cromer, Lord 99
Crowe, B.L. 102-3
Culture and education 77, 81-3, 93, 97, 154, 171, 218, 251, 253, 265-6, 275-6, 282, 291-2, 308, 316-17, 320, 344, 354, 360, 365, 369, 372, 379, 387, 395, 399, 423, 455, 459
Cyprus 264, 309, 333, 337, 349, 351, 353, 355, 360, 371, 384, 395, 428, 431, 439-41, 443, 447, 452, 466-7
Atilla Line 333
tripartite talks on (1974) 333
Czechoslovakia 4, 13, 17, 20, 25-6, 31-2, 51, 111, 158-9, 173, 205, 212, 243, 292, 338, 378, 409, 446, 451, 459, 465-6, 468, 477
Prague declaration (1972) 22, 28-9, 106, 475

Dahlhoff, G. 347
Dahrendorf, Prof. R.G. 346
Daily Mail, The 310
Darwin, H.G. 49, 107
Daunt, T.L.A. 18
Davignon, Viscount E. 9, 203, 240, 257, 388, 408-9, 434
Davignon Procedures
see European Political Cooperation
Demirel, S. 466
Deniau, J-F. 17

Denmark 5, 16, 42, 64, 153-4, 156-7, 161, 165, 174, 186, 190, 193, 195-6, 243, 273, 284-5, 290, 314-15, 334, 339, 357, 366, 370, 373, 378, 391-2, 394, 408, 412, 421, 432-3, 459
Folketing 16
Deryabin, Y.S. 309
Détente 2, 4-7, 13, 15, 17, 25, 32, 41-2, 50, 56, 110, 112, 121, 129, 145, 159, 166-7, 177-82, 185, 190, 205, 213-14, 222, 270, 274, 278, 287, 297, 304, 318, 322, 324-5, 327, 329, 339, 341, 357, 372, 388, 397, 417, 424, 431, 434, 440-1, 448, 451, 455, 460-3, 465, 468, 470-1, 473, 476-8
Dickie, J. 310
Diplomatic and Commonwealth Writers' Association 310
Dobbs, J.A. 4, 159
Dobrosielski, M. 244, 283
Dobrynin, A.F. 58, 99-100, 102, 419-20
Douglas-Home, Sir A. 15, 21-3, 38, 40-1, 56-8, 60, 62, 70, 87, 89, 91, 94, 98, 114, 116, 120-1, 128, 131-2, 136, 152-5, 157-8, 160, 162-5, 168, 173, 176, 179, 187-8, 191, 193, 195, 201, 203-4, 206, 209-10, 213, 220, 225-6, 230, 234, 237-8, 241, 243-4, 248, 250, 261
visit to Moscow (1973) 210, 224
Dubinin, Y.V. 174, 194, 234-5, 239, 244, 266, 345-6, 372, 393, 398-400, 405, 407-8, 411-13, 425, 438, 445, 448
Ducci, R. 370, 408
Dulles, J.F. 475

Economic Commission for Europe (ECE) 3-4, 12-13, 25, 31, 109, 117, 133-4, 303, 457, 460
Edes, J.M. 180, 198, 211
Egypt 232
Ekholm, G. 444-5
Elliott, T.A.K. 84-9, 91, 94-5, 98, 104, 114-16, 118-26, 131-2, 136, 146-8,

Elliott, T.A.K. cont'd
>150-1, 156, 160, 163, 168, 173-5, 178, 180, 191-2, 196-7, 199, 204-5, 210, 213, 222-3, 225, 249, 252, 254, 261-2, 265, 268, 281-2, 286-90, 293-4, 301, 309, 317-19, 324, 326-9, 464, 469

Environment 77, 171, 217, 303, 308, 320, 446-7, 457
Ernemann, A. 376
Estonia 107
Eurogroup 69
European Atomic Energy Community
>*see* European Community/Communities

European Coal and Steel Community
>*see* European Community/Communities

European Community/Communities (EC) 2, 5, 7, 9, 13-14, 17, 23, 26, 30-1, 33, 35, 38, 58, 64-9, 77, 85-8, 90, 96, 101, 103, 109, 111-12, 125, 134-5, 141, 145-7, 149, 152, 154-7, 162, 165, 167-70, 172-3, 175, 184, 186-7, 189-90, 192-204, 206-12, 217, 219-20, 223-4, 230-5, 239-40, 242-4, 246, 248-50, 252, 255-9, 262, 264, 267-8, 272-5, 277, 279, 282, 284, 286-7, 289-90, 293, 295, 300-3, 306, 310-15, 321-4, 326, 330-2, 334, 336-7, 342, 344, 346-7, 349-51, 357-62, 364, 366-70, 373, 375-8, 382, 388, 390-6, 404, 407, 410, 414, 421-2, 428-9, 432-5, 442, 444-7, 449, 451-2, 454, 457, 466, 468, 476-7
>Commission 9, 86, 156, 190, 193-5, 203, 206-8, 217, 303, 346, 375-6, 392, 403, 414, 444, 452-3, 457
>Common Agricultural Policy 30
>Common Commercial Policy 13, 149, 193, 207
>COREPER 193-4, 207, 210
>Council 208

CSCE Ad Hoc Group 9, 65, 68, 75, 84, 125, 133, 135-6, 141, 156, 171-2, 193-5, 201, 203, 206-7, 209, 230, 242, 265, 271, 274, 286, 369, 376, 429
>European Atomic Energy Community 5
>European Coal and Steel Community 5
>Ministers 248, 331, 347
>Offer at CSCE 193-4, 201, 203, 206-9, 302
>Presidency 157, 165, 172, 193, 217, 219, 230, 233, 242, 258, 267, 322, 361, 370, 407, 432, 440, 444
>Treaty of Rome (1957) 30, 64

European Economic Community (EEC)
>*see* European Community/Communities

European Political Cooperation (EPC)
>Political Committee (Political Directors) 9, 11-12, 14, 19, 21, 33, 35-6, 42, 50, 58-9, 62, 64-72, 74-5, 77-8, 80-3, 84-6, 98, 104, 123, 125-7, 131, 133, 141-2, 155, 157, 172, 193-5, 201, 203, 206-7, 231-3, 241, 243, 246, 249, 258, 260, 267-8, 271-4, 285, 288, 290, 293, 307, 309, 311-13, 331, 335, 339-40, 346, 360-1, 363, 368-71, 373, 375-7, 386, 388, 390-4, 407-9, 415, 431, 433
>CSCE Sub-Committee 9, 19-20, 24, 33, 50, 65, 71, 74, 84, 87, 97, 110, 120, 152-8, 165, 168, 188, 194, 198, 201, 230-2, 238, 243, 271-3, 286, 316, 331, 360-1, 363, 368, 370, 376-7, 390-1, 393-4, 407

Fadeyev, N.V. 208
Fall, B.J.P. 24, 53, 73, 75, 85, 91-2, 101, 103, 107-8, 110-12, 123-4, 137, 146, 159, 163, 168, 172, 187, 194, 198, 201, 210, 222, 254, 256-7, 277-8, 289, 292, 294, 296, 299, 302,

Fall, B.J.P. cont'd
306, 321, 339, 342-4, 347, 351,
361-3
Farace di Villaforesta, A. 343-4,
353, 356, 360
Ferraris, L.V. 196
Fielder, Dr. M. 180, 375, 387, 444,
447
Figaro, Le 190
Figgis, A. St. J. 331, 345, 353, 356,
361, 372, 395, 403, 406-7, 423,
433-4, 438
Financial Times 338
Finland 152, 156, 163, 174, 183, 198,
205, 275, 282, 298, 300, 321, 326,
329, 334, 384, 407, 426, 433, 436-
7, 439, 442, 447, 452, 455, 464-5,
467-8
Fenno-Soviet *communiqué* (1974) 246
Finlandia Hall 464
Fitzgerald, Dr. G. 164
Ford, G.R. 341, 388, 415, 465-7
Foreign Press Association (FP) 36
Fourcade, J-P. 432
France 8-9, 11, 16, 19, 30, 35-6, 38-9,
41-5, 47-8, 64, 66, 70, 80-2, 85-6,
90, 92-3, 95-7, 99, 102, 104, 107,
110, 112, 115-16, 119, 123-7, 129-30,
133, 135, 139, 141-3, 145, 148, 151,
153-8, 160-2, 164-5, 167, 173-5, 186,
190, 195-6, 201-4, 207, 210, 212-13,
215-16, 219, 224-5, 231-2, 236,
239-43, 249, 257-8, 263, 270-2,
276, 282, 284, 289, 292, 295, 311-
14, 322, 328, 336-7, 341, 344-5,
349-50, 352, 359-60, 364-72, 375,
377-9, 382, 386, 389-92, 394-5, 400,
404, 406-7, 411, 421, 427, 429,
432-4, 437, 439, 442, 446, 451,
459
Fretwell, M.J.E. 133

Gaja, R. 36, 147
Galloway, W.J. 34
Galsworthy, Sir A. 368

Garvey, Sir T. 220, 236-8, 260-2,
287, 289, 294, 327, 329, 419, 461,
474, 479
Gaspari, D. 337-8
Gauci, V.J. 429
**General Agreement on Tariffs
and Trade (GATT)** 134, 303,
395
Genscher, H-D. 296, 308, 329, 420
**German Democratic Republic
(GDR/DDR)** 2, 4, 8-9, 12, 14,
24, 26-8, 30-2, 41, 84, 92-3, 132,
143, 158, 173, 239, 242, 276, 291,
296, 317, 345, 348-50, 354, 365,
375, 386, 409, 450, 465, 471-3, 475
**Germany, Federal Republic of
(FRG)** 2, 4, 8-9, 19-20, 22, 25-6,
64, 96, 106-7, 132, 149, 153-5, 157-
8, 161-2, 193, 201, 207, 210, 219,
223, 230-2, 234, 236, 239-40, 242-
3, 249, 257-9, 263-4, 267, 272, 276,
278, 289-90, 295-6, 298, 310, 317,
322-3, 328-9, 336, 338, 346-7, 349,
359-60, 365-6, 369-73, 377, 380,
383, 386, 389-90, 395-6, 400, 413,
420-1, 425, 427-8, 430-3, 436, 441,
444, 451-2, 456, 465-6, 470-2, 475
(*see also* Berlin)
Baden-Württemberg elections (1972)
36
Bundestag 36
Eastern Treaties 181, 231, 470,
472
North Rhine-Westphalia elections
(1975) 364
Ostpolitik 2, 20, 37, 99, 364
Gibraltar 107, 155, 165, 196, 204, 240,
259
Gierek, E. 466
Giscard d'Estaing, V. 282, 386,
388, 463, 465
meeting with Mr. Brezhnev at
Rambouillet (1974) 386
Godber, J. 21
Goodall, A.D.S. 310
Gordon, J.K. 133, 136, 180

Goulding, M.I. 237, 250
Graber, P. 46
Graham, J.A.N. 102, 104
Gray, J.W.D. 173, 180
Grechko, A. 178
Greece 42, 44, 65-6, 85, 189, 196, 333, 355, 366, 395, 427-8, 443
Greek communist party 338
Greenhill, Sir D. 18-19, 21, 27, 29, 61
Groll, G. von 116, 158, 196, 230, 293
Gromyko, A.A. 21, 58-9, 109, 147-8, 157, 159, 161-2, 164-6, 214, 220, 235-6, 246, 261, 277-9, 287, 294-5, 320-1, 334-5, 339-40, 350, 372, 378-84, 397, 406, 409, 412, 419, 429, 436-8, 448, 461, 463-5
Guardian, The 24
Guest, M.R.J. 163
Gvishiani, J.M. 462

Haig Jr., Gen. A.M. 57
Harmel Report (1967) 42
Harmel, P.C.J.M. 42
Hartman, A. 285, 383, 420
Hattersley, R.S.G. 284, 373, 391, 423-4, 426, 429, 454
Heath, E.R.G. 35-6, 39, 90, 99-100, 235-7, 246, 250
Helskov, N. 408
Henderson, J.N. 2-3, 230, 259
Hibbert, R.A. 8, 41, 106, 349
Hildyard, D.H.T. 187-8, 191-3, 198, 201-7, 209-11, 221, 234, 238, 240-2, 244, 248-9, 254, 257, 260-6, 269, 281-2, 286, 288, 291, 297-301, 307, 309, 311, 313, 315-6, 333, 335-6, 343-5, 347, 358-61, 363-5, 367, 371-2, 385-7, 389, 393-400, 405-8, 410, 412-14, 419-23, 428, 430, 433, 435, 437-40, 443, 447-8, 451-2, 454, 464
Holder, Miss J.A. 163
Holdgate, Dr. M.W. 182
Holy See 318, 413, 416-17, 464
Honecker, E. 465, 471-3

Human contacts 120, 154, 171, 177, 181-3, 185, 192, 207, 214, 218, 221, 223, 235--6, 249, 251-2, 266, 273, 275-7, 282, 291, 299, 316, 319-21, 324, 333, 343, 345-6, 348, 353, 356-7, 362, 364, 369, 387, 395, 399-402, 407-12, 415-17, 423, 458, 462, 465, 475
family reunification 298-9, 308, 310, 316, 343-4, 353, 356, 360, 477
freer movement 7, 10, 14, 32, 39, 42, 47, 50, 55, 61, 65, 70-3, 77-8, 82, 84, 103, 110, 118, 121, 138-9, 141, 143, 181, 214, 218, 225, 242, 250-1, 278, 320, 322, 328-9, 331, 356, 402, 409, 458, 473
marriage 218, 291, 299, 343, 353, 356, 360, 458
tourism 400-1, 457
Human rights 345
Hungary 13, 31, 158, 325, 338, 349, 375
Husak, G. 465-6
Hutchinson, Miss P.M. 49
Huydecoper, J.L.R. 196
Hyland, W.G. 60, 103

Iceland 65, 164, 264
Iloniemi, J. 436
Industrial cooperation 189, 208, 303, 320
Information 154-5, 165, 171, 178, 181-3, 185, 187, 190, 192, 207, 214, 218, 223, 236, 240-2, 247, 250-1, 253, 265-6, 273, 275-7, 282, 291, 299, 308, 314, 316, 319-20, 322, 324, 331, 343, 345, 348, 354, 356-7, 360, 362, 395, 397-400, 402, 407-10, 413-16, 423, 455, 458, 462, 478
jamming of radio 54, 111, 121, 316, 356, 417, 424, 458
journalists 154, 218, 253, 314, 331, 354, 387, 390, 398-402, 405, 410-11, 413, 416, 418, 452, 459, 477-8
magazine proposal 54, 82-3, 121, 154, 185, 218, 220, 253

Information cont'd
television 154, 185, 220, 253, 400, 410, 418
Inter-Parliamentary Union (IPU) 12, 109
conference (1973) 109
International Court of Justice (ICJ) 164
Ireland, Republic of 5, 67, 106, 131, 144, 164, 207, 231, 258, 263, 273, 302, 312, 350, 352, 361, 366, 371, 375, 412
Ismay, Lord 62-3
Israel 160-1, 163, 165, 173, 232-3, 274
Italy 19, 42, 44, 47-8, 50, 64, 77, 88, 92, 115-16, 123-4, 126, 129-31, 138, 145, 147, 153-6, 161-2, 165, 167, 173, 186, 190, 193, 196, 198, 207, 212, 215, 239-40, 242-3, 250, 258, 287, 309, 311-12, 360, 366, 368, 370, 378, 389-90, 407, 421, 427, 431-2, 434, 440, 459, 466

Jackson, H. 375
James, A.G. 36, 273, 287
James, C.M. 1, 18
Japan 64
Jews 111, 179, 329, 375, 464
Jobert, M. 164, 224, 246
Jodko, T. 387

Karamanlis, C. 466
Karjalainen, A. 163
Kastl, J. 245-6
Kawan, L. 207, 375, 387, 414, 444
Kay, J.C. 180, 206, 210, 265
Kekkonen, U.K. 8, 163, 246, 450, 464, 466, 468-9
Kharlov, M.A. 174
Khrushchev, N.S. 236, 474
Killick, Sir J. 3, 21, 23, 33, 59, 61-2, 70, 72, 146-51, 157-8, 164, 176-8, 217, 220, 222, 224-5, 235, 262, 284, 286, 325, 337, 340, 347, 358, 361-3, 367, 382-3, 385, 393, 401, 408-9, 423, 426, 441, 455

Kingswell, J.A. 435-7
Kissinger, Dr. H.A. 34, 56-60, 99-100, 102-3, 217, 258-62, 277-80, 287, 301, 304-6, 308, 311, 323-5, 329-31, 334-5, 339-40, 383, 391, 396, 409, 411, 414-15, 419-20, 436-8, 452
message to Mr. Callaghan (1974) 277
***Komitet Gosudarstvennoi Besopasnosti* (KGB)** 176
Kondrashev, S.A. 411, 413
Koster, H.J. de 18
Kosygin, A.N. 464
Kovalev, A.G. 166, 174, 257, 297, 385, 387, 389, 393, 397-8, 405-6, 411, 413-14, 421-2, 428, 430-2, 434, 436-9, 441-3, 448
Krasin, V.A. 176-8
Kreisky, Dr. B. 179
Kuznetsov, V.V. 59

Lambert, Miss S.J. 439
Lange, H.M. 63
Latvia 107
Laver, P.M. 320, 348, 366, 372, 395, 402, 411, 442
Leahy, H.H.G. 163
Ledwidge, B.W.J. 58
Lever, P. 39, 75, 96-7, 153, 172, 342
Lewty, D.I. 338
Liechtenstein 144, 318
Liechtenstein, Henri Prince of 144
Liedermann, H. 364
Lipatti, V. 434, 447
Lithuania 107
Lloyd, Maj-Gen, R.E. 60
Logan, D.A. 313, 339, 342, 432
Lucas, R. 116, 136
Lugon, J. 444
Lunkov, N.M. 21-3, 59, 61-2, 70, 72, 235-7, 283, 294-5, 310, 371-3, 419-22
Luns, Dr. J.M.A.H. 68, 306
Luxembourg 64, 67, 258, 290, 309, 421

Macedonia 26
Mackintosh, M. 60
Macmillan, H. 52
Macovescu, G. 431
Maitland, Sir D. 301
Makarios, Archbishop 333, 429, 466
Mallia, C.J. 439
Malta 63-4, 77, 139-40, 144, 160-7, 174, 205, 215, 264, 286, 309, 318, 371, 384, 392, 396, 407, 429, 431-9, 443, 453, 458, 464
   Anglo-Maltese Defence agreement (1964) 64
Maltsev, V.F. 88-9
Malyorov, M. 176
Mansfield, M. 39, 64
Maresca, J.J. 432
Marsden, W. 210, 302
Marshall, P.H.R. 206, 301
Martino, Prof. G. 63
Mawhinney, B.M. 107
Maxey, P.M. 163, 173, 180, 194, 199, 205, 210, 213, 234, 247, 272-3, 326
McAuliffe, V.A. 340, 342
McLaren, R.J.T. 50, 73, 75, 87, 101, 107, 129, 173, 175, 179, 245, 254, 256, 264, 268, 305, 329-30
McNally, T. 391
Mediterranean 49, 64, 71, 77, 90, 93, 97, 134, 139, 156, 160-2, 165, 167, 173-5, 190, 215, 232-3, 249, 255, 266, 273, 287, 308, 353, 371, 392, 396, 429, 431, 434-9, 453, 457
Mellbin, S.G. 196
Mendelevich, L.I. 94, 128, 131, 160, 166, 174, 198, 205, 210-12, 255, 262, 270, 283, 287-8, 292-3, 300, 309, 333, 345, 348, 350, 359, 365, 372, 382-5, 404-6, 411-12, 422, 428, 436, 441-2, 447-8
Metternich, Clement Wenceslas Prince von 325
Meyer, K. 135, 156
Middle East 77, 93, 139, 160, 162, 248, 259, 274, 409, 429, 458

1973 war 232
Millard, Sir G. 46-8, 183
Miller, D.I. 180, 292, 316
Ministry of Defence (MOD) 43-4, 60
Mintoff, D. 64, 139, 143, 160-2, 165, 396, 429, 431, 435-7, 464, 466
Miranova, Ms. Z.H. 174
Mitterrand, F.M.M. 282, 289
Molotov, V.M. 475
Monde, Le 176
Morgan, H.T. 351, 361, 363, 375, 390-1, 393, 401, 408-9, 423, 426, 430
Moro, A. 47, 49, 388, 441-2
Morocco 233
Most Favoured Nation (MFN) 93, 97, 134-5, 203, 217, 274, 302-4, 308, 320, 353, 356, 359, 374-6, 386-7, 395, 403, 444-6, 451
Murrell, G.D.G. 177, 235, 289-90
Mutual and Balanced Force Reductions (MBFR) 2-3, 6-7, 15, 17-18, 37-9, 42-5, 48, 56-61, 72, 76, 90, 96, 103, 114, 125, 128, 139, 153, 189, 202, 217, 224, 226-7, 229, 236, 251, 270-1, 323, 328, 337, 339-42, 373, 439, 465, 472, 476, 478
Mutually acceptable conditions (MACs) 299, 316, 343-4, 354, 360, 364, 367, 369, 458

Nash, K.T. 60
Nesterenko, A.Y. 59
Netherlands 42, 64, 115, 153, 155, 161, 165, 173-4, 186, 190, 193, 196, 212, 219, 235, 240, 242, 244, 249, 255, 258, 272, 279, 311, 314, 322, 336, 340, 360, 368-70, 373, 382, 397, 404, 407-9, 412, 415, 420-1, 427-8, 433-4, 452
Neutral and non-aligned states
   package proposal (1974) 329, 344, 346
New Zealand 56

Nineteen Eighty-Four 291

Nixon, R.M. 34-5, 37, 41, 56-7, 64, 90, 147, 159, 237, 278-9, 282, 293, 295, 304, 307, 311, 322-3, 341

Nixon-Chou *communiqué* (1972) 39

Noble, B.P. 338

North Atlantic Treaty Organisation (NATO) 2-12, 16, 19, 21, 23, 25, 28, 30, 35-7, 39, 42-50, 53, 56, 58-60, 62-9, 71, 73-83, 85-6, 88-93, 95-6, 98, 100-5, 107, 111-14, 120-1, 129, 133, 137-8, 140-1, 147, 150, 152-6, 162, 167-8, 172-3, 180, 184-6, 190, 192, 196-7, 199, 202-4, 206-9, 216, 219, 223-4, 227-9, 232, 239, 242-4, 246-9, 252, 257, 263-4, 267-9, 271, 273, 277, 279-81, 284-6, 289, 293-5, 297-8, 301, 305-6, 308-13, 315, 320, 322-3, 330, 332, 334-7, 340, 344, 346-7, 350-1, 353, 357-8, 360-2, 365-6, 371-3, 377-8, 388-9, 393, 396-7, 404-7, 409-11, 414, 418-23, 427-9, 434-5, 437-8, 441-2, 446, 449, 451-2, 454, 475-6, 458

North Atlantic Council (NAC) 1, 7, 25, 58, 63, 73, 228, 252, 277, 304, 311-15, 330, 332, 340-2, 351, 363, 376-7, 388, 405, 432

Senior Political Committee (SPC) 73, 88, 95, 97, 112, 129, 153, 172, 228, 245, 269, 280-1, 311, 314, 330, 340, 342

Northern Ireland 20, 107, 111, 180, 262

Norton-Taylor, R. 24

Norway 5, 42, 44, 58, 64-7, 95, 115, 123, 161, 174, 190, 196, 226, 229, 242-3, 261, 309, 314, 334, 336, 373, 377, 443

Odeen, P. 60

Oder/Neisse line 26

Oplinger, G.G. 34-6

Organisation for Economic Co-operation and Development (OECD) 12-13

Organisation of Petroleum-Exporting Countries (OPEC) 232

Overton, H.T.A. 57

Pakenham, M.A. 310

Palliser, Sir M. 393

Palme, O.J. 289

Peaceful coexistence 100-1, 108, 462

Peaceful settlement of disputes 48, 76, 92-3, 107, 111-12, 123-4, 131, 171, 173, 183, 189, 192, 197, 200, 202, 204, 216, 231-2, 248, 297, 352, 355, 357, 435, 456

Pearson, L.B. 63

Peck, Sir E. 25, 36, 58, 62, 69-71, 226, 271, 280-1, 294, 304, 306, 311, 332, 341, 376

Penney, J.A. 258

Petric, J. 27, 29

Pike, M.E. 199

Podgorny, N.V. 246

Poland 13, 26, 31, 36, 158, 187, 190, 205, 234, 239-40, 242, 251, 261-2, 278, 283, 286-8, 316, 325, 345, 451, 475

Pompidou, G. 237, 261, 282

Popplewell, P.J. 369, 374, 376

Portugal 65, 156, 196, 283, 396, 439, 461, 463, 466, 473, 477

Portugese communist party 461, 463

Pozharski, V.S. 134, 414

Pravda 176-7, 371

Prendergast, W.B. 311

Preston, P.S. 185

Principles 1-2, 7, 10-11, 26-7, 38-9, 46-7, 59, 63, 70, 73, 75-6, 83, 92-3, 95-7, 99-102, 104-8, 111, 113, 116-18, 122-4, 126, 128-9, 131-2, 135, 138-9, 141, 145, 155, 157-8, 181, 183, 188-92, 198, 202, 205, 209, 211, 215-16, 218, 221, 223, 225, 228, 231, 234, 241-2, 249-52, 254-5, 257, 259, 261-3, 265-6, 268, 275, 278, 287-9, 293, 297-8, 300, 306-9,

Principles cont'd
311, 314, 318-19, 333, 347, 349-52, 355, 359, 364, 366, 368-9, 380, 382, 386, 388-9, 394, 402, 405-6, 411, 414, 423, 427, 430-1, 440, 450, 453, 455-6

declaration of 153, 155, 183-4, 190, 196, 200, 223, 230, 258, 263, 265, 268, 296, 299-300, 319, 321, 348-9, 351, 354-5, 359, 368-9, 379, 381, 384-5, 394, 399-400, 402-3, 405-6, 427, 430-1, 455-6, 458, 465, 469, 472

inviolability of frontiers 5, 24, 92, 96-7, 106-7, 117, 120, 131-2, 147, 159, 180, 202, 210-13, 215, 231, 236-7, 241, 250, 254, 257-66, 268, 272, 275, 277-8, 281-2, 290, 296, 319, 355, 379-80, 425, 450, 455-6, 465, 472

non-intervention 107, 126, 128, 131, 135, 297-8, 300, 307, 319, 456, 466

non-use of force 200, 213, 216, 231, 248, 250, 352, 355, 430, 450, 456

peaceful change of frontiers 211-13, 231, 237, 241, 257-65, 272, 296, 319, 355, 368, 372, 378-9, 382-3, 385-7, 389, 394, 398, 402, 430-1, 450, 452, 456, 472, 475

self-determination 185, 231-2, 297, 349, 351, 355, 359, 364, 450, 456, 458

territorial integrity 76, 106-7, 131-2, 202, 212-13, 250, 355

Quadripartite Rights and Responsibilities (QRR) 264, 349, 352, 368, 384, 386, 389, 394-5, 397-8, 401-2, 404, 411, 414, 427, 430-1, 434, 436, 438-9, 455

Quadripartite agreement 470-4, 479

Radio Free Europe (RFE) 54, III, 121, 317, 417, 424, 459

Radio Liberty 54, III, 121, 317, 417, 459

Ramsbotham, Sir P. 279-80, 284, 330

Ramsey, A.J. 48

Rapacki, A. 25

Reeve, R. 180, 423

Residence Amat (Geneva) 347-8

Rippon, A.G.F. 17

Rodman, P. 57

Rogers, W.P. 41, 43

Romania 9, 11, 13, 25, 27-9, 31, 35, 76-7, 83, 85, 112, 116, 124, 127, 129-30, 132, 134, 143, 152-3, 158-9, 166, 173-4, 181, 189, 200, 202, 214, 216, 227, 231, 248, 266, 274, 285, 292, 338, 345, 349, 351-3, 365, 373, 385, 389, 392, 395, 400, 413, 415-16, 418, 425, 427-8, 430-1, 434, 436, 438-9, 442, 450, 453, 456, 459, 469

Bucharest Declaration (1966) 29

Roper, J.C.A. 422

Royle, A.H.F. 163

Rutten, C. 408-9

Saint Pierre, Abbé de 48

Sakharov, Dr. A. 176-9

Saliba, E.V. 162

San Marino 164, 318, 464

Sauvagnargues, J.V. 320-1

Scheel, W. 47, 162, 164, 258-60, 278-9

Schmidt, H.H.W. 44, 296, 374, 388, 465

Schmidt-Pauli, Dr. E. von 279

Schumann, M. 41, 49

Science and technology 189, 217, 303, 308, 320, 354, 387, 446-7, 457

Scott, K.B. 50, 53-4

Scott-Barrett, Maj-Gen. D.W. 470, 474

Semenov, Y.A. 210-13, 237, 408

Sexy Bar (Dipoli) 137

Sherer, A.W. 313-15, 331, 334-6, 377, 398, 414, 419, 436-7

Sheridan, R.G. 55

Shitikov, A.P. 53, 150
Short, E. 147
Simakov, V.I. 174
Simpson, W. 147
Sinton, W.B. 331
Smirnovsky. M.N. 21-3
Soames, Sir C. 208
Soares, M. 463
Solzhenitsyn, A.I. 176-8, 245
Sonnenfeldt, H. 60, 102, 256, 279-81, 284-5
Sorsa, 144
Soviet Academy of Sciences 176
Soviet Union (USSR) 5-7, 13, 22, 24-5, 28, 30-4, 36, 42, 52, 60, 64, 73, 83, 91, 97, 99-100, 107-8, 112, 143, 146-7, 149, 152-3, 155-62, 164-70, 173-92, 196-202, 204-6, 210-17, 219-21, 223-9, 231, 234-43, 245-6, 248, 250-2, 254-68, 270-1, 273, 276-83, 285-90, 292-310, 312-25, 327-9, 331, 333-41, 343-6, 350, 353-62, 364-89, 391, 393-431, 433-4, 436-53, 455-9, 461-3, 468-72, 475-9
  agreement with United States on prevention of nuclear war (1973) 159
  Anglo-Soviet Consultative Committee 52
  April Plenum of the Central Committee (1973) 178
  Communist Party of the Soviet Union (CPSU) 6, 147, 397, 475
  dissidents 176-7, 179, 182
  draft declaration 99, 158-9, 214-16
  Fenno-Soviet *communiqué* (1974) 246
  Politburo 178, 236
Soye, de 445-6
Spaak, P-H. 63
Spain 106, 139, 160-1, 164-5, 174, 189, 257, 259, 270, 345, 349, 351, 427-8, 439
Staden, B. von 35-6, 39, 41
Staercke, A.M. de 62, 314
Stage I 152-8, 160, 163, 165-7, 173, 181, 243, 317, 450, 464-5

Stage II 153, 165-8, 170, 173, 175, 177-86, 192, 198, 205, 211, 215, 222, 224, 230, 233-4, 238, 246, 252, 256, 258, 260, 272, 277, 279-81, 283, 287, 289-90, 292-3, 301-2, 305-6, 309-10, 313, 317, 321, 329-33, 347, 356, 359-60, 363-4, 370-1, 374, 393, 395-7, 406, 409, 419-20, 426, 430, 434, 436, 438, 447-8, 464, 466
  global approach 400, 404-10, 412, 415-16, 423
Stage III 167, 182, 184, 205, 220-1, 224-5, 243, 245-6, 249, 252, 254-7, 261, 268, 274, 277-9, 283, 285-6, 289-90, 292-5, 304-6, 311, 318-19, 321, 328, 333, 338, 341-2, 361, 371, 373, 377, 379, 382, 388, 390, 392, 394-7, 399-400, 405-7, 409-10, 414-15, 419-21, 426, 429-33, 435, 437-8, 440, 442, 447, 449, 452, 454, 461, 463-6
Stalin, J.V. 474
Staples, H.A.J. 24, 50, 54, 81-2, 129, 172, 245, 254
Stark, A.A.S. 168
Stewart, M. 15, 56, 109
Stoel, M. van der 364
Strategic Arms Limitation Talks/Treaty (SALT) 17, 56-7, 63, 261, 323, 328, 409, 468
Streator, E. 256, 314
Streltsov, M.N. 278
Sub-Committees/Commissions
  see Baskets I, II and III
Sully, Duc de 48
Sutherland, I.J. 419, 455, 461
Sutterlin, J.S. 102
Sweden 12, 46-9, 59, 76, 120, 141, 143, 174, 183, 189, 238-40, 270, 276, 282, 289, 334, 336, 384, 423, 427, 434, 439, 445-6, 453
Switzerland 11-12, 46, 48-9, 59, 76, 89, 92, 107, 111, 120, 124, 131, 141, 143-4, 169, 173-5, 183, 187, 189,